The Changing Administrative Law of an EU Member State

Domenico Sorace • Leonardo Ferrara •
Ippolito Piazza
Editors

The Changing Administrative Law of an EU Member State

The Italian Case

Springer

G. Giappichelli Editore

Editors
Domenico Sorace
University of Florence
Florence, Italy

Leonardo Ferrara
University of Florence
Florence, Italy

Ippolito Piazza
University of Florence
Florence, Italy

ISBN 978-3-030-50779-4 ISBN 978-3-030-50780-0 (eBook)
https://doi.org/10.1007/978-3-030-50780-0

This Springer imprint is published by the registered company Springer Nature Switzerland AG.
The registered company address is: Gewerbestrasse 11, 6330 Cham, Switzerland

Contents

Chapter 1
Introduction: The Changing Administrative Law of an EU Member State—The Italian Case

Domenico Sorace, Leonardo Ferrara, and Ippolito Piazza

This book aims to present the evolution of Italian administrative law in the context of the European Union. The chapters provide an overview of Italian administrative law, focusing on the main changes that have occurred in recent decades.

At the origin of the volume, there is the editors' intention to offer foreign scholars a useful tool to understand the current characteristics of the Italian administration. For this reason, the analysis carried out is based not only on the transformations induced by national dynamics but also, and above all, on the consequences of the European integration process on national administrative law. The authors describe these transformations, with the awareness of how the events have gone elsewhere.

The time horizon of the authors was mostly the last 50 years, approximately. However major changes had been set in motion, on the one hand, by the Constitution of the Italian Republic, entered into force in 1948 (but implemented only after some years and subsequently amended) and, on the other hand, by the European Treaties, starting from the Treaty of 1957 establishing the European Economic Community.

Hence the book shows the modifications on the administrative law imposed by the Constitution and produced by the law of the European Union, mainly by way of regulations and directives and also by means of soft law. These modifications are technically analyzed and some aspects critically discussed.

However, these factors are not the only ones that have been considered in the volume. Some inherent dynamics of the law of public administration are taken also in account, particularly pertaining the relations between administrative law and private law. The evolution of the administrative justice has been thoroughly examined, as well as the expansion of regulation and the increasing legal protection of individual rights. It was necessary to consider even the novelties induced in the law of the public administrations by the growing role of technique: intended both as

D. Sorace · L. Ferrara · I. Piazza (✉)
University of Florence, Florence, Italy
e-mail: domenico.sorace@unifi.it; leonardo.ferrara@unifi.it; ippolito.piazza@unifi.it

D. Sorace et al. (eds.), *The Changing Administrative Law of an EU Member State*,
https://doi.org/10.1007/978-3-030-50780-0_1

specialized knowledge (think, in particular, of the field of economics), and as a set of technologies capable of influencing the organization and the procedures of public administration. Finally, administrative law is inevitably conditioned by the social and economic pressures for innovation that periodically arise in our societies.

All these factors, of course, generally are not isolated, but more often they are concomitant and complementary. The chapters of the book—while maintaining a legal approach—also consider the influence of these economic, social, cultural and technological factors. That is why this book is not just a handbook of administrative law but offers an in-depth analysis of the most relevant issues for the Italian public administration today.

In the first part, the book covers some general themes: the comparison between the Italian integration of the nineteenth century and the contemporary European integration; the discipline of the procedures and organization of public administrations; the public budgets; the administrative justice; the public services; the digital administration; the process of juridification.

The second part is focused on specific topics instead: the role of law in the construction of cultural identity; public intervention in the economy; regulation of the banking sector; cohesion and subsidiarity; public employment; healthcare management; civil protection; local government.

In the end the last chapters host some comments of non-Italian scholars, stimulated by the reading of previous essays.

The book shows on the whole the picture of a law largely Europeanized that however preserves meaningful national features. This, after all—not the total homologation of the law of the Member States—is to be regarded as the aim of the European Union and that is why the comparison between the law of these states can be quite interesting.

Part I
General Issues

Chapter 2
The Plurality and Diversity of Integration Models: The Italian Unification of 1865 and the European Union Ongoing Integration Process

Roberto Cavallo Perin and Gabriella M. Racca

Contents

Abstract Analysed in this chapter are the characteristics of two main integration processes that Italy has experienced. Firstly, the country's unification as a nation more than 150 years ago. Secondly, and more recently, together with other EU Member States, the constitution of a Legal Order. In both cases, the integration process is not meant to be homogeneous as far as various entities and activities are concerned, nor is it based mainly on general and abstract rules. Rather, it relies on administrative acts and different forms of administrative cooperation.

The administrative integration process involving different contexts within unified Italy as a kingdom, from 1865, shows recurring asymmetry because of multiple levels of integration needed—something which was achieved by involving many different institutions in the process. Likewise, the ongoing European Union integration process is not resulting from one single, but from a number of parallel relationships among various institutions working in different sectors, and pursuing integration by designing and following their own path and timing.

In the newly unified Italy the administrative integration process was not always structural (as for ministries, etc.). Also, it was only functional at times (as for the

R. Cavallo Perin (✉) · G. M. Racca
University of Turin, Turin, Italy
e-mail: roberto.cavalloperin@unito.it; gabriella.racca@unito.it

D. Sorace et al. (eds.), *The Changing Administrative Law of an EU Member State*,
https://doi.org/10.1007/978-3-030-50780-0_2

authorities of each jurisdiction, central banks, etc.). However, functional integration was arguably no less effective than structural integration. The 1865 Unification Laws of Italy, in fact, have been thoroughly studied and praised, and rightly so, despite the fact that their impact onto the newly unified country was limited because of their abstract definition, which required subsequent asymmetrical activities by administrative bodies to put them into practice, thus make them effective.

Examining the approach adopted by the Italian administrative bodies after 1865 as a case study, we may argue that only closer cooperation between today's national and European institutions would allow them to succeed in pursuing integration as a shared goal. All this regardless of whether that integration should take place through traditional instruments (such as the controls that used to be performed by the Prefect in Italy, but are now a prerogative of the EU Court of Auditors) or network organisations (such as ETCGs, transnational purchasing groups, or cross border central purchasing bodies).

A parallel between the two different administrative integration processes outlined here will be drawn and discussed in this chapter.

2.1 The Integration Process in Italy 150 Years Ago and in Europe Now: Parallels and Asymmetry

Nobody compares the physical ability of a youth with the maturity of an elderly person. Nonetheless, it may be worth taking into account Italy's long and challenging experience of integration with the more recent process being undertaken by the European Union to find similarities and differences through appropriate comparisons.

That is why understanding the relation between two main integration processes that Italy has experienced can bring to the fore the complexity of issues faced in the past and arising in the present. Italy's first integration process stemmed from the birth of the country as a nation in 1861–1865.[1] The second one (more recent and still in progress) involves the participation of Italy as a Member State of the European Union.

Although a lack of complete symmetry among the different sectors and institutions can be observed within the integration processes being discussed here, both of them can be regarded as aimed at meeting relevant needs in the historical periods in which they saw inception.

Over the last 20 years administrative law has seen many sectors and institutions become subject to the EU discipline, and in some cases the integration process is evident. Aside from leading to the creation of the Euro as single currency, the EU discipline—either conceived as a detailed discipline with specific provisions such as

[1]L. 17.03.1861, n. 4761, on the Italian Kingdom, and the law of Administrative Unification: l. 20.03.1865, n. 2248, all. A-F.

directives and regulations, or as a discipline based on principles—has been of great importance for agriculture, the environment, public procurement, health, education, and many activities of general economic interest.

Conversely, undeniable is the inexistence of common provisions on administrative procedure despite the fact that attempts have been made to create them.[2]

The same applies to the effectiveness of administrative acts and norm on public assets.[3] Also evident is the absence of common provisions on contractual obligations.[4] The same applies to European business activities.[5]

All these subject matters would have been relevant also for public administrations.[6]

The absence of a common disciplinary framework for the aforementioned domains is even more noticeable because public and private law (*alias* administrative and commercial law at the heart of public or private law for economics) are generally perceived as the pillars of the juridical unity to pursue within the European market.[7]

The EU single market has always been considered to have a shared juridical culture, deriving either from legislative or judicial sources. Such a single market should thus be ruled by a shared discipline envisaging exemptions and exceptions, but not depending on the nationality of companies, individuals, and/or territoriality.

---

[2]The EU Parliament's resolution 15.1.2013 provided recommendations to the Commission for an EU legislation on administrative procedures (2012/2024(INL)). See also the subsequent European Parliament resolution, 9.06.2016 for an open, effective and independent European administration, (2016/2610(RSP)).

[3]Cfr. *ReNEUAL Model Rules 2014* and in particular Hofmann et al. (2014), de Leonardis (2016), Craig (2013), Galetta (2011), Della Cananea (2009), Glaser (2014), Stelkens (2014) and Harlow (2006).

[4]On the unfinished European Civil Code see Alpa (2007), Ciatti (2012), Schulze and Stuyck (2011) and Cámara Lapuente (2003); for a purpose of an "alternative model of the EU's constitution", on common provisions see Dawson and de Witte (2015). For exceptions see the *Vienna Convention on the Sale: United Nations Convention of 11 April 1980*, ratified by law 1.12.1985, n. 765; Directive n. 1999/44/CE, of the European Parliament and the Council 25.5. 1999; Ajani (2012), Alpa et al. (2012), Sánchez-Lorenzo (2013) and Ragno (2008).

[5]On the so-called *Lex mercatoria*, on the sectors see Directive n. 2006/123/EEC of the European Parliament and the Council 12.12.2006, *Bolkestein*; Directive n. 2011/83/EU of the European Parliament and the Council, *on consumers*; Directive n. 2006/112/EEC of the Council 28.11.2006, *on VAT*; art. 54, § 2, TFEU; Directive n. 2012/30/EU of the European Parliament and the Council 25.10.2012, *on the safeguard of shareholders and third parties towards limited companies*; Directive n. 2009/133/EEC of the Council 19.10.2009, *fiscal regime for mergers, divisions, etc and for the transfer of incorporation of SE or SCE*; on anti-discrimination: Directive n. 2000/43/EEC of the Council 29.6.2000 *on race or ethnic group;* Directive n. 2000/78/EEC of the Council 27.11.2000, *on employment and working conditions*; Directive n. 1999/70/EEC of the Council 28.6.1999, *on fixed-term work contracts AGREEMENT CES, UNICE e CEEP*; Directive n. 2011/7/EU of the European Parliament and the Council 16.2.2011, *on delays on commercial transactions*. Finally, see Gnes (2012); for a global perspective on the role of the EU in the global economy, see Alesina et al. (1997); more recently Spolaore (2014) and Jowell (2008).

[6]Cimini (2016) and Craig (2011).

[7]For an historical reconstruction see Alesina et al. (1997).

It should be remarked, however, that the non-homogeneity noticeable at a closer analysis of the integration process in exam, cannot be regarded as a normal feature of any integration process.[8] As already mentioned, since its unification 150 years ago Italy has experienced an integration process seeing many "parallel" interpretations of the same 1865 Civil Code being kept in force for almost 60 years by the High Courts (*Corti di Cassazione*) in Turin, Florence, Naples, Palermo, and Rome, the latter from 1878 (R. d. 24 March 1923, No. 601).

2.2 Administrative Integration and Plurality of Unifications

Similar tools and models recur in the two integration processes under scrutiny.

First and foremost, mention should be made of the designation and greater relevance of the institutions responsible for the implementation and management of a new comprehensive legal order—a phenomenon that could be observed at first in the Kingdom of Italy, and later on in the European Union. In both cases new institutions driving a unification process have been juxtaposed to pre-existing ones.

Meanwhile the transition into the new legal order has been made possible thanks to the 'little steps' forward that were taken by administrative authorities, either in Italy or in the European Union. The reason underpinning that kind of operating mode is essentially structural, and directly owes to the theory of judicial acts of Continental public law.

The effectiveness of Italy's post-unification legal order owes to its concrete definition, which historically pertains to the administrative or judiciary system rather than legislation itself. Being an ensemble of abstract norms, the latter actually follows or precedes the concrete evolution of a legal order dictated by administrative acts or judicial facts.

Actually, the Italian laws on administrative unification followed the unification the Public Administration authorities such as ministries and their central and peripheral bodies, for instance the Ministry of Internal Affairs, Foreign Affairs, Public Works, Agriculture, and Industry and Commerce.[9]

The effective unification of the aforementioned institutions was implemented—following purging or voluntary adhesion—by newly appointing staff who had already been employed in pre-existing states.[10]

Furthermore, local public authorities were subjected to governmental control while embassies were either suppressed or merged. Al this was achieved through

[8]For the identification of the enhanced cooperation procedure (art. 20 TEU and art. 326 ff. TFEU) as an useful tool of differentiated integration: Fabbrini (2013). For a theorical approach see Pierson (1994), Sandholtz and Stone Sweet (1997) and Spolaore (2013, 2014).

[9]Cudia (2016).

[10]Cassese (2014, 2016), Cassese et al. (2017), Melis (2015), Sandulli and Vesperini (2011) and Calandra (1978).

concrete administrative acts, which opened way establishing new ministerial institutions and a new system of local authorities was therefore originated.[11]

Administrative acts thus became tools for the integration of newly appointed personnel once working for the states existing before the unification of Italy. That often entailed relocating people throughout the territory of the Italian Kingdom, which contributed to fostering national identity as well as a sense of belonging to a shared culture.[12] Such a phenomenon appears to have been happening within the European Union too.[13]

From a theoretical standpoint, integration through the administrative system can be regarded as a process driven by institutional relationships, or better by a plurality of unifications of different institutions.[14] Such an interpretation allows us to understand why there is frequent asymmetry within an 'alignment' pursued to implement a comprehensive legal order effectively and timely. Actually, what we can observe is not one single relationship between legal orders, but rather a series of parallel relationships between institutions (and consequently their legal orders).

Each of them experienced a *reductio ad unitatem*, more or less marked as a result of an aim of political and territorial cohesion that may vary depending on the role played by the institutions in question (European Central Bank [ECB], European and national Courts of Auditors, etc.) and the sectors in which they operate (finance, agriculture, etc.), respectively.

Therefore, it may be appropriate to describe unification as a plurality of processes of integration (involving ministries, local authorities, etc.) accompanied by a plurality of *reductio ad unitatem* processes. All this not has not always taken place structurally (as for ministries, etc.), but sometimes only functionally (involving judicial bodies, central banks, etc.) as the latter mode is not less effective than the former.

It should be added that it may not be necessary to define a specific sequence of procedural phases of the integration process in that the legal order arising therefrom

[11]Royal decree (r.d.) 11.1.1861, *Aumento della pianta numerica degl'Impiegati del Ministro dell'Interno*, in *Celerifera*, 2394-2395; r.d. 6.11.1861, *Nuova pianta del Personale del Ministero degli Affari Esteri*, in *Celerifera*, 2179; r.d. 14.02.1861, *Nuova pianta numerica e stipendi degli Ufficiali ed Impiegati nel Ministero della Pubblica Istruzione*, in *Celerifera*, 589-590; r.d. 20.1.1861, *Nuova pianta numerica degl'Impiegati del Ministero di Grazia, Giustizia ed Affari Ecclesiastici*, in *Celerifera*, 490-49; r.d. 21.12.1860, *Pianta organica e Quadro di riporto del Personale del Ministero dei Lavori Pubblici*, in *Celerifera*, 241-245; r.d. 8.3.1861, *Aggiunta alla pianta numerica del Ministero di Agricoltura, Industria e Commercio*, in *Celerifera*, 525-528; r.d. 5.1.1861, *Nuova pianta numerica del personale dell'amministrazione centrale delle Finanze*, in *Celerifera*, 433-435. Iudica (2016), Gagliardi (2009), Chiariello (2016) and Apicella (2016).

[12]Grüner (2016), De Vinci (2016) and Melis (2004).

[13]See EUCJ, 9.9.2003, C-285/01, *Burbaud c. Ministère de l'Emploi et de la solidarité*. Gagliardi (2009); annotation of judgements, Kessler (2003), Icard (2003), Pongérard-Payet (2003), Muir (2003), Luby (2004) and Weiler (2012); more precisely, Drumaux and Joyce (2018).

[14]Aside from the aforementioned civil jurisdiction it is worth mentioning the unification of the Italian banks of emission (1893), which, after the unification of the Italian Kingdom, kept into existence five issuing institutions for 32 years. See Luzzatto (1968) and Costa Cardol (1989).

is something original, inextricably linked to the historical period in which it sees inception, and peculiar of the institution it relates to.

Italy's 1865 unification laws are bear witness to the most famous episode of the Italian administrative integration process. Those laws, which would have opened way to configuring the Italian institutions over the years, are still rightfully celebrated although they only provided the abstract definition of unification.[15]

2.3 Asymmetric Effectiveness of Administrative Integration Within Different Relevant Sectors in the EU

In 1971 the EU issued their first Procurement Directives, which in Italy would become a law only 6 years later (law 8 August 1977, No. 584).[16] The complexity of the Italian regulatory system on procurement, however, required a much longer period (more than 20 years) for the effective implementation of the aforementioned directive. Actually, the main changes in the Italian procurement system owe to the European Union Court of Justice (EUCJ).[17]

The EUCJ, in fact, provided an interpretation of the directive and "configured, in accordance with the European legal culture" some important legal institutions (i.e., bodies governed by public law) and concepts (i.e., in-house providing mode, cooperation between public administrations, relevant market; public service and goods providers; construction and/or public service concession, and other). All this with a view to clarify and better define the EU Procurement Directive so that it could be implemented effectively in all the EU Member States.

By providing an interpretation that is reminiscent of the "the best pages in the book of history" of the Constitutional Courts of the EU Member States' National, the EUCJ proved being able of thoroughness and innovativeness, which are necessary to successfully pursue any integration process.

---

[15]Benvenuti (1969). See also *Amministrare*, Issue no. 1/2015, entirely dedicated to the administrative unification laws, with contributions by Aimo (2015), Bonini (2015), Tosatti (2015), Mori (2015), Soresina (2015), Merusi (2015), Polsi (2015), Consito (2016), Tigano (2016) and Papadopoulou (2017) regarding the theories that have developed concerning the democratic legitimacy of the European Union. For a critical view of the theory of the triple legitimacy in Europe and its relationship with the participation of the (European) citizen, see Weiler (2017). On the role of citizens, see Van de Walle (2018); Regulation n. 1408/1971/EEC of the Council 14.6.1971, *on social security of workers (employees and self-employed persons) and their families moving within the Community*.

[16]Directive n. 71/304/EEC of the Council 26.7.1971; Directive n. 71/305/EEC of the Council 26.7.1971, later law 8.8.1977, n. 584.

[17]Directive n. 92/50/EEC of the Council 18.6.1992, public procurement of services; Directive n. 93/37/EEC of the Council 14.06.1993, public procurement of works; Directive n. 93/36/EEC of the Council 14.06.1993, public procurement of supplies. Racca (2014b), Racca and Cavallo Perin (2014) and Ponzio (2016).

Indeed, the legislative and judicial integration in question is generally regarded as one of the most successful and advanced, and other sectorial aspects are also praiseworthy. Nonetheless, still low is the percentage of contracts above the EU relevance threshold (20%) in Italy.[18] Furthermore, the EU cross-border participation is also negligible (1.6%).[19]

Far from being structural, the reason underpinning such an outcome depends on the nature of the administrative acts and on the role of the functions in charge of defining the organizational framework of the Member States within the EU legal order: because the EU directives are general and abstract while the EUCJ's judicial acts only apply as case-law, the jurisdiction in question can be implemented effectively only to some extent.[20] The integration process actually depends on the public administrations, managing the procurement process (outsourced) and defining the threshold of each contract (thus deciding whether it is within the scope of the EU directives). Consequently, the implementation of the European single market is impacted by public administration demand and policies. Integration in relevant markets, in fact, essentially depends on the cooperation among national public administrations and EU institutions through administrative cooperation leading for example to the creation of cross border public demand sides and other aggregated public demand strategies.[21]

[18]EU Commission, Commission staff working paper, *Evaluation Report: Impact and Effectiveness of EU Public Procurement Legislation*, I, http://ec.europa.eu/internal_market/publicprocurement/docs/modernising_rules/er853_1_en.pdf, 27.

[19]EU Commission, *Communication from the commission to the European parliament, the council, the European economic and social committee and the committee of the regions*. Making Public Procurement work in and for Europe, COM(2017) 572 final, Strasbourg, 2017, http://eurlex.europa.eu/legal-content/EN/TXT/PDF/?uri=CELEX:52017DC0572&from=EN.

[20]Racca (2015).

[21]For the affirmation of an "obligation to cooperate" on national central administrations (art. 197 TFEU): Directive n. 2006/123/EC of the European Parliament and the Council of 12.12.2006, on *internal market services*, wh. no. 105, art. 29, par. 1°; Art. 17, Regulation n. 450/2008/EC of the European Parliament and the Council of 23.04.2008, *Community customs code*; Racc. 2009/524/EC of the Commission of 29.06.2009, *measures to enhance the functioning of the internal market*. See Lottini (2012), Lafarge (2010) and Sutherland (1992). See art. 298, TFEU on the existence of an "*open, effective and independent*" *European administration*. See D'Angelo (2016) and de Leonardis (2016); European Parliament, *Towards an EU Regulation on Administrative Procedure*?, 2010 in http://www.europarl.europa.eu/RegData/etudes/etudes/join/2010/432743/IPOL-JURI_ET(2010)432743_EN.pdf.

2.4 Integration Among Public Administrations: Organizational Capacity and Principle of Subsidiarity

Since the unification of Italy, many institutions and rules have remained nearly the same.[22] In the public procurements sector a European set of rules, not at all standing aloof from the cultures of the Member States, has emerged.

As mentioned earlier, the "in house providing mode", the "administrative cooperation",[23] the "aggregation of public procurement", and the "concession of works and services and all the forms of suppliers selection" all represent continuity in administrative law culture, which stemmed in national contexts yet has flourished in a European field of knowledge.[24]

Indeed, the Public administration's organizational capacity is a key factor in pursuing and achieving the EU cultural goals steered toward integration. Public administrations may also play a significant role in market integration, to some extent, through the innovation of their contractual strategy and the reconfiguration of their purchasing power.[25]

The EU Directive forbidding Member States to prohibit to use the framework agreements of another Member State thus implies the possibility for a national Public administration to apply such provision effectively, and reshape their cross-border procurement strategy.[26] Such a general and abstract provision, however, requires administrative acts to be issued by contracting authorities so as to meet public needs or demand, and define the EU Member States' procurement strategies.

The cooperation among the Public administrations of different Member States can take place in various ways, for example it may be occasional or permanent, convention-based or structural as happens with European Groups of Territorial Cooperation (EGTC).[27] Aside from ECTCs, cooperation is also possible through "other established entities under EU law" or "bodies governed by public law".[28] It should be remarked that this kind of cooperation is likely to require to overcoming legal and language barriers, and also the applicability of a national law which is not

---

[22]See the "*Europeanization of administrative law*": Schwarze (2012) and Harlow (2006). The purpose is to find common principles and values to create a global administrative law of the EU, which is "generally regarded as the most sophisticated of international political regimes, possessing the most developed transnational legal order."

[23]Artt. 6 and 197 TFEU. Auby and Dutheil de La Rochère (2014a, b), Chiti (2010, 2011) and Bassi (2004).

[24]See Cavallo Perin (2014) and Merusi (2013).

[25]Such as the subdivision in national lots noticed to all the participating undertakings, which are encouraged to search for synergies with others: law 17.2.1884, artt. 3, 38. Rostagno (1887) and Harlow and Rawlings (2007).

[26]Directive n. 2014/24/EU, art. 39, § 2. Ponzio (2016) and Racca (2014a, 2015); D.Lgs 18 April 2016, n. 50, art. 43.

[27]Directive n. 2014/24/EU, art. 39, § 5. Cavallo Perin and Racca (2016).

[28]See the case of the *European Health Public Procurement Alliance—EHPPA*, consortium created under French law in 2013 in order to facilitate cooperation and exchange of information.

that in force where the contract shall be fulfilled.[29] The effectiveness of a legal order and above all its level of integration, therefore, essentially depends on the organizational capacity of the public administrations involved in its sphere of application.[30]

Organizational capacity and the principle of subsidiarity apply as requirements to national and EU public cooperation networks as well.[31] This entails that the competences of each institution that is part of a network shall be defined. And also that the appointment of any institution as subject managing functions or services depends on their suitability, which is to be measured based on the aforementioned principles (Art. 5, TEU; Art. 118, paragraph 2, Constitution of Italy).

In a broader view, the cooperation among different national and/or European public administrations with relevant competences can give shape to networks operating in different sectors of interest. Although to a different extent, integration among Public administration is desirable in every sector, as is the legitimization of the action of each institution involved. The latter shall be regarded as part of a network, defined either by a national legal order or the European one.

A correct assignment of competences underpins the efficiency and efficacy of any action aimed at pursuing public policies. Above all, it actually puts into practice the legal order based on which competences are given, thus determining its effectiveness. Public administrations of the Member States may therefore turn into public organizations under the aegis of the European Union while still being national Public administrations.[32]

It should also be remarked that the effectiveness of the EU legal order, as well as that of every EU Member State, can be achieved with no need to have the same level of integration of public administrations within each relevant sector.[33]

From a juridical standpoint, the EU legal system implies that the capacity and subsidiarity of national organizational structures must be attained in the pursuit of

---

[29]Directive n. 2014/24/EU, wh. no. 73, recalling Regulation n. 593/2008/EEC, on the applicable law for contractual obligations, so-called Rome I. See. Racca (2014c) and Ponzio (2014). Regulation n. 1082/2006/EEC of the European Parliament and the Council 5.7.2006, in *OJEU*, amended by Regulation n. 1302/2013/EU of the European Parliament and the Council 17.12.2013 (in force from 22.6.2014). Carrea (2012), Cocucci (2008), Dickmann (2006) and Engl (2007).

[30]Racca and Cavallo (2011), Cudia (2016), Portaluri (2016), Primerano and Lamberti (2016) and Dimopoulos (2004).

[31]Case law: i.e., EUCJ, 8.02.2018, C-144/17, Lloyd's of London C. Agenzia Regionale per la Protezione dell'Ambiente della Calabria; EUCJ, 30.01.2017, C-360/15 and C-31/16, College van Burgemeester en Wethouders van de gemeente Amersfoort C. X BV; EUCJ, 20.12.2017, C-277/16, Polkomtel sp. z o.o. C. Prezes Urzedu Komunikacji Elektronicznej.

[32]Nigro (1957). On European administration as an "integrated organisation" of national and Union administrations see Saltari (2007), Porchia (2008), Chiti (2013), Franchini (2013) and Cimini (2016). The "administrative capacity" of national administrations "to implement European law" is a "matter of common interest" (art. 197, TFUE); cfr. Chiti (2010).

[33]Agriculture, currency, healthcare, education, consumer protection. D'Angelo (2016), Romeo (2016), Racca (2017, 2018) and Cavallo Perin and Racca (2016).

European Union policies (Art. 5, TEU).[34] The lack of organizational capacity of a national institution justifies the application of the principle of subsidiarity either through the attribution of competence from a specific organization or through EU public cooperation networks.

2.5 Administrative Protection of Fundamental Rights in the Integration Processes[35]

The administrative protection of individual rights is an example of integration among public institutions within the EU that has recently concerned healthcare and education in particular (Charter of Fundamental Rights EU, Art. 14 and Art. 35; Art. 6 TEU).

In the EU the legal and institutional protection of the rights to healthcare and education beyond borders has been regarded as resulting from the freedom of movement within the EU, granted to workers at first, and then to Member State citizens (Art. 45 TFEU and Art. 20 and 21 TFEU).

As mentioned in an earlier paper, it has been argued that the right of EU citizens to access good healthcare and education has been granted by means of legal instruments typical of the "Common Market",[36] no matter whether as an unwanted or unavoidable effect.[37]

The 'freedom of movement' right has been granted to workers and service providers (supply side) applying the non-discrimination principle (demand side).[38] That implied granting those people the right to access healthcare and education in

[34] *Ex multis*, EUCJ, 7.02.2018, C-304/16, The Queen (app. by American Express Company) C. The Lords Commissioners of Her Majesty's Treasury, 43; EUCJ, 20.12.2017, C-81/16 P, Regno di Spagna C. CE, 20; EUCJ, 6.09.2017, C-643/15 and C-647/15, Slovakia and Hungary C. Council, 38 ss.; EUCJ, 2.06.2016, C-27/15, preliminary question, Do. Po., and EUCJ, 8.09.2016, C-225/15, Pi.Pi. C. CRGT.

[35] Donato (2016); See on the concept of irrelevance among legal orders: Santi Romano (1918); for the different individual rights see Habermas (2015), Lehning (2001) and Spolaore and Wacziarg (2009).

[36] *Amplius* Cavallo Perin (2013).

[37] For the overcoming of the *status of* "marketbürger" by the European citizen: Ferrari (2007). The references above are linked to a monumental jurisprudential work—at first by the Court of Justice—which has acknowledged to European citizens the opportunity to get education and healthcare anywhere in the Europe Union. Thus, taking increasing advantage of an Internal Market or of a soft competition not only between institutions but even between the different systems existing in the Member States, according to an institutional occurrence opened to new interpretation the laws of the Treaty on the Functioning of the EU (TFEU, Art. 2 paragraph 5; and Art. 6).

[38] *Inter alia*: Iliopoulou (2007), Gagliardi (2012), Vesperini (2011), O'Leary (2011), Barnard (2010), Spaventa (2007) and Condinanzi et al. (2006).

their Member State of destination.[39] As a result, the "portability of social rights" in the EU territory entitles all European citizens to have accession to the services granted in the Member State where they may move into.[40]

The EU competence on areas of actions such as healthcare and education is limited to "carry[ing] out actions to support, coordinate or supplement the actions of the Member States", as set out in the Treaty on the Functioning of the European Union (TFEU, Art. 6).

Nonetheless, the EU competence should be interpreted as the faculty to put in place anything that is missing—in terms of healthcare and education—in the Member States by supporting them so as to make them able to provide for what they cannot grant on their own, but could do by relying on a network of organizations selected by the EU. In this perspective, the EU competence to provide for support, coordination, and supplement where needed, allows for a selection of institutions to be joining the network.

The Public Administration has been required to improve the effectiveness of their action in new ways. For instance, by ensuring the coexistence of different communities within their territory so as to foster development and enable each and every individual to exercise their fundamental rights.[41] Now as ever, administrative acts building on the analysis of 'big data' and adopted by a good, efficient, and far-seeing

---

[39]*European Health Strategy*, COM (2007) 630 of 23.10.2007; Art. 22, Regulation n. 1408/71/EEC of the Council 14.6.1971, on social security of workers and their family members; art. 20, Reg. 883/2004/EEC of the European Parliament and the Council 29.4.2004, social security systems; Dir. 2011/24/EU of the European Parliament and the Council 9.3.2011, *rights of patients to transboundary healthcare*. See EUCJ, 28.4.1998, C-158/96, *Kohll* c. *Union des caisses de maladie*; C. giust., 12.7.2001, C-157/99, *Smits e Peerbooms* c. *Stichting Ziekenfonds VGZ e Stichting CZ Groep Zorgverzkeringen*; EUCJ, 16.5.2006, C-372/04, *Watts* c. *Bedford Primary Care Trust*; EUCJ, 19.4.2007, C-444/05, *Stamatelaki* c. *Organismos Asfaliseos Eleftheron Epangelmation (OAEE)*; EUCJ, 5.10.2010, C-512/08, *Commission* c. *France*; EUCJ, 5.10.2010, C-173/09, *Elchinov* c. *Natsionalna zdravnoosiguritena kasa (NZOK)*. See Saitta (2016) and Costamagna (2011); EUCJ, 13.2.1985, C-293/83, *Gravier* c. *City of Liege*; EUCJ, 21.6.1988, C-39/86, *Lair* c. *University of Hannover*. From the affirmation of the economic freedom of movement of goods, capital and persons – the EU supranational legal order, of the Single Market, has certainly created the right of people to obtain everywhere the typical social rights to education and healthcare. Cfr. Conticelli (2012) and Cerrina Feroni (2012); for a first systematic overview on the issue: Consito (2009), Esteban et al. (2012) and Montalvo and Reynal-Querol (2005).

[40]Monti (2010) and Consito (2012). European accreditation affirms a responsibility of the EU for the quality of this recognized services and, consequently, EU provides also for a selection of national organizations capable of ensuring "a high level of human health protection" (TFEU, Art. 168, paragraph 2), "quality education" (TFEU, Art. 165, paragraph 1), "the development of a European dimension of Education" (TFEU, Art. 165, paragraph 2), aimed at "the improvement of public health, the prevention of illness and diseases and the elimination of sources of danger to physical and mental health" (TFEU, Art. 168, paragraph 1, 2nd sentence).

[41]Taylor (2001).

Public Administration can prevent and settle conflicts.[42] That may ultimately lead to actually ensuring the fruition of individual rights.[43]

These days some remarks set forth in the Italian Constitution, therefore, appear as true as ever: to avoid prejudice to the constitutional legal order, the Public administration as a whole and its constituent institutions shall not keep being inadequate for a long time (Const., Art. 118, paragraph I) otherwise maladministration may become systemic (Const., Art. 97, paragraph II). The key role of the Public Administration in protecting fundamental rights must thus be acknowledged: only the potential and concrete effectiveness of Public Administration can lead to the effectiveness of the constitutional legal order as a whole.

It has been affirmed that there is no good Public Administration without a Constitution (Italian Const., Art. 97, paragraphs I and II).[44] Nonetheless, we may also argue that there is no Constitution without good Public Administration, which shall essentially be regarded as a capable and efficient organization turning abstract yet fundamental rights into reality.

References

Aimo P (2015) Comuni e Province, funzioni e controlli (all. A). Amministrare, Issue no. 1/2015, pp 7 ff

Ajani G (2012) Un diritto comune europeo della vendita? Nuova complessità. Contr. e impr. pp 71 ff

Alesina A, Spolaore E, Wacziarg R (1997) Economic integration and political disintegration. National Bureau of Economic Research, Working paper no. 6163, pp 24 ff

Allegretti U (1993) voce Imparzialità e buon andamento della pubblica amministrazione. In: Dig. disc. pubbl., vol VIII. Torino, pp 139

Allegretti U (1996) Amministrazione pubblica e Costituzione, Padova, pp 70 ff

Alpa G (2007) Il diritto privato europeo: significato e confini del sintagma. In: Capilli G, Alpa G (eds) Lezioni di diritto privato europeo, Padova, pp 3 ff

Alpa G, Conte G, Perfetti U, von Westphalen FG (eds) (2012) The proposed common European sales law – the lawyers' view. Munich

Apicella EA (2016) Pubblico impiego: poteri organizzativi e gestionali. In: Cavallo Perin R, Police A, Saitta F (eds) L'organizzazione delle pubbliche amministrazioni tra Stato nazionale e integrazione europea. Pisa University Press, Pisa, pp 149–168

Auby JB, Dutheil de La Rochère J (2014a) Avant-Propos. In: Auby JB, Dutheil de la Rochère J (eds) Traité de droit administrative européen. Bruylant, Bruxelles, p 14 ff

[42]On the State as "protagonist of the 150 years" with the performance of provisions and the exercise of functions "at the service of development": Melis (2015).

[43]Cfr. Ranelletti (1904), Chiappetti (1973) and Benvenuti (1994).

[44]Allegretti (1993, 1996). In the sense which emphasises "the standpoint of the administration as interest to service or anyway as objective result which all offices must strive to achieve" see Trimarchi Banfi (2007). In general, on the right to a good administration see Chevalier (2014), Rabinovici (2012), Trimarchi (2011), Ponce Solé (2011), Galetta (2010) and Chiti (2005).

Auby JB, Dutheil de La Rochère J (2014b) Introduction: Degré de convergence de droits administratifs dans le creuset du droit européen. In: Auby JB, Dutheil de la Rochère J (eds) Traité de droit administrative européen. Bruylant, Bruxelles, p 1283 ff
Barnard C (2010) The substantive law of the EU, the four freedoms. Oxford University Press, Oxford, p 422 ff
Bassi N (2004) Gli accordi fra soggetti pubblici nel diritto europeo. Milan
Benvenuti F (1969) Mito e realtà nell'ordinamento amministrativo italiano. In: Benvenuti F, Miglio G (eds) L'unificazione amministrativa e i suoi protagonisti. Vicenza, pp 75
Benvenuti F (1994) Il nuovo cittadino (1994), and later in Scritti giuridici, vol 1, Vita e pensiero, Milan, 2006, pp 844
Bonini F (2015) Comuni e Province, circoscrizioni (all. A). In Amministrare, Issue no. 1/2015, pp 55 ff
Calandra P (1978) Storia dell'amministrazione pubblica in Italia, Bologna, pp 33
Cámara Lapuente S (ed) (2003) Derecho privado europeo. Madrid
Carrea S (2012) La disciplina del gruppo europeo di cooperazione territoriale (GECT) tra diritto dell'Unione europea, autonomia statutaria e diritto internazionale privato: un tentativo di sintesi. Dir. comm. internaz, pp 611 ff
Cassese S (2014) Governare gli italiani. Storia dello Stato. Il Mulino, Bologna, p 54
Cassese S (ed) (2016) Research handbook on global administrative law. Elgar, Cheltenham
Cassese S, von Bogdandy A, Huber PM (2017) The administrative state. Oxford University Press, Oxford
Cavallo Perin R (2013) Crisis del Estado de Bienestar. El Papel del Derecho Administrativo. In: Piñar Mañas JL (ed) Crisis económica y crisis del Estado de Bienestar. El Papel del Derecho Administrativo, Madrid, pp 155 ff
Cavallo Perin R (2014) Conclusion. In the conference Appalti Pubblici: innovazione e razionalizzazione. Le strategie di aggregazione e cooperazione europea nelle nuove Direttive, Roma, Council of State, 14.5.2014, in Ius Publicum Network Review, http://www.iuspublicum.com/repository/uploads/18_11_2015_18_40_Atti_del_Convegno_Consiglio_di_Stato_14_05.pdf
Cavallo Perin R, Racca GM (2016) La cooperazione amministrativa europea nei contratti e servizi pubblici. Rivista italiana di diritto comunitario XXVI(6):1457 ff
Cerrina Feroni G (2012) Pubblico e privato nella erogazione delle prestazioni sanitarie. Italia, Germania, Svizzera a confronto. Munus, pp 65 ff
Chevalier E (2014) Bonne administration et Union européenne. Bruylant, Bruxelles, p 167 ff
Chiappetti A (1973) L'attività di polizia. Aspetti storici e dogmatici. Padova
Chiariello AM (2016) L'organizzazione centrale dello Stato ed il modello ministeriale. In: Cavallo Perin R, Police A, Saitta F (eds) L'organizzazione delle pubbliche amministrazioni tra Stato nazionale e integrazione europea. Pisa University Press, Pisa, pp 223–264
Chiti E (2005) Il principio di buona amministrazione. In: Chiti E, Franchini C, Gnes M, Savino M, Veronelli M (eds) Diritto amministrativo europeo – Casi e materiali. Giuffrè, Milan, pp 39–40
Chiti E (2010) Trattato di Lisbona. La cooperazione amministrativa. Giorn. Dir. Amm., 241–245
Chiti MP (2011) Lo Spazio amministrativo europeo. In: Studi in Onore di Alberto Romano, vol I. Editoriale Scientifica, Napoli, p 168
Chiti E (2013) La costruzione del sistema amministrativo europeo. In: Chiti MP (ed) Diritto amministrativo europeo. Giuffrè, Milan, p 45 ff
Ciatti A (2012) Postilla sull'attitudine unificatrice del diritto privato dell'Unione europea. Contr. e impr. Europa, pp 180 ff
Cimini S (2016) L'evoluzione dei caratteri degli enti pubblici. In: Cavallo Perin R, Police A, Saitta F (eds) L'organizzazione delle pubbliche amministrazioni tra Stato nazionale e integrazione europea. Pisa University Press, Pisa, pp 365–388
Cocucci V (2008) Nuove forme di cooperazione territoriale transfrontaliera: il gruppo europeo di cooperazione territoriale. Riv. it. Dir. pubbl. comunit., pp 891 ff

Condinanzi M, Lang A, Nascimbene B (2006) Cittadinanza dell'Unione e libera circolazione delle persone. Milan, p 24 ff
Consito M (2009) Accreditamento e terzo settore. Naples
Consito M (2012) L'immigrazione intellettuale. Verso un mercato unico dei servizi professionali. Naples, pp 124 ff
Consito M (2016) Modelli organizzativi d'integrazione europea: il diritto di asilo e la libera circolazione (dell'asilante). In: Cavallo Perin R, Police A, Saitta F (eds) L'organizzazione delle pubbliche amministrazioni tra Stato nazionale e integrazione europea. Pisa University Press, Pisa, pp 579–596
Conticelli M (2012) Privato e pubblico nel servizio sanitario. Milan, pp 76 ff
Costa Cardol M (1989) Ingovernabili da Torino. I tormentati esordi dell'Unità d'Italia. Mursia, Milano, p 210
Costamagna F (2011) I servizi sociosanitari nel mercato interno europeo. L'applicazione delle norme dell'unione europea in materia di concorrenza, aiuti di Stato e libera circolazione dei servizi. Napoli, pp 200 ff
Craig P (2011) Integration, democracy and legitimacy. In: Craig P, de Burca G (eds) The evolution of EU law. Oxford University Press, Oxford, p 17 ff
Craig P (2013) A general law on administrative procedure, legislative competence and judicial competence. Eur Public Law 19:503
Cudia C (2016) Pubblica amministrazione e valutazioni tecniche: profili organizzativi. In: Cavallo Perin R, Police A, Saitta F (eds) L'organizzazione delle pubbliche amministrazioni tra Stato nazionale e integrazione europea. Pisa University Press, Pisa, pp 321–342
D'Angelo F (2016) I modelli organizzativi e la coamministrazione. In: Cavallo Perin R, Police A, Saitta F (eds) L'organizzazione delle pubbliche amministrazioni tra Stato nazionale e integrazione europea. Pisa University Press, Pisa, pp 535–554
Dawson M, de Witte F (2015) From balance to conflict: a new Constitution for the EU. Eur Law J 22(2):204–224
de Leonardis F (2016) Tra leggi di unificazione del 1865 e legge europea sul procedimento amministrativo. In: Cavallo Perin R, Police A, Saitta F (eds) L'organizzazione delle pubbliche amministrazioni tra Stato nazionale e integrazione europea. Pisa University Press, Pisa, pp 511–533
De Vinci G (2016) L'effetto unificante delle relazioni sindacali sull'evoluzione organizzativa delle pubbliche amministrazioni. In: Cavallo Perin R, Police A, Saitta F (eds) L'organizzazione delle pubbliche amministrazioni tra Stato nazionale e integrazione europea. Pisa University Press, Pisa, pp 169–188
Della Cananea G (2009) Procedural due process of law beyond the state. In: Von Bogdandy A, Wolfrum R, von Bernstorff J, Dann P, Goldmann M (eds) The exercise of public authority by international institutions: advancing international institutional law. Springer, Heidelberg, p 965
Dickmann R (2006) Il gruppo europeo cooperazione territoriale (GECT). Foro Amm. CDS, pp 2902 ff
Dimopoulos A (2004) The common commercial policy after Lisbon: establishing parallelism between internal and external economic relations?. In: Croatian Book of European law and policy, vol 8
Donato L (2016) La riforma delle province e le forme di cooperazione tra i comuni. In: Cavallo Perin R, Police A, Saitta F (eds) L'organizzazione delle pubbliche amministrazioni tra Stato nazionale e integrazione europea. Pisa University Press, Pisa, pp 389–406
Drumaux A, Joyce P (2018) Leadership in Europe's public sector. In: Ongaro E, Von Thiel S (eds) The Palgrave handbook on administration, p 121 ff
Engl A (2007) Future perspectives on territorial cooperation in Europe: the EC regulation on a European grouping of territorial cooperation and the planned council of Europe third protocol to the Madrid outline convention concerning euroregional co-operation groupings. European diversity and autonomy papers, pp 5 ff

Esteban J, Mayoral L, Ray D (2012) Ethnicity and conflict: an empirical studi. Am Law Rev 102 (4):1310–1342
Fabbrini F (2013) Enhanced cooperation under scrutiny: revisiting the law and practice of multi-speed integration in light of the first involvement of the EU judiciary. Leg Issues of Econ Integr 40(3):197
Ferrari E (2007) L'uguale libertà del cittadino europeo: linee di frattura della corrispondente concezione nazionale di uguale libertà. Riv. trim. dir. pubbl., pp 931
Franchini C (2013) L'organizzazione amministrativa dell'Unione europea. In: Chiti MP (ed) Diritto amministrativo europeo. Milan, pp 256 ff
Gagliardi B (2009) "Al servizio dell'integrazione": il funzionario pubblico europeo. In: Cavallo Perin R, Police A, Saitta F (eds) L'organizzazione delle pubbliche amministrazioni tra Stato nazionale e integrazione europea. Pisa University Press, Pisa, pp 555–578
Gagliardi B (2012) La libera circolazione dei cittadini europei e il pubblico concorso. Napoli, pp 18 ff
Galetta DU (2010) Diritto ad una buona amministrazione e ruolo del nostro giudice amministrativo dopo l'entrata in vigore del trattato di Lisbona. Dir. amm., pp 601 ff
Galetta DU (2011) Procedural autonomy of EU member states: paradise lost? Springer Science & Business Media, London
Glaser MA (2014) Les relations entre administrations pour l'exécution du droit de l'Union. In: Auby J-B, de la Rochère JD (eds) Traité de droit administrative européen. Bruylant, Bruxelles, p 437 ff
Gnes M (2012) I privilegi dello Stato debitore. Milano, pp 159 ff
Grüner G (2016) Il Prefetto e l'organizzazione amministrativa periferica dello Stato. In: Cavallo Perin R, Police A, Saitta F (eds) L'organizzazione delle pubbliche amministrazioni tra Stato nazionale e integrazione europea. Pisa University Press, Pisa, pp 343–364
Habermas J (2015) Democracy in Europe: why the development of the EU into a transnational democracy is necessary and how it's possible. Eur J Int Law 21(4):546–557
Harlow C (2006) Global administrative law: the quest for principles and values. Eur J Int Law 17 (1):208, par. VI
Harlow C, Rawlings R (2007) Promoting accountability in multilevel governance: a network approach. Eur Law J 13(4):542–562
Hofmann HCH, Schneider JP, Ziller J (eds) (2014) ReNEUAL model rules on EU administrative procedure, book II – administrative rulemaking, ReNeual, www.reneual.eu
Icard P (2003) Le concours d'accès aux écoles de l'administration contesté. Recueil, Le Dalloz, pp 2851
Iliopoulou A (2007) Libre circulation et non discrimination, éléments du statut de citoyen de l'Union européeenne, Bruxelles
Iudica G (2016) L'unificazione attraverso l'organizzazione. In: Cavallo Perin R, Police A, Saitta F (eds) L'organizzazione delle pubbliche amministrazioni tra Stato nazionale e integrazione europea. Pisa University Press, Pisa, pp 107–126
Jowell J (2008) The global economy and the rule of law, Global Law Summit, London, 2015
Kessler F (2003) Formation professionnelle: reconnaissance des diplômes étrangers par les écoles administratives françaises. Revue de jurisprudence sociale:949–951
Lafarge F (2010) Administrative cooperation between member states and implementation of EU law. Eur Public Law 16:597 ff
Lehning PB (2001) European citizenship: towards a European identity?. Law and philosophy. Kluwer Academic Publishers, Berlin
Lottini M (2012) From 'Administrative Cooperation' in the application of European Union law to 'Administrative Cooperation' in the protection of European rights and liberties. Eur Public Law 18:128 ff
Luby M (2004) Chronique de jurisprudence du Tribunal et de la Cour de justice des Communautés européennes. Journal du droit international:584–586
Luzzatto G (1968) L'economia italiana dal 1861 al 1894, Torino, pp 48 ff

Melis G (2004) Gli impiegati pubblici. In: Melis G (ed) Impiegati. Torino, pp 20–21
Melis G (2015) Fare lo Stato per fare gli Italiani, Bologna
Merusi F (2013) Integration between EU law and national administrative legitimacy. Ius Publicum Network Review, n. 2
Merusi F (2015) Consiglio di Stato (all. D) e abolizione del contenzioso (all. E). Amministrare, Issue no. 1/2015, pp 225 ff
Montalvo JG, Reynal-Querol M (2005) Ethnic polarization, potential conflict and civil war. Am Econ Rev 95(3):16 ff
Monti M (2010) A new strategy for the single market – at the service of the European economy and society. Report to the President of the European Commission José Manuel Barroso, 9 May 2010, 62–63
Mori S (2015) Sicurezza pubblica, diritti (all. B). Amministrare, Issue no. 1/2015, pp 91 ff
Muir E (2003) Libre circulation des personnes. Arrêt "Burbaud". Revue du droit de l'Union européenne (3):766–769
Nigro M (1957) L'edilizia popolare come servizio pubblico (Considerazioni generali). Riv. trim. dir. pub., pp 183 ff
O'Leary S (2011) Free movement of persons and services. In: Craig P, de Búrca G (eds) The evolution of EU law. Oxford University Press, Oxford, p 499 ff
Papadopoulou L (2017) 'All Good Things Come in Threes': from a double to a triple democratic legitimacy of the European Union. In: Papadopoulou L et al (eds) Legitimacy issues of the European Union in the face of crisis. Hart Publishing, Oxford, pp 61–94
Pierson P (1994) The path to European integration: a historical institutionalist perspective. Program for the study of Germany and Europe, Working paper no. 5.2
Polsi S (2015) Lavori pubblici (all. F). Amministrare, Issue no. 1/2015, pp 287 ff
Ponce Solé J (2011) EU law, global law and the right to good administration. In: Chiti E, Mattarella BG (eds) Global administrative law and EU administrative law. Relationships, legal issues and comparison, Part 2, pp 133 ff
Pongérard-Payet H (2003) Emploi dans l'administration publique. Reconnaissance mutuelle des diplômes et concours de la fonction publique. Europe, 356, Nov. Comm., pp 23–25
Ponzio S (2014) Joint procurement and innovation in the new EU directive and in some EU-funded projects. Ius Publicum Network Review, n. 2/2014, http://www.ius-publicum.com/repository/uploads/20_03_2015_13_12-Ponzio_IusPub_JointProc_def.pdf
Ponzio S (2016) L'integrazione organizzativa europea nel settore degli appalti pubblici. In: Cavallo Perin R, Police A, Saitta F (eds) L'organizzazione delle pubbliche amministrazioni tra Stato nazionale e integrazione europea. Pisa University Press, Pisa, pp 597–624
Porchia O (2008) Principi dell'ordinamento europeo. La cooperazione pluridirezionale, Bologna
Portaluri G (2016) Il principio d'imparzialità e i modelli organizzativi. Le autorità amministrative indipendenti. In: Cavallo Perin R, Police A, Saitta F (eds) L'organizzazione delle pubbliche amministrazioni tra Stato nazionale e integrazione europea. Pisa University Press, Pisa, pp 301–320
Primerano G, Lamberti L (2016) Il principio di efficienza ed i modelli organizzativi: le agenzie amministrative. In: Cavallo Perin R, Police A, Saitta F (eds) L'organizzazione delle pubbliche amministrazioni tra Stato nazionale e integrazione europea. Pisa University Press, Pisa, pp 283–300
Rabinovici I (2012) The right to be heard in the charter of fundamental rights of the European Union. Eur Public Law 18(1):149 ff
Racca GM (2014a) Nuove prospettive per l'aggregazione dei contratti pubblici nel contesto europeo. In: Fernandez Acevedo R, Valcarcel Fernandez P (eds) La contratacion publica a debate: presente y futuro. Civitas, Cizur Menor, pp 455–492
Racca GM (2014b) Presentation in the conference Appalti Pubblici: innovazione e razionalizzazione. Le strategie di aggregazione e cooperazione europea nelle nuove Direttive, Roma, Council of State, 14.5.2014, in Ius Publicum Network Review, http://www.iuspublicum.com/repository/uploads/18_11_2015_18_40_Atti_del_Convegno_Consiglio_di_Stato_14_05.pdf

Racca GM (2014c) Joint procurement challanges in the future implementation of the new directives. In: Lichère F, Caranta R, Treumer S (eds) Modernising public procurement: the new directive. Djøf publishing, Copenhagen, p 225 ff

Racca GM (2015) Le centrali di committenza nelle nuove strategie di aggregazione dei contratti pubblici. In Italiadecide Rapporto 2015, Bologna, pp 489 ff

Racca GM (2017) Gli accordi fra amministrazioni pubbliche: cooperazioni nazionali ed europee per l'integrazione organizzativa e l'efficienza funzionale. Diritto amministrativo XXV(1):101 ff

Racca GM (2018) The role of the third parties in the execution of public contracts. In: Folliot-Lalliot L, Torricelli S (eds) Oversight and challenges of public contracts. Bruylant, Bruxelles, p 415 ff

Racca GM, Cavallo PR (2011) Organizzazioni sanitarie e contratti pubblici in Europa: modelli organizzativi per la qualità in un sistema di concorrenza. In: Pioggia A, Civitarese Matteucci S, Racca GM, Dugato M (eds) I servizi sanitari: organizzazione, riforme e sostenibilità. Una prospettiva comparata. Maggioli Editore, Rimini, pp 193–215

Racca GM, Cavallo Perin R (2014) Corruption as a violation of fundamental rights: reputation risk as a deterrent against the lack of loyalty. In: Racca GM, Yukins CR (eds) Integrity and efficiency in sustainable public contracts. Balancing corruption concerns in public procurement internationally. Bruylant, Bruxelles, pp 23–48

Ragno F (2008) Convenzione di Vienna e diritto privato europeo. Padova

Ranelletti O (1904) La polizia di sicurezza. In: Orlando VE (ed) Primo trattato completo di diritto amministrativo italiano, vol IV. Milan, pp 263, pt. I

Romeo A (2016) Il modello dell'azienda per le amministrazioni pubbliche. In: Cavallo Perin R, Police A, Saitta F (eds) L'organizzazione delle pubbliche amministrazioni tra Stato nazionale e integrazione europea. Pisa University Press, Pisa, pp 407–420

Rostagno F (1887) Contabilità di Stato, Corso Teorico-Pratico sull'attuale sistema contabile del Regno d'Italia, Milan, 36

Saitta F (2016) L'organizzazione delle pubbliche amministrazioni e lo Stato nazionale: i profili evolutivi. In: Cavallo Perin R, Police A, Saitta F (eds) L'organizzazione delle pubbliche amministrazioni tra Stato nazionale e integrazione europea. Pisa University Press, Pisa, pp 37–66

Saltari L (2007) Amministrazioni nazionali in funzione comunitaria. Milan, pp 23 ff., and 249 ff

Sánchez-Lorenzo SA (2013) Common European sales law and private international law: some critical remarks. J Private Int Law 9:191 ff

Sandholtz W, Stone Sweet A (1997) European integration and supranational governance. J Eur Public Policy 4:298 ff

Sandulli A, Vesperini G (2011) L'organizzazione dello Stato unitario. Riv. trim. dir. pubbl., 2011, p 47 ff

Santi Romano (1918) L'ordinamento giuridico, Pisa. 2nd ed. 1946, then in L'ultimo Santi Romano, Milan, 2013, p 138 ff

Schulze R, Stuyck J (eds) (2011) Towards a European contract law. Munich

Schwarze J (2012) European administrative law in the light of the Treaty of Lisbon. Eur Public Law 18:285 ff

Soresina M (2015) Sanità pubblica (all. C). Amministrare, Issue no. 1/2015, 179 ff

Spaventa E (2007) Free movement of persons in the European Union, barriers to movement in their constitutional context. Alphen Aan Den Rijn, pp 113 ff

Spolaore E (2013) What is European integration really about? A political guide for economists. J Econ Perspect:125–144

Spolaore E (2014) The political economy of European integration. In: Badinger H, Nitsc V (eds) Handbook of the economics of European Integration. Routledge, p 3 ff, https://sites.tufts.edu/enricospolaore/files/2012/08/The-Political-Economy-of-European-Integration.pdf

Spolaore E, Wacziarg R (2009) War and relatedness. National Bureau of Economic Research, Working paper no. 15095

Stelkens U (2014) Vers la reconnaissance de principes généraux paneuropéens du droit administratif dans l'Europe des 47? In: Auby JB, Dutheil de la Rochère J (eds) Traité de droit administrative européen. Bruylant, Bruxelles, p 731 ff

Sutherland P (1992) The internal market after 1992: meeting the challenge. Report presented to the Commission by the High Level Group on the functioning of the Internal Market, 28.10.1992

Taylor MC (2001) The moment of complexity. Emerging network culture. The University of Chicago Press Book, Chicago, p 245 ff

Tigano F (2016) Organizzazione dell'ordine pubblico. In: Cavallo Perin R, Police A, Saitta F (eds) L'organizzazione delle pubbliche amministrazioni tra Stato nazionale e integrazione europea. Pisa University Press, Pisa, pp 265–282

Tosatti G (2015) Sicurezza pubblica, organizzazione centrale e periferica (all. B). In Amministrare, Issue no. 1/2015, pp 91 ff

Trimarchi M (2011) L'art. 41 della Carta europea dei diritti fondamentali e la disciplina dell'attività amministrativa in Italia. Dir. amm, pp 537 ff

Trimarchi Banfi F (2007) Il diritto ad una buona amministrazione. In: Chiti MP, Greco G (eds) Trattato di diritto amministrativo europeo, vol I. Giuffrè Editore, Milan, p 52

Van de Walle S (2018) Explaining citizen satisfaction and dissatisfaction with public services. In: Ongaro E, Von Thiel S (eds) The Palgrave handbook of public administration and management in Europe. Palgrave Macmillan, London, pp 227–241

Vesperini G (2011) Vincolo europeo e diritti nazionali. Milan, pp 67 ff

Weiler JHH (2012) In the face of crisis: input legitimacy, output legitimacy and the political messianism of European integration. J Eur Integr 34:826

Weiler JHH (2017) United in fear – the loss of Heimat and the crises of Europe. In: Papadopoulou L et al (eds) Legitimacy issues of the European Union in the face of crisis. Hart Publishing, Oxford, pp 359–378

Chapter 3
Evolution of the Principles and Rules on Administrative Activity

Carlo Marzuoli

Contents

Abstract The chapter analyses the most significant aspects of the evolution of the discipline of administrative action and relations between public administration and citizens in Italy, over the last 50 years. The changes concern the conception of the public interest and administrative discretion, the implementation of the principle of legality, the centrality of the administrative procedure, the wider use of powers and acts of private law, the rules designed to allow greater efficiency in the exercise of various types of control of private activities, the "new" rights (participation in the

C. Marzuoli (✉)
University of Florence, Florence, Italy

D. Sorace et al. (eds.), *The Changing Administrative Law of an EU Member State*,
https://doi.org/10.1007/978-3-030-50780-0_3

procedure, transparency of public administration, the right of access), and the civil liability for unfair damages. The author points out that there are still shortcomings and contradictions in Italian administrative law, but that it is deeply changed and improved, because it is more respectful of the values of the Italian Constitution and of European Union law.

3.1 Introduction

The most important administrative laws of the Kingdom of Italy (1861) were issued in 1865. Those were Law No. 2248 of 22 March 1865, including seven attachments, and Law No. 2359 of 25 June 1865, on expropriation on grounds of public utility.

Such laws were the subject of the Centenary Conference held in Florence in 1965. In the past century, two events of great significance took place: firstly, the transformation of the Italian State from monarchy to republic (1946) with the signing of the new Constitution (1948); and secondly, the gradual establishment of European legal systems (1951–1957).

Yet by 1965, 17 years after the new Constitution was introduced and eight since the Treaty of Rome, administrative law, as it concerns powers, acts and activities, remained unchanged from the tradition inherited from the laws of 1865. Regarding the aspects in question, the Constitution was largely bypassed, despite many scholars having highlighted its particularly innovative character. As for Community law, this had yet to gain any significant presence and therefore received little attention.

The next 50 years were characterised by a slow but continuous discovery and penetration of the principles and norms of the Constitution (first) and of European Law (later). There are two basic paths, and they cross often: the reconsideration of the institutions and fundamental notions of administrative law (with respect to administrative power, procedure, relations with citizens and new rights and responsibilities) and the use of private law models for governing the activity of public administrations.

The most influential points of reference are: the principle of legality; the principle of sound administration (Article 97 of the Constitution), the principle of impartiality (also Article 97 of the Constitution); the principle of publicity and the principle of transparency; the principle of due process; the principles of reasonableness, proportionality and reliability; the principles of good faith and of correctness; the principle of subsidiarity; the principle of *neminem laedere* (not causing unjust damage unto others, Article 2043 of the Civil Code); the principles of Community law (today European) to which the fundamental law regarding administrative activity refers, Law No. 241 of 7 August 1990 (*New rules concerning administrative procedure and right of access to administrative documents*).

Many of those principles derive from tradition, but have seen more extensive and incisive developments; others are new or relatively new; some are written (as in the aforementioned Law No. 241/1990),[1] while others are not. They come to the fore at different times, sometimes slowly, other times more quickly thanks to legislative intervention and the rulings of judges by which they are made explicit (or created) and translated into "living" law: the Constitutional Court, the European Courts (Court of Justice and General Courts, the European Court of Human Rights), administrative judges (Council of State and Regional Administrative Courts, the Court of Auditors to some extent), the Supreme Court and ordinary judges. Factors that differ but which, setting aside any conflicts and shortcomings, all lean towards the configuration of a "Law of Public Administrations" following the title of a known handbook.[2] The following paragraphs give a brief outline of the most significant moments and issues concerning the evolution in question, before highlighting the current trends.

3.2 Private Interests, 'Public' Interest, Administrative Discretion; the Shift in Focus from Act to Procedure

Administrative discretion has taken on a role that is more complex, but at the same time more truthful and useful.

The Constitution attributes importance to conflicting rights and interests, such as national sovereignty, but it also limits national sovereignty to ensure "peace and justice among nations" (Article 11 of the Constitution); freedom and security; health, environment and economic development ("sustainable" development); economic freedoms and social rights; balanced budgets and public services, and much more. The public interest that must be satisfied in individual events and in the exercise of individual powers does not exist in nature. Rather, it is the result of a choice, with an ever-increasing number of variables; it stems from a comparison between innumerable interests, both public and private, and the administration has an obligation to take into account all relevant interests in a reasonable and proportionate manner.

The centre of the decision-making moment expands and moves. Originally the focus was on the final administrative act, whereas now it is shifting towards the administrative procedure. Administrative procedures have always been around. Some were very detailed and complex, such as those pertaining to expropriation for public utility (introduced with the aforementioned Law No. 2359/1865), or to public property, planning law or public contracts. In the 1930s, several scholars

[1] Or even in regulations concerning certain activities and entities, as in Law No. 180 of 11 November 2011 (*Rules for protecting the freedom of enterprise. Company statute*), which, on the subject of relations between public administrations and companies, cites (Article 9): the "principles of transparency, good faith and effectiveness of access to administrative documents, information and services"; the "criteria (...) of economy, effectiveness, efficiency, timeliness, impartiality, equal treatment, proportionality and publicity", of reduction or elimination, and "where possible" of "formal and bureaucratic burdens".

[2] Sorace (2000).

recognised the importance of the notion of procedure,[3] and in 1940 a fundamental study was published[4] which allowed for further progress. However, the substantial importance of the procedure[5] was only fully acknowledged after the signing of the Constitution. Procedure became an intrinsic feature of administrative power; the term "principle of procedure" was coined with the idea that every administrative power has a procedural side. This was to provide a way in for affected parties and their assessments, needs and requests, and to make the reasons behind administrative decisions both transparent and visible, with the resulting implications in regard to checks (administrative, judicial, public opinion) and protection. In short, procedure emerged as the most appropriate foundational approach to introducing general rules on administrative activity.

3.3 Introduction (by Law) of the General Procedure Model (1990); Cornerstones (Time, Conclusion Method, Dedicated Office)

In 1990, thanks (also) to the commitment of scholars of administrative law, including Mario Nigro, President of the Commission appointed to set-up the project,[6] the general rules on administrative procedure were finally issued in the form of Law No. 241/1990. The turning point was important both per se, and because it opened up a path that could not be stopped. With the regulation of procedure, as well as several other highly important aspects (agreements, § 5), general regulations on the essential nature of powers and acts of the administration would become inevitable. This happened 15 years later with Law No. 15/2005, which introduced new provisions within that law (as we will see).

The cornerstones of the model. Three points of relevance, not just procedurally but substantially, in that they affect important aspects of the relationship between administration and private individuals.

In the past, procedures could last indefinitely, with no given date of conclusion except in individual cases; the affected party was forced to take further steps in order for a conclusion date to be set (invitation to act), which was essential, among other things, to be able to seek protection from a judge. The implicit measure was also deemed admissible with a certain ease, i.e. taken from an act intended for a different effect or even deduced from a fact. Finally, in the absence of an established legal rule, one could often conclude—by interpretation—that justification was not necessary for certain types of acts.

[3]Forti (1931) and Miele (1933).

[4]Sandulli (1940).

[5]Benvenuti (1952), Giannini (1961, 1970), Pastori (1964), Berti (1975) and Cassese (1970).

[6]Nigro (1990).

The new law changes the picture. Each procedure must have a pre-fixed term (Article 2); the procedure must conclude (principle of the "express measure", Article 2) with the issuance of a measure corresponding to the specific power exercised (but the same law provides for extended exceptions, § 8); the act must be justified, with the exception of regulatory acts and general acts for which justification may be given but is not required (Article 3).

Such justification and the measure expressed represent the codification of principles created by case law. However, the provision on the term is new.

It enables affected parties to know when the uncertainty deriving from the pending procedure will end. Not only that: on conclusion of the procedure, the affected party is able to appeal to the court seeking the issuance of a measure and to request compensation for any damage caused by the delay, the latter being introduced more recently (now Article 2-*bis*).

The opening of the procedure to the affected parties (to be discussed, § 4), the complexity of the situations to be faced, the heterogeneity and conflict (often) of the interests to be satisfied and the principle of impartiality mean the preliminary phase and the decision-making phase need to be kept as separate as possible. At the same time, there is a need to create a new type of office: the officer in charge of the procedure (Articles 4 et seq.). This officer is tasked with implementing and governing preparatory and preliminary activities[7] and keeps all loose ends together to prevent the distribution of activities between offices from causing delays and inefficiencies (Article 4 et seq.).

Meanwhile, it is important to encourage and facilitate contact between the administration and affected parties if effective participation is to be achieved, while it is equally important to designate a person, and not some vague office, to whom any questions regarding the pending procedure may be addressed. This is the other face of the procedure manager; to this end, government organisation is regulated in such a way that the employee assigned to the role is identified automatically.

The manager concludes the preliminary phase and issues the results; if the body responsible for issuing the final measure intends to depart from the results, it must justify its decision.

The set of rules governing the preliminary investigation is small, and derives mainly from the principles and tasks of the procedure manager. Impartiality (Article 97 of the Constitution) requires gathering all necessary elements to reach a lawful and appropriate decision (if the power is discretionary). However, the principle of sound administration must also be taken into account and the law itself prohibits aggravation of the procedure. The gathering of preliminary elements is governed by the principle of inquisition. The administration must establish—beyond the connection to what is indicated by the parties involved—the facts to be ascertained and the means to prove them, save any contrasting legislative indications. However, the role of the principle tends to diminish, especially in proceedings initiated by a party.

[7]This office may be the same body responsible for issuing the act.

Opening up the procedure to affected parties and offering them the opportunity to become equally involved are grounds for extending the costs of introducing and proving any facts of interest to them.

The situation differs in part when it comes to independent administrations: the preliminary phase is widely regulated, especially with regard to consultation, participation and defence phases.

3.4 The Players Involved: Administrations and Private Entities (Participation)

Besides in certain procedures (e.g. concerning penalties, urban planning), the main player has typically been the holder of power, i.e. the administration or multiple administrations (§ 8).

With Law No. 241/1990, implementing the principle of "due process" and the participation of individuals and communities, the administration's decision is open to participation of the affected parties. Individuals become active players in the procedure, having the right to intervene and to represent their interests. However, this model does not apply to procedures for issuing "regulatory, general administrative, planning and programming" acts or to tax procedures: in these cases, their specific governing laws are applied (Article 13).

The new players fall into one of two categories depending on how their interests relate to the power exercised by the administration.

Those with directly affected interests (e.g. the recipient of the measure) have the right to participate and to receive a specific procedure commencement notice (Article 7). And for proceedings initiated by a party, they are entitled to an additional notice. On conclusion of the preliminary phase, the administration, should it consider there to be "grounds preventing acceptance of the claim", before deciding, must communicate such grounds to the affected party so that he may reassert his reasons prior to the final decision (Article 10-*bis*).

Then there are those whose interests are not directly affected but who may be harmed by the issuance of the measure (Article 9): these entities may participate, but are not entitled to receive a procedure commencement notice. It should be noted that those with widespread interests (i.e. interests held separately by multiple individuals: an interest in protecting the environment, health, etc.) may participate, but on the condition that they form committees or associations.

Implementation of these rules faced significant resistance. The administrations were not prepared; the available resources had not been increased to meet the new demands and an adequate administrative culture was still lacking. And several case law guidelines from the administrative judge helped to support these practices.

In the system described, the ordinary citizen ("*quisque de populo*") has no place. The original text of the Nigro Commission provided for a "public inquiry", i.e. holding assemblies that were open to all, but this proposal was not accepted.

However, anyone is allowed to participate in sector proceedings—especially on environmental matters—in implementation of European directives and international agreements or according to regional laws, laying down forms of public consultation and public inquiry.[8]

Law No. 241/1990 also provided that those involved in procedures may enter into agreements with the administration; participation in the process can also become participation in the constitution of the act: see the following paragraph.

3.5 An Alternative to the Unilateral Administrative Act: Exercising Administrative Power Through Agreements

The issuance of an act is the standard form of concluding procedures. This explains why we find, in the original text of Law No. 241/1990, a provision of particular interest with respect to acts.

Administrative power is generally characterised by having effects on other subjects without the need for their consent. However, since the nineteenth century, in pursuing the public interest, the administration in some cases adopted acts that would require private-party consent (for example, concessions of public services, concessions of state property, acts which make up the public service relationship, etc., town planning agreements). The traditional principle that public power could not be the subject of an agreement with private parties prevented (especially in case law) such events from being classed as contractual events. This allowed the administration to maintain a position of supremacy over the ensuing legal relationship and to retain in particular broad powers of revocation (see § 6). The most followed concept was that of the "concession contract": for example, the relationship between an administration granting the use of part of a beach (state property) and the private beneficiary required to pay a fee was governed by two acts: a unilateral administrative act (the decree of concession) and the contract (under which certain obligations were established between the parties). The contract was legally dependent on the administrative concession act, meaning that by revoking the unilateral act the administration could terminate the relationship. This is in the absence of a general principle providing for compensation, which would only be made possible through a specific set of regulations.

From the 1960s on, a legal culture increasingly inspired by constitutional values, the supporting role of the principle of legality, a public interest seen as increasingly conforming to the Constitution (§ 2), as well as certain norms and principles of

---

[8]Legislative Decree No. 152 of 3 April 2006 (*Rules on Environmental Matters*), Articles 24, 24-*bis*; Legislative Decree No. 50 of 18 April 2016 (*Public Contract Code*), Article 22. A particularly interesting model is also given in Tuscany Regional Law No. 46 of 2 August 2013 (*Regional public debate and promotion of participation in the drafting of regional and local policies*).

European Law, led to a reduction of government privileges. And Law No. 241/1990 substantially overturned the traditional principle discussed above.

Article 11 states that administrative discretionary power exercised through the procedure may end either with the issue of the unilateral administrative act or, preferably, with the signing of an agreement with the private parties concerned (except in certain proceedings).[9] The agreement may be of a "replacing" nature (producing the same effect as the unilateral administrative act) or "supplementary" (predetermines the discretionary content of the administrative act which must then be issued in execution of the agreement itself). "To guarantee the impartiality and sound administration of the administrative action" it must be preceded "by a resolution of the body (...) responsible for adopting the measure" and "must be properly supported" (Article 11 of the law cited above).

The agreements are subject, "unless otherwise provided, to the principles of the civil code regarding bonds and contracts, where compatible" (Article 11 of the law cited above). However, the law expressly provides that, for reasons of public interest, the administration may invoke "unilateral termination" (considered an administrative act of revocation, § 6). In any such case it shall be required to pay "indemnity" for any detrimental damages caused to the private party (Article 11 of the law cited above).

Finally, a more widespread use of consensus in relations between administrations—a system well known and accepted for some time—is allowed both for the performance of public works (scheduling agreements, recently opened to the participation of private individuals)[10] and for "governing the collaborative performance of activities of common interest" (as stated in Article 15).

3.6 A Second Step: Introduction (by Law) of General Rules Governing Powers and Unilateral Acts of the Administration, in Particular Powers of Supremacy

The administration and its activity have always been subject to the principle of legality, to be understood according to two distinct profiles: (a) the need for a law to acknowledge the existence of an administrative power of supremacy, describing its basic aspects (assumptions, purpose, competence, procedural elements: principle of typicality); (b) the obligation to pursue the aims indicated by the law, irrespective of the nature of the activity to be carried out.

---

[9]Such as the proceedings for issuing "regulatory, general administrative, planning and programming" acts as well as tax procedures (Article 13 of the law cited above).

[10]The agreements have highly complex objects; they are used to coordinate and organise different skills in relation to the pursued goal and for making decisions that could alter specific acts pertaining to individual administrations.

In 1965, at the time of the Centenary of Law No. 2248 of 22 March 1865, this principle had not yet been properly implemented. There was a need not only to adopt a general procedure model (§§ 3-4), but also to address other issues.

As a result of the 2005 amendments (§ 3) there is now a set of general regulations governing the validity of the measure (Article 21-*bis*, 21-*quater*) and the power of the administration to suspend it (Article 21-*quater*), as well as the power to forcibly fulfil (Article 21-*ter*), without the intervention of the judge, the obligations imposed by a previous measure (destruction of illegal work, collection of administrative fines, etc.). This last power is not a normal feature of the administrative measure but a power in its own right, which exists only in the cases provided for by law.

Also laid down are two general powers that clearly underline a position of supremacy (of privilege) of the administration: the power of revocation (Article 21-*quinquies*) and the power of automatic annulment (Article 21-*nonies*).

According to tradition, a discretionary administrative act was, by nature, deemed revocable for reasons of expediency by the same body that issued it. This is without compensation, except in individual cases. Scholars and case law had limited the extent of that power: it (usually) referred to acts that generated lasting relationships and gave greater weight to the principles of reliability and proportionality. But such power was still too broad and, in any case, devoid of a regulating provision under which it would be assigned to the administration. This is no longer the case: the power in question is the subject of a specific legislative provision (the aforementioned Article 21-*quinquies*), is more limited, and in any case carries a compensation in relation to "damages" suffered by the private party.

The same guideline applies to the power of automatic annulment. This power, assigned to the body and referred to its own administrative act which is deemed unlawful, requires two conditions: the illegitimacy of the act and the feasibility of annulling it. Thus it is a discretionary power. Even this power was considered to exist beyond specific statutory provisions; an act merely had to be an administrative act—and not even a discretionary one—in order to be used. A further significant aspect was that there was no given deadline for annulment. Today there are general legislative foundations, several specific regulations and, above all, a deadline. This must be "reasonable", in accordance with criteria already applied by case law, and must not exceed (in certain cases) 18 months. There is still no provision on compensation.

3.7 Public Intervention and Private Entity Activity: Recourse to the Replacement of Authorisations with Powers of Successive Control

The principle of subsidiarity requires that public authority intervention with respect to individual freedoms and activities is admissible only if necessary for reasons of public interest, and with as little interference as possible.

Where there are specific and exhaustive regulations over the conditions required for the exercise of activity, the model consisting of a declaration by the interested party in lieu of an authorising measure—a model already present in the legislation—has been increasingly used, including in implementation of European law. Today, the most relevant example of this is the "*Segnalazione certifica di inizio attività-Scia*" (Certified notice of commencement of activity, or "SCIA") (Article 19 of Law No. 241/1990, cited above). Once the declaration has been communicated, along with any technical certifications by private professionals, activity may commence. The administration will quickly be able to ascertain whether the legal requirements are met and, if not, may order the situation to be rectified (if possible) or the cessation of activity and restoration of the original situation. Once this term has elapsed, the only power left for the administration to use is that of automatic annulment, which requires (as mentioned) an assessment not only of legitimacy, but of suitability.

This model presents several problems. This is not a "technical" simplification (such as the elimination of objectively superfluous documentary or procedural obligations), but an alternative distribution of risk between conflicting interests, i.e. a choice of policy. The authorisation system is largely set up for the protection of the public interest entrusted to the administration: where there is no authorisation, even if its refusal is unlawful, the activity cannot be carried out. However, the system in question favours the interest of the person looking to carry out the activity. But not without limits: the law prevents application of the model when it comes to public interests of particular importance (landscape and environmental constraints, security, citizenship, etc.).

However, there is no shortage of doubts. There is the issue of other potential parties, holders of an interest that conflicts with the exercise of the activity. The authorisation model contains a measure (the authorisation) that they can challenge; in the new model, there is no such measure. So they now have to take further steps: in short, the pathways to protection are more complicated.

There's more: in reality, there are risks for those directly affected. The issuance of authorisation in fact means greater assurance that the intended activity will be compliant with the law. This is certainly more reassuring, as it gives the administration recourse to the power of automatic annulment. Under the "SCIA" model, there is no such provision.

3.8 The Need for Results: Complexity of the Administration, Administrative Dysfunction and 'Simplifications' (Silence, Procedural Simplifications, Conference of Services)

Evolution has placed more focus on the principle of sound administration. Public institutions that fail to meet their targets generate distrust and detachment. In recent decades the formula of the "result-focused" administration has become widespread. There have been repeated legislative interventions, especially in pronounced cases where administrations have faced material difficulties caused by a decline in human and financial resources. Recalled below are several events that can be variably traced back to this perspective, and which can be assessed in very different ways: silences, procedural simplifications, and "decision-making" rather than merely preliminary conferences of services.

Silences.

Administrative silence in response to private sector claims has posed serious problems. In the absence of a term for the conclusion of a procedure, the first requirement was to know how to transform silence, or inertia, into something legally relevant in order to appeal to the judge. At the time of the Centenary, there was still no satisfactory solution.

It took many years for a real change to take place, with an amendment to Law No. 241/1990, when the legislator expressly established that the expiry of the term mentioned above (§ 3) automatically implies the formation of a legally relevant silence (Article 2).

The second requirement concerned the significance to be attributed to the silence.

In proceedings initiated by a party, tradition placed the claimant at risk of dysfunction and attributed to the silence the refusal of the requested measure. In the eighties, with the model becoming increasingly widespread and eventually the main point of reference, "*silenzio assenso*" emerged, equating silence to acceptance of the application (Article 20).

The risk of administrative dysfunction is again shifted from the person directly affected to the public interest and to other parties to the proceedings. This again raises issues already seen (§ 7). If the proceeding concerns specific public interests (health, cultural and landscape heritage, defence, cases in which European law imposes a formal measure, and many others), assent by silence does not apply; opposing parties may appeal against it, but the lack of a measure implies a lack of support, and it may be more difficult to dispute what happened; the administration retains powers of automatic annulment and even of revocation (which raises even more doubts); without an express measure, it is not easy to invoke reliability.

Finally, it should be noted that extending the scope of application of the silence (denial or assent) is a form of reneging on the promise according to which the procedure concludes with an express decision (§ 3).

Silence related to acts within the proceeding.

In the context of a wider trend aimed at simplifying the procedure, other hypotheses have been introduced. Of particular note are the opinions and technical assessments some administrations are required to make within a proceeding.

To avoid paralysis of the proceeding, if an opinion is not received within the agreed term, the proceeding must or may continue, depending on the different hypotheses (Article 16 of Law No. 241/1990). Once again: none of this applies when it comes to opinions concerning public interests of particular value (environment, landscape, health).

Technical assessments (Article 17 of the law cited above) must be obtained regardless, and may be requested from another public institution or from university institutes.

Decision-making conference of services ("*Conferenza di servizi decisoria*").

Another route for an administration to put together a measure is through a decision-making conference of services, aimed at coordinating and expediting the exercise of public powers (Articles 14 to 14-*quinquies*). It is a fragmented and complicated set of regulations. The basic (simplified) aspects are outlined below.

In order to carry out an activity or to construct a (complex) project, it is often necessary to obtain acts and secure decisions that fall under the jurisdiction of multiple bodies or public entities. The administration primarily affected arranges a conference to which each affected administration is called to participate. The procedure is regulated in such a way as to favour seeking a shared solution, e.g. stipulating that the dissent of one or more administrations shall not prevent the conclusion of the procedure. Dissent is particularly important if it is expressed by an administration that holds public interests of special importance ("*protection of the environment, landscape/territory or cultural heritage or protection of public health and safety*", Article 14-*quinquies*) and may be overcome by referring the matter to the Council of Ministers.

As can be seen, regulating the procedure can sometimes result in derogating from the ordinary distribution of responsibilities between administrations. This poses delicate problems, especially when the entities involved are public bodies with constitutionally guaranteed autonomy.

A specific position of assent by silence between administrations and public service operators was introduced in 2015 (Article 17-*bis* of Law No. 241/1990). It concerns acts of varying importance (assents, agreements or clearances); competent administrations must provide their consent within a certain term. Once the term expires, consent is understood to be given. Where there is a lack of agreement between state administrations, decision-making duty passes to the President of the Council and to the Council of Ministers.

The law in this case does not reproduce the limit imposed by significant public interests: the only limitation is the fact that, in specific cases, the European Law imposes a decision through an express measure.

This model raises many doubts in terms of its scope of application, especially with respect to the conference of services (which reproduces many aspects).

3.9 The Current Face of the Invalidity of the Administrative Act (Nullity, Invalidating Illegitimacy)

The system of invalidity of the administrative act was based on illegitimacy/annullability, and therefore on the issues of incompetence, violation of the law and abuse of power, as provided in Law No. 5992 of 31 March 1889, marking the emergence of the administrative judge.

Nullity was a doctrinal creation, adopted in reference to the commission of private party acts (contracts, above all: lack of essential elements, violation of mandatory norms). Norms that referred to it were rare and were often thought, despite using the term "nullity", to provide for annullability.

This was (and still is) a further consequence of the principle of supremacy. The administrative act pursues the public interest (a greater interest), therefore it must remain in effect until it is annulled by a given authority (the administration itself or the judge).

Since 2005 the picture has changed.

A positive regulation on nullity exists. This is useful per se. However, the provision (Article 21-*septies* of Law No. 241/1990) follows the situation having emerged from case law and, with respect to the protection needs of private parties, according to some makes it worse.

Yet the newest and most important point is one based on the traditional principle of preservation of legal acts and that of the "result-focused" administration.

The provision (Article 21-*octies* of the law cited above) states that not all legitimacy issues are grounds for annulment, i.e. there are "non-invalidating violations".

When the measure is adopted "*in violation of the rules on the procedure or on the form of the acts*", it must not be annulled in the presence of these conditions: if the act pertains to the type of non discretionary acts and it is "*clear*" that "*the decision content could not have been different from the one specifically adopted*". Moreover, if the violated provision is that on the notice of commencement of the proceeding, the act, even where it is of a discretionary nature, it must not be annulled if the administration "*demonstrates in court that the content of the act could not have been different from the one specifically adopted*".

The provision prioritises the need to uphold the substantial result, if it appears to comply with the law. These are in fact said to be "formal" issues. Yet, sometimes, the rules of procedure are attributable to specific rights, such as the provision requiring notice of commencement of the procedure. Thus the problem emerges of finding some form of reaction that protects these rights.

3.10 Transparency and Rights of Access

The general principle that characterised the legal system under ordinary legislation was professional secrecy, besides special secrets such as state secrecy. Professional secrecy was applied in an exasperated manner. It often forced the recipients of a measure to lodge an appeal without first knowing the elements (facts, documents) based on which the administration had made its decision.

With the right of access to administrative documents introduced by Law No. 241/1990 (Articles 22 et seq.), another reversal occurred: secrecy became the exception, and *knowability* the rule.

However, the regulation in question attributed the right of access only to those who had an individual interest in being aware of documents that were not public per se.

Once the barrier to secrecy fell (save some exceptions), one of the most delicate issues concerned the theory whereby the conflict was not, in fact, with the administration. The administration could be in a position of indifference with respect to the requested document, whereas the real affected party was the private entity to which the document referred (another participant in a competition, a neighbour seeking to build, etc.).

The subsequent adoption of the general framework for the protection of privacy (now Legislative Decree No. 196/2003) introduced some level of order. Prevalence was given to the right of access, except where the document contained "data likely to reveal a state of health or sex life" ("super-sensitive" data); in this second case, the right of access prevailed only "where the legally significant situation for which protection was sought with the request for access to administrative documents was at least equivalent to the rights of the affected party, or consisted of a right of personal status or any other fundamental or inviolable right or freedom" (Article 60 of Legislative Decree cited above and Article 24 of the cited law).

However, this right of access did not adequately fulfil the principle of transparency (the administration as a 'glass house') as it limited the right of access to subjects with individual interests. The ordinary citizen was not entitled to demand access, except in cases provided for by industry laws, and especially those related to the environment.

The legislator is then supposed to intervene with the aim of preventing and containing corruption. Indeed, it provided for a series of cases in which data and documents held by the administration must be published (Legislative Decree No. 33 of 14 March 2013, *Restructuring of regulations concerning the right of public access and the obligations of publicity, transparency and dissemination of information by public administrations*). This is the best system for implementing the principle of transparency. Anyone has the right (right of "*public access*") to take legal action to demand that the data be published (Articles 3 and 5.1 of the aforesaid decree).

The law, however, cannot provide for all data meriting publication. It therefore introduced, with reference to the US Freedom of Information Act model, another type of "*public access*" (Article 5.2): the right of anyone to be informed of any additional data and information held by the administration beyond that required to be published, notwithstanding certain limits. And it is the administration that must assess whether or not such limits exist, on a case-by-case basis.

3.11 Principles Governing the Relationship Between Administrative Acts and Powers and Private Acts of the Administration

The administration exercises its activity with administrative powers or with the capacity and powers of private law; it may pursue the public interest through activities and acts of private law. It has already been seen that principles of the Italian Civil Code can even help establish the framework of the act concluding the process for exercising a public power (agreements, § 5).

There are two fundamental problems: for any given act of the administration or of a private entity exercising an administrative activity, it must be ascertained whether it is under administrative or private law, as well as identifying, assuming it is an act of private law, any administrative rules and principles connected to it.

The legislation broadened the use of the unilateral act of private law by the administration and broadened the use of consensual models. This took place in the field of administrative organisation, transforming the employment arrangement of many categories of civil servants into a working relationship governed by private law, along with a general amendment to Law 241/1990. This, following the additions made by the aforementioned Law No. 15/2005, restructured the entire framework of relations between administration, administrative act and private law.

The pattern is thus (Article 1(c)1-*bis*): (a) the "*authoritative*" act is always an administrative act; (b) the non-authoritative act, i.e. a type of act that can be issued by any private individual, is to be classified as an act of private law, "*unless the law provides otherwise*". Thus, non-authoritative acts are in principle of a private nature.

But the situation is more complex than it appears. The significance and the usefulness of the notion of "authoritativeness", for the purpose of the problem at hand, are increasingly debated. Meanwhile, private law acts are nearly always adopted in relation to administrative procedures; one of the most notable cases, also under European law, is that of public contracts (project procurement, works, services, supplies). The general characteristic principles and criteria of the administration are set out in Law No. 241/1990 for general administrative action. This raises the question concerning their relevance and their implications when the administration handles private law acts. Finally, in Italy, the nature of the act is often relevant to determine whether jurisdiction lies with the administrative judge or the ordinary judge, and this aspect can (although it should not) affect the answer to the question regarding the nature of the act.

3.12 Civil Liability for Unfair Damage and a Victory for Civilisation

In addition to contractual liability, the administration is also traditionally expected to hold non-contractual civil liability. Any unlawful act attributable to the administration carries the obligation to pay compensation for the damage. Since 1948 this has been guaranteed by the Italian Constitution; according to Article 28, the State and all public bodies are responsible for damages caused to citizens by their officials and employees.

In the past, the scope of responsibility was very small.

One early obstacle derived from a common interpretation of the sphere of administrative discretion. In individual cases (for example, damage caused by non-maintenance of roads, damage from public service activities, general damage from material activities of administrations), some aspects of the issues to be addressed were considered discretionary and their presence was considered to obstruct the assignment of blame. As a result, the administration was exempt from liability.

This attitude has changed gradually over the years, and especially in the second part of the last century; there is one prevailing view which, based on the rights afforded to citizens under the Constitution, specifically identifies areas in which there is discretion, on an individual basis.

The second obstacle, far more radical and broader in scope, concerned the distinction between individual right and legitimate interest within the Italian legal system. Compensation would apply only to violations of individual right, not those of legitimate interest. However, the legitimate interest is the individual situation that typically exists in relations with the administration when it exercises public powers and in particular discretionary powers. Thus, the illegitimacy of the administrative act had no effect on the compensation for damages, except in some infrequent cases.[11] Conclusion: a large part of administrative activity was removed from civil liability. This was a further manifestation of the traditional idea of the natural primacy of public interest, and not of a primacy admissible only if founded by and within the limits of the law.

In the early 1960s, the issue of compensability following the violation of legitimate interests had begun to draw attention, yet case law in particular showed no signs of change. In the years that followed, in light of a further examination of constitutional principles following the gradual introduction of principles and norms

[11]These were cases in which the administrative act sacrificed an interest which, before the act was issued, was to be qualified as an individual right: for example, the right of an owner subject to a decree to occupy his property. In such cases, if the act was illegitimate, its annulment could be obtained from the administrative judge. The annulment took effect *ex tunc*; therefore—it was said—following the annulment, the situation reverted to an individual right and was thus compensable. What occurred could in fact be legally qualified as a *de facto*, untitled occupation, as if it had been done by any private individual.

of European law, as a result of the legislation, and in particular Law No. 241/1990 and the introduction of the procedural model mentioned above, the relationship between private individuals and the administration began to change. The relationship was increasingly characterised by the principle of legality, along with consequent reduction of the principle of authority to an extent compatible with the rule of law; the attribution or recognition of new rights; and a different conception of the relationship between the weight of public interest and the weight of private interests.

The criticisms became heavy. In 1999, the United Sections of the Italian Supreme Court passed ruling No. 500, overturning the guideline followed up to that point rendering the violation of a legitimate interest compensable, which was later consolidated by the legislation.

However, the Supreme Court set a limit to prevent the mere illegitimacy of the act from being sufficient to assign responsibility to the Administration. The general norm of reference (Article 2043 of the Civil Code) requires the element of negligence; the judge found that, when the damage resulted from an unlawful administrative act, the illegitimacy per se was not equivalent to the presence of negligence. Negligence required additional elements of proof.

The near-20 years of this century represent our first experience under this new principle and with the various issues that have arisen, especially with respect to the attribution of negligence (i.e. of what it may consist) which, by virtue of European law and the case law of the European Courts, is sometimes not required, and to the identification and quantification of damage. In any case, another story has begun. Once the legitimate interest is accepted as compensable, the question begs itself as to whether the distinction at the heart of the issue—between individual right and legitimate interest—is still useful, and if so, to what extent.

3.13 Where We Are

There are many other issues and aspects that need to be addressed. I am referring to the transformations brought about by changes concerning administrative organisation; by the distinction (since the nineties) between policy and administration; by the broad use of regulations, directives, guidelines and standards; by the privatisation of employment for most civil servants; by the introduction (under European law) of the public law body model; by the creation and multiplication of independent authorities; by the use of public companies; by the increasing impact of "technical" aspects and bodies; by the certifying role adopted by private professionals; by the [ongoing] "digitisation" of the administration, and by the various and often debatable "short cuts" with which we have tried to simplify or enlighten the governance of administrative activity (§§ 7-8).

But we can't do it all. We can only try to summarise and bring to light the underlying trends.

Here's a first. All activity, powers and acts of the administration are subject to constitutional principles and, to a much broader and deeper extent, European law, compared to our reference point (1965). The points raised in the previous paragraphs show that the system as a whole seems to be stabilised, notwithstanding some undesirable political upheavals in relations between (or within) the States of the Union.

From having the central administrative power as the authority (as an expression of supremacy over citizens) we have shifted to seeing administrative power as merely a function (dutiful exercise of powers and activities in the interest of citizens, where authority is only a means to an end), and this first and foremost translated into the centralisation of procedure.

These perspectives have increasingly placed focus on the conviction that administrative law should be viewed as the rights granted to citizens by the Constitution, by European law and by national laws. It is significant that the introduction of the general model of administrative procedure has led to the creation of specific rights, such as procedural rights (to receive a procedure commencement notice, to participate, to meet deadlines), or to the assignment of other rights, such as that of access to administrative documents (generally provided, even in the absence of a pending procedure). It is even more significant that many of those rights and others referred to above (§ 12) are confirmed in what will later become European law: we need merely look at the "*Right to good administration*".[12]

Meanwhile, this progress and this rebalancing between administration and affected parties raises the issue of equal treatment, with a position that goes against tradition: that of individual obligations to the administration with respect to their activity during proceedings and their relationship with the administration (obligations of correctness, truthfulness and good faith).

A second trend is the gradual intertwining of administrative law and private law. § 11 mentioned the widespread use of private law norms and principles. The problems still under discussion are many, and vary in scope. Many scholars believe that the use of private law powers could over-sacrifice the "functional" nature of administrative activity (i.e. its use for other public purposes), and it could simultaneously reduce guarantees for citizens. This would be due to the lower limits applicable to private law powers with respect to discretionary power and to the more widespread (legal) irrelevance of interests which, in the traditional framework of administrative law, would be relevant: for example, those of the opposing party, of the holder of the widespread interest and of potentially any other subject.

Other scholars note that private law is also changing: individual freedom is not what it was in the past (having become increasingly limited by fairness, good faith, abuse of rights), while industry laws (consumers, users) provide for rules aimed at

[12]Article 41 *Charter of Fundamental Rights of the European Union:* Every person has the right to have his or her affairs handled impartially, fairly and within a reasonable time (...) This right includes: the right of every person to be heard, before any individual measure which would affect him or her adversely is taken; the right of every person to have access to his or her file (...); the obligation of the administration to give reasons for its decisions. (...) 3. Every person has the right to have the Community make good any damage caused by its institutions or by its servants in the performance of their duties.

rebalancing the position of the weaker party. Private law also avoids granting privileges to the administration without a legal basis (being non-justifiable, of which there have been many in the past), providing greater stability and mutual responsibility in relations between the administration and those involved, and thus making it an appropriate instrument for ensuring the sound performance of the administration.

It is an open discussion, but a change has already occurred. At least in terms of administrative activities, traditional "Administrative Law" has been replaced, as anticipated (§ 1) by the "Law of Public Administrations". It is a law that unites the principles, norms and concepts of common private law with those of special law. But unlike in the past, special roles carry a different tone and other implications: they are now derived, limited and governed by the rules and constitutional values that govern the relationship between citizens and public authorities.

This representation seems to be the most current and the most useful. The extent to which the legal role according to its representations (the "ought") matches the actual course of events poses another problem altogether.

References

Benvenuti F (1952) Funzione amministrativa, procedimento, processo. In: Benvenuti F (ed) Scritti giuridici, vol II. Giuffrè, Milano, 2006

Berti G (1975) Procedimento, procedura, partecipazione. In: Studi in memoria di Enrico Guicciardi. Cedam, Padova

Cassese S (1970) Il privato e il procedimento amministrativo. In: Archivio Giuridico

Forti U (1931) «Atto» e «procedimento» amministrativo. In: Studi di diritto pubblico in onore di Oreste Ranelletti, vol I. Cedam, Padova

Giannini MS (1961) Lezioni di diritto amministrativo. Roma

Giannini MS (1970) Diritto Amministrativo, vol II. Milano

Miele G (1933) Alcune osservazioni sulla nozione di procedimento amministrativo. In: Miele G (ed) Scritti giuridici, vol I. Giuffrè, Milano, 1987

Nigro M (1990) Il procedimento amministrativo fra inerzia legislativa e trasformazioni dell'amministrazione (A proposito di un recente disegno di legge). In: Nigro M (ed) Scritti giuridici. Giuffrè, Milano, 1996

Pastori G (1964) La procedura amministrativa. Introduzione generale. In: Pastori G (ed) Scritti scelti. Jovene, Napoli, 2010

Sandulli AM (1940) Il procedimento amministrativo. Giuffre, Milano

Sorace D (2000) Diritto delle amministrazioni pubbliche. Una introduzione, I edn. Il Mulino, Bologna

Chapter 4
Unity and Fragmentation: The Italian Public Administration

Aristide Police

Contents

Abstract The public Administration is moving towards models in which a single center of government is replaced by a myriad of other ones inhabited by a variety of actors, relationships and interactions. New centers were born both on the world or continental plan and at national and local level, where there is an increase of the importance of subnational governments such as regions, municipalities and especially large cities. To facing a growing importance of the local dimension, as a place of citizenship, identity and subjectivity, the traditional model of administration based on institutional centralization and hierarchical relations, no longer seems sufficient to tackle problems related to the complexity and fragmentation of the modern society. In fact the model of traditional hierarchy, in which a single subject—the institution responsible for decisions—intervened in the formulation and implementation of public policies, is replaced by a network model based on the cooperation between the multiple public and private entities, State and *non-State* actors who appeared on the scene. The tendency, new and unstable, is that of a territorial rebalancing of political powers and of their actions, as well as the relations between politics and society. This essay, referring to the Italian experience, will focus on models of public

A. Police (✉)
L.U.I.S.S. University, Rome, Italy
e-mail: apolice@luiss.it

D. Sorace et al. (eds.), *The Changing Administrative Law of an EU Member State*,
https://doi.org/10.1007/978-3-030-50780-0_4

management, in a process of isomorphic type, behaviors and organizational structuring typical of the private sector along with other hybrid organizational forms based on intermediation and trust policies. The theme of governance and its effects will be finally taken into consideration at the level of local governments and policies that the latter are called to deal with and manage.

4.1 Preface

According to a common definition in Italian Administrative Law, the public Administration as an administrative organization identifies a 'pre-established structure composed of offices, and corresponding powers' (Scoca 2001). The definition is based on the realistic consideration according to which every human community expresses not just its own interests, but also the interests of its individual components. Because each of these interests deserves to be nurtured and protected to an equal degree, there is a need to create certain structures specifically designated for the purpose (Sorace 2018). The series of structures created to satisfy the interests of a human community constitutes what is commonly defined as the public or administrative organization. The dimension of the organizational systems responsible for the protection of interests of the general public depend on the greater or lesser complexity of the human community to which they relate. This applies despite the fact that administrations always present the same basic organizational structures, which are conventionally usually referred to as public 'offices'. The series of offices, created to achieve the collective public interests, thus form the public *apparatus*.

The public administration can therefore be defined as a series of Offices (i.e. basic structures) responsible for performing the administrative function, namely an activity intended to take care of public interests. More specifically, the expression 'public administration' indicates that system of authorities, agents and bodies to which the general legal system entrusts the protection of the public interests. This generates a coordinated system of people and resource organized to achieve certain general objectives (Giannini 1970).

According to Article 1 (para. 2) of Legislative Decree no. 165 of 30 March 2001 within the administrative Organization have to be included 'all State administrations, including institutes and schools of all kinds and levels and educational institutions, independent State corporations and administrations, Regions, Provinces, Municipalities, Mountain Communities and their *Consortia* and Associations, Universities, Independent Public Housing Agencies, Chambers of Commerce, industry, crafts and agriculture and their Associations, all national, regional and local non-economic public Authorities, the Administrations, Institutions and Entities within the National Health System, the Agency for Public Service Bargaining Representation and the Agencies regulated by Legislative Decree no. 300 of 30 July 1999'.

For the purposes of this paper, it should be noted that the Italian administrative Organization has profoundly changed over time (Cassese 1982). From an original design that tended to bring the organization of the public Administration within the general framework of the State, it has gradually moved towards a pluralistic system, which, rather, makes a distinction between the State and non-State administrations. This latter term, in particular, indicates the administrative organization that is not directly controlled by the State, but by other subjects that still have a public function.

Therefore, this essay will be focused on these transformations rather than on the analysis from a structural view point of the aspects relating to the morphology of each administrative body, and it will be an inquiry into the causes of the evolutions of their internal and external dynamic relationships. A journey along the path that starting from a single public Administration (coming out from the unification process of the Country in a single Nation and in a single State) is running towards a significant fragmentation into many public Administrations (if not a fragmentation of the Nation and of the State) (Giannini 1979; Cassese 1993).

The analysis that will be developed in the following pages regards the dramatic change occurred to Italian public Administration starting from the analysis of transformations on the ground of governance. To facing a growing importance of the local dimension, as a place of citizenship, identity and subjectivity, the traditional model of public Administration based on institutional centralization and hierarchical relations, no longer seems sufficient to tackle problems related to the complexity and fragmentation of the modern Society (Benvenuti 1996). The model of traditional hierarchy, in which a single subject intervened in the formulation of/and policy implementation—the public institution responsible for decisions—is replaced by a network model based on the cooperation between the multiple public and private entities, State and non-State actors who appeared on the scene (Cerulli Irelli 2004).

Starting from 1980s, a new way of doing government emerges and a different conception of public Administration is affirmed, where the models of behavior and the influences of the institutional context assume relevance in defining the same administrative organization (March and Olsen 1989).

There are different forms and models of governance: from those that are more market-oriented to those originating from the Community that are based on a different type of authority and different relationships, as well as on a different conception of public action (Powell 1990; D'Albergo 2002).

This essay, referring to the Italian experience, will analyze the models of new public management adopted by the public Administration, in a process of isomorphic type, behaviors and organizational structuring typical of the private sector along with other hybrid organizational forms that are based on intermediation and on so-called trust policies (Pollit and Bouckaert 2004).

Finally, the theme of governance and its effects will be taken into consideration at the level of the local governments and at the level of policies that the latter are called to deal with and manage.

4.2 The Organization of the Public Administration in the Italian Constitution

A short background of the Constitutional framework within which this process is taking place is in any event necessary for a better understanding of the current evolution of the Italian model of public Administration.

The Constitution of the Italian Republic does not contain many provisions that relate directly to the administrative organization. The few provisions that deal with the issue, however, allow to reconstruct a model of administrative organization, based on the breakdown of the public system taken as a whole, and characterized by the coexistence of State and non-State public bodies. Article 5 of the Constitution firstly enshrines the ‘principle of autonomy’, confirming that ‘The Republic, one and indivisible, recognizes and promotes local autonomies, and implements the fullest measure of administrative decentralization in those services which depend on the State (Esposito 1954). The Republic adapts the principles and methods of its legislation to the requirements of autonomy and decentralization’ (Ambrosini 1944; Bartole and Mastagostino 1971).

To fully understand the meaning of this provision, it is necessary to read it in conjunction with Article 114 of the Constitution, whereby ‘The Republic is composed of the Municipalities, the Provinces, the Metropolitan Cities, the Regions and the State’ (para. 1), notwithstanding the fact that the ‘Municipalities, Provinces, Metropolitan Cities and Regions are autonomous entities having their own statutes, powers and functions in accordance with the principles laid down in the Constitution’ (para. 2) (Berti and De Martin 2002; D’Atena 2001).

On the basis of the combined provisions of the Constitution stated above, it emerges clearly that the Republic is divided into Regions, Provinces and Municipalities, which are all equivalent to the State. It follows that these public entities may be (and, in fact, often they are) the holders of a specific political and administrative policy, which might even conflict with that of the State. This is important in relation to the issue of the administrative organization (Giannini 1972). The reaffirming of the principle of autonomy in fact means that the general administrative organization must necessarily adapt to the many institutional entities in which administrative policy is developed and it must therefore be structured according to a model based on the principle of pluralism (De Martin 2006, 2007; Mangiameli 2002).

The picture described above has moreover been enriched following the amendment to Title V, Part Two, of the Constitution, where it is stated that the ‘Municipalities, Provinces and Metropolitan Cities carry out administrative functions of their own as well as the functions assigned to them by State or by regional legislation, according to their respective spheres of competence’ (Article 118, para. 2 of the Constitution). They are also recognized as having ‘revenue and expenditure autonomy’ (Article 119 para.1 of the Constitution) so that they can ‘fully finance the public functions attributed to them’ (para. 3)¸ and ‘their own assets, which are allocated to them pursuant to general principles laid down in State legislation’ (para. 2) (Vandelli 2010).

That said, it should in any case be noted that the constitutional model of the administrative organization is not precisely depicted, and, in fact, an analysis of the individual provisions of the Constitution shows at least three different models of Administration (Guarino 1977; Giannini 1988).

The first model has been taken from a systematic reading of Article 95 of the Constitution, whereby the 'Prime Minister conducts and holds responsibility for the general policy of the Government. The Prime Minister ensures the coherence of political and administrative policies, promoting and coordinating the activities of the Ministers'. These latter are in turn 'collectively responsible for the acts of the Council of Ministers and they are individually responsible for the acts of their own ministries'.

Article 95 of the Constitution therefore seems to authorize a reading of the relationship between the executive power and the administrative organization in terms of a strict subordination, including in organizational terms, of the latter to the former (Zanobini 1938; Virga 1958).

If we analyze Article 97 of the Constitution, however, the public law theory reaches different conclusions. According to the provision in question, 'public offices are organized according to the provisions of law, so as to ensure the efficiency and impartiality of administration'. This constitutional provision seems to assert a principle diametrically opposed to that enshrined in Article 95, namely the principle whereby the administration is rigidly subject only to substantive law. In organizational terms, the application of the principle of legality under Article 97 of the Constitution must make it possible for public systems to perform their functions adequately, avoiding any influence by political powers (Scoca 2017; Sciullo 2014).

The picture described above then became even more problematic with Italy's membership of the European Union. There are currently many sectors of the Italian Legal System where administrative decisions are no longer made internally, but, rather, at EU level. This has inevitably resulted in the creation of organizational structures, in which EU and national levels overlap in the joint performance of administrative activities (Bulmer 1994).

This organizational model, correctly defined as the 'EU Administration', obviously clashes with the other two models already examined.

Finally, the organizational model of the public Administration that emerges from the Italian Constitution is a composite, polycentric model, in which numerous centers coexist in the development of administrative strategies. The Italian Constitution applies the principle of institutional pluralism and it confirms the existence of a range of institutional entities, both State and non-State, in which administrative policy intended for the governance of the community can be formulated (Berti 1968; Benvenuti 1956).

4.3 The Complexity of the Administrative Organization

The Entities entrusted with the administrative functions and the provision of public services can ideally be distributed on a horizontal line articulated by functions and skills and, at the same time, on a vertical line articulated by territorial competences, a line that starts from central Administration and branches off to peripheral units and local territorial bodies. However, the distribution of entities by territorial jurisdiction does not determine hierarchy or autonomy relationships which, instead, depend on the nature of the administrative entities.

At national level, the management of public functions and services is entrusted: (a) to the State whose organization is divided by functions and depends directly on the Government and the Ministries; (b) to national public bodies (*Enti pubblici*); to administrative agencies (*Agenzie amministrative*); (c) to independent Authorities (*Autorità amministrative indipendenti*); (d) to Companies with public ownership (*Società pubbliche*) (Torchia 2009; Franchini and Vesperini 2015).

At regional level, the management of public functions and services is entrusted: (a) to the Region whose organization is divided by functions and it depends directly on the Regional Government; (b) to other public bodies: administrative Agencies and Companies with regional ownership; (c) to local or territorial offices of the State administration and/or other national administrative structures.

At municipal level, the management of public functions and services is entrusted: (a) to the administrative structures of Municipalities (*Comuni* or *Città Metropolitane*), Provinces, and Other minor local Authorities; (b) to other public bodies, administrative Agencies and Companies with municipal or local ownership; (c) to local or territorial offices of the State administration and/or other national administrative structures.

This picture highlights the fragmentation of the Public Administration, which is further complicated by the multiplicity of the organizational structures of the single Entities. The administrative entities can, in fact, take the form of: (a) a Ministry or Department, the main organizational units of the state administration controlled directly by the Government; (b) a national public Entity (*Ente*), generally with legal personality, its own management bodies (usually a president and a board of directors appointed by the government), autonomy in directing its offices and setting management objectives, while supervision and political address depends on the government; (c) an Administrative Agency, with no legal personality, but with budgetary, organizational and functional autonomy and with its own management bodies (general manager, management or management committee) and internal control (board of auditors, management control body), subject to the power of direction and supervision of the competent minister who agrees on the objectives and results to be achieved, the financial resources, the procedures for verifying the operating results; (d) an independent Administrative Authority that is characterized not only by the management autonomy of independence from political power; (e) a local public Entity with functional autonomy which is characterized both by sectoral specialization and by the limited competence of a given territorial area; (f) a local public territorial Entity (Regions, Provinces, Municipalities, Cities) which is characterized by the high degree of autonomy being the directing bodies elected directly by citizens or through secondary elections; (g) public Companies (Scoca 2017).

The complexity of the public Administration and its articulation at the State, Regional and Local levels led to the creation of coordination structures (the Unified Conference, the State-Regions and State and local Governments Conferences) (Antonini 2009; Anzon 2002).

4.4 Flexibility and Fragmentation: Towards a New Model

The great changes brought about by historical and structural factors that are happening in the contemporary Italian society on the ground of Governance put us ahead of one question to be explored: that is, if we are witnessing the disappearance of the function of the public Administration and the undeniable loss of weight of the public Administration itself; or, rather, if we are witnessing a process—difficult and impervious, but also full of opportunities—of reconversion of the role and public functions of the public Administration. Do we assist to the irrecoverable decline of the State or, more simply, are we facing with one of its own transformations towards new arrangements? The decline of the monopoly of politics and administration of the national State, in Italy, nourishes the debate on the new models of regulation of public policies and on the transition from *Government* systems to *Governance* systems (Mayntz 1999).

The *formula* "from government to governance", as it is well known, indicates the process that leads to the weakening of the traditional bases of political power and of the institutional force of the Nation State as well as the disappearance of the powers of government of the public Institutions that have operated, especially in the last century, according to one topical logic and based on rigid schemes and self-referential drift. The emptying of the State due to one of his internal restructuring that loses on the ground the centralization of functions towards one greater articulation and fragmentation of government functions, on the ground supranational and local level (Moreau Defarges 2003; Pierre and Peters 2000; Kooiman 1993).

In the Italian experience, *Government*, which contains all the elements of a vision of the traditional and static bureaucracy, considered as a set of institutions and as a model of hierarchical and centralized government, is deeply in crisis (De Valles 1931; Forti 1948).

At the beginning of the twentieth century, the public Administration appeared as a perfect machine. The Public bureaucracy with its rational organization well embodied together with the great industry from the vertical and integrated hierarchy and rationality. An organizational model founded on simple and clear rules that punctuate each behavior and action, were the fundamental elements to guarantee the maximum predictability of the action with respect to the environment (Melis 1996; Nigro 1966).

In the era of mass production, growth and industrial development, the mechanical and rational model of the public Administration found its legitimacy: Companies and public Administration could be organized like aseptic machines, incontrovertible.

The same people were considered to be like mechanisms, gears that contributed to the functioning of the system, obeying the orders imposed from above. It was the era of mass democracy, of low-skilled labor force, which overlooked the business world for the first time since the second industrial revolution, often farmers from agriculture and immigrants (Weber 1922).

This model, which over time has been changing and also applying in distinct manner, depending on the contexts and individual administrative cultures, obviously fails to have the same reason to be in the post-industrial era, in a phase of the cycle defined as fragmentary in which the society is characterized by being de-structured, individualized and increasingly differentiated. This process is very well perceived in the Italian experience that is moving to a new model of public Administration based on the concept of "administrative flexibility" that is the result of the changes underway in the economic, productive and social system (Sepe et al. 2003).

The new Italian *Scenario* is that of a public administration that expands and it expands both to horizontal level, creating new Services and new Sectors of public policies, and vertically through the push towards the regionalization of public powers with the creation or greater responsibility attributed to local Government, and the globalization with the creation of supra-national Government (Cassese 1985).

This is how it was born a galaxy of semi-autonomous Institutions that rises problems of integration in consideration of the profound differentiation in terms of legal forms of action and purpose: a new set of institutional Bodies and sectorial Policies, connected in a loose way (Bobbio 2002).

This process of evolution is accompanied by the process of streamlining, which affects it same entrepreneurial world, at least in the industrialized countries, and that involves the public administration that tends to "lose weight" and to imitate behaviors typical of the private and that we could say in short, it becomes post-bureaucratic. This is why, also in the Italian reforms of the last two decades, we began to speak, of "new management" (or "privatization") of the administrative Organizations and of the administrative action, along with the processes of contracting out and outsourcing the provision of goods and services. Actions of imitation of the traditional entrepreneurial model that, while investing the public Administration and its organization, seldom are able to produce more quality and cost-efficient results; these new models instead of focusing on quality, flexibility and cooperation, often reinforced bureaucratic mechanisms and procedures, hierarchies and decision-making processes top-down (Di Gaspare 1995).

The Italian rhetoric of these past years tended to envisage this passage as "a moment of change" from the old *Government*, set on hierarchical values and authoritative to the new *Governance*, based on the values of competitiveness, efficiency—effectiveness—economy and self-government (Cerulli Irelli 2017). As if the new public management was implicitly good, while the old one was implicitly bad.

The concept of *Governance*, in addition to be among the most abused and ambiguous one and to enclose distinct meanings, in itself it does not contemplate, in fact, a positive action or successful results of regulation, but on the contrary, these last ones must be continually searched and prosecuted according to the institutional configuration within which the *Governance* itself finds space. Furthermore, among the Italian Scholars, it is necessary to be very careful not to reduce the concept of *Governance* to a managerial technique, strictly adhering to the descriptive plan to avoid an ideological drift (Falcon and Marchetti 2013).

4.5 Rhetoric, Mythologies and New Model of *Governance*

To understand the changes occurred and ongoing in the Italian public Administration it seems necessary an analysis of the rhetoric of administrative models and public action regimes. Behind the new adjustment models, in fact, there are cognitive and cultural dimensions, systems of shared beliefs, rhetoric and "*rational mythologies*" that are at the basis of regulatory provisions, interpretative processes and social construction. Rhetoric that also declined in practical knowledge and instrumental solutions giving life to competitive and sometimes even incompatible models, often used as theories absolute, as one best way. Rhetoric that have followed over time up to now and which have made changes from the terrain of languages and communication codes (Bobbio 1995).

After the war, in years of reconstruction, the theme of the bureaucratic reform of the public Administration was the password transmitted by the political classes through a legal language. The reforms took place through the adoption of new regulations and it was precisely on this rational legal basis that the legitimacy of this model was founded. The parameter to evaluate the administrative action was that of the legal appropriateness (the compliance with the law) and the strict adhesion to the rule became, in fact, the goal to pursue (Melis 1996; Marongiu 1988).

Malfunctions, bureaucratic slowness, ritualism were the consequent corollaries. This model, well described by the metaphor of the pyramid whose regulation was of type bureaucratic-hierarchical, was based on authority and institutional centralization. Rigidity and immobility have been recognized and criticized as negative characteristics of the model, equally prominence has never been given to quality, on the contrary positive, like continuity, impartiality, neutrality, honesty and a high attention to the equity of the relations with citizens (Scharpf 1993).

For all the 1960s and 1970s, instead, there was a rhetoric that exalted all that it was public intervention and planning: the superiority of the State ownership of the enterprise oriented towards social aims represented an undisputed common place. The language used was in this case of an economic nature while the renewal of the public Administration found its rhetoric in the speeches related to programming State. The model was that of a planned administration, an administration that provided services and public services, through the nationalization of private industries (electricity, railways, etc.), re-launching the idea of the State ownership. A model that already, giving broad background to all the available resources, contained in itself the prodromes for the emergence of the next corporate model of public Administration. In this model, attention stands out the apology to what is public: during the glorious thirties the State maintains the reins of command and controls are still firm (Treves 1977).

Starting, however, from the 1980s, with the emergence of neoliberal conservative policies in Great Britain and in the United States begins the crisis of the public that appears to be over and put on the other hand in favor of all that is private initiative. The effects of these policies in the following decade in Italy led to containment of public spending, reduction in welfare spending and policies, in favor of a boost to privatization of public production activities and the liberalization of monopolies.

This change of attention is explained not only on the ground of economic policies measures adopted as a response to the critical situation in public finance, but also starting from a different conception of the individual and his aspirations oriented towards achievement of a higher degree of autonomy (Giannini 1959). In the context of public Administration this push towards everything that is private, finds its own equivalent in the "managerial model" process, or in the imitation within the Public Sector of *criteria* and principles of a business type, not only in those sectors directly involved in the production and supply of goods and services to citizens, but also in areas such as the justice, taxation, security.

The form of the relationships is no longer dual or predominantly dual; it now fits the figure of the supplier that radically changes the relationship between public Administration and citizens. From the culture of legality and planning it passes to that of the result, which increases the functions of public control to the detriment of the provision of services and autonomy, reducing the citizen to customer and consumer and at the same time exalting the attention of the public Administration in his comparisons as a reference point to be taken into consideration (Benvenuti 1994).

Currently the model proposed by the rhetoric is that of a shared or participated Administration or a style of policy that favor horizontal networks, partnerships. A deliberative style that pushes, beyond the citizens and shareholders towards inclusiveness, a series of specific and widespread stakeholders. In fact, different operative and operational *formulas* are developed, administrative procedures oriented towards partnership, negotiation and mediation between public and private subjects that target citizens, understood not as individuals but as a Community (Cassese 2001).

The goal becomes that of solving problems, overtaking a perspective oriented to the control of the instances of the reference groups. The rationality on which these changes are based has procedural nature and it insists on transversality, dialogue and horizontal connection to carry out projects specific on defined subjects, otherwise poorly integrated and disarticulated. Rhetoric becomes crucial for the speeches related to the promotional functions of the public Administration, citizens' requests for participation and the push for self-government of civil society. None of the models has been made in a pure way, however, in the documents related to the reforms of the public Administration and in the structures of public Organizations. These models play an important role in creating the rhetorical dimension of the Reform. Even those who support a particular cultural vision must confront the forces of tradition, *inertia* and harsher opposition (Donolo 2006).

In fact, statements, decisions and actions often diverge. To make innovation, in fact, it is necessary the rhetoric with its hierarchical character of relationship and transmission from top to bottom meetings, dialogues, exchanges ideas with the persuasion that is the discourse that comes from below with its characteristics of uncontrolled subjectivity. The change is not only dictated from the outside and from above but it is recognized and shared also by the organizational base (Bifulco and de Leonardis 2002; Bifulco and Vitale 2005).

If indeed the regulatory change is programmable, relatively timely and it leads to the approval of norms with the consequences that the prescriptiveness implies (above all initially), the socio-cultural change is a long-lasting process that requires local practices processed to respond to a change from the environment or from within administration. Cultural innovation is like a local interpretation of a message inspired by center or another local area and therefore it is configured as a "testing" process, verification, reinterpretation and correction, learning and only at the end of this complex process one can speak of acquisition aside administration. The rhetoric of change, in fact, for its hierarchical nature of social relationship that moves along the high/low line even if it can be systematic and coherent in the treatment of issues, however it is born "alien" and difficult to internalize by the organizational subjects. It is for these reasons that to speak today of participation (there are now many devices that are put in place and that they involve a multiple universe of subjects. Think of Tables, *Consortia*, Authorities, mixed public private Agencies that were born in Italy or still to Agreements, Pacts, Cards, Conventions, etc.) *per se*, while certainly expressing a new conception of administrative action and of the relations between the public Administration and the citizens, it is not necessarily an index of innovation and change of the public Administration *tout court*. In fact, it is necessary to check in practice the conditions, effects and the nature of these paths, the institutional framework in which participation and inclusiveness are implemented and of course the role of the public Administration and the change trigged by these processes (Benvenuti 1994).

4.6 Negotiation vs. Regulation in the New *Governance*

Although the managerial model is currently inspiring the reorganization of many sectors of the public Administration and the redesign of the same public function in Italy, there is no doubt that many of such experiences based on a participatory model are taking place especially in certain areas (local) and for certain matters of public policies, such as urban redevelopment, welfare policies, the cultural sphere, the local development, etc.

It is very interesting to question on what are the main changes that have favored this change in the styles of regulation of public policies by pushing the public Administration to adopt increasingly and in a massive way these models of "inclusive" type rather than others (Rhodes 1997).

After the international crisis of the 1970s there was an interruption of the economic development which had started after the Second World War which resulted in the Welfare State crisis (in its configuration of the Keynesian State of a universalistic kind). The crisis of the Welfare State manifests itself according to three new *Scenarios*: as a fiscal crisis, a crisis of effectiveness and a crisis of equity.

The first, due to a disproportion between the increased and unexpected demand for public goods and services by citizens, due to the increase in risks and social economic insecurity, and the increasing costs to support it. This is a financial crisis, which has deprived the State of many of its governmental abilities and, inevitably, it has determined a reduction in public spending and a search for alternative ways to achieve economic savings. From this very reason there was a relevant growing interest towards private and individualistic solutions as well as the recognition of the economy and of the market as a superior mechanism for allocating resources (Police 2002; Le Galès 2002).

The second crisis is related to the performance and effectiveness of public welfare Institutions whose responses did not manage neither to eliminate old poverty and to contain new ones, nor to produce services fit to citizens' expectations and needs.

This crisis has led to a loss of legitimacy of the centralized administrative model and top-down decision-making structure, resulting in a swing of public policies and legislative reforms towards outsourcing and other solutions entrusting services to the private sector and to the no-profit sphere. The direct consequence of this crisis was also the sharpening of symptoms of dissatisfaction and loss of confidence of citizens towards the public Administration considered inadequate to give specific and concrete answers (Bobbio 1996).

Finally, the equity crisis affecting the related difficulties in the fair redistribution of resources that have contributed to further undermining the legitimacy of public welfare institutions (and in a second stage of the public Institutions at large).

The welfare state crisis undoubtedly reverberates on the rethinking of the role of the State central government and its public function; both in the direction of saving public resources from one side and, on the other side, of an expansion of new forms of responsibility involving the civil society and the market, which begin to erode decision-making spaces, once exclusive prerogative of the central State. Naturally the solutions adopted by the various Countries were different, according to the assertion of different ideologies. The neoliberal one in the Anglo-Saxon world (the U.S. with President Reagan and Great Britain with the Baroness Thatcher's Government at the very end of the 1970s and at the beginning of 1980s) introduced economic policies finalized to minimize the influence of the State, delegating to the market with its competitive mechanisms many functions, up to the answer of the continental European countries that have tried the way of the welfare mix or welfare community or forms of cooperation between state, market and third sector. In the Italian perspective this change was softer (and very distant from the neoliberal rhetoric), but the shift towards the market and the private sector was significant as well.

Another important factor that encouraged changes in styles of regulation, going in the sense of greater integration and cooperation, was undoubtedly the influence and the orientation expressed by great transnational subjects towards the nation States.

The OECD and the European Union, in a context of scarcity of resources and increasing complexity of the problems, exerted pressures of both type cognitive and normative, pushing the different Countries to adopt new tools and rules geared towards governance and involvement of external actors (Benington and Geddes 2001). The goal these Institutions wanted to achieve with the introduction of such kind of post-bureaucratic regulation of public policies was to "reduce uncertainty of decision and implementation processes [in order to] make public programs not only less expensive and more effective, but also more governable" and to do that the road that was indicated was the one leading towards the experimentation of "technologies" of decisions making and management more appropriate than those adopted during the welfare State years.

Finally, the evolution of the administrative State was accompanied by the change that involved public policies that have been looking for greater legitimacy, effectiveness and relevance to the problem solving: a new culture of the performance. The citizens were now asking to solve problems; the evolution of policies accompanied that of the administration of the State, with a greater importance and role of a negotiated public function in the satisfaction of social demand of public goods and services.

The elements that influence this relationship, the future of public policies and the change of role of the State and of the public function are changes that influenced the Italian public Administration as well as the world scene. This globalization process implies and has led to the erosion of the powers and autonomy that the nation States inherited from modernity. This process was a boost to the "marketization" of the public Administration and to the dramatic shift to administrative models adapted by imitation from the economic sphere, such as liberalization policies, legislation on privatization and commercialization of the public function and the creation of private markets once exclusive monopoly of public supply of goods and services.

The processes of Europeanization, that like earlier mentioned have included national Administrations in networks and multi-level transnational Institutions, favored the implementation of these complex and integrated programs, policies and constraints (Richardson 1996).

The complexification of public policy actors and the push towards subsidiarity, along the periphery-center institutional axis, was made possible through the creation of hybrid models, plots and networks involving a multiplicity of different public Subjects and Entities. In this process of transformation that connects strictly the evolution of public policies with the need for innovation of the public Administration, took place reductions and enlargements of the Public Sector (the public *Arena*), involving regulation as well as the public planning activities. The policies that require, in fact, greater integration to respond to the increased complexity of the society and of the collective needs were transforming the national public Administration (and the Italian public Administration was no exception to this process) to become more and more articulated, multi-purpose, multilevel and able to incorporate social interactions and inclusive practices (Bassanini and Castelli 2008; Castelli 2011). This of course changes their nature and their quality: they will always be more integrated, complex, interdependent and global, but also aimed at enhancing the value and the ability of the subjects to the self-enactment, on the principles of subsidiarity and sustainability (Cassese 2001).

The Public Function was changing in the same direction in this period, simply removing and canceling the old conception of a centralized administrative State and the bureaucratic management model. More than a crisis of the Public Function we should speak of evolution. The classical model established in the past century was, in fact, replaced by a constellation of organisms differentiated by types and functions, strongly intertwined with economic, social, technical and scientific tools (Scoca 2017).

The unitary model of the State bureaucracy evolved in a post-bureaucratic model; organizational forms and network organizations are proliferating while we assist to the multiplication of the levels of Governance and of practices of intermediation, listening, sharing, negotiation with the actors of society. The idea underlying this design is that the interrelation, the strategies of the actors can lead to the development of participatory forms open, oriented towards cooperation and the creation of beneficial trade for participants. Although starting from different endowments the participants recognize each other, accepting the rules of comparison and acting in a non-collaborative situation at least in regulated competition, they could give rise to positive common game.

On the other hand, it is easy to understand that in a highly complex society on the field of processes, characterized by a growing interdependence of the levels of Government (Barbera 1973) and the emergence of a plurality of actors, the old authoritative way and of the vertical command, as well as not very effective resulted without any political legitimacy. A "new Citizen" was born (Benvenuti 1994).

In a globalized *era*, the solution of problems was not necessarily ascribed to regulatory models in which the market paradigm prevails: on the contrary, the more uncertainty is present, the more it will be necessary in fact to regulate trough *consensus*, to negotiate solutions. And what stands out in the new *panorama* is precisely the strong interdependence between the public Subjects and Institutions involved in the networks and the Citizens: intensity and repetition of the relationships, which go in the direction of building shared maps, languages and common codes as well as new organizations that put themselves at the service of these new opportunities and needs. In this new configuration of the network State thus emerge new structures of Government, interorganizational networks in which the public administration, explicitly in turn from different levels of Government, takes on new roles and functions depending on the case, the ability and the context of the actors, acting as an Actor among others in situations in which self-regulation prevails, is the case of those "public schemes by default"; as a third actor, *super partes* that coordinates, orients, values and supports a certain model of Governance based on the inclusion of Citizens, on deliberative methods and on encouragement and the development of the Society self-organization or more simply by de-contributing to the Public Function and taking care only of procedural staging and bureaucratic rituals like formalization of rules on decisions already taken in other contexts (Cassese 2001).

Let us proceed with order by analyzing more closely the Italian experience of Governance and the other *Scenarios* that it opens for public Administration.

4.7 Coordination vs. Fragmentation: The Task of the Italian Administration

It has to be clarified, in relation to the innovation strategies adopted by the public Administration, if in the Italian experience Governance can be considered in all respects the emerging political response of the State to the critical situation described above and then an attempt to redefine the borders and the role of public administrative action in the Society or simply the unintended consequence of such crisis due to technological, social and economic transformations and their effects on the environment and on the quality of life and work.

In the first case, the Governance, in its Community sense, could be a "challenging" paradigm to be opposed both to the Government and to the model based on a Governance linked to the private interests (of which new public management and Anglo-Saxon neoliberal policies have brought forward). A Governance, understood as a trust-based and oriented network Community, it could be a sort of European response based on equity and on the principle of the exclusivity that would be opposed to the managerial style American model, based on the principles of efficiency, economy and management particularly attentive to internal organization and more specifically technical aspects.

Giving response it is not an easy task, because, as already hinted, the concept of Governance, as well as making use of different meanings, can be ambiguous and therefore easily misunderstood.

The theory of political Governance established after the Second World War was coming from the experience of Governments that aspired to orientate explicitly and towards defined objectives socio-economic development of their Countries. The themes around which they developed were those of growth and implementation of public policies; but the initial perspective was the vertical one, from above, in substance the Legislator's point of view. Rapidly the European Countries passed from a simple concept of governance to that of Governability, with the attention given not only to the subjects of the policies but rather to the recipients of these, considered the failures and resistance encountered in the implementation of public policies. At first born as "management theory" in Germany or "political leadership" in England, with the time, the concept of Governance changed semantically with respect to its origins emphasizing the cooperative nature and coordination. This process was highlighted also in Italy by Administrative Law Scholars.

The coordination and cooperation in Governance is understood as a new style of cooperative Government that differs from that based on hierarchical control. In this sense it would be based on the interaction of the State with non-state Actors, both public and private within decision-making networks. With this concept the centrality of the State weakens as a center of political control, leaving space to alternative forms of "Governance of Society" such as market principles and horizontal self-organization.

It is from here that the different ways of coordination of individual actions, considered primary forms of construction of the social order, were taken into account by Italian public Administration. Even if we are in the period of the early 1980s, when the policies of neoliberalism took hold by promoting deregulation and privatization processes to foster growth and increase of economic efficiency, it has to be noted that in the Italian studies on public Administration and Governance equal interest rose the cooperative and horizontal forms of social self-regulation and production of policies with respect to the hierarchy and principles of the market. In the mid-1980s, in fact, the key words of the theoretical debate, more often recalled, were those of decentralization, cooperation and network to emphasize any aversion to hierarchical power. It soon became clear, however, that to entrust the resolution of problems to public/private networks and social self-regulation was not a universal model for public Administration, it did not bring always benefits but sometime could make more complex and further fragmented the scene.

This awareness made possible another important reflection on public Administration that led to see the State not so much as a weakened element, with reduced managerial capacity, but simply as an organism that was going through, in a vision of a polycentric society, a change of its traditional form. It was very evident, in fact, that social self-regulation could work well only within a framework of Institutions established or recognized by the State and that the Institutional framework itself not only legitimized these relationships but it could encourage them. Hierarchical control of the State and self-regulation would therefore not be contrasting tools and principles, but rather a combination that could strengthen the effectiveness of the administrative action.

With the emergence of globalization, the scenarios naturally became more complex, because other Subjects and new Institutions came into play; the political coordination at international level, compared to the European one, incapable to delineate "any subject capable of directive power" and lacking "any institutionalized frame for almost the very object of this political driving effort".

If before changes related to Europeanization and globalization, the concept of Administration and Governance were extended to include the nuances of meanings that emerged over time, but remained circumscribed and well delimited, today with the advent of the transnational dimension, we are facing a real Paradigm shift, whose contours are struggling to be clearly outlined. If on a national level the State more than being delegitimized acquires new roles and different functions, in the international public *Arena*, and especially in the European public *Arena*, it really loses control capacity due not only to the "sale" of legislative and regulatory powers, but above all due to the integration of European societies and markets and the gradual dissolution of national economic boundaries.

Naturally it should be considered here also the theme of the relationship between democracy and Governance, whose connections are very relevant as it is sadly confirmed by the recent European political *scenario*, but this task is out of the scope of this Essay. The only aspect that we can emphasize, about participatory processes, is the *focus* on horizontal cooperation as a new form of democratic legitimacy of policies networks, outlining the importance of the degree of representation of private subjects within these networks. Perhaps, the difficulty of representing the specific needs of the Individuals today makes us consider these networks, in which different and opposing political interests meet, a "modern and smoother form of representation of interests".

It has to be recognized of course the tensions between the different types of representation of interests, to avoid the risk to exalt the processes from below through models of old corporatism, which protect the interests of one part, without worrying about the common good.

Finally, globalization opens up the *scenario* to many Governance regimes that coexist together with their structures and processes. Recent Studies develop to the point of envisaging an encroachment of paradigm, the modern State undergoes a turn towards a style more cooperative: as we have already noted, networks bloom everywhere and there are many experiences and experiments of deliberative practices. Understanding public Administration and Governance as that set of transformations that have to do with intensification and dissemination of participatory practices that are closely linked to processes of multiplication of the levels and of the Actors, to the principle of activation and to the territoriality of policies, the main terrain of experimentation.

If the public Administration trough Governance does not in itself lead to one contribution to the solution of the problems of coordination and fragmentation of the social and institutional structures, as the rhetoric used could make one think, at the same time Governance can become an instrument of innovation of social interactions and games between the Actors lighter than the old authoritative way of governing administrative problems, provided that it is not read or used as a tool to weaken the Public Function.

What is going to affect the success are, in fact, elements such as the institutional regulatory framework in which it is to be implemented, the role played by the public Institutions present—at a national and local level—and the presence of devices oriented to the growth and development of resources, both economic and social, of self-organization present in society. And this could be true also in the Italian experience.

Naturally, a government that does not consider society as pure object or Citizens as its subjects, but based on strong interactions, on processes more than on procedures, on the mobilization of resources and subjectivity.

Let's now proceed with the analysis of the Italian experience by focusing on the different arrangements and configurations that this can take in the context of a post-bureaucratic public Administration.

4.8 The Path Towards a Multicentric and Transnational System of Governance

As previously noted, the change of public Administration is moving towards models in which a single center is replaced by a myriad of other centers or suburbs, inhabited by a variety of actors, relationships and interactions that trace the outlines of a great network whose relational modality is negotiating and/or deliberative. If the transition from Government to Governance shifts the accent to the bottom, the question that arises is at what stage is positioned the "Entry Level" of a possible actor, a question that is linked to legitimate local interests aimed at maximizing utility or to the oriented social visions to a solidarity and expressive spirit. To give an answer to this question, we need to go back to the ways and intensity of delegation of government functions regarding the three periods that the models of regulation of public action have passed through.

These three periods are characterized by being representative of cultural models as well on which each phase is founded: the first appears to be characterized by centralization institutional and hierarchical relations. This model of government is based, in fact, on standardized administrative procedures considered valid regardless of the results and legitimized by the presence of a formal authority. The relationship between the political party and the administrative part, between who decides and who implements it is functionally separated and hierarchical. From the point of view of the set-up and of the institutional instruments there is one hierarchical distribution of skills and the progressive reduction of discretion e decision-making autonomy in the lowest positions of the organizational institutional pyramid. Authoritative and legal checks are carried out with sanctions. The alternatives to this model of Government are found in the two models that Governance declines according to two different visions: the market and the Community.

The second period is based on institutional decentralization and subsidiarity based on the comparison and on the convergence between the utilities of the actors: this model therefore assumes the subsidiarity logic that is based on the coincidence of the utility of individual actors and only subsequently on collective subjects and entities. The responsibility in this case would coincide with interests while inter-institutional and inter-organizational relations are well founded on the negotiation partnership and on an equal relationship between those who take decisions and those who are in charge of their implementation. For the structure and the institutional instruments, we are in the presence of a regulation bottom-up type involving stakeholders in decision-making processes, resorting to short-term forms of contracting to limit costs and forms of assessment of the results of the processes. This model, in fact, is based on the one hand on the outsourcing of public functions, privatization, internal markets and controls, and on the other, on the attributions of autonomy and managerial tools to the management that comes to acquire, at least on the paper, problem solving and diplomatic-negotiating skills.

Finally, the third phase is characterized by a model of the reticular type founded, however, on a sharing of values from part of the network actors starting from a shared mission. In this model we are in the presence of contexts that favor and incentive behaviors based on interaction and coordination as well as the formation of common languages, codes and knowledge. The social capital that comes valued and promoted through policies facilitates the establishment of negotiating styles, participatory and cooperative.

In the same public Administration, the distinction so clear between technical professionals and political leaders is held together through the continuous research of integration between decision, execution and sharing of driving functions. This trough an involvement both of the recipients of the interventions and of those who, in the process of planning of objectives and plans, deal with the implementation of services.

The risks to which these models meet are different from each other.

Apart from the first based on the Government model whose problems have been extensively dealt with in the previous paragraphs, in the Governance of market-oriented networks, the Italian experiences of public Administration report that the main disadvantages are those related to the difficulty of representative Institutions to play a role important driving, the weakening of attention to the interests of the most marginal in favor of private consolidated interests, to the difficulties of preventing actions of freeriding, to the lack of transparency in informal processes due also to the widening of the responsibility between these complex structures, uncertain effectiveness at costs of *ex post* rationalization methodologies for decisions and evaluation of the results and finally an excessive risk of standardization and an abnormal increase in supply flexible institutional tools.

At the same time, the main risks in which trust-based networks are governed, very strong in the Italian experience, are those of the decision-making stall due to the fragmentation of powers, on one hand, and the danger of the opportunism of those participating, on the other, of the difficulties of predetermining the trend implementation processes and legitimize the intervention of a higher authority for unlock any stasis situation. Another big risk is that in the contexts more disintegrated with scarce social capital, situations of weakening occur or indifference towards the common goods, with the consequence of an increase in the range of the territorial inequalities supported by a different weight of Community resources. These networks also need leaders not only of instrumental quality but also able to involve and to enhance local actors and actions. High transaction costs of participation in shares for each player and difficulty in successfully implement these processes on a national and not just local scale, conclude all the main disadvantages of the model.

The two post-bureaucratic models of the Italian experience of public Administration, here synthetically outlined, configured both as reticular systems, are distinguished according to their different cultural orientation: the first founded on the idea of the market and therefore on the private interests, while the second oriented to the community and therefore based on the value of trust.

The cultural change of the models of regulation is of course profoundly influenced by structural, political and economic factors as well as by specific situations local both in territorial terms (national and regional level) and in terms of policies specificity of sectoral policies. Thus, for example, neoliberal market-oriented policies and convinced proponents of the self-regulating capacity are contrary to any regulatory intervention and distribution of politics: their goal is in fact to free the market from all constraints that limit development skills. Such market-oriented policies are often accompanied by forms of governance and tools that favor public-private partnerships, different co-decision tables types of networks involving private actors, negotiation practices promoted by the institutions, strategic planning of cities. On the front of public institutions, the new public management, in its original Anglo-Saxon model and its continental translation, constitutes the corresponding strategy for administrative reform that has not been adopted only by the Countries that carried out one conservative politics, but also from those of the center-left politics as it has been in the Italian recent history; a model flanked by more open models, less hierarchical in formulation and implementation of public choices.

Relations between local, national and transnational governments are based on a new and unstable *equilibrium*: the tendency is that of a territorial rebalancing of political powers and of their actions, as well as the relations between politics and society. Multicentric and transnational systems of Governance weaken capacity of the State of regulating and allocating, pooling the Authority, through different intertwining of power, between political, social and State governments, but also transnational Actors such as multinationals and intergovernmental Organizations. Involving civil society is considered, in the Italian experience, useful to legitimize socially and politically decisions and decision-makers, as well as to increase the effectiveness of policies. A search for social *consensus* emerges with regard to the structural changes of economic type and other key reforms. The same Cities, as we will see, put in practice diversified strategies to confront the challenges of globalization introducing more local and global connections in policies and governance than in the past.

However, it is necessary to pay attention and to distinguish the two opposing models of public Administration and of "governing": one that aims aggregation of Actors, focused on negotiations between interested parties to compete with each other; the other that has, instead, as an objective the integration, hinged on institutions and their ability to bring out actors, identities and political capacities—of citizens in first place—around a system of social meanings, values and norms shared.

During the years, in Italy, many spurious models of Regulation and structuring of Public Action which hybridize and recompose the three ideal models described above in a hybrid manner appeared and were put in place. Market and Community, utilitarianism and trust therefore mix and generate tensions and ambiguities that must be monitored especially in the phases of the processes of creation of *Arenas* and deliberative spaces. However, these tensions do not constitute elements necessarily dysfunctional: they could, in fact, reveal opportunities to put in the field and experience the ability of actors to create hybrid forms that enhance and experience errors in the field and exploit learning skills beyond the boundaries cast models, prescriptive and unilateral models proposed by the rhetoric of the moment.

4.9 Rule of Law, Social Welfare and Performance: Reembracing Unity

As for Italy, founded on an administrative culture that belongs to the legalistic *Rechtsstaat* model typical of the Napoleonic tradition, while traditionally the State plays a central role in society, the involvement of the Citizens is limited. Attitudes towards managerial models have been different and even contradictory among themselves: we have gone from the refusal to the acritical acceptance within an apparent redefinition of the boundaries between bureaucratic logics based on a culture of legal type and managerial logics. The public Administration, already in difficulty in dealing with issues related to deregulation, it is, in fact, today totally unprepared to face the complexity that develops when the need arises consolidating competition and the market. This also explain the persistence of a mix of administrative cultures that combine legalistic culture and managerial culture.

On the other hand, Italy is also known for having always been characterized, since the first years of the unification of 1861, for a variety of administrative traditions that existed within the different local Kingdoms and Sates. It is therefore difficult to understand what kind of reform and administrative framework we are facing and this especially in the last years when we had in power many Governments with an unstable and temporary character. The result was that of a fragmentary nature of the interventions and of a coming and going of reforms before announced and then canceled by following Cabinets, that generated a situation equally fragmented. Faced with the crisis of the State, of representativeness and of the politics also in Italy started in the 1990s, at a very intense period of reform legislation. The problem of the reorganization of the public Administration has become pressing and central within the public debate from the point of view of one review of administrative functions, of the administrative organization and of the rationalization of resources, the fight against waste, of the simplification of regulations, of the modernization of the legal system.

A simplification was then outlined in the context of the size of the activities of the public Administrations. In particular, a streamlining and a rationalization of administrative processes, of operational practices that it really has changed the face of the public Administration, compared to the past, also because we are not treated only with amendments to the legislation in question or introduction of computerization, but of a real cultural change that has affected the established, traditional practices, taken for granted.

The introduction of an evaluation system related to the efficiency, the use of resources and the effectiveness of the interventions, the separation between political function and management functions and an allocation of greater responsibility and managerial tools and privatization of the employment relationship for civil servants complete the framework of the public Administration reform implemented in Italy in those years. Responsibility, flexibility, result, evaluation and objectivity are all terms belonging to the rhetoric of the 1990s.

In truth the impression is that of a rift between reformist aspirations and reality: despite the call to the market and the isomorphic tendencies towards the business world, the public administration, from the organizational point of view, does not seem to follow, for many characteristics, that much declaimed objectivity. Let's just think about the theme of the careers linked to merit or the conditions of the workers both in terms of the content of the work from the point of view of remuneration, professional mobility, skills, etc. And the same recursive discourses on the need to reform the public also confirm this Administration that all governments reiterate, as well as the climate of mistrust that demonizes massively public Administration, services and personnel and which further strengthens an outsourcing oriented logic, as the only model to solve complex and persistent problems.

These modernization processes are grounded also on the idea of a Citizen to whom the public Administration must give answers. The innovation that emerges from the reforms of the last decade is certainly the attention paid to the Citizen as a subject that enters fully into the panorama of decisions concerning public action. The major focus on increasing the protection of citizens' rights—in the first half of the 1990s at the level of norms, in fact, the "rights of citizenship"—went hand in hand with the commitment to focus on the "result" of the administrative action. Therefore, the idea that prevailed in the first ninety years of the last century is the one of a public Administration that is on a higher level than its own interlocutors whether they are employees or citizens or private organizations, essentially one unilateral conception of public action based on hierarchical relationships. It changes also the role (and functions) of the State, passing from management functions to regulation functions also thanks to the European Union influence. The authoritative nature of the actions of the public Administration has been lost to strengthen the negotiating nature. And it is precisely in this direction that also the role of the Citizens gains space.

The basic elements on which the reforms have played are mechanisms that follow a more strictly managerial logic typical of Companies, elements of modernization that have facilitated the streamlining and flexibility of the public Administration and elements that have exalted the participation among the different subjects of Governance especially in some sectors such as health, social welfare and culture, environment, education. Of course in the face of all these changes that have brought to exalt a results-oriented administration, the risk of losing on the ground impartiality and the principle of equality always lurks, where above all flexibility, trust relationships, models management have favored façade modernization, increasing *phenomena* of cronyism and dependence of public Administrations on politics.

As we have seen, therefore, the Italian *panorama* of administrative systems is very varied and it can be noted for its hybrid character.

Moreover, the idea that the market cannot self-regulate and therefore also a rethink of the role of the State towards those regulatory functions, apparently more modern with respect to those in charge of management, in fact they were also very criticized especially by the supporters of deregulation. This change of perspective was certainly urged by the situation of economic and social *crisis* that pervades all states: starting from terrorist attacks to the concrete consequences of financialization of economy, the crisis of representativeness, the resurgence of feelings of nationalism and localism and the conflicts of civilization between nationalities, religions, etc. The growing and unprecedented need of security and the new social demands for inclusion alarm the democratic-liberal institutions that show increasing difficulties to keep everything under control. The immense trust towards the market seems today to fade even for the most avid supporters that are going to support better deregulation rather than deregulation *tout court*, even proposing solutions that provide for forms of new protectionism both in economic field—commercial than social. The organizational paradigm of mold managerial that prevailed in the 1980s and 1990s begins to show the first cracks while its greater utility in the field becomes the impossibility of using it in a public policy context as an external element and as a critical *stimulus*.

If the national administration has to support the European process and the pressures that come from it, in the sense of a lightening of the Administration from more points of view, it is also true that a redevelopment of the same forms of intervention is needed and therefore, rather than less State, as the liberal recipes themselves propose, we must aim rather on a different State able to operate according to a negotiating style in the design of new regulation systems, to reembrace a new kind of unity of our public Administration.

4.10 The Quest for the Ideal City and Its Public Administration

The nation-State, at least in the typical configurations of industrial modernity, has definitively lost its ability to structure and dominate the flows, the groups, to organize institutions, to impose its culture and thanks to the globalization of the economy, but also of information and culture, this has effects also in the institutional field. New centers of Government were born both on the world or continental plan, and at national and local level where there is an increase of the importance of subnational Governments such as Regions, Municipalities and especially large Cities.

The emerging paradox is that the State, on one hand, seems to be too big to give the right answers to the problems and contingent emerging needs at the local level, on the other hand it is too small and with little force to weigh on globalized scenarios and to control supranational economic actors. This *scenario* opens space for a radical renewal of the role of local governments and Cities which find themselves at the center of a dialectic double tension: on one hand the global dimension and the local one, on the other the push for cooperation and competition. Local administrators today find themselves managing a series of problems that decentralization and the tendency towards differentiation of public policies has poured into the Territories, often with few resources, pressed by Citizens and interests organized that have higher and higher expectations. At the same time, we do not have to forget that the destinies of the Cities are often played at the *supra-local* level, supranational but also continental and in any case in an increasingly global perspective.

It was born between local Actors and local Governments the possibility to elaborate forms of particular Governance and to organize themselves also as subjects of European Governance since the Cities become poles of aggregation and privileged representation of interests, groups, associations, organizations, inhabitants. If on the one hand these *Scenarios* are opened, on the other it is evident that these processes of aggregation, relationship, choice, conflict, representation create fragmented situations that require the political capabilities of administrators and the local Government of the cities called to deal with burning issues once centrally regulated, for example related to economic development, poverty, pollution, etc.; cities that are also considered incomplete local societies just to underline the linking of the strategies of the groups and of the local actors to the wider transformations of the context.

If it is true that local Governments are characterized by the smaller size and from financial and functional limits imposed by central Governments, at the same time, they result to be strategic for many reasons. The first concerns the democracy: local governments still seem to be the bulwark of these principles, certainly characterized by a closer relationship with Citizens. Even in Italy it is the national level that comes recognized by Citizens as the real space for comparison with its decisive political weight: it is here, in fact, that the most important choices of life are questioned beyond the concreteness of the issues faced at a local level. Up front even in this awareness, Cities are still active to stimulate debate linked to local issues and to revive democracy by promoting mechanisms and procedures of direct participation of citizens: despite the political crisis of the 1990s, in fact, also in Italy there are several initiatives of city conferences, of *referendum* of popular initiative, tables and participation meetings. The forms of participation can still be very different from each other: there are those requiring an advisory opinion to Citizens, associations and organizations, those that instead ask the subjects to enter into the merits of the projects presented, negotiating with the Administration to formulate entirely concrete proposals and those involving citizens to evaluate and discuss a public policy.

Other reasons that highlight the importance of local Government are the production of services to Citizens, the search for innovation that is incentivized precisely for the same proximity to the Citizens and the fact that the local dimension is considered a priority because yes intertwined with other levels of government especially in public policy. Finally, the relevance also at the supranational level of the local Government to the detriment of the national, due to decentralization and globalization. Decentralization that is not but occurring only against the micro dimension, but also towards society itself through a withdrawal of the State, especially for certain public policies, which they give way to market mechanisms, to individuals or to the third sector.

Policies at the local level are also undergoing various changes. Priorities change because they are central to local development rather than local policies only to the social and to the territory tout court; change the way services are managed, from "rowing" to "steering" by entrusting services to third parties purpose of streamlining and giving flexibility; and, finally, it changes the relationship with the Citizens often participating in some choices. With respect to public policies, the three main axes that, in any case, move to local level are precisely those mentioned related to economic development, welfare and al territory. In fact, they find wide space after the exhaustion of the Keynesian *social status* model, the reduction of state allocations and the increasing competitiveness between Cities, in a globalized *scenario*, all those policies linked to the promotion and growth of the territory. Cities become leader, trying to exploit also relationships and resources of possible local partners to improve their positioning and competitive advantage. It is the success of marketing strategies territorial planning, strategic planning, the various papers that ratify pacts for the sustainable development between Cities at European level, of promoting the image of cities that try to attract talent and capital. The strategies to improve have multiplied the attractiveness to the outside, they have made the cities more interesting and the argument is not valid only for large cities of historical or artistic interest, but also for smaller towns until some time ago not valued from this point of view.

Faced with this trend by one part of the risk is to feed even more fractures, divisions and inequalities between different levels of citizenship, on the other hand the attention to the valorization of cities and their assets, if made with certain criteria that are those of involvement, sharing, participation, respect for the city and its inhabitants, in a logic of learning and reflection, are certainly interesting elements.

These trends that lead to enhance economic instruments, strategies and visions due to the diffusion of the new public management have taken roots in Italy, a major change for a Country in which the structure is soaked and strongly based on the administrative rule of law. This new anti-bureaucratic conception of the model of local Government that considers that the public Administration must “steer” rather than “row”, set the main rules and objectives and delegate the service production function.

It is at the local level that these post-bureaucratic pushes find fertile ground to be experimented also with the risk of incurring further fragmentation of services and of the social fabric of the cities themselves, with relative loss or weakening of the scope egalitarian and universalist towards the strengthening of a vision and management based on the privatism. Despite these trends and the associated risks, the increased role of Local Governments that see their powers, their autonomy and their responsibilities increased towards the Community in a general context, however, that diversifies and becomes more complex.

The development of such processes finds both ideal reasons and practical ones: the search for *consensus* that seeks to obviate even the weak electoral legitimation and to prevent conflicting moments and deep disagreement by one hand, on the other hand the attempt to make the Citizens responsible for choices that concern them more closely. This is the case, for example, of urban regeneration which in Britain has seen it development of a participated urbanism which then spread as a model in the great European Cities because without the consent of the citizens is much more difficult, if not impossible, to make certain choices necessary to change the territory and improve the life of Cities.

Probably, the quest for the ideal public Administration in Italy found the right path in the Government of the Cities: a new quest of the Ideal City for a new Italian Renaissance.

References

Ambrosini G (1944) Autonomia regionale e federalismo. Edizioni italiane, Roma

Antonini L (2009) Il regionalismo differenziato. Giuffrè, Milano

Anzon A (2002) I poteri delle regioni dopo la riforma costituzionale. Il nuovo regime e il modello originario a confronto. Giappichelli, Torino

Barbera A (1973) La regione come ente di governo. Politica del diritto

Bartole S, Mastagostino G (1971) Le regioni. Il Mulino, Bologna

Bassanini F, Castelli L (2008) Semplificare l'Italia. Stato, Regioni, enti locali, Passigli, Firenze

Benington J, Geddes M (2001) Local partnerships and social exclusion in the European Union – new forms of social governance. Routledge, London

Benvenuti F (1956) L'organizzazione impropria della P.A. Riv. trim. dir. pubb. 968

Benvenuti F (1994) Il nuovo cittadino. Tra libertà garantita e libertà attiva. Marsilio, Padova

Benvenuti F (1996) Disegno dell'Amministrazione italiana. Linee positive e prospettive. Cedam, Padova

Berti G (1968) La pubblica amministrazione come organizzazione. Cedam, Padova

Berti G, De Martin GC (2002) Il sistema amministrativo dopo la riforma del titolo V della Costituzione. Luiss, Roma

Bifulco L, de Leonardis O (2002) Pratiche e retoriche dell'intermediazione amministrativa. In: Battistelli F (ed) La cultura delle amministrazioni fra retorica e innovazione. Editore Franco Angeli, Milano

Bifulco L, Vitale T (2005) La contrattualizzazione delle politiche sociali e il welfare locale. In: Bifulco L (ed) Le politiche sociali. Temi e prospettive emergenti. Carocci, Roma

Bobbio N (1995) Tra due Repubbliche. Alle origini della democrazia italiana. Donzelli, Roma

Bobbio L (1996) La democrazia non abita a Gordio. Studio sui processi decisionali politico-amministrativi. Franco Angeli, Milano

Bobbio L (2002) I governi locali nelle democrazie contemporanee. Laterza, Roma-Bari

Bulmer S (1994) The governance of the European Union: a New Institutionalist approach. J Public Policy 13(4):351–380

Cassese S (1982) Il sistema amministrativo italiano, S.S.P.A. Istituto Poligrafico dello Stato, Roma

Cassese S (1985) Le trasformazioni dell'organizzazione amministrativa. Riv. trim. dir. pubb. p 374

Cassese S (1993) Rapporto sulle condizioni delle pubbliche Amministrazioni. Dipartimento della Funzione Pubblica, Roma

Cassese S (2001) L'Arena pubblica. Nuovi paradigmi per lo Stato. In: Riv. trim. dir. pubb., p 601

Castelli L (2011) L'organizzazione amministrativa delle regioni. In: Mangiameli S (ed) The italian regionalism in the path of the federal State. Springer, Heidelberg

Cerulli Irelli V (2004) Il nuovo assetto dell'amministrazione, relazione presentata al Convegno L'attuazione del Titolo V della Costituzione, Varenna, 16–18 settembre 2004, in www.federalismi.it

Cerulli Irelli V (2017) Lineamenti di diritto amministrativo. Giappichelli, Torino

D'Albergo E (2002) Modelli di governance e cambiamento culturale: le politiche pubbliche fra mercato e comunità. In: La cultura delle amministrazioni fra retorica e innovazione. Editore Franco Angeli, Milano

D'Atena A (2001) L'Italia verso il federalismo. Taccuini di viaggio. Giuffrè, Milano

De Martin GC (2006) Unitarietà della Repubblica e pluralismo delle istituzioni politiche: l'organizzazione delle Regioni. In: Labriola S (ed) Studi per il 60° della Costituente. Laterza, Roma-Bari
De Martin GC (2007) Le tendenze centralistiche nella organizzazione amministrativa delle Regioni prima e dopo le recenti riforme costituzionali. In: Studi in onore di Leopoldo Mazzarolli, vol II. Cedam, Padova
De Valles A (1931) Teoria giuridica dell'organizzazione dello Stato. Cedam, Padova
Di Gaspare G (1995) Organizzazione amministrativa. In: Dig. pubbl., vol X. Utet, Torino, p 513
Donolo C (2006) Il futuro delle politiche pubbliche. Bruno Mondadori, Milano
Esposito C (1954) Autonomie locali e decentramento amministrativo nell'art. 5 della Costituzione. In: La Costituzione italiana. Saggi. Cedam, Padova
Falcon G, Marchetti B (2013) Pubblico e privato nell'organizzazione e nell'azione amministrativa. Cedam, Padova
Forti U (1948) Teoria dell'organizzazione e delle persone giuridiche pubbliche. Jovene, Napoli. Giannini MS (1958)
Franchini C, Vesperini G (2015) L'organizzazione. In: Cassese S (ed) Istituzioni di diritto amministrativo. Giuffré, Milano, p 83
Giannini MS (1959) Autonomia Pubblica. In: Enciclopedia del diritto, vol IV. Giuffrè, Milano
Giannini MS (1970) Diritto amministrativo, vol I. Giuffré, Milano
Giannini MS (1972) Il decentramento amministrativo nel quadro dell'ordinamento regionale. In: Atti del III Congresso di studi giuridici sulla Regione. Giuffré, Milano
Giannini MS (1979) Rapporto sui principali problemi dell'Amministrazione dello Stato. Dipartimento della funzione pubblica, Roma
Giannini MS (1988) L'amministrazione pubblica dello Stato contemporaneo. Cedam, Padova
Guarino G (1977) L'organizzazione pubblica. Giuffré, Milano
Kooiman J (1993) Modern governance: new government – society interactions. Sage, London
Le Galès P (2002) European cities. Social conflicts and governance. Oxford University Press, Oxford
Mangiameli S (2002) La riforma del regionalismo italiano. Giappichelli, Torino
March JG, Olsen JP (1989) Rediscovering Institutions. The organizazional basis of politics. The Free Press, New York
Marongiu G (1988) L'attività direttiva nella teoria giuridica dell'organizzazione. Cedam, Padova
Mayntz R (1999) La teoria della Governance: sfide e prospettive. Riv. Italiana di Scienza Politica 29 (1):3–21
Melis (1996) Storia dell'Amministrazione pubblica italiana. 1861–1993. Il Mulino, Bologna
Moreau Defarges P (2003) La Gouvernance. Presses Universitaires de France, Paris
Nigro M (1966) Studi sulla funzione organizzatrice della pubblica amministrazione. Giuffré, Milano
Pierre J, Peters BG (2000) Governance, politics and the state. St. Martins Press, New York
Police A (2002) Federalismo "asimmetrico" e dequotazione dell'eguaglianza: le fragili fondamenta della cittadinanza amministrativa. Dir. econ. 489
Pollit C, Bouckaert G (2004) Public management reform. A comparative analysis. Oxford University Press, Oxford
Powell WW (1990) Neither market nor hierarchy: network forms of organization. Res Organ Behav 12:295–336
Rhodes RWA (1997) Understanding governance. Policy networks, reflexivity and accountability. Open University Press, Buckingham
Richardson J (1996) European Union: power and policy making. Routledge, London
Scharpf FW (1993) Coordination in hierarchies and networks. In: Scharpf FW (ed) Games in hierarchies and networks. Analytical and empirical approaches to the study of governance institutions. Campus Verlag, Frankfurt a.M., p 125
Sciullo G (2014) L'organizzazione amministrativa. Principi. Giappichelli, Torino

Scoca FG (2001) La pubblica Amministrazione come organizzazione. In: Mazzarolli L et al (eds) Diritto Amministrativo, vol I. Monduzzi, Bologna, p 451
Scoca FG (2017) Diritto Amministrativo. Giappichelli, Torino
Sepe S, Mazzone L, Portelli I, Vetritto G (2003) Lineamenti dell'amministrazione italiana (1861–2002). Carocci, Bari
Sorace D (2018) Il diritto delle pubbliche amministrazioni. Una introduzione. Il Mulino, Bologna
Torchia L (2009) Il sistema amministrativo italiano. Il Mulino, Bologna
Treves G (1977) L'organizzazione amministrativa. Utet, Torino
Vandelli L (2010) Il sistema delle autonomie locali. Il Mulino, Bologna
Virga P (1958) L'organizzazione amministrativa. Ediz. Universitarie, Palermo
Weber M (1922) Wirtschaft und Gesellschaft, 1922, trad. it. Economia e società, 1961. Edizioni Comunità, Milano
Zanobini G (1938) Corso di diritto amministrativo Vol. III L'organizzazione amministrativa. Giuffré, Milano

Chapter 5
The New Functions of Public Budgets

Antonio Brancasi

Contents

Abstract The chapter investigates the most relevant legislative transformations affecting Italian regime of public finance in the last 50 years. Moving from the effects caused by the introduction in 2012 of the balanced budgetary rule in the Constitution, it deals with the impact of this rule on both the accounting standards and the local finance.

5.1 Introduction

It can be said that the current structure of public finance and its system of governance is the result of transformations and reforms having occurred over the last 50 years. Prior to the early 1960s, a significant lack of mobility had kept alive legislation

Antonio Brancasi was deceased at the time of publication (1947–2018)

A. Brancasi (✉)
University of Florence, Florence, Italy
e-mail: domenico.sorace@unifi.it

D. Sorace et al. (eds.), *The Changing Administrative Law of an EU Member State*,
https://doi.org/10.1007/978-3-030-50780-0_5

dating back to the 30s, which primarily used bureaucratic systems to regulate the preparation and management of budgets, ultimately highlighting the need for unifying coordination tools at that level for the financial activity of the state. A need that was met through the system of accountants, who were (and still are) placed in each ministry (Central Accounting Offices, now Central Budget Offices) but were (and still are) employed by the General Accounting Office (Ministry of the Treasury and now also of Economy and Finance).

Only since the 1960s has a form of governance over public finance been implemented in a progressive and increasingly sophisticated manner, and at a political level and no longer limited only to the state. These reform measures were intended to tackle four types of problems, sometimes separately and sometimes jointly, in addition to the far more recent adaptation of the legislation to the Fiscal Compact. And it is precisely around these five reforms that the remainder of this discussion is based.

5.2 Centred Budgetary Decision-Making and Balancing

The starting point consisted essentially of the pre-constitutional regulation which, upon approval of the state budget law, did not allow Parliament to make informed decisions regarding the forecast public finance trend for the new year. It is also true that the constitution reserved the preparation of budgets and their submission to the Houses for the government, rolling the various parts of the budget into a single design. However, the fact remains that giving the government sole legislative discretion over the budget has never nullified (and still does not nullify) the authority of the Houses to amend proposals submitted by the government. Primarily though, the rational use of such powers, being fully aware of the consequences, was affected by the manner in which the Houses proceeded to examine and approve the state budget. Indeed, at that time the State budget was divided into multiple laws, each relating to an individual ministry, for which the government's proposal, while consistent in its singular nature, was broken down in multiple bills which, given the bicameral composition of Parliament, were submitted at the same time, with half going to each House. The result was that each House made its decision without having first reviewed the overall picture in terms of revenue and expenditure for the new year. So much so that, even though a summary of the budgetary balances was attached to the Ministry of the Treasury's budget, only the House to which the bill for that ministry was submitted for initial review was able to keep track of the macro consequences of individual decisions.

It should also be added that the Constitution of 1948 regulated these aspects in a provision which, though concise (Article 81), would later help prioritise consideration of the overall balancing of public finance for decisions having financial ramifications. However, the fact is that this provision was scarcely read and therefore often circumvented. Significantly, in this sense, the obligation per the expenditure laws to indicate all financial means used to cover expenditure referred solely to those expenses affecting the budget already approved for the current year, and was not considered to apply to those laws which assigned expenses to future budgets, in which they were thus required to be reported. It was accepted that the laws, in instituting new or greater expenses or reducing revenue, could provide for the coverage of such charges by authorising the government to issue public debt securities; the consequence was that the total amount of debt was ultimately the sum of specific and partial decisions, rather than the subject of a specific decision regarding this essential balancing aspect.

It was in the mid-1960s that we began to be aware of the issue of the rationality of decision-making processes and of their vital role in reviewing and making public finance decisions on a macro-scale. The multiple budget laws are consolidated into a single act, whose draft law is submitted for initial review in alternate years to one of the two Houses: this allows each House to simultaneously examine and assess all the forecasts of the ministries, and to do so bearing in mind the summary table indicating the various budgetary balances contained in the Ministry of the Treasury's forecasts.

Along the same lines, another important change was the position taken by the Constitutional Court in favour of an in-depth review of the constitutional provision concerning the obligation of financial coverage. It was stated (Ruling No. 1 of 1966) that this obligation applied to all laws that introduced new or increased expenditure or which reduced revenue regardless of the financial year in which such effects would enter into force, including, for example, any increased costs that may be applied to future financial years, which would therefore have to be reported in future financial statements.

However, it was with Law No. 468 of 1978 relating to the state (and previously Law No. 335 of 1976 relating to the regions) that the need to rationalise the decision-making process in public finance underwent a systematic overhaul which, as well as modifying the rules inherited from the pre-constitutional era, had the task of regulating issues that had not been previously recognised.

The central point of this new system was that the decision to resort to the financial market must be made on approval of the budget, and once such decision was made was the state authorised to issue public debt. This limited jurisdiction had three closely related consequences. The standard laws could no longer authorise the issuance of debt to provide coverage for any unforeseen charges, as was previously the case. Debt was used solely to fund the budget, and it is in this, and in the same resources provided by the debt, that the standard laws may be able to cover their charges. The total debt amount is subject to a particular express decision to be made in consideration of the overall compatibility of public finance and, more generally, of financial markets. This then takes over the previous system, under which the total debt was the summary result of multiple decisions made over time in the event of and with reference to sector-specific measures.

The decision on balancing left to the budget (and based largely on the extent of the recourse to the financial market) was accompanied by the introduction of tools that would ensure a consistent supplementation of the system. On the one hand, the introduction of the multi-year budget next to the annual budget helped fill the limited and inadequate outlook with respect to financial forecasting. On the other hand, the same multi-year budget served to support the Constitutional Court's in-depth review of the financial coverage obligation: in fact, the various laws would have found a reference in the multi-year projections for this budget attesting to the sustainability of the charges assigned to future financial years.

Subsequent reform efforts took on the task of refining this tool, while leaving untouched the central point of assigning balancing decisions to the budget. More specifically, it has been provided that draft laws must be accompanied by a technical report documenting the financial implications of the act, while the legislative process has been regulated to give prominence to such reports.

5.3 Overcoming Budgetary Rigidity and Expanding Its Decision-Making Space

Budgetary rigidity essentially refers to the impossibility for budgetary decisions to freely allocate resources and to the consequent legal need of having to give them a specific allocation, or the impossibility of doing so in the absence of regulations governing the activities such resources would target. This is not meant to refer to the inevitable constraints deriving from operations during previous years: clearly, the decisions made on such occasions must be kept in mind for subsequent financial statements, whenever they have consolidated legal positions in third parties. Rather, it is in reference to the constraints that budgets may face in pre-existing decisions which, rather than being operations-related (i.e. adopted in the performance of previous financial statements), have the function of regulating and planning financial activity under the same budget. Constraints that can be both positive, in the sense that one of the two acts (the budget) is required to conform to the other (the regulation), and negative, in that the former is not available—or at least does not have the same effects—in the absence of the latter.

This problem is certainly present in the European legal system which, in terms of negative constraints, for example, requires the existence of a basic act as the basis for expenditure: it is provided in particular that "The implementation of expenditure shown in the budget shall require the prior adoption of a legally binding act of the Union providing a legal basis for its action and for the implementation of the corresponding expenditure in accordance with the regulation referred to in Article 322, except in cases for which that law provides" (Article 310.3 TFEU).

The standard in principle provides a translated summary of the provision of the Financial Regulation (Article 49) which, for the implementation of appropriations entered into the budget, requires the prior adoption of a basic act "by the legislative authority" which takes "the form of a regulation, a directive, a decision". However, it should be recalled that the Financial Regulation had in turn incorporated a consolidated ruling of the Court of Justice stating the need, in order to have access to expenditure, not only a substantial budgetary allocation but also, in the case of "significant actions", a substantial secondary legal basis. The Court then deducted the "non-significant actions" from this rule, which it indicated as those inherent to preparatory activities for the adoption of a basic act and which it justified stating their legal grounds lay in the power of initiative which the Treaty assigned directly to the Commission. The Financial Regulation then laid down an extensive series of cases in which expenses could be incurred in the absence of a basic act: all expenses for the implementation of acts conferring general and implicit powers (Article 49(6)).

Although based on its wording the regulation concerns expenditure, i.e. budget management rather than the budget itself, it also indirectly limits the budget, precluding its function of allowing for expenditure in the absence of a basic act and allowing it to authorise expenditure only in relation to activities which the institutions of the Union are permitted to carry out by another act.

The positive constraint is when the non-budget act (which may be the basic act but could also be an addition thereto) regulates not only activity, but also expenditure; this happens because the typical structure of the budget, which distinguishes it from other acts, allows for a complete identification of the contents of its specific provisions and those of any other legislative acts governing expenditure. Such a situation typically occurs in two cases: one where the act directly determines the amount of expenditure required during a certain period, and one where the amount of expenditure is indirectly determined by the way in which the activity is regulated, e.g. granting third parties the right to financial services. Both phenomena occur at the EU level, where the first type of expenditure is expressly provided for by inter-institutional agreements between the Parliament, Council and Commission on budgetary governance and sound management, which state that (legislative) acts concerning multi-annual programmes "contain a provision in which the legislative authority lays down the financial framework for the programme"; while the second type of expenditure is found in the concept of expenditure recognised by the same inter-institutional agreements as necessary to "enable the Community to meet its obligations, both internally and externally, under the Treaties and acts adopted in accordance therewith".

Acts with such content pose the problem of whether (and to what extent) they are able to constrain the budget. At European level, at one time, the affirmative answer was achieved by the concept of compulsory expenditure, which the EC Treaty referred to as "expenditure necessarily resulting from the Treaties or from acts adopted in accordance therewith" (Article 272). The inter-institutional agreement between Parliament, the Council and the Commission of 6 May 1999, where it concerns improvement of budgetary procedure, referred to it as "expenditure as the budgetary authority is obliged to enter in the budget by virtue of a legal undertaking entered into under the Treaties or acts adopted by virtue of the said Treaties". It should be noted that the category of compulsory expenditure at the time carried additional consequences (not relevant at this point) concerning the form of government and relations between Parliament and Council.

The distinction between compulsory and non-compulsory expenditure was abolished by the Lisbon Treaty, such that the positive budgetary constraint of not being able to disregard what was established by previous legislative acts would seem to have failed. In actuality, for acts "likely to have appreciable implications for the budget", the TFEU requires assessment of the possibility of funding the related expenses (Article 310(4)). Clearly the law does not refer to acts on expenditure management, as that would encounter the issue of ascertaining the existence and capacity of a relevant budget allocation (this is taken from Article 310(2) and Article 317(c)(1) of the TFEU).

Rather, it refers to acts governing non-budgetary expenditure, and the required assessment can certainly concern merely the feasibility of the rule (i.e. the possibility of financing what is established by the act so as to avoid decisions that cannot then be implemented due to a lack of resources). But beyond that, the clarification that this assessment must serve to "maintain budgetary discipline" (Article 310(4) TFEU) suggests that it is also intended to safeguard and protect decisions either adopted or pending with respect to the budget. In other words, it could be said that there is such a need for protection since the budget is required to include these expenses, because if this constraint did not exist, there would be no need to protect a budget that may determine the size of appropriations regardless of what is established by the other acts.

This problem has also affected the Italian legal system and was resolved directly by the Constitution of 1948 (Article 81(3)), providing for both the negative constraint of not being able to authorise expenses related to activities that the administration is not already entitled to carry out under normal laws, and the positive constraint of not being able to modify or disregard provisions contained in other laws, with the consequent requirement to report as appropriations those amounts corresponding to what was established by the financial content of other laws.

The positive constraint ended up making the budgetary decision too rigid, having negative ramifications on the possibility of governing the trend of public finance. Indeed, in the moment the budget was established, it was inevitable that there would be a trend of such a scale that it became incompatible with the pursued balancing targets and, even still, the budget could not be used to make the necessary adjustments by modifying the current legislation. This issue was overcome with the precautionary introduction of the financial law (later converted, without significant modifications, to the law of stability): the solution was to support the budget law and its procedures with a law (the financial law) which, classed as a normal law, was removed from the positive constraints placed on the budget. However, the solution created more problems than it solved, as by ensuring the approval of the budget it accompanied it would ultimately take on all the tensions typically associated with public finance, as well as being subject to a multitude of measures, often laid down by micro-sector interests, which rather than helping to keep public finance trends under control would make doing so more difficult. In view of this, the content of this law had to be limited, establishing which type of measures could not be adopted through it. These limitations were introduced by an ordinary law, i.e. on the same level as the one to be limited, so the guarantee of their observance was simply inserted into the legislative procedure rules which allowed the President of the House, to whom the law was submitted for first reading, to declare the inadmissibility of any provisions in conflict with the restrictions in question.

Today the situation is quite different, even if the outcomes are very similar. Constitutional Law No. 1 of 2012 repealed the provision of the 1948 Constitution which assigned both upper and lower limits to the budget (Article 81(3)). But it would be erroneous to assume this meant that the budget law could be freely invoked without limitation; this discussion we will leave for later, following the constitutional reform of 2012.

5.4 Placing Quantitative Limitations on Budgetary Movement

The starting point was largely unbalanced since the quantitative limits placed on budget size and balances applied only to institutions other than the state (not least for municipalities, provinces and regions), leaving the state entirely unaffected.

Those institutions were (and still are) subject to a number of static and dynamic quantitative constraints. The former followed a naturally stable trend and helped demarcate the institutional sphere of autonomy of the entity: think of the rule whereby debt to be budgeted for must not consist of financial charges exceeding a certain percentage of the ordinary income (or taxes) of the institution; think also of the imposition (made official by the constitutional reform of 2001 but already present in the ordinary state legislation) of the principle of the golden rule whereby recourse to debt is permitted only to cover investment expenses. Meanwhile, the dynamic constraints tended to be limited in duration since they were established in relation to the contingent needs of the economic situation: the main example of this type of constraint is the "Internal Stability Pact", whereby the financial activity of institutions was determined by their attainment of European targets for containing general government deficit and based on the idea that any sanctions imposed by the EU for violations of the prohibition of excess deficits would have been imposed by the state against those bodies having violated the Pact.

In the case of the state, the starting point concerned the absence of quantitative limitations on public finance and the related financial balances. Such limitations, forecasting the coverage of new or greater expenses, had in fact existed since the 1948 Constitution, but this rule was introduced solely for non-budgetary laws, meaning it carried no limitation whatsoever for determining total revenues and expenses and establishing debt amounts.

At one time even the state itself found no form of market influence in these decisions since it was able to ascertain the cost of its debt independently, while still taking into account the monetary consequences of such decision. The residual buyer principle was in force until 1981, according to which the Bank of Italy would buy all the government debt securities that had not been placed on the market at the time they were issued. This rule was accompanied by an issuance system in which the Treasury established the amount of securities to be placed along with their price and interest rate, with the understanding that if the yield offered was unattractive to investors and if part of the issue was not placed, it would be absorbed by the Bank of Italy. In other words, the Treasury unilaterally determined the cost of its debt and, in doing so, it also determined the portion of debt that would be financed by the creation of a monetary base, as absorbed by the Central Bank.

In 1981 the Bank of Italy "denounced" this rule in order to assert its autonomy of assessment in relation to the amount of money to be placed on the market through the purchase of public debt securities (the so-called divorce between the Bank of Italy and the Treasury). As a result, the placement system for public debt securities also changed: since the Bank of Italy no longer guaranteed the purchase of unplaced securities and reserved the decision of whether to finance public expenditure on the basis of independent assessments relating to the need for monetary stability, the placement of securities would be done through an auction system. The Treasury would establish the amount of securities to be issued and their interest rate and would leave the price to be set by the market, such that the entire amount of securities would be placed, albeit sometimes at very low prices (meaning lower revenues for the issuer) and with very high returns.

As of 1981, the Treasury was no longer able to establish the cost of its debt, but was still able to fund itself (within certain limits) and determine the creation (to the same extent) of a monetary basis by the Bank of Italy. The system of advances which the Bank of Italy was required to grant in the exercise of state treasury management remained in place; advances on which the Bank of Italy had no margin of discretion since they were payable up to the maximum legal limit (14% of expenditure entered in the budget) and at a rate also established by law (1%).

The EU took things a step further, with the Maastricht Treaty imposing certain harmonised legal measures on Member States following the creation of the single currency. These are the current Articles 123 and 124 TFEU, which on the one hand allow National Central Banks (NCB) to act as treasurers for their respective states and national administrations, but at the same time they prohibit them from granting overdraft facilities on accounts in the name of such entities and from purchasing public debt securities on the primary market (i.e. at the time of issue). The aim of these prohibitions is to ensure the full autonomy of National Central Banks in view of their conversion into operational instruments of the European Central Bank (ECB) such that they cannot be forced, on the basis of national government guidelines, to adjust their decisions in terms of monetary base creation to public demand, rather than to the need for monetary stability.

In the late 1980s, using the financial law (later the law of stability), legal constraints were surreptitiously placed on the scale of expenses for the state, with particular reference to increases in current expenses. As already mentioned, the function of this law was to accompany the budget law so as to avail of what was precluded for the latter, making it possible in practice to modify other laws to make their provisions consistent with the financial balance pursued. This was made possible since the financial law (later the law of stability), despite being part of the legislative procedure of the budget law and fully involved in the proceeding, was considered a normal law, unlike the budget, and as such was subject to the normal regime laws, including the obligation to indicate the coverage of its anticipated charges. The artifice allowing legal constraints to be placed on the amount of expenditure drew on the fact that this law was assigned to make a number of decisions that had previously been made by the budget, without encountering any limitations whatsoever. The transfer of these decisions from the budget law to the financial (later stability) law and the system governing the financial law allowed for the imposition of financial coverage for expenses that were previously uncovered, since they were made through the budget. Moreover, this coverage obligation was in this case put together in highly specific terms with respect both to the object, as it was limited only to current expenses, and to the usable means of coverage, drawing on the improvement in the trend of certain budget balances versus the previous financial year.

Achieving a systematic system of constraints and limits on financial equilibrium, even at the expense of the state, required a constitutional reform (Law No. 1 of 2012) implementing the Fiscal Compact, but we will discuss this in later paragraph.

5.5 The [Failed] Attempt to Establish an Effective Decentralisation of Public Finance ('Fiscal Federalism')

The starting point in this case was the 1948 Constitution which, in regard to the matters of interest here, mentioned not the municipalities and the provinces, but only the regions.

Regarding the municipalities and provinces, Article 128 merely proclaimed their autonomy, but "within the principles established by the general laws of the Republic which determines their functions". As such it was the state laws, with no limitation found in the Constitution, that would establish the nature and the type of resources available to those entities and the powers they were granted. In fact, the tax reform of the early 1970s introduced the complete centralisation of the tax levy, abolishing the taxes previously applied to institutions and replacing them with state transfers. Transfers which were commensurate with the proceeds of the abolished taxes as reported before they were abolished. The absence of systems for adjusting these statutory transfers replacing the eliminated local taxes, at least to inflation, led to a serious financial crisis affecting institutions, driving up their debt, which was addressed by state support interventions whose regulation was characterised by complete instability.

In the case of the regions, meanwhile, their financial autonomy was recognised but, besides having dependence on the laws of the Republic, this did not afford any real power of taxation as it provided only for internal taxes, suggesting that the regions were considered merely as revenue holders. Such internal taxes were later recognised only in special circumstances and in a limited number, with some regions allowed to set the rates within a state-imposed range.

The 1948 Constitution fully acknowledged the significant imbalances so characteristic of Italy and, to ensure less developed regions did not lack the necessary resources to carry out their functions, state financial transfers with a balancing function became essential. In this respect, the Constitution provided for a fund to be allocated according to the reduced wealth of the affected communities, along with an additional fund to finance actions to eliminate these imbalances, promoting a greater development of less favoured regions. Ultimately, except for the over-generalised provisions on internal taxes which failed to recognise an outright tax authority, the system outlined by the Constitution appeared fairly balanced since the established purposes of the two funds served to limit the state's discretion. The fact is that the 1948 Constitution model completely blew up, not so much because of the violation of its provisions, but because additional funds were created of an amount that was established sporadically and whose management was often delegated to the ministries of the specific sector concerned. This all meant that the types of revenue envisaged by the Constitution, which were not wholly guaranteed, remained largely insignificant at the amount levied, with most funds coming from other types of income whose regulation was typically unable to provide adequate guarantees in terms of their amount, stability and distribution criteria.

The scenario tends to change drastically when we look to the second half of the 1990s as a result of the legislative measures introduced to improve the autonomous aspect of the legal system under the existing Constitution. A trend that was later developed with the constitutional reform of 2001, which completely rewrote Section V of the Constitution dedicated specifically to the system of autonomy.

On the financial side, there were a variety of changes. First of all, the new constitutional provisions no longer concerned just the regions, but attributed the same financial autonomy to minor territorial entities (municipalities, provinces and metropolitan cities). They also granted tax authority to the institutions: their income system was based on internal taxes which, while under state laws on coordination, had to regulate how tax was applied; alongside internal taxes, there was participation in the tax revenue generated by the respective communities. These two types of revenue, both designed to make sure the entity had continued access to the wealth generated by its community, were inevitably destined to produce maximum financial inequality given the sharp imbalances that characterised the economy and the varying ability to pay taxes of different parts of the country. Specifically to prevent such outcomes, a balancing provision was introduced in favour of territories with a lower tax capacity. Its function, at least in the way it was intended, would ensure supplementary state transfers to those entities that were unable to cover the standard expenses incurred through the exercise of their assigned administrative duties from their internal taxes and their share of local tax revenues. This introduced another new regulation, with respect to the original system from the 1948 Constitution, from which indications can also be drawn in relation to the amount of resources to be guaranteed to each institution.

The goal of the 2001 reform has not really been achieved, to which there have been at least two contributing factors. Firstly, the inability to fully oppose non-balancing positions, intended to ensure as much of the wealth as possible would be kept where it was generated, ended up distorting the reform, preference being given to the compromise solution of ensuring balancing solely to fund state-regulated functions by establishing essential levels of service to be guaranteed under a system of equality throughout the national territory. But beyond that, the failure of the reform was also down to its intrinsic limitation of creating a static system without contemplating rules to address the change, such that the advent of the crisis, starting from the end of the first decade of the 2000s, made the model blow up completely and the state, using its power of financial coordination, freely granted the institutions financial autonomy.

5.5.1 The Constitutional Reform of 2012 and the Implementation of Fiscal Control: The System As a Whole

The four thematic strands seen so far, which have polarised the development of the sector since the 1960s, later converged into a systematic structure with the constitutional reform of 2012 (Law No. 1 of 2012) implementing Fiscal Control. As is known, this required that all signatory States incorporate the European budgetary rules into their national law, following procedures of their choosing, i.e. by constitutional reform or by ordinary law with power over other laws. Unlike other jurisdictions, Italy followed the first approach, with the new Article 97 requiring that all administrations ensure "the balancing of budgets and the sustainability of public debt" "in accordance with EU law". The quantitative constraints on budgetary policy are therefore the same, in terms of scope (general public administrations understood as a single unit) and content (a specific balance of budgets and a specific maximum amount of debt), as those imposed by the European Union on Member States.

These two rules established by the new Article 97 of the Constitution, namely the balancing of budgets and the sustainability of public debt, must be interpreted "in coherence" with the legal system of the European Union. This has a dual meaning: firstly, the quantities to which they refer are the same as those considered by the prohibition on excess deficits, such that balance must be understood as the net level of debt/net credit; secondly, the limit on such quantities is the same as that set by the European Union and is therefore expressed in terms of the ratio to GDP.

And in fact the balance rule is articulated in terms of the net debt/credit shown in the consolidated financial statement of the public administrations, to be calculated by correcting the effects of the economic cycle after accounting for any one-off or temporary measures. The size of this balance, which is the rule to be followed, is that indicated for each year of the period in question by the financial and budgetary planning documents (which according to Law No. 196 of 2009 consist primarily of public finance decision-making) and must be such as to ensure "at least the achievement of the medium-term objective", as provided by the Stability Programme and which, for States whose debt is not significantly less than 60% of GDP, according to the Fiscal Compact must be placed between the balance or surplus and with a deficit no greater than 0.5% of GDP. Quantifying the balance constraint through financial and budgetary planning documents and through the Stability Programme is therefore a national policy decision. However, it is one that must be shared by the Council of the European Union and, more importantly, it must remain within the limits established "by the law of the European Union and by international agreements on the matter" (i.e. by the Six-Pack and the Fiscal Compact, respectively).

Both the set balance limit and the medium-term objective may be temporarily exceeded in the circumstances allowed by the Six-Pack, i.e. during severe economic recessions and extraordinary events outside the control of the state (such as major disasters and serious financial crises). The decision to adopt such measures lies with the government, which consults with the Commission and proposes the measure to Parliament, in addition to the duration of the exemption, the exclusive purposes for which the funds are to be used and the plan to restore the balance limit and, consequently, the medium-term objective. The decision of the Parliament must be made by absolute majority of the members of both Houses.

Regarding the second rule established by the new version of Article 97 of the Constitution for public administrations, i.e. the sustainability of public debt, a single reference is made to European Union law, which means a reduction in overall debt by one-twentieth per year, with the corrections envisaged by the Six-Pack.

Ultimately, a complete transposition of the European rules into the Constitution; however, it would be erroneous to consider that this reintroduction (through a kind of formal reference) of the same constraints imposed by the EU legal system adds nothing to them and is useless and without consequence. In fact, the European rules are quite particular because they are not supported by any jurisdictional control, so the constitutionalisation of these rules is intended to give them a judicial protection that is not provided at European level. In short, a solution that could be seen as an alternative to modifying the Treaty and extending the jurisdiction of the Court of Justice to observing the prohibition on excess deficits and the Stability and Growth Pact.

However, to achieve this result, namely jurisdictional control (evidently of our constitutional court) over the observance of European constraints, it must be possible to determine the contribution made by each budget to their observance or violation. In other words, these constraints, applying to the entire sector of public administration, must be implemented in terms of constraints applied to each institution, such that any sanction of their violation also helps ensure implementation of the European rules. This brings to light the overall structure of the reform which, through the new version of Article 81 of the Constitution, regulated the balance between revenue and expenditure of the state budget, while the amendment to Article 119 of the Constitution established rules for regions and local authorities.

It should also be noted that the last point of the reformed Article 81 and Article 5.3 of Constitutional Law No. 1 of 2012 provide for the adoption of a law to be approved by an absolute majority of the members of each House, the contents of which are listed in a level of detail that is unusual for a constitutional law. More specifically, this law is designed to specify the new constitutional rules regarding items listed by the Constitution itself; the listing of contents is not without consequence since the provisions of the law approved by absolute majority have the force to impose themselves on subsequent laws, and can act as standards interposed with the Constitution, to the extent that their content relates to that provided by the Constitution.

This specification of new constitutional rules was implemented by Law No. 243 of 2012, intending to further reinforce its provisions by stipulating that any repeal, modification or exemption thereof can only be made expressly. It laid down new constitutional rules for the entire sector of public administrations so as to integrate the principles established by the reformulated Article 97 of the Constitution, structuring them into rules applied to individual budgets by specifying the provisions of the reformed Articles 81 and 119 of the Constitution, in the case of the state, regions and local authorities, and expanding the scope of the administrations specifically affected by the reform in the case of non-territorial entities.

In addition to quantitative rules, the constraint imposed by Fiscal Compact on the Member States also concerned the establishment of an independent national body to monitor compliance with these rules. This body was governed by Law No. 243 as cited above, to which this task had been delegated by the constitutional amendment.

5.5.2 Continued: Quantitative Rules on Individual Budgets

The limitations set for the department as a whole are laid down in rules for individual institutions by the financial and budgetary planning documents which, in establishing the overall balance for the sector (in terms of net debt/credit of the effects of the economic cycle, after accounting for one-off and temporary measures), must do so not only for each year of the period in question, but by spreading it across the various sectors that make up the department. The same mechanism is envisaged for the overall debt sustainability rule, whose reduction target for the entire public administration department (namely one-twentieth per year) is divided, by the financial and budgetary planning documents, among the various sectors that make up the department. In other words, a distribution of the overall limit between the various bodies but which is not fully available to the legislator, once the consolidated size has been ensured and used to meet the medium-term objective set by the Stability Programme. Yet it is the same constitutional reform, supplemented by Law No. 243 as cited above, that must determine the balance limits for each sector of the department and to thereby constrain the distribution of the overall limit.

This is provided for in the reformed Article 81 with respect to the state budget. According to the constitutional provision, the recourse to debt is allowed only under certain conditions, and is forbidden outside of these circumstances (point 2 of the reformed Article 81). In this case, the terminology used does not refer to individual debts but rather, based on the general principle of the necessary "coherence with the EU system" (as stated in Article 97 of the Constitution), talks about debt as a balance, i.e. as net indebtedness, and the provision requires the equalising of this balance, which, being the difference between the final revenues and the final expenses after accounting for financial transactions, does not prevent public debt contractions as necessary to renew maturing securities.

Overall there are two different cases in which a negative balance of net debt is possible: effects of the cycle, on the one hand, and authorisation of the Houses in the presence of exceptional events, where the scope of any anti-cyclical policies is bound to differ depending on which of the two required conditions is used to resort, by derogation, to debt. If it is simply an adverse phase in the economic cycle, there is no need for any authorisation adopted by absolute majority of the Houses, while debt recourse procedures must be limited to providing only the funds necessary to offset the lower revenues and higher dead weight costs (i.e. deriving from current legislation) brought about by the negative cycle. However, if exceptional events do occur, they must be assessed by the Houses by an absolute majority and the recourse to debt is without limitation. In the first case, the funds yielded by the debt, in addition to covering the increased expenses, would be used to offset the lower revenues, making them available for any type of expenditure. In the second case, such funds can only be used in the ways established by the Houses themselves in authorising the debt, where they find no constraints (e.g. inapplicability of the golden rule principle) in doing so.

For the budgets of regions and local authorities, there is the reworded Article 119 of the Constitution and the provisions of Chapter IV of Law No. 243 cited above (as amended by Law No. 164 of 2016). The new Article 119 of the Constitution confirms that funds provided by debt transactions can only be used in investment costs, adding however that such operations are in any case permitted "on the condition that the balance of the budget is respected for all entities of each region". In other words, at the regional level (and therefore including the same region in question), deficit institutions must pay (and for the same amount) institutions in surplus.

The constraints that the Article 119 of the Constitution establishes for regions and local authorities take no account of the effects of the economic cycle, such that the possibility of entities resorting to debt remains the same regardless of any negative or positive cyclic performance, despite the effects of an economic expansion or recession being felt on the revenues of regions and local authorities and the costs of many social safety nets being borne by these institutions. The possibility of derogating from balance constraints under exceptional circumstances is also only afforded to the State. In light of this, Law No. 243 cited above establishes that, in such situations, the state must help fund, through transfers to the regions and local authorities, the essential levels of basic services and functions to the extent provided in the financial and budgetary planning documents, taking into account the effects produced by the negative cycle on the institutions' revenue and expenditure. Logically, in a positive cycle, a reverse mechanism is envisaged, with the institutions required to pay any savings and higher revenues they obtain to the state for inclusion in the provision for the amortisation of state securities. The provision of these financial transfers from the centre to the periphery and vice versa is based on the idea that the effects of the cycle must rebound entirely on the state budget, even where they actually concern the revenue and expenses of the regions and local authorities. In short, during a negative cycle, it is only the state that can indebt itself and the extent to which it may do so takes account of the effects of such a situation on the revenues and expenses of the regions and local authorities. Logically, therefore, it should pass on to those entities the funds it has obtained precisely because of their financial situation.

Law No. 243 cited above, unlike Constitutional Law No. 1 of 2012, which makes no express provisions in this respect, also provided balancing rules for non-territorial public administrations which must ensure, both in terms of budget estimates and final accounts and of both accrual and cash-based systems, a non-negative balance between final revenue and final expenditure. Such entities are not able to calculate balances and adjust them based on the effects of the economic cycle, while they also lack the rules, provided for regions and local authorities, on transfers to or from the state in relation to negative or positive effects of the cycle.

5.5.3 Continued: The Content of the State Budget

From the abolition of the original point 3 of Article 81 of the Constitution by the constitutional reform, one could draw the conclusion that the budget law is now assimilated to any other law and is subject to the same legal system. An assimilation that would raise the question of relationships with other laws and, in particular, the question of whether or not it is able to disregard the financial provisions of other laws. Another question that arises concerns the persistence of the intrinsic limit of the budget law of not being able to authorise expenses related to activities that the administration is not already entitled to carry out under normal laws.

The answer to all these questions is deferred by the law reform to be adopted by an absolute majority of the members of each House, who, among other things, must determine what the content of the budget law can and should be.

Law No. 243 of 2012 has, first of all, absorbed into the budget law the content of the law of stability, as provided by Law No. 196 of 2009 in place of the original financial law. The new budget law must comprise two sections, the first of which, of a regulatory nature, having the same content as the law of stability, while the second section corresponds to the "tabular" part of the standard budget law.

The fact that the content of the regulatory part, that once was the content of the law of stability and even prior of the financial law, is governed by provisions interposed with the Constitution is quite relevant for at least two reasons.

Firstly, it must be remembered that the phenomenon of the "*omnibus* financial laws" has made it necessary to limit the type of rules that can be included in the "possible" content of these laws; a requirement that was addressed with different solutions which, as provided by ordinary laws, were however sanctioned only at the level of the *interna corporis* of the parliamentary procedure, which allowed the Chairpersons of the Houses to declare as inadmissible any rules of the financial law (later of the law of stability) that were not related to what could be its content. Law No. 243 cited above constructs these limitations in terms substantially similar to that provided in Law No. 196 cited above, since the provisions of this part of the budget law must be functional to the objectives of the economic and financial planning documents; must take effect after the 3 years considered by the budget; cannot provide for legislative powers or measures of a local or micro-sectoral nature; and cannot be of a regulatory or organisational nature. What changes is the effectiveness of these limitations, since the fact of being provided for by rules interposed with the Constitution implies that their violation foreshadows a real constitutional violation.

Secondly, it must be remembered that in addition to their "possible" content, the laws of stability (and even before the financial laws) had a "necessary" content that consisted, inter alia, of determining budget balances and, in particular, setting the maximum level of recourse to the financial market. Such decisions were thus reserved for these laws, but this was done through ordinary measures that would probably not have prevented another law from increasing the recourse to the financial market established in the decision on the budgetary manoeuvre. Law No. 243 cited above proposes the same sphere of exclusive jurisdiction in favour of the budget law, whose first section must determine the balances and the maximum limit of recourse to the financial market, while the second section must establish the maximum amount of government securities net of those to be repaid. Again in this case, what changes is the effectiveness of this jurisdictional reserve, which, being established by interposed rules, is bound to make any non-budgetary legal provisions having budget-impacting content constitutionally unlawful.

As for the so-called "tabular" part, between the two orders of constraints that derived from Article 81.3 of the Constitution (that of not being able to authorise expenses related to activities that the administration is not already entitled to carry out under normal laws, and that of not being able to modify or disregard provisions contained in other laws), Law No. 243 cited above confirmed the former and modified the latter, albeit in line with what already occurred with the aforesaid Law No. 196. The need for expenses authorised by the budget to relate to activities that the administration is already entitled to carry out follows the clarification that budgetary forecasts must be "formed on the basis of current legislation" (Article 15.3). The possibility of disregarding the provisions of other laws, however, lies between two orders of limitations. This possibility can only consist of a reformulation of financial quantities, which means that only those provisions of actual expenditure laws (those which determine the amount of the foreseen expenditure without requiring the administration to be involved) may be disregarded—and not provisions that create expenditure mechanisms (such as those which grant subjective rights to obtain financial services from the administration). Furthermore, this possibility must be exercised "under the conditions and within the limits provided by state law".

The budgetary law regulation concludes with the provision under the new Article 81 of the Constitution, which subjects "every law" and no longer "any other law" to the obligation of financial coverage; a norm which, in the 1948 wording, referred only to those non-budgetary laws, such that the scope of the change lies in imposing the obligation of coverage also to the budget law. The meaning of this is not easy to understand since the budget law now faces quantitative constraints directly from the regulation on "recourse to debt", which, in reality concerning "net debt", has the primary goal of actually limiting the budget. Consequently, as long as the costs make up the "net debt" balance, such a problem of mandatory coverage should not even arise as it would be impacted by the limitations imposed on that balance. All this is to say that the budget law is intrinsically covered to the extent that the net debt balance resulting from its provisions complies with the constraints discussed, while in the event that such compliance is not present—even prior to a violation of the coverage requirement—an infringement of these constraints would be found. Probably the only recognisable effect from extending mandatory coverage to the budget law is the application to it (and in particular to its first section) of the coverage methods which require, first and foremost, the quantification of expenses and a technical report accompanying the relevant draft law and any amendments.

Chapter 6
The Administrative Jurisdiction in Italy: The Path Toward a Speciality to Serve Full Protection of Rights Against Public Authority

Gian Domenico Comporti

Contents

Abstract This essay analyses the evolution of the administrative justice in Italy by remarking the change, begun in the end of the last century and improved with the entry into force of the 2010 Code of Administrative Trial, toward a system of full protection of rights and interests harmed by the public power. A relevant stage of such evolution is also the dialogue established with the European Court of Human Rights and the European Court of Justice: the resulting dialectic between different systems, indeed, may lead to re-interpret and update in a critical sense the traditional speciality of the public administration and its judge.

G. D. Comporti (✉)
University of Siena, Siena, Italy

D. Sorace et al. (eds.), *The Changing Administrative Law of an EU Member State*,
https://doi.org/10.1007/978-3-030-50780-0_6

6.1 A Long Season of Ambiguous Justice

Administrative jurisdiction is a polysemous concept commonly used to indicate all the means—such as administrative and judicial appeals—provided by a legal system "in order to ensure the conformity of administrative action to laws".[1]

The Italian system of administrative jurisdiction has had complex origins and has been characterized by an ambiguous nature.

Being born by a gradual detachment from the ordinary *jurisdictio*, this system is the result of an experimental workshop having its main grounds in the fervour of French Revolution and the impassive rationalism of 1800s Napoleonic reforms (28 Pluviôse of year VIII). Such experiment, due to the distinction between active administration—that is the unilateral exercise of authority free from "any delay due to litigation and collegial discussion"[2]—and administrative disputes—capable to satisfy citizens' demand for justice through a review over administrative acts—has finally led to define the two main terms which have dialectically fostered the modern form of administrative State: authority and justice.

Since then, the evolution of remedies has proceeded along with the postulate—of historical and cultural rather than legal origin—that administrative jurisdiction cannot be organized outside the structures of the public authority in a system deriving from the French model—as the Italian one is. Thus, such evolution has been marked by a frantic search for a balance between two conflicting poles: discretion of administrative bodies and freedom of citizens.

The first footstep has been the "abolitionist" trade-off choice of 1865, which was firstly conceived as a bold liberal project to subject the whole public administration to the jurisdiction of ordinary courts as well as any private citizen, but has actually maintained the Council of State in its double role of special judge over certain mandatory subjects and conflicts of jurisdiction.

Such process has continued with the Crispi reform of 1889: instead of rebuilding the foundations of the system, this reform has just completed it by establishing the Fourth Section of the Council of State—with authority to invalidate unlawful acts for the sake of administrative legality and against the bias of the political address set by the majority—beside the jurisdiction of ordinary courts—with authority to check facts at issue and to award damages.

The Constitution of the Republic of 1948, despite outlining a unitary system of jurisdiction based upon the protection of individuals (Articles 24, 103 and 113), has finally accepted the dualism inherited from the past, namely the presence of a special jurisdiction for public authority to ensure the "justice within administration" (Article 100 of Constitution) through the judgement over special types of rights (the so-called legitimate interests) and with the further provision of exclusive jurisdiction over ordinary rights of individuals in "particular matters specified by the law" (Article 103, paragraph 1 of Constitution).

[1]Nigro (1983), p. 21.

[2]Romagnosi (1814), p. 19.

Therefore, a long season has passed without any breaking point since the beginnings, as the trade-off formulation of Article 7 of 2010 Code of Administrative Trial (CAT) may ultimately prove.

Neither any exception can be found in the creation of Regional Administrative Courts (RAC) in place of Provincial Councils during the 1970s decade,[3] as long as it is true that such reform has been implemented mostly in the perspective to enhance a pluralist and autonomist model of State. As result, the novelty of a first instance court at hand of citizens, while has increased their chances for direct challenge against all administrative acts and, as such, the frequency of their access to the jurisdiction, on the other hand has not brought a radical change in the previous system of rights protection. Rather, it has resulted in a useful instrument to unveil the flaws of such system.

Hence, laying on the background of a systematic approach—more focused on the theoretical perspective of conflicts in public authorities' organization rather than the practical dimension of procedures and development of remedies fitting the evolution of individuals' interests—a real "historicist myth"[4] has finally gained a foothold by stating that administrative jurisdiction, on the grounds of the "positive result of the test run by history"[5] and the prestige by this way acquired, has proved to be an institution "necessary in any time and in any system".[6]

6.2 A Conflicting Authority in the Perspective of Balances Within the Legal System

The key word marking such long season has been the idea of conflict, conceived as a guarantee for the constitutional autonomy of the public administration and its special jurisdiction. Its purpose was to prevent ordinary courts from carrying out any review over the acts of a public authority, with respect to which the ultimate judge could be only the King with his sovereign prerogatives. Such idea has become reality into the legal form of conflict of powers, originally provided as a preferential and extraordinary means reserved only to public authority for avoiding any interference by judges. This footprint has characterised all the subsequent evolution of this instrument, once that it has been transferred from the field of relationships between public authorities to the area of conflict of jurisdictions. Its transplant into the Code of Civil trial Procedure (CCP) in the 40s has removed such privilege indeed, making the conflict of jurisdiction a common instrument available to all litigants within a trial;

[3]Declared unconstitutional by the sentences of the Constitutional Court 22.3.1967, No. 30, and 20.4.1968, No. 33.

[4]García de Enterría (2010), p. 45.

[5]See para. 1 of the Report to the special Committee provided by the General Assembly of the Council of State on June 30th 1946.

[6]Romano (1932), p. 4.

notwithstanding, the evocative sense of a system of balances laying in the background and influencing the developments of the procedure has remained unaltered.

In this context it should be natural that the solution of issues on jurisdiction were considered as an essential check over the organisational and systematic prerequisites of the court seised in the case to exert its authority. Therefore, such issues would have affected the final decision on the merits beyond any limit, due to the power of courts to raise them *ex officio* in any state and grade of the proceeding (Article 37 of CCP). The question of the recognition of the proper court to settle the case—defined by some authors as a real "torment"—has then become prevailing over the substantive matter of the case itself. Indeed, while in private disputes the award in favour of one litigant means that he has a right to be protected in accordance with substantive laws, the protection of citizen's rights in disputes against the public authority, on the contrary, has been artificially de-structured in distinct steps, the first of them being the formal classification of the action and the object of the claim.

The uncertain recognition of the court having authority on the case has pushed authors and judges to examine several applicable parameters to solve the question (*petitum*, as the object of the claim; *causa petendi*, as the entitlement to the claim). At the end, the choice has been toward an arrangement in line with the theory of reduction of rights affected by authority—even if unlawfully exerted. Such choice, based upon the general distinction between situations of lack of authority—corresponding to individual rights fully protected under ordinary jurisdiction—and wrongful exercise of authority—corresponding to legitimate interests protected under administrative jurisdiction—has led to fragment remedies into a dualist set, made of separate and reciprocally-excluding compartments, which has shown to be largely ineffective in the reality.

Along this path the administrative courts have become specialised in judging over the existence and the validity of authoritative acts. Since, a stabilization of some characteristics of the administrative trial, starting from the primacy of annulment. Such action, bringing essentially to a negative remedy—that is, the elimination of the act—and thus allowing the administrative body to exert again its authority, has appeared to be the most appropriate in order to safeguard the autonomy of the public authority from the power of review held by judges. At the same time, less regard has been paid to other remedies, such as the mere declaration and the condemnation, which have been developed only in marginal cases of absence of the authoritative act (such as in the cases of so-called "silence-breach" of the duty to provide with an authoritative act)[7] or absence of administrative discretion (such as in the so-called "equal relationships", wholly regulated by the law).[8]

In this context it is extremely significant that some effectiveness has been recovered only in two areas lying outside the ordinary trial of cognisance, which

---

[7]Conceived by the Council of State since its General Assembly held on May 3rd 1960, No. 8, in *Giur. it.*, 1960, III, 257.

[8]Typically those regarding the economic claims of the public servants, analysed since Council of State, Section V., 1.12.1939, n. 795, in *Giur. it.*, 1940, II, 37.

are respectively: the proceeding for precautionary measures, which has been progressively extended[9] to atypical remedies capable to better ensure an urgent and interim protection of new interests to pretention; and the proceeding for administrative compliance, where the idea of a final judgement, which is at the same time open to reviews on facts, has been experimented jointly with the potentialities of a cooperation between the judge and the *ad acta* commissioner. However, these further developments have just proved, even if implicitly, the limits of the ordinary trial of cognisance.

6.3 From the Jurisdiction (on the Legality) of the Authority to a Jurisdiction for the Protection of Interests Harmed by Public Authority: The Centrality of Actions

A different backdrop has taken place in the end of the last century, in line with a general trend of "reshaping" the administrative jurisdictions which has affected many European countries.[10]

An important factor in such change of paradigm has been the European law, as implemented within Italian domestic law by renewing the model of exclusive jurisdiction.

European Law, besides inducing an intense dialogue among Courts—to be analysed hereafter—has played a key role especially in the field of public procurement contracts. Indeed, the provision of full and effective remedies[11] for the sake of developing open and competitive markets in public procurements has reduced the procedural autonomy of EU Members States and has pushed forward the introduction of compensatory remedies[12] and the redefinition of atypical precautionary measures.[13]

---

[9]Starting from the sentence of Constitutional Court on 28.6.1985, No. 190, in *Foro it.*, 1985, I, 1881.

[10]García de Enterría (2010), p. 55.

[11]The first directive on review procedures (Directive n. 89/665/CEE) already aimed that reviews ought to be taken "effectively and, in particular, as rapidly as possible" (Article 1) and imposed to Member States to provide comprehensive measures, including urgent and interim ones, "with the aim of correcting the alleged infringement or preventing further damage to the interests concerned", up to the invalidation of unlawful decisions and the award of damages (Article 2).

[12]As it has happened with Article 13 of Legislative Act February 19th 1992, No. 142. As courts have noted, "in this way it is admitted for the first time in the Italian law the right to compensation deriving from administrative acts which violate legitimate interests (as interests of competitors within a public tender offer normally are)" (see Cass., S.U., 10.11.1993, No. 11077, in *Foro it.*, 1994, I, 3138.

[13]As set out in Article 3 of Legislative Act July 21st 2000, No. 205, amending the Article 21, para. 7, of the Legislative Act No. 1034/1971. A similar trend had already been anticipated by the UE case law, with the decisions of the Court of Justice Case 19.6.1990, *Factortame*, and Case 21.2.1991, *Zuckerfabrik Südertihmarschen AG*.

By the other point of view, exclusive jurisdiction has not merely extended its scope, since 1998,[14] to entire sets of subject matters (such as public works, public contracts, land planning), but also has become the chance to centralise into administrative trial all the remedies available to citizens—included compensation[15]—against any form of public authority (even when such authority is carried out in way of fact, and so by indirect exercise).[16]

The subsequent intertwining of judicial actions and judging techniques has shaken the rather peaceful system previously in force and has paved the way to significant developments, resulting in two convergent directions.

The first one has regarded the compensatory remedy and has taken place within the period of time elapsed between the memorable judgement No. 500/1999[17] and the likewise important judgement No. 30254/2008,[18] both ruled by the Joint Sections of Corte di Cassazione. In that specific context, the issue on interplays between action for invalidation and claim for damages has not only become the starter of a vibrant debate—mostly ideological—between the two jurisdictions, but also the chance to reconsider the different types of remedies in view to realise a full relief of harmed interests. The withdrawal from a purely abstract and geometric approach, due to a newer perspective refusing formalism and focusing rather on the essence of remedies, has shifted the attention to the instrumental and subjective nature of jurisdictional protection of rights and legitimate interests (both regarded with equal dignity). Such new approach is better comprehensive of all "the different remedies available to the authority of different judges" and, furthermore, leads the person whose interest has been violated to take the centre stage: this person "not only has the right to choose whether to start proceedings or not, but also to choose the type of action (. . .) in order to react to the fact that his substantive interest (. . .) has been left unsatisfied".[19]

The other direction of change, in line with the first one, has moved from the acknowledgment of full and comprehensive remedies accorded by various courts and the resulting convergence of their respective methods to work. Such approach

[14]As effect of Articles 33 and 34 of the Legislative Decree March 31st 1998, No. 80.

[15]As set out by Article 35 of the previously cited L.D. No. 80/1998.

[16]As pointed out by these important decisions: Const. Court, 6.7.2004, No. 204, in *Foro it.*, 2004, I, 2594, and Const. Court, 11.5.2006, No. 191, *ivi*, 2006, I, 1625.

[17]See Cass., S.U., 22.7.1999, n. 500, in *Foro it.*, 1999, I, 2487, which has admitted the compensation of damages deriving from unlawful administrative acts, considered as such to be violating legitimate interests.

[18]See Cass., S.U., 23.12.2008, No. 30254, in *Foro it.*, 2009, I, 731, which has rejected the theory stating that the award of damages must be conditional upon the prior invalidation of the administrative act. Such theory was held up by Council of State (General Assembly) 22.10.2007, No. 12, in *Foro it.*, 2008, III, 1, on the assumption of an indefectible "nature of appeal of the action before the administrative court, which has the authority (. . .) not only to annul the act, but also to conform the administrative action in order to ensure a satisfactory and lawfully balance between the two interests at stake".

[19]As it can be read in Cass., S.U., No. 30254/2008.

has led to review the very notion of jurisdiction, to be conceived no more as expression of the authority to judge over certain disputes, but instead as a unitary "public service"[20] given by multiple courts which do not belong to separate spheres anymore, but rather concur together to ensure, "on the basis of distinct authority, a more adequate answer to the claim for justice".[21]

These developments has generated some relevant and converging effects. Firstly, it has grown up the awareness that the primary goal of the process "is to fulfil the right of the parties to have a positive or negative response on the object of the dispute (...) *justice is justice on the merits*".[22] Then, the pivotal role of the claims brought by the parties has replaced the focus on the powers of the judge. As consequence, an "erosion of the *ex officio* principle on jurisdiction issues and a favour for the different rules concerning the court authority, which are based on the choice of the party to raise the issue and are precluded by behaviours of implicit acquiescence, formerly considered as irrelevant",[23] have occurred. These are actually the grounds laid down by Article 9 of CAT, which limit only to the first instance the authority of the court to find *ex officio* its lack of jurisdiction. The same provisions rule also that, in the second instance, the issue on jurisdiction must be raised by means of a specific appeal against that part of the judgement stating on or implying it. Furthermore, we may account a relevant convergence of the two high courts, due to an in-depth analysis of the respective research offices (Office for Rulings Record of the Corte di Cassazione and Studies Office of the Council of State), on the inadmissibility of an appeal relying upon the lack of jurisdiction, if such appeal is filed by the plaintiff whose claim has been rejected in the merits as result of the first instance. This rule implies indeed that the correct recognition of the court having jurisdiction in the case, despite concerning a general interest of the system beyond individuals, does not convey anymore an imperative value of the process worth to be defended at expense of other values, such as order and celerity of the proceedings.[24] Justice, as it is increasingly regarded as a scarce resource to be administered properly for the collectivity, is now seen in its practical and relational extent within the specific case

---

[20]As it can be read in Cass., S.U., 9.10.2008, No. 24883, in *Foro it.*, 2009, I, 806, on the implicit judgement over the question regarding jurisdiction.

[21]See Const. Court 12.3.2007 No. 77, in *Foro it.*, 2007, I, 1009, on *translatio iudicii.*

[22]Cass., S. U., 6.3.2009, No. 5456, in *Foro it.*, 2009, I, 3047.

[23]See again, on the wave of a new interpretation of Article 37 CCP pushed for by the cited Cass., S. U., No. 24883/2008, Cass., S.U., No. 5456/2009, cit. This heading has been acknowledged, on the side of administrative law, by the Article 9 of CAT and incisively by Council of State, Section VI, 26.3.2015, No. 1595.

[24]See Cass., S.U., 20.10.2016, No. 21260, in *Foro it.*, 2017, I, 966. The principle has been confirmed by Cass., S.U., 19.1.2017, No. 1309, in *Foro it.*, 2017, I, 1277, with regard to the trial on retirement-welfare accounting and, finally, by Council of State (General Assembly), ord. 28.7.2017, No. 4, which has held up the withdrawal of reasoning relying upon a generic concept of "process abuse".

and, consequently, is understood to the very purpose of ensuring a quick and "appropriate satisfaction to the request for relief"[25] brought by the harmed claimant.

The reform of administrative trial regulation enacted with the Legislative Decree No. 104 on July 2nd 2010—having, among others, the purpose to update the set of remedies "capable to reach the needs of the winning claimant"[26]—has sealed the above mentioned developments. Furthermore, it has fostered an in-depth analysis of the administrative jurisdiction matter by a point of view which had been so far unexplored: the plaintiff's powers to shape the process. Consistent with the principle that process must provide any possible action in order to enforce claims arising from a controversy, the administrative trial has overcome the traditional boundaries of the action for invalidation and has opened to different and atypical remedies (see Articles 30 and following of CAT),[27] allowing to judge to adopt all useful measures to protect the alleged right (Article 34, para. 1, lett. "c" of CAT). Such renewed toolbox is now recalling a very sense of full jurisdiction, projecting the authority of the court—even if in theory—beyond the limited scope to ascertain the legality of an administrative act. Actually, such authority may encompass the whole administrative relationship at dispute—as far as the circumstances in the case and the nature of claims allow that.

In one century, the logic of conflict lying at the base of the binary model of remedies, as inherited by the liberal order, has therefore passed on the torch to a monist-inspired dualism, according to which different courts are nowadays committed to a common and service-oriented duty. At the same time, the Corte di Cassazione has been promoted to the role of ultimate authority, to ensure not only the external architecture of the constitutional system and the separation of jurisdictions, but also the means by which every judge enforce the forms of rights' protection enabled by the system.

6.4 The Proceedings: The Claim and Its Conditions

The improvement of administrative jurisdiction described above has led to strengthen the powers of litigants to control the subject matter of the dispute and to deal with its proceedings in a satisfactory manner. However, this trend is not always consistent with other leanings that likewise aim, even if in a broad sense, to enhance accessibility to the trial. Beside the common effect of increasing the chances

[25] As the Court said in the famous CIR-Fininvest case: Cass., Section III; 17.9.2013, No. 21255, in *Rivista di diritto processuale*, 2014, p. 26.

[26] As stated by Article 44, para. 2, letter b), n. 4, of the Legislative Act June 18th 2009, No. 69; see now the provision of Article 34, para. 1, of CAT.

[27] These aspects of the new system of actions are well focused by the decisions of Council of State (General Assembly), 23.3.2011, No. 3, in *Corriere giuridico*, 2011, 979, and Council of State (General Assembly), 29.7.2011, No. 15, in *Foro it.*, 2011, III, 501. See also Cass., S.U., 9.3.2015, No. 4683, in *Urbanistica e appalti*, 2015, 787.

to review any wrongful use of authority, distinct cases should be looked at by different perspectives indeed. It is now worth to analyse them in detail.

By one side, we can first account a rising mindset in favour of "safeguarding the chances to access the process and its final decision in the merits". This line of thinking considers "those outcomes allowing the judge to discharge the trial" for proceeding issues as "not prevailing".[28]

In such context, a jurisdictional review increasingly focused on the substantive elements of the authority rather than the formal ones—both procedural or organisational—becomes very important. As a matter of fact, the Article 21-*octies*, para. 2, of the Legislative Act no. 241 of August 7th 1990[29]—as it prevents the invalidation of due acts for infringement of legal provisions concerning forms or internal proceedings—has already shaped the role that lacks of legality may play within the review judgement, in view of their influence onto the revised act to be adopted by the administration.[30]

Furthermore, there are two other relevant trends to examine in the same perspective. By one side, the administrations' authority to arrange the *res controversa* by removing the challenged act is reviewed more severely. It is noted, indeed, that an *ex officio* annulment justified on formal or procedural issues (for instance: lack of an open session to examine tenders for awarding a public contract) may be unsatisfactory to the harmed interest and should not allow a no-further-proceeding sentence, because this could "hinder the judgement of other significant grounds of appeal" (such as those "capable to produce stronger effects toward the potential award of the contract", as it could be, for instance, a ground of appeal entailing the exclusion of other competitor).[31] By the other side, the rising of "brief" or "simplified" judgements (Article 74 of CAT), justified for reasons of processual economy, has been shepherded by the principle that the conclusive point of fact to focus the judgement upon—with possible overcoming of other grounds of appeal—must appear the most appropriate "to definitively settle the dispute" rather than quickly close the trial.[32]

In such context, the importance of the claimed subject-matter principle has been recently confirmed by the General Assembly of the Council of State, with special reference to the controversial matter of judicial overcoming of appeal grounds. Apart

[28]Council of State, Section IV, 9.1.2014, No. 36.

[29]Regulation of administrative proceedings and right to access to administrative documents.

[30]In this direction, for instance, some judges have stated that such provision has confirmed previous rulings "aiming to assess the actual interest into the appeal, which is denied whenever the claimant cannot expect a different decision by the public office, even as result of a repetition of the act" (Council of State, Section VI, 16.5.2006, No. 2763).

[31]Council of State, Section VI, 2.10.2007, No. 5086, which has wrongly moved from a supposed priority to examine formal lacks capable to affect the whole administrative proceeding, considering the statement that "the administrative trial is subject to the claimed subject-matter principle, being it intended to protect claimant's rights and interests and not merely to carry out an impartial control over the administration and its alleged mistakes".

[32]As stated, ultimately, by Council of State (General Assembly) 27.4.2015, No. 5, in *Giur. it.*, 2015, 2192.

from cases of brief judgements, annulment for lack of authority, overcoming for logic and preliminary issues (for instance: alternative or conditional grounds of appeal) or reasons of economy (the so-called "promptest grounds":[33] see cases of grounds already assessed and rejected, or upholding for lack of fair hearing), it has been ruled that the gradation of appeal grounds, if duly and clearly set by the plaintiff, binds the court to follow such order, even if this could "lead to outcomes not perfectly fitting with public interest and legality".[34] One of these outcomes, indeed, may be to provide the winning claimant with a stricter constraint onto the administration for the repetition of the act.

More ambiguous tendencies show up, instead, when organisational issues and public interests of particularly sensitive nature are involved.

By the first point of view, the positive reception of direct appeals against acts has been better marked out when such review causes an indefinite break in administrative proceeding.[35] It has been noted indeed that acts having a constraining effect on the administrative action (such as proposals or opinions) have the scope to safeguard the "distinction of roles, functions and authority" of certain bodies and hence they are not deemed to define the procedure: as consequence, courts has stated that only the final act of the proceeding is appealable, being it the actual expression of the authority and the reference for any review of its grounds.[36] Moreover, when judges have examined the impact of authority issues on the questions of gradation and overcoming of appeal grounds,[37] they have held up a subjective interpretation of the provision set by the Article 34, para. 2, of CAT—provision preventing the court to rule over administrative powers not yet exercised. Particularly, they have regarded such powers as "those unexercised by the relevant authority or that body called upon to exert its powers in the relevant administrative sub-system". On the basis of this reasoning, defaults concerning authority or compulsory proposals or opinions have been regarded so seriously that the plaintiff's right to gradate the appeal grounds has

[33]Also conceived by civil courts as a selective criterion of the "most evident, plain and promptest reason to lead to a decision, regardless whether based on proceedings issues or in the merits", whose enforcement "is able to ease the activities of investigation and drawing of the reasoning" (see Cass., S.U., 12.12.2014, No. 26242, in *Foro it.*, 2015, I, 862, regarding contracts invalidation).

[34]Council of State (General Assembly), No. 5/2015, which finally finds the "overcoming of the traditional case-law rule – mainly concerned with a consistent protection of public interest (. . .) – stating that it is always up to the court to set the order of consideration of appeal grounds, based on their substantive relevance (. . .) which is not modifiable by the mere request of the plaintiff".

[35]What really matters being "the preclusion of the following progression of the proceeding", as stated by Council of State, Section VI, 9.6.2005, No. 3043; Council of State, Section V, 2.10.2000, No. 5224.

[36]Council of State, Section IV, 28.3.2012, n. 1829, which also excepts the cases where the administration: (a) does not proceed any further, remaining silent before the request of the party; (b) notifies the interested party of the constraining act with adverse opinion, thereby assuming such act as its own.

[37]This question is hardly debated among courts, after the 2010 CAT has not confirmed any provision similar to the one set by Article 26, para. 2, of the RAC Act, which imposed to refer back to the relevant authority in case the issue on authority was accepted.

been limited, being the court prevented from "set rules for an administrative body which has not exerted its *munus* yet".[38] In such cases, generic principles ("protect the legality of administrative action and underlying public interests") and sensitive needs to keep the judiciary system efficient (that is, to limit the "excess of protection, often resulting in very abuses of process") ultimately prevail over protection of individual rights, forcing the plaintiff to choose between the two: not to raise any issue concerning the authority of the public office (and other similar issues), or raise them being aware that they cannot be gradated.

With regard to requisites of actions (that is, entitlement and interest of the plaintiff to bring the action), it should be noted that the common attitude to widen the access to jurisdiction has not always been consistent with the utmost protection of the harmed claimant's interest (that is, the subjective point of view of judicial relief). In many cases, indeed, general interests related to the community or the sector which the plaintiff was operating within had to be accounted as well.

The growing relevance of collective and general interests[39]—as much as third parties' interests involved in administrative proceedings—has led the law-in-practice to hold the *vicinitas*—adopted in the 1970s to settle cases on building constructions[40]—as a flexible indicator of the connection (in several respects: by space, by association or membership, by function) between individual interest and the context affected by public authority. In this way, the larger is the objective or subjective range of conflicting interests, the more is deemed sufficient a bare "display of potential harm"[41]—if not a simple link to "matters or values of constitutional rank", such as environment.[42] In such cases, indeed, the position of the claimant is connected with a broader interest to govern properly certain areas of the legal system.[43] In this special regard, we should finally account a growth of special statutory entitlements to plead for protection of general interests, such as freedom of competition and regular course of public contracts market:[44] here, the trial clearly

[38]See Council of State (General Assembly), No. 5/2015, cit.

[39]Such as those regarding, for instance: appropriate land planning, environmental protection, consumer protection, efficiency of public offices and public concessionaires, competition and economic regulation, electoral rights, gender equality compliance.

[40]Council of State, Section V, 9.6.1970, No. 523, in *Giur. it.*, 1970, III, 193. Such selective test, based upon the "housing settlement" of the facing householder, has progressively expanded to include any form of "lasting relationship" with the interested area and, therefore, has been regarded as a flexible assessment relying upon "the nature and the dimension of the building (...), its purpose, its impact on the urban context and the outcomes (...) on the quality of life of those who, being residents, workers or similar", live in the area (Council of State, Section V, 20.2.2009, No. 1032, with regard to the opening of a mall).

[41]Council of State, Section V, 28.7.2015, No. 3711.

[42]Council of State, Section IV, 9.1.2014, No. 36.

[43]As it has been stated, for instance, by Council of State, Section IV, 7.5.2015, No. 232 and 6.2.2017, No. 491 with regard to the "interest in the regular course of competition, in order not to unlawfully harm the interest of another competitor in the same market".

[44]The reference is to Article 21-*bis* of the Legislative Act No. 287 on October 10th 1990, as introduced by the Article 35 of the Law Decree No. 201 of December 6th 2011, n. 201 and

overrides the principle that invalidation is at disposal of the claimant and then is conceived as the instrument to bridge over the failures of those pre-trial administrative proceedings which should ensure, by public enforcement, the regulation of crucial values of the system.[45]

6.5 A Review Over Administrative Discretion Hardly Facing with Facts at Issue

A judge having an effective authority to remedy defaults of administrative proceeding, in view to ensure a full relief to the interests involved within, is definitely approaching an appeal-based model. This model is actually typical of other legal systems, all having the common ambition to fully ascertain the facts at issue and the assessments made by the administration. In this regard, it should be recalled the domestic experience of "own jurisdiction", exercised by the Council of State since before the Italian unification and then converged into the "jurisdiction in the merits" enacted by the Crispi Act of 1889: such experience, particularly, has been characterised by a full-extent authority of the court to ascertain facts at issue in order to get from them, rather than from internal documents of the proceeding, the reference for the proper administrative decision. The modern rule of *full jurisdiction*, as laid down in Articles 6 and 13 of ECHR and Article 47 of the Charter of Fundamental Rights of the EU, is ideally in line with that experience. Indeed, the Court of Strasbourg reads those provisions as giving the full and autonomous authority to judge over "all the points at issue",[46] in order to tackle and settle[47] "every relevant issue, in fact or at law, for the final decision".[48]

Such a proximity of legal and cultural sources from different times and places—all nourished by shared goals and common procedures, all aiming to guarantee civil liberties—leads us to distance from a sort of doctrinarism, which has marked many of the most widespread approaches to the matter of public authority. Therefore, it is

converted into Legislative Act No. 214 of December 22nd 2011, which empowers the Antitrust Authority to challenge general administrative acts, regulations and other provisions enacted by any public administration when they infringe competition rules. Furthermore, after the abrogation of the so called constraining recommendation set out by Article 211 of the Legislative Decree No. 50 of April 18th 2016 (Public Contracts Code-PCC), a similar instrument is now available to ANAC (Anti-corruption Authority) to challenge public offers for tenders and other provisions infringing the rules on public contracts (see the new Article 211, para. 1-*bis* and 1-*ter*, of the PCC, as introduced by Article 52-*ter* of the Law Decree No. 50 of April 24th 2017, No. 50 converted into Legislative Act No. 96 of June 21st 2017).

[45]Council of State, Section V, 30.4.2014, No. 2246, in line with Const. Court, 14.2.2013, No. 20.

[46]See ECHR, case 23.6.1981, *Le Compte, Van Leuven and De Meyer v. Belgium*, para. 61.

[47]"Point by point, without ever having to decline jurisdiction when replying to them or ascertaining various facts", as stated by ECHR, case 17.4.2012, *Steininger v. Austria*, para. 50.

[48]ECHR, II, case 13.2.2003, *Chevrol v. France*, para. 83.

time to proceed with new critical eyes to the recognition of "boundaries demarcating the limit of administrative discretion—not reviewable—and the limit of jurisdiction".[49]

Firstly, we should be aware that only a thin line divides "the intellectual process of verifying the internal logic and consistency of the reasoning behind the challenged act and the process resulting in a choice among several evaluative options, more or less arguable, related to the merits of the administrative action at dispute".[50] Secondly, it should be accounted a margin of uncertainty due to the contrast between formal statements and real outcomes of decisions, as well as to some kind of suggestive wording (such as the distinction between "hard/soft" or "external/internal" review) which presume to rationalise the many cases of administrative discretion. On this background, we can argue that the said limit now depends on whether the assessments made by the administration is questionable or not. In such trajectory, the equation "merits equals technical discretion" has been superseded and the same assessments are now reviewed by the standpoint of "appropriateness of technical criterions and applicative process".[51]

This said, once we shift from the mere description to the analysis of the judicial review—with special reference to the actual development of proceedings and their interactions with the trial—it should be noted that all relevant facts, as well as requirements set by the law, are generally capable to be ascertained and judged by the court. Exceptions may regard those choices marked by a strong political colour, due to democratic representation concerns. Even the more complex facts regulated by independent authorities tend to pass through the review process, given that the principle of effectivity prevents the court—when facing a technical complexity, or when the assessment behind the regulatory choice is hard to understand—from judging by appearance. On the contrary, the court has the "duty to go beyond appearances and verify the inner reasonableness of the choice adopted".[52]

The core of genuine choices—that is, the merits—is covered by a prerogative for the administration instead. Such prerogative, however, is no more intended in a general sense; on the contrary, it must be observed in a "circumstantial" perspective, that is, by accounting the whole context of timing, facts and inquiries as well as their

[49]See Cass., S.U., 16.1.2014, No. 774, arguing about a path finally opened by the evolutionary spirit of European law and "marked by the respect of two fundamental principles: fullness of rights protection (...) and proportionality, all aimed to limit the unreviewable administrative discretion".

[50]As said by Cass., S. U., 8.3.2012, No. 3622. Echoes of the mindset that firmly disapproves a model of review against assessments are clearly notable. This mindset is often revealed when jurisdiction issues are under judgement: see, for instance, Cass., S. U., 17.2.2012, No. 2312 and Cass., S. U., 20.1.2014, No. 1013. In the same direction, Council of State, Section VI, 14.8.2013, No. 4174, in *Foro it.*, 2014, III, 173, states that the review over arguable assessments of facts should be limited to symptomatic cases of misuse of powers, "being unnecessary to compare the public interest and the actual interests pursued by the administration".

[51]As clarified since the important decision of Council of State, Section VI, 9.4.1999, No. 601, in *Foro it.*, 2001, III, 9.

[52]Council of State, Section VI, 19.1.2016, No. 165, in *Giornale dir. amm.*, 2016, 684.

developments in the case. After all, the Article 31, para. 3, of CAT (as referred to by Article 34, para. 1, lett. c, of CAT) adopts the same perspective, as it extends such review—at the trial stage—to the claimed subject-matter in cases of inaction and denials by the administration.[53] It may well happen, as a matter of fact, that the inquiry carried out during the administrative proceeding entails a reduction or even a depletion of the estimated range of choices, so that only one of the potential decisions remains adoptable; no more room for any discretion or assessment is left over. The judgement in favour of the plaintiff may as well outline a "pathway" that constraints such choice, once the challenged administration has to repeat the act.[54] In this regard we should note that administrative trial is still curbing the general rule that judgement covers both the claimed and claimable facts. At the same time, extreme theories arguing that a negative judgement prevents the administration from any repetition of the act have not gained consensus. Hence, it is possible that facts or circumstances already accounted, but improperly appraised as a whole,[55] are reconsidered for new assessments or in-depth analysis—in accordance with the principles of autonomy and responsibility of administration, as ensured by the "remand" rule set out in Articles 88, para. 1, lett. f) and 112, par 1, of CAT. Despite these remarks, however, it is a fact that the renewal of the administrative proceeding is actually subject to "precise limits and constraints".[56]

Thus, apart from infrequent cases of precise rulings, which preclude the appraisal of elements already deemed as neutral or irrelevant,[57] in the ordinary cases of judgements based upon formal lacks, inadequate statement of reasons or breach of instrumental and in-proceeding duties,[58] the judicial ascertainment of relevant facts is constraining on the administration. New assessments of such facts and circumstances should not be carried out seeking for "whatever ground" or just repeating arguments that have already been judged as inadequate.[59] On the contrary, they must show the "acknowledgement of evident and serious mistakes in the previous assessment", in accordance with principles of sound administration, fairness and good faith.[60] Furthermore, arguments such as the principle of effective protection, or the need for every trial to result in a definitive settlement of the case, have supported the so called "tempered *one shot*" theory, according to which the administration, once its first decision of denial is annulled, has the duty to re-examine "the matter in its

[53]Council of Administrative Justice (CAJ), jurisd. Section, 15.9.2014, No. 541.

[54]Council of State, Section IV, 7.4.2014, No. 1625.

[55]Council of State, Section IV, 22.1.2013, No. 356.

[56]Council of State, (General Assembly), 15.1.2013 n. 2, in *Urb. app.*, 2013, 952.

[57]Council of State, Section IV, n. 1625/2014.

[58]That is, all situations that Council of State, (General Assembly), 9.6.2016, No. 11, in *Foro it.*, 2017, III, 186, has defined—borrowing a concept of private law—as "obligations of means", so excluding any power of the judge to replace the discretional authority of the administration and reach the result expected by the citizen.

[59]*Ibid.*, para. 6.2.4 of the decision reasoning.

[60]Council of State, (General Assembly), No. 2/2013, cit.

entirety and to raise immediately every question deemed to be relevant, so that after its new assessment it cannot issue other negative decisions, even if based on facts not yet examined".[61]

Such thinking represents the highest achievement coming out of the interaction between trial and administrative proceeding, as concerned by European law too, and definitely shows that a reception of the *full jurisdiction* rule relies mostly on the integrity and responsibility of every player involved in the case, rather than on abstract concepts.

These leanings of the administrative jurisdiction toward a full-extent authority of review put the *quaestio facti* at the centre of the trial. As consequence, the focus shifts on the investigation. Although some provisions of CAT (Articles 63 and 64) acknowledge the claimed subject-matter principle, such investigation still suffers some lacks: (a) considering that the trial rotates around the beginning petition and the final decision, there is no specific stage and judge for the research of evidence; (b) cultural issues still restrain from using the same means of proof provided for the civil trial.

With regard to the first point, it should be noted that administrative trial has traditionally a concentrated structure and there is no judge appointed to settle all issues on proceedings and proofs since the beginnings of the trial. Therefore, apart from some appreciable initiatives taken by single RACs Presidents at a local stage, the proof of facts briefly described in the appeal petition (Article 40, lett. c, of CAT) is limited, in view of the chamber session for precautionary measures (Article 55 of CAT) or the public hearing for the brief discussion of the case (Article 73 of CAT).

With regard to the second point, we can see that investigative practices are frequently characterized by an uncontrollable use of *ex officio* powers by the judge, who still keeps the role of "lord of the evidence". As consequence, litigants tend not to engage into offering an alternative version of facts and technical aspects of the case and thus their initiative in investigative activities gradually dry up. Moreover, the documentary evidence is still pivotal both in the CAT system and in the practice, despite the action for annulment has been flanked by other types of action (such as condemnation to pay damages or to provide) which clearly refer to elements lying outside the proceedings file.

Relevant signs of such layout are: a reluctant attitude toward informal questioning; the actual disuse of inspective powers as to Articles 63, para. 2 of CAT and 118 of CCP; the rare use of testimonial evidence—allowed in the written form only, as set out in Article 63, para. 3 of CAT—which is sometimes downgraded to the "mere *prima facie* evidence, only capable to legitimate the *ex officio* powers of the judge", or even deemed equivalent to an *affidavit*, because of the common criminal liability in case of perjury;[62] finally, the cold approach towards the technical

---

[61]Council of State, Section IV, 31.3.2015, n. 1686.

[62]See Council of State, (General Assembly), 20.11.2014, No. 32. In the same direction, see Council of State, Section V, 23.2.2015, No. 863. Tar (RAC) Lombardia, Brescia, 25.6.2015, No. 1240, while analysing the admissibility of testimonial evidence (in a case of denial of the residence

expertise—already limited by the CAT to cases where it is considered necessary (Article 63, para. 4, of CAT)—which represents however an important means of investigation in order to acknowledge, in cross examination with litigants-appointed experts, any specialised notion that is still unknown to the administration but is nevertheless necessary to settle autonomously and directly all questions at issue. Not less important is the way courts reach a settlement of claims when judging on damages: by one side, the judgement of pecuniary condemnation is restricted (by the Article 34, para. 4, of CAT) to ascertain the *an debeatur* and to set out rules to calculate such damages,[63] leaving the parties negotiate over their amount and the terms of payment; by the other side, despite the judicial review broadens to the area of torts and shares its general rules on burden of proof, case law frequently shows that the measure of liquidated damages is not aligned with the real circumstances of the case, but rather depends on presumptive and abstract table-based criterions.

The general impression left by the above addressed trends is that any limitation to the claimant's powers to define the subject matter of the trial results, as a matter of fact, into an obstacle to giving the judge a full-extent authority of review over facts. As consequence, traditional arguments in favour of administrative jurisdiction's speciality risk to be perpetuated. Such arguments indeed, as much as they depend either on the alleged informality and quickness of the proceedings or on the presumed awareness and expertise of the judge, clearly derive from the old and out-of-date model of internal jurisdiction—as well as other models of jurisdiction being too close to administration.

---

permit), has pointed out that it must be strictly necessary in order to prove circumstances not included within the reasons of the act and not otherwise acknowledgeable.

[63]Sometimes (as in the case settled by C.G.A.R.S. Section I, 7.11.2017, n. 479) the reasoning is totally vague, so that the initiative for an "indemnity offer", to be examined by the creditor, is left to the administration. Seemingly this is a replacement of the indispensable role of the court and, moreover, it raises some issues in the compliance stage by requiring further ascertainment. It is not casual that judges address it as a "so called "generic" condemnation (. . .) regarding the *an*" (C.G.A. R.S., Section I, 5.6.2016, No. 131). The model is taken from the Article 278 of CCP, but someone seems to overlook that the Article 34, para. 4, of CAT "assumes that the right to damages must be fully ascertained in all its elements and only its measure may be estimated by either the same judgement or, afterwards, through a negotiation to be carried out by the parties in accordance with to the rules set by the court" (Council of State, (General Assembly), 8.10.2009, No. 5; Council of State, Section IV, 25.6.2010, No. 4126).

6.6 Attempts of Dialogue Between Courts in a Multilevel System and the Alarm of a Large-Scale Litigation of Objective Nature

The 2010 enactment of CAT has marked the access of administrative jurisdiction into an open legal system, inspired by principles arising from both the evolving frame of the Constitution and the European law (Article 1 of CAT). Hence, different types of remedies are shifted outside their original environment, with its influences of historical and cultural nature, and project themselves in a multi-level system made of national and international players, where judges take on a central role.

In such changing context, the enhancement of technical solutions takes place through various forms of "dialogue" between courts from different legal systems. This exchange can be addressed as a genuine case of *judicial borrowing*.

We have already noted the tight "confrontation through standardisation" that has characterised the internal dialogue between the civil and the administrative jurisdictions.

Other forms of debate regard national courts, the European Court for Human Rights and the European Court of Justice instead.

On the first side, we should note the trend in private property protection against administrations which unlawfully seize lands for building public facilities. Since 2000, a series of judgements by the Strasbourg Court[64] have pointed out that the "fair balance"—as defined through procedures laid down by law—between the public interest and the respect of fundamental rights (protected in the form of "right of respect" for own possessions, as to Article 1 of ECHR's First Protocol) has been broken by the domestic rule of acquisitive occupation as created by courts.[65] Such rule has become part of our law since 1983, in order to legitimate several *extra ordinem* practices carried out by many local administrations (in other words, *de facto* deprivations of private properties beyond any procedure laid down by law for their expropriation). It resulted in a new form of forced conveyance into the public hand based on a tort—the construction of the public facility—to be rebalanced through compensation to the owner for the economic value of the property. Since then, many attempts to delimit and distinguish various cases have been done, as well as to *ex post* legitimate misconducts of administrations—in the form of acquisition of the land occupied and used for public purposes.[66] Such conducts, indeed, were justified at least on the grounds of a prior appraisal of interests at stake, formally performed through the preliminary proceeding of public use declaration of the facility. However, after several attempts of resistance by

[64]The reference is to the famous judgements of ECHR on 30 may 2000, issued in the cases *Belvedere Alberghiera s.r.l. v. Italia* and *Carbonara e Ventura v. Italia*, in *Foro it.*, 2001, IV, 233.

[65]This rule, which is hardly contested by both private and public law doctrines, has been created by the judicial decision of Cass., S. U., 26.2.1983, No. 1464, in *Foro it.*, 1983, I, 626.

[66]After the rules previously in force were declared unconstitutional by the Const. Court 8.10.2010, No. 293. Now the rules are laid down by the Article 42-*bis* of the D.P.R. 8.6.2001, No. 327.

national courts, both the Joint Sections of Corte di Cassazione (in 2015)[67] and the General Assembly of the Council of State (in 2016)[68] have finally recognised that such rule could not survive any longer. As consequence, they have classified the abusive occupation and transformation of private property within the general scheme of "lasting torts", to be treated under the common rules. That is to say, they do not cause any transfer of private property into public hands but only generate a liability of the administration for damages occurred to the owner.

If the dialogue with the law of the Convention has then brought a *destruens* effect on some contrasting ideas of our domestic law, the trends concerning the *pars construens* of the reasoning adopted in different jurisdictions do not show the same consistency and clarity. Indeed, there is a contrast between: (a) the civil judge, who stresses on the owner's freedom to choose for either the claim for restitution of property (after its restoration, and with faculty to claim damages) or the claim for an amount of damages equivalent to the lost value (and this claim is regarded as a surrender of ownership on such property); (b) the administrative judge, who is more inclined, instead, to enforce traditional remedies against the public authority in order to push for a further administrative action, which is regarded as the only one aimed to find the final settlement of the contrasting interests and, so, the proper remedy for individuals.[69] This is all happening like in a screenplay which is difficult to understand, not only for reason of different approaches and styles of judgement, but particularly because of the match between two different cultures in thinking remedies. And in this match, as a matter of fact, the administrative trial is still regarded as the proper place where administrative action (whether lacking or affected by mistakes) is rescued and then stimulated to ponder, within the course of lawful proceedings, fair expectations of individuals.

Even the Strasbourg Court case law concerning administrative fines with substantive nature of penalties[70] raises a general question on how to allocate rationally the guarantees of defence between the administrative stage—progressively conforming to judicial proceedings principles—and the trial stage, which is required—such as a kind of ideal continuity of the two stages—to provide point by point, with full authority, on the merits of penalty measures affecting citizens' rights. Leaving apart both technical aspects of very complex matters, such as banking and financing, and interpretative stretches that frequently affect forensic

[67]Reference is to Cass., S. U., 19.1.2015, No. 735, in *Foro it.*, 2015, I, 436.

[68]See Council of State, (General Assembly), 9.2.2016, No. 2, in *Foro it.*, 2016, III, 185.

[69]See the recent and important decision of Tar (RAC) Calabria, Section Reggio Calabria, 12.5.2017, Np. 438, in *Foro it.*, 2017, III, 415, which has dissociated from the "old trend" as to the cited sentences of Joint Sections No. 735/2015 and General Assembly No. 2/2016, motivating that the "judiciary function would actually become an ancillary instrument in the hands of individuals' discretion".

[70]Strict tendency enforced since the decision of ECHR, case 8.6.1976, No. 5100/71, *Engel e altri v. Paesi Bassi*, in *Foro it.*, 1977, IV, 97, and confirmed, more recently, by ECHR, Section II, case 4.3.2014, No. 18640/10, *Grande Stevens e a. v. Italia*, *ivi*, 2015, IV, 129.

strategies,[71] it is the "systematic" effect of a purpose-driven concept of court—aiming to best enforce the Convention guarantees on fair trial—that leads to challenge categories (such as administrative proceeding and trial) and distinctions (such as administration vs. jurisdiction) resulting from long and complex evolutionary paths within different countries.

Moreover, it is significant—this time, on the side of European law—the current debate with reference to public contracts. A contrast of opinions has recently occurred on a specific question, that is the order to be followed by the court in addressing two mutually exclusive appeal petitions (the main one and the incidental one), when they both challenge the counterpart's right of action and thus aim to make his petition dismissed as inadmissible. By one side, the preliminary ruling of ECJ pursuant to Article 267, para. 3, of the TFUE has been used as a safety valve, in order to outsource the solution of internal debates arising out of divergent rulings within the highest court.[72] It has then become the additional instrument at the service of nomophylactic function, insofar as any simple Section of the Council of State, when dissenting from the General Assembly's opinion, is enabled to call *ex officio* for a ruling by the EU Court—which is regarded as binding to settle the case—without referring again the question to the internal nomophylactic body.[73] On the other side, such a closer dialogue with a court that addresses the matter of public procurement contracts by the macro-perspective of traditional freedoms (free movement of goods and services, freedom of establishment) has entailed a juxtaposition of different views on the purposes of the trial. One of these views indeed, in the perspective of a "subjective" jurisdiction, is inclined to restrict entitlements to claim for repetition of the administrative proceeding—in the sense that only "the appellant who has regularly taken part to the public tender has the right to claim either his "final" goal, that is the achievement of the contract firstly obtained by his competitor, or alternatively (and often subordinately) his "indirect" goal, that is the invalidation of the whole tender and its consequent repetition".[74] Such view has been facing with another one, according to which all appellants are equally entitled to claim for the exclusion of other competitors—if and when the administration

[71]As admitted by Cass., Section I, 30.6.2016, n. 13433, arguing that "a proper application of Convention principles brings not to an indeterminate standardisation" of legal concepts, "but to a wise use of the *distinguishing*", even in the view of the "substantive and pragmatic approach arising out from European Court decisions".

[72]Such debate is well remarked by the contrasting positions of Council of State, (General Assembly), 10.11.2008, No. 11, in *Foro it.*, 2009, III, 1, and Council of State, (General Assembly), 7.4.2011, No. 4, *ivi*, 2011, III, 306,with regard to relevant interests to bring the action.

[73]These are important principles asserted by the ECJ, Grand Section, 5.4.2016, case C-689/13, *Puligenica*, in *Foro it.*, 2016, IV, 324. An attempt to read such decision rationally and in coordination with national rules has been done by Council of State, (General Assembly), 27.7.2016, n. 19, in *Foro it.*, 2017, III, 309.

[74]Such statement has been confirmed also by Council of State, (General Assembly), 25.2.2014, No. 9, in *Foro it.*, 2014, III, 429, which has remarked—even acknowledging the principles stated by ECJ., Section X, 4.7.2013, C-100/12, *Fastweb*—that "it is not acceptable to validate an exegesis of the rules on conditions of the action that brings to a derogatory jurisdiction of objective scope".

commences a new proceeding, after finding that "one of the irregularities which leads to exclude both the successful tenderer and the competitor challenging the appointment (...) likewise affects other bids".[75]

Finally, as attempt to solve the problem, the new Code of public contracts[76] has introduced a provision (in Article 120, para. 2-*bis*, of CAT) that puts on any participant the burden to challenge immediately the admissions to the tender of other competitors, so creating a "super-special" judicial proceeding which exclusively serves the correct setting-up of competition within the tender before the examination and comparison of bids:[77] a judicial proceeding of clearly objective nature, where the judgement does not regard the right of the participant to win the tender and obtain the contract, but instead is focused over a new kind of formal interest, that is the ascertainment of a lawful access of competitors to the procedure for their selection. The paradoxical outcome is that the pragmatism and essentiality sought by EU law, which points towards a general goal of economic nature (that is, the interest for an open market), imply a certain underestimation of national rules on judicial proceedings, as well as their role of serving the protection of rights. Neither the addressed tendency seems to regard only the specific matter of admissions to/exclusions from selection, as proved by our internal case law. Some decisions, taking the cue from those new provisions of law, extend the area of cases (considered so far as exceptional)[78] where administrative acts with general and preliminary content, such as public calls for tender, may be immediately challenged even on the grounds of the choices of selection criteria or the provision of unclear rules that

[75]See the recent Council of State, Section V, ord. 6.11.2017, No. 5103, which has acknowledged a conflict of rulings within the same case law and has therefore referred again to the General Assembly the question on whether the judge—within a trial for invalidation of a public tender—must examine the main petition together with the incidental one aiming to exclude the former, "even if other competitors, whose bids have not been challenged, have joined to the public tender and if it is verified that irregularities claimed as grounds of appeal affect only the challenged bids". The General Assembly, with the decision 11.5.2018, No. 6, has referred the question to ECJ for preliminary ruling.

[76]Approved with Legislative Decree No. 50 on April 18th 2016.

[77]Council of State Section III 23.11.2016 No. 4994, in *Giur. it.*, 2017, 175. Such procedure has been criticised by authors, economic operators and specialised lawyers. At the beginning it has been deemed compatible with the Directive no. 89/665 and the article 47 of the Charter of Nice, even if under the condition that the administrative acts to be challenged within 30 days must be duly notified and accompanied by a "report of the relevant reasons, being capable to ensure" that the interested recipients become aware of the alleged violation of EU law (ECJ, sect. IV, ord. 14.02.2019, case C-54/18, par. 32). Finally, the procedure has been repealed by the Law Decree No. 32 of April 18th 2019, article 1 (par. 22 and 23), with reference to the trials commenced after the entry into force of the converting Law No. 55 of June 14th, 2019.

[78]At least found, since Council of State (General Assembly) 29.1.2003 No. 1, in those "clauses which hinder the admission of the participant to the selection", such as those concerning the "subjective requisites of candidates", or those which put "absolutely unintelligible or evidently unproportioned burdens" having regard to the tender, and "substantially imply that the participant cannot access the tender and the proceeding must stop".

make too difficult to submit a valid offer.[79] So, by this way, increasing the rate of trials of objective nature, given that they serve the correct regulation of administrative proceedings.[80]

Finally, it is exactly the delicate issue of markets regulation that reveals the trend of a jurisdiction being lured into the area of relevant economic litigation. Such trend is due to the usual awareness of administrative judge in promoting himself as the key advocate for general and currently sensitive interests. That leads him outside the area of mere remedial function—which is typical of the trial—to step into the field—already populated and guarded by various sector authorities—of mediation and regulation of social conflicts.

Some reasons related to specialization and expertise, together with the need for certainty and stability of settlements—particularly perceived by operators of those sensitive sectors, which are moreover affected by cyclical crises—jointly plot to create special forms of justice "for" the market: that is, with the purpose to guarantee the proper functioning of those economic contexts crossed by stresses of particular intensity and relevance, rather than the protection of rights and interests of players operating "in" the market. Such justice "for" the market is then attracted into a peculiar and rarefied environment, crossed by pressures and needs at a systemic level, whose government is demanded, in the first instance, to expert regulators of various origin and authority. Sometimes the way such regulators perform their task is recognised as a "para-jurisdictional", or at least "neutral" role, for reason that they are mostly unbound from the political-elective circuit and, thus, from the influence of policies expressed by the government in charge. In fact, as some examples in the fields of antitrust, supervision on public procurements, fines in banking and finance sectors and measures to resolve bank crises may show, the administrative jurisdiction, called upon as the most proper place for review, is led to take on a position that, if not fungible, is at least collateral or subordinated to sectorial authorities, to the extent its contribution to ascertain and settle the case risks to be cut down of the specific and fundamental ability to appraise directly and autonomously the relevant facts of technical nature, and tends to be limited to the mere handling of a proceeding (however, extremely simplified and boosted) whose purpose is only to offer an *ex post* and *ab externo* legal framework to set the case within. Being a judge "for" the market, in this perspective, then risks to mean working "for" the public authority entitled to resolve problems within the relevant sector, so conferring to its decisions the official blessing of stability.

---

[79]In such direction, see for instance Council of State, Section III, 2.5.2017, o. 2014, and Tar (RAC) Lazio, Roma, Section III *ter*, 13.12.2016 No. 12439.

[80]The relevant question has been recently addressed—following to the call for ruling by Council of State, Section III, ord. 7.11.2017, n. 5138—by the General Assembly with its decision No. 4 on 26.04.2018. Such decision, pursuant to general principles on conditions for petition laid down in Articles 24 of Constitution and 100 of CCP (as referred to by Article 39, para. 1, of CAT), has considered preferable the opinion that "the competitor who has applied to participate to the tender is not entitled to challenge those clauses within the public call which do not imply his exclusion, so precluding him with certainty from the participation".

The cited examples show that "dialogue" is a generic and polysemous word, scarcely evocative by itself of a commonly acceptable meaning and univocal course. It must be declined in different forms according to the context where the confrontations between courts, interests at stake and recalled factors of ideological and cultural nature take place. It is however certain that the "exchange of sensitiveness and reasoning" (Calabresi 2013, p. 21) laying down these dynamics make easier to understand that the season of specificity and stability of administrative experiences, with all their paradigms as shaped in every national context, have definitely passed. At the same time, it urges the need for a critical update of the reasons lying at the base of speciality for administration and its jurisdiction.

6.7 Conclusion: A Special Jurisdiction Serving the Full Protection of Citizens' Rights

The preceding analysis may prove two points. Firstly, that in over fifty years from the 100th anniversary of the unified administrative laws,[81] the administrative judge has lost its original role of administration controller and has become a stronghold for the protection of interests harmed by public authority. Secondly, such change has occurred due also to the encounter with EU law: this is the sign that sooner or later some "fundamental" needs emerge within all judicial systems of various countries, encouraging mutual exchanges even between the respective systems of remedies, beyond the difference of paths and technicalities of the respective histories.

It is by now a widespread trend among European countries the affirmation of dualistic frameworks for rights protection, based however on increasingly common basis.

By one side indeed, the UK monistic system, at first with the introduction in 1997 of the *application for judicial review*, and then with the 2007 reshaping of *Administrative Tribunals* into mostly jurisdictional bodies, has experienced the establishment of special judges and proceedings for the arrangement of litigation in public law matters; by another side, the most dualistic of systems (that is, the French one) has acknowledged the progressive convergence of the two traditional rails of *contentieux objectif pour excés de pouvoir* and *contentieux subjiectiv de pleine jurisdiction* toward a common system of full protection for citizens. At the same time, the proliferation of jurisdictional bodies of hybrid-nature, both at European and global level, is a sign of the evolution in the forms of rights protection, even in highly technical and complex matters such as banking and finance. And this evolution tends to overcome the canonical distinctions inherited by an antagonistic view of common law systems (mostly unitary) and *règime administratif* systems (mostly binary).

[81] Celebrated in 1965 in the city of Florence and sponsored by the High Patronage of the President of the Republic.

In a landscape where national specificities related to the role of the State tend to decline and influences from higher levels play as "transplants facilitators and emulation stimulators",[82] common models lose their characteristics and reshape themselves in unknown forms. A dualism of purely abstract and conflicting nature, such as the one inherited by the liberal era and recalling different views of substantial and processual relations, then becomes obsolete. Its place is taken by a dynamical and evolving coexistence of various forms of *spécialisation* and *professionnalisation*[83] in organizing and managing a set of remedial powers, now governed by almost uniform principles.

In this scenario with complex frames, the combined dialectical effect of traditional concepts such as objective-subjective and general interests-individual interests tend to be understood in new terms, s they represent the latitude of values that mark the jurisdiction, in a general sense, as a service: that is, effectivity of remedies within a fair trial (progressively shaped in a subjective sense) and efficient organisation of courts' work (in view of general interests of the system).

By its side, the "speciality" of administrative jurisdiction becomes a mere sign of the different matter at the core of litigation against public authority. It is seen and understood, in a positive sense, as a peculiar ability to find those solution which best capture the processual dimension of the relationship between citizen and administration.

Of course, different mindset and particular awareness in judging, which are a legacy of the historical and political tradition of every system, result in the survival of differences within the judicial practice, largely depending on whether court law tendencies are more or less deferent toward the administration and the values that it represents. In this sense it may be understood the paradox of the domestic administrative judge, whose increased rate of success in finding review techniques against the public authority is negatively compensated by tendencies that limit his powers of ascertainment, distance his horizon from the real substance of the conflicts and hinder the full development of an independent ability to observe and resolve matters at issue.

The *trade-off* between the two tendencies is even more stressed by the seen pressure—partly of supranational source—for a litigation that disregards the practical dimension of conflicts concerning ordinary life problems and touches significant as well as abstract questions of economic and social nature, whose management forces toward peculiar forms of coexistence with regulatory and supervisory authorities of the relevant sector.

Hence, the traditional "practical reason" of administrative jurisdiction, more than evocating an unsustainable mindset of free judging—as claimed and guarded in accordance with systematic coordinates, which are external to the process—must be

[82]Cassese (2017), p. 597.

[83]As remarked by the Observatoire des Mutations Institutionalles et Juridiques (OMIJ) de l'Université de Limoges, in the 2007 research entitled *La justice administrative en Europe*, Presses Universitaires de France, Paris, 2007, 20.

reinterpreted, instead, under the sign of a sophisticated ability to face with modern schemes an old challenge: that is, ensure within trials against administration a professional specialisation, to the full service of those who aspire to relieve detrimental effects of unsatisfactory relations with public authority.

References

Calabresi (2013) Il mestiere di giudice. Pensieri di un accademico americano. Alberico Gentili Lectures (Macerata, 19–21 marzo 2012), a cura di Barbisan B., il Mulino, Bologna

Cassese (2017) Monismo e dualismo giudiziario. Storia e prospettive, in Riv. trim. dir. pubbl., 583

García de Enterría E (2010) Le trasformazioni della giustizia amministrativa. Un cambio di paradigma? (Italian translation by Masera S. R.). Giuffrè, Milano

La justice administrative en Europe (2007) Presses Universitaires de France, Paris

Nigro M (1983) Giustizia amministrativa, III edn. il Mulino, Bologna

Romagnosi G (1814) Instituzioni di diritto amministrativo, da Cesare Orena Stamperia Malatesta, Milano

Romano S (1932) Le funzioni e i caratteri del Consiglio di Stato, in Il Consiglio di Stato. Studi in occasione del centenario, I, Istituto Poligrafico dello Stato, Roma

Chapter 7
Administrative Citizenship and Public Services: Is the Constitutional Project Still Possible in the Perspective of the Union?

Alessandra Pioggia

Contents

Abstract The contribution aims to investigate if public services are still the tool for the establishment of a community and an administrative citizenship, also in an European dimension. Public services, indeed, are not only functional to respond to the needs of the community, but also serve to "form" that community, giving body to the administrative citizenship of its members. In the perspective of European law, a service, however, before being an instrument for the transformation of society, is a productive economic activity. Behind this position there is a precise idea of public service: not as a place where the relationship between institutions and the community is realized in a choice, even political, but as "product". A project of society and European citizenship needs a Public sphere that had a role that goes beyond the simple intermediation between users and business, and a real European budget that redistributes the burden of ensuring a certain level of social services for all.

A. Pioggia (✉)
University of Perugia, Perugia, Italy
e-mail: alessandra.pioggia@unipg.it

D. Sorace et al. (eds.), *The Changing Administrative Law of an EU Member State*,
https://doi.org/10.1007/978-3-030-50780-0_7

7.1 "Administrative Citizenship"

"Administrative citizenship" is a concept that allows us to look at the legal system from an interesting viewpoint. The formula includes, in fact, both the dimension of the community (citizenship), and that of public institutions (administration). At the same time, it is a concept that emphasizes the idea of citizenship not as a presupposition of relations with public institutions, but as a result of the relationship with them (Bartolini and Pioggia 2017).

The constitutional provision that best encapsulates this "other" idea of citizenship is that found in Article 3, which, in its second paragraph, states: "It shall be the duty of the Republic to remove those obstacles of an economic or social nature which constrain the freedom and equality of citizens, thereby impeding the full development of the human person and the effective participation of all workers in the political, economic and social organisation of the country".

This is a revolutionary provision for the era in which it is formulated, which marks the transition from the rule of law to the social state of law (Supiot 2013, p. 28). It does in fact establish a new category of rights, which impose organizational duties on the public sphere, since in order to be satisfied need services and provisions (Costa 1997). They are "social rights", which by their affirmation realize the principle of real equality and provide a juridical answer to the limits of formal-only equality (Marshall 1973).

Through Article 3, the Italian Constitution commits the Republic to making a social transformation, which has as its main player its administration and as a double result the full development of people and their active participation in the political, economic and social organization of the country. The way in which this second result is formulated and the three dimensions of participation are connected, in turn, with Article 2 of the Constitution, which, after recognizing that people have "inviolable rights", requires each person to fulfill the "imperative duties" of a solidarity also declared as "political, economic and social".

The goal of participating in the organization of these three dimensions and the duty to do so, dedicating their energies to the common good, define the idea of citizenship that is not a starting point (as belonging to the State by birth), but the point of arrival of an individual liberation, which, in turn, allows for a restitution of solidarity. Everyone is born as a "person", but becomes a citizen, through the relationship with an administration that taking care, instructing and supporting the individual, allows him or her to be realised and to participate in the life of the community to which he or she belongs.

The idea of citizenship as a result of the active commitment of the Republic in removing the obstacles that society puts before the complete and equal fulfilment of the person is also the result of the history of our country.

The Italian State, formed in 1861 with territorial unification, immediately has to confront the profound social, economic, cultural and linguistic differences that divided the peninsula. If political citizenship (understood as belonging to the state) arises with unification, administrative citizenship (understood as belonging to a community, not only political, but also economic and social) is a much later achievement.[1]

The Constitution of 1948 renews this objective in the cultural atmosphere that followed the Second World War, in discontinuity with both the fascist experience and the liberal state, and establishes a social project that puts the person and his/her development central to its organisation. The deep and convinced rejection of the idea of the instrumentality of the individual to the State and the overturning of this paradigm, through the recognition of the instrumentality of public institutions for the full realization of the person, open the road to the affirmation of administrative citizenship in the meaning that is first illustrated (Di Nucci 2002).

The implementation of the constitutional system has not been immediate, nor without contradictions.

The welding between the centrality of the person, the solidarity pact and the project of society is questioned almost immediately due to some economic policy choices sensitive to the pressures of "international" liberalism, choices also determined by the inclusion of Italy in the western bloc and by adhesion to the Bretton Woods Agreement. All this has given new vigor to an individualism deeply rooted in Italian culture, with the result of tightening borders between social groups (Allegretti 2012) and of postponing the full realization of the welfare state to an indefinite future.

Significant is the interpretation of many of the most revolutionary constitutional norms, throughout the 1950s, as merely programmatic norms, not susceptible to immediate implementation, but in need of complex legislative translation, in turn, the object of discretionary political choices.

Alongside the slow process of adaptation of the "political" institutions to the constitutional project, starting from the 1960s, is the transformation of the administration, which represents the "public" engine of the new society envisaged by the Constitution. Thus emerge the first major public bodies for the management of economic services, such as electricity and telephone, and, in the 1970s, two fundamental social services are reformed: the health service, with the establishment in 1978 of the National Health Service, and that of social care services, which in 1977 gone under regional responsibility, for regulatory and planning level, and municipal, with regard to provision.

The season of the 1970s and early 1980s marks the consolidation of a service administration in Italy, aimed at satisfying the needs of people within the perspective of their full development. It is significant, for example, that while the National Health Service is formed, at the same time an aspect of the provision of mental

[1]Noted in this regard are the words of Massimo d'Azeglio, Italian politician, academic and painter, who lived between the end of 1700 and the early part of the second half of the 1800s, who, after Italian Unification in 1861, said the renowned phrase: "Fatta l'Italia, bisogna fare gli italiani" ("We have made Italy, now we must make Italians"). In reality, Massimo d'Azeglio had in mind the need for a moral rebirth of the Italian populace, seen as weak and corrupt, but his words have been interpreted as an affirmation of the need to construct a sense of national belonging that did not represent the automatic result of territorial unification.

health services is profoundly transformed. The Italian story of the closure of mental hospitals is well-known (Foot 2014), motivated precisely by the fact that it was an organizational system of the health service that contrasted with the dignity of the person and such as to be an obstacle rather than support for his or her full development. The organizational redefinition of psychiatry is exemplary of how public service is understood as an instrument of emancipation of the person in the perspective of his/her full participation in the life of the community.

The history of our country and the constitutional system of administrative citizenship that derives from it, provide interesting example also in the perspective of European citizenship. For now, the latter is a notion of variable content, which has an albeit limited, political dimension, but which is still too fragile in its administrative dimension (Shaw 1997). If the Italian events teach us something, it is that in order to "make the Europeans" we need institutions that take on responsibility for removing the obstacles that prevent people who are in a "unified" territory from becoming a community.

The following considerations aim to focus attention on the main way through which the institutions of the Republic fulfil their commitment to remove the obstacles that effectively hinder the full development of the human person: public services. The idea is to try to reread the concept of public service starting from its function as an instrument of administrative citizenship, to verify if the evolution of its regulation, which is deeply influenced by European law, is consistent with this function or, instead, if it has taken a different direction.

7.2 The "Political" Dimension of Public Services

The existence of suitable services to meet the development needs of individuals and communities, but above all the public organization of them, has been recognized, also historically, as the "source of a more solid sense of belonging to the community and constitution of citizenship" (Sordi 2002).

In the perspective of citizenship, the public organization of the service appears, in fact, central. As we have just considered, the purpose of the service is not only to provide a useful service to the community, but the higher one: to ensure that the satisfaction of the need becomes an instrument of individual emancipation that enables the person to participate fully in the life of the community.

This applies in particular to services that meet rights which are most immediately tied to personal development, such as education, assistance, work-related services, and of course, health, but there is no doubt that it also invests the function of many other services, such as transport, the distribution of electricity, gas, water, etc ... These are in fact opportunities for the construction of an equal community in which basic needs are met and in which the resources are used with responsibility so as to preserve the environment and the resources themselves, also for the future community. This creates a link between service and community and makes the first an instrument that contributes to the formation of the second.

In this perspective, the qualification of some services as public serves to signal not only the nature of the subject who assumes the responsibility to provide them (a public subject, for the note), but their function and, consequently, their organization.

The public quality of services, which is normally associated with the idea of an activity that the public sphere recognizes as necessary to meet the needs of the community, in this way, is defined in a more precise and, at the same time, more profound way. Public services are not only functional to respond to the needs of the community, but also serve to "form" that community, giving body to the administrative citizenship of its members.

The function of the service is also reflected therefore, on choices relating to its organization. It is not enough that the service exists, it is also necessary for its organization to be coherent with the project of the full development of the person (and construction of the society of citizens) of which he or she is a part. When faced with public services, to put it in the words of the Constitutional Court, "*organization and rights are mirrored aspects of the same matter, one and the other, implying and conditioning each other. There is no organization that, directly or at least indirectly, is not aimed at rights, just as there is no right to a service that does not condition the organization.*"[2]

In this perspective, thus we can say that the decision on how a service will be organized also affects the idea of citizenship and of community and is therefore properly and deeply political choice.

Of course this does not mean that it must be the political power that manages the service. In our country there have been experiences of the presence of figures of political legitimacy at the top of the structures that provide services and they have not been successful. This happened, for example, in the case of the management of health services which, until the 1992 reform, took place through bodies managed by the municipalities, participating with their own political representatives. The penetration of political and electoral interests in the decisions of real management gave rise to irrational solutions from an operational point of view and to growth in expenditure, which soon appeared unsustainable. This led to a reform[3] that separated the political decision about the service from its real management, clarifying what the role of the former should be and valuing its function of building citizenship through rights.

The organizational choice that affects the way in which the right will be satisfied is necessarily entrusted to the political bodies, given it constitutes a piece of the constitutional project of transformation of society. To remain in the field of health services, there is no doubt, for example, that the way in which the moment of acquiring a patient's informed consent should be organized belongs to this type of

---

[2]Constitutional court. 338/1998 (Translated by the author).

[3]The so-called second reform of the national public health service, began with Law 421 of 1992 and essentially enacted with legislative decrees 502 of 1992 and 229 of 1999.

decision. The recent law on the matter,[4] with the ruling that "the time in communication between doctor and patient constitutes cure time"[5] has created a "political" choice in the organisation of the service, consistent with its function as an instrument for the fulfilment of a social right.

Highlighting a political dimension of the choice of organization of the service that satisfies social rights does not prevent us considering the service from an economic point of view, but places this second perspective in a, let us say, subsequent and subordinate position.

7.3 The "Economic" Dimension of Services in the European Perspective

The question I wish to ask here is whether the function of public services in the constitutional project is still possible in the perspective of the European Union.

The answer is neither simple nor unequivocal. The first thing to say is that the European community legislation does not come with a social dimension (Giubboni 2003). In the evolution of the Treaties, the Community system acquires increasing sensitivity for this aspect, but despite the adoption in 2017 of the "European Pillar of Social Rights", the almost exclusively national setting of the rights to services still stands today. This is, however, inevitable, given the characteristic of expensive rights (not only in economic terms, but also in organizational terms) of social rights, which is ill-suited to the functions of European community institutions and the size of the European budget.

From this derives the lack of a notion of a uniform public service (Sorace 2010), for which European legislation recognises a number of notions (services of general interest, services of general economic interest, non-economic services of general interest, services of public utility, social services of general interest, etc.) that intersect the national ones of public service, but which from time to time take into consideration a specific profile, isolating it from context and making it object of a regulation that never directly concerns the service.

My feeling is that this fragmentation of the notion of service in a plurality of profiles, each individually invested by a regulation that does not take into consideration the public service in its overall dimension of tool for the realization of a society project, leads to loosening the connection between public choice and idea of community. In particular, public services are no longer the place in which the political dimension of that project finds space, but become the field of application of different disciplines, where services are fragmented into a kaleidoscope of profiles and risk losing their sense.

---

[4]Law 219 of 2017.

[5]Article 1, paragraph 8 (Translated by the author).

From a system perspective, the alarm has already been raised on how the focus on the "expensive" aspect of services is seriously running the risk of transforming them into levers of economic rebalancing, in the context of the financial stability of the monetary union (Bilancia 2014; Brunkhorst 2014).

But there are other aspects that threaten the survival of the public sense of service and that derive from the cultural roots on which the system of the Community first and the Union second is built and from the logical priority of the economic dimension over the "political" one.

In the perspective of European law, a service, before being an instrument for the transformation of society, is a productive economic activity.

It is significant that Article 14 of the Treaty on the Functioning of the European Union, after citing the importance of services for the social economic cohesion of Europe, consigns to the States and the Union the task of ensuring their conditions of operation, essentially from an economic and financial point of view.

It is a starting point that defines the basic features of the subject of regulation, a starting point, with respect to which the public service profile presents itself as an addition, an adjustment that, within the limits of proportionality, affects a mechanism which finds its very origin in the market and its physiological dynamics. In other words, the service is intended as an economic subject, to which the public qualification is added, without modifying its nature at root.

All this is evident in the way in which the European system identifies "services of general economic interest", within the broader category of "services of general interest".

The progressive extension of the notions of economic activity and of business undertaking has in fact produced the consequence for which, in effect, almost all the services of general interest result as also of general *economic* interest.

Economic activity, in light of the jurisprudence of the Court of Justice, must be understood as "any activity consisting in offering goods and services on a given market" (Pavel Pavlov and Others, 12.09.2002, C-180/98, C-184/98), regardless of the legal nature of the subjects carrying out the activity. In fact, the classification of "undertaking" has been extended by judges to "every entity engaged in an economic activity, regardless of the legal status of the entity and the way in which it is financed" (Court of Justice Klöchner-Werke AG Hoesch AG, 13.07.1962, C-20/61 and Hoefner and Elser, 23.04.1991, C-41/90). The fact that the entity in question also carries out non-economic activities does not preclude this classification (see, for example, MOTOE, 1.07.2008, C-49/07).

To this must also be added the irrelevance of the fact that the service is paid directly by the user who benefits from it or by others. In the field of services, the law has clarified, in fact, that where services are usually provided against remuneration, the activity of the provider must be considered an economic activity, even if the service is not paid directly by those who benefit from it.

The consequence of all this is that "Almost all services offered in the social field can be considered 'economic activities' within the meaning of Articles 43 and 49 of the EC Treaty" (Implementing the Community Lisbon programme: Social services of general interest in the European Union. Communication from the Commission. *COM (*2006*)* 177).

7.4 The Service of General Economic Interest as a Paradigm of Public Service in Europe

Considering its extension also in the field of services that meet social rights, the notion of service of general economic interest is particularly important for understanding the vision of service held by European legislation (Sorace 2010).

The service of general economic interest is an activity that the market performs or could perform against payment, but which is not actually fulfilled under conditions that the administration holds as necessary to satisfy the needs of the community.

The inadequacy of the market justifies, therefore, the introduction of corrections proportionate to the purpose to be achieved.

But what kind of corrections are they? What kind of intervention does the European regulatory system envisage in order to guarantee the function of general interest of the service?

The peculiarity of the regulation of the service of general economic interest is resolved, in fact, in the exceptions to the rules of competition, legitimized by the impediment that their full application would exercise on the mission entrusted to the undertaking in charge of managing the service. Even the mission of public service is defined by difference from an entrepreneurial root: it implies the provision of services that an undertaking, if it were considering its own commercial interest, would not assume or would not assume to the same extent or under the same conditions (Article 2, EC Reg. 1307/2007).

The setting remains that of the undertaking that provides a service in exchange for remuneration and the public dimension is limited to the fact that it is possible to grant it advantages in the productive economic system.

The discipline of state aid is paradigmatic in this sense.

In the case of services, as is well-known, transferrals to an undertaking which are configurable in terms of compensation for public service obligations are excluded from the prohibition of state aid.

Let us take the case of a service provided by an organization (qualified as an undertaking, regardless of its public or private nature, solely due to provision of services against payment, also indirect) directly in charge of the service (i.e. not selected through a selective procedure). In a hypothesis like this, we are faced with a public service, entrusted to an essentially public organization. Well, even in this case the acceptable level of compensation for service charges in order not to incur the prohibition of state aid must be "determined on the basis of an analysis of the costs which a typical undertaking, well run" would have to bear to fulfill these obligations, taking into account the relevant revenues as well as a reasonable profit margin (Altmark, 24.07.2003, C-280/00).

With a prediction such as this, the cultural primacy of the business economic model over any other form of service organization is evident. Functional optimality belongs to the organizational system of the productive undertaking and onto this, additional obligations and perfectly compensable features can only be grafted.

This last aspect also tells us much about the specialty of a service as public: the difference between the provision of a service that is consistent with entrepreneurial and market logic and the provision of a public service, designed to be functional for the pursuit objectives of general interest, is completely and exactly monetizable.

The crux of the argument is not, as has been thought and could continue to be thought, the idea of "market failure", but further back, in the identification of "what" the market cannot do.

As is well-known, the position of the European Union has always been one for which specific obligations for public services can not be attributed to an activity that is already provided or can be provided satisfactorily and on terms (such as price, objective quality characteristics, continuity and access) consistent with the public interest as defined by the State. Behind this longstanding and consolidated position there is a precise idea of public service: not as a place where the relationship between institutions and the community is realized in a choice, even political, that originates from a vision of society and social progress, but as "product" with particular characteristics. At the base there is, in fact, a product-provision that already exists or that must be built according to typical business logic. This is where the corrections are grafted, which make it functional for satisfying the needs that the public sphere deems in need of satisfaction.

7.5 What Is Lost by Neglecting the "Political" Dimension of the Service?

Considering public services from a predominantly economic point of view produces at least two consequences.

The first is the cultural renunciation of the possibility that the relationship between public institutions and the community, which is built through service, can give rise to something radically different from what can arise through the dynamics of supply and demand typical of the market. We are reluctant to imagine a product from scratch, in which even non-monetizable needs, so to speak, can be satisfied.

The second consequence is also an exclusion, an absence, which this time concerns the organizational dimension of the service. The logical primacy of the entrepreneurial organization, starting from which necessary corrections are introduced to ensure some characteristics of the product, shifts the user's guarantees on the latter, neglecting the way in which the service is provided. This is entirely consistent with the idea of private service, but could, in some cases, not be completely so for the public service. Indeed, as we have said, its function is more complex and can not be resolved solely in meeting the single need through a single performance. It represents the element of a larger design, which aims at the full realization of the human person.

Public services often consist of services to enjoy with which one enters into a deep relationship with the organization that provides them, a relationship in which other fundamental rights and freedoms are also involved (relating, for example, to self-determination, dignity, freedom of expression, social wellbeing, etc ...). The care of these "other" rights can not be limited to "non-violation", but, since it is entrusted to a public service, which has as its ultimate goal the establishment of the community, it must make an effective contribution to the full development of the person.

This "high" function of the service finds less and less space to express itself, also due to a national legislation that has embraced the economic logic of service.

Since the 1990s, in Italy, as in much of the rest of Europe, a season of privatization has opened, which has transformed the organization of many service providing entities and initiated the process of outsourcing public services, reducing margins for their direct management by the administrations. The assignment of services to private undertakings also affects the modalities of their organization. The organization becomes the way in which the private manager guarantees a revenue from the management of the service. The contract with the administration concerns mainly, if not exclusively, the service product and its characteristics. The way this is provided is the space in which the private undertaking makes economic choices that maximize profit.

An interesting example is the management of the school meals service.

In many municipal administrations, this service has been managed for many years with the participation and even with the operational contribution of parents and, indirectly, the community of users. In these experiences, knowledge, participation, social growth, solidarity, education and health resources have been shared, which, in addition to guaranteeing a service, contributed significantly to the path of full development of the people involved and to their "participation in the political, economic and social organization of the country". Throughout the last decades, in most of the municipal administrations, management outsourcing choices have prevailed, constructed upon a purely economic assessment, putting the costs in relation to the service provided. This has led to the assignment of the service to a few large private companies that can supply quality services saving on organizational costs and that, in most cases, have excluded users from the production process. The service continues to be provided (perhaps even with lower costs), but the spaces have been reduced and in some cases have disappeared in which "other" rights are guaranteed and so too the relationship between public sphere and community that contributed to the realization of the society project described by the Constitution.

In cases like this, as in all those in which the administration reduces its role to mere intermediary between users and the private undertaking supplying the service, an important function of the service is renounced, one in which it is configured as a useful tool not only for meeting the needs of the community, but also to build that community, through the full administrative citizenship of its members.

7.6 Public Institutions and Service Organization

To what has been considered so far, it could be objected that public institutions always have the possibility of organizing certain services handling them directly and not entrusting them to private undertakings. This is the case, for example, of the health service, which, in our country, as in others, does not act, in principle, as an undertaking (as explicitly recognized by the Court of First Instance of the European Communities for the Spanish health service in the Fenin case, 04.03.2003, lawsuit T-319/99). What follows from this, also in terms of service provision, type of service, and relationship with the organization, has been well highlighted by a recent jurisprudence which has described in a particularly effective manner the way in which organizational choices of the service, its functioning and the right it aims to satisfy are interconnected within the framework of a larger design.

We can refer here to a section of a ruling with which the administrative judges (Council of State)[6] has indicated with great clarity what is the way in which the organization of the health service must work in its relationship with the person. After recalling how satisfying the right to health is also a means by which the Republic contributes to the realization of the personality of the individual, the judges reconstructed the duties of the health organization so as to understand in them much more than the simple dispensation of a medical service. That which is due to the person in the relationship with the health organization is an activity "that goes from receiving the patient to understanding his/her requirements and needs, from listening to his/her requests to the diagnosis of his/her illness, from the doctor/patient consultation to the initialising and development of a shared therapeutic strategy, to the formation of informed consent to the implementation of planned and desired treatment". But the particularly significant section of the sentence is that in which the judges clarify how all the services due to the patient fit into "a path that is above all existential, even before curative" that has "in the identity dimension of the patient, in his person and in the pursuit. of his psycho-physical well-being, its fulcrum and its goal". As can be seen, in a case like this, this is far beyond the recognition of rights to a service, fully involving the service and its organization in the constitutional project of the full development of the person. The provision of the service becomes part of what the Council of State defines as an "existential path" that has as its fulcrum and end the "identity dimension"[7] of the person.

It therefore remains an area for the marked specificity of some public services, at least when these are directly provided by a public administration.

To this consideration, although correct, I wish to add two observations.

The first is that to think that the sole way to allow the public service to maintain its dimension as a tool for accomplishing a social project is to entrust it to an organization even subjectively public, is misplaced and, to some extent, anti-historical. In fact it involves the renunciation of staking a space for a political project for the many

[6]Cons. Stato, sez. III, sent. n. 4460/2014.

[7]Translations by the author.

services that have already been entrusted to private individuals or organizations of entrepreneurial characteristics. Public decision can and must have a role that goes beyond the simple intermediation between users and business and that concerns, above all, the conception of the way in which the service should be organized and provided, even when the task of providing it will be entrusted to a private undertaking.

The second observation is that even when a service is directly provided by the public administration, this does not protect it from the cultural prevalence of economic logic, which can also act as an "external" factor in the organization of the service.

An example in this regard can be again observed in the health services.

The European discipline on cross-border healthcare[8] has been conceived as a measure to protect the freedom to provide services in the internal market, thus in an entirely economic perspective of guaranteeing free exchange. The original restrictions on the faculty to be reimbursed for treatment taken abroad are considered, in fact, the source of a competitive economic disadvantage for private healthcare operators in the member countries, compared to national suppliers (in Italy, the National Health Service). Their removal therefore aims to eliminate an obstacle to the freedom to provide services.

If, for the purposes of applying the discipline of state aid, the national health service can not qualify as an undertaking, for the purposes of the freedom to provide services in the internal market, it is instead set in competition with other operators which no doubt can qualify as undertakings..

The consequences for a public health service such as ours are various. The most significant of these is certainly the sustainability of the service and the damage that such sustainability can suffer from the potential underutilization of national public facilities. This is a future perspective, but not necessarily so far ahead.

Another possible consequence regards the loss of the relationship between service and community. Thinking of public services as a tool for the realization of a social project connects the person with the public power, to which the Constitution has entrusted the task of removing the obstacles that effectively prevent the full realization of the individual. Thinking instead of public services as economic provisions, puts emphasis on the relationship between the user and the provider, which can also be an undertaking. In this way political responsibilities towards the community remain in the shade and with them the function of social services in guaranteeing real equality. In this cone of shadow, new forms of inequality can nestle. Just think, to stay with the latter example, of the new freedom of healthcare that looms in the discipline of cross-border care and of the new inequalities in the instruments of knowledge, not only economic but also cultural, that it hides.

---

[8]EU Directive n. 24 of March 9, 2011.

7.7 Which European Administrative Citizenship?

Even the profiles of so-called European social citizenship do not shift from this framework. As is known, the logic is that of non-discrimination based on nationality for access to service provision. It is not a matter of transnational social solidarity (Azoulai 2010), but of extension of the rights of the user borne by the host State. In a period of economic crisis, such as that under way, the weight of internal migration can be perceived as unsustainable and therefore a source of reduced protection for national citizens (Guzi and Kahanec 2015). The example of Brexit demonstrates how this type of citizenship is not functional to the creation of a community, but rather the opposite, contributes to its disintegration (Deakin 2016).

Solidarity needs communities to redistribute the burdens of creating a social project and, from the perspective of the Union, it needs a real European budget that redistributes the burden of ensuring a certain level of social services for all. In the so-called European social citizenship there is nothing like this (Giubboni 2016). If some hope, with regard to a possible liberation of the social solidarity circuits from their "national roots", had arisen, the European crisis has inexorably pushed it back (Giubboni 2018).

The initial question therefore returns: are public services still the tool for the establishment of a community and an administrative citizenship?

The answer, in my view, today is more negative than positive, and the risk is that the function of services in the construction of citizenship is progressively and fully dissolving.

The great absentee in this context is the political dimension of the service, its being an instrument of a social design, even before the fulfilment of an obligation of service provision assumed in a user relationship. This absence is also evident in what has been called "the 'jurisprudentialization' of political order"[9] (Azzariti 2009), to describe a process of progressive technicalization and political neutralization of the legal systems, particularly evident in the European legal system.

Without a project of society, citizens, transformed into users, lose their political interlocutor, present themselves alone before the undertaking that provides the services and recourse to justice becomes the only possible exercise of administrative citizenship.

References

Allegretti U (2012) Gli apparati organizzativi e la democrazia, in Rivista AIC, Associazione Italiana Costituzionalisti, 4/2012, www.rivistaaic.it

Azoulai L (2010) La citoyenneté européenne, un statut d'intégration sociale. In: Cohen-Jonathan J (ed) Chemins d'Europe. Mélanges en l'honneur de Jean Paul Jacqué. Dalloz, Paris, p 1

[9]Translation by the author.

Azzariti G (2009) Verso un governo dei giudici? Il ruolo dei giudici comunitari nella costruzione dell'Europa politica, in Rivista di diritto costituzionale, 3

Bartolini A, Pioggia A (2017) Le cittadinanze amministrative. Percorsi e prospettive dell'amministrazione tra diritti e doveri a 150 anni dalle leggi di unificazione amministrativa. In: Bartolini A, Pioggia A (eds) Cittadinanze amministrative, A 150 anni dall'unificazione amministrativa italiana a cura di Domenico Sorace e Leonardo Ferrara, vol VIII. FUP, Firenze, p 9

Bilancia F (2014) Crisi economica e asimmetrie territoriali nella garanzia dei diritti sociali tra mercato unico e unione monetaria, in Rivista AIC, Associazione Italiana Costituzionalisti, 272014, 2, www.rivistaaic.it

Brunkhorst H (2014) Collective Bonapartism – democracy in the European crisis. German Law J 15 (6):1177

Costa P (1997) Alle origini dei diritti sociali: "Arbeitender Staat" e tradizione solidaristica. In: Gozzi G (ed) Democrazia, diritti, costituzione. I fondamenti costituzionali delle democrazie contemporanee. Il Mulino, Bologna, p 277

Deakin S (2016) Brexit, labour rights and migration: why Wisbech matters to Brussels. German Law J 17(Brexit Supplement):13

Di Nucci L (2002) Alle origini dello stato sociale nell'Italia repubblicana. La ricezione del Piano Beveridge e il dibattito nella Costituente. In: Sorba C (ed) Cittadinanza. Individui, diritti sociali, collettività nella storia contemporanea. Ministero beni e attività culturali (Ministry of Cultural Heritage and Activities), Roma

Foot J (2014) La "Repubblica dei Matti". Franco Basaglia e la psichiatria radicale in Italia, 1961-1978. Feltrinelli, Roma

Giubboni S (2003) Diritti sociali e mercato. La dimensione sociale dell'integrazione europea. Il Mulino, Bologna

Giubboni S (2016) Cittadinanza europea, libertà di circolazione e solidarietà transnazionale: un riesame critico, in Politiche sociali/ Social policies, n. 1, 182

Giubboni S (2018) Free movement of persons and transnational solidarity in the European Union (EU) – a melancholic eulogy. In: Civitarese Matteucci S, Halliday S (eds) Social rights in Europe in an age of austerity. Routledge, London, p 273

Guzi M, Kahanec M (2015) Socioeconomic cleavages between workers from new member states and host-country labour forces in the EU during the Great Recession. In: Bernaciak M (ed) Market expansion and social dumping in Europe. Abingdon, New York, p 120

Marshall TH (1973) Class, citizenship and social development, with an introduction by SM Lip set. Greenwood Press, Westport (Connecticut)

Shaw J (1997) Citizenship of the Union: towards post-national membership?, in Jean Monnet Working Paper 6/97

Sorace D (2010) I servizi "pubblici" economici nell'ordinamento nazionale ed europeo, alla fine del primo decennio del XXI secolo, in Diritto amministrativo, 1

Sordi B (2002) Servizi pubblici e concorrenza: su alcune fibrillazioni tra diritto comunitario e tradizione continentale, in Quaderni fiorentini, 582

Supiot A (2013) Grandeur et misère de l'État social. Fayard, Collège de France – Paris

Chapter 8
The Rise of Technological Administration and the Ragged Route Towards a Digital Administrative Law

Stefano Civitarese Matteucci

Contents

Abstract The chapter focuses on the 'invasion' of technology into the functioning of public administration and how it affects the 'political quality' of its decision-making. The latter constitutes the main source of legitimation of administrative authorities by linking their action to an accountable representative, which is traceable, in turn, to the fundamental constitutional rule that entrusts the government to the parties with the confidence of the Parliament. By focusing on digital administration, the chapter explores new ways of functioning and accountability, and then, of legitimacy of governmental activity as opposed to political accountability. Within this scenario, it discusses how and to what extent e-government and automation are changing both the functioning of public administration and some doctrinal traditional concepts of administrative law.

8.1 Technology, Politics, and the Law

Within a research project which aspired to chart change, challenges, and the direction of development of the Italian public administration in the twenty-first century at the turn of 150 years from its foundation as the executive apparatus of the Italian

---

S. Civitarese Matteucci (✉)
University of Chieti-Pescara, Pescara, Italy
e-mail: s.civitarese@unich.it

D. Sorace et al. (eds.), *The Changing Administrative Law of an EU Member State*,
https://doi.org/10.1007/978-3-030-50780-0_8

unitary state, one cannot doubt that technology and expert knowledge must be at the forefront. In fact, over the last half century the problems posed to the public sector and administrative law by the impressive evolution of science and technology are a matter of constant investigation and concern in the literature.[1] Government and its apparatuses, as a social institution, although being guided by the rule of law and the duty to abide by political directions, are not immune to social change, which over the years in question has been huge. The society of information and technology as upgoing ordering principles both of polities and individuals are nowadays highly debated issues. The same fate of democracy may depend on what use societies will make of communication and information technology.

Before such a wide horizon the same issue of the relationship between law and technology is usually conceptualised as a chapter of the troubled relation between the former and such normative disciplines as politics, ethics, and economics as long as they seek to regulate, withstand and direct the 'boundless puissance' of 'technics'. On another note, both law and economics can be conceived as 'techniques' in their own right, being this a requirement for them to be treated as autonomous subjects of knowledge. Then, if we assume 'technics' as technical domain at large, any instrument which enables us to change reality belongs to it. From this standpoint the frequent juxtaposition between law and technology sounds perplexing. This view entails that law—far from being just a technique to guide human behaviour—has (ought to have) a substantive content to counter the substantive content that technology would enjoy in the contemporary world, that is the "end of an unlimited growth of its power . . . of its capacity to achieve end goals".[2]

Taking on such a debate requires to undertake ethical-normative commitments to import one or another theory of justice into the concept of law. This is a truly important debate, but I will leave it in the background and limit myself to investigating one of the most evident recent grounds of change of the functioning of public administration in relation to technological development, namely the so-called digitalization goal.

One of the outstanding issues which this topic entails is whether and to what extent the 'invasion' of technology into the functioning of public administration undermines such a fundamental, albeit slippery, character of it as the 'political quality' of its decision-making. The latter constitutes a sizable part of the legitimation we are prepared to acknowledge to administrative authorities by linking their action to an accountable representative, which is traceable, in turn, to the fundamental constitutional rule that entrusts the government to the parties with the confidence of the Parliament.[3]

[1]See Bromley (2002).

[2]Severino (2012).

[3]The difficulty to reconcile the political content of administrative decision-making with the constitutional mandate to bureaucrats to be impartial is patently showed by the endless discussion on the extent to which a 'spoil's system' is desirable and lawful in the Italian context. See Carboni (2010).

However, another completely different form of accountability and legitimation rooted in the specific technocratic nature of the relevant authority seems to have emerged. This is vested, in other words, in the specific technical-specialized competence of the persons in charge of leading such authorities and making decisions. The sizeable increase over the last half century of the number of such authorities, particularly but not exclusively in the field of market and financial regulation, supposedly placed out of the majority-minority dynamic, might be interpreted as a sign of the advance of technology at the expense of politics.[4]

This is of course highly problematic, because it entails that specialised knowledge, *qua* 'technics', must prevail over allocative interest choices. This is the case, for example, for monetary choices, conceived as politically neutral and for this reason entrusted on 'independent authorities' (the Central Banks), which are almost immune from political accountability. The main point of contention is whether such technical choices can be deemed authentically so rather than a way to make political decisions migrate to unaccountable spheres.

This course towards neutrality and efficiency as the outcome of technology applied to public administration is the typical mark of the process of digitalisation. I do not claim that the rise of independent 'technical' authorities and the progression towards an ICT administration are pieces of the same 'design', however one can detect a common element of change along the line of the 'liberation effect' from politics that technology and expert knowledge promise.

By focusing on digital administration, one has the best chance to explore new ways of functioning and accountability, and then, of legitimacy of governmental activity as opposed to political accountability. Within this grand scenario, the chapter aims to discuss how and to what extent 'digitalisation' is affecting and should affect the functioning of public administration.

Two questions constitute the thread of the chapter. The first is to what extent we can still make sense of 'digital administration' as distinct from a traditional way of administrative organisation. We are undoubtedly going through a transitional era even though our daily experience teaches us that a great deal of the Italian bureaucracy keeps on working according to the 'dusty files' culture celebrated by some great nineteenth century novelists. It is hardly deniable though that within a few years the 'administrative transactions' could be ordinarily digital and thus the 'code of digital administration' and the 'code of public administration' become one. With the Public Administration Reorganisation Act (of Parliament) n. 124 of 2015, a comprehensive reform of the organisation of Italian public administration (PA) has been set in motion in which, according to the then Italian Minister for Public Administration Marianna Madia, "digitalisation is *the* means to change the State at long last and not simply one among many others. This is why it represents the heart of the reform".[5]

---

[4]Civitarese Matteucci and Torchia (2017).

[5]See at http://www.corrierecomunicazioni.it/pa-digitale/39379_marianna-madia-il-digitale-cuore-della-riforma-pa-basta-indugi.htm (last visited 4 September 2018).

Secondly, we wonder whether and to what extent by changing the means of communication within the public administration arena the substance of interactions which occur thereabout changes too. In a way this is the old issue of the relationship between form and substance, where the first now bears the semblance of a powerful technology. This is a question which especially besets public law scholars. Although it depends on the scope of the application of ITC to public administration, it is not too audacious to foresee the extreme scenario of the replacement of human decisions with AI ones, which, thanks to the Internet, can store and elaborate a huge amount of information. In such a case we would have a 'technical' decision replacing a 'political' one. It is not clear, though, whether recent reforms by bringing forward digitalisation pave the way for automated decision-making too. On this specific point, the GDPR recently passed by the EU, might be interpreted as somewhat hindering, or braking, such an outcome.

The chapter is structured as follows. In the ensuing section some terminological and conceptual clarifications are offered, viz. the notions of 'online public services' and *e-government* taken in an incremental perspective. I contend, namely, that the transactional dimension of e-government is to be conceived as the main goal to pursue as being somehow completer and more desirable than the informative dimension only. The third section deals with the impact, both quantitative and qualitative, of e-government upon government and public administration, especially regarding the level of diffusion of e-government also in light of the 'digital agenda' policy. The fourth section sheds light on some analytical and conceptual aspects of the impact of the use of the ICT on the structure and functioning of public administration, particularly by taking on the so-called re-engineering of bureaucratic processes and automated decision-making, while the fifth section offers some final remarks.

8.2 Conceptual and Terminological Clarifications

First of all, we need to delimitate the phenomenon we want to enquire about, to which I will indifferently refer as ITCs or e-government. It has evolved across the years, moving from the advent of the computer with the employment of simple software to the design of complex informatics, to cloud computing.[6] The phenomenon of e-government has a global nature. It concerns all the states and it has been the object of an ever-growing attention by scholars of different social and political fields. Suffice it to think of the collection of cases analysed in the book 'Comparative E-government' edited by Christopher Reddick (Springer, 2010) or of the several volumes (21) in the series *Public Administration and Information Technology* by the same Reddick for Springer.

[6]Osnaghi (2013).

According to one widely acknowledged conceptual framework e-government can be described as a bi-dimensional phenomenon.[7] The first one regards the level of technological sophistication, in a system of coordinates ideally placed on the x-axis, the second the type of interaction between the recipients and the service, ideally placed on the y-axis. As to the latter, they regard the relationships between government and individuals about social or other benefits, political rights, and business as well as those between government and public servants and between different public authorities. By service I mean here "online service", expression which stands for the peculiar manner of interaction between providers and users whilst the actual content of such services includes any administrative task, namely—employing a traditional Italian doctrinal distinction—both 'functions' (PA prerogatives) and services in the strictest sense. A quite comprehensive definition of online service states it is "an activity or a series of activities, of a more or less intangible nature, which result in an exchange between a provider and a client where the subject of the transaction is an intangible good".[8]

The level of sophistication, the x-axis, can in turn be articulated in five stages, from one to five: information, bi-directional communication, transaction, integration, and political participation.[9] They are the first four that refer more closely to public administration for the latter prevalently concerns the issue sometimes evoked in terms of e-democracy. It goes without saying, however, that e-democracy is significant to admin law as well. Article 9 of the Code of Digital Administration (CDA) establishes that administrative authorities should favour as much as possible any use of new technologies which is able to enhance citizens' participation in the democratic process and facilitate the enjoyment of political and civil rights both individually and collectively.

Some Italian literature in the 80s, embracing an optimistic view of the then dawning relationship between ICTs and democratic institutions, envisaged that the development of informatics would be the turning point for a change in the relationships between public institutions and citizens—within which admin law had to be adjusted as well—inspired to a full and authentic democratisation bolstered by the direct participation of people in government.[10] At the beginning of the 90s the advent of the Internet led a number of authors to consider it as the best solution to the old issue of the lack of quality and quantity of representation that impairs liberal democracies.[11] In such a climate several governmental programmes to boost e-government assisted by conspicuous investments were implemented.[12] Such

[7]Hiller and Bélanger (2001).

[8]Batini (2013).

[9]One can find a similar classification in the Guidelines of 2011 regarding how to set up the institutional websites of any public administration issued pursuant to article 4 of the Directive n. 8/2009 of the Minister for the Public Administration and Innovation.

[10]Berti (1986).

[11]Johnson and Post (1996) and Santos (2007).

[12]Morison (2003).

Panglossian views are nowadays far less popular among scholars as their auspices have been proven largely unattainable until now.[13] Due to such failures, the present mainstream view, which can be named pragmatic, purports that technology has nothing particularly new to offer to democracy but reinforce the existing practices and political and social institutions.[14] Along with such conceptions a third coexists, which has been defined dystopian, where ICTs are viewed as a means of massive danger both to democracy and basic freedom up to their destruction.[15] Taking heed of such major concerns, the dominant pragmatic approach appears to be the most relevant if we focus on public administration. This is slippery terrain, however, because most of the times such an approach is all but neutral and in fact the rise of e-government has very often been associated with those positions that consider technology as an arrow in the sheath of the new public management (NPM) ideology. For example, to such ideology belongs the idea that ICTs might reduce negative externalities caused by the formalisation of administrative decisions into strictly legalised procedures.

Among the other four levels of e-government sophistication, the information stage essentially concerns in the Italian legal system the creation of the institutional website pursuant to article 53 CDA, which establishes that institutional websites shall operate through a network which complies with principles of accessibility, enhanced usability, and availability and be disabled people friendly, complete and clear in information, inter-operational, reliable and easy to use. The second level, relating to bi-directional communication, consists of a non-fully complete form of interaction with the users because it does not include any online transaction. It contemplates an exchange of information between officials and users. It is possible that online forms have to be filled in, but the service is provided in an ordinary way. This is still a 'documentary' stage, whilst transaction and integration are the levels of sophistication where the service is appropriately online and ICTs operate in a 'meta-documentary' way.[16] In such cases one can speak of a digital procedure in the specific meaning that the decision which shapes a particular legal relationship is operated through the website, namely by using data elaborating software which produces that decision. In many cases such transactions—for example the payment of a fine—do not seem to appear that different from what happens in e-commerce. In other cases, more complex administrative decisions are dealt with, such as permits or benefits. The difference between the transaction and integration stages regards the fact that in the latter a thorough transformation of back-office practices is pursued, so in a sense the stress is more on specific organisational tools. There is in the literature

[13] Schafer (2006), Longford and Patten (2007). From a broader perspective, however, we cannot ignore that one of the most impressive political European phenomena of recent years, the surge of Five Stars in Italy, is founded on 'Rousseau', a decision-making Interned-based platform. See Deseriis (2017).

[14] Agre (2002), Longford and Patten (2007).

[15] Koops (2008).

[16] D'angelosante (2017).

the idea that the integration stage would imply a proper shift from a bureaucratic-centred concept to a citizen-centred concept of public administration, where, that is to say, both the organisational and service dimensions would adapt according to the users' needs.[17]

Considering the other dimension of the phenomenon at hand—which looks at the recipients of e-government—a point stands out as regards the sophistication scale, which is whether the passage from the information stage to the transactional stage is to be considered a sort of progress towards the achievement of "true" e-government, as if, in other words, the higher the sophistication the fuller digital citizenship is. This seems to be the NPM approach, whose model is e-commerce and whose paramount value is efficiency. Such an approach may have influenced policy implemented by the EU commission in agreement with Member States between 1999 and 2006, which clearly show a trend to privilege the e-commerce/transaction side. In this period indeed, one notes a sizeable increase in supply of online services, which reached 70% in 2007.[18] However, this was not accompanied by an analogous rise in the employment of online services by the users. Viz. a clear asymmetry persists in Europe between supply and demand of e-government in favour of the former. The "Digital Agenda Targets Progress Report" (Digital Agenda Scoreboard) of June 2015 speaks about a slow increase in e-government. The use of e-government services, measured on the quantity of online forms submitted (only 25% of which is indicated as complete), has risen from 38% to 47% in five years. Such data constitute the average between remarkably differentiated situations in each Member State. As for Italy—which is among the countries at the bottom of the list (third last)—the figure is little more than 10% and it has not seen change across the five-year period.

Those who simply do not have access to the Internet, a number, by the way, which is constantly dwindling, constitute a sub-cluster of people who do not benefit from online e-government. The mentioned Digital Agenda Scoreboard refers to the Internet as a "success story" and in fact at the level of the Union the percentage of Internet users reaches 75%. However, in the majority of the Member States around a third of the population do not access the Internet. This group includes disadvantaged people who are the most likely candidates to access social services aimed at fostering their social inclusion such as education, social assistance, job activation, etc.

8.3 Digital Agenda and the Principle "Digital First"

From what discussed in the previous section emerges that one of the key-points concerns the quantitative and qualitative incidence of e-government on government and public administration. Although there are not exhaustive studies regarding the

[17]Tat-Kei Ho (2002).

[18]Codagnone and Osimo (2010).

Italian situation, surveys and reports exist as regards the international context. When talking of ICTs and public institutions the literature refers to two aspects or at least the following stand out. The first regards the level of diffusion of e-government and therefore the success of digital agenda initiatives. The second, much more meaningfully, regards the analysis and evaluation of the practices which are brought about by the use of such technologies. In this section we deal with the first point, while the second will be addressed in the following section. There is a further aspect on which we will turn in section five which concerns the identification of the possible scenarios deducible from the legal rules which accompany the introduction of such technologies and that affect central notions of administrative law such as decision-making and procedure.

As to the first aspect, a sort of paradox lurks here. On the one hand, the pervasiveness of ICTs seems to exert its influence on the very structure of social and institutional models, as much so that it is familiar to refer to our historical time as the digital era. On the other hand, they are phenomena which require a specific governmental implementation, without which, that is to say, change barely takes place. In other words, one cannot say that politics is merely superseded by technology if choices, plans and investment are needed to make e-government become an ordinary practice and if such choices are not neutral towards the model of e-government one wishes to pursue. It seems that the employment of ICTs may enhance or emphasise the features of certain ideal-types or models of public administration, but it does not constitute a model per se. It is somewhat evident, anyway, that such a digital era yields new asymmetries and disequilibrium. One of the so-called digital divides regards in fact the chasm between the traditional functioning of public administration—suffice it to mention the time issue—and new modalities of socio-economic interaction which develop thanks to the internet.

Governments are expected to be able to detect and acquire remarkably complex and sophisticated operating systems and make them functional and—as the experience of some UE Member States shows—one should not take for granted that such an ability is just a function of the amount of resources invested.[19]

It is in such a framework that "digital agenda" initiatives are to be located. At the level of the EU, the Digital Agenda for Europe, launched within the Europe 2020 strategy, has got broader scope than the digitalisation of PA, for it mainly regards economic growth and employment to be pursued in seven priority areas and 101 actions. Among the most prominent objectives there is the adoption of a new and stable regulatory framework for broadband, the creation of specific infrastructure for digital public services and the increase in digital skill. As mentioned before, the level of achievement of such goals by all Member States is yearly measured in the Digital Agenda Scoreboard where Italy is among the strugglers. The Italian Digital Agenda aims at filling this gap.

Another figure, more comprehensive and refined than the Scoreboard, the Digital Economy and Society Index (DESI) (http://ec.europa.eu/digital-agenda/en/desi)

[19]Keen (2010).

provides more precise data regarding each country. This is a composite index, developed by the European Commission, with the purpose of assessing the growth of the Member States towards a digital economy, which considers a cluster of factors dealing with five dimensions: connectivity, human capital, Internet use, integration of digital technology, and digital public services.

In the DESI report for 2018 Italy, with Romania, Greece, and Bulgaria, has the lowest scores on the index. Among the factors that determine such a result there is scarce connectivity, due to the little availability of fast Internet connections, paucity of digital skill and generally a limited use of the Internet. 31% of Italians have never used the Internet and the wariness towards online transaction is still widespread. Only 42% of habitual Internet users use online banking and only 31% trade online. All such factors bounce back on the development of e-government and influence the dimension of online public services, which although closer to the EU average is however underdeveloped. The report pins down the lack of digital skill among bureaucrats as an explanation of this condition.

What the Italian CDA has promised for a decade, that is to say that central and local public administration shall rethink their organisation and operational way in light of new ICTs to "secure the availability, management, access, transmission, storage and fruition of information in digital modality" is far from being achieved. Another actual issue is that the CDA—which have already been amended many times—provides for the adoption of a sizeable number of measures of implementation through a variety of sources—such as regulations, ministerial decrees, guidelines, technical rules—most of which have not been issued yet.[20] The delegated legislation, Act 26 August 2016, n. 179, passed by the government pursuant to article 1 of the Public Administration Reorganisation Act (of Parliament) n. 124 of 2015 tries to face this problem by bestowing most of such a technical regulation upon the governmental Agency for Digital Italy.

The same article 1 of the PA Reorganisation Act—pompously headed "digital citizenship"—aims at changing and integrating the CDA in order to further strengthen the centrality of digital administration. Particularly committing is the wording of article 1, par. b), which introduces the new principle "digital first". Digital first means that by adopting digital technology on a large scale, administrative procedures and back-office practices have to be redefined and simplified to seek quick decision within certain time and transparency towards both citizens and corporations. It is uneasy to see, however, how the formulation of new principles—allegedly more convincing than the previous ones—can per se make the Italian Digital Agenda more effective.[21] Article 3 of the CDA, in turn, provides citizens and corporations with a new right to the use of ICTs when they communicate

[20]'Monitoraggio dell'attuazione dell'Agenda digitale italiana del Servizio Studi della Camera', 20 March 2015, n. 159 http://documenti.camera.it/Leg17/Dossier/Pdf/TR0270.Pdf.

[21]The main provisions concerning the Italian Digital Agenda can be found in the following law decrees: D.L. n. 83 del 2012 (c.d. "Crescita"); D.L. n. 179 del 2012 (c.d. "Crescita 2.0"); D.L. 69 del 2013 (c.d. "del Fare"); D.L. n. 90 del 2014 ("Semplificazione e trasparenza amministrativa ed efficienza degli uffici giudiziari"); D.L. n. 133 del 2014 (c.d. "Sblocca Italia").

with public administration.[22] Thereby such a right refers only to the information level. We wonder whether article 1.1 of the PA Reorganisation Act, which delegates the government to reform ample sectors of the organisation of public administration, by broadening the scope of this right to enable citizens and corporations to have access to all data, documents and services now refers to the transactional stage as well. The report which accompanies the cited act of delegated legislation emphasises that the principle which inspires the reform is to put digital rights first so that—one can argue—processes of digitalisation of PA should be treated as the object of an obligation to fulfil them. This delegated legislation amends the CDA by establishing that PA makes its services (so apparently all its activity) digitally available and providing for a 'public class action' in case an administrative authority does not comply with such 'obligations'. The idea of broadening the scope of digitalisation to any 'service' coupled with attributing a right to have PA to comply with such an organisational requirement may seem the best way of making sure that e-government becomes at last ordinarily practised.[23]

There are, however, a number of downsizes to this scheme. Firstly, one has to wonder whether and to what extent we can actually speak of a right-obligation relationship, as such judicially enforceable. The provision of a class action is far from decisive to this regard, as in Italian law it is a tool—available either to any consumers or their associations—conceived as a way to assess that either public services comply with the obligations set out in the consumer charters and qualitative and economic standards or that providers do not fail to adopt such charters or other framework regulations. Administrative courts are just allowed to issue recommendations to make amends of the mismanagement of the service if that is the case and provided that the action recommended does not negatively affect public finance. It is extremely difficult to fathom how such a pattern can be adapted to the sort of 'obligations' at hand. Anyway, it is even more difficult to reconcile this action with the protection of specific individual digital rights and it is implausible that administrative courts would interpret these 'rights' as enabling individuals either to challenge PA to perform digitally or to impugn decisions not digitally processed/made as procedurally biased. An actual possibility is that the class action will become concretely available if and when the above-mentioned governmental Agency issues technical standards and quality levels for PA to comply with. This will occur, though, when digitalisation has already gone well forward.

Secondly, the same alleged extension of the right from the communication to transaction stage makes the notion of digital rights as proper rights even more implausible. It is then more plausible as well as desirable to interpret the reference to "rights" in a moral sense, linked in fact to citizenship, hence as the content of a

[22]This discipline resembles the Spanish's one as set up by the Act of Parliament n. 11 of 2007, where a right to communicate with PA through electronic means has been established. See Delgado (2009).

[23]See, however, the following section as regards the limitations that EU law establishes concerning fully automated decision-making.

principled political activation. We should not be too preoccupied with this rhetorical resort to the language of rights—which we are well used to in recent times—in so far as it is not taken in the wrong way. It can become harmful in fact if one wants to interpret it as empowering the courts to manage the policy behind such 'rights'. To be fair the same idea of a right to an indeterminate digitalisation of administrative activity is disputable for the reasons we have expounded above.

Leaving rights aside, it is more likely that the Italian struggle with digital agenda has to do with cultural and technological structural problems, which one should look into and cope with before investing on programmes which risk remaining manifestos.[24] Administrative and administrative law cultures represent in turn but a fraction of such structural problems. The paramount question regards, thus, how the use of ICTs interacts with practices and modes of functioning of PA.

8.4 Re-Engineering Bureaucratic Work and Automating Decision-Making

Taking heed of what we have expounded so far regarding the fundamental characteristics and impact of e-government on PA, we can now turn to discuss the specific question of the so-called re-engineering of bureaucratic work and automated decision-making.

We can conceive the organisational dimension both in narrow terms and with reference to the decision-making process. Two are, then, the most relevant factors of such a 'mature' or enhanced stage of e-government. It is often said that e-government programmes aim at 're-engineering' administrative procedure at the integration stage, where, that is to say, the design of organisational patterns and manner of decision-making (also involving different authorities and even citizens and corporations) is embedded in one point of access only. Re-engineering should take on the challenge to reorient the organisation and practice of PA around users' needs by reforming procedural rules so as to conceive them as centred on the delivery of service rather than the exercise of power. One should bear in mind that such a shift of the barycentre of administrative procedure is neither neutral nor simply derived from the different technology employed. The idea of a user centrality can be instrumental both to the corporatisation of PA—which was dear to the first rise of e-government—and opposite ideas such as administration democracy, ameliorative participation, etc. Digitalisation can empower either of such objectives, but, while it remains important to choose one, the fact stands that our present knowledge suggests that ICT is somewhat parasitic of existing models of PA rather than a factor which changes their fundamentals.

Having said this, the transformation of the information vector from paper and ink to bits plays a major role in the dissemination of information necessary to determine

[24] Harshly critical remarks are made by De Michelis (2013).

a course of action. Through digital technology information can be centralised, on the one hand, and easily shared and analysed among several units, in this way decentralised, on the other hand. It is supposed that this process of centralisation-decentralisation of information ensures both more transparency and accountability of officials.[25]

In the Italian legal system, the discipline of the 'digital file' pursuant to article 41 CDA seems to embody such an idea. All acts, documents and data that pertain to a certain procedure, irrespective of who has produced them, have to (should) be collected in a digital file which has to be directly accessible by all the authorities involved in that procedure. Still more comprehensive, for it affects the subjective dimension of PA, is the solution adopted in the Spanish legal system, where the legislation has set up an 'electronic site of public administration' which is meant to be a virtual room for carrying out administrative tasks, thereby trying to change the perception that citizens have of public administration as a complex web of inaccessible offices. The law establishes a specific link between the 'electronic site' and the discharge of administrative duties as well as between the former and a specific legal responsibility to act on the part of certain public bodies.

Such coordination-cooperation between different public authorities seems to generalise the precept of "points of single contact".[26] In the political science literature this issue is often treated under the label of joined-up government.[27] Although there are those who underline the problems of a holistic concept of PA where vertical and horizontal integration (which absorbs even private parties in the unit which operates as the access point) risks confusing duties and accountability,[28] the idea that this approach yields positive outcomes tends to prevail. Sharing tasks and duties between different administrative units should discourage self-regarding behaviours, boost greater transparency in reciprocal interactions and greater accountability relating to a common achievement.[29]

This re-engineering notion has been embedded in the Danish legal system by coining a new 'Principle of Administrative Law by Design' as a result of a number of opinions issued by the Parliamentarian Ombudsman office. The principle spells out that the whole process of developing, programming, using and disposing of digital administration must ensure its integration with the relevant legislation and unwritten principles of administrative law.[30] This precept is especially important when dealing with decision-making systems, where "the citizen's legal position is predetermined by the interpretation of the regulations laid down in the algorithmics".[31] Here human

---

[25]Petrakaki (2010).

[26]Article 6 of the Directive 2006/123/EC of 12 December 2006 on 'services in the internal market'.

[27]Pollitt (2003).

[28]Zouridis and Bekkers (2000).

[29]Cole and Fenwick (2003), Illsley et al. (2000), Curthoys and Eckersley (2003).

[30]Motzfeldt (2017). Denmark is a world leading country regarding e-government and indeed it occupies the first position in the Digital Economy and Society Index.

[31]H.M. Motzfeldt, cit., 743.

activities are replaced by bestowing ICT with a number of automatic operations.[32] This too is deemed to bring about greater transparency, the foreseeability of outcomes, time certainty, ease of control, strong accountability and the possibility that procedures are looked after by personnel lacking specific professional skill once the software has been set up and appropriately instructed.

In the Anglo-Saxon area the downsizes of such a shift from human to algorithmics are usually addressed from the perspective of the lawfulness and fairness of automated decision-making. A ground-breaking report of the Australian Administrative Review Council of 2004,[33] which led in 2007 to issuing a best practice guide by the Australian Ombudsman, aired a number of concerns regarding automated decision-making.[34] This report acknowledged that the use of 'expert systems',[35] whilst important to improve public administration performance and make savings, had to be attentively assessed to ensure their compatibility with the core administrative law values that underpin a democratic society governed by the rule of law. To this purpose it put forward as many as 27 guiding principles, the first seven of which directly relating to the basic characteristics and values of administrative law. The most relevant precepts were based on the distinction between 'making a decision' and 'helping a decision maker make a decision'. The first case should be restricted to decisions involving non-discretionary elements, whilst, when expert systems are used to assist an official in exercising his or her discretion, the systems should be designed so that they do not fetter the decision-maker in the exercise of his or her power by recommending or guiding the decision-maker itself to a particular outcome. Both these alternatives were deemed to require a statutory recognition of the use of computer programmes, even though the report mentioned views that this would not be necessary because such programmes are simply tools. Equally, the delicate power to override a decision made by or with the assistance of an expert system should be legislatively provided for and disciplined.

As has been noted, also in the UK the issue of the legal basis of automated decision making is still to be dealt with.[36] In Le Sueur's view the fact that there are specific provisions that expressly allow for decisions to be "made or issued not only by an officer of his acting under his authority but also (a) by a computer for whose

---

[32]By automated decision-making one means "breaking down a decision to a set of 'if then' rules and criteria: a decision is understood as an algorithm (a sequence of reasoning) that selects from predetermined alternatives. An 'inference engine' can systematically check whether the condition of a rule is met; if so, it can 'conclude' that the consequent of that rule applies" [Le Sueur (2016)].

[33]Administrative Review Council, 'Automated Assistance in Administrative Decision Making: Report to the Attorney-General', Report No 46 (2004) available at http://www.arc.ag.gov.au/Documents/AAADMreportPDF.pdf.

[34]'Automated Assistance in Administrative Decision-Making' http://www.ombudsman.gov.au/__data/assets/pdf_file/0032/29399/Automated-Assistance-in-Administrative-Decision-Making.pdf.

[35]In the report an 'expert system' is defined as a "computing systems that, when provided with basic information and a general set of rules for reasoning and drawing conclusions, can mimic the thought processes of a human expert".

[36]Le Sueur, see at note 32.

operation such an officer is responsible" [Social Security Act 1998 (c. 14) Ss. 2–3], in spite of a rather loose approach in English admin law to the need for specific legislative authority for executive action, may be interpreted as a legal necessity for an express legal basis for automation.

As regards this we can note that, for example, in the Spanish legal system there is a general provision referring to administrative action carried out via an information system appropriately set up so as to make sure that the intervention of a person is not necessary.[37] This ample clause seems not to exclude from its semantic scope any typology of decision and thereby is open to any technological evolution in the realm of artificial intelligence. The question is that such a general and apparently unconditional acknowledgment of automated decision-making, while formally meets the requirements of the rule of law, risks turning out to be too thin a safeguard of the above-mentioned administrative law values. The best way, the one however implied in the Australian Administrative Review Council report, should be to require a specific legal authorisation referring to each and every type of decision-making.

As regards this, the fundamental legal source to be considered within the EU is currently the GDPR,[38] whose art. 22 prohibits any "decision based solely on automated processing, including profiling, which produces legal effects concerning him or her or similarly significantly affects him or her".[39] By using the word "solely" this provision seems to rule out a purely automated decision-making system but not a decision support system, where the ultimate decision-maker is still a human being. However, the border between these two situations is vague. In the 'Article 29 Data Protection Working Party's' view, "if someone routinely applies automatically generated profiles to individuals without any actual influence on the result, this would still be a decision based solely on automated processing".[40]

The same article 22 establishes, as a way of exception to the said prohibition, that a decision based solely on automated processing is lawful if it is "authorised by Union or Member State law to which the controller is subject and which also lays down suitable measures to safeguard the data subject's rights and freedoms and legitimate interests".[41] Interestingly, this provision conjures up both the

[37]Delgado (2017), at note 4, 287–288.

[38]Regulation (EU) 2016/679 of the European Parliament and of the Council of 27 April 2016 on the protection of natural persons with regard to the processing of personal data and on the free movement of such data, and repealing Directive 95/46/EC (General Data Protection Regulation), OJ 2016 L 119/1.

[39]The analogous provision in the previous EU legislation (Directive 95/46/EC) has sometimes been interpreted by the Member States as a right to opt-out rather than a prohibition Veale and Edwards (2018), Korff (2002) but the guidelines issued by Article 29 Working Party (A29WP), *Guidelines on Automated individual decision-making and Profiling for the purposes of Regulation 2016/679* (WP 251, 3 October 2017). https://perma.cc/ 3X54-2DGC, are adamant in interpreting the provision at stake as providing for a prohibition.

[40]A29WP, *Guidelines*..., at note 39, 399.

[41]The provision stems from French law which inspired article 15 of the Data Protection Directive which responded "to fears in the early days of digitisation that automated, and hence potentially inscrutable and unchallengeable, decisions might prejudice access to important facilities such as

recommendation discernible in the Australian Administrative Review Council report, that a specific legal authorisation to algorithmic decisions referring to each and every type of decision-making should be mandatory, and the concern of Danish administrative law regarding a specific design for any particular instance of a proper automated decision-making programme.

Summing up, EU law tolerates either national general provisions implementing decision support systems or specific provisions regarding the automated processing of certain types of decisions.[42] Evidently, though, this does not touch upon the line drawn by the Australian report as to the distinction between discretionary and rule-bound decisions. This report holds that, when the operation to be undertaken is solely a matter of rule subsumption, the benefits of automated decision-making would overcome its drawbacks.[43] Le Sueur elaborates on this point by observing that automated decision-making might achieve more consistent implementation of written law than can be done by human officials: "automation based on the application of objective criteria holds out the promise of legal certainty (like cases are treated identically), the elimination of bias, ensuring that no irrelevant considerations are taken into account, and that all relevant factors are included. To this extent, automation can be regarded as enhancing the rule of law".[44]

One can think, therefore, that the scenario of an automated procedure fulfils the Weberian ideal of a bureaucrat utterly dispassionate and fully accountable as long as he or she is part of a hierarchy that abides by a rigidly pre-set protocol.[45] Yet, there is another side to consider. Within such a perspective, other benefits which the functioning of complex organisations can provide thanks to non-conformist behaviours—the ones that Luhmann called useful illegality—get lost. In Luhmann's view an unlawful behaviour is one that harms formal expectations. From a systematic

credit, housing or insurance. In practice, the provision was little known and largely unused" (Veale, Edwards at note 37).

[42]It is fitting to note that when automated decision-making is admissible the GDPR (articles 13–15) provides for rights of information and access in favour of the affected parties amounting to "meaningful information about the logic involved, as well as the significance and the envisaged consequences of such processing for the data subject". Such rights, though, seems to only guarantee general and *ex ante* explanation regarding "the system functionality, including the general logic (such as types of data and features considered, categories in the decision tree), purpose or significance" but not *ex post* explanation on the "rationale, reasons, and individual circumstances of a specific automated decision" Wachter et al. (2017).

[43]A formidable theoretical challenge lurks here, which revolves around the characters of legal interpretation and whether or to what extent AI can mimic human mind, provided this is desirable. Should not we seek to avoid human bias after all? Normally, however, the interpretation of the legal rules to apply is laid down in the algorithmics and in this way it is still a human artefact in the form of text-oriented, or *in abstracto*, interpretation as opposed to fact-oriented, or *in concreto*, interpretation (Guastini 2005). Somehow, the difference between text-oriented and fact-oriented interpretation relates to the distinction between *ex ante* and *ex post* explanation discussed in the previous note.

[44]See at note 32, 190.

[45]What is missing of the ideal Weberian's bureaucrat is the intimate adhesion to a bundle of values and skills which inform bureaucracy as a profession.

perspective, though, behaviours which we can classify in a sort of grey area between legality and illegality can be nonetheless useful, even though they frustrate formal expectations.[46] Luhmann provides some examples, such as following rules on the grounds of prohibited reasons or goals, abiding by the law but not within the time allowed, flouting habitually obsolete rules or rules whose application can harm more important interests etc. All these are unlawful but useful behaviours as they imply adaptive strategies which favour creative behaviours and adaption to a continually changing environment. One can look at this phenomenon from the perspective of the broader context in which an official has to decide. There is a sizeable amount of literature which, building on the work of Lispsky, suggests that administrative decision-making is informed by an ampler set of cultural values than the bureaucratic-legal ones.[47]

Purportedly, automation would get rid of such aspects of the functioning of administrative organisations, shifting the focus from the exercise of a kind of interstitial discretionary power accompanied by adaptive behaviours, which imply responsiveness for the use of some kind of contextual evaluation, to a form of accountability which turns into the technology employed. Relating to this there is another aspect discussed by Le Sueur, that is the chance that automated decision-making will favour a trend to design decision-making systems that hinge on bright line rules and reduce or eliminate the margins of discretion expressly or implicitly conferred by the law.[48]

As to automated *discretionary* decision-making, it is generally agreed that algorithmics should be avoided and digitalisation confined to a supportive function. As we have seen the Australian Administrative Review Council's view was that automation of discretion collides with the administrative law values of lawfulness and fairness, even though expert systems can be used as an administrative tool to help officials exercise their discretion. The allure of such systems is that they are able to face the greater issue of information age, that is to deal with the innumerable amount of information available to the decision-maker, burdened with the nearly impossible task of selecting what is relevant,[49] which implies he or she is able in a relatively short time to assign meaning to such data in a certain context and structure it. But such a function of an expert system should not be pushed up to replace a human decision-maker.

The most intriguing question concerns the reproducibility through computing of mental processes which occur when a political choice is made, that is to say to ponder facts and interests to reach a correct decision whatever the meaning of a correct decision might be. In such a circumstance the issue is not only—and not

[46]Luhmann (1964).

[47]Lipsky (1980) and Halliday (2004).

[48]The point is disputed. Buffat (2015), in reviewing the relevant literature detects tow opposite attitudes. which she labels respectively 'curtailment thesis' and 'enablement thesis', and calls for more empirical research on the topic.

[49]Klapp (1982).

much—the one regarding the ability to build ‘smart systems’ but also to penetrate into the decision theory, which with particular regard to public organisations has long contended that decision-making processes can be encapsulated in a sequence of pre-set steps, such as choice of the most appropriate course of action, implementation of the decision, and assessment of its effects. There are many other factors at stake, even of an emotional nature and it is not certain that their possible eradication from decision-making by entrusting it to software yields the best possible course of action.[50]

However, scholars in the field of artificial intelligence applied to legal systems have long claimed that software-agents can be autonomy-furnished, viz. possessing the ability to detect connections with the organisational referring framework, choosing whether or not to abide by a rule, and establishing how to pursue individual and social goals within certain normative constraints.[51] In other words they would be able to do things such as “exegesis, hermeneutics, legal interpretation, and scientific theorisation” and stimulate the emotional component which is part of dialectic reasoning, founded on typical features of human societies such as debate and discussion in the effort of attributing meaning to things.[52] In such an interdisciplinary area of research as the one regarding simulation of dynamic systems it is believed that we are not far away from the possibility to transform “intuitive policy making into model-based policy design”.[53] A ‘guru’ of contemporary physics thinks that in the middle of the twenty-first century the era of “emotional robots” might be blossoming.[54]

8.5 Conclusive Remarks

It is clear that if this is the direction that the systems of public decision-making will take, then current concepts of accountability and justiciability of administrative decisions will require a complete revision.

The idea that we can limit ourselves to updating our traditional notions does not sound truly satisfactory. In a way, if we look at these problems from the familiar perspective of legal concepts we can apparently continue to rely on the received ‘fictional legal notions’ (*fictio iuris*). In fact, it is sufficient to impute the artificial will of a software to a public body—in turn a *fictio iuris* itself—and thereby to a public authority to which the former belongs. This point, in other words, regards that

[50]Simon (1983), Lerner et al. (2015).

[51]Rubino and Sartor (2008) and Lucatuorto and Bianchini (2009) claim that e-government discretional decision-making, facing the reasonable and proportional comparison of competing private and public interests, could be supported by Artificial Intelligence tools.

[52]Op. Loco ult cit.

[53]Pruyt (2015).

[54]Kaku (2011).

special juridical attitude called doctrinal constructivism (dogmatic) which aims at mapping certain areas of law by employing a specifically constructed language.

Continental scholars, influenced by early German nineteenth century doctrinal constructivism, have long elaborated specific legal notions made out of the consolidated precepts of doctrinal tradition to describe such new phenomena. Namely, such key-notions of administrative law as 'organ' and 'administrative act' would not suffer from their being adapted to explain such things as the digitalisation of administrative decisions and the creation of virtual offices. Indeed 'organs' (those particular administrative units which are able to formally express the will of a public authority) can continue to be regarded as administrative units awarding legal powers which affect third parties, and 'administrative acts' as those declarations made by an 'organ' that, by using the power conferred to it, produces any specified legal effect. In this way we can straightforwardly make sense of a 'digital organ' and a 'digital administrative act'. In other words, the fictional nature of such legal concepts fits the even more fictional nature of digital administration. As has been highlighted, the will which an administrative act embodies it is not really a will of a human being, it is instead always a "procedural will":[55] an administrative organ, irrespective of it being an office composed either of human beings or electronic agents, always comes to issue a declaration of will, judgment, knowledge or wish in order to implement a legal provision with the goal of taking care of public interest.

One wonders, though, what is the actual heuristic value of conceptual constructions which are capable of containing so very different substances, in other words of remaining unaffected by such a huge change of institutional practices as the one by which a human decision shifts into a 'robot' one. In fact, the notion of 'delegating' a decision to an automated system raises a number of unique problems, which cannot be faced by merely updating our fictional legal notions. For instance, just mentioning a couple, who at the end of the day should be identified as the 'decision-maker'? We cannot take for granted that it is the computer itself rather than the programmer, the policy-maker, the authorised operator. Moreover, is the concept of conferring a power by means of a rule appropriately used in this circumstance? As has been pointed out, unlike human agents, a computer software can never truly be said to act independently of its programmer or the relevant administrative authority.[56]

References

Agre PE (2002) Real-time politics: the internet and the political process. Inf Soc 18:311, 317
Batini C (2013) Un'introduzione ai servizi di e-government. Amministrare 23:38
Berti G (1986) Diritto e Stato. Riflessioni sul cambiamento. Cedam, Padova
Bromley DA (2002) Science, technology, and politics. Technol Soc 24:9–26

[55]Delgado, at note 37, 299; Giannini (1981).

[56]M Perry and A Smith, 'iDecide: the legal implications of automated decision-making' (FCA) [2014] FedJSchol 17, available at http://www.austlii.edu.au/au/journals/FedJSchol/2014/17.html.

Buffat A (2015) Street-level Bureaucracy and E-government. Public Manage Rev 17:149–161
Carboni N (2010) changing relationships between politicians and Bureaucrats in contemporary democracies: an empirical analysis of the Italian experience. Int Public Manage Rev 11:90–109
Civitarese Matteucci S, Torchia L (eds) (2017) La tecnificazione della pubblica amministrazione (Technologisation of Public Administration). Firenze University Press, Firenze
Codagnone C, Osimo D (2010) Beyond i2010. E-Government current challenges and future scenarios'. In: Nixon PG, Koutrakou VN, Rawal R (eds) Understanding E-Government in Europe. Routledge, Oxford, p 39 fig. 3.1
Cole M, Fenwick J (2003) UK local government: the impact of modernisation on departmentalism. Int Rev Adm Sci 69:259–270
Curthoys N, Eckersley PM (2003) E-Government. Routledge, Oxford, pp 227–257
D'angelosante M (2017) La consistenza del modello dell'amministrazione 'invisibile' nell'età della tecnificazione: dalla formazione delle decisioni alla responsabilità per le decisioni'. In: Civitarese S. Torchia L, p 320
Delgado IM (2009) Las notificationes electronicas en el procedimiento administrativo. Tirant lo Blanch, Valencia, p 63
Delgado IM (2017) La riforma dell'amministrazione digitale: un'opportunità per ripensare la pubblica amministrazione'. In: Civitarese S, Torchia L, above, pp 287–88
Deseriis M (2017) Direct parliamentarianism: an analysis of the political values embedded in Rousseau, the 'operating system' of the five star movement. JeDEM 9(2):47–67. http://www.jedem.org
Giannini MS (1981) Istituzioni di diritto amministrativo. Giuffré, Milano, p 292
Guastini R (2005) A sceptical view on legal interpretation. In: Analisi e diritto P. Comanducci, Guastini R (eds) Maggioli, Rimini, 142
Halliday S (2004) Judicial review and compliance with administrative law. Hart, Oxford, p 100
Hiller JJ, Bélanger F (2001) Privacy, strategies for electronic government. E-Government Series Pricewaterhouse Coopers Endowment for the Business of Government, Arlington
Illsley B, Lloyd G, Lynch B (2000) From pillar to post? A one-stop shop approach to planning delivery. Plan Theor Pract 1:111–122
Johnson DR, Post D (1996) Law and borders: the rise of law in cyberspace. Stan Law Rev 48:1367 et seqq
Kaku M (2011) Physics of the future. Penguin Books, London, p 83
Keen J (2010) Integration at any price: the case of the NHS national programme for information technology. In: Margetts H, Hood C (eds) Paradoxes of modernization; unintended consequences of public policy reform. Oxford University Press, p 138
Klapp OE (1982) Meaning lag in the information society. J Commun, pp 57–60
Koops B (2008) Criteria for normative technology: the acceptability of "code as law" in light of democratic and constitutional values. In: Brownsword R, Yeung K (eds) Regulating technologies: legal futures, regulatory frames and technological fixes. Hart, Oxford, p 158
Korff D (2002) EC Study on Implementation of Data Protection Directive, Report, Cambridge (UK) September, p 119
Le Sueur A (2016) A Robot Government: automated decision-making and its implications for parliament. In: Horne A, Le Sueur A (eds) Parliament: legislation and accountability. Hart, Oxford, p 184
Lerner JS, Li Y, Valdesolo P, Kassam KS (2015) Emotion decision making. Ann Rev Psychol 66:799–823
Lipsky M (1980) Street-level bureaucracry: Dilemmas of the individual in public service. Russell Sage Foundation, New York
Longford G, Patten S (2007) Democracy in the age of the internet, Univ New Brunswick Law J 56:5
Lucatuorto P, Bianchini S (2009) Discrezionalità e contemperamento degli interessi nei processi decisionali dall'Amministrazione digitale. Ciberspazio e diritto 10:41–58
Luhmann N (1964) Funktionen und Folgen formaler Organisation, Duncker & Humblot Berlin, p 304, V chap. I.3

Michelis G (2013) Agenda digitale: di cosa si sta parlando? Amministrare, pp 69 et seqq
Morison J (2003) Online government and e-constitutionalism. Public Law 14:15
Motzfeldt HM (2017) The Danish principle of administrative law by design. Eur Public Law 23:739–754
Osnaghi A (2013) A, Pubblica amministrazione che si trasforma: "Cloud Computing", federalismo, interoperabilità Amministrare 59
Perry M, Smith A (2014) 'iDecide: the legal implications of automated decision-making' (FCA) FedJSchol 17, available at http://www.austlii.edu.au/au/journals/FedJSchol/2014/17.html
Petrakaki D (2010) Accountability in the context of E-Government. In: Nixon PG, above, p 100
Pollitt C (2003) Joined-up government: a survey. Polit Stud Rev:34–49
Pruyt E (2015) From building a model to adaptive robust decision making using systems modeling. In: Janssen M, Wimmer MA, Deljoo A (eds) Policy practice and digital science. Integrating complex systems, Social Simulation and Public Administration in Policy Research, Springer, p 90
Rubino R, Sartor G (2008) Source norms and self-regulated institutions. In: Casanovas P, Sartor G, Casellas N, Rubino R (eds) Computable models of the law. Springer, pp 263–274
Santos B (ed) (2007) Democratising democracy: beyond the liberal democratic canon. Verso, London
Schafer B (2006) Democratic revival or E-Sell Out? A Sceptic's Report on the State of E-Governance in the UK' Report to the XVIIth International Congress of Comparative Law, July, 9–11
Severino E, Technics, Nihilism, Truth (2012) Phainomena XXI/82-83, p 111
Simon HA (1983) Reason in human affairs. Stanford University Press, Stanford
Tat-Kei Ho A (2002) Reinventing local governments and the e-government initiative. Public Adm Rev 18:434–444
Veale M, Edwards L (2018) Clarity, surprises, and further questions in the Article 29 Working Party draft guidance on automated decision-making and profiling. Comp Law Secur Rev 34:400
Wachter S, Mittelstadt B, Floridi L (2017) Why a right to explanation of automated decision-making does not exist in the general data protection regulation. Int Data Privacy Law 7:76–99
Zouridis S, Bekkers V (2000) Electronic service delivery and the democratic relationships between government and its citizens. In: Hoff J, Horrocks I, Tops P (eds) Democratic governance and new technology. Routledge, Oxford, p 132

Chapter 9
The Juridification Process in Italy and the Influence of EU Law

Luca De Lucia and Barbara Marchetti

Contents

Abstract This chapter describes the juridification process and its implication for Italian administrative law. First, it briefly analyses some tools—many of them permanent—aimed at relieving and simplifying the Italian legal environment. It then goes on to examine the paths that juridification has followed in some areas: bioethics, sport, food safety and environment. In addition, it illustrates the role of the Courts, the legislature, and the administration, and the tools each of them have used (binding norms, general principles and soft law) to explain how some interests have received legal protection. The chapter furthermore deals with juridification in connection to the EU integration process. In particular, it analyses, on the one hand, the influence that supranational law and other institutional measures (e.g. country-specific recommendations) exert on some areas of the Italian administrative legislation and, on the other hand, the effects that the multilevel dimension of

L. De Lucia
University of Salerno, Salerno, Italy
e-mail: ldelucia@unisa.it

B. Marchetti (✉)
University of Trento, Trento, Italy
e-mail: barbara.marchetti@unitn.it

D. Sorace et al. (eds.), *The Changing Administrative Law of an EU Member State*,
https://doi.org/10.1007/978-3-030-50780-0_9

jurisdictionalisation has on one specific aspect of the Italian system of administrative justice.

9.1 Introduction

The term juridification is polisemantic: for example it can be understood as "the proliferation of law", or as the tendency towards an increase in (formal) law within the social dynamics, or as the expansion of judicial power.[1] In this chapter, the term is used to indicate two different, but connected, issues.[2] First, the quantitative and qualitative increase in legislative provisions relating to areas previously not subjected to legal regulation or at any rate subjected to a less dense legal regulation (so-called legification). Second, the judicial activity which, on the one hand, regards increasingly important areas (at times with a political dimension) of collective life and, on the other hand, allows for the judicial protection of individual and collective interests previously of no legal importance (so-called jurisdictionalisation).[3]

Obviously, legification and jurisdictionalisation can be either convergent or diverging processes. For instance, Courts can start protecting an interest that in the past was irrelevant for the law and that the legislature subsequently chooses to subject to a legal regulation: this has occurred in Italy with the locus standing of individuals for the protection of the environment.[4] On the other hand, Courts can operate in an "orthopaedic" way by broadening the scope of a legal provision (e.g. the standing to bring an application for judicial review of the decisions of the Competition authority addressed to other undertakings)[5] or on the contrary by reducing it (e.g. the case-law on the standing of individuals in city planning litigations).[6] Moreover, it can also happen that the legislature cancels out or corrects the effects of the judicial activity: this has occurred, for example, with the case-law of the Supreme Court (Corte di Cassazione) regarding the compensation for damages

---

[1]For a synthesis of the possible meanings of the word juridification see Blichner and Molander (2008), pp. 36–54.

[2]Voigt (1980), pp. 18–23.

[3]However, juridification has also a third dimension. It is the so-called bureaucratisation, namely the extension of the administrative competences on the economic and social life. As such, the bureaucratisation involves the autonomy (legally recognised or factually practised) of the executive bodies (Galligan 2007, p. 295). Consider for example the discretionary, technical, normative and programming tools of the public administration (see e.g. Taruffo 1987, p. 581 ff.). This paper does not face specifically this topic.

[4]Consiglio di Stato, adunanza plenaria, judgment 19.10.1979, No. 24 and subsequently Art. 13, Law 8 July 1986, No. 349.

[5]E.g. Consiglio di Stato, sezione VI, judgment 14 June 2004, No. 3865.

[6]E.g. Consiglio di Stato, sezione V, judgment 9 June 1970 No. 523 and Corte di Cassazione, Sezioni Unite, judgment 25 October 1982 No. 5530.

caused by an unlawful administrative decision, which was later scaled down by a legislative provision.[7]

Juridification today has different features from those it had some decades ago, when it constituted the key to the interpretation of the transformation of the relations between the state and the society (and its self-regulation dynamics).[8] Nowadays, its structure is far more complex and derives from the multilevel dimension of the legislative and judicial powers.[9] Actually, legification encompasses not only the EU legislation but at times also international and global regulation.[10] Equally, jurisdictionalisation comprises at least three levels: Italian Courts, those of the European Union, and the Court of Human Rights. In the light of their composite nature, the factors of juridification can give rise to far more complex dynamics than those mentioned above. For instance, conflicts between Courts of different levels can occur, as well as convergence between the national legislature and a supranational Court at the expense of the domestic Courts.

From a different perspective, in Italy, similar to that of other Countries,[11] legal regulation has very wide dimensions: detailed legislative provisions regulate almost all spheres of life.[12] This situation—which has been named in various ways: e.g. the "crisis of the law",[13] the "trap of laws"[14] or "Penelope's shroud"–[15] obviously produces many negative consequences.[16] The quantitative aspect has qualitative consequences, as the legislation assumes the form of fragmentary and patchy

[7]According to the Supreme Court: (1) the ordinary Courts have the jurisdiction over these litigations (Corte di Cassazione, Sezioni Unite, judgment 22 July 1999, No. 500); (2) the previous action for the annulment of the administrative decision was not a condition for taking the damages action (e.g. Corte di Cassazione, Sezioni Unite, order 13 June 2006, No. 13659). On the contrary, according to the subsequent legislative discipline: (1) the jurisdiction over these litigations relays on the administrative Courts (Arts. 7 and 30, Legislative Decree 2 July 2010, No. 104; previously Legislative Decree 31 March 1998, No. 80); (2) even though it is not mandatory, the previous action for the annulment of the administrative decision is highly recommended by the code of administrative trial (Art. 30, par. 3, Legislative Decree 2 July 2010, No. 104).

[8]Habermas (2017), pp. 1022–1046; Teubner (1987).

[9]See for all Ferrarese (2015).

[10]See for all Cassese (2016).

[11]With regard to France, see Conseil d'État (2016).

[12]See recently Cassese (2018).

[13]This expression is actually quite old (see e.g. Carnelutti 1930, pp. 424–429): see, for a more recent study, Modugno and Nocilla (1989), p. 411 ff.

[14]Mattarella (2011).

[15]Natalini and Tiberi (2010).

[16]"The crisis of the legislative quality shows itself both with normative inflation and the poor clarity, contradiction, lack of generality and abstractness of rules with the consequent uncertainty surrounding their application": Quote from the President of the Supreme Administrative Court (Consiglio di Stato) in the speech for the inauguration of the Judicial Year 2016 (the speech is also available on: https://www.giustizia-amministratva.it/cdsintra/wcm/idc/groups/public/documents/document/mday/mjcx/~edisp/nsiga_4150149.pdf consulted on the 18th March 2018).

interventions (as the expression of sectorial and corporative interests),[17] often characterised by an excess of detail. This, on the one hand, gives rise to the increasing interference of the legislature in the social sphere and, on the other hand, to the uncertainty of the rules governing specific areas (and consequently to difficulties with their observance). The result of this—apart from a rise in the bureaucratic burden and the expense for the citizens and firms—is an increase in administrative discretion and of judicial litigations.[18]

The causes behind this situation are numerous. First of all, sociological, technical and administrative factors have to be mentioned: "(. . .) the complexification of the world—linked to the acceleration of technological progress, to the opening of the borders and to the emancipation of individuals towards the traditional conception of the family and the society—leads to the complexity of the law".[19] This derives from the manifold expectations (of general character and of groups) expressed by the society (which are often followed by specific public policies) and therefore from the necessity to adapt the current legislation to the technological, economic and social progress.[20] Political and media factors must also be taken into consideration: In the face of the reduction of financial resources, the law can represent (at least apparently) an efficacious answer to given problems and constitutes an irrefutable proof that a political action has been undertaken.[21] Finally, each legislative intervention potentially triggers a self-generating process, as it is based on the modification of previous legal provisions and often requires the enactment of further legal regulations (and this causes the necessity of interpretation by the Courts).[22]

These brief remarks demonstrate that more extensive research on this topic should focus on the entire Italian legal order, on its internal and external dynamics and on the possible criteria for interpreting this changing reality. This chapter—which is essentially addressed to scholars of other countries—has a more limited scope, as it describes only some more recent problems of juridification, which are directly linked to Italian administrative law.

First, it briefly analyses some instruments—many of them now have a permanent nature—aimed at relieving and simplifying the Italian legal environment (par. 2). It then goes on to examine the paths that juridification has followed in some areas. The illustration of the role of the Courts, the legislature and the administration and the instruments they have used (binding provisions, general principles and soft law) should explain how some interests had received legal protection (par. 3). Moreover, the chapter deals with juridification in connection to the EU integration process. In particular, it analyses, on the one hand, the influence that supranational law and other institutional tools (e.g. country-specific recommendations) exercise on some areas of

[17]Bombardelli (2015), pp. 996–997.

[18]Bombardelli (2015), p. 985 ff.

[19]Conseil d'État (2016), p. 14.

[20]Celotto and Meoli (2008), where further references.

[21]Conseil d'État (2016), p. 15; Celotto and Meoli (2008), Mattarella (2011), p. 21 f.

[22]Conseil d'État (2016), p. 15; Bombardelli (2015), p. 998 f.; Mattarella (2011), p. 21 ff.

the Italian administrative legislation (par. 4.1.) and, on the other hand, the effects that the multilevel dimension of the jurisdictionalisation has on one specific aspect of the Italian system of administrative justice (par. 4.2.). Brief general remarks conclude the chapter (par. 5).

9.2 Public Policies with Regard to Legification

Thanks also to the activity of supranational institutions,[23] Italy has elaborated specific policies aimed at simplifying and rationalizing its legal environment.

This subject is highly complex, since it involves the theory of the sources of law. It is therefore not possible to focus on this issue here. With regard to the state competences,[24] however, we can mention, without considering the instruments of de-legification[25] and those aimed at insuring the good quality of the legislation,[26]

(a) the unified mix codes aimed at gathering together legal and regulatory provisions related to homogenous areas[27] (which however have caused many applicative problems)[28] and
(b) the compilatory unified codes, aimed at gathering together the legal provisions relating to homogenous areas and at insuring the logic and systematic coherence of the respective legal disciplines.[29]

Codification is another important mechanism,[30] which is used constantly by the legislature.[31] Codes are legislative decrees which have two specific characteristics:

---

[23]See e.g. OCDE (2011, 2013).

[24]Regarding the recent trends of the regional legislation, see Camera dei deputati (2017).

[25]Art. 17, Law 23 August 1988, No. 400; Art. 2, Law 24 December 1993, No. 537; Art. 20, Law 15 March 1997, No. 59 (which provides for the so-called annual law for simplification): see Celotto and Meoli (2008).

[26]See e.g. Di Benedetto et al. (2011).

[27]Art. 7, Law 8 March 1999, No. 50 (as emended by the Law 24 November 2000 No. 340). On the basis of this law six unified mix codes have been enacted. They relate to the compulsory purchase (Decree of the President of the Republic 8 June 2001, No. 327), building activities (Decree of the President of the Republic 6 June 2001, No. 380), the circulation and residence for nationals of Member States of the European Union (Law 18 January 2002, No. 54), costs of judicial proceedings (Decree of the President of the Republic 30 May 2002, No. 115), criminal records, register of administrative fines depending on the commission of a criminal offence (Decree of the President of the Republic 14. November 2002, No. 313) and public debt (Decree of the President of the Republic 30 December 2003, No. 398).

[28]See e.g. Celotto and Meoli (2008).

[29]Art. 17-*bis*, Law No. 400/88, inserted by Art. 5, Law 18 June 2009, No. 69.

[30]See in general Mattarella (2011): third part.

[31]Nowadays many codes are in force. See e.g. the code for data protection (Legislative Decree No. 196/2003), electronic communications (Legislative Decree No. 259/2003), for cultural goods and the landscape (Legislative Decree No. 42/2004), for industrial property (Legislative Decree

"a) the substantial reform of the legislative regulation of the area concerned, taking into account the criteria of simplification (e.g. the lightening of the bureaucratic burdens) and of "de-regulation"; b) the systematic collection of all the legislative provisions regarding a specific area".[32]

Moreover, Article 14 of the Law of 11 November 2005, No. 246 provides for a different instrument: the so-called "slim down laws" mechanism. According to this complex procedure, the state government had firstly to identify the state legal provisions in force and the incoherence and antinomies within the various areas. Afterwards, with specific legislative decrees it had to identify the legal provisions enacted before 1 January 1970, which had to remain in force, whilst the others had to be considered as being abrogated.[33] The implementation of this policy led to the abrogation of about 30,000 legislative acts; on the other hand, it has caused considerable uncertainties as to whether individual pieces of legislation have remained in force.[34]

Recently, however, the government has interpreted the aim of legal simplification in a different, more pragmatic manner. The starting point is that what matters above all is not only the enactment (or the abrogation) of the legal provisions, but the effective reduction of the bureaucratic burden on citizens and firms. Consequently, the state government, the regions and the municipality representatives have carried out an intense coordination activity in order to progressively simplify the administrative action in five areas: digital citizenship, welfare, health, taxation, the construction sector, and undertakings.[35]

The path towards the simplification and rationalization of the legal order is obviously very hard. For this reason the actions carried out have not always produced results that match up to expectations. From this perspective, scholars unanimously propose a more intense use of the legislative techniques, which could surely improve the normative environment.[36] One positive fact must be underlined, however. For over 20 years the general belief has been that juridification should be governed using specific tools: in fact, each parliamentary majority has had its own

No. 30/2005), for the digital administration (Legislative Decree No. 82/2005), for the protection of consumers (Legislative Decree No. 206/2005), for assurances (Legislative Decree No. 209/2005), for the environment (Legislative Decree No. 152/2006), for the tourism (Legislative Decree No. n. 79/2011), for the public procurement (Legislative Decree No. 50/2016), for the third sector (Legislative Decree No. 117/2017), for the Corte dei Conti procedure (Court of Auditors: Legislative Decree No. 174/2016), for the civil defence (Legislative Decree No. 1/2018).

[32]Celotto and Meoli (2008).

[33]Bombardelli (2015), p. 1009 f.

[34]See for all Ainis (2014).

[35]This is the so-called Agenda for Simplification 2015–2017, that is an agreement concluded between the national government, the regions and the representatives of the provincial administrations and of the municipalities; see also the Agenda for the Simplification for the triennium 2018–2020.

[36]On this matter, see, for instance, Federalismi.it, No. 3/2018, which is in fully devoted to the sources of law and to the role of the Parliamentary committee for legislation.

policy on this matter.[37] If this is the case, it is normal that the political orientation of each individual government (and the corresponding conception of the relations between the state and the society) influences the modality of these actions.[38]

9.3 Juridification in Italy: Examination of Some Fields

To understand the features and scope of juridification processes in the Italian legal system it could be useful to analyse certain fields and interests. Thus, we can understand the techniques of the juridification process and which are its implications.[39]

It was said above that by the juridification of an area or an interest one not only means the occupation of legal provision—be they the product of the legislature or the result of the creative work of Courts—of virgin territories, i.e. free so far from law, but one also means the phenomenon of change in techniques and intensification of legal regulation.[40]

If you look at the last 50–60 years of Italian history, the first phenomenon is, in fact, very rare: you find it, for example, for the legal protection of animals or, in some respects, in bioethics, for which you have a real passage of certain interests from what was legally insignificant to what is legally significant. For many other goods or areas, on the contrary, there is mainly a process of juridification of the second type, that is changes or movements in the intensity and scope of regulation. In this case, it can be said that the good or the interest already found protection or legal regulation, but what changes over time is the type and intensity of this regulation, and therefore the guarantees and tools used to protect it.

Four different substantive fields are considered here, chosen for their heterogeneity and observed in consideration of the plurality of juridification techniques and implications produced: bioethics, sport, food safety and the environment.

9.3.1 Bioethics

The juridification of bioethics finds its main cause in scientific and technological development: it is technology and science applied to biomedicine that transform

[37]Duilio (2013).

[38]For a different perspective on this matter, see also Conseil d'État (2016), p. 15.

[39]See Marchetti and Renna (2016).

[40]Blichner and Molander (2008), p. 38.

interests that have been hitherto legally insignificant (de facto interests) into legally protected and justiciable rights.[41]

Moreover, the juridification process concerning this matter has, in Italy, peculiar characteristics, not detectable in other fields of the legal system; in fact, it seems to avoid legislative techniques by favouring the role of another actor, the judicial one. The juridification is accomplished, therefore, not so much through legislative provision but above all through jurisdictionalisation.

There are at least two reasons: on the one hand, the speed of technological developments makes it difficult for legislature to intervene, also due to their inability to decide matters with a highly political and divisive impact. On the other hand, the personal and individual character of claims, together with the urgency of protection, makes it natural to seek the consideration of the Courts, the natural interpreters of the protection claims not yet positively regulated.

This means that the few statutes or laws produced by the legislator are often subsequent to the Courts' case law, which anticipates and predetermines their content, drawing them from constitutional principles and general categories of law.[42]

The jurisdictionalisation of bioethics also has two consequences, one positive, the other negative. On the one hand, this is a juridification conducted with a case-by-case approach, tailored to the specific circumstances of the single case; on the other hand, this path can be a harbinger of a certain degree of uncertainty and unpredictability. The legislative process, in turn, presents peculiar characteristics in this matter: the Italian Constitutional Court, in fact, in some rulings of 2002, 2009 and 2014 (judgments 282, 151 and 162), has actually clarified how the discretion of the legislature in this context must be conditioned and oriented by science, according to a principle of scientific reasonableness of the law.[43]

Conclusively, not only are the Courts the first actors of the juridification in bioethics, but the legislative role appears also conditioned by a fundamental dialogue with medical science, whose contribution becomes a necessary condition of its constitutional validity.

9.3.2 Sport

Sport is a paradigmatic field for investigating the process of juridification as a transition from a sectoral regulation to a regulation that is relevant for the State legal order. The rules of sports activity, in fact, are initially an expression, both in Italy and in other European countries, of self-regulation (of private associations and organisations) which is irrelevant to the State.

---

[41] Casonato (2012), p. 16; on biolaw's features see also Casonato (2017), pp. 81–95; on the legal implications of technical developments see. Brownsword et al. (2017).

[42] Cortese and Penasa (2016), p. 169.

[43] Bin (2006), p. 1; Gemma (2006), p. 33; Penasa (2009), p. 817.

Therefore, they did not interfere with the rights recognised and protected by the State, but they exhausted their regulating function within the sectoral sport order in which they were produced.

The private and sectoral nature of sport rules and the initial State indifference[44] have allowed the build-up of a self-regulated world sports system,[45] which aimed at regulating international competitions and making the sports results comparable in different countries.

However, two processes of juridification intervene on this scenario: the first takes place in the first half of the twentieth century, as a result of the national legislature, and the second is the product of the legal pressures produced by European Union law in the last decades of the same century.

With the process of juridification, which starts in the Fascist period, a partial "publicisation" of sports' rules and orders takes place: private bodies with regulating functions are brought back into the public sphere and put under the control of the Government, through the publicisation of the Italian National Olympic Committee (CONI) and the administrativisation of some of their acts.[46]

A second juridification process is pushed by the European Union during the 1970s and 1980s. Two factors drive it: on the one hand, the need to control the doping phenomenon, through the adoption of national laws implementing EU measures (starting with Law 1099 of 1971 and ending with Law 376 of 2000).[47] On the other hand, the increased economic significance of competitive sport activity requires a law regulating professional sports (Law 91 of 1981) within the framework of Community treaties on economic freedoms (starting from the Court of Justice's 1995 ruling on the well-known Bosman case).[48]

The increased economic weight of sports also pushes towards a redefinition of the boundaries between sports system and State legal order: the decisions taken by sports bodies having a significant economic impact on the life of the members, bringing the latter to sue State Courts for judicial protection, and the Courts accord them protection when sport decisions are relevant in the State legal order.

The uncertain and controversial line between the two systems leads to a new legislative attempt to define the two territories in 2003 (Law Decree No. 220, converted into law No. 280 of 2003).[49] The same Constitutional Court, in 2011, recognises the relevance for the State system of all those sports decisions that, preventing (definitively) access to sports competitions or affiliation to a

---

[44] Manfredi (2016), p. 318.

[45] On the sports global regulation see Casini (2010).

[46] Marchetti (2003), p. 960; Morbidelli (1994), p. 171.

[47] Bonini (2014), p. 395.

[48] EU Court of Justice, judgment 15 December 1995, C-415/93 (Union royale belge des sociétés de football association and Others/Bosman and Others), EU:C:1995:463.

[49] Manfredi (2007), Massera (2008), p. 113; Ferrara (2010), p. 491; Goisis (2007), Napolitano (2004), p. 1153.

federation, can limit fundamental rights, including the right to associate and to express one's personality, and certain patrimonial rights relevant for the State.[50]

The attraction of sports in the orbit of State and European Union law is therefore the result of the recognition of sport as a social and economic phenomenon that is much more complex than at the time of its first sectoral self-regulation, and that is able to impact on a variety of public interests—the protection of health, labour, freedom of association, economic freedoms—relevant to the general system and likely to affect the economic freedoms guaranteed by the EU Treaties.

9.3.3 Food Safety

Food safety has been regulated for a large part of the twentieth century for protecting health and fighting fraud.[51] The juridification of this field has, however, intensified and expanded since the end of the twentieth century because of the need to guarantee new multiple interests connected to it: in addition to health, it became necessary to give legal protection to agriculture, environment, trade, consumer protection and worker safety. The juridification process resulting from the emergence of these interests and the impact of food safety on world trade and the European Union single market has multiplied the levels of norms production. On the one hand, key players in juridification have become the World Trade Organization (WTO) and the Codex Alimentarius Commission (CAC), on a global scale; on the other hand, a central role has been assumed by the European Union, which through regulations 178/2002 and a harmonisation legislation has established a new framework of rules applicable throughout the territory of the Union.[52]

Moreover, at a sub-State level, the Italian Constitution grants Regions concurrent legislative powers on the matter, thus determining the possibility that, next to a State legislation, there will be an additional layer of internal regulation.[53] In addition to the plurality and multi-level actors, the rules on food safety have also seen an extension in a horizontal sense, aiming to cover every different profile having some impact on food safety, from labelling, to technological development, from environmental implications to packaging and advertising.

The horizontal extension, combined with the complexity of a multi-level legislation, determines coordination defects and possible inconsistencies.

Alongside the process of legalisation, sometimes anticipated by Courts, the process has led to the creation of new administrations, tasked with carrying out

[50]Italian Constitutional Court, judgment 11 February 2011, No. 49, commented by Manfredi (2011), p. 688.

[51]Ramajoli (2016), p. 395; Ramajoli (2015), p. 271. See particulrly health laws T.U. (Royal Decree 27 July 1934, No. 1265) and Law 30 April 1962 No. 283.

[52]Alemanno (2007), Ansell and Vogel (2006), p. 237; Bevilacqua (2012) and Capelli et al. (2006).

[53]Borghi (2012), p. 26.

technical assessments of risk: at the European level, the Food Security Agency has been created to operate in a network with similar authorities instituted at the national level. However, in Italy an authority with equivalent features has not yet been created, and risk assessment is attributed to a National Committee for Food Safety established at the Ministry of Health.[54]

As is well known, while the European agency and the corresponding national authorities are called upon to carry out the technical assessments, other administrative authorities (Commission and Government of the Member States) have to adopt the discretionary management risk decisions, trying to balance public health and environmental interests, on the one hand, and economic and commercial trade interests on the other.

9.3.4 Environment

We can trace different stages in the environment's juridification process, corresponding to the different meanings assigned to "environment" over time. At first, it has been the subject of fragmentary disciplines concerning related activities or interests (health, urban planning, landscape) outside a univocal constitutional framework of reference. This step, which occupied a consistent period of the last century, failing to consider the environment as a good to protect as such, failed to create the necessary institutional and organisational framework for environmental protection.

The second step of the juridification process starts when the environment finds its definitive recognition as a unitary good, first in the constitutional jurisprudence,[55] and then in the law of the European Union.[56] This evolution produces, on the national level, the establishment of the Ministry for the Environment in 1986 (with Law No. 349; it was later renamed the Ministry for the environment and the protection of the territory and the sea in 2006) and the adoption of specific legislative acts for environmental protection, among which the 2006 Environmental Code (issued by Legislative Decree No. 52); at the EU level, it is primarily affirmed by the Court of Justice (judgments of 7 February 1985 in Case C-240/83 and 20 September 1988 in Case C-302/86), which defines it as an "imperative requirement" conditioning economic freedoms; and it grows exponentially later with the Union's enlargement and the extension of its competences. First it is included in the Single European Act, later its relevance is reflected at the institutional level, with the creation of the European Environment Agency (regulation 1210/90). Therefore, it receives its definitive consecration in the Maastricht Treaty as a principle of sustainable development, and lastly, with the Amsterdam Treaty, it

[54]Gabbi (2012), p. 241.

[55]Giannelli (2016), p. 284.

[56]Mazzamuto (2009), p. 1571.

becomes a fundamental goal of the EU (Article 3)[57] The inclusion of the environment among the subjects of concurrent competences, enshrined in the Lisbon Treaty, definitively attributes to the EU institutions the role of fundamental actors of environmental juridification.

At the national level, the juridification process has several implications in terms of rights and interests related to environmental protection. Generally speaking, the juridification of an interest or a good creates new justiciable rights: interests that were previously legally insignificant find protection in administrative decision-making and before the Courts.

In the case of the environment, moreover, it has been observed that the creation of rights is also accompanied by the creation of duties in the name of the principle of solidarity based on Art. 2 of the Italian Constitution.[58]

Furthermore, environmental protection also determines, at the level of administrative action, the applicability of peculiar tools and techniques that are at least partly an exception to ordinary paradigms.

In light of the international obligations deriving from the Aarhus Convention, in fact, environmental administrative proceedings and related decisions must be subject to rules on transparency, participation and access to judicial protection, which present obvious special traits and which are justified by the need to ensure the most widespread control over administrative acts having an impact on the environment.[59]

The juridification of the environment, therefore, does not imply only the definition of binding rules and standards applicable to everybody; nor is it limited to conferring instruments and tools for demanding their respect by affected individuals, as usually occurs. It also aims at the creation of widespread legitimate interest that promotes environmental protection regardless of the injury of a specific individual actionable right, thus achieving its "objectification".[60]

9.4 Juridification and European Integration

The construction of the European Union is first and foremost the result of legal integration and owes a lot to the work of the Court of Justice, which has literally "built" the pillars on which the EU legal system is based.[61] If we add to the Court of Justice's creative role the intense legislative activity of the EU, the significant

[57]Blanke (2013), p. 157; Burns and Carter (2009) and Giuffrida (2012).

[58]Fracchia (2013).

[59]On Aarhus Convention's implication on Italian administrative law see Macchia (2006), p. 639; Goisis (2012), p. 91; Delsignore (2013), p. 734; Romano (2012), p. 1691.

[60]Romano (2017), p. 19.

[61]Accetto (2012), p. 79.

influence of European Union law on the juridification processes of the Member States becomes clear.

This section examines some of the EU's influences on Italian legification and jurisdictionalisation processes.

9.4.1 Legification

The first thing to bear in mind is that EU law intervenes in the national juridification whenever the regulation of Member States intercepts European-wide interests. The examples are countless and concern all the hypotheses in which the interest regulated at the state level crosses the economic freedoms protected by the Treaties or, more generally, the objectives underlying the action of the European Union. In general, different types of relationships can be singled out between the EU and the national legal process: at least three hypotheses can be abstractly identified.

The first, which we could call incremental, is when the European Union produces rules that result in a more intense legalisation (or a new juridification) of an activity that was previously governed by national rules or was not regulated. The second, which could be roughly defined as "zero-sum legalisation", is when the European Union intervenes directly in the regulation of an activity, decreeing at the same time its national de-juridification.[62] The third hypothesis is that the European Union lacks any competence in regulating the matter, producing only indirect influences on national law.

We see an example of the first type in the field of food safety and sport. Both these sectors were respectively subjected to national and sectoral regulation, but the complexity and the increased economic relevance of interests involved led to a European Union juridification, first through the EUCJ judgments and then through the adoption of organic regulations aimed at harmonising the Member States' legislations. An example of the second type is represented by the Community rules introducing the liberalisation of some economic activities that were previously subjected, at the national level, to public control.

Here European juridification has the effect of partially de-juridificating the field: it is the case of the directive 2006/123 (so-called services directive), which has the effect of eliminating permissions for economic activities which were nationally required. In this case, we can also speak of de-bureaucratisation.

An example of the third type is bioethics. Here the process of juridification can be said to be partially influenced by the supranational context: it remains, in fact, entrusted mostly to the discretion of national actors, whether they are legislative or judicial and the European Union does not overlap its jurisdiction with the national one.[63]

---

[62] Savino (2015), p. 232.

[63] See Cortese and Penasa (2016), p. 176.

In the first and second examples EU law's impact on the national juridification process is explained by the undisputed economic relevance of regulated interests: there is no doubt, in fact, that the Europeanisation of national law is the consequence of the need to make Member States' legal systems compliant with European economic freedom protection.[64] Conversely, the European Union role in bio-law—as we saw—is still limited, although some European competences can be found every time that economic EU interests are intercepted (for example, genetic manipulation patentability, cross-border health services, clinical research regulations).

A final observation concerns the content of EU juridification. As is known, European law for a long time aimed at binding member States to achieve certain objectives without indicating the means to achieve them. According to the Court of Justice jurisprudence, since the Rewe case (in Case C-45/76), it was the Member States that established the means and procedures to be followed in order to ensure the effective application of European Union law (the so called procedural autonomy principle).

This procedural indifference no longer appears, however, as a constant feature of European law because the law, in this respect, seems to have changed. It is the case of public procurement for works, supplies and services: here, alongside a regulation imposing values such as openness, non-discrimination, equal treatment and competition in public procurement procedures since the 1970s, the Union has promoted (remedies directive No. 66 of 2007) a framework of procedural rules and remedies which constitutes a model for protection of tenderers in all Member States. It has its cornerstones in the institution of independent review bodies having the power to annul awarding decisions and to grant interim measures; it also provides for compensation of damages when these damages are the consequence of the rules' violation and establishes some cases in which the contract has to be declared ineffective because of the unlawful award decision.

This regulation, imposed on the Member States for contracts above a certain value, has been implemented in the Italian system also for contracts of lower economic value, giving rise, in this sector, to a judicial review procedure that is accelerated and differentiated from the ordinary one.

Consider again the field of competition: it is an area in which the European Union has its own substantive rules (Articles 101 and 102 TFEU) and its own antitrust authority, which is the EU Commission. However, since enforcement of EU law is ensured by a network of national authorities, a recent proposal for a directive (ECN plus) shows the growing interest of EU law in the procedural framework within which national regulatory authorities operate. More specifically, the new proposed rules require States to grant antitrust authorities more extensive investigative and decision powers, adequate tools for a stronger cooperation within the network and a minimum standard of independence for regulatory authorities, thus occupying an area, the procedural one, generally left to the Member States' autonomy.

[64] See Torricelli (2015), p. 248.

Moreover, this step is deemed necessary to ensure a level playing field for economic operators within the European common market, given that 85% of the European antitrust decisions are enacted not by the Commission itself, but by the national authorities connected in the network. Then a procedural difference in NCA powers can result in a differentiated treatment of economic operators that potentially puts at risk the objective of a uniform and effective application of European competition rules.[65]

Conclusively, not only does the European Union law interfere in the substantial regulation of interests, conferring rights and obligations founded on EU legal provisions, but it also increasingly regulates the way in which these new interests must be procedurally protected, any guarantee that must be assured to them and the way in which administrations have to operate when they enforce EU law.

Lastly, it should not be forgotten that the national juridification process can be triggered or conditioned by European Union law not only as a result of hard law (directives and regulations), but also as a consequence of soft law (White Books, recommendations, open method of coordination—OMC),[66] which can guide or lead, even to a different degree from State to State, national reforms necessary to align with European goals.

It is the case of the Council recommendation of 11 July 2017 on Italy's 2017 National Reform Programme: in addition to containing budgetary targets, it identifies specific actions to be taken, including reducing the length of the civil trial through efficient management of procedures and rules; strengthening the fight against corruption; reforming public employment; improving the efficiency of public enterprises; adopting and implementing rapidly competition law, and removing the remaining restrictions on competition.

It is also the case of the past Mandelkern Commission of 2001 and the Action Plan to simplify and improve the regulatory environment of June 2002.[67]

It is evident that such acts can trigger new national juridifications in the areas of reference, albeit through alternative channels to the traditional ones in which acts having binding and general effects are adopted.

9.4.2 *Jurisdictionalisation*

The Court of Justice represents an extraordinary factor in jurisdictionalisation, at times accompanying this national phenomenon and at times superimposing its action. We tackle here only one aspect of this problem, which originated from recent

[65] On the principle of procedural autonomy see Galetta (2009); on the proposed EU Directive on the European Network competition plus (ECNplus) see Ghezzi and Marchetti (2017), p. 1013.

[66] Falkner et al. (2005), Trubek and Trubek (2005), p. 343; Jacobsson (2004), p. 14; Terpan (2015), p. 68; Craig (2012), p. 181.

[67] For a comment see Corletto (2005), p. 15.

judgments of the Court of Justice in the field of public procurement. This allows a brief examination of some similar dynamics, which have, however, a purely internal nature.

The starting point is that according to Italian law, administrative Courts cannot examine the lawfulness of the challenged administrative decisions in the general interest. On the contrary, their review must be aimed at ascertaining the validity of the claim in the interest of the applicant.[68] In the field of public procurement this means that a firm, who participated in a tender procedure and was ranked second, is entitled to challenge the decision awarding the public contract in the administrative Court, in order to ask for the reassignment of the contract in their favour.

The Court of Justice, however, has recently clarified that according to the EU law regulating this area, the national Court must protect not only the interest of the applicant to obtain a particular contract "directly in the same procedure", but also the "indirect" interest that a new public procurement procedure is launched, in which the applicant (and the other bidders) can participate.[69] In other words, in these cases, the administrative process has to ensure not only the possibility for the claimant to achieve directly a legally valuable benefit (i.e. the award of the particular contract), but also a hypothetical one (i.e. the launch of new tender procedure).[70]

The result of this is that the administrative process is subject to a potential functional transformation: moving from being an instrument to satisfy a direct interest of the applicant, to becoming an opportunity to check the lawfulness of the administrative action (irrespective of the direct protection of the rights of the private parties).[71] This is after all the declared objective of the EU legislature: "when undertakings do not seek review, certain infringements may not be corrected . . .".[72]

Jurisdictionalisation can be seen clearly: in these cases, the goal of ensuring the effective implementation of EU law implies the extension of private interests, which can be protected by the administrative Courts[73] and consequently the extension of the role of these Courts. Ultimately, thanks to the sectorial EU legislation and the case-law of the Court of Justice, in the field of public procurement in Italy there is a

[68] Consiglio di Stato, adunanza plenaria, judgment 7 April 2011, No. 4.

[69] Court of Justice, judgment 5 April 2016, C-689/13 (Puligienica), EU:C:2015:693; see also the judgment 4 July 2013, C-100/12 (Fastweb), EU:C:2013:448. In Italian literature, see e.g. Villata (2015), p. 826 ff.; Ferrara and Bartolini (2014), p. 918 ff. In Italian case-law, see for e.g. Consiglio di Stato, sezione V, order 6 November 2017, No. 5103.

[70] Consiglio di Stato, sezione V, judgment 20 July 2017, No. 3593, par. 14.

[71] Consiglio di Stato, adunanza plenaria, judgment No. 4/11.

[72] Recital 6 of the Council Directive 89/665/EEC of 21 December 1989 on the coordination of the laws, regulations and administrative provisions relating to the application of review procedures to the award of public supply and public works contracts (consolidated version). It must be remembered that since its origin, the Community legal order has recognised rights in favour of individuals and firms (so-called private enforcement), as "The vigilance of individuals concerned to protect their rights amounts to an effective supervision in addition to the supervision entrusted by Articles 169 and 170 to the diligence of the Commission . . .": Court of Justice, judgment 5 February 1963, Case 26/62 (van Gend & Los), EU:C:1963:1: see for all Wilman (2015).

[73] Consiglio di Stato, sezione V, judgment 20 July 2017, No. 3593.

special administrative process, which departs considerably from the constitutional principles of the administrative justice.[74]

However, this is not the only trend towards jurisdictionalisation in the Italian legal order. As a matter of fact, especially in the last decade, in addition to the legislative and judicial extension of locus standi in administrative matters,[75] many legal provisions have been enacted, which, irrespective of EU law, allow actions be brought before the administrative Courts by a number of private subjects for the protection of general interests.

Suffice to recall the legal standing of environmental associations (which was provided for by the national legislature long before it was imposed by European law)[76] and the provisions that allow associations and collective bodies to go to Court to protect public or collective interests (e.g. the landscape, the territory of nature reserves or nature parks)[77] or to protect interests of certain categories (e.g. consumers, enterprises).[78] In addition, according to the law, citizens or associations can now take action to counter the inefficiencies of public administrations or bodies that supply public utilities.[79] But the examples do not stop there. Indeed, mention should also be made of the cases of *actio popularis* established by the law[80] (amongst which the recent regulation of civic access to documents stands out)[81] and

---

[74]Bartolini (2014).

[75]E.g. Consiglio di Stato, Adunanza Plenaria, judgment 7 April 2011, No. 4 (para. 37).

[76]See Art. 18, par. 5, Law 8 July 1986, No. 349 (Instituting the Ministry of the Environment); Art. 309 and Art. 310, Legislative Decree 3 April 2006, No. 152 (Environmental Code).

[77]Art. 146, par. 11, Legislative Decree 22 January 2004, No. 42 (Cultural Heritage and Landscape Code); Art. 13, par. 2, Law 6 December 1991, No. 394 (Framework Law on Protected Areas). See also Art. 11, Law 11 August 1991, No. 266 (Framework Law on Volunteer Work). In doctrine, see Manfredi (2014), p. 520 ff.

[78]For example, for consumers, see Art. 139 ff., Legislative Decree 6 September 2005, No. 206 (Consumer Code), on which see for all Manfredi (2014), p. 522 ff. and Cudia (2012), p. 239 ff. Regarding the Chambers of Commerce and the CNEL [National Council for Economics and Labour], see Art. 4, Law 11 November 2011, No. 180 (Provisions for the Protection of the Freedom of Enterprise), on the basis of which trade associations represented in at least five Chambers of Commerce or the CNEL, together with their local branches, have the legal standing to bring actions before the Court to protect both the interests of all those belonging to the same professional category, or to protect similar interests concerning only some economic subjects.

[79]Legislative Decree 20 December 2009, No. 198, for which see Cudia (2012), p. 286 ff.

[80]See, for example, the popular action regulated by Art. 9 Legislative Decree 18 August 2000, No. 267 (Unified Code on Local Authorities), concerning Court cases that citizens can bring in the event of the omission of taking a legal action on the part of provinces and municipalities. See also the popular corrective action regarding the elections for local government, provinces, regions and the EU Parliament, now regulated under Art. 130, Legislative Decree 2 July 2010, No. 104 (Code of Administrative Court Procedure). See for all, Cudia (2012), p. 239 ff.: Astone et al. (2010).

[81]See the new wording of Art. 5, Legislative Decree 14 March 2013, No. 33, as amended by the Legislative Decree 25 May 2016, No. 97 (containing the re-ordering of the legal discipline regarding the right of civic access to public documents and the obligation for publicizing, transparency, and diffusion of information by public administrations), on which see e.g. Galetta (2016), p. 1019 ff.

the possibility of taking legal action in front of the administrative judge granted by the legislature in favour of some administrative authorities (and in particular the National Competition Authority[82] and the National Anti-Corruption Authority[83]) against other public administrations.[84]

While the jurisdictionalisation carried out by the Court of Justice and the EU legislature aims at the improving the effectiveness of EU law, that carried out by Italian legislature is based on different and more complex grounds. The assumption is usually that public administrations are either unwilling or unable to pursue certain public interests (both national and European) or to reach adequate quality standards in the actions they take.[85] This (social and institutional) mistrust of the public administration has led the legislature on the one hand to limit the administrative behaviour through increasingly analytical legal regulations and, on the other hand, to multiply the cases of locus standi for judicial review when it concerns the protection of public interests.

Even though these transformations are still limited to specific areas, they move anyway towards the narrowing of role of the public administration of mediating between different social actors and identifying the general interest. Should these trends be consolidated, it is likely that it would lead to a social model focused on judicial confrontation at the expense of political mediation, which in Italy traditionally is called public interest.

9.5 Conclusive Remarks

Juridification is necessary and in part inevitable. It is a continuously expanding process both in Italy and in other countries. Some factors, such as technological and scientific development and the privatisation of certain activities, impose changes over time in the degree, extension and intensity of legal regulation. We have seen that juridification is the result of numerous, interconnected and multi-level processes. Depending on the interest concerned, the regulation can be global, influencing that at supranational level, which in turn orients national, regional and local regulation. Far from being linear and harmonious, these mutual impacts can lead to overlaps, inconsistencies, and uncertainty regarding competences and illogicality.

In this situation, the Italian legal order has reacted with specific policies aimed at making the normative system more rational and comprehensible. However, these

---

[82]Art. 21-bis, Law 10 October 1990, No. 287 (Competition and Fair Trading Act): see e.g. Pace (2013), p. 785 ff.

[83]Art. 211, Legislative Decree 18 April 2016, No. 50 (Public contracts code).

[84]See e.g. Art. 37, par. 2, lett. No. Decree-Law 6 December 2011, No. 201 (converted into Law No. 214/2011) with reference to the Authority for the Regulation of Transport. See also Art. 6, par. 10, Law 9 May 1989, No. 168 (Instituting the Ministry of Education, University and Technologic and Scientific Research). On this subject, see Cerulli Irelli (2014), p. 341 ff.

[85]See De Lucia (2017), p. 1 ff.

policies have not always been successful; often the legislature has acted according to the "old" techniques, producing pieces of legislation that are fragmented and of difficult interpretation.

In the face of these uncertainties, that continues to characterise the Italian legal order, a central role is played by the (administrative) Courts. The Courts, in fact, act as stabilizer in three respects: by managing a large number of litigations efficiently; by ensuring the coherence of the legal order also in relation to the transformations induced by EU law; and by tackling very complex problems (also with political impact), which the public administration seems unable to solve satisfactorily. In this context, the weak link here seems, therefore, to be the public administration, which—not always through faults of its own—has difficulties in contributing effectively to managing legal complexity and consequently in representing a reference point for the citizens and the economic system.

References

Accetto M (2012) The influence of EU law on national legal systems. In: Maas C (ed) Juridification in Europe. Europeans Liberal Forum, Den Haag, p 79
Ainis M (2014) La semplificazione complicante. Federalismi.it
Alemanno A (2007) Trade in food regulatory and judicial approaches in the EC and the WTO. Cameron May, London
Ansell C, Vogel D (2006) What's the beef? The contested governance of eu food safety. Massachusetts Institute of Technology, p 237
Astone F, Manganaro F, Tassone R, Antonio SF (eds) (2010) Cittadinanza ed azioni popolari. Rubbettino, Soveria Mannelli
Bartolini A (2014) L'adunanza plenaria torna sul ricorso incidentale escludente – Una decisione poco europea, Giornale di diritto amministrativo 918 ff
Bevilacqua D (2012) La sicurezza alimentare negli ordinamenti giuridici ultrastatali. Giuffrè, Milan
Bin R (2006) La Corte e la scienza. In: D'Aloia A (ed) Bio-tecnologie e valori costituzionali. Il contributo della giustizia costituzionale. Giappichelli, Turin, p 1
Blanke H-J (2013) Article 3 (The objectives of the European Union). In: Blanke H-J, Mangiameli S (eds) The treaty on European Union (TEU). A commentary. Springer, p 157
Blichner LC, Molander A (2008) Mapping juridification. Eur Law J 14:36–54
Bombardelli M (2015) Semplificazione normativa e complessità del diritto amministrativo, in Dir. pubbl., 985
Bonini S (2014) Doping, Enc. Dir., Annali, vol. VII. Giuffrè, Milan, p 395
Borghi P (2012) Diritto alimentare italiano e integrazione europea. Riv. Dir. agrario 26
Brownsword R, Scotford E, Yeung K (2017) The Oxford handbook on law, regulation and technology. Oxford University Press, Oxford
Burns C, Carter N (2009) Environmental policy. In: Jones E, Jones A, Weatherill S (eds) The Oxford handbook of the European Union. Oxford University Press, Oxford
Camera dei deputati, Osservatorio sulla legislazione, Rome, 2017, vol. II (the survey is also available on: http://www.camera.it/application/xmanager/projects/leg17/file/RAPPORTO_SULLA_LEGISLAZIONE_2015-2016_VOLUME_II.pdf, consulted on the 5.2.2017)
Capelli F, Klaus B, Silano V (2006) Nuova disciplina del settore alimentare ed Autorità europea per la sicurezza alimentare. Giuffrè, Milan
Carnelutti F (1930) La crisi della legge, Rivista di diritto pubblico 424–429
Casini L (2010) Il diritto globale dello Sport. Giuffrè, Milan

Casonato C (2012) Introduzione al biodiritto. Giappichelli, Turin
Casonato C (2017) 21st century biolaw: a proposal. Biolaw J I:81–95
Cassese S (ed) (2016) Research handbook on global administrative law. Edward Elgar
Cassese S (February 2018) Troppe norme (spesso inutili). Corriere della Sera
Celotto A, Meoli C (2008) Semplificazione normativa (dir. pubbl.), Digesto discipline pubblicistiche, vol. II. UTET, Turin, p 806 ff
Cerulli Irelli V (2014) Legittimazione "soggettiva" e legittimazione "oggettiva" ad agire nel processo amministrativo. Diritto processuale amministrativo, 2014, 341 ff
Conseil d'État (2016) Étude annuelle 2016 – Simplification et qualité du droit, Paris
Corletto D (2005) La semplificazione dei procedimenti autorizzatori. In: Falcon G (ed) Il diritto amministrativo dei Paesi europei tra omogeneizzazione e diversità culturali. Cedam, Padua, p 15
Cortese F, Penasa S (2016) Dalla bioetica al biodiritto: sulla giuridificazione di interessi scientificamente e tecnologicamente condizionati. In: Marchetti B, Renna M (eds) La giuridificazione, op. cit., 169
Craig P (2012) EU administrative law. Oxford University Press, Oxford, p 181
Cudia C (2012) Gli interessi plurisoggettivi tra diritto e processo amministrativo. Maggioli, Rimini
De Lucia L (2017) Locus Standi and distrust of the public administration. A comparison of three models. Rev Eur Adm Law, 1
Delsignore M (2013) La legittimazione delle associazioni ambientali nel giudizio amministrativo: spunti dalla comparazione con lo standing a tutela di environmental issues nella judicial review. Diritto processuale amministrativo, 734
Di Benedetto M, Martelli M, Rangone N (2011) La qualità delle regole. Il Mulino, Bologna
Duilio L (ed) (2013) Politica della legislazione, oltre la crisi. Il Mulino, Bologna
Falkner G, Treib O, Hartlapp M, Leiber S (2005) Complying with Europe. Harmonisation and soft law in the member states. Cambridge University Press, Cambridge
Ferrara L (2010) Giustizia sportiva, ad vocem. In: Enc. Dir., Annali, vol III. Giuffrè, Milan, p 491
Ferrarese MR (2015) Diritto sconfinato. Inventiva giuridica e spazi nel mondo globale. Laterza, Bari-Rome
Fracchia F (2013) Introduzione allo studio del diritto all'ambiente. Principi, concetti e istituti, Editoriale scientifica, Neaples
Gabbi S (2012) Dieci anni di EFSA: l'Autorità europea al cuore del sistema europeo per la sicurezza alimentare. In: Ricci C (ed) La tutela del diritto alla sicurezza e qualità degli alimenti. Giuffrè, Milan, p 241
Galetta D-U (2009) L'autonomia procedurale degli Stati membri dell'Unione europea: "Paradise Lost"? Giappichelli, Turin
Galetta D-U (2016) La trasparenza, per un nuovo rapporto tra cittadino e pubblica amministrazione: un'analisi storico-evolutiva, in una prospettiva di diritto comparato ed europeo, Riv. it. dir. pubbl. comun., 1019 ff
Galligan DJ (2007) Law in modern society. Oxford University Press, Oxford
Gemma G (2006) Giurisprudenza costituzionale e scienza medica. In: D'Aloia A (ed) Bio-tecnologie e valori costituzionali. Il contributo della giustizia costituzionale. Giappichelli, Turin, p 33
Ghezzi F, Marchetti B (2017) La nuova proposta di direttiva Ue in materia di Rete europea della concorrenza e la necessità di un giusto equilibrio tra efficienza e garanzie. Riv. it. dir. pubbl. comun 5:1013
Giannelli A (2016) Ambiente. In: Marchetti B, Renna M (eds) La giuridificazione. Firenze University Press, Florence, p 284
Giuffrida R (ed) (2012) Diritto europeo dell'ambiente. Giappichelli, Turin
Goisis F (2007) La giustizia sportiva tra funzione amministrativa e arbitrato. Giuffrè, Milan
Goisis F (2012) Legittimazione al ricorso delle associazioni ambientali ed obblighi discendenti dalla Convenzione di Aarhus e dall'ordinamento dell'Unione europea. Dir. proc. amm., 91
Habermas J (2017) Teoria dell'agire comunicativo, vol II. Il Mulino, Bologna
Jacobsson K (2004) Soft regulation and the subtle transformation of States: the case of EU employment policy. J Eur Soc Policy 5

Macchia M (2006) La compliance al diritto amministrativo globale. Il sistema di controllo della Convenzione di Aarhus. Riv. trim. dir. pubbl., 639
Manfredi G (2007) Pluralità degli ordinamenti e tutela giurisdizionale. I rapporti tra giustizia statale e giustizia sportiva. Giappichelli, Turin
Manfredi G (2011) Gruppi sportivi e tutela endoassociativa. Giur. cost., 688
Manfredi G (2014) Interessi diffuse e collettivi (diritto amministrativo). In: Enciclopedia del diritto. Annali VII. Giuffrè Milan, p 520 ff
Manfredi G (2016) Lo sport. In: Marchetti B, Renna M (eds) La giuridificazione. Firenze University Press, Florence, p 318
Marchetti B (2003) Lo sport. In: Cassese S (ed) Trattato di diritto amministrativo, vol I. Diritto amministrativo speciale. Giuffrè, Milan, p 960
Marchetti B, Renna M (eds) (2016) La giuridficazione. Firenze University Press, Florence
Massera A (2008) Sport e ordinamenti giuridici: tensioni e tendenze nel diritto vivente in una prospettiva multilaterale. Dir. pubbl., 113
Mattarella BG (2011) La trappola delle leggi. Molte, oscure, complicate. Il Mulino, Bologna
Mazzamuto M (2009) Diritto dell'ambiente e sistema comunitario delle libertà economiche. Riv. it. dir. pubbl. comun., 1571
Modugno F, Nocilla D (1989) Crisi della legge e sistema delle fonti. Diritto e società p 411 ff
Morbidelli G (1994) Gli enti dell'ordinamento sportivo. In: Cerulli Irelli V, Morbidelli G (eds) Ente pubblico ed enti pubblici. Giappichelli, Turin, p 171
Napolitano G (2004) Caratteri e prospettive dell'arbitrato amministrativo sportivo. Giornale di diritto amministrativo, p 1153
Natalini A, Tiberi G (eds) (2010) La tela di Penelope. Primo Rapporto Astrid sulla semplifi cazione legislativa e burocratica. Il Mulino, Bologna
OCDE (2011) Reviews of Regulatory Reform: Regulatory Reform in Italy 2001. Paris
OCDE (2013) Better Regulation in Europe: Italy 2012, revisited edition, Paris, 2013
Pace LF (2013) La legittimazione dell'AGCM a ricorrere avverso i provvedimenti della p.a. ex art. 21-bis l. 287/1990 e la violazione delle norme sugli aiuti di Stato, in Id., Dizionario sistematico del diritto della concorrenza. Jovene, Neaples, p 785 ff
Penasa S (2009) La "ragionevolezza scientifica" delle leggi nella giurisprudenza costituzionale. Quad. cost., 817
Ramajoli M (2015) Dalla food safety alla food security e ritorno. Amministrare, 271
Ramajoli M (2016) La sicurezza alimentare. In: Marchetti B, Renna M (eds) La giuridificazione. Firenze University Press, Florence, p 395
Romano MC (2012) Interessi diffusi e intervento nel procedimento amministrativo. Foro amm. Cons. Stato 6:1691
Romano MC (2017) Oggettivizzazione della tutela giurisdizionale amministrativa in Germania. Impulsi europei, riflessioni comparate e punti di convergenza. In: Cerulli Irelli V (ed) La giustizia amministrativa in Italia e in Germania, Quaderni di diritto processuale amministrativo. Giuffrè, Milan, p 19
Savino M (2015) I caratteri del diritto amministrativo europeo. In: De Lucia L, Marchetti B (eds) L'amministrazione europea e le sue regole. Il Mulino, Bologna, p 232
Taruffo M (1987) Note sui modi della giuridificazione. Politica del diritto 581 ff
Terpan F (2015) Soft law in the European Union. The changing nature of EU law. Eur Law J 21:68
Teubner G (1987) Juridification – concepts, aspects, limits, solutions. In: Id (ed) Juridification of social spheres. Walter de Gruyter, Berlin
Torricelli S (2015) L'europeizzazione del diritto amministrativo italiano. In: De Lucia L, Marchetti B (eds) L'amministrazione europea e le sue regole. Il Mulino, Bologna, p 248
Trubek DM, Trubek LG (2005) Hard and soft law in the construction of social Europe: the role of open method of co-ordination. Eur Law J 11:343
Villata R (2015) Finale di partita. Diritto processuale amministrativo, 826 ff
Voigt R (1980) Verrechtlichung in Staat und Gesellschaft. In: Id (ed) Verrechtlichung. Athenäum, Königstein, pp 18–23
Wilman F (2015) Private enforcement of EU law before National Courts. Edward Elgar

Part II
Specific Issues

Chapter 10
The Italian Legal Order and the Making of a National Cultural Identity

Edoardo Chiti, Gianluca Gardini, and Aldo Sandulli

Contents

E. Chiti (✉)
University of Tuscia, Viterbo, Italy
e-mail: edoardo.chiti@unitus.it

G. Gardini
University of Ferrara, Ferrara, Italy
e-mail: gianluca.gardini@unife.it

A. Sandulli
Luiss University, Rome, Italy
e-mail: asandulli@luiss.it

D. Sorace et al. (eds.), *The Changing Administrative Law of an EU Member State*,
https://doi.org/10.1007/978-3-030-50780-0_10

Abstract This chapter explores the variety of regulatory techniques and processes through which Italian law has tried to shape Italian cultural identity. Although the chapter aims to provide an account of the evolution of such techniques and processes, the historical perspective is also used to understand the current situation and to reflect on possible future developments. The underlying thesis of this research is that the shaping of Italian cultural identity over the last 50 years encapsulates a dialectic between unity and pluralism. Within such overall framework, the investigation discusses the political and administrative measures adopted in three different groups according to sector: (1) art, cultural heritage, and media; (2) education; and (3) language. Study of these sectors shows that the Italian legal order has not always been successful in guiding cultural processes. More often than not it has been content to support them or to attempt to contain them, leaving it to developments in society to limit the scope of regulation and not the reverse.

10.1 The Questions

This chapter explores the variety of regulatory techniques and processes through which Italian law has tried to shape Italian cultural identity, understood as the overall set of values, beliefs, and traditions through which a plurality of individuals and groups are reciprocally interlinked in a broader society. The perspective of this research is mainly historical: we aim to provide an account of the evolution of the public law instruments used by the Italian political and administrative bodies to shape national cultural identity over the last 50 years, to identify the forces at work in this process, and to explain its overall dynamics. The historical perspective, however, is used not only to reconstruct the process so far, but also to understand the current situation, which should be seen as only one step in a wider historical process. The historical approach also provides the basis for reflection on possible future developments.

The underlying thesis of this chapter is that the shaping of Italian cultural identity over the last 50 years reflects and encapsulates a dialectic between unity and pluralism. The choices of Italian political and administrative bodies in a number of important policy areas have promoted this dialectic as a fundamental internal tension within the national cultural identity. This is true, for example, of the legal framework governing the relationships between central government and local communities, the rules regulating the main cultural activities, legislation governing linguistic interaction between those within the legal system, and the discipline governing the relationships between Italian culture and those of other European countries.

We examine here the measures adopted by political and administrative institutions in three different groups according to sector: (1) art, cultural heritage, and media (Sect. 10.2); (2) education (Sect. 10.3); and (3) language (Sect. 10.4). Study of these sectors shows that the Italian public institutions have been only partially successful in building and shaping national cultural identity, which is to some degree the product of the measures adopted by the public institutions in what is sometimes conceived as a top-down, even paternalistic project on one hand, and partly the product of the free and spontaneous will of Italian society on the other. In reality, the Italian legal order has not always been successful in guiding cultural processes. More often than not it has been content to support them or to attempt to contain them, leaving it to developments in society to limit the scope of regulation and not the reverse. The picture that emerges from our investigation also points to a number of unresolved tensions that the legal order needs to acknowledge and control rather than passively accept.

10.2 Art, Cultural Heritage, and Media

10.2.1 The 'Cultural Policy' of the Fascist Regime: The Nationalisation of Culture

Reflection on the macro-field that includes art, cultural heritage, and the media cannot but follow the historical perspective of cultural processes as a whole, which will be considered here as a supporting structure on which to graft further reflection on the three specific sectors in question.

A suitable starting point would thus be the origins of contemporary culture. In the eighteenth century, culture was confined to literature, the figurative arts, theatre, and classical music as phenomena reserved to the elite, but in the nineteenth, the concept of culture broadened out to include the forms of expression, inclinations, styles, and tastes of the emerging sections of society. In turn, 'the legal order reacted with measures aiming to protect the sensibilities of the general public, guaranteeing the preservation of the state of affairs and the affirmation of the dominant styles of the time'.[1] It was during this phase that the concept of 'mass culture' began to take shape, expressed—together with the traditional forms—through publishing, with the spread of the main national newspapers and the birth of the popular novel, together with the entertainment business, with the opening up of theatres to the lower classes.

Fascism later went to great lengths to establish the (also) cultural identity of the new political community: Mussolini's government, in fact, took upon itself the role of guide and controller of the culture and cultural identity of the Italians. Not surprisingly, the Bottai laws on the protection of art and natural beauties came into effect at that time (laws 1089 of 1.6.1939, and 14972 of 9.6.1939 respectively), introducing the new idea of the 'social function of property',[2] and still bearing the traits of an elitist interpretation focused on excellence (works of art are protected on

[1]Donati (2016).

[2]Ragusa (2011), p. 256.

account of their value and rarity, while only places of 'uncommon beauty' can be subject to protection). Art especially was the focus of Mussolini's attention.

In the space of a couple of decades, the 'cultural policy' of the Fascist regime seized control of the major areas of cultural interest (the protection of works of art, the safeguard of natural beauties and the landscape, restoration, museums, exhibitions, modern art, and artistic education) and, as with the public administration, it attempted to bring them within the political goal of 'Fascistising' the Italian State. The fundamental idea behind the whole design was that conflicts between private and public interests could not be countenanced, as the former were to flow neatly into the superior all-encompassing interest of the Nation.

In order to give impetus to the cultural policy of the Fascist nation and the Italian people, in 1937, the Ministry of Popular Culture (MinCulPop) was set up under the initial leadership of Edoardo Alfieri, succeeded by Alessandro Pavolini in 1939, and, from 1943 onwards, by Gaetano Polverelli. MinCulPop 'marks the transition from the early Fascist control of high culture and intellectuals, through agitation and subversion, to a policy of integration and normalisation through the construction of two myths: the cult of the Duce as a popular hero and the creation (already largely brought to fruition) of an ordered, vigorous, and excellent New Italy that invited its citizens to lead peaceful, sober and moral existences'.[3] But the regime did not stop at organisational and institutional reforms: it embarked upon a policy of patronage through what was known as direct intervention in culture, aiming to bring a range of activities, services, and tasks that would not otherwise have been spontaneously performed by private individuals into the public sphere. Direct intervention was achieved through the creation of a complex of public bodies with the aim of correcting weaknesses in the market: the State used these bodies to intervene in the various phases of the cultural arena, as well as in the preparatory and secondary activities connected with them.

With this in mind, and with the aim of transforming the press into a power at the service of the regime, in 1935 the Government decided to set up the ENCC, the Italian cellulose and paper agency, which was entrusted with the task of promoting the development of paper production, with the additional purpose of protecting Italian companies from foreign competition. At the same time, a subsidy mechanism was set in motion to grant direct subsidies to publishers, which quickly took the form of 'insurance' for publishing (without distinction between types of undertakings). These funds were made available with a view to fostering pluralism in the field of information, supporting new publishers in their access to, or continuing presence on, the market. In reality, government aid generated, if anything, what has been defined as 'the illusion of pluralism in the field of information',[4] which, in the years to come, would justify constant interference by the public authorities in the exercise of fundamental freedoms, such as freedom of the press and commerce.

---

[3]Donati (2016).

[4]Magri (2016).

The Fascist years were also characterised by the spread of new forms of expression (the first cinema had opened in Pisa in 1905) and new means of communication (the Italian Radio-communication Union made the first radio broadcast in 1924), in a perspective that, for the first time, highlighted the close connection between cultural events, technical innovation, economic structures, and the role of institutions. It was during the Fascist period that the public authorities implemented an extensive policy of both indirect and direct support for the entertainment industry: the regime considered it a means of cultural propaganda, and the State, on the one hand, supported it with direct subsidies, while favouring, on the other hand, the transformation into 'national' public bodies of a number of private ones that were deemed important for the purposes of Fascist cultural education. By virtue of Royal Decree n. 1767 of August 7, 1925, the National Institute of Ancient Drama, founded in 1914, became a national institution, and few months later, with Royal Decree-Law n. 1985 of November 5, 1925, the Film Education Union became the 'moral entity of public law' named Istituto Luce, with the vocation of the 'dissemination of popular culture and general education through film screenings [...] distributed for charitable purposes and to spread national and patriotic propaganda'. During the same period, a number of other bodies were set up to control the entertainment industry, especially film (e.g., the *Ente Nazionale Industrie Cinematografiche*—ENIC), considered the warhorse of cultural propaganda.

10.2.2 The Republican Legal Order: An Open Cultural Policy and the Dialectic Between Homologation and Diversity

The nationalisation of culture, and State aid for the production and dissemination of artistic and creative production did not, however, represent the only vision of mass culture to emerge at that time. Gramsci opposed the 'official' view of culture and saw folklore as the purest expression of the 'world- and life view' of some specific social classes.[5] Gramsci focused on the creative power of social dynamics, opposing the dominant culture by slipping into any empty spaces that this may leave and expressing 'a series of often creative and progressive innovations, determined spontaneously by ways and conditions of life in the process of development that are in contradiction to, or simply different from, the morality of the ruling strata'.[6]

The clash between Fascist interventionism and Gramscian spontaneism would blend through the constitutionalising of culture, which implies a condition of 'active neutrality' on the part of the State towards cultural and artistic activities,[7] almost as if to underline the position of equidistance and ideological impartiality that public institutions must assume in a democracy when determining the artistic-cultural value

[5]Gramsci (1975), p. 2311.

[6]Gramsci (1975).

[7]Rimoli (2003).

of a work or product or in selecting the ones to be promoted and supported from among those considered valuable. The liberal-democratic model promotes a 'policy of culture' 'open to all men of culture',[8] as opposed to ideological and elitist 'cultural policy'. In this context, the task of public institutions is to remove not only the material obstacles but also the psychological and moral barriers to the development of a free and open culture, as 'the former hinder or impede the circulation and exchange of ideas, and contact between people of culture. The latter hinder and make difficult, or even dangerous, the formulation of a solid conviction through the falsification of facts or flawed reasoning, or still yet through various kinds of pressure on the individual conscience'.[9] Cultural production on an industrial scale, which began to take shape in the mid-1950s with the launch of national television broadcasting, tried to satisfy public demand, bringing culture closer to people, but at the same time it betrayed the Gramscian idea of 'popular culture' rooted in history and traditions.

However, applying a production approach to manifestations of thought inevitably leads to the standardisation of creativity and the homologation of tastes, as well as the risk of the alienation and infantilising of consumers,[10] a phenomenon particularly evident in public service broadcasting in the late 1960s. At that time, the RAI's educational project, which had previously excelled in public information and cultural programmes, revealed an inability to give a voice to the secular and nonconformist minority who sought the opportunity to participate in the political and institutional life of the country. There is no doubt that, together with the spread of knowledge and information, in addition to the acquisition of new linguistic resources by a still illiterate population, fragmented into a thousand different dialects and popular traditions, the RAI contributed to the emergence of a high degree of cultural homologation, moving towards widespread trivialisation.[11] The cultural stereotype proposed and propagated by the RAI in its first decade of life embraced only one of the many identities of the country and did not reflect the call for renewal, the cultural restlessness, and the turmoil taking place in civil society at the time.

However, alternative currents of ideas were developing in parallel to the mainstream: 'cultural subsystems marked by difference, proposing original styles and topics, often antagonistic to the common norm'. This is how the pluralism of cultural systems is born, within which, as Weber observed,[12] everyone is given the opportunity to identify in a way that is no longer underground or secret but, on the contrary, can display pride at belonging and being special. Essentially, it is precisely in mainstream culture that cultural pluralism and multiculturalism are rooted. Paradoxical as it may seem, the massification of cultural output and the pluralism of forms of expression are closely connected in Western, especially Italian, history.

[8]Bobbio (2005).

[9]Bobbio (2005), p. 23.

[10]Adorno (1959), p. 21.

[11]Bettetini (1990).

[12]Weber (1917).

What is more, experts feel that mass cultural products perhaps increase the risk of infantilising consumers, lowering their critical thinking skills, but at the same time they make culture available to social categories that would otherwise be excluded, thus sensitising people to themes and scenarios of which they previously had no knowledge.[13] Thus, the Gramscian gap between mass culture and popular culture is diminished in the name of substantive democratisation in terms of access to knowledge and creativity.

10.2.3 The Dialectic Between Centralism and Local Autonomy

In the 1970s the dialectic between homologation and cultural diversity gradually came to be flanked by the dialectic between central and local authorities. In some sectors (for example, the protection and fruition of cultural heritage), regional authorities began to seek a greater role in the regulation, financing and, in part at least (regarding everything not left to the Provinces), in the planning and coordination of activities, while the Municipalities gradually became cultural 'administrative centres', directly granting subsidies and increasingly managing initiatives and cultural activities on their own.

The difficulty of decentralising cultural policies and, therefore, adapting the government of the sector to the new 'plural State' is particularly evident in the entertainment sector. In this context, from the early 1970s, developed the 'spread of initiatives by local authorities as producers, organisers and distributors, and especially by municipalities through permanent theatres set up and financed through the so-called 'optional expenditure mechanism''.[14] The close of the decade saw a process of rethinking the administration and regulation of entertainment in line with the reform trend that affected the entire institutional and administrative system at the time: decentralisation and privatisation. This dual dialectic (centre-autonomy on one side, public-private on the other) would turn into a structural issue, becoming the hallmark of the entire sector. Suffice it to say that, in terms of decentralisation, after the approval of Presidential Decree n. 616/1977, almost all the Regions approved numerous legislative measures to support the various forms of entertainment with funding only slightly lower than what the State provided. Regarding privatisation, after years of unsuccessful efforts, legislative decree 367 of 29 June 1996 made the transformation of entities of prime national interest operating in the music sector into private law foundations compulsory, and with it the specification of the public and private entities that would be involved: this was an opening up to private individuals that clearly favoured a solution to the rigidity of public organisation and the entrepreneurial management of entertainment. But all dialectic is naturally made

[13] Eco (1964).

[14] Barbati (2016).

up of continuous oscillations, of stops and starts. Thus, legislative decree 386 of October 20, 1998, which established the Ministry of Cultural Heritage and Activities, granting it the relevant powers previously assigned to a specific Department at the Presidency of the Council of Ministers, represented a setback in the move towards territorial autonomy typical of the closing decade of the twentieth century. The legislative pendulum swung back, bringing substantial re-centralisation of the 'entertainment' sector, once more at ministerial level, under the jurisdiction of two separate directorates-general: one for live entertainment and the other for the cinema.

Like that of entertainment, the regulation of cultural heritage traditionally hinges on a State-Autonomy dialectic.[15] The reform of Part V of the Constitution itself, while emphasising the distinction between protection and valorisation, aims to 'constitutionalise' a series of powers reserved to local authorities in the field of cultural heritage. In reality, this distinction has never been clear, and for over a decade, recourse to instruments of coordination and interinstitutional cooperation has been the leitmotif of the model for the distribution of administrative power between the State, the Regions, and the local authorities, confirming the difficulty of defining with any certainty their respective areas of competence in the field of cultural heritage.[16] From this point of view, the 2004 Code of Cultural Heritage and Landscape does not seem to be a step forward towards the decentralisation of powers: although it theoretically introduces the procedure for transferring State ownership of the cultural heritage to the local authorities, the limited number of transfers actually carried out shows, if anything, the substantial failure of 'federalist' logic in this sector.

10.2.4 The Present Day and Ongoing Transformation

The contemporary postmodern era has brought with it some new elements that profoundly affect Italian culture, the first of which is the slow and laboured construction of Europe's cultural identity. Those who recognise as truly European only the cultures of those peoples who share the common heritage of Greek thought, Roman law, and the Christian faith, find themselves in opposition to those who, on the contrary, deny that these characteristics alone constitute European identity, underlining how the very idea of 'Europe' is based on constant and fruitful contamination with other cultures.[17] The fierce debate on the inclusion of an explicit reference to Christian values in the preamble to the draft European Constitution, later transformed into a mention of the Union's 'cultural, religious and humanistic heritage', is nothing more than a reflection of the ever-dormant tension between these opposing visions of European identity. Various formulae have been proposed

[15]Sau (2016).

[16]Cammelli (2011).

[17]Crépon (2006).

to solve this seemingly irremediable tension: on the one hand, there is 'republican nationalism',[18] which envisages the formation of a community-based civil conscience resulting from a progressive and spontaneous rapprochement of the original cultures, different traditions, and specific vocations that make it up. It is only thanks to the construction of a collective identity and awareness (and to the extent that this will happen) that European statehood can be achieved. On the other hand, there is 'constitutional patriotism',[19] which sees the sharing of common constitutional values, able to bring about a shared feeling among its peoples as the only possible condition for the creation of a European federation. In this perspective, therefore, the creation of a European demos follows rather than precedes the construction of community institutions that can be the driving force for the affirmation of 'a new community or a new form of supranational democracy'.[20]

Secondly, one of the main innovations of the contemporary age is the transition from analogue to digital technology, from which the phenomenon of 'technological convergence' originates. This shift leads to the 'progressive dematerialisation of cultural products, which are now migrating incessantly towards their digital versions and, at the same time, are shared by millions of people often with no consideration for copyright law, intellectual property, and thus the remuneration of creative work'.[21] The contemporary debate on new rights, and consequently new forms of discrimination, starts from these premises: access to the Internet is invoked by some as a constitutional right of the individual, and the States must address this in order to avoid modern phenomena of discrimination.

The solution to the problem of discrimination linked to new technological rights is not only to break down the digital divide, the technological infrastructure gap, but also to reduce the knowledge divide, i.e., the knowledge gap that separates experienced Internet users from the digitally illiterate. The latter, precisely because of their inability to use the technology, are deprived of considerable cognitive and participatory opportunities. The problem is therefore cultural as well as material: the cost, the age-related lack of familiarity with the medium, and the conviction that one can live without the Internet after all are factors that lead a significant proportion of the Italian population not to use it.

For this reason, the same logic should apply to the Internet as the reasoning underlying public intervention in support of merit goods: the State cannot fail to spread Internet culture and its value among its affiliates, regardless of the demand for access expressed by consumers as they are meritorious in themselves, producing social inclusion and a series of positive externalities. 'It is not enough to build a motorway, a metaphor often used for broadband: it is also necessary to publicise its

---

[18]Isensee (1989).

[19]Habermas (1998).

[20]Ponzano (2010).

[21]Donati (2016).

use, to facilitate the purchase of cars and to set up driving courses so that driving licences can be accessible to all'.[22]

On the other hand, it has been noted that the phenomenon of digitisation generates a different approach to the search for and fruition of culture: 'while up to now our culture has evolved with the search for relevant information based on discussed and successively shared criteria, today this selection is up to individuals who may be lacking solid third-party criteria, such as the validation and conservation of what is solid and relevant'.[23] Debate among scholars is heated on this point too: some authors deny that the Internet can be an example of 'realised pluralism' because information available online is often of poor quality and is moulded upon the expectations of users by companies in the audio-visual market, so that genuine pluralism cannot be said to exist.[24] Undoubtedly, unreliable and incomplete news circulates on the web, and often the data flows, the so-called big data, trigger an 'information overdose' that increases uncertainty rather than dissipating it.[25] The real risk is that ideas are transformed into consumer goods on the Internet, and for this purpose they are specifically manipulated to make them attractive and therefore more likely to be purchased by those willing to pay for them. Others, on the contrary, believe that these distortions are not sufficient to disprove the existence of a 'realised pluralism' on the Internet, which, being open, offers a sounding board to a multitude of ideas in such a way that any wholesale reduction to just one voice would appear unrealistic.[26]

Moreover, not all the content circulating on the Internet is put there by businesses; on the contrary, the characteristic of the Internet is the chance it offers to anyone to make their voice heard and to exercise the right to speak without particular technical difficulties or the problem of scarce resources, which, at least originally, was a constraint of the broadcasting system. As the Italian Constitutional Court has pointed out, discussing this issue with regard to radio and television, pluralism of information does not guarantee knowledge but an opportunity for citizens to 'be able to make their own judgements, taking into account different points of view and conflicting cultural orientations' (Court of Justice, n. 112, 24–26 March 1993). This is certainly an opportunity that the Internet can offer, and from this point of view, pluralism creates an opportunity rather than a promise of enrichment.[27]

There is room in this gap between realised and artificial pluralism for intervention by the public regulator: on the one hand, the State must create the conditions for the free dissemination and correct reception of information on the virtual circuit; on the other hand, the State is required to ensure that the exercise of the freedom of expression of thought on the Internet does not stifle the rights of others, by providing

---

[22]Massari (2016).

[23]Donati (2016).

[24]Manetti (2012).

[25]Mantelero (2012).

[26]Massari (2016).

[27]Massari (2016).

consistent and proportionate sanctions. 'After gaining access to the Internet, in fact, citizens can legitimately petition the State, demanding that enjoyment of the medium be free from harmful interference and that the spontaneous pluralism of the Internet not be sacrificed to the benefit of market interests'.[28]

The issue of technological neutrality, also highlighted with reference to the transition from paper to digital printing, can correspondingly be approached from a critical point of view, however. In today's society, and particularly among the younger generations, a 'series of social habits are emerging that risk "killing off" the press'.[29] The triumph of 'post-alphabetic' or paperless information raises a question about the role that the printed press should play in a pluralistic society, 'precisely because we are, today as never before, in an era marked by a multiplication, diversification and simplification of the channels of access to information'. The newspaper, unlike television broadcasting and online information, 'is the only one that leads to reflection and in-depth reasoned criticism', stimulating a cognitive process in the individual that other media do not impose.[30] Thus, the right to buy a newspaper is different from the right to watch television or access the Internet. This is why, faced with predictions about the end of the press and the book, a dilemma about the position of the public regulator also arises. The pluralism of information, traditionally invoked to favour support for the printed press, is highlighted here to counter the idea of the withdrawal of the public authorities from their support of the publishing sector. According to this reading, in fact, the 'death' of the printed press in no way leads to the 'death' of the cultural function of the medium, and if, on the one hand, legislation to protect the press may now seem anachronistic, on the other hand, precisely for the sake of the pluralism that has always been a beacon on the horizon of media regulation, legislation that does *not* protect it seems equally intolerable: 'The withdrawal of the legislator in the name of 'technological neutrality' from the regulation of the press would harm, rather than support, the freedom of public opinion'.[31]

A similar argument, on the other hand, can be made for broadcasting activity, which requires the active presence of the State to create a public broadcasting service able to act as a counterweight to the interference of political and economic power in the cultural education of citizens. Public service broadcasting plays an important role in the protection of cultural diversity, as well as in the affirmation of a people's identity, and it is unthinkable that this sensitive area be abandoned to market dynamics without the leadership of the State or adequate public regulation.[32] We see from this then that in these areas 'net neutrality', invoked as a panacea for all the ills of online information, is still a long way off.

---

[28]Massari (2016).

[29]Magri (2016).

[30]Magri (2016).

[31]Magri (2016).

[32]Gardini (2016).

10.3 Education

10.3.1 The Role of Education in Building National Identity

Education was the great driving force behind the construction of Italy's national identity: what has been achieved over the 150 years since national unity has been done, for the most part, in the schools. Whereas Italy was united as a result of war and traumatic events, the Italians were formed, in terms of identity, especially through public education over the subsequent decades.

The period in which national unity took place—the nineteenth century—coincided with the temporal juncture in which free and compulsory public education was spreading throughout Europe as an expression of the public function of education and, therefore, as a duty of the State rather than a means of spiritual and moral elevation of the individual and a means of achieving social equality. The State School came into being between the second half of the nineteenth and the first half of the twentieth century, and was essentially considered as a means for creating the structure (along with, and by means of, the dissemination of a shared language and the bare rudiments of knowledge) of a patriotic feeling and the spirit of national unity, as well as—especially during the 20 years of Fascist rule—the affirmation of a politically and socially oriented culture of the State, and education with the same objectives; a means of creating generational change for the ruling upper-middle class elites, with consequent constraints on egalitarian ideals and merit as a means of social mobility.

After the Second World War—following the entry into force of the Republican Constitution, but also with the spread of pedagogical ideas from overseas—schooling began to be seen as an instrument of democratic growth: a process of mass education gradually developed across the peninsula, first at secondary, and then at high-school level. The Constitution, of course, rests on the pillars of the freedom of teaching and the right to education, with the corollary of the obligation of the Republic to establish state schools of every kind and level, as well as free elementary education and the possibility of reaching the highest levels of study on the part of the able and deserving, despite their lack of material wealth, as well as the freedom of institutions and private individuals to set up schools (with a right to equal treatment). In this way, a constitutional framework based on a national education system resulting in a balanced alchemy between the public and private sectors was envisaged. This framework has made possible the development of education as a social right, implementing the principle of substantial equality and (at least potentially) developing a particular form of autonomy: the functional autonomy of schools and universities.

In virtue of this new constitutional equilibrium (and alongside the awareness of the close link between the level of education and the economic and social development of a nation) the trend has undertaken a specific trajectory: (a) the transition from State school to a widespread and integrated education system with a polycentric and ownerless structure within which, given the need to privilege the so-called hinges of the model (the general rules and the essential service levels are set by the State in accordance with constitutional principles), the Regional and Local Authorities have gained in importance, but above all, the autonomy of educational institutions and universities was recognised in the 1990s; (b) the transformation of education from a public civil service to a public social one for compulsory individual use, centred on the object of the service and therefore on the central importance of the person rather than the public entity providing the service; (c) the increasing interpenetration and flexibility of the boundaries between the traditional forms of education (school, university, vocational training), so that, linked by special 'bridges', a one and triune education system has developed.

In the wake of the affirmation of education as a right, the idea of school and university as a community has emerged, regarding social formation in which personalistic, pluralistic, and solidarity-based principles are laid down; school and university are recognised as the *loci* of full expansion of the principles of equality and solidarity.

Regarding education as a system built on the opposing relationship between the unitary general fabric and the autonomistic principle expressed in specific relation to schools and universities, the latter have been defined in terms of a functional juridical body, through which the full manifestation of functional autonomy is permitted and constitutionally guaranteed for universities, but which is implicit in the Constitution also in relation to schools.

From the public service perspective, schools and universities have long had to address not so much the private market viewpoint and therefore a struggle to occupy spaces there but the idea of improving performance in order to elevate the person through a sort of collaborative competition and from the point of view of the education system, which contemplates public and private equality coexisting in the harmonic equilibrium envisaged by article 33 of the Italian Constitution referred to above: a public initiative that the Constitution deemed necessary and direct, the freedom of the private sector to provide education, not something to be limited, but to be conveyed. The public sector has an incentive to improve performance; the private sector is constrained by public service obligations. All this is in line with the best meaning that can be attributed to the concept of merit in terms of an education that is not based on wealth but that guarantees access to the highest levels of education by the able and deserving, taking into account the point made above, namely that the higher the level of education within a country, the greater its wealth will be.

10.3.2 Revising the Established Paradigm: The Relationship Between Centralism and Autonomy

Over the last 25 years, a number of sometimes contradictory and asymmetric tendencies have emerged that have contributed to reshaping the general picture once more, forcing us, if not to admit a move backwards with respect to the trajectory described so far, at least to review the basic paradigm that has marked development since the Republic was founded.

This is particularly true in certain areas: the relationship between centralism and autonomy, the relationship between the public and private sectors and the influence of competitive mechanisms in the context of a social right, and the relationship between European and national law in terms of education.

First of all, in part because of the economic crisis that has aggravated a situation of heavy cuts in education in Italy and that had already begun before 2008, there has been a limit or, at least, an attempt to 'set constraints' on the right to education, deeming it a financially conditioned social right.

In this, it must be recognised that the Italian Constitutional Court has acted as a breakwater. One example is judgment no. 80/2010, clearly stating that the education service should not be based on purely organisational, organic, or financial efficiency, but should be orientated and suited to the specific characteristics of the persons entitled to education. The education of disabled people was therefore considered as a fundamental right of the constitutionally protected person and should thus be considered as a priority over the possible budgetary or organisational aspects of the activity of schools.

It is not just the right to education that runs the risk of being limited by the legislator. Freedoms that run parallel to this right such as freedom of teaching and freedom of scientific research are also exposed to new and greater dangers than in the past. These freedoms were originally conceived and built upon as a defence against the interference of public power. They were created to guarantee the necessary protection of an intangible sphere regarding teachers with respect to government powers. Subsequently, the problem of denominational schools and universities has come to the fore in recent decades—we refer in particular to the Cordero case or, more recently, *Lombardi Vallauri*, also addressed by the European Court of Human Rights—and, therefore, in this respect, the conflict between the freedom of the schools and universities on the one hand, and freedom of teaching and freedom of scientific research on the other. Today the problem appears in a different perspective: since non-State actors with mainly profit-making aims are also present on the scene (especially in the university sphere), it is necessary to verify how these freedoms (especially scientific research, but also teaching) can coexist with conceptions of the university that are not entirely consistent with the traditional idea of *universitas* accepted by the Italian Constitution.

As far as the relations between the centre and forms of autonomy are concerned, the last few years have seen a sort of parabolic evolution of autonomy. As mentioned above, the trend in the 1990s was to extend autonomy in the field of education (with regard to both territorial autonomy and, above all, the functional autonomy of schools and universities). In recent years, there has been a shift in the opposite direction, moving away from a logic centred on a national education system as a compound administration in a pluralistic sense towards a return to centralism with the MIUR at its apex (although, as far as the university is concerned, this is a 'star-shaped centralism' with a political point, the MIUR, a technical point, the ANVUR, and a financial point, the MEF, as well as 'corporative' points, the CRUI and the CUN, often taking antithetical positions).

The complex jigsaw puzzle of the distribution of legislative power in article 117 of the Constitution was resolved in a sort of regressive centralism, involving a strong erosion of the powers of the Regions, the failure to implement financial autonomy, and the failure to define the essential levels of services. This also happened because the Constitutional Court decidedly endorsed the return of central authority. The ruling that constituted a watershed in this sense is of course n. 200/2009, which, in addition to posing serious problems in terms of the organisation of the sources, legitimised the idea of national planning for the education system, within the limits of the general norms on education, thus strongly affecting the powers of the Regions (especially those under ordinary statute).

If this is essentially how the relational framework between the State and the Regions looks, the education system ought also then to be based on the relationship between the centre and the functionally autonomous bodies. Within the framework of the national education system, the model requires the centre to only impart political direction, leaving the educational institutions to provide the service themselves. In this case too, however, functional autonomy has also been subjected to some marked limitations. The legislative approach has been to strengthen the umbilical cord between the heads of schools, the universities, and the MIUR with intermediate bodies such as the regional school offices on the one hand, and the CRUI on the other. This sort of vertical governance has led to the significant weakening, both in schools and universities, of the role of the collegial bodies in a framework in which the latter have great difficulty in connecting with the territory in a productive manner due to the current economic crisis.

The parabolic course of functional autonomy can be clearly observed through the legislation n. 240/2010 (the so called *Gelmini* legislation). Thanks to this legislation, there has been a move away from the autonomy of universities with no accountability (university autonomy was handled with little sense of accountability) towards the outright removal of said autonomy in the first years of the twenty-first century. Article 1 of the *Gelmini* law opens with a promising statement: ‘Universities are the primary centre of free research and free education within their respective systems and are places of learning and the critical processing of knowledge; they operate, organically combining research and teaching, for the cultural, civil, and economic progress of the Republic’. But the next paragraph immediately introduces a provision that, in substance, reduces the autonomy of universities. And this elimination takes place in respect of certain decisive aspects of university structure, while autonomy survives in certain aspects that are painstakingly applicative, to be addressed by the senior management of the universities. All this became very significant when the university statutes were drawn up, drafted as they were under the aegis of the ministry.

The situation has changed once again with the recent so-called Good School Reform (Legislation no. 107/2015), which seems to be moving in the direction of giving new strength to the autonomy of educational institutions and, in particular, the heads of schools, in a relationship of active dialogue with families, discovering bottom-up participation anew. This could lead to the rediscovery of functional autonomy, perhaps with a new lease of life, but in a framework of greater responsibility than in the past, also for universities. One might therefore envisage the start of a ‘second effort’ in the pluralistic and polycentric direction of autonomism. But, as mentioned above, it will largely depend on how the reform is implemented, and, in this respect, the first 2 years of implementation have produced very disappointing results.

10.3.3 The Relationship Between the Public and Private Sectors

We have also seen the introduction of competitive mechanisms in the field of education and especially in higher education in the last few years. Such mechanisms should be used with caution and good sense in the context of public services. The question is whether they can contribute not to the construction of an education market but to the improvement of the institutional system.

In the constitutional framework of the national education system described here, public educational institutions must be faithful to their nature, and it ought to be unthinkable to transform them into firms or enterprises, jeopardising their role as contributors to the social cohesion of a community as a place of inclusion and social equity. Once the public nature of the public institutions has been firmly established, it is then possible to integrate private schools into a pluralistic system on an equal footing, and at this point they could also follow their agendas, or even business activities, with the aim of making money. Consequently, the role of the private sector and that of private funding cannot change the role of the state school but can be seen as a mechanism for virtuously improving the system.

With specific regard to universities, one of the most significant risks is that of redefining the concept of university beyond constitutionally established boundaries. State universities have coexisted with non-State universities for many decades and have found a balance and harmony in their *modus operandi*. However, a plethora of non-State universities have sprung up over the last few years, with consequences well worth studying.

Some of their competitive mechanisms have a significant impact on the overall physiognomy of the system and must therefore be calibrated and applied with caution: one example is the evaluation of research and teaching and other phenomena that have been given too much importance insofar as they can have consequences beyond the education system, such as the much-debated legal value of the degree, whose abolition would create more problems than it would solve.

10.3.4 The Relationship Between National and European Legislation

Lastly, there is the European dimension, that is also increasingly permeating the education sector and that strengthens the pluralistic and polycentric framework;

nevertheless, it also introduces new variables to the system. At the European level, for example, education moves more closely alongside policies promoting and guaranteeing effective EU citizenship and making the European socio-economic system more competitive as a whole.

This is coming about through the 'development of quality education', a goal in which the Union itself plans to play a facilitating role, committing itself to encouraging cooperation between States and to putting in place any appropriate supporting action, possibly complementing in a wholly spontaneous and independent way what they propose to do in this sense. The fact that this incentive is presented through recommendations and communications does not mean, however, that the European initiative is less effective, not least because of its 'mixed' methodology, which is heavily influenced by the logic of other social sciences (in particular, economics) characteristic of European action.

In fact, to say that the Union can address the question of education in terms of quality is tantamount to establishing: (a) that the supply is measurable according to criteria that are external to the Member States and will inevitably have to do with the Union's systemic objectives, and (b) that any such measurement will be important both for specific supranational support, where appropriate, and with a view to facilitating or making the achievement of these general objectives even more effective'. This is, in theory, soft law, but, in concrete terms, these are policies that require alignment with the parameters set by the Union: the so-called open method of coordination.

European education policy and the benchmarks that derive from it, which now have an important influence on the development of national policies, are firmly geared towards four main objectives: the 'efficiencyisation' of education (i.e., the need to pursue indicators of system efficiency), 'school beyond school', and the strategy of results (i.e., abandoning a policy of self-referencing and comparison with demand coming from other policies), the welfare of knowledge (which implies the functionalisation of education to European needs and, therefore, the redefinition of educational purposes), and the redefinition of value assumptions.

This leads, in certain circumstances, to a clash between these objectives and parameters and the indications found in the national constitutional provisions, particularly those concerning how the national legislator sometimes implements European soft law.

10.4 Language

10.4.1 A Question Neglected in Legal Studies

Language is the third and last sector for consideration in this overview of the regulatory techniques and processes through which the Italian legal order has contributed to shaping the Italian cultural identity. The language used by the subjects and institutions of the political order is, in fact, a fundamental component of national cultural identity. By regulating linguistic interactions between subjects and institutions of the political order, law may define membership (e.g. when it identifies one or more official languages within the legal order and when it establishes a link between language skills and citizenship). It may also address social conflicts (as in the case of the protection of linguistic minorities) and structure and stabilise institutional relations (e.g., when it regulates the linguistic interactions between public administrations and the addressees of administrative action).

Despite the importance of linguistic interactions in the broader processes of building national identity, Italian legal studies have paid scant attention to the ways in which the legal system has attempted to govern and direct such interactions. Even 60 years after Alessandro Pizzorusso's pioneering writings,[33] there have been very few legal studies on the regulation of linguistic interactions: some important examples include Giovanni Poggeschi's important volume on language rights and duties,[34] research on the interpretation and translation of law, and some studies of the language of the European administrative networks.[35] The impression is that jurists struggle to take on a vast and complex field of research that they see as an intricate set of issues. A new attempt to do so has recently been made in a volume edited by the authors of this chapter; it contains a section addressing the legal choices regarding a number of problems concerning language and the way these choices have influenced the processes of construction of Italian cultural identity and how it changes.[36] This volume offers three main keys to interpretation that are worth attention here.

10.4.2 The Regulation of the Use of Language for the Purpose of Civil and Political Integration: Three Historical Phases

The first concerns the historical evolution of the ways in which the Italian legal system has regulated the use of language as an instrument of civil and political integration. The question is addressed by Matteo Gnes, who asks whether the Italian order has regulated the use of language for the purpose of the civil and political integration of individuals in the national community, what purposes it has pursued, what instruments it has used, and what effects its measures have produced.[37] His position is that the existence of a common language is, as such, a factor in the civil and political integration of individuals within a community. From this perspective, language is not so much (or not only) a tool for carrying out concrete activities but

---

[33]Pizzorusso (1957).

[34]Poggeschi (2008).

[35]Chiti and Gualdo (2008).

[36]Chiti et al. (2016).

[37]Gnes (2016).

one of the characteristic elements in the idea of nation, in line with the traditional approach of constitutional studies. This leads the author to examine the ways in which the political institutions of a unified Italy have addressed the question of Italian as the language of the Italian nation over the years.

Gnes traces a complex history, drawing on a wealth of studies on the history of the Italian language. He makes reference to Tullio de Mauro's fundamental work, recalling that at the time of the Unification, Italian was a 'foreign language in its home country'.[38] Historical, cultural, social, and political factors rendered the linguistic situation very complex, making the affirmation of Italian as a national language somewhat remote. Thus, whereas in post-revolutionary France the use of dialects was forbidden, and use of the French language was promoted and made obligatory across the board, in Italy, according to de Mauro's classic reconstruction, different forces were at work. On the one hand, emigration abroad, urbanisation, and the roles of bureaucracy and the army contributed to the reduction or rejection of dialect. On the other hand, the growing importance of the educational institutions and political organisations, the press and the mass media, coupled with recognition of the use of Italian as a factor in lessening class differences, favoured the development of a shared language. In this phase, therefore, the legal system operated in various ways to promote the use of a common language. Its actions were, however, almost always indirect, insofar as the promotion of Italian as a national language was neither at the heart of any linguistic policy recognisable as such, nor did it represent the explicit aims of the various regulations on the subject, which in many cases even expressly established linguistic regulations open to the use of languages other than Italian (e.g., permission for members of the Chamber of Deputies to use French). The slow spread of Italian as a national language was the result, rather, of the combination of social pressures, functional requirements, and the mostly unexpected consequences of the public policies of the new State.

The second phase in the historical process of promoting Italian as a national language began with the birth of the Fascist regime, which developed a genuine linguistic policy consisting of a war on the use of dialect terms, ethnic minority languages, and foreign borrowings. Anti-dialect policy, Gnes recalls, was most virulent in schools, where the use of dialects was opposed not only in their spoken forms, but also as literary languages. The battle against the languages of ethnic minorities was mainly addressed to South Tyrolean and Julian languages and led to extremely punctilious linguistic regulation that envisaged, for example, the forced Italianisation of place names and hotel signs. The onslaught against foreign borrowings resulted in a wide range of measures of various kinds, including a ban on 'exoticisms' and the obligation to replace them with Italian equivalents. On the whole, it was a contradictory policy, strongly oriented towards the promotion of Italian as a national language on the one hand but undermined internally by an evidently authoritarian logic, on the other.

---

[38] De Mauro (2015).

The third and final phase began with the new constitutional order. Probably as a reaction to excessive Fascist language policy, the Constitution, as is well known, does not expressly name Italian as the 'official language' of Italy. Recognition of Italian as an official language is, however, to be found in sources of constitutional rank, such as the statutes of the Special Regions and numerous ordinary laws, as well as, implicitly, the Constitution itself, as the Constitutional Court has recognised. Beyond the formal definition of Italian as the national language, the system has developed what Gnes defines as 'fragments' of a linguistic policy consisting of a variety of relatively autonomous and markedly fragmented actions, capable of influencing, each in its own specific field of operation, the linguistic behaviour of the various actors within the legal order and promoting the use and recognition of Italian as a national language. Key areas are: the education sector, where the aim of spreading the Italian language is expressed, the role of language in relations with the public administration, the mass media, the position of foreigners, the dissemination of the Italian language abroad, and the use of foreign languages.

Taken as a whole, these actions show how the lawmakers have been, and continue to be—especially in recent years—particularly committed on the linguistic front, making choices that regulate the linguistic behaviour of the subjects of the legal order, fostering the use of Italian as the language of the national community. However, the actions taken do not indicate a uniform design. The policies implemented mainly respond to the need to solve contingent problems; they lack a sense of planning or, when they aim to make fundamental choices, they struggle to operate as a set of functionally unitary actions.

10.4.3 A Specular Phenomenon: The Evolution of the Protection of Linguistic Minorities

While Gnes examines how Italian law has regulated the use of language in terms of the civil and political integration of individuals, promoting Italian as the language of the Italian nation, another chapter in the same volume edited by Chiti, Gardini, and Sandulli[39] looks at whether, and if so how, Italian law has regulated the position of minority linguistic communities.[40] The basic assumption of the investigation is the same as that of Gnes: there is an essential link between language and community insofar as language expresses identity and belonging. For Gnes, however, language reflects the identity of a national community. In Poggeschi's essay, on the other hand, the possibility is mooted that, alongside the national language, there may be languages that give a voice to minorities and that can establish relations of various, even conflictual kinds, with the national language.

[39]Chiti et al. (2016).

[40]Poggeschi (2016).

The author observes that there have always been linguistic minorities in Italy, from the time of Unification to today. What has changed is the legal standing of their languages. The evolution of this regulation reflects in some way that of the guidelines sometimes followed by the law on the question of Italian as a national language. Thus, in the liberal age, the absence of any institutional policy clearly aimed at promoting Italian as a national language was reflected in a substantial tolerance or indifference to the languages of the linguistic minorities. Fascist language policy, strongly oriented towards the affirmation of Italian as a national language led, on the other hand, to the practical repression of minority languages. In the Republican order, the fragmentary series of policies for the promotion of Italian as the language of the national community have gone hand in hand with the recognition of the linguistic rights of minorities, in line with the requirements of a system called upon to foster the coexistence of unity and pluralism, also amid the growing pressure of international and European obligations. However, the current regulatory framework is far from complete. In order to deal with the increasingly complex problems posed by the social changes taking place today, not least the migratory phenomena triggered by the numerous regional crises, the law has to assess the possibility of extending its remit beyond the protection of the languages of historical minorities, addressing issues such as the protection of dialects, the protection of the languages of immigrants, and developing ways of studying foreign languages.

10.4.4 The Language Regime of the Italian Administrative System

The regulation of language in terms of civil and political integration and that of linguistic minorities are the two main instruments through which the Italian legal order has influenced the processes of construction and change in the linguistic component of Italian cultural identity. Alongside these two types of regulation, however, there are others that are more limited in scope but no less important. One of these is the regulation of linguistic interactions involving public administrations.

The traditional discipline of this type of linguistic interactions reflects a fundamental tension: on the one hand, the legal order, since Unification and throughout the twentieth century, has promoted Italian as the language of the national administrative system; on the other hand, in line with the pluralistic principle established by the Constitution, multilingualism, meaning the coexistence of more than one language or several varieties of the same language in the same community, has always been a hallmark of the practice and work of Italian bureaucracy and its interaction with the citizens, regardless of the formal legal provisions.

It is interesting, however, to observe the ongoing transformations of this established model. The Italian administrative system is involved in an increasing number of relations with the administrative systems of other States and international and supranational bodies, the most important of which is the European Union. This European and global openness leads national administrations to form various relationships with the administrations of ultra-state bodies and with the administrations and citizens of other countries. In this new context, which has developed over the last three decades, there is a proliferation of linguistic, oral, and written interactions between actors speaking and writing in different languages. The Italian regulations on the use of language in the national administrations are changing to take into account the growing European and global importance of their activities and the new network of interactions.[41] In particular, two main groups of disciplines are being developed. The first is that of the disciplines promoting the use of languages other than Italian by national administrations when carrying out activities of European and global relevance: one example is that of soft law measures requiring the knowledge of English and other foreign languages in order to hold certain positions in the military administration, given its participation to different types of international operations; another example is that of the measures encouraging the internationalization of the Italian academic system, which implies research and teaching in foreign languages. The second is the disciplines that promote the use of both Italian and foreign languages, exemplified by the use of foreign languages in the elementary education system for different purposes, including integration of foreign students in the school community.

These two sets of disciplines do not encapsulate two opposing approaches: they rather occupy different points along a continuum between two poles, that of the exclusive promotion of the use of Italian and that of the exclusive promotion of the use of a foreign language. The regulations that have developed in recent years either tend towards one of the two extremes, that of the exclusive promotion of the use of a foreign language, or else they identify intermediate formulas, but there are no instances of the law promoting the exclusive use of Italian by national administrations without also providing for the use of other languages. The emergence of these regulations is due to a variety of factors, some of which are functional, such as the ability to carry out administrative activities, and some of which are political. An essential role, however, is played by the strictly linguistic aspects of interactions, such as the actors involved in each channel used, the degree of formality, the various balances between the different linguistic functions, and, in particular, between the communicative and symbolic functions.

Arguably, the emerging linguistic regimes establish a specific balance between unity and linguistic pluralism, privileging the latter. On the one hand, English is recognised as the vehicular language of the national administration alongside or in competition with Italian when carrying out activities of European or global prominence. On the other hand, the importance of foreign languages other than English, including rare ones, is recognised for certain specific types of administrative activities. The tendency to foster linguistic pluralism to the detriment of unity is not something new in the history of the Italian administrative system, given that

[41] Chiti and Favilla (2016).

multilingualism has always been a feature of the practice and activities of Italian bureaucracy in its interactions with private actors. What is new, however, is the variety of languages used by administrations, beyond Italian with its varieties, dialects, and historical minority languages, to the languages of speakers and administrations of other countries.

The current developments are highly problematic. The main issue is the impact of these developments on the role of Italian as a language for the national administration. Admittedly, the increasingly widespread use of languages other than Italian, especially English, in ever more numerous contexts, raises legal problems and carries with it the risk of the structural and functional regression of Italian. In assessing the implications of the new language regulations, however, excessively rigid interpretations of the constitutional framework must be avoided, proposing solutions that do not equate to the mere removal of current developments, considering that these developments also have consequences on the way the Italian administrative system operates.

10.4.5 A Set of Tensions

This brief outline of the ways the legal order regulates linguistic interactions within the national community is fairly indicative. Since its transformation in a Republic, the Italian polity has avoided addressing questions of language *en bloc*. The solutions offered in response to the various questions can very rarely be ascribed, even *a posteriori*, to any sort of broader and more complete language policy. Action has always been partial, as a response to specific contingencies, and has sometimes been inconsistent.

It comes as no surprise, therefore, that analysis of the different solutions developed does not reveal a clear and unambiguous design regarding the relationship between unity and linguistic pluralism. What emerges, rather, is a set of tensions. Italian is not generally promoted as the language of the national community, but through *ad hoc* acts and without developing any real linguistic policy with evident means and goals. There is therefore a drive towards unity, but it is a weak one. There is also a drive towards linguistic pluralism, guaranteeing the position of linguistic minorities and the use of foreign languages by the administration, but the enhancement of pluralism remains woefully incomplete, because there are no suitable means to face the most recent social developments such as the formation of immigrant language communities. In general, the promotion of pluralism does not seem to take into account the numerous implications of the choices made, especially with regard to the role of Italian as a national language. It cannot be said, therefore, that the Italian Republic has succeeding in constructing and directing the linguistic dimension of Italian cultural identity.

References

Adorno T (1959) Dissonanze. Feltrinelli, Milano
Barbati C (2016) Lo spettacolo nella storia istituzionale italiana. In: Chiti E, Gardini G, Sandulli A (eds) Unità e pluralismo culturale. Firenze University Press, Florence, p 325
Bettetini G (1990) L'Italia televisiva chiama davvero l'Europa? In: Rath CD, Davis HH, Garçon F, Bettetini G, Grasso A (eds) Le televisioni in Europa, I, storia e prospettiva della televisione nella Repubblica federale tedesca, in Gran Bretagna, Francia e Italia. Edizioni della Fondazione Giovanni Agnelli, Torino, p 237
Bobbio N (2005) Politica e cultura, 1955. Torino, Einaudi
Cammelli M (2011) Pluralismo e cooperazione. In: Barbati C (ed) I soggetti. Barbati C, Cammelli M, Sciullo G (eds) Diritto e gestione dei beni culturali. Il Mulino, Bologna
Chiti E, Favilla ME (2016) Il regime linguistico delle amministrazioni nel processo di apertura europea e globale del sistema amministrativo italiano. In: Chiti E, Gardini G, Sandulli A (eds) Unità e pluralismo culturale. Firenze University Press, Florence, p 251
Chiti E, Gualdo R (eds) (2008) Il regime linguistico dei sistemi comuni europei. Multilinguismo e monolinguismo nell'Unione europea, Quaderno n. 4 della Rivista trimestrale di diritto pubblico. Giuffrè, Milano
Chiti E, Gardini G, Sandulli A (eds) (2016) Unità e pluralism culturale. Firenze University Press, Florence
Crépon M (2006) Altérités de l'Europe. Galilée, Paris
De Mauro T (2015) Storia linguistica dell'Italia unita, III edn. Laterza, Roma
Donati D (2016) Cultura popolare e ordinamento giuridico. In: Chiti E, Gardini G, Sandulli A (eds) Unità e pluralismo culturale. Firenze University Press, Florence, p 425
Eco U (1964) Apocalittici e integrati: comunicazioni di massa e teorie della cultura di massa. Bompiani, Milano
Gardini G (2016) RAI e servizio pubblico radiotelevisivo: la 'cultura italiana' in equilibrio tra unità, pluralismo e mercato. In: Chiti E, Gardini G, Sandulli A (eds) Unità e pluralismo culturale. Firenze University Press, Florence, p 291
Gnes M (2016) La lingua come fattore di integrazione civile e politica. In: Chiti E, Gardini G, Sandulli A (eds) Unità e pluralismo culturale. Firenze University Press, Florence, p 195
Gramsci A (1975) Lettere dal carcere, 1936, vol III. Einaudi, Torino
Habermas J (1998) (1996) Die Einbeziehung des Anderen. Studien zur politischen Theorie, Frankfurt, trad. it. Ceppa, L., L'inclusione dell'altro. Studi di teoria politica. Feltrinelli, Milano
Isensee J (1989) Abschied der Demokratie von Demos. In: Schwab D, Giesen D, Listl J, Strätz H-W (eds) Staat, Kirche, Wissenschaft in einer pluralistischen Gesellschaft. Duncker & Humblot, Berlin, p 705
Magri M (2016) La disciplina dell'editoria quotidiana e periodica. In: Chiti E, Gardini G, Sandulli A (eds) Unità e pluralismo culturale. Firenze University Press, Florence, p 375
Manetti M (2012) Il pluralismo informativo tra vecchi e nuovi media. In: Mazzeschi RP, Del Vecchio A, Manetti M, Pustorino P (eds) Il diritto al pluralismo dell'informazione in Europa e in Italia. Rai Eri, Roma, p 239
Mantelero A (2012) Big data: i rischi della concentrazione del potere informativo digitale e gli strumenti di controllo. Diritto dell'informazione e dell'informatica:135
Massari G (2016) L'avvento di Internet: accesso al mezzo e ai contenuti digitali. In: Chiti E, Gardini G, Sandulli A (eds) Unità e pluralismo culturale. Firenze University Press, Florence, p 399
Pizzorusso A (1957) Lingue (uso delle), Novissimo digesto italiano, vol IX
Poggeschi G (2008) I diritti linguistici. Un'analisi comparata. Carocci, Roma
Poggeschi G (2016) Unità nazionale e pluralismo culturale: l'evoluzione dello status giuridica delle minoranze linguistiche dall'unità d'Italia ad oggi. In: Chiti E, Gardini G, Sandulli A (eds) Unità e pluralismo culturale. Firenze University Press, Florence, p 231

Ponzano P (2010) Identità europea e cittadinanza dell'Unione. In: Baruffi MC (ed) Cittadinanza e diversità culturale nello spazio giuridico europeo. Cedam, Padova, p 15

Ragusa A (2011) Alle origini dello Stato contemporaneo: politiche di gestione dei beni culturali e ambientali tra Ottocento e Novecento. Franco Angeli, Milano

Rimoli F (2003) L'arte. In: Cassese S (ed) Trattato di Diritto Amministrativo, II edn. Giuffrè, Milano, s.p. II, 1513

Sau A (2016) Il contributo della disciplina sulla tutela e valorizzazione del patrimonio culturale alla costruzione dello Stato unitario. In: Chiti E, Gardini G, Sandulli A (eds) Unità e pluralismo culturale. Firenze University Press, Florence, p 355

Weber M (1917) 2010, Il politeismo dei valori. Brescia, Morcelliana

Chapter 11
Administrative Unification and Public Intervention in the Economy

Maurizio Cafagno and Francesco Manganaro

Contents

Abstract Within the context of administrative unification and public intervention in the economy, the Authors analyse the effects on the Italian public administration of the shift from the aim to create a state and a national market to that of taking part in the creation of a single and super-national market. The analysis is carried out through a historical reconstruction with a view to examining a number of issues. Thus, the

In writing up the paper, which presents the results of shared reflection, Maurizio Cafagno drafted sections I and III, Francesco Manganaro sections II and IV.

M. Cafagno
University of Insubria, Varese, Italy
e-mail: maurizio.cafagno@uninsubria.it

F. Manganaro (✉)
Mediterranea University of Reggio Calabria, Reggio Calabria, Italy
e-mail: francesco.manganaro@unirc.it

D. Sorace et al. (eds.), *The Changing Administrative Law of an EU Member State*,
https://doi.org/10.1007/978-3-030-50780-0_11

analysis highlights how the determination of rules of conduct does not always lead to the desired outcome due to the peculiar nature of the market, concluding with a warning that the only remedy remains the constant evolution which needs constant interventions, especially with the aim of improving those administrations that intervene in the economic area in a professional manner.

11.1 Introduction

This paper sets out to describe and discuss some of the transformations that have affected the Italian public administration, in the transition from the objective of creating a state and a national market to that of participating in the creation of a single supranational market.

The argumentation will be divided into two parts: the first part sets the background and will describe, in inevitably cursory terms, the evolutionary path followed by the models of public intervention in the economy.

The second part, with a critical approach, will focus on variables that, in our opinion, have limited the effectiveness of public intervention in the economy.

The argument will follow two directions, selected from among the several that may in principle deserve further study.

The first, thinking of a strict administration between rules and the market, will try to show how, in the name of a not always relevant need to protect the competition, the internal order has wrongly ended up with the shattering of the action of the public administration, in the guise of economic actor, through an overabundance of constraints, rules and consequent exceptions, not at all justified by a correct reading of the principles and the European norms, which ironically it had intended to implement.

This excess not only weakened and flattened the administration, instead of unifying it, but it also ended up compromising the achievement of the underlying substantial objective of strengthening the single market.

This reflection will start from the subject of public contracts and then move on to critically reviewing the subject of concessions and public or mixed enterprises, in the varied forms experienced by the processes of liberalization and privatization.

The second line of argument intends to highlight factors of weakening and transformation of the public administration which have emerged, rather than from the reflective needs of control of the officials, from the objective difficulty of the legal system to keep up with the rapid and sometimes unexpected movements of the market.

Attention will be paid to situations in which the changes in the administration would seem more due to the crucial detachment with which the economy, globalizing or transforming itself, threatens to move away from the law or imposes a prompt refinement of legal responses aimed at preventing or mitigating a growing multitude of possible market failures.

11.2 Background

11.2.1 The Difficult Relationship Between Law and Economy

Looking at history, the idea prevails that the economy has its own rules that the law cannot really influence.[1] The market always needs the law,[2] at least to limit the influence of monopolistic companies.[3]

Even the classical liberals of the English school believed that public intervention was necessary at least in order to guarantee the defense of property rights and to define the rules of exchange. For Adam Smith, the "natural" freedom of the market needs a minimum of state guarantees: the proper functioning of the institutions, the jurisdiction, the protection against external invasions. So even for a liberal like John Stuart Mill, a laissez-faire approach in the market needs at least the public functions of justice and security. It is, therefore, a common opinion that the market can develop within an institutional framework governed by public law, while substantial differences remain regarding the specific influence that public measures can exert on the economy.[4] The opposite extreme theories, according to which the market is able to operate alone or, on the contrary, there can be strict economic planning, are not substantiated.

History shows that some form of economic regulation is always necessary, and its results can be useful[5] or harmful for economic development: an example of the former type in Italy is the support to the economic boom of the Sixties, while an example of the latter is the failure of economic planning.

This idea is confirmed in the European legal area. There was a transition from the single national market, created with the national unification of 1861, to the European single market: the role of public state actors in the economic field has changed, but public intervention for the survival of the market is not reduced.[6]

11.2.2 The Historical Development of Public Intervention in the Economy in Italy

The laws of national unification of 1865 extended Piedmont's legislation to the new unitary State. This created a national state and a single market.[7] The protectionist

[1]Merusi (2013).

[2]Irti (2004) and Ciocca (2012).

[3]D'Alberti (2008).

[4]Picozza and Ricciuto (2013) and Di Gaspare (2015).

[5]Mazzucato (2014).

[6]Aimo (2015).

[7]Calandra (1978) and Nigro (1980).

measures that were introduced favored the rising industrialization of the North of the country, creating a clear division with the South.[8]

The new unitary State proceeded to the partial sale of assets more for the need to recover economic resources than for a liberal ideological conviction aimed at reducing the owner-State. Without creating new public entities, the first unitary state, through fiscal policy and public budgets, introduced some forms of control over the economy, in order to achieve the unity of the market, protecting it from external interventions.

At the beginning of the twentieth century, the nascent unitary state needed new public entities to create infrastructures for investments. The State Railways Company was created in 1905. The idea of universal public service began to spread, and therefore the increase in spending implied that "finance from simple means ends up prevailing over the ends of the same modern state".[9]

In the post-World War I phase, the needs of reconstruction stimulated the creation of public actors to support production. After the great crisis of 1929, public holding companies (such as IRI, ENI, EFIM) were created. The new and ambiguous category of public economic bodies was introduced for them, i.e. real commercial enterprises regulated by private law, but subjected to the publicistic discipline only because they were created by law. With the public economic bodies the instrumentation of public subjects is completed, through which the State intervenes in the economy: Ministry, special company, public holding company.[10] With these new instruments, the State was introduced into the market no longer through rules, but directly as a producer of goods and services.

The promulgation of the Constitution of the Republic of 1948 opens a new chapter of public intervention. It consolidated a mixed economy in which public and private property coexist, functionalized to social utility. Property changes from an absolute right to enjoy and dispose of the thing (Article 463, Civil Code 1865) to a right subject to obligations (Article 832 of the current Civil Code).

Article 41 of the Constitution establishes the freedom of private economic initiative,[11] but also in this article the various souls of the constituents are revealed, since the economic initiative of private individuals cannot be contrary to social utility and is always subjected to programs and controls.

In the 1960s and 1970s the improvement of economic conditions was propelled by the development of industrial production and manufacturing, due to the initiative of a part of Italian entrepreneurship, strongly supported by substantial state subsidies. There is a new type of public intervention in the economic field in which, in addition to the producer State, there is a financing state that helps and supports development. In those years, the welfare state is created, with mass education and the universal health and social security system.

---

[8]Cassese (2012a, b).

[9]Orlando (1940).

[10]Merusi (2012).

[11]Trimarchi Banfi (1992).

The birth of the European Union creates the conditions for a decline of the state organization of many productive sectors subject to the rules if the supranational organization.[12]

In the 1980s the crisis of public intervention was widely felt and therefore the search began for different remedies from the past, whose effectiveness, however, eventually turned out to be lower than expected. Public spending increased excessively not only for the extension of the welfare state, but for political clientelism, which led to unnecessary waste, and its harmful consequences became evident soon. The crisis of large management bodies (IRI, ENI, EFIM)—often due to pathological deviations such as the creation of black funds for political parties—marked the definitive involution of a mode of public intervention in the economy.

The crisis manifested itself in the early 1990s. It was first of all a political crisis, epitomized by the judicial inquiry that became informally known as "Mani Pulite" (i.e. "Clean Hands"), which was reflected in public intervention in the economy due to the evident overlap between state public bodies and political parties.

However, there was a radical change in the laws on public administrations with an impact on public expenditure management bodies. With the law n. 241/90 on the procedure, the administrative function became a shareholder and the subject of agreements with private parties, with the law n. 142/90 on the reform of local authorities, the function of government—including economic development—which up to that point had been an exclusive prerogative of the state, became shared with local authorities; this law also introduced a new model of intervention in the economy, through mixed companies for the management of local public services.

The discipline on public procurement, in line with European legislation, involves a broad liberalization of contractual instruments such as public-private partnership[13] or competitive dialogue, innovative institutes compared to the traditional public management of the sector.

The awareness of the unsustainability of the public debt and the orientation to the single European market led to the first timid attempts at privatization and liberalization.[14]

The need to separate policy from management transforms the producing State into a regulatory state, which is no longer a producer of goods and services, but an arbitrator that dictates rules for the market.[15] This decisive factor contributed decisively to the Community law, which sees in the financing state (for example, with state aid) a danger for a market that is open to competition.

These were the years of real or alleged liberalization and privatization, of the reform of the banking system, of the modification of the public accounting system,

[12]Sorace (2013a, b).

[13]Cafagno et al. (2013).

[14]Torricelli (2016).

[15]Lazzara (2017).

of the opening of the local public services market, of the creation of a large number of independent administrative Authorities.[16]

This eventually led to the great crisis of 2008, which according to some observers was due to a lack of control of the law on banking financial transactions. This serious crisis could not be tackled with public investment policies for the substantial accumulated public debt, which was compounded by the total failure of policies pursuing liberalization and the opening of local public service markets. The awareness of being before a systemic and not only contingent crisis urged us to think more carefully about new ways of sustainable development, in a renewed relationship with the natural environment, the object of economic exploitation that is no longer sustainable. The global contradictions of a world in which the alleged global unity of the market is countered by profound inequalities between developed, emerging and underdeveloped areas, were thus exploding. The disruptive effects are evident in the large-scale migrations of entire populations that not only flee from wars, but are also looking for better living conditions.

Europe's response to this systemic crisis cannot be achieved through traditional models of development support, such as using more or less liquidity, controlling interest rates, and even a more or less drastic reduction of public debt does not appear to be decisive, as evidenced by the continuation of the crisis.

11.3 Critical and Reconstructive Profiles. Direct Intervention: Administration As an Economic Actor

11.3.1 Impartiality, Efficiency and the Single Market

The central topic of this stage of reflection lends itself to a quick schematization, which is offered immediately in the interest of clarity.

We have already noted that the paradigm of the "regulatory State"—situated within a European framework that in general does not oppose mixed economies and proclaims indifference with respect to the regime of property—does not prevent the administration from playing an economic active role, but it requires respect for principles and constraints to prevent it, by negotiating or self-producing [or by designing formulas that are positioned in the middle of the two options], distorts competition and raises barriers to free movement.[17]

In this logic, the goal of the removal of obstacles to free movement and the objective of the protection of competition certainly foreground—possibly in Italy more than elsewhere—the urgency to tackle problems that the economic lexicon would define "agency", internal of the administrative apparatus.[18]

---

[16]Cintioli (2017).

[17]Carullo (2005, p. 225), Ciocca (2006, p. 19), Corso (2007, p. 279), La Spina and Majone (2000), Ogus (2000, p. 19) and Trimarchi Banfi (2014, p. 26).

[18]Brosio (1989), Coase (1989, p. 167) and Fama and Jensen (1989, p. 213).

It is well known that an asymmetric distribution of information, along the chain of command of public organizations, creates conditions that are conducive to opportunism, which in turn can induce bodies and administrative officials to pursue unfair advantages—to the detriment of collective utility—when there is a question of drawing on common resources.[19]

These practices concern the European Union not only, and not primarily, as an immediate reason for the waste of taxpayers' money, but rather as factors of market pollution and as a cause of disincentive for economic operators to participate in trade on a global scale.

In light of incidents that all too often fill the pages of our newspapers and of the alarming reports that the courts of accounts or supervisory authorities periodically disseminate, it becomes even superfluous to stress that the problem is very serious and should not be underestimated.

However, it must be considered that inefficiency is a no less fatal barrier when it comes to the development of economic exchanges.

The inefficient conformation or improper use of the means with which the administration operates on the market fatally erode the surplus that the economic transactions are able to generate, reducing their attractiveness and thus compromising the interest of companies in taking part and the inclination of investors to cross national borders.

Effective policies for the promotion and safeguarding of free circulation and competition, in the various areas of direct intervention, therefore postulate the subjection of public administrations or their emanations to a regime capable of combining impartiality and efficiency and of reconciling their potential frictions.

We now intend to show that, by virtue of a superficial and stereotyped reading of European principles, administrative and judicial practice and even internal legislation have tenaciously supported, in a large part of the period on which we are called to reflect, a questionable inclination to reduce the issue of the protection of competition to that of the impartiality of the administration, systematically underestimating the issue of efficiency.

This distortion of perspective has affected the whole structure and administrative action causing serious deterioration and fragmentation rather than unification, to the detriment of the opening of the market.

We will start from the cross-sector of the competitions to illustrate this claim.

Once the underlying misunderstanding has been clarified, a few examples will suffice to show that it reoccurs similarly in terms of public enterprises and models of management of public services.

[19] Moe (1989, p. 25), Napolitano and Abrescia (2009, p. 203) and Lindsay (1989, p. 377).

11.3.2 Contractual Procedures

The discipline of the tenders—shaped by a process of osmosis with the rules in force since the early 1970s, the era in which the initial directives relating to public works and supply contracts were issued—reflects the conflict between competing needs concerning the establishment of a single market.[20]

Simplifying, we can say that the discipline contains two souls; the oldest is a legacy of the original national accounting regulations, while the most recent one derives from European law.[21]

The former interprets bankruptcy mechanisms and transparency rules as tools to control spending decisions and administrative conduct.[22]

Observed in this perspective, the race, metaphorically speaking, acts as a "cage", that compensates for the inevitable deficits of post-control checks—aggravated precisely by the information asymmetry that disadvantages the public institution in the relationship with its employees—through the preventive and precautionary imposition of strict decision-making protocols, aimed at neutralizing the danger of undue conditioning.

Assuming that it would be illusory to attempt to govern and control the conduct of the officials through the verification, *a posteriori*, of the results achieved, a rigorous proceduralization of the mechanisms of choice, *a priori*, rises to a degree useful to prevent referees, bearing in mind that administrations are still structures that interact with reality through the acts and behaviors of their bodies and agents.[23]

This logic leads us to consider the procedural rigidity that is less desirable than the freedom to evaluate the officials and, therefore, the possibility of an opportunistic exploitation of the information advantage they hold, to the detriment of the institution and the community.

By adopting the second and alternative visual angle—so far enhanced by economic reflection rather than by legal doctrine—the insolvency procedures lend themselves to being investigated not only as control mechanisms, but also as means of efficient allocation of goods, that is, in a way, as devices for controlled emulation of competitive dynamics.

Striving to distil and artificially reproduce, within the procedure, the typical interactions of a competitive market, may allow the public client to exploit the antagonism between the aspirants to mitigate a second problem of information asymmetry. This second problem is qualitatively different, and is due to the cognitive weaknesses that may cause opportunism of the potential counterparts and

[20]Comporti (2011), Ledda (1982, p. 317), Pericu (2009a, b, p. 631) and Sorace (2013a, b).

[21]Cafagno (2001) and Picozza (2010, p. 29).

[22]Ledda 1982, p. 317) and Giannini (1981, p. 459).

[23]Rizzo (1994, p. 7) and Doni and Mori (2011, p. 41).

private operators, rather than public officials, to the potential detriment of the community.[24]

If the first approach introduces a favor criterion to eliminate discretion, this second point of view pushes in the opposite direction.

As a matter of fact, the rich interdisciplinary scientific production specialized in market design and auction designation explains that an efficient modeling of selective procedures requires a flexible adaptation of the competition rules to the characteristics of the auctioneer, of the participants, of the involved transactions, of the reference market. So the theory invites us to be wary of resorting to rigid and undifferentiated procedural stereotypes.[25]

However, control instances of the officials' work (who argue for the severity of selective mechanisms) and efficient modeling objectives (which instead look favorably at flexibility)—which are all coherent purposes with the promotion of competition, undermined both by the partiality of the client and the inefficiency of public bargaining, which makes exchanges unattractive—can find a relatively easy combination when it comes to preparing the final wording of simple and standardized contracts, since in these cases the influence of procedural design on the final result is still limited.

On the other hand, the two visions enter into conflict and problems arise as the complexity of the economic transactions involved increases, specifically when tenders prepare the ground.

A solid literature shows that, as the client administration moves away from the area of standardized contracts—something that happens, for example, with concession assignments or private, contractual or institutional public partnerships—the strengthening of a goal, at internal of the race, may involve the frustration of others.

It is sufficient to mention, very briefly, that mechanical and formal procedures, which nevertheless prevent the actors involved from learning from one another and from moderating unknowns and risks, in preparing complex contracts, can inhibit the willingness to compete even more seriously, that transmitted by the suspicion that administrative discretion should be subject to manipulation.[26]

Along the lines of the famous essay that Oliver Williamson dedicated to the issue of competition for the market, in view of the assignment of services under the natural monopoly regime,[27] it is worth adding that, when the conclusion of complex transactions is at stake, which presuppose highly idiosyncratic investments and very long-

[24]Dimitri et al. (2006), Klemperer (1999), Schmidt and Schnitzer (1997, p. 97) and Wolfstetter (1995, p. 367). Please also consult the online essays at http://www.market-design.com/library-general.html.

[25]Klemperer (1999), Vickrey (1961) and Schmidt and Schnitzer (1997).

[26]Bajari and Tadelis (2006), Cafagno (2001), Doni (2005, p. 307), Klemperer (1999) and Schmidt and Schnitzer (1997, p. 97).

[27]Williamson (1986a, b, p. 485).

term commitments, the rigidity of tenders promises to prove ineffective, as well as inefficient.[28]

In these situations, the execution of procedures which are as rigid and formal as possible, far from exorcising the discretionary power, simply ends up postponing the exercise at the time of the execution of the agreed commitments, moving the problems of control of the officials and collusive phenomena on even more difficult terrain.[29]

In the face of this tension between objectives, Italian law and practice have long overdrafted the idea that in the name of the more cautious respect for European regulations, the need to limit discretion, which is useful for preventing the arbitrariness of officials, must in any case prevail.

In the history of Italian discipline, the now repealed general law on public works (framework law 11 February 1994, No. 109) has offered perhaps the most representative example of the setting.

This was, in fact, a law passed at the height of the so-called "tangentopoli" crisis, which brought about some investigations of the judiciary in the 1990s on corruption, which was rife within a fraudulent system that connected politics and entrepreneurship.

Having emerged from the most acute phase of the scandal, the subsequent legislation[30] has mitigated the mistrust of the bureaucracy, but it has continued to conceive the procedural constraints of the public contracts as instruments aimed at limiting and regulating the power of choice of administrative officials.

But this is not the philosophy espoused by European law.

To realise this, it is sufficient to consider the level of elasticity of the procedural options that European law makes available to public clients according to the assignment of services or uncommon work, innovation partnerships and concessor relationships.

These examples of non-standardized contractual cases are united by the tendency to mobilize resources that are generally in force, often giving positions that are even monopolistic, and therefore have marked distributional effects and offer higher average benefits than a common contract.

---

[28]Also read the report of the AGCM on Competition and regulation in public utility services, AS026, of July 1, 1994, at the address http://www.agcm.it/, p. 26. Cf. Crocker and Masten (1988, p. 327), Goldberg (1997, p. 342) and Laffont and Tirole (1993).

[29]The Report on the fight against corruption COM (2014) 38 final, Annex 12—Annex on Italy—p. 12, reports that, according to the empirical studies and reports of the Court of Auditors, "in Italy corruption is particularly lucrative in the post-award phase" and often, after formally unassailable tenders, "the quality of the work is intentionally compromised in the execution phase" (our translation). On the subject you can also read the so-called Cassese report, Parliamentary Acts XIII Legislature—Chamber of Deputies, Report of the Study Committee on Corruption Prevention, presented to the Speaker of the Chamber on October 23, 1996.

[30]In particular, the previous contract code, Legislative Decree 163/2006, with the annexed implementing regulation.

The increase in expected annuities obviously exacerbates the danger of the desire to unduly constrain the prosperous public choices.

If European law deems the prevention of favoritism or corruption to be a priority, according to the long perpetuated vision in Italy, it would be reasonable to expect, in all these cases, a crackdown on procedural constraints and the further narrowing of discretionary power.

In contrast, however, European law has legitimized flexible methods of selection, which even widen discretion.

There are many examples, such as the previous jurisprudence with which the Court of Justice in 2004 overturned art. 21 of the aforementioned Merloni law.[31]

This rule decided—in the face of a community discipline that, by adjusting the methods for evaluating offers, gave the contracting authorities the task of choosing between the lowest price criterion and the economically most advantageous bid—to establish a priori preference for the first method, because by its nature it is suitable for minimizing administrative discretion.

The European judge disapproved, clarifying that the presumption of transforming competitive procedures into a sort of straitjacket, within which to imprison economic estimates and evaluations, in the name of the need to watch over the bureaucracy, does not respond at all to genuine and appreciable objectives safeguarding the market.[32]

Furthermore, the interpretative communication of the European Commission of 2000 on the concessions,[33] while crediting the existence of an obligation to "compete", in compliance with transparent, non-discriminatory, proportionate, previously established criteria, has nevertheless considered "the grantor free to choose the most appropriate award procedure, [...] depending on the characteristics of the sector concerned".[34]

More generally, a declared propensity to relaunch the elasticity of the selective methods has informed the European institutions since the program of rationalization of the contractual legislation initiated with the Commission's communication of March 1998 on public procurement in the European Union. This process began with a motion of dissatisfaction with the fruits collected until then, due to the "complexity of the legal framework and the rigidity of its procedures", to then announce the intention to "simplify the former and make the latter more flexible".[35]

The revision program first advanced with the reorganization rules of 2004 and, in 2014, with the remarkable step marked by the approval of three new directives on the

---

[31] Court of Justice, Second Chamber, 7 October 2004, Case C-247/02.

[32] See par. 39 and ff. of the motivation of the sentence.

[33] Communication on the concessions of 12 April 2000.

[34] The Opinion of the Economic and Social Committee "Strengthening the law of concessions and public-private partnerships (PPP)", of October 19, 2000, commented on that first act of address even deprecating the absence of an explicit invitation to prefer competitive negotiated procedures, judged to be more suitable to cope with the high degree of uncertainty that generally distinguishes concession assignments.

[35] Commission Communication of 11 March 1998, COM (98) 143.

assignment of concessions and tenders, in the ordinary sectors and in the special sectors, which stand out precisely because they promote flexibility and granting credit to the discretion of the clients.[36]

The new national public contracts code, that has been recently approved [D. Lgs. 50/2016] seems to have finally aligned with European reasoning, adopting rules that enhance and legitimize the use of forms of plastic trading interaction, which postulate an intense exercise (at least on paper) of discretionary power.

Exemplary institutions include preliminary market consultations (articles 66-67), pre-commercial contracts (Article 158 c.2), the innovation partnership (article 65), the negotiated competitive procedure (Article 62 and Article 123), the flexible selection criteria prior to concession assignment (Article 171 paragraph 7), the aforementioned competitive dialogue (Article 64).

It is almost superfluous to add that, in order for the updated theoretical bases to be translated into practice, the effective cooperation of administrative officials is essential, as they are usually required to choose the procedural solutions offered by the legislation.

It is sufficient to consult the database of the TED service[37] to verify the extent to which flexible procedures have been used in the last 5 years, such as competitive dialogue and negotiated competitive procedures, above-threshold, comparing the local situation to that of countries such as France, Germany and England, to take note that—despite legal openings and theoretical opportunities—the effective availability of Italian public administrators to cover little tested procedural trajectories, under the looming threat of claims by the Court of Auditors or of judicial complications, remains drastically limited. The new code of contracts has planned an ambitious work of rationalization and requalification of public demand, but one can assume that, beyond the incipient numerical and quantitative adjustments, the process of staff training and the effective acquisition of expertise and administrative skills necessary for the management of problematic and innovative procedures will require time and cultural changes, also in the methods of judicial review.

11.3.3 In-House Providing, Public Enterprises, Mixed Companies

The phenomenon of public entrepreneurship involves a multitude of subjects and topics—ranging from liberalization, to privatization, to the various areas of public

[36]The 42nd recital of Directive 2014/24/ EU begins with the statement that "it is essential that contracting authorities have more flexibility in the choice of a procurement procedure that provides for negotiation" and it is plausible "that a more extensive use of these procedures also increases cross-border trade". Thanks to the new rules governing procurement in the ordinary sectors, there is the possibility of using the competitive negotiated procedure.

[37]Tenders Electronic Daily, online version of the Supplement to the Official Journal of the European Union, for public tenders and concessions, at http://ted.europa.eu/TED/search/search.do.

utilities, to mixed capital companies, to special societies, to instrumental societies, to singular societies, to societies in charge of the management of local services—whose extensive and complex discipline, segmented into sectors that are at times very specialized, would be impossible to properly summarize here.

Among the most interesting and debated cross-cutting issues is the definition of the operating limits of the so called in-house provision.

The developments of Italian law, in recent decades, would seem to coincide with the propensity to periodically oscillate between extremes, misaligned, in excess or in defect, from European coordinates.

It should be immediately emphasized that, in principle, European law does not oppose the option of public self-production, in the same way as a priori judgments.

The administrations also have the right to utilize the market, negotiating, are free to choose the alternative of self-production, if necessary assuming the role of company.[38]

European law requires compliance with tender constraints, in the first case, while it requires compliance with the general principles for the protection of competition, to which private companies are subject, in the second case.

The two economic models and the corresponding legal regimes (negotiation and self-organization) remain logically and formally distinct in the EU legal system.[39]

The possibility of choosing between the two alternatives, on an equal footing, is now explicitly established by the "principle of free administration of public authorities", codified by art. 2 of the new directive on administrative concessions.[40]

In short, supranational rules do not prescribe that the public administration should resort to the market; more simply, they prescribe the execution of competitive procedures when it decides to resort to the market, which does not exactly happen when it prefers to self-produce.[41]

---

[38]Brosio (1988).

[39]Dugato (2013, p. 855).

[40]Article 2 of Directive 2014/23 / EU of 26 February 2014, on the awarding of concession contracts; in jurisprudence, see for example Court of Justice, Grand Chamber, 9 June 2009, in case C-480/06, according to which "a public authority can fulfill the tasks of public interest upon it through its own instruments without being obliged to resort to external entities not belonging to its services and may also do so in collaboration with other public authorities"; this is compliant, among the many precedents, with the Court of Justice, 6 April 2006, in case C-410/04; Court of Justice, Sec. I, 11/1/2005 n. C-26/03; among the interpretive documents confirming the orientation, Communication from the Commission on the "application of Community law of public procurement and concessions to institutionalized public-private partnerships", C (2007) 6661, Brussels, 5 February 2008.

[41]European Commission, Communication on "Application of Community law of public procurement and concessions to institutionalized public-private partnerships", C (2007) 6661, Brussels, 5 February 2008, cited: "in Community law, the public authorities are free to carry out their own business or entrust it to third parties, for example to mixed capital entities set up as part of a public-private partnership. However, if a public entity decides to involve a third party in the exercise of an economic activity under conditions constituting a public contract or a concession, it is necessary to comply with the provisions of Community law applicable in the matter". Cf. Contessa (2014).

It has been rightly observed that the legislative and jurisprudential clarification of the assumptions to which the configurability of the in-house is subordinated, made by the European legislator and jurisprudence in the decades between the famous Teckal[42] judgment and the approval of the 2014 directives, cannot be read as an index of prevention towards the institute [or, symmetrically, preferably for alternative solutions], being animated by the very different purpose of tracing the boundary line that marks the transition from the area of the exchange ratio to that of self-production, in order to moderate uncertainty and prevent circumvention, but without undermining the freedom of administrations to choose.[43]

Compared to these simple coordinates, management practices and regulatory constraints, in the Italian legal system, have alternated actions and reactions united by the difficulty in finding the right balance.

The report for 2015 of the Autonomy Section of the Court of Auditors, on "the participated bodies of local authorities"[44]—one of the many documents that can be consulted, for a similar order of evidence—offered a cross-section of the experience gained by five thousand institutions that leaked a use of in-house assignments [or self-styled] to say the least unbridled, in fact.

According to the results obtained[45] "out of a total of 26,324 reports" of custody examined,[46] less than five hundred were based on tenders. These are striking numbers which, together with the figures that measure the economic results, undoubtedly indicate a problem.

Nonetheless, within the theoretical framework, which is still summarized by the principle of free administration, it would have been reasonable to expect that the orderly response to the phenomena of abuse was substantiated by a more accurate monitoring of the use of the in-house procedure, in practice, rather than in preliminary rulings.

But even here, as happened after the season of the scandals that over the last century have swept the subject of contracts, the awareness of the gaps that have made the excess possible has periodically provoked legislative or jurisprudential reactions tending to the extreme opposite.

Thus—again proceeding from examples close in time—the art. 4 of the d.l. n. 138/2011, in an effort to curb the use of in-house provision in the management of local services of economic importance, has a priori limited the operational scope

[42]Court of Justice, 18 November 1999, case C-107/98.

[43]Contessa (2014), Sorace (2010, p. 20) and Trimarchi Banfi (2012, 2013).

[44]Autonomy Section, resolution no. 24/sezaut/2015/ FRG; the document is drafted for the purpose of the report to Parliament, pursuant to art. 7, co. 7, l. June 5, 2003, n. 131.

[45]Through a survey that involved 4935 bodies.

[46]A situation in the equivalent substance is represented by the report for the year 2014, Court of Auditors, Autonomous Section, resolution no. 15/sezaut/2014/ frg.

of the institute much more than would have been licensed by an objective reading of European standards.[47] The subsequent legislation has perpetuated a contrary attitude, moving from a policy of abrupt prohibitions to a policy of dissuasion, based on measures of disincentivation.[48]

A similar closing attitude, according to many commentators, has inspired the draft decree on the management models of local public services of economic importance, designed in implementation of the Madia law and then abandoned, as a result of the ruling of the Constitutional Court that delegated law.

Recent addresses of the administrative magistracy[49] have drawn inspiration from these provisions to support—in the footsteps of the Plenary Meeting n. 1 of 2008[50] and of the sentence of the Constitutional Court 325/2010—that the institute of in-house providing integrates "before a model of organization of the administration, an exception to the general rules of Community law, which require the award of public procurement through the tender".

In fact, these are ideas that echo the questionable philosophy, critically examined some pages above, which has misapplied the discipline of contracts.

The stereotyped use of European decisions on the protection of competition, to limit the in-house procedure, ended up in this way acting as a safe-conduct to regulatory or interpretative operations which, on closer inspection, are rather an expression of distrust in the management administration and its officials.[51]

By widening the view to the larger audience of public holdings, it is possible to see in the restless and chaotic vortex of internal legislation and jurisprudence the signs of a perplexing difficulty, also on this side, to reconcile instances of government of discretion and instances of efficient use of the economic instrument.

---

[47]The sentence of the Constitutional Court n. 199 of 20 July 2012 has overturned the rule, as repetitive of provisions abrogated just the year before, at the end of a referendum consultation, without however calling into question the choice of limitative merit of the in-house procedure and indeed recalling, in the opposite direction, what had already been stated in the judgment of 17.11.2010, n. 325. Cf. Trimarchi Banfi (2012, p. 723) and Caputi Jambrenghi (2012, p. 123).

[48]On the reasons for the change, Camporesi (2015). In this direction, for example, the "crescitalia" decree was promoted—with the endorsement of the Constitutional Court (see judgment of March 20, 2013, No. 46) in regulating the bonuses intended for cost limitation policies in the field of public services (Cocco 2013). In the different sector of the supply of assets and capital goods, some recent rules on spending review have shown an even more radical closure towards the self-production scheme.

[49]Council of State, Sec. III, 7/5/2015 n. 2291; the sentence is published in the online magazine Law of Public Services, http://www.dirittodeiservizipubblici.it.

[50]Where indeed it is stated (point 8 of the grounds) that "the in-house procedure, as constructed by the jurisprudence of the community, seems to represent, rather than a model of organization of the administration, an exception to the general rules of the law".

[51]Obviously there is no lack of jurisprudential pronouncements of a different sign. For example, Council of State, Sec. III, 24 October 2017, n. 4902, affirmed "the ordinary and non-exceptional nature of in-house assignment, using the conditions" and that the "decision of the administration, if justified, escapes the legitimacy of the administrative judge, save the hypothesis of macroscopic misrepresentation of facts or manifest illogicality".

The matter is vast and intricate and, since the underlying thesis should be sufficiently clear, we prefer to refrain from delving into the details, while instead proposing some brief considerations by way of summary.

The literature on this subject points out that the decline of the season of interventionism in economics, with its vocation to political leadership and to welfareism, has in no way reduced the phenomenon of public participation.

On the contrary, starting from the 1990s the varied processes of liberalization and privatization triggered by the pressure of European law have been accompanied by a phenomenon of proliferation of special or instrumental companies.[52]

These trends have over time increased both the number of participated structures [which, according to the ISTAT report published in December 2014, amounted to 11,024 in 2012][53] and their typological variety.[54]

The study that Assonime[55] conducted in 2008 on the "Principles of reorganization of the legal framework of public societies" identified—as a schematization that certainly does not do justice to the wide variety of the phenomenon—at least three groups of mutations (in turn distinctions and substitutions), on the part of companies in public hands engaged in business activities: companies that have real public functions, companies that provide instrumental services, and in-house companies.[56]

Many official reports—for example the aforementioned Court of Auditors' report on "the participated bodies of local authorities"[57]—warn that in this flourishing propagation of forms and organizational articulations, the corporate instrument has often been the objective of forcing protective rules of competition or avoiding public finance constraints, especially at the local level.

Driven by the usual reflection, the system has tried to limit the elusive impulses with further special rules or with interpretative solutions derogating from the common code rules.

In the name of the need to prevent arbitrations or waste—in spite of the lack of tolerance of European law for the adulteration of corporate law, which is the expression of the rulings of the Court of Justice in the matter of golden share— a dizzying succession of rules, often episodic, issued without an overview, has varying degrees and, depending on the case, limited the autonomy of private law of public bodies or promoters, circumscribed the operating scope of the investee companies, subject to the insolvency regime the recruitment of personnel, subjected the directors

---

[52]Chiti (2009), Clarich (2010), Dugato (2013), Scoca (2005, p. 239), Goisis (2006, p. 2961), Ibba (2011), Pizza (2007) and Valaguzza (2012).

[53]ISTAT, the public subsidiaries in Italy, December 22, 2014, at www.istat.it.

[54]Marcovecchio (2012, p. 104).

[55]See the critical evaluations of Assonime, *Principi di riordino del quadro giuridico delle società pubbliche,* September 2008, in www.astrid-online.it.

[56]Clarich (2009) and Marcovecchio (2012, p. 104).

[57]Deliberation n. 24 / sezaut / 2015 / FRG, cit.; see also Chamber of Deputies, Research Department—Department of Budget, Societies with public participation, Dossier n. 337, 4 April 2012, in http://documenti.camera.it/leg16/dossier/Testi/bi0506.htm.

of the company to the jurisdiction of the Court of Auditors, contingent on their fees, limited recourse to arbitration procedures, pressed for the publicizing of controls.

This chaotic situation has given rise, according to a critical thought not without arguments, "to a legislation whose application appears sometimes uncertain, rich in difficulties, which has obfuscated the chain of responsibilities – as a consequence above all of the difficulties it has produced in legal interpretation – at the exact moment in which it intended to expand them".[58]

There is no point in dwelling on the indisputable fact that the distortion of the code model, the bundling of legal constraints on choices that should normally fall within the entrepreneurial autonomy, according to market assessments, the uncertainty generated by the fragmentation and confusion of the legislative and jurisprudential framework are all serious obstacles to the efficiency of management.

Encouraged by the growing confusion, even in this matter the Italian legislator has produced a last-minute effort to rationalize.

The law 7 August 2015, n. 124, for the reform of the public administration, has in fact delegated to the government the approval of a Consolidated Law for the reorganization of the discipline of public holdings.

This time the delegation was implemented and the text was actually approved [D. Lgs. 19 August 2016 n. 175, supplemented by Legislative Decree 16 June 2017 no. 100].

The legislative operation deserves undoubted appreciation, but it is too early to offer a judgment on the relative results.

11.3.4 Conclusion

The conditions for some short observations appear to be ripe at the end of the section.

Looking at a more or less remote past, the analysis conducted intends to show the inconsistency of the claim to conform the intervention of the PA, as an economic actor, to the logic of supremacy of the objectives of limiting discretion, without regard for efficiency.

When at stake are non-trivial economic operations, when a certain threshold of complexity is overcome, there is no quantity of rules that can act as a surrogate to a capable official.

The attempt to replace competences with instructions is a futile operation doomed to failure, which European law does not encourage at all.

As the Nigro commission clearly stated, in presenting the unprecedented proposal to combine, within the general law on the procedure, the principle of informality of the administrative action to the serious exploitation of the institute of the person in

[58] Antonioli et al. (2015).

charge of the procedure, simplification and professionalization are two sides of the same coin, two ingredients of a single solution.[59]

Similarly, the inflation of norms or constraints and official's deresponsibilization are two sides of the same problem.

Aware of this link, the green paper on the modernization of procurement, which contributed to the preparation of the directives approved in 2014,[60] has rightly warned that the valorisation of flexible procedures must necessarily be accompanied by a strengthening of the competences and negotiation skills of the administration.[61]

In this sense, the mitigation of the factors of weakness and fragmentation of public intervention, in the investigated economic sectors, passes through investment policies that are functional to the redevelopment of administrative personnel, to complement and counterbalance spending cuts and organizational aggregations.

It is also urgent to refine the measures to prevent the phenomena of waste or corruption that are not resolved in the habitual [ineffective] consolidation of rules and procedural constraints.

The decision to enhance the soft law tools, renouncing the heavy regulatory apparatus that served as a complement to the previous code of contracts, together with the strengthening of the tasks and guidance functions of A.N.A.C., envisaged by Legislative Decree No. 50/2016, would seem to be symptomatic operations of the desire to relax legal constraints and to give dynamism to the market and public commissions, but a more balanced development of rules and competences remains for the moment a goal to be achieved.

11.4 Critical and Reconstructive Profiles: Evolution of the "Regulatory State"

11.4.1 The Changing Object of the Regulatory State

An issue to be explored is the difficulty in which the regulatory state is found by the nature of the object treated, i.e. the market.

The constitution of the European single market, in the context of the broader globalization of the economy, leads to a market without a state, both because the supranational market overlaps with the national market and because the global economy is without legal rules, for the inexistence of a level of world government.

---

[59]Nigro (1966) and Cafagno et al. (2013, p. 493).

[60]COM (2011) 15 Def.

[61]The Economic and Social Committee, in its opinion delivered on 13 July 2011 on the same Green Paper, has in its turn remarked (Section 3.6.4) that "the negotiation of contracts, especially if complex, requires (...) that the buyer has a considerable skill set. The introduction of a general negotiated procedure will have to be accompanied by a series of measures aimed at ensuring that purchasers can have staff with the necessary skills and experience".

What unites the two phenomena is the flight of the economy from the national regulation and, consequently, a modification of the public administrative structures. And yet national states continue to participate in regulating the economy through a variety of public entities, such as ministries, agencies and independent administrative authorities.

We limit ourselves to examining three particular issues: (a) the lack of legal rules in the global economy; (b) the rules of a supranational market; (c) the sectorialization of the regulatory discipline at the national level.

11.4.2 The Lack of Legal Rules in the Global Economy

The flight of the economy from regulation is evident in the globalized institutional system due to the weakness of international institutions and the overlap between differentiated legal systems, such as state or supranational sections (WTO, WHO, etc.). And so the law cannot cope with a globalized economy.

It is a stateless economy, in the sense that regulation is impossible due to the nature of the object being treated. It is the terrain of large financial transactions, international commercial agreements, different tax policies that encourage or discourage industrial investments.

And even the big issues related to the survival of the planet, such as the protection of the environment, end up being the subject of agreements without effective normative value, since the economic considerations of the subscribing countries prevail. Global economic law is therefore not a homogeneous whole, as it consists of "producers of rules and decisions and intersections between different legal, national and ultra-national legal systems".[62]

The problematic point is how in a globalized economy without legal rules supranational or state systems can continue to exist that regulate the economy in their limited territorial boundaries.

Global events affect the economy more than state and supranational regulations. Therefore, the crisis of the Western stock exchanges may be due to the diminished Chinese production, but also to facts apparently not very related to the economic field: it was, for example, shown how the trend of an international football match can influence the behavior of investors on the financial market.

11.4.3 The Regulation of the European Single Market

The development of the European single market has given the European Union an increasing number of new ways of intervening in the economy. The transformation

[62] D'Alberti (2008, p. 134).

of the State from producer to regulator is not a necessity imposed by the accession to the European Union, since what matters for the European legislator is to guarantee competition where there is also a public entity producing goods and services. Indifference as to the producer or manager does not mean that European legislation does not take into account the asymmetries to the advantage of former monopolists or fictitiously subject to privatization. What we want to point out here is a further evolution of the process of unification of the European market, which takes powers and functions away from the national states with modifications to the state administrative apparatus, leading to a qualitatively different intervention by the Community institutions.

One of the clearest expressions is the regulation of the financial and banking markets, increasingly deeper after the Basel III agreement, which provides for a progressive transition to the European regulation and banking supervision, in implementation of a project for European Banking Union.[63]

In this context, a decisive role is played by the European Central Bank (ECB), whose broad functions appear increasingly distant from traditional institutional relations.[64] Not only there is an extension of the powers conventionally assigned by the Treaty, but also new methods of control over central banks and, ultimately, the fiscal policies of national states. There is no legal justification for the control powers exercised by the ECB on independent subjects such as central banks. One cannot explain the democratic legitimacy of a technical body capable of binding national parliamentary assemblies on the sustainability of public budgets. It is a transfer of functions to a technical subject without a real federal option of the States that make up the Union. The concern expressed by national constitutional courts and constitutional doctrine provides evidence that this is a slippery road.

The fact remains—for the state administrative organization—that this form of regulation involves the reduction of the functions of the state administrations, as happens in the specific case of the Bank of Italy.

From this point of view, it also explains the control over expenditure exercised by the European Court of Auditors, in agreement with the national courts of auditors, especially through the financial audit, which makes it possible to verify compliance with the financial parameters of the Union and of the balance of public budgets, which contribute to the formation of the consolidated account.[65] Any unification of different systems requires control of the market and prices, which is possible only by governing the monetary base, public expenditure, and the exchange rate. In the case of the Union it is clear that the single lever of the single currency—which was not adopted by all the countries of the Union—could not guarantee the unification of the market. The strengthening of financial and monetary policy, as well as the introduction of the fiscal compact and the principle of budgetary balance are pieces of a mosaic that is not yet complete.

[63]Siclari (2017a, b).

[64]Zatti (2017).

[65]Siclari (2017a, b).

It is however undeniable, as regards the profile of the national administrative organization, that the ascending process of the functions has led to reductions/suppressions of functions and/or competences of national public entities.

11.4.4 The Sectorialization of the Regulatory Discipline at the National Level

A third issue to be examined is that relating to the wide regulatory activity remaining within the state administration, despite the supranational unification.

The transition from the producer state to the regulatory state is founded in our system on the doctrine of the state that is called "light" or "withdrawal" of the State also in the name of a horizontal subsidiarity, often intended as a substitution of private entities in services related to public responsibility or, on the contrary, as public intervention in cases of insufficient activity of the private subjects.[66]

The same notion of regulation was, moreover, the object of a difficult definition by the Italian doctrine, divided between a broader notion, which includes all the antitrust activity, and a more precise notion, which concerns only the specific actions of the independent authorities equipped with regulatory functions.[67]

From the point of view of the state administrative organization, some of the numerous independent administrative authorities established in our legal system are increasingly becoming governed: this is the case of the Competition Authority and the market, for regulatory powers and regulators of Consob, as well as for the exceptional regulatory, regulatory and sanctioning force now attributed to the National Anti-Corruption Authority.[68]

The fragmentation of regulation is due to the excessive sectoralization of the independent administrative authorities and to the constitutional reform of 2001, which gave the Regions some legislative competences regarding networks and services, also fragmenting the normative discipline on public funding.

However, in the single sectors subject to regulation, the uniform discipline dictated by the administrative authorities realizes a new normative and organizational centralization.[69] It will then be the administrative judge, who has jurisdiction in matters of litigation on the economy, to judge the application of the rules introduced by the independent administrative authorities, despite the type of judicial assessment on the "weak" merit against the specialty of the powers of the Authorities.[70] The fact remains of a high judicial dispute, unmatched by other European States, also due to the substantial lack of confidence in regulation.

---

[66]Manganaro (2014, p. 45).

[67]Lazzara (2017).

[68]Cintioli (2017).

[69]Manganaro (2010, p. 23).

[70]Tropea (2017).

11.4.5 New Perspectives

The analysis carried out demonstrates how the regulation of the market is still today the main form of relationship between public subjects and economic initiative.

As regards the structure of the national administrative organization, it produces differentiated effects: supranational structures that replace national subjects; intersections between national bodies and the European Union; new and greater powers of national administrations, such as independent administrative authorities.

One point should be emphasized in particular as regards the administrative organization.

If the economy escapes a normative discipline intended as a definition of rules of conduct, what makes the difference in terms of effectiveness and efficiency cannot be the determination of the rules, but the methods of implementation of them by the administrative structures, to leave open the reflection if the model or its implementation is wrong.[71]

The enlargement of legislation is not an adequate response to the needs of well-being and economic and social growth, which underlie public intervention policies in the economy. This is evident proof of the inefficiency and corruption of the public procurement sector, despite the presence of a thousand articles contained in the Code of public contracts and in the related regulation.

Inequalities, inefficiencies and illegal conducts originate from the different implementation of the same rules by administrative structures that are too different across the national territory and throughout Europe, with the consequence that the "inequality of administrative capacity inevitably affects the operation of a homogeneous market and the competitiveness of companies".[72]

Focusing only on the idea of better and more precise regulation is not sufficient, since a normative view does not resolve the question of a different and asymmetric implementation of it.

A substantial investment of economic resources is necessary for the structures and training of the personnel of the public administrations in charge of managing economic facts in a professional manner. It is therefore necessary to implement organizational measures that go from the qualification and/or reduction of the purchasing centers up to the best use of European funding often lost due to design or management ineptitude.

The only productive investment of the country would be a public administration that is able to be the engine of economic and social development.

[71]Trimarchi Banfi (2012).

[72]Napolitano (2011).

References

Aimo P (2015) L'unificazione amministrativa [legge 20 marzo 1865, n. 2248] e l'evoluzione post-unitaria. Comuni e Province, funzioni e controlli [All. A], in Annale ISAP, 23/2015

Antonioli M, Goisis F, Maltoni A, Perfetti LR (2015) Manifesto per una riforma di sistema delle società a partecipazione pubblica. Diritto dei servizi pubblici, 9 marzo 2015, www.dirittodeiservizipubblici.it

Bajari P, Tadelis S (2006) Incentives and award procedures: competitive tendering vs. negotiations. In: AA.VV (ed) Handbook of Procurement, a cura di N. Dimitri, G. Piga, G. Spagnolo. Cambridge University Press, Cambridge

Brosio G (1988) Perché esistono le burocrazie pubbliche? Elementi per una teoria positiva dell'organizzazione del settore pubblico. In: Economia Pubblica

Brosio G [a cura di] (1989) In: AA.VV. La teoria economica dell'organizzazione, Quaderni di "problemi di amministrazione pubblica", n. 13. Formez, Il Mulino, Bologna

Cafagno M (2001) Lo stato banditore. Giuffrè, Milan

Cafagno M, Botto A, Fidone G, Bottino G [a cura di] (2013) In: Aa.Vv. Negoziazioni pubbliche. Scritti su concessioni e partenariati pubblico-privati. Milano

Calandra P (1978) Storia dell'amministrazione pubblica in Italia. Bologna

Camporesi R (2015) Il piano di razionalizzazione delle società partecipate locali nella legge di stabilità 2015. Diritto dei servizi pubblici, gennaio 2015, http://www.dirittodeiservizipubblici.it

Caputi Jambrenghi V (2012) I servizi pubblici: dal monopolio alla concorrenza. In: Aa.Vv (ed) Il contributo del diritto amministrativo in 150 anni di Unità d'Italia, a cura di M. Spasiano. Editoriale scientifica, Napoli, p 123 ff

Carullo A (2005) Lezioni di diritto pubblico dell'economia. Cedam, Padova, p 225 ff

Cassese S [a cura di] (2012a) La nuova costituzione economica. Bari, p 9

Cassese S (2012b) L'Italia: una società senza Stato? Il Mulino, Bologna. cap. I

Chiti MP (2009) Carenza della disciplina delle società pubbliche e linee direttrici per un riordino. www.astrid-online.it

Cintioli F (2017) L'Autorità garante della concorrenza e del mercato e il suo ruolo unificante nell'ordinamento. In: Cafagno M, Manganaro F (eds) L'intervento pubblico nell'economia (a 150 anni dell'unificazione amministrativa italiana), a cura di L. Ferrara, D. Sorace. Firenze University Press, Firenze

Ciocca P (2006) Come funziona, e non funziona, una economia di mercato. In: Aa. Vv (ed) Economia per il diritto, a cura di P. Ciocca, I. Musu. Bollati Boringhieri, Torino, p 19 ff

Ciocca P (2012) Centocinquant'anni: per una 'teoria della storia economica' d'Italia. Rivista di storia economica 1:9 ff

Clarich M (2009) Società di mercato e quasi – amministrazioni. Dir. amm. 2:253 ff

Clarich M (2010) Le società partecipate dallo Stato e dagli enti locali fra diritto pubblico e diritto privato. In: Guerrera F [a cura di] Le società a partecipazione pubblica. Torino, p 1 ff

Coase RH (1989) La natura dell'impresa. In: Brosio G [a cura di] Aa.Vv. La teoria economica dell'organizzazione, Quaderni di "problemi di amministrazione pubblica", Formez n. 13. Il Mulino, Bologna, p 167

Cocco G (2013) L'in house providing fra giustizia amministrativa e Corte Costituzionale. Diritto dei servizi pubblici, 5 luglio 2013, www.dirittodeiservizipubblici.it

Comporti GD [a cura di] (2011) In: Aa.Vv. Le gare pubbliche: il futuro di un modello. Editoriale Scientifica, Napoli

Contessa C (2014) L'in house providing quindici anni dopo: cosa cambia con le nuove direttive, novembre 2014, www.giustizia-amministrativa.it

Corso G (2007) Liberalizzazione: le premesse di diritto europeo. Istituzioni del Federalismo 2:279 ff

Crocker KJ, Masten SE (1988) Mitigating contractual hazards: unilateral options and contract length. Rand J Econ 19:327 ff

D'Alberti M (2008) Poteri pubblici, mercati e globalizzazione. Bologna, p 85

Di Gaspare G (2015) Diritto dell'economia e dinamiche istituzionali. Milano
Dimitri N, Piga G, Spagnolo G [a cura di] (2006) In: Aa.Vv., Handbook of procurement. Cambridge University Press, Cambridge
Doni N (2005) L'affidamento mediante gara di contratti pubblici: l'importanza della reputazione. Pol. econ.: 307 ff
Doni N, Mori PA (2011) Appalti pubblici e discrezionalità: problemi e soluzioni secondo la teoria economica. In: Aa.Vv (ed) Le gare pubbliche: il futuro di un modello. Editoriale Scientifica, Napoli, p 41 ff
Dugato M (2013) Le società a partecipazione pubblica. Giornale dir. Amm. 8–9:855 ff
Fama EF, Jensen MC (1989) La separazione della proprietà dal controllo. In: Brosio G [a cura di] Aa.Vv. La teoria economica dell'organizzazione, Quaderni di "problemi di amministrazione pubblica", Formez n. 13. Il Mulino, Bologna, p 213
Giannini MS (1981) Istituzioni di diritto amministrativo. Giuffrè, Milan, p 459 ff
Goisis F (2006) Imprese pubbliche. In: Diz. dir. pubbl. Cassese, IV. Giuffrè, Milan, p 2961 ff
Goldberg (1997) Regolamentazione e contratti amministrati [trad. it.]. In: Aa.Vv (ed) Concorrenza, monopolio, regolamentazione, a cura di D. Grillo, M. Cossutta. Il Mulino, Bologna, p 342 ff
Ibba C (2011) Le società a partecipazione pubblica: tipologie e discipline. In: Ibba C, Malaguti MC, Mazzoni A [a cura di] Le "società pubbliche". Torino, p 1 ff
Irti N (2004) L'ordine giuridico del mercato. Laterza ed, Bari
Klemperer P [a cura di] (1999) In: Aa.Vv. The economic theory of auctions, vol. I e II. Edward Elgar, Cheltenham
La Spina A, Majone G (2000) Lo Stato regolatore. Il Mulino, Bologna
Laffont JJ, Tirole J (1993) A theory of incentives in procurement and regulation. The M.I.T. Press, Cambridge
Lazzara P (2017) La funzione regolatoria: contenuto, natura e regime giuridico. In: Cafagno M, Manganaro F (eds) L'intervento pubblico nell'economia (a 150 anni dell'unificazione amministrativa italiana), a cura di L. Ferrara, D. Sorace. Firenze University Press, Firenze
Ledda F (1982) Per una nuova normativa sulla contrattazione pubblica. In: Aa.Vv (ed) Studi in onore di Antonio Amorth, vol. I, Scritti di diritto amministrativo. Giuffrè, Milan, p 317 ff
Lindsay CM (1989) Una teoria degli enti pubblici. In: Brosio G [a cura di] Aa.Vv. La teoria economica dell'organizzazione, Quaderni di "problemi di amministrazione pubblica", Formez n. 13. Il Mulino, Bologna, p 377
Manganaro F (2010) La giustizia innanzi all'Autorità garante della concorrenza e del mercato. Il dir. dell'econ. 1:23 ff
Manganaro F (2014) Le amministrazioni pubbliche in forma privatistica: fondazioni, associazioni e organizzazioni civiche. Dir. amm. 1–2:45 ff
Marcovecchio VA (2012) Presenza e diffusione delle società pubbliche nell'ordinamento italiano. Il diritto dell'economia 25(78):104 ff. [2-2012]
Mazzucato M (2014) Lo Stato innovatore. Laterza ed, Bari
Merusi F (2012) La disciplina pubblica delle attività economiche nei 150 anni dall'Unità d'Italia. In: Spasiano M [a cura di], Aa.Vv. Il contributo del diritto amministrativo in 150 anni di Unità d'Italia, Editoriale scientifica, Napoli, p 185 ff
Merusi F (2013) Il sogno di Diocleziano. Il diritto nelle crisi economiche. Torino
Moe TM (1989) La nuova economia dell'organizzazione. In: Brosio G [a cura di], Aa.Vv. La teoria economica dell'organizzazione, Quaderni di "problemi di amministrazione pubblica", Formez n. 13. Il Mulino, Bologna, p 25 ff.
Napolitano G (2011) Le norme di unificazione economica. Riv. trim. dir. pubbl. 1:97 ff
Napolitano G, Abrescia M (2009) Analisi economica del diritto pubblico. Il Mulino, Bologna, p 203 ff
Nigro M (1966) Studi sulla funzione organizzatrice della pubblica amministrazione. Giuffrè, Milan
Nigro M (1980) Il governo locale, I, Storia e problemi. Roma
Ogus A (2000) La regolazione dei servizi privatizzati. In: Aa. Vv (ed) I servizi a rete in Europa, a cura di E. Ferrari. Cortina, Milano, p 19 ff

Orlando VE (1940) Diritto pubblico generale. Milano
Pericu G (2009a) La disciplina degli appalti pubblici in Italia. In: Scritti scelti. Giuffrè, Milan, p 631 ff
Pericu G (2009b) Privatizzazione e servizio pubblico. In: Scritti scelti. Giuffrè, Milan, p 833 ff
Picozza E, Ricciuto V (2013) Diritto dell'economia. Giappichelli, Turin, p 65 ff
Pizza P (2007) Le società per azioni di diritto singolare tra partecipazioni pubbliche e nuovi modelli organizzativi. Giuffrè, Milan
Rizzo I (1994) I contratti nella Pubblica amministrazione: considerazioni metodologiche per una verifica empirica. Econ. pubbl.:7 ff
Schmidt KM, Schnitzer M (1997) Methods of privatization: auctions, bargaining and give-aways. In: Giersch H (ed) Privatization at the end of the century. Springer, Berlin, p 97 ff
Scoca FG (2005) Il punto sulle c.d. società pubbliche. Dir. econ.:239 ff
Siclari D (2017a) La regolazione bancaria e dei mercati finanziari: dalla 'neutralizzazione' dell'indirizzo politico sul mercato all'unificazione europea. In: Cafagno M, Manganaro F (eds) L'intervento pubblico nell'economia (a 150 anni dell'unificazione amministrativa italiana), a cura di L. Ferrara, D. Sorace. Firenze University Press, Firenze
Siclari D (2017b) Corte dei conti e istituzioni superiori di controllo. In: Cafagno M, Manganaro F (eds) L'intervento pubblico nell'economia (a 150 anni dell'unificazione amministrativa italiana), a cura di L. Ferrara, D. Sorace. Firenze University Press, Firenze
Sorace D (2010) I servizi pubblici economici nell'ordinamento nazionale ed europeo, alla fine del primo decennio del XXI secolo. In: Aa. Vv (ed) La regolazione dei servizi di interesse economico generale, La regolazione dei servizi di interesse economico generale, a cura di E. Bruti Liberati, F. Donati. Giappichelli, Turin, p 10 ff. and 20 ff
Sorace D [a cura di] (2013a) In: Aa. Vv. Amministrazione pubblica dei contratti. Editoriale scientifica, Napoli
Sorace D (2013b) L'amministrazione europea secondo il Trattato di Lisbona. Diritto pubblico 1:167 ff
Torricelli S (2016) Le privatizzazioni nelle gestioni dei servizi pubblici. Dalla unitarietà alla disgregazione dei modelli, in this Volume
Trimarchi Banfi F (1992) Organizzazione economica ed iniziativa privata e organizzazione economica ad iniziativa riservata negli artt. 41 e 43 della Costituzione. Politica del diritto 1:3 ff
Trimarchi Banfi F (2012) Procedure concorrenziali e regole di concorrenza nel diritto dell'Unione e nella Costituzione [all'indomani della dichiarazione di illegittimità delle norme sulla gestione dei servizi pubblici economici]. Rivista italiana di diritto pubblico comunitario 5:723 ff
Trimarchi Banfi F (2013) Il principio di concorrenza: proprietà e fondamento. Diritto amministrativo:15 ff
Trimarchi Banfi F (2014) Lezioni di diritto pubblico dell'economia. Giappichelli, Turin, p 26 ff
Tropea G (2017) Il giudice amministrativo, giudice dell'economia. In: Cafagno M, Manganaro F (eds) L'intervento pubblico nell'economia (a 150 anni dell'unificazione amministrativa italiana), a cura di L. Ferrara, D. Sorace. Firenze University Press, Firenze
Valaguzza S (2012) Società miste a partecipazione comunale. Ammissibilità e limiti. Giuffrè, Milan
Vickrey W (1961) Counterspeculation, auctions, and competitive sealed tenders. J Finance 16(1):8 ff
Williamson O (1986a) Le istituzioni economiche del capitalismo, trad. it. Franco Angeli, Milan
Williamson OE (1986b) La gara per la concessione di sfruttamento di un monopolio naturale. In: Le istituzioni economiche del capitalismo, trad. it. Franco Angeli, Milan, p 485 ff
Wolfstetter E (1995) Auctions: an introduction. J Econ Surv 10(4):367 ff
Zatti F (2017) Il controllo della BCE sulle economie nazionali. In: Cafagno M, Manganaro F (eds) L'intervento pubblico nell'economia (a 150 anni dell'unificazione amministrativa italiana), a cura di L. Ferrara, D. Sorace. Firenze University Press, Firenze

Chapter 12
Regulation of the Italian Banking Sector: From the 1936 Banking Law to the European Banking Union

Marcello Clarich

Contents

Abstract The article traces the evolution of the regulation of banks in Italy from the banking law of 1936 to the recent changes made at European level with the banking union project. Until the 1980s the banking system was characterised by a low level of competition combined with a high level of stability. Banking crises were resolved with the guidance of the Bank of Italy without causing losses to depositors. Following the implementation of the banking union, the regulatory model changed radically. The resolution of failing Italian banks, monitored at European level, has also become more complex due to a strict interpretation of state aid rules by the European Commission. To cope with the new scenarios, Italian banks are likely to have to strengthen or merge.

12.1 Introduction

Economic and financial crises, from that of the 1930s to the most recent in 2008-2011, have reinforced the belief that banks are special companies to be subjected to public regulation. Indeed, unlike companies operating in other sectors

M. Clarich (✉)
The Sapienza University of Rome, Rome, Italy
e-mail: marcello.clarich@uniroma1.it

D. Sorace et al. (eds.), *The Changing Administrative Law of an EU Member State*,
https://doi.org/10.1007/978-3-030-50780-0_12

(e.g. manufacturing or construction), the failure of a bank not only affects shareholders, creditors and employees. A large bank in crisis can compromise the solvency of other banks that are healthy but are also significantly exposed to the insolvent bank on the interbank market. This triggers the so-called domino effect, which compromises the stability of the entire financial system. The consequences can be devastating for the economic system as a whole, which sees credit flows essential to the healthy growth of non-bank companies dry up.

For these reasons, all economically developed countries have implemented financial and banking legislations for many decades, overseen by supervisory authorities with very strong regulatory, inspection, authorising and disciplinary powers.

The Great Depression of the Thirties also caused the collapse of major credit institutions in Italy that were saved thanks to state intervention. In an institutional response, a banking law was issued in 1936 which formed the legislative foundation for the public regulation and oversight of credit institutions, entrusted primarily to the Bank of Italy, for more than fifty years.

At the European level, the supervisory role and the practices followed by the Bank of Italy helped manage banking crises by preventing them from contaminating the system as a whole and giving security to savers facing the risk of losses. The primary objective of stabilising the credit system has for decades been the 'compass' that has guided supervisory activity. To that end, the banking law attributed broad discretionary powers to the top bodies of the credit system so as to allow national regulators to shape the structure of the market by limiting the territorial expansion and operations of supervised banks ("structural oversight"). Prior to the breaking of European law towards the end of the last century and in the years that followed the 2008 financial crisis, the goal of improving the competitiveness of the banking market has played a secondary role.

The banking law of 1936 also contained a directive component, making it possible to coordinate and guide banking activity towards economic or industrial policy objectives set by the government. This component was in line with the legislation of the 30s, driven by corporatism and the expansion of public interference in economic sectors to the detriment of the freedom of enterprise.

Unlike what happened in other countries (in particular Germany), the directive component of the banking law affected the actions and practices of supervisory authorities for a long time.

The scenario changed in the fourth quarter of the last century and in more recent years following the application of European credit guidelines that have led to at least two paradigm shifts. Firstly, the banking sector has opened up to greater competition following the creation of a single European market, which establishes a level playing field for business. The directive component of the 1936 banking law and the attribution of the system of largely discretionary powers to the top authorities proved incompatible with the context of promoting competition. Secondly, as a reaction to the 2008 financial crisis and the years that followed, supervisory roles over large banks and roles overseeing the prevention and resolution of banking crises were devolved to European institutions, and in particular to the European Central Bank, rather than to individual Member States.

In anticipation of conclusions, the shifts in the regulatory environment have deeply affected the role and powers of national regulatory authorities and have made it more difficult to save national banks affected by the crisis. In some cases, for the first time in many decades, even savers suffered losses, as will be discussed, in application of the new European rules on the so-called "bail-in".

From a more general point of view, the evolution of the banking and financial regulations of the last fifty years—as has occurred in many other sectors of the Italian administrative system—has been marked by two main trends.

The first is the 'Europeanisation' of rules and systems, with the passage from a closed regulatory and governance system on a strictly national level (and even separate to some extent from the general legislation) to a system based on European rules, with European regulators having gradually reduced the role of nation states. This has meant a significant transfer of sovereignty to supranational institutions, without these being anchored to democratically legitimate mechanisms that would ensure they are fully accredited in the eyes of the electorate and public opinion.

The second trend concerns the gradual "depoliticisation" of duties which, as will be discussed, had ultimately fallen at the hands of government politicians at least until the 1980s. European regulators have been set up independent of national governments, placing emphasis on technology and on the objectivity and uniqueness of the public interest entrusted to them (currency stability, sound and prudent management of banks).

To grasp the particular characteristics of the Italian model compared with the experience of other systems, the evolution of the regulatory system needs to be retraced in a more analytical manner up until the most recent years.

12.2 The First Phase Leading Up to the Banking Law of 1936

As already mentioned, the banking law of 1936,[1] which followed the similar German law of 1934, for decades formed the foundation on which the system of supervision over credit institutions operating in Italy was governed. It in fact remained in force until the Consolidated Banking Act was approved by Legislative Decree No. 385 of September 1st 1993.

It also consolidated the special status of the banking enterprise with respect to other commercial enterprises, which had already begun to establish itself in previous decades. The 1882 Code of Commerce classed "banking operations" as "acts of commerce" and those who habitually carry them out "merchants". Specific rules

[1]R.D.R. No. 375 of March 12th 1936. On the evolution of banking regulations see Nigro (1972), Vitale (1977), Vignocchi (1974) and Capriglione (1978).

applied to just six institutions authorised to issue banknotes, i.e. bearer instruments designed to serve as legal tender in the payment system.

The need to establish a special statute for the banking enterprise emerged following periodic banking crises (1892–1893, 1907, 1921), in some cases due in part to a perverse interweaving between politics and business.

This saw an initial response in 1926 through several regulatory measures. Firstly, the Bank of Italy (established in 1883) was granted the right to issue banknotes, consolidating the monetary and lender functions of a central bank into a single institution.[2] Secondly, an initial regulation was introduced to protect savers. This gave the Ministry of Finance powers of prior authorisation over banking activities and opening branches. The Bank of Italy took on supervisory functions over all credit companies and institutions (including savings banks).[3] Special requirements were introduced for banking enterprises (minimum capital, mandatory reserves, minimum ratio of assets to deposits) aimed at preventing bank collapses.

A more detailed set of regulations for the credit sector was only introduced following the crisis of 1929, which overwhelmed major Italian banks operating according to the mixed bank model (having significant shareholdings in industrial companies).

These were saved through indirect state measures applied through public bodies such as the *Istituto di Liquidazioni* (Liquidation Institute) and later the *Istituto per la Ricostruzione Industriale* (Institute for Industrial Reconstruction, IRI) established in 1933.

In Germany, the big banks (*Grossbanken*) were bailed out in 1932 thanks to direct state intervention, resulting in their "socialisation" and "quasi-statisation". However, unlike events in Italy, once the most challenging phase of the crisis was over they were put back in the hands of private shareholders within just a few years.[4]

The banking law of 1936[5] firstly set out a top structure for a single and consistent banking system. It was headed by an interministerial committee (*Comitato Interministeriale per il Credito ed il Risparmio*, CICR) entrusted with credit oversight, the Ministry of the Treasury and, above all, the Bank of Italy. The latter assumed a direct supervisory role over credit companies (operating in short-term credit) and credit institutions (specialising in medium- and long-term credit) which it

[2]R.D.L. No. 812 of May 6th 1926.

[3]R.D.L. No. 1511 of September 7th 1926 and R.D.L. No. 1830 of November 6th 1926. Savings banks, set up for charitable purposes and to promote the spirit of saving among grass-roots classes, had gradually taken on the characteristics of actual banks and had been bound by special regulations since the end of the nineteenth century (Law No. 5546 of July 15th 1888).

[4]Pohl (1982), p. 274.

[5]With the structural changes implemented in the immediate post-war period, in particular through Legislative Decree of the Provisional Head of State No. 691 of July 17th 1947, which replaced the original Committee of Ministers with the Interministerial Committee for Credit and Savings and entrusted bank oversight to the Bank of Italy, in place of the defunct *Ispettorato per la difesa del risparmio e per l'esercizio del credito* (Inspectorate for the Protection of Savings and for the Use of Credit).

exercised through extremely broad prescriptive, authorising and disciplinary powers. Having a system overseen by an interministerial committee composed of the leading politicians from the affected ministries guaranteed a close-knit relationship with the government in general. This created a link between bank activity and the general objectives of economic and industrial policy.

Secondly, the banking law of 1936, while protecting multiple credit entities (ordinary banks, cooperative banks, savings banks, public-law credit institutions, rural and specialised sectoral banks), also subjected them to a common regime under firm public control. The custodianship of public savings and credit activity were defined as "duties of public interest" and as such justified heavy restrictions on the freedom of business and even saw banking categorised as a public service.

The banking company's special status under the banking law was outlined in general terms by the provisions contained therein and was developed in more detail by regulatory acts and supervisory instructions issued by the Bank of Italy. In this respect, there has been talk of "administrativising" the banking regulations entrusted to administrative systems with broad discretionary powers so as to influence the structure of the market and the operations of individual credit institutions (known as "structural supervision").

More specifically, the issuance of authorisation to conduct banking activities required a discretionary assessment by the Bank of Italy in relation to the specific situation of the target market in terms of sufficiency or insufficiency of services offered to savers and businesses and an appropriate level of competition. Rather than just a standard authorisation, this was an all-out administrative concession to carry out a public-sector activity, based on the definition given in the banking law mentioned above, as a task of public interest rather than as a business activity.

The Italian public law doctrine[6] rebuilt the credit system as a special legal system (*ordinamento giuridico sezionale*), independent and partly derogatory from the general (statutory) system in which private entities operate. The banking law in fact introduced all the proper elements of such special legal system: multiple regulated entities, namely different types of credit companies and institutions granted access to the legal system through an admission procedure by a public body (the bank authorisation issued by the Bank of Italy); a public authority or a system of public authorities placed at the top of the system (CICR, Ministry of the Treasury, Bank of Italy) with regulatory and supervisory duties; a set of special rules largely issued directly by the authorities in charge of the sector (internal regulations of the system, such as instructions from the Bank of Italy); a system of special administrative penalties for violation of the rules imposed by the system's top bodies and a system of domestic justice, also internal to the legal system. The duties assigned to the Interministerial Committee for Credit and Savings also include having to resolve claims brought by affected entities against the Bank of Italy's provisions.

[6]See Giannini (1940), p. 707.

The public-sector aspect of the banking system was also accentuated by the fact that most banks were not set up as joint-stock companies but as public entities.

According to their specific legislative classification, these were in fact known as public-law credit institutions (including some of the major Italian banks such as Banca Nazionale del Lavoro, Banco di Napoli and Banco di Sicilia) and special credit institutions. But even savings banks, established in the nineteenth century as a spontaneous emanation of civil society at the local level, had been subject to controls specifically intended (especially under the aforesaid 1888 law) to make jurisprudence classify them as public bodies. The large commercial banks (Banca Commerciale, Credito Italiano, Banco di Roma), following the bailout in the aftermath of the 1929 crisis, remained, albeit in the official role of a private company within state lines. Their shares were in fact held by a public body (IRI), which retained them even once the crisis had been overcome.

12.3 From the 1948 Constitution to the 1980s

The 1948 Constitution, which is still in force today, had no immediate impact on the banking law of 1936.

Firstly, the general constitutional provision on the subject of economic initiative (Article 41) legitimises control and planning regimes intended to guide and coordinate economic activity for social purposes.

Secondly, another more specific provision on the promotion and protection of savings reiterates that it is the duty of the Republic to coordinate and control credit activity (Article 47).

Finally, the Constitution places no specific limits on public property in general (Article 42) or on that of private companies. Indeed, in some areas (public services, monopoly situations) it allows for the nationalisation of individual companies or categories of companies (Article 47). With a banking system already dominated by public banks, introducing this latter provision with regard to the banking system would have made little sense. However, it could have justified actions to nationalise the large banks in France in the aftermath of the Second World War and replicated on an even larger scale in the early 1980s.[7]

Ultimately, the constitutional framework was perfectly in line with the general directive structure of the banking law of 1936. This was certainly not the case with the German Basic Law of 1957 (*Grundgesetzt*), as interpreted by constitutional case law, which guarantees freedom of enterprise from direct measures of public authority. Indeed, in the banking sector, the banking law of 1934 also gave supervisory authorities broad discretion over issuing bank authorisations based on the needs of

[7]This refers to Laws 45-015 of December 2nd 1945 and 82-155 of February 11th 1982, which turned over to the public 36 banks, representing 87.6% of all assets. See, respectively, Laufenberger and Ducrus (1955), p. 481; Vasseur (1982), p. 220.

the local market and the economy as a whole (so-called market demand or *Bedurfnissprufung*). In the period following the Basic Law of 1957, a legislative amendment from 1961 codified and enforced reasons for denial of authorisation based on strictly technical grounds (insufficient assets, directors failing to meet professional requirements, etc.).[8] In Germany, it took a wholly internal evolution to change the approach of the banking law in line with the ordoliberal approach of the overall economic constitution.

In the decades that followed, at least up until the 1980s, the regulatory framework established by the banking law of 1936 ensured the stability of the banking system through the operational activity of the supervisory authorities, at the cost of a certain degree of immobility, inefficiency and a structural segmentation of the market.

Firstly, the functional specialisation of credit institutions was maintained on the grounds of a clear demarcation of the areas of operation of credit companies providing short-term commercial credit, fuelled by overnight deposits, and of special credit institutions dedicated to offering medium- and long-term credit financed by bond issues of an equal period of validity. Furthermore, as a reaction to the failure of the mixed bank model, a ban was placed on overly close interactions between banks and industries.

Secondly, from a subjective point of view, the distinction was maintained between the types of credit companies listed in the 1936 banking law (joint-stock company, cooperative, public bodies), which also precluded processes of aggregation dictated by dimensional growth. The prevalent importance of public banks remained unchanged.

Thirdly, the banking market remained divided between local markets and the national market: the former with a strong presence of regional banks specialising in small savings accounts and financing smaller companies (rural banks, cooperatives and savings banks), the latter populated almost exclusively by the largest credit institutions.

Essentially, the structure and the evolution of the banking market was mainly dependent not on the functioning of the mechanism of competition, but on the administrative decisions of the supervisory authorities. For example, for many years they did not allow for the opening of new branches, which had to be done in line with a national plan.[9] The Bank of Italy even had the power to order the closure of bank branches in pursuit of a more rationalised territorial distribution. Even the ban on different savings branches cohabiting the same square was only removed in 1962.

The extent of the powers attributed in particular to the Bank of Italy allowed it to influence the operational and strategic decisions of the banks by acting informally (known as "moral suasion"). Even crises affecting certain credit institutions were

---

[8]See Mayer (1981), p. 4.

[9]This refers, for example, to the national plan for the opening of new branches approved by the CICR on January 6th 1978.

resolved through operations carried out under the direction of the Bank of Italy without any direct impact on savers.

This Italian experience has elements similar to those of the English one. Supervisory activity, especially over the major London banks, was in fact exercised by the Bank of England essentially through informal contacts and consultations. And this was under a highly embryonic legislation (the Bank of England Act of 1946), containing a single provision that granted the Bank of England the power to request information, make recommendations and, with authorisation from the Ministry of the Treasury, issue orders to banks.[10]

Ultimately, the culture and practices of banking oversight for a long time focused on ensuring the stability of the credit system, preventing in particular the systemic effects of crises, and on protecting the interest of savers who, in the decades following the introduction of the banking law, had suffered no direct losses. Competition in the banking market was of secondary interest, even if the absence of competitive pressure led to a lack of efficiency and a lower propensity to innovate.

12.4 The Consolidated Banking Act of 1993

In the 1980s, the frame of reference gradually evolved to necessitate an overhaul of the regulatory framework, resulting in the adoption of the Consolidated Banking Act of 1993.[11]

The change was brought about by multiple factors. A closed and inefficient market such as banking in the long run favoured the emergence of new financial intermediaries (in particular in the securities, leasing and insurance markets) outside the credit system that could offer alternative financial products to bank credit. These new intermediaries began to take up operational space from credit institutions which, due to regulatory constraints, were unable to expand the range of services they offered. This provided a boost to bank de-specialisation through the gradual lifting of constraints and legislative and administrative restrictions.

At the same time, many credit institutions formed multi-functional groups in order to expand their product and service offerings. This was done through the acquisition of controlling interests in non-bank companies (leasing, factoring, mutual funds, trusts, etc.) which fell outside the scope of bank supervision. Thus emerged the need for regulations on the consolidated supervision of banking groups, both where a bank assumed the role of parent company and where a bank held the position of subsidiary (Legislative Decree No. 356 of November 20th 1990).

The approval of several European directives then proved decisive, first and foremost with Directive No. 77/80/CEE of December 12th 1977, transposed to the

[10]See Pringle (1973), p. 114 examining the advantages and disadvantages of moral suasion.

[11]For developments leading up to the Consolidated Banking Act and its enforcement, see Costi (2012).

Italian system with Presidential Decree No. 350 of June 27th 1985 regarding bank authorisation. Under the new regime, the granting of authorisations was subject to objective technical criteria, expunging all administrative discretion, linked to an assessment of the "economic needs of the market". This facilitated access to the banking market by new credit institutions and helped overcome the directive approach of the banking law.

Of an even greater impact was Directive n. 89/646/CEE of December 15th 1989, transposed to the Italian legal system by Legislative Decree No. 481 of December 14th 1992, which introduced the principle of mutual recognition. Credit institutions were allowed to provide their services in all Member States through subsidiaries, or even directly. Meanwhile, the oversight of foreign branches and activities carried out in other countries was left to the supervisory authority of the home state (principle of "home country control"). The principle of equivalence of bank authorisations was dependent, under the same Directive 89/646/CEE and in other more specific directives that followed, on a minimum harmonisation of the conditions of exercise of banking activity. In this perspective, Legislative Decree No. 481/1992 went beyond the principle of functional specialisation, introducing the universal bank model, making the distinction between the different categories of companies and credit institutions less relevant.

The de-specialisation of the legal structures of the banks was fostered through the conversion of banks established as public bodies into a joint-stock companies. To this end, Law No. 218 of July 20th 1990 (known as the "Amato law") introduced two mechanisms to achieve this result: the direct conversion of banks already having a corporate foundation into joint-stock companies, and the divestment of the bank by the public body and its transfer to a newly-formed company whose shareholding is retained by the public body as a holding company. This second route was followed in particular by savings banks, which took on the status of non-profit organisations (known as "banking foundations") operating in cultural, scientific and social fields. The dividends from the holding in the transferee bank generated funds that would be allocated to disbursements and other measures in the target sectors of activity.

The so-called "cold privatisation", namely the conversion of the legal structure of the banks from a public entities to joint-stock companies, also formed the premise for the so-called "hot privatisation" operations, namely the transfer of packets of control of the original public owned joint-stock companies to private entities. This paved the way for aggregations, as were even unofficially encouraged by the supervisory authorities, aimed at overcoming the sub-optimal size of many credit institutions with strong recoveries of efficiency. Following a complex restructuring process through mergers and incorporations, the major Italian banks (in particular Banca Intesa and Unicredit) took on a size comparable to that of the large banks that have been ever-present in countries such as Germany and France. This enabled them to operate successfully in the context of a single market for banking services offered at the European level.

In a minority of cases, banking foundations fully disposed of their holding in the transferee banking company to concentrate on their non-profit activities. In most cases, they maintained (and still maintain) minority holdings in banking companies resulting from processes of aggregation.[12] This enables them to serve as permanent shareholders in conjunction with other banking foundations which also hold minority shares in the same banking company.

Of significance in a more general context is Antitrust Law No. 287 of October 10th 1990, approved with a considerable delay compared to other European countries and which represented a turning point in relations between the state and the market. Indeed, the law elevated the public interest in the protection and promotion of competition, which for decades had held a space in European treaties with a dedicated implementation by the European Commission.[13] A wide range of powers to ascertain violations and isasue penalties were assigned to a new public institution, the Italian Competition Authority, responsible for applying the new legislation horizontally across all economic sectors.

However, the new legislation contained an important exception with reference to the banking and credit sector. Primary jurisdiction for exercising the new powers was in fact given to the Bank of Italy, after obtaining a non-binding opinion from the Italian Competition Authority (Article 20).[14] As such, particularly in regard to control over bank mergers, the Bank of Italy retained the ability to assess and balance the interest in competition and in stability. Only in 2005, once the so-called savings law was enacted (Law No. 262 of December 26th 2005), was the credit sector also placed back under the primary jurisdiction of the Italian Competition Authority.

Ultimately, as a result of this evolutionary process, banking companies have become full-fledged companies, exposed to competition stimuli and subject to public oversight solely to guarantee their stability and to prevent systemic risks ("prudential supervision"). The soiled directive approach of the 1936 banking law was thus expunged. The culmination of this trend is the Consolidated Banking Act, which brings into the system all the innovations introduced in the previous period.

In a nutshell, the Consolidated Banking Act above all sets out the targets pursued in exercising the powers granted to credit authorities (Interministerial Committee for Credit and Savings, Ministry of Economy and Finance, Bank of Italy): the healthy and prudent management of supervised subjects and the overall stability, efficiency and competitiveness of the financial system (Article 5). Furthermore, supervisory powers must be exercised "in accordance with the provisions of the European Union" (Article 6), thus creating a direct and permanent link with the European level.

Secondly, it explains the "enterprise nature" of banking activity, consisting of the custodianship of public savings and the exercise of credit activity (Article 10.1), thus

---

[12]Today around one third of the 88 banking foundations have completely disposed of their shares.

[13]Only in 2001, following a reform of the Constitution, was the protection of competition given constitutional status as a matter reserved for state legislative sources in determining the scopes of state and regional legislative jurisdictions.

[14]See, on Article 20 of Law No. 287 of 1990, Siri (1993), p. 391.

excluding any public sector connotation. It is reserved for "banks" (paragraph 2), no longer divided into categories and types governed by their own rules.

In line with this vision, the Bank of Italy's issue of banking authorisation is dependent on the fulfilment of a number of conditions strictly regulated by law (legal form of a corporation or cooperative, minimum paid-up capital, requirements of professionalism, integrity and independence of directors, etc.) (Article 14.1). This ruled out all real administrative discretion and thus the possibility of assessing interests other than that of the "sound and prudent management" of the bank (point 2). The Bank of Italy, however, retains technical margins of appreciation, for example when assessing the initial activity programme presented on submission of an application for authorisation.

The Consolidated Banking Act also gives credit authorities broad regulatory powers in the form of regulations, general administrative acts and supervisory instructions designed to regulate the main aspects of banking activity. For example, the requisites of integrity for those with significant holdings in banks and the requisites of professionalism, integrity and independence of those who perform administrative, management and control functions at banks are established by regulations of the Minister of Economy and Finance, after consultation with the Bank of Italy (Articles 25 and 26). Furthermore, fundamental aspects such as capital adequacy, risk containment, available shares, administrative organisation and internal controls, as well as information to be made public, are subject to general provisions of the Bank of Italy issued in compliance with resolutions of the Interministerial Committee for Credit and Savings (Article 53).

The Consolidated Banking Act then outlines a complex system of oversight for banks and banking groups under the Bank of Italy vested with extensive administrative powers (authorising, auditing, disciplinary) (Article 53 et seq.). In the event of a crisis or irregularity, the Bank of Italy may subject the banks to extraordinary administration by appointing one or more extraordinary commissioners (Article 70). In the event of an irreversible crisis, the Bank of Italy may force administrative liquidation, which follows a specific procedure that is different from ordinary bankruptcy proceedings (Article 80 et seq.). The Bank of Italy also exercises supervision over financial intermediaries which are required to register on a special list (Article 106).

Finally, the Consolidated Banking Act contains a number of provisions aimed at guaranteeing the transparency of the contractual conditions in relations between banks and customers (Article 115 et seq.).

Ultimately, since the approval of the Consolidated Banking Act, banks have permanently assumed company status, albeit that of a special company subject to a number of obligations and constraints based on the primary objective of ensuring the stability of the banking system.

The developments following the Consolidated Banking Act have kept the new approach unchanged. In particular, the so-called Savings Law No. 262 of December 28th 2005, issued in reaction to the bankruptcies of several industrial companies (Cirio and Parmalat) which had caused huge losses for savers, adjusted certain aspects of the Bank of Italy's organisational structure and created closer links between Italy's financial authorities (Articles 20, 21 and 22). Similarly, Law No. 33 of March 24th 2015 made the conversion of cooperative banks with assets in excess of €8 billion into joint-stock companies mandatory as part of the de-specialisation of the legal forms of banks, as provided in the Consolidated Banking Act. The same strengthening of the powers of the Bank of Italy, as a result of the transposition of Directive 2013/36/EU by Legislative Decree No. 72 of May 12th 2015, did not alter the structure of relations with supervised banks.

12.5 Developments After the 2008 Financial Crisis

The global financial crisis that broke out in 2008 hit the Italian economic and financial system heavily, and led to a change in its institutional structure through the devolution of regulatory and administrative powers at the European level towards the banking system.

In the period from 2007 to 2014, the crisis led to a 9.1% drop in national gross domestic product and a 30% decline in investments, having significant effects in terms of reducing the standard of living for large swaths of the population and increasing the gap between social classes.[15] A decade later and Italy is one of the few European countries that has still to recover its pre-crisis gross domestic product level. Europe's economic recovery over the last few years is comparatively slower in Italy, with significant divergences between the more economically developed areas of central and northern Italy and the less developed areas of central and southern Italy.

During the very early years of the financial crisis, the Italian banking system seemed more robust than that of other European countries in which, in order to avoid systemic crises, extraordinary support measures were approved in the form of recapitalisations of crisis-hit institutions using public money, state loans and guarantees, etc. Italian banks did not keep high-risk financial assets (or "toxic assets") in their balance sheets and were less exposed to systemic risks than banks in other European countries, which were more directly involved in the development of global finance.

To authorise the bailout of many European banks through extraordinary measures of direct intervention (recapitalisation) or indirect intervention (guarantees and loans) by the states, the European Commission, in a communication on state aid approved in 2008,[16] at the low-point of the crisis, significantly relaxed the

[15]See Macchiati (2016), p. 15. As for the standard of living, it need only be considered that twenty years ago an Italian earned an average of $1500 less than a German in one year, whereas in 2014 that difference was almost $10,000. And Italy's economic advantage over Spain has also declined over the same period from $5000 to $1700. Unlike most European countries and the USA, Italy was hit harder by the recent crisis than it was by that of the 1930s: see Toniolo, currently in publication.

[16]OJ C 270 of October 25th 2008. On the subject of state aid, see Pera et al. (edited by) (2017).

application of the applicable rules on the Treaty on the Functioning of the European Union.[17]

The European Commission thus authorised measures in favour of banks with very short deadlines, without requiring the preliminary drafting of restructuring plans for the recipient bank aimed at minimising the anti-competitive impact and causing no losses to savers and, in particular, holders of subordinated bonds. Many banks in major European countries benefited from public support using a massive amount of public resources, equivalent to several points of GDP.[18]

Meanwhile in Italy, at a very early stage, the government authorities and the leading banks' top management did not see the need for capital strengthening measures to mitigate insolvency risks. Only in four cases were public support measures put in place. The main example was the case of Monte dei Paschi di Siena, with reference to which in 2009 the Italian government approved several urgent measures to increase the capital endowment by underwriting special bonds for an amount of €1.9 billion (known as the Tremonti Bond, named after the Minister of Economy and Finance at the time).[19]

Compared to what happened in other countries, the Italian banking crisis turned out to be severe, and particularly since 2011 due to two destabilising causes. Firstly, the market fallout or growing financial difficulties affecting many Italian industrial companies (especially small- and medium-sized companies) increased the excess of non-performing loans in the balance sheets of creditor banks.[20] For some banks, one exacerbating factor were the overly expansive credit policies and with a high concentration of risk. In order to cope with the losses they had to draw on assets, many of which had fallen to levels below the minimum set by supervisory regulations. Capital increases were often required, at a time when it was not easy to find investors willing to take what were perceived as high risks. Banking foundations with minority shareholdings in the largest Italian banks committed a great deal of resources to this end.

Secondly, Italian banks, whose portfolios contained large numbers of Italian government bonds, saw the value of their investment decline due to the drop in the price of securities in light of the perceived risk of default of the Italian state among

[17]The Commission relied on Article 107.3 of the Treaty on the Functioning of the European Union, which authorises the issue of aid in exceptional circumstances in order to remedy a crisis affecting the economy of a Member State.

[18]As a result of the support measures adopted by German banks, public debt in Germany increased €225 billion from 2009 to 2015. See Giunta and Rossi (2017), p. 182.

[19]In implementation of Legislative Decree No. 185 of January 29th 2008. This issue was authorised according to procedures, criteria and conditions contained in the Ministerial Decree of February 25th 2019. Similar securities were underwritten by the state in favour of Banco Popolare, Banca Popolare di Milano and Credito Valtellinese.

[20]On the banks' expansive credit policies (with an average growth of over 8% in the period from 2000 to 2008), the vulnerability of Italian companies during the economic downturn and the growth of impaired loans, which in June 2016 amounted to €191 billion net of budgetary provisions, see Giunta and Rossi (2017), p. 171.

international investors. This was due to the imbalances in public finance and the loss of confidence in the ability to repay public debt. The sovereign debt crisis made the Italian banking crisis even more critical. A perverse loop was created to be self-feeding, since the bank bailouts from the injection of public funds only served to exacerbate the imbalances in public finance and increased the spread of newly-issued public securities, making the securities held by the same banks depreciate even further.[21]

However, unlike events resolving the banking crises in other countries during the initial aftermath of the 2008 crisis, the bailouts and support measures issued in favour of Italian banks in recent years, as we will see, turned out to be far more complex. This is also due to the change in the institutional framework at European level and a more rigorous interpretation of the Treaty rules on state aid by the European Commission.

As for the change in the European regulatory framework, as the initial response to the 2008 crisis, the European Banking Authority (EBA) was set up in 2011, its primary functions being to regulate and disseminate good supervisory practices in the banking industry. It forms part of the European System of Financial Supervision (ESFS), which comprises three sister authorities in the financial, insurance and banking sectors. The system also includes the European Systemic Risk Board (ESRB). The European Banking Authority, while not providing direct supervision over banks, promotes, through the adoption of binding technical standards and guidelines, the "Single Rulebook", a homogeneous framework of rules designed to ensure a level competitive playing field and to protect savers, as well as harmonising supervisory practices.

Beginning in 2014, a more ambitious reform process began under the name of the "Banking Union", which is still being developed.[22]

Firstly, in 2013, a new banking oversight model was introduced in response to the worsening of the crisis in 2012, giving the European Central Bank direct supervisory powers over the major credit institutions of individual Member States. A new body, the Single Supervisory Mechanism, has been set up within this.[23]

Italy's largest banks have been drawn Europe's centralised oversight system, while the Bank of Italy, traditionally holding top supervisory functions by virtue of the Consolidated Banking Act, has seen its role reduced to that of organisational and functional support with respect to the powers of the European Central Bank.

The latter has established a supervisory style, based in part on rigid performance and risk assessment indicators, which has significantly changed the relationship between supervised and supervisory banks. For many years in Italy, the oversight

[21]On the interweaving between banking risk and sovereign risk see Bini Smaghi (2013), p. 111; Bruni (2017), p. 87.

[22]On the Banking Union see Chiti and Santoro (edited by) (2016); Barucci and Messori (edn.) (2014).

[23]See Regulation (EU) No 1024/2013, adhered to by the Italian legal system with Legislative Decree No. 223 of November 14th 2016.

by a single authority—the Bank of Italy—had nurtured a high level of customer trust in the stability of the banking system and was based on a culture that was "*relatively stable over time and known*" to reassure even the markets.[24]

The change in the institutional framework with the creation of the Single Supervisory Mechanism has made it more difficult for the government and banks with weakened assets to engage in dialogue with the European institutions (the Commission, as well as the European Central Bank) to try and identify the most adequate solutions to prevent or resolve crises.

A second regulatory change is the introduction of a new set of European regulations for resolving banking crises through the "Single Resolution Mechanism", which came into force at the beginning of 2016.[25] The Single Resolution Mechanism introduces tools for the prevention (resolution plans, etc.) and resolution of banking crises, ensuring they do not lead to systemic effects. The new mechanism provides for intervention measures which, from the most recent analysis, may also require forms of public support, albeit in compliance with the principles on state aid. The new functions have been assigned to a new apparatus, the "Single Resolution Board", which must operate in close connection with the European Central Bank and the Commission.

The new regulation is based on the principle that, as a rule, bank bailouts must be implemented through the use of private funds, to be provided by shareholders and holders of subordinated loans (known as a "bail in"). Even in cases where public support measures ("bail outs") are needed to prevent systemic crises likely to put the entire national financial system at risk, these must be reduced to a minimum by eliminating the value of the shares and other securities held by private investors.

The application of new rules, in particular those requiring the involvement of subordinated securities, has not been staggered over time—as was proposed—in the sense that they refer only to issues of securities after the entry into force of the new regulations. As such, in Italy, as well as in other Member States, large categories of investors have for the first time in many decades had to bear significant losses as a result of banking crises (for example in the case of Banca Etruria).

A third component of the Banking Union process, consisting of rules on deposit guarantee schemes, is the subject of a new directive.[26] Meanwhile, the most critical issue of the sharing of risk and burden not just nationally, but at the European level, still remains unresolved. This is due to resistance from several Member States, whose electorates are not willing to concede the massive use of public funds (paid for by taxpayers) to that end.

Regarding the application of the rules of the Treaty on state aid in the most recent phase, the Commission issued a communication in 2013, replacing that of 2008,[27]

---

[24]See Giunta and Rossi (2017), p. 185.

[25]See Directive 2014/59/EU and Regulation (EU) No 806/2014, adhered to by the Italian legal system with Legislative Decree No. 180 of November 16th 2015.

[26]See Directive 2014/49/EU transposed by Legislative Decree No. 30 of February 14th 2016.

[27]OJ C 216/01 of July 30th 2013. On state aid communications, see Clarich (2017).

which reinstated a more rigorous interpretation of the legislation. Accepting that the financial crisis has become less severe, even if yet to be fully overcome, the Commission has made the procedure for approving state aid measures launched by Member States less viable. More specifically, it has given its consent to the adoption by banks of measures to support a restructuring plan aimed at minimising the outlay of public money, while at the same time reducing anti-competitive impact, such as not to undermine the position of competing banks not affected by the crisis. The new Communication is thus based on the principle, as reiterated and developed by the new regulations for the resolution of banking crises, that losses must first be absorbed by shareholders and holders of subordinated loans.

The repercussions of the adjusted regulatory framework on the Italian banking system have been quite significant.

Firstly, during the crisis affecting Banca Tercas, which was put into extraordinary administration by the Bank of Italy, an attempted recovery in 2014 through a capital increase paid up by the Interbank Deposit Protection Fund was met with opposition from the European Commission. The Commission in 2015 considered that the operation had been carried out in violation of state aid rules with a request for repayment of the amount (€265 million). This is since the Interbank Deposit Protection Fund, though funded by bank contributions, operates under the dominant influence of the Bank of Italy.[28] The Commission's decision was the subject of a judicial appeal before the European Court of Justice.

Secondly, in 2015, after going into crisis, four small- or medium-sized banks (Banca Marche, Banca Popolare dell'Etruria and Lazio, Cassa Risparmio di Ferrara, CariChieti) were put into extraordinary administration by the Bank of Italy. It then put forward crisis solutions to ensure their operational continuity. However, for the first time in many decades, losses were absorbed not only by shareholders, but by savers holding subordinated bonds.[29]

Thirdly, after the crisis affecting two Veneto banks (Banca Popolare di Vicenza and Veneto Banca), the European authorities in 2017 did not consider there were systemic risks such as to justify resolution according to the new rules. The two institutions were placed into liquidation in 2017 following the standard procedures established by the Consolidated Banking Act. However, in order not to allow a destruction of value that would interrupt business continuity, the business complexes

---

[28]See European Commission Decision C(2015) 9526 final of December 23rd 2015. The European Commission has deemed that even if the Fund is set up with private resources, it is still recognised by the Bank of Italy (Article 96-*ter* of the Consolidated Banking Act) and its actions are imputable to the Italian State. In fact, Fund membership is mandatory for banks and the actions of the Fund are subject to approval by the Bank of Italy.

[29]Decree Law No. 183 of November 22nd 2015 introduced the institutions resolution, ensuring business continuity through the creation of four new institutions to which the healthy corporate component was sold, but with the entire investment value of the shares and subordinated bonds eliminated and a recapitalisation measure adopted by the National Resolution Fund, supplied by contributions from Italian banks. In 2017, the banks in question were absorbed by UBI Banca S.p.a. for the symbolic price of one Euro.

were transferred in a block to the Italy's largest bank (Banca Intesa). This took place as part of a complex operation which also required the Commission's approval of substantial state aid to Banca Intesa in order to prevent an excessive impact on Veneto's regional economy, in which the two institutions had a very significant presence.

Finally, in the case of Monte dei Paschi di Siena, numerous attempts have been made to resolve the crisis (caused largely by the amount of non-performing loans) through increases in capital (the last unsuccessful attempt coming in late 2016), as necessary following the failure to overcome the stress tests conducted on all European banks by European and national supervisory authorities. With the crisis worsening, the Italian government passed a decree law (No. 237/2016) containing public support measures for liquidity and capital, from which Monte dei Paschi di Siena was able to benefit. Moreover, the bank has been afforded recourse to an instrument for cases of non-irreversible crisis pursuant to the new regulation on resolving banking crises known as precautionary recapitalisation, authorised by the European authorities. It has required the injection of more than €8 billion in public funds and has led to the state assuming the role of the bank's controlling shareholder. The sharing of charges among subordinated loan holders has been reduced to a minimum through a complex system of exchanges between shares of which the bondholders have become holders of newly-issued ordinary bank bonds.

In all of the cases indicated thus far, the negotiations between the Italian and European authorities have been particularly complex, with occasional misunderstandings and tensions that have seen some media coverage. The losses suffered by groups of small investors have had an impact on public opinion and on the electorate, with negative consequences in terms of consensus towards incumbent governments.

12.6 Concluding Notes

The transition from an essentially national banking oversight model, based on a culture of stability, to a European model more oriented to the culture of competition has radically changed the context in which Italian banks operate.

First and foremost, the institutional leaders have changed, with the emergence of new European institutions according to the model of independent authorities. European regulation has become predominant. Administrative powers with respect to individual credit institutions (authorising, prescriptive, disciplinary powers) have also largely stepped out of the national perimeter. At the same time there has been an increased "de-politicisation" of decision-making processes, which are no longer entrusted to political decision-makers (Ministry of Economy and CICR), placing emphasis on technology which appears to have consolidated in numerous areas of public regulation over the last fifty years. Bank oversight and the powers connected to it have lost their political and administrative discretionary status designed to guide and shape the market, retaining only the technical component behind assessments entrusted to the new European bodies.

Assessment of the capital strength of banks has become far more rigorous (under the new "stress test" regulations). The asset strengthening of many Italian banks has required a considerable amount of private fund-raising in the form of capital increases. The accumulation of impaired loans in the balance sheets of many banks has proven (and to some extent still is) a factor of weakness in the Italian banking system.

All this has happened in a context in which public finance imbalances resulting from commitments assumed by the Italian state within the so-called European Fiscal Compact have been left unresolved. As such, the recurrence of the perverse mechanism between the sovereign debt crisis and the banking crisis cannot be ruled out in the future. At the European level, there are discussions on how to introduce new risk mitigation rules as a precursor to creating European-level risk sharing mechanisms, in a context where solidarity between Member States with more stable finances with respect to difficulties affecting other Member States with precarious budgetary situations does not find sufficient consensus.

In a system of common rules, centralised oversight at European level and a rigorous application of state aid regulations, the Italian banking system could see further developments. In particular, this could see concentration processes involving big national banks (such as Banca Intesa and Unicredit) in order to better equipping them to face a competition that is becoming increasingly stiff at the European and global levels.

References

Barucci E, Messori M (ed. 2014) Toward the European Banking Union, Firenze
Bini Smaghi L (2013) Morire di austerità, Bologna
Bruni F (2017) L'unione bancaria e dei mercati dei capitali, in Vv. Aa., Europa – sfida per l'Italia, Roma
Capriglione F (1978) Intervento pubblico e ordinamento del credito, Milano
Chiti M, Santoro V (ed. 2016) L'Unione bancaria europea, Pisa
Clarich M (2017) Sostegno pubblico alle banche e aiuti di stato, in Giurisprudenza Commerciale
Costi R (2012) L'ordinamento bancario, Bologna, V ed
Giannini MS (1940) Osservazioni sulla disciplina della funzione creditizia, in Scritti giuridici in onore di Santi Romano, Padova
Giunta A, Rossi S (2017) Che cosa sa fare l'Italia, Bari
Laufenberger H, Ducrus B (1955) La nationalisation des banques. Illusions et réalité, in Revue de Science et de Législation Frinancière
Macchiati A (2016) Perché l'Italia cresce poco, Bologna
Mayer H (1981) Das Bundesaufsichtsamt fur das Kreditwesen, Düsseldorf
Nigro M (1972) Profili pubblicistici del Credito, Milano
Pera A, Prosperetti L, Siragusa M (ed. 2017) Oltre la crisi: regolazione, concorrenza e aiuti di Stato nei settori bancario e finanziario, in Concorrenza e Mercato, vol 24
Pohl M (1982) Konzentration im Deutschen Bankwewen (1848–1980), Frankfurt
Pringle R (1973) Banking in Britain, London
Siri M (1993) L'applicazione delle regole di concorrenza nel settore bancario, finanziario e assicurativo, in Banca, impresa e società

Toniolo G (forthcoming) Le due crisi nel mondo: un breve confronto, Relazione al Convegno su "La società italiana e le grandi crisi economiche 1929–1936", Sapienza University of Rome – 26–28 novembre 2016

Vasseur M (1982) La nationalisation des banques, in Actualité juridique droit administrative

Vignocchi G (1974) Il servizio del credito nell'ordinamento pubblicistico italiano, Milano

Vitale P (1977) Pubblico e privato nell'ordinamento bancario, Milano

Chapter 13
Cohesion, Subsidiarity and Organization: The Experience in EU and Italy

Pier Luigi Portaluri

Contents

Abstract The contribution examines the role of public-private partnership in the Italian cohesion experience. We're used to talk about political and administrative cohesion in a spatial sense, intertwined to the territorial dimension. Indeed, cohesion can be seen also under a social profile, where private people can carry out the public functions in a horizontal subsidiarity relation with the public Administration.

So, the analysis conducted above this instrument can lead to a special profile of it: the partnership between the public and the private parties, indeed, leads to a number of economic and social advantages. Privates can carry out the public functions with their own finances and investments; and they can do even better than the public bodies, having positive social effects from their action.

Partnerships are a concrete application of the principle of subsidiarity, foreseen by Art. 118 of our Constitution in its *horizontal* meaning, that is the relation between the public and the private parties of a deal that can carry out the public tasks without burdening (*exclusively*) on public funds and—more in general—on public efforts. Administration and civil society can cooperate in order to guarantee the supplying of goods that cannot be usefully produced by market competition, which has the negative fold of excluding weakest subjects from the enjoyment of essential goods. The public-private partnerships have not only an economic positive fold,

P. L. Portaluri (✉)
University of Salento, Lecce, Italy
e-mail: pierluigi.portaluri@unisalento.it

D. Sorace et al. (eds.), *The Changing Administrative Law of an EU Member State*,
https://doi.org/10.1007/978-3-030-50780-0_13

but above all a social positive influence by guaranteeing the well-being of the population.

13.1 Introduction

During the studies for the 150th anniversary of the administrative unification laws in Italy, I headed the scientific unity of the University of Salento on the theme of the political-territorial cohesion.

In a more specific sense I looked after my fellowship studies on the different aspects of this wide and ambiguous concept, focusing on the political-territorial cohesion as the prism of the relationship between Italy-state-level and both EU and the system of local autonomies.

The studies took their start from the given idea that both at EU and regional/local level economic cohesion does not evolve in a similar way in all territories: on the contrary, people take often disadvantages from their local position (depressed, peripheral Regions, isolated or not-well-connected countries, etc.) and market regulation by itself does not have the capacity to compensate these differences and inequalities.

13.2 Territorial Cohesion in EU

One of the ways in which the objective of economic and social cohesion is believed to be achieved is to entrust *ad hoc* legal entities with certain development initiatives that transcend the strictly regional sphere—that is, sub-state administrative entities—thus favouring the positive aggregation between public and private subjects, from a cooperative and subsidiary point of view for purposes of common interest.

Starting from this point of view, my contribution[1] in the aforementioned 150th anniversary studies has aimed to explain how territorial cohesion policies can help to a more equal development in EU, analyzing the coordination tools (e.g.: GEC, GECT, CoR, *etc.*) set by European Institutions to carry out the goal stated by the current Art. 174 TFEU.[2] Within the European Union's policies, the establishment of

[1]Portaluri and De Giorgi Cezzi (2016).

[2]Art. 174 TFEU: "1. In order to promote its overall harmonious development, the Union shall develop and pursue its actions leading to the strengthening of its economic, social and territorial cohesion.

2. In particular, the Union shall aim at reducing disparities between the levels of development of the various regions and the backwardness of the least favoured regions.

3. Among the regions concerned, particular attention shall be paid to rural areas, areas affected by industrial transition, and regions which suffer from severe and permanent natural or

macro-drivers for ultraregional cohesion can make it possible to channel economic resources to functionally aggregated bodies (set up *ad hoc*), which share a certain project idea in a framework of legal co-regulation (EU's, state, regional), without compromising the autonomy of the constituent institutions of the Republic (Art. 114, Constitution), which, indeed, could recover tasks and operational capabilities in their horizontal dimension, as a form of rebalancing due to "crushing" suffered on the vertical plane.

In this way, a first mark can be fixed: EU policies addressed to disadvantaged Regions look at realizing territorial cohesion both through their involvement in decisional and legislative processes and the allocation of special funds for them. That's the reason why territorial cohesion and the so-called Regional policy are often overlapped: they're intertwined.

Yet at a cursory glance it's hard to dispute that the territorial cohesion has a close connection to the economic purpose of the development: but it's not just related to a purely economic aspect. The concept has multiple components and dimensions that make it difficult to be focused: there are a myriad of institutional, political and even academic definitions of "territorial cohesion". It comes from the fact that already the term "territorial" derives from "territory": and the latter has not only a spatial sense.[3] On the contrary, "territory" is connected to space, sovereignty, citizenship, jurisdiction and—over all—administration limits: so the "cohesion" (often used in the sense of "convergence", that sounds like an approach among different territories) must be intended in many different ways, all interlaced and interdependent. It should be enough to think that no political cohesion (or "unity", if you prefer) is possible without a solidarity economic effort or even a creation of a social community: the three pillars of EU cohesion policy (political, social and territorial) are indivisible, indeed.

The noble intent of the EU of converging the territories of the member States and equally level their economy through a sustainable development, helping depressed Regions, could have no effects if not measurable: so the challenging task now is to set parameters that could measure the level of territorial cohesion trends in a selected territory. There's a need to use quantitative and qualitative indicators (such as, for example: productivity, employment rate, criminality rate, inter-municipal cooperation, eco-efficiency, waste treatment, accessibility to infrastructures, city ranking, road density, telecommunications infrastructures, etc.) to improve understanding and to closely monitor the trends: these data should be balanced in a way that the holistic notion of Territorial cohesion could become measurable.

---

demographic handicaps such as the northernmost regions with very low population density and island, cross-border and mountain regions".

[3]From the conception of the territory as a political space, we have moved on to a conception of territory as functional to the achievement of financial stability and to the pursuit of objectives of a predominantly economic nature. The enhancement of the functional dimension, moreover, is not unknown even to our system, which, for its part, has encouraged the development of interlocalius aggregations with legislation, for the frenzied truth and, often, disorganic (and not at all successful). See Luchena and Manfrellotti (2017).

In this regard, there are positive signs towards the elaboration of methodologies which can provide a solid ground to analyse territorial cohesion, namely within the ESPON Programme (*European Observation Network for Territorial Development and Cohesion*), launched in 2002 by the European Commission, with the expectation to support applied research and studies on territorial development and spatial planning, in support of policy development.

Indeed, the need for measuring territorial cohesion is twofold. For one, a widely accepted method of measuring territorial cohesion would help to reduce its scientific misunderstanding, and to engage the academic community in producing useful studies, which could be of vital importance to better understand and correct territorial imbalances. Secondly, at the political level, the territorial cohesion concept could be discussed in a more concrete and focused way. In both cases, the need for the elaboration of aggregated territorial cohesion indicators is of crucial importance, as this would allow for the design of a concrete indicator. Such an indicator could measure the territorial cohesion in a certain period of time, thus permitting the measurement of territorial cohesion trends in general and in all their main dimensions: so the territorial cohesion could seriously taken at the center of the political agenda of the EU, especially now that global economy tends to clear local realities, that vice versa are the new point of strength of the European Union.

13.3 Cohesion in the Italian Experience

We can say our Country has a historical virtue on the research of cohesion: this was, after all, the goal of the administrative unification laws of 1865. But history told us that Italy couldn't hit the target: the profound efforts to establish coordination tools between the State and the local levels have faced some challenges with the Regional experience—born in 1970—that caused the multiplication of institutional subjects to be involved in the decisional processes.

But, more in general, Administrative law is in continuous transformation, being the right inherent in the evolution of society: nevertheless, however much it may evolve, the fundamental pillars can never be overwhelmed unless the concept of the rule of law is overturned. In fact, administrative law is characterized by the law that governs the organization and activity of subjects who must take care of public interests, interests that represent the reason of life of these entities, and which regulates the methods of protection of private individuals who they can, if necessary, collide with these subjects, who always act for the realization of public interests.[4]

The great changes in political and legal context—the well-known Constitutional reform of Title V in 2001—have caused abandonment of the traditional administrative subjects and a contemporary newborn form of cooperation between public and private: the so-called *partenariato* ("partnership", in a certain way). This kind of

[4]See Dipace (2016).

partnership constitutes the operative mode of cohesion in Italy (so-called "funzione-compito"),[5] so the target could be reached (so-called "funzione-scopo"):[6] cohesion becomes in a while the function, the objective that guides the operations of public administrations.

The identification of the target has a notable importance in the public-private partnerships (that constitute the correspondent for the italian *partenariato*): we must remember that public administration is ruled by the principle of legality; when the public activity is carried out by a private, this principle continues to be in act, but in a different way. It consists in a finalization of the activity: the "funzione-scopo", indeed.

This finalization leads the public administration to choose the instrument to carry out its scope: this instrument could be even a contract for public-private partnership. The issue is that, in Italy, the public-private partnership contract[7] can be atypical[8] in its form, but not in its target (always public and unavailable by the administration or the private party).

13.3.1 Public-Private Partnership and Cohesion

What's the role kept by public-private partnership (or PPP) in Italian cohesion policy? The answer to this question is yet to come, but the evolution of this institute in the Italian administrative law could be an attempt to tell it.

The well-known PPP is widely considered as "a sort of *brave new world* in the realization of public interventions",[9] but it suffers a difficulty due to the classic antagonism between public and private interests, almost always directed to divergent targets.

---

[5]That's a concept involving the characteristics of the administrative activity, that is typed and formalized in its contents, fixed by the law.

[6]This is a concept tied to the goals kept by the public administration: the administrative activity is always directed to a public interest or carries out a public task.

[7]The so-called partenariato contrattuale: there's a distinction between public-private partnership and "institutional" public-private partnership (so-called partenariato istituzionale).

[8]According to Dipace (2016), that the atypical contract is the main instrument used by the partnership is derived from some considerations. Just think of the multifunctional role played by the private entity and the complex allocation of financial risk, which may involve several subjects, to infer that in our legal system there are no contractual models capable of regulating and composing all the interests at stake. Often complex negotiations are necessary, sometimes transfused into a single contract, sometimes in several contracts linked to each other by a functional link. These are contracts characterized by the absence of a specific discipline that identifies the structure and function, which are instead established in concrete, from time to time, by the contracting parties with the negotiation of the individual aspects of the transaction. Only flexible instruments allow to regulate in detail the complex operations, so the absence of discipline is not penalizing.

[9]Manfredi (2014).

So, the advantages deriving from the new governance of the public administration—that approaches business models in action and organization—are to be balanced with the disadvantages of the potential conflicts between the private and the public parties of the partnership.[10]

Even the European Union warned the Member States from considering public-private partnership as a sort of "miracle":[11] successful PPPs require an effective legislative and control framework which ensures that each partner recognizes the objectives and needs of the others; such an accepted methodology is necessary to ensure efficient application and to benefit from the recognized advantages for the public and private sector.

But in Italy this model is deemed to encounter many difficulties: there's a kind of scepticism in importing it, due to the traditional way of managing public interests maintained by the Administrations. But there's a hope: if we look in the past, one of the greatest authors[12] in Italian administrative law used to criticize the import of foreign models, but he considered also the benefits deriving from the foreign influence on our administrative law.[13] Similarly, the general unbelief for the public-private partnerships must leave place to a genuine consideration of the benefits of this way of managing public interests:[14] this, above all, keeping in mind that the PPPs are a foreign model and they have to be transposed in the Italian context.

They constitute an instrument for the Administration through which it can deal with private investors in a public contract. In this way, it's possible to note the erosion of some of the "reassuring" categories which the '800's dogmatic has handed over to us, produced by the process of economic, juridical and political integration experienced by the Old Continent from the Second World War to today. Among the categories that are beginning to shatter, bending before the unifying force of Community law, there is the (un)clear split between the public and private sectors. This gave rise to the reflection on the "new" contractual category of the public private partnership. In this way of relations between the two extremes of the public/private dichotomy, a way has been identified to stimulate the involvement of the members of the social and economic complex in the tasks aimed at satisfying collective needs.[15]

---

[10]Manfredi (2014).

[11]*Green Paper of the European Commission, 2004: European Commission Green Paper on public-private partnerships and Community law on public procurement and concessions, COM (2004) 327 final.*

[12]Benvenuti (ed. 2006).

[13]Benvenuti spoke about the administrative unification laws of 1865: they were the result of the import of French and Belgian models.

[14]This goal can be reached through a full awareness of PPPs' characteristics: their limits, their criticalities, and above all, the need to adapt them to the normative and organizational context of the Italian administration. See Manfredi (2017).

[15]Loo Gutíerrez (2014).

The origin of this model is located in the so-called "welfare State's crisis":[16] it turned out that the economic failure of the States had led to the renunciation of States to hold the monopoly of the public services that couldn't be anymore afforded by public funds.

On the contrary, awareness has been gained that private individuals are able to set up complex organizations aimed at obtaining funding, planning, executing and managing complex and relevant infrastructural projects and works. Private individuals today are a valid alternative for carrying out the technical, organizational and financial activities necessary for the execution of the works and plants required for the provision of public services.[17]

So, the public-private partnerships contribute to dissolve the split between two different worlds, two different ways of thinking and acting: the public sector can use the benefits from the private parties and vice versa.

But the most important thing, here, is the dogmatic value of the PPPs and their application of the principle of subsidiarity, cited in our Constitution,[18] that leads to cohesion: the public/private dichotomy is deemed to be solved.[19] In the reflection on the models adopted by the public-private partnerships there is, in fact, the intention to bring to unity the aims of the public power and the techniques of the juridical relations of its specular opposite, that is, the non-power of the private. In PPPs, the intent to renounce the unilateral imposition of their own determinations, the paradigmatic and distinctive technique of the administration of the State, is clear in order to take advantage of the public interest gained by the private sector.[20]

The potentiality of this instrument has led the European Union to sustain it: the development of partnerships is one of the clearest results of the progressive elimination of the aforementioned dichotomy between public law and common law, both in the contractual PPP and in the "institutionalized" PPP.[21] The reflections on PPPs are one of the fundamental stages of the commitment undertaken by the European Commission in the realization of the unique market. This effort has been carried out by trying to remove the obstacles to freedom of establishment and the freedom to provide services, particularly in the public procurement market, since this market and the "neighbour" of services of general interest are characterized by being among the most regulated and far from the rules of the game of competition.[22] This is due to the fact that "public enterprises have long lived undisturbed in a sort of shadow of

---

[16]Ullman (1998).

[17]Loo Gutíerrez (2014).

[18]Art. 118 Cost.

[19]See Heidemann (2009). See also Horwitz (1981) and Mnookin (1981).

[20]See Loo Gutíerrez (2014).

[21]The fundamental distinction, as identified by the EU Commission in the Green Paper of 2004, is between the contractual partnership, which finds, that is, its foundation in a negotiation relationship (the typical example is represented by the concession) and the partnership institutional, which is instead based on the establishment of a distinct legal entity in which the public and private subjects participate (the reference clearly goes to mixed companies). See Chiti (2009).

[22]See Loo Gutíerrez (2014).

European competition policy. Only in the last twenty years the Commission has rediscovered and rigorously applied the provisions on state aid and the rules on competition to the public services sector".[23]

In this way, the rules of competition and the free market take on the role of values aimed at achieving other goals, which would derive, as a corollary, from their implementation, also in the sphere of public services, belonging to a sector of long-held economy "excluded" from policies to promote free competition, which were gradually becoming established on the basis of the provisions of primary sources of European law.

The existing connections, on the one hand, between (effective) competition, (free) market and public services and, on the other hand, the modalities assumed by their production, supply and choice of its producers and/or providers are highlighted by the aforementioned European Commission Green Paper on public-private partnerships and Community law on public procurement and concessions, COM (2004) 327 final, which is one of the culmination of the long road taken by the Commission in its attempt to introduce clarification supranational level regarding this economic sector, public procurement and concessions.

For the EU Commission, the term PPPs refers to "forms of cooperation between public authorities and the world of business which aim to ensure the funding, construction, renovation, management or maintenance of an infrastructure or the provision of a service". The partnership is normally characterized by four elements: "(1) the relatively long duration of the relationship, involving cooperation between the public partner and the private partner on different aspects of a planned project; (2) the method of funding the project, in part from the private sector, sometimes by means of complex arrangements between the various players. Nonetheless, public funds—in some cases rather substantial—may be added to the private funds; (3) the important role of the economic operator, who participates at different stages in the project (design, completion, implementation, funding). The public partner concentrates primarily on defining the objectives to be attained in terms of public interest, quality of services provided and pricing policy, and it takes responsibility for monitoring compliance with these objectives; (4) the distribution of risks between the public partner and the private partner, to whom the risks generally borne by the public sector are transferred. However, a PPP does not necessarily mean that the private partner assumes all the risks, or even the major share of the risks linked to the project. The precise distribution of risk is determined case by case, according to the respective ability of the parties concerned to assess, control and cope with this risk".

The European Union uses the PPPs to force the openings of the public service and the "special or exclusive" rights that kept it at the shelter of competition, allowing its entry into this "market":[24] this technique could lead to a greater cohesion of the EU, by the public-private partnership in Italy.

[23]Clarich (2003).

[24]Symptoms of the growing attention of the EU to the public-private partnerships are also the Communication from the Commission to the European Parliament, the Council, the European

And—pay attention—public-private partnership is a juridical concept even though it's not defined in the EU Directive 2014/23/EU: this is even more valid in the Italian context, where the legislative instrument for public contracts—the Code of Public Contracts, legislative decree 18th April 2016, No. 50—gives a formal definition to these partnerships[25] and fixes a general discipline of their use in the public tasks.[26]

This is, above all, the aspect of great novelty in respect of the former legislation, that didn't provide any general discipline, but only fixed some detailed norms for specific kind of public-private partnership (i.e. project financing, *etc.*). The new form of internal legislation—even without a definition of PPPs in the Directives of the EU—has a potential of development under the constitutional principle of subsidiarity: that indicates, in its horizontal meaning,[27] the retreat of public intervention and the simultaneous expansion of spaces reserved for private parties.[28]

Why public-private-partnerships, horizontal subsidiarity and cohesion (above all, social cohesion) are so intertwined? We can refer to a doctrine[29] that sees horizontal subsidiarity as a profile of the more complex solidarity principle, also present in our

---

Economic and Social Committee and the Committee of the Regions on Public-Private Partnerships and Community Law on Public Procurement and Concessions, COM/2005/0569 final; the European Parliament resolution on public-private partnerships and Community law on public procurement and concessions (2006/2043(INI)); the Commission interpretative communication on the application of Community law on Public Procurement and Concessions to institutionalised PPP (IPPP), 2008/C 91/02; the Green Paper on the modernisation of EU public procurement policy—Towards a more efficient European Procurement Market (COM 2011, 15).

[25]Art. 3, lett. eee), legislative decree No. 50/2016 defines ""contratto di partenariato pubblico privato", il contratto a titolo oneroso stipulato per iscritto con il quale una o più stazioni appaltanti conferiscono a uno o più operatori economici per un periodo determinato in funzione della durata dell'ammortamento dell'investimento o delle modalità di finanziamento fissate, un complesso di attività consistenti nella realizzazione, trasformazione, manutenzione e gestione operativa di un'opera in cambio della sua disponibilità, o del suo sfruttamento economico, o della fornitura di un servizio connessa all'utilizzo dell'opera stessa, con assunzione di rischio secondo modalità individuate nel contratto, da parte dell'operatore. Fatti salvi gli obblighi di comunicazione previsti dall'articolo 44, comma 1-bis, del decreto-legge 31 dicembre 2007, n. 248, convertito, con modificazioni, dalla legge 28 febbraio 2008, n. 31, si applicano, per i soli profili di tutela della finanza pubblica, i contenuti delle decisioni Eurostat".

[26]Artt. 179 ss., legislative decree No. 50/2016.

[27]The principle of subsidiarity has a vertical and a horizontal dimension: according to the first, the administrative functions belong to the Municipalities and the higher levels of government intervene as the lower ones fail to carry them out. At the opposite, subsidiarity is understood in a horizontal sense with reference to the particular relationship between the State and the citizens, both as individuals and in their social formations, for which state intervention is reduced to a minimum to the advantage of the ever wider autonomy recognized to private individuals in the carrying out public tasks.

[28]Dipace (2016).

[29]Libertini (2015).

Constitution at Art. 2[30] and—at the EU level—in the Treaty of Amsterdam at Art. 2.[31]

According to this doctrine, there are some goods that cannot be produced only by market competition. "It would be easy to be tempted by a Decourbertinian idea, so a well-ordered competition would cement overall solidarity (as it is traditionally said to happen with joint participation in sports competitions). But it would be a liar idea: apart from the consideration that it does not work well even for sports competitions, nor for the competition between individuals within stable organizations, even less this idea could work for competition between companies. This is a race in which losers are normally destined to disappear; and the defeat of the losing party brings with it not only the loss of capital, but also the sacrifice of the stakeholders (workers, in the first place), which on those enterprises had aimed, either by will or by necessity".[32]

The good results of market economy in terms of allocative efficiency are not equal to a general well-being of the population: not happiness, or even social cohesion. That's why some goods have to be produced or supplied by public entities: when they can't afford them, private parties can serve with their know-how and—above all—their funds, carrying out public tasks.

Therefore, a sort of chain has been created: solidarity principle needs to be realized—among other instruments—by the horizontal subsidiarity; public-private partnerships are an instrument of subsidiarity that can realize solidarity and—through it—cohesion and, more generally, a diffuse well-being.

13.4 Organization Forms and Cohesion in Italy. Nods

But the Italian experience tells us of the difficulties to apply the rule of cohesion at the organization level (so-called "funzione-ufficio"):[33] while the target suggests a *unicum*, a convergency, organization of public administration has a disrupt structure,

[30]Solidarity is an integral part of European constitutional experiences, as the founding value of the great cultures at the roots of Western thought, namely the Greco-Roman and the Christian. See, among others, Lombardi Vallauri (1981).

[31]The solidarity principle is one of the founding principles of the legal system of the European Union, as expressed by the aforementioned art. 2: this consideration derives also from the jurisprudence of the Community in terms of subjective legal situations. The apparent disregard of the Union for social rights stems from the fact that the way in which the latter are understood is closely linked to the historical and juridical experience of the individual States; apparently, it has been said, because the Treaty, if, on the one hand, does not renounce to affirm the value of solidarity, puts it, on the other hand, the realization to the sensibility of the different juridical experiences. See Luchena and Manfrellotti (2017).

[32]Libertini (2015).

[33]That's a concept tied to the organization: it links to the activity attributed to an office or an office complex. For the classification among "funzione-scopo", "funzione-compito" and "funzione-ufficio", see Modugno (1966).

too complex, reticular and confused. But there's also a general legislative favor for non-institutional spaces for confrontation, consultation, participation and cooperation, to put relevant interests together and get a good administrative action that keeps control also on the weakest territorial interests.

About this, we have to remark that, according to the traditional administrative doctrine, organization is not only a serving profile of the administrative action: on the contrary, it is a precious prefiguration of the activity of the public administration.[34]

In this perspective, every decision on the (upstream) plan of the organization necessarily reacts—and decisively—on the identification of the alternative decisions that can and must be assumed on the (downstream) level of the activity: the organization therefore, it is not only an external frame of limitation, but also and above all an internal measure of the direction of administrative action.[35] Therefore, the organization has a direct reflection on the administrative action: that's also the main thinking of a traditional well-known doctrine.[36]

It turns out that our State level recognizes local autonomies and always tries to find a way to protect depressed zones—the case of our *Mezzogiorno* is an example—and keeps in mind the goal of cohesion by the institution of an *ad hoc* Minister—*Ministero per la Coesione territoriale e il Mezzogiorno*—assisted by an other institutional administrative figure: an Agency (*Agenzia per la Coesione territoriale*).

Despite the creation of the abovementioned figures, cohesion cannot be said reached: and probably the State level is the real responsible of this current failure. There's where we can find the great misalignment between administrations and their functions: and the example is hidden in all those figures that justify their existence by creating the function, almost forgetting that "first the function, second the office".

In the Italian experience territorial cohesion has above all an administrative sense, connected to the historical context of this Country: it emerges in the relationship among government levels, in respect to the principles stated by Art. 118 Cost; the economic effect—also present—is a side effect, connected to the efficiency of local autonomies. By strengthening it, Italy can be a territory where cohesion can be effectively realized.

13.5 Conclusions

The necessary approach in this contribution has been directed to create a link between the concept of territorial, social and economic cohesion and some of the traditional institutions of Italian administrative law.

---

[34]Nigro (1966).

[35]Monteduro (2016).

[36]We're talking about Feliciano Benvenuti. See, on his works and way of thinking, Cortese (2017).

We have seen that cohesion is a concept known since the intervention of European Union with its Treaties, for it is now present in Art. 174 TFEU; but also we have to face the fact that this concept is not at all stranger for Italian law: some of the traditional principles of our administrative law are just directed to guarantee cohesion policies.

One of these: the principle of subsidiarity, present in Art. 118 of our Constitution. We have analyzed it in its *horizontal* meaning, that is the relation between the public and the private parties of a deal that can carry out the public tasks without burdening (*exclusively*) on public funds and—more in general—on public efforts. Administration and civil society can cooperate in order to guarantee the supplying of goods that cannot be usefully produced by market competition, which has the negative fold of excluding weakest subjects from the enjoyment of essential goods. The public-private partnerships have not only an economic positive fold, but above all a social positive influence by guaranteeing the well-being of the population.

Also, cohesion can be reached by the correct application of the principle of organization of the public Administration: even if some difficulties have been noted because of the "shredded" offices and competences, often disorganised in our system. The principle of organization is the valve that allows the administration to pursue the goal of cohesion. Do not be amazed at the influence that the organizational factor can have on the activity: as noted above, the organization itself prefigures the activity. The administrative function—fundamental trait that guides the conduct of the actions by the public authorities—also regulates the organization: that changes—or may change—based on the objectives of public interest that the legislator sets out from time to time. The greatest difficulty, however, lies in choosing the organizational modality more suited to achieving the goal of cohesion, because unfortunately our country has not distinguished itself for organizational clarity or effectiveness.

References

Benvenuti F (ed. 2006) Mito e realtà nell'ordinamento amministrativo italiano, now in Id., Scritti giuridici, III, Milano, 2006, pp 2733 ss

Chiti MP (2009) I partenariati pubblico-privati e la fine del dualismo tra diritto pubblico e diritto comune, in Id. (ed) Il partenariato pubblico-privato. Concessioni, Finanza di progetto, Società miste, Fondazioni, Napoli

Clarich M (2003) Servizi pubblici e diritto europeo della concorrenza: l'esperienza italiana e tedesca a confronto, in Rivista trimestrale di diritto pubblico

Cortese F (2017) L'organizzazione amministrativa e le autonomie territoriali nel pensiero di Benvenuti, in Riv. trim. dir. pubbl., n. 1/2017, pp 73 ss

Dipace R (2016) Il partenariato pubblico privato nel diritto amministrativo in trasformazione. In: Longobardi N (ed) Il diritto amministrativo in trasformazione. Per approfondire, Torino

Heidemann M (2009) Private law in Europe – the public/private dichotomy reviseted. Eur Bus Law Rev 20

Horwitz MJ (1981) The history of public/private distinction. Univ Pa Law Rev 130

Libertini M (2015) Concorrenza e coesione sociale, in Persona e mercato, 2015, pp 53 ss., published on http://www.personaemercato.it/wp-content/uploads/2015/01/Libertini.pdf
Lombardi Vallauri L (1981) Corso di filosofia del diritto, Padova
Loo Gutíerrez M (2014) I principi di sussidiarietà e solidarietà nel partenariato pubblico-privato contrattuale, Roma
Luchena G, Manfrellotti R (2017) Brevi riflessioni in tema di governance plurilivello e aggregazione funzionale fra soggetti pubblici e privati. Il caso dei Fondi strutturali, in Rivista AIC – Osservatorio costituzionale, 2/2017
Manfredi G (2014) La valorizzazione del patrimonio culturale: modelli organizzativi e strumenti. La "Fondazione la Grande Brera", il partenariato e la panacea di tutti i mali, in Aedon, 2/2014, online
Manfredi G (2017) I modelli organizzativi nell'amministrazione dei beni culturali tra mito e realtà. In: Astone F, Caldarera M, Manganaro F, Saitta F, Saitta N, Tigano A (eds) Studi in memoria di Antonio Romano Tassone, Napoli
Mnookin RH (1981) The public/private dichotomy: political disagreement and academic repudiation. Univ Pa Law Rev 130
Modugno F. (1966), voce Funzione, in Enc. dir., XVIII, Giuffrè, Milano, pp 301 ss
Monteduro M (2016) Le figure soggettive ed i modelli organizzativi sperimentati dall'ordinamento italiano in relazione alle politiche europee di coesione territoriale. In: De Giorgi Cezzi G, Portaluri PL (eds) La coesione politico-territoriale, Firenze
Nigro M. (1966) Studi sulla funzione organizzatrice della pubblica amministrazione, Giuffrè, Milano
Portaluri PL, De Giorgi Cezzi G (2016) La coesione politico-territoriale: rapporti con l'Europa e coordinamento Stato-autonomie. In: De Giorgi Cezzi G, Portaluri PL (eds) La coesione politico-territoriale, Firenze
Ullman CF (1998) The welfare state's other crisis: explaining the new partnership between nonprofit organizations and the state in France, Bloomington (Indiana)

Chapter 14
Public Employment Reform: The Difficult and Controversial Abandonment of the Public Model

Alfredo Corpaci

Contents

Abstract The chapter deals with the reform of public employment in Italy, which began in the 1990s, with the aim of overcoming the traditional difference between the public employment regime and that of private employees. The author analyses the history of the reform process, characterized by the succession of rules more or less similar to those of private employment. The work takes into account the jurisprudence of the Constitutional Court, according to which a balance must be found between the public and private models, so as to respect the constitutional principles of impartiality and sound performance of the public administration. Today, Italian public employment law is still seeking such a balance.

14.1 A Major and Highly Challenging Reform

The 1990s were a decade of significant change in the Italian administrative system. These included the reform of the traditional "pubblico impiego", now considered an archaic expression for designating work in public administrations.[1]

[1]Rusciano (2015), p. 1.

A. Corpaci (✉)
University of Florence, Florence, Italy
e-mail: alfredo.corpaci@unifi.it

D. Sorace et al. (eds.), *The Changing Administrative Law of an EU Member State*,
https://doi.org/10.1007/978-3-030-50780-0_14

For a long time there was no doubt that employment relationships fell under public law, with multiple elements thought[2] to rule out all uncertainty: the public nature of one of the parties to the arrangement, the public goal pursued by the two parties in entering into it, the nature of the job (focusing on achieving the goals of the public body), and the public powers of supremacy to which it gives rise. The matter was therefore referred to administrative law scholars, with respect to teaching and scientific research, and to administrative lawyers and the administrative courts, with respect to judicial protection.

If we consider that the reform[3] sought to remove the matter from administrative law and administrative courts and hand it over to labour law, and to the labour courts for disputes, it appears to be no exaggeration to describe it as the "most important change" of Italian administrative law in the twentieth century.[4] So much so that in the first legal journal dedicated to privatised public employment, the editor (a labour lawyer) spoke of it as a "revolution of culture, conceptual instrumentation, and language".[5]

At the same time, however, the radical shift and the significance of competing interests portended complexities and difficulties of a path which in fact turned out to be "laced with ambiguity and heading backwards".[6] This is clear in view both of its duration of more than twenty-five years (the reform process which began in the early nineties is still under way) and of its fluctuating trend, marked by continuity but also by variations that lend to equivocal interpretations.[7]

14.2 The Project: Bringing Public Employment Under Labour Law

The reform is related to a situation of financial, organisational and managerial crisis in which impacted the public administration after the second world war.

As summarised by a study on Italian bureaucracy from national unification to the present day,[8] in the 1960s, while developing a modern and dynamic economic system, the way of being and functioning of the administrative apparatus represented a "ball and chain around the foot of development" rather than an aid. Civil servants at

---

[2]Zanobini (1958), p. 265.

[3]On the sector reform, see Saitta (2016), pp. 37 et seq.; Apicella (2016), pp. 149 et seq.

[4]Cassese (1997), p. VII. Rusciano (2015), p. 1, speaking of a "mass-scale" reform, 2015: 1.

[5]Carinci (1998), p. 4.

[6]Cassese (1997), p. VII.

[7]In light of the long legislative process Carinci (2013), p. 534, expresses the opinion that both the original way of understanding privatisation, as a reconditioning of the entire world of work to a "common home", and the push in that direction have failed, giving way to a renewed diversity of regulation between public employment and private work.

[8]Melis (2015).

the time were characterised by a lack of dynamism and propensity for innovation, low productivity, not great professional skills, disproportionately southern origin and territorial distribution, age ranges that showed a predominance of elder people over youth, accompanied by a formalistic training brought about by a selection process that clearly favoured legal matters.[9]

The need to remedy so many critical issues would compel part of the political forces and trade union organisations, backed by a sector of the doctrine, to develop a radical reform project of the traditional Italian system of public employment.[10]

In this respect, since the early twentieth century, an *ad hoc* regulation had been developed for civil servants of the state, which differed from that for private work. The law[11] subjected it to a broad set of rules. This included appointments, obligations, promotions, conflicts, transfers, leave, resignations, penalties, disciplinary proceedings, and dispensations from service. A clear difference thus emerged with respect to employment under private parties, which was poorly regulated on the legislative side and largely left to free agreements. This difference was linked to the idea that work performed on behalf of the public administration, being instrumental to the fulfilment of its duties in the interests of the community, could not be independently regulated by parties in the exercise of freedom of negotiation. Instead, it required to be regulated by acts of public authority and focused to the public interest. This would come full-circle in 1923 as the litigation on the matter was assigned to the administrative courts.[12]

This gradually led to consider the civil servant, rather than a worker paid for his job, a part of the administrative system. This view was widely shared even after the adoption of the Republican Constitution, since many found confirm of it in different provisions of the basic charter.

Based on the idea that work is a component (personal element) of office organisation, it was seen as necessary to reserve its regulation *to legislative act*s (since this reserve is established for the office organisation by the Article 97 of the Constitution so as to ensure the sound performance and impartiality of the administration) and maintain it subject to a public regime.

In support of this, reference was made to other varied provisions relative to the special traditional regime: these include the regulation stipulating equal conditions

---

[9]Melis (2015), pp. 63 and 26–27.

[10]See D'Antona (1998). The idea of privatising government jobs not associated with the exercise of public powers, keeping under public law only those to whom such exercise was or could be entrusted (directors), had been put forward around the end of the 1970s by the then Minister for Civil Service, M.S. Giannini, one of the most revered university professors of administrative law: see "Rapporto sui principali problemi dell'Amministrazione dello Stato", submitted to the Houses on 16 November 1979.

[11]Issued in 1908 (R. Decree No. 693) was the first consolidated text of laws on the status of civil servants, Article 1 of which divided them into three categories: administrative, accounting and order, with the employees in each category sorted by skill level, then by type if of the same skill level, and then by seniority if of the same skill level and same type.

[12]See R.D. No. 2840 of 30 December 1923.

of access to public office in accordance with the requirements set out by law (Article 51 of the Constitution), and which in principle requires selection by competition (Article 97); that which places civil servants at the "exclusive service of the Nation" (Article 98); that which requires citizens entrusted with public duties to fulfil them with "discipline and honour", taking an oath in the cases established by law (Article 54); and that which sets out the responsibilities applicable to officials and employees of the state and public entities (Article 28).

However, as the years passed the position that public employment was irreducible to "*ordinary*" subordinate work would be accompanied by a contrasting notion that the legal category of public employment had now been stripped of any constructive utility, requiring a restructuring that would focus on the employment contract.[13] On the other hand, the system's most critical issues were attributed to its alleged speciality, starting from its wide regulation by statutes which, driven by *corporate* claims, led to an opaque dispensation of legal and economic benefits in favour of one micro-category or another (to the point that it became known as the "jungle" legislation). At the same time, it led to rigidity and a formalistic application of rules and principles whose proclaimed and abstract functionality to the public interest actually drew attention away from the aspects of efficient management and productivity.

Meanwhile, it was questioned that the application of labour law could be impeded by the constitutional text.[14] The Constitution sees work as being of meaningful value[15] and is treated such that it cannot be reduced, in the public sector, to merely an internal component of office organisation and thereby subject to the regime which Article 97 refers to administrative organisation. However, it must be added that Article 97 does not imply a legislative regulation for all the aspects of the working relationship. In turn the other constitutional provisions, above mentioned, laying down behaviours, obligations or responsibilities for certain civil servants, do not imply a public status as such, given that these may be translated into duties, obligations and constraints inherent to a relationship keeping the characteristics and the object of the employment relationship subject to labour law.[16]

These reflections and considerations led to the drafting of a reform project in the early 1990s aiming to dismantle the legal and judicial system of public employment.

---

[13]Rusciano (1978).

[14]On this point see Orsi Battaglini (2007a).

[15]It was observed by Orsi Battaglini (2007b), p. 1361 that in the Italian constitutional system, "the ethical-political emphasis and the individual and collective protection of work are certainly placed (. . .) on a higher plane not comparable with that of the principles (sparse and ambiguous, among other issues) relating to public administration".

[16]Otherwise, by assigning to constitutional norms the function of ensuring civil servants and public workers go about their duties impartially and in the pursuit of the common good, those individuals are placed in a "*different body*" from other workers. Their activity is seen as an object of service set up in pursuit not of the employer's interests, but of the public interest, in accordance with specific constitutional rules "that require a particular level of professionalism such as to ensure the quality of the service provided to citizens" (Racca 2009, p. 253. See also Cavallo Perin 2009).

The traditional separation between public and private work would disappear through their unification under the same discipline (that set out by the provisions of the civil code and other *private laws*), the contractualisation of relationships, and the reassignment of judicial protection to the ordinary labour court. The administration was assigned the role of a contractual party, restructuring its position and powers in a way much like those of a private employer (no longer public powers but managerial powers). Naturally, this restructuring also applied to the other party to the relationship—the worker, whose position and subjective legal situations were no different from those of a private sector employee (individual rights protected by the ordinary judicial authority, no longer downgraded by the exercise of ruling public powers).

The reform project affects an enormous part of public employees, with the exception of certain categories still subject to the previous public system: ordinary, administrative and accounting magistrates (given the need to protect their autonomy and independence in light also of the reserve to constitutional law on the judicial system), state lawyers and *solicitors* (traditionally associated with magistrates), military personnel and police forces (given the particular emphasis on the constraints of subordination and discipline), general state officials and their equivalents (given their preposition to top offices of the state public administration), and diplomatic and prefectural staff (given their preposition to offices in representation of the state both abroad and domestically). The public regime will also be maintained for university professors and researchers, pending a planned review of their status.[17]

Moreover, the legislative unification is not absolute, but is offset by the application of "limits associated with the pursuit of general interests at which the organisation and action of public administrations are aimed".[18]

The reform placed many expectations on the application of the regime and the provisions of common labour law and its dynamics: first and foremost, the abandon of the regulatory and remunerative "jungle" created by the previous system, with improvements in operational and expenditure control processes, as well as an increase in productivity and organisational efficiency.

Significantly, the reform project would draw strong opposition from the Council of State,[19] citing what it saw as an insurmountable obstacle in that work activity for public administrations also consists of the performance of public duties. Thus, the position of the public administration cannot be reduced to a private interest in ensuring the performance of work, but rather, the public interest to the correct performance of public duties must be considered as pre-eminent. According to the Council of State, privatisation would have only been possible for those systems and/or for those groups of personnel that were not assigned public functions.

[17]See Article 2.5 of Legislative Decree No. 29 of 3 February 1993.

[18]Article 2.1(a) of Law No. 421 of 23 October 1992.

[19]Council of State, General Assembly, opinion no. 146 of 31 August 1992, in Foro It., 1993, III, 4 et seq.

14.3 The Fluctuating Evolution of Legal Framework

Burdened by heavy reservations since the outset, the reformist design has been implemented through constant dialect between different points of view. The numerous regulatory measures introduced since 1992 have had a fluctuating trend in one direction or the other, and are typically passed over multiple phases.

At first, privatisation was still moderated by a broad application of public law. For example, all aspects pertaining to office organisation were kept under public regime. Multiple restrictions were placed on the role and on the scope of collective bargaining,[20] and there were numerous cases in which employees of public administrations were subject to a different set of regulations to those employed privately. As already mentioned, only certain lower-ranked executives were put on contract; the rest remained subject to the previous public regime.[21]

Several years later, a new enabling law[22] followed that would extend privatisation: on the subjective side, extending it to all executives;[23] on the objective side, extending the regulatory harmonisation between public and private employment and reducing the application of public law to a single part of office organisation.

The reserve for public sources and, more generally, the application of public law was limited to one area referred to as the macro-organisation,[24] beyond which the administration was called to operate "with the capacity and powers of a private

---

[20]Governed by a broad legislative framework the contract structure, the contracting parties (for the national negotiations, public administrations are legally represented by a specific agency), the procedure and the signing of contracts.

[21]Based on concerns expressed in the literature (Rusciano 1978, p. 327) regarding the extent to which the private work regime was attributable to top officials fully involved in the exercise of administrative powers, for which the functional element was *considered to absorb subordinate duties.*

[22]Law No. 59 of 15 March 1997, "Government Delegation for the assignment of duties and tasks to the regions and local authorities, for public administration reform and for administrative simplification."

[23]The public system remains firmly in place for the categories, listed above, excluded from privatisation. As for executives, according to the Constitutional Court, the Constitution does not provide—except for magistrates—any guarantee of autonomy to be implemented by law through a special legal status (Order No. 11 of 30 January 2002 and, previously, Ruling No. 313 of 25 July 1996). A position that was criticised since it would weaken the leadership with respect to politics and government.

[24]This includes laying down basic guidelines for the organisation of offices, identification and methods for filling senior positions, and the overall determination of organic resources (see Article 2 of Legislative Decree No. 80 of 31 March 1998, amending the previous regulation laid down by Legislative Decree No. 29 of 3 February 1993, according to which public administrations are generally regulated by law, regulations or organisational acts).

employer".[25] This reference to the "capacity" and to the "powers"[26] of the private employer also generally applies to the management of labour relations, and appears to support the radical change brought about in terms of the type of power under which the administration *performs its duties*. All acts governing the labour relationship are an expression of the managerial power given in Article 2104 of the Civil Code, which includes the multiple conformative, specific, evaluative, control and disciplinary powers, among others, of the employer. All relevant acts are to be considered not as administrative acts in exercise of special ruling powers of the administration, but rather as being implementation of private-sector negotiating powers.

As for the extension of harmonisation, the convergence of public- and private-sector work was maximised, reducing the need for special regulations and reinforcing the role of and the spaces for collective bargaining.[27] Particularly illustrative of the current orientations is the introduction *of a preferred standard concerning the source of the contract,* on the repealability of legal, regulatory or statutory provisions by contracts or collective agreements.[28]

It should however be noted that even when the guideline on legislative unification was at its most prevalent, several special provisions still remained unaffected. One need only recall the requirement for administrations to guarantee their employees "equal contractual treatment";[29] the stipulation that any violation of mandatory provisions concerning worker recruitment and employment (including the restrictive rules on fixed-term contracts) shall under no circumstance result in permanent employment given the Article 97 of the Constitution which requires public competition;[30] or, in the case of a de facto assignment to higher duties, the exclusion that such assignment may become final (in contrast to Article 2103 of the Civil Code); or, moreover, the specific regulations pertaining to conflicts, accumulation of employment and positions. Indeed, as repeatedly emphasised by the Constitutional Court,

---

[25]See Article 4 of the aforementioned Legislative Decree No. 80 of 1998.

[26]In the previous version of Article 4 of Legislative Decree No. 29 of 1993, the formula used referred exclusively to the "powers" of the private employer.

[27]Article 43 of the aforesaid Legislative Decree No. 80 of 1998, removing the exclusions laid down in the previous regulations, curtly provides that "collective bargaining takes place on all matters relating to employment and union relations".

[28]"Any legal, regulatory or statutory provisions that introduce guidelines for employment whose applicability is limited to employees of public administrations or to categories thereof may be waived by subsequent contracts or collective agreements, with the repealed part no longer applicable unless the law expressly states otherwise" (provision introduced by Article 2 of Legislative Decree No. 80 of 1998, cited above).

[29]The requirement that individual employment relationships of private personnel are to be contractually regulated (Article 2.3 of Legislative Decree No. 165 of 2001) should be read in conjunction with the provision that requires equal treatment. Since the worker has the right to the same treatment as other workers vis-à-vis the administration, the individual employment contract, beyond its role of establishing the relationship, has no regulatory scope since the application of different treatments is not permitted.

[30]See Constitutional Court No. 89 of 27 March 2003.

the process of legislative unification is limited by the special nature of the employment since "the public administration still retains – even under a newly formalised contractual relationship – a specific connotation (...) [given] the specific nature of the public employment for which Article 97 of the Constitution legitimises a differentiation of treatment compared to private work".[31]

Although, as we have seen, there was a certain point in history characterised by a containment of special regulations, it was followed by a trend reversal. Law No. 15 and Legislative Decree No. 150 of 2009 turned the relationship between law and collective bargaining on its head, reinforcing the role of the law and considerably extending its scope of application.[32] In this sense, the change in the clause previously allowing collective bargaining to re-appropriate spaces improperly occupied by legislative re-applications is largely symbolic. With the provisions of 2009, this is allowed only where it is expressly permitted by law. Alongside this, the scope of collective bargaining is generally determined by an ambiguous and reductive formula,[33] while all special rules laid down by law are to be classed as "*imperative*" *(mandatory)*, nullifying any contrasting contractual clauses.

Then there are many specific exclusions to the intervention of collective bargaining. Several are added to those already provided for in the previous legislation,[34] including exclusions relating to managerial prerogatives, as well as the assignment and revocation of managerial duties.

Beyond the above exclusions, for certain matters, bargaining is allowed but only within the limits provided for by law. This is the case with disciplinary matters which are subject to the most detailed regulations, which not only leaves no room for bargaining but puts stringent constraints on the exercise of managerial powers. Meanwhile, the government is entrusted to draw up a "code of conduct"[35] for public employees which is considered a "source of disciplinary responsibility". This brings

[31]See, for example, Constitutional Court No. 82 of 27 March 2003 and No. 146 of 16 May 2008.

[32]The widening of the scope of legislative application and of the limits and constraints imposed both on collective bargaining and on managerial autonomy follows the apparent inadequacy of the regulation on negotiating sources and the specific exercise of managerial powers in some areas, including discipline, increased productivity, assessment and reward.

[33]In modifying the previous regulations it is established that "the rights and obligations directly relevant to the employment relationship" are to be determined by collective bargaining, as it may be inferred that the organisation of work and the related employer powers are outside its scope.

[34]With Delegated Law No. 421 of 1992 (Article 2.1(c)), the following points were reserved for regulation by law: (1) legal responsibilities pertaining to individual operators in conducting administrative procedures; (2) bodies, offices and procedures for their assignment; (3) basic principles of office organisation; (4) selection procedures for access to employment and starting work; (5) organic roles and resources; (6) guarantee of the freedom to teach and professional autonomy in educational, scientific and research activities; (7) regulations on responsibility, conflicts and cases of prohibition of accumulation of employment and public positions.

[35]See Article 1.44 of Law No. 190 of 6 November 2012. The given purpose of this code, approved by Decree of the President of the Republic, is to "ensure the quality of services, the prevention of corruption, and compliance with the constitutional duties of diligence, loyalty, impartiality and exclusive commitment to upholding the public interest".

us back to a unilateral set of regulations (the code is established as a regulation with a direct disciplinary scope), which has led to talk of "re-publicising certain aspects of the public administration employment relationship (...) [justified by the fact that] the public interest and the public law authority are constitutionally essential to govern the employment relationship of those entrusted with overseeing public duties".[36]

However, the view that the application of a special set of legal rules amounts per se to the restoration of the public system does not seem to be widely shared. Special rules do not necessarily imply a specificity of the subject matter. And, moreover, the most recent developments (as we will discuss) show signs of a shift towards a structure more in-keeping with the initial spirit of the reform, and which is in line with the position of the Constitutional Court.

14.4 The Integration of Law and Collective Bargaining in the Constitutional Court's Case Law

The Constitutional Court has played a key role in solving some delicate constitutional issues brought about by the privatisation of public employment. It is of particular relevance, in this sense, the statement that Constitution does not require the status of public employees to be provided by a primary law. This eliminated the conflict between public employment and the structural form of private labour. At the same time, the Court affirmed the need for an "even application" of both legislative and contractual sources in order to ensure a "proper balance" between the values of impartiality and sound administration expressed by the Constitution.[37] The solution outlined above has been the subject of clarifications and criticisms in a broad case law. Particularly, in reaffirming that the application of private labour law to public employment does not violate the Constitution per se,[38] the Court did not fail to

[36]Carloni (2013), pp. 384–385. Article 17 of the code of conduct lays down "the minimum duties of diligence, loyalty, responsibility and proper conduct that public employees are required to observe". Such duties, free of the stress and redundancy that at times taint their definition, can be read as legal obligations of a contractual relationship relating specifically to the performance of the work in question, as with the duties of diligence and loyalty provided for in Articles 2104 and 2105 of the Civil Code.

[37]According to the Court, the balance between impartiality and sound administration should be pursued with "a set of legally reserved regulatory aspects" and deferring to civil law those which do not concern the exclusively public moment of administrative action (see ruling no. 309 of 16 October 1997).

[38]Constitutional Court, ruling no. 11 of 30 January 2002.

penalise solutions deemed disrespectful of what is required by the "specificity of the relationship"[39] and the need for "the pursuit of general interests".[40]

Meanwhile, a particularly significant ruling was passed recently on collective bargaining in the public sector.[41] Called to pass judgement over the legislation providing, since 2010, for a prolonged suspension of collective bargaining, due to demands to reduce public spending, the Court ruled out the illegitimacy of legislative measures restricting contractual and wage dynamics. The Court also refused the argument of the unequal treatment of public employees to private ones. On the same occasion, the constitutional judge confirmed that public work and private work "can not be considered one and the same thing" and that differences remain, even after the privatisation of public employment. However, according to the Court, considering the "pivotal role" of collective agreements to be acknowledged also in the public sector, is to be regarded as being in violation of the Constitution a system placing a block on collective bargaining when it assumes a structural nature (as in this case).

Set against a legislation that reduced its role, the Court ri-affirmed the value of a system in which collective bargaining plays a major role in synergy and dialectics with primary law. The collective agreement "effectively and transparently covers the opposing interests of the parties and contributes to the effective implementation of the principle of proportionality of pay, acting on the one hand as an instrument for ensuring equal treatment of workers and, on the other, as a driving force of productivity and merit". Thanks to its multiple roles in public employment, collective bargaining involves a complex net of constitutional values (Articles 2, 3, 36, 39

---

[39]See the case law on the rule of public competition, which the Court deemed constitutionally applicable in regard to so-called career progression, meaning "access to a new job with bigger responsibilities" (see, inter alia, Constitutional Court No. 273 of 23 July 2002). Also deemed symbolic were the Court's rulings on executives, highlighting the need for "specific guarantees" not only to protect them as employees, but first and foremost to ensure the effectiveness of constitutional principles aimed at protecting public interests. Introduced in this light, for example, were the rulings indicating as constitutionally unlawful the system for the automatic termination of any executive office that does not uphold fair process, with the automatic replacement of executives who fail to verify achieved results (see Constitutional Court Rulings 103 and 104, both of 23 March 2007).

[40]The Constitutional Court (Ruling 351 of 24 October 2008) has deemed the provision granting solely compensatory protection to any unfairly dismissed public executive as constitutionally unlawful. In regard to this last legislation, the Supreme Court also noted that the modulation of protections in the context of contracted public employment requires that the legislator consider interests differently to private employment such that, whereas in the private sector "the employer's power of dismissal is limited to the purpose of protecting the employee, in the public sector the power to terminate employment is shrouded in guarantees and limits that are imposed not only in the interest of the person to be dismissed, but – above all – to protect the more general collective interests (...), [thus highlighting] not Article 41, sections 1 and 2, but Article 97 of the Basic Charter" (Supreme Court, Labour Section, No. 11868 of 9 June 2016). In line with the above considerations, Article 21 of Legislative Decree No. 75 of 2017, with a provision that clearly differentiates the public from the private sector, established that in cases of cancellation or declaration of nullity of the dismissal, all public administration employees (executives or otherwise) are protected by the ruling of employment reinstatement, as well as the payment of compensation.

[41]See Ruling No. 178 of 23 July 2015.

and 97), within a framework of protections backed by numerous supranational sources; thus, the suspension of negotiation and contractual procedures is admissible only for limited periods of time and can not be extended *ad libitum*.[42]

Ultimately, the constitutional Court upholds the virtuosity of a system whose structure and governance is open to integration between legislative source and collective contractual dynamics, in the direction of a moderate application of the principles and instruments common to private employment. This does not exclude, anyway, the appropriate diversifications.

14.5 The Most Recent Developments: A Balance Between Administrative and Labour Law

With respect to more recent developments, reference must be made to the legislative delegation to the government for regulating employment with public administrations per Law No. 124 of 2015,[43] and its implementation.[44] The agreement signed in 2016 between the Minister for Simplification and Public Administration and the Trade Union Confederations and the collective labour agreements for public employees launched over the last few months should be considered in combination.

First of all, it should be pointed out that, since the beginning of the privatisation process, the application of private law in the management of work in public administrations has never been questioned, with the very clear and unambiguous reference to the capacity and powers of the private employer.

It was also noted that a privatisation limited to managerial processes ultimately marks the "failure of the reform ideal".[45] And indeed, it must be agreed that a heavily unbalanced structure in the relationship between legislative and negotiating source,

[42]Following the ruling of illegality by the Constitutional Court, on 23 December 2017, after a freeze on collective bargaining lasting several years, ARAN (Agency for Public Service Bargaining Representation) and the trade unions signed a draft 2016–2018 national labour contract for the central functions department. Not only did this agreement have an economic impact, but it affected trade union relations (promoting the institutions of union participation and updating matters of supplemental bargaining) and many regulatory aspects (absences, permits and leave, work hours, holidays, disciplinary codes, flexible employment, etc.). The resumption of national collective bargaining has been strengthened by a relative attenuation of the regulatory limits by Legislative Decree No. 75 of 2017, although numerous specificities remain in the regulation of employment and their respective protections. In this respect, the reference to the public interest as a justifying element of a specificity does not always seem appropriate (as in, for example, the rule whereby in the event of cancellation of a disciplinary penalty due to lack of proportionality the judge is given the power to recalculate the fine, taking into account not only the severity of the actions but the "specific public interest violated").

[43]See Article 17 of Law No. 124 of 7 August 2015.

[44]See in particular Legislative Decree No. 75 of 25 May 2017.

[45]Romeo (2012), p. 717.

in the mix common/specific regulations, as well as in the connotative elements of special rules, is not coherent with a fully privatised model.[46]

However, the most recent developments allow for a corrective understanding of certain excesses. With the agreement mentioned at the beginning of the paragraph, the government has undertaken to rebalance the relationship between sources, recognising that the public sector needs a serious overhaul that cannot be achieved in the absence of robust labour relations which, as occurs similarly in the private sector, help to raise productivity levels. This results in a strengthening of the role and an extension of the scope of collective bargaining, considered "as a natural place for the regulation of the employment relationship, workers' rights and guarantees, as well as the organisational aspects by which they are directly affected".

These aims have been partially implemented in Legislative Decree No. 75 of 2017. Regarding the relationship between law and collective bargaining, it is certainly notable the restoration of the formula that in principle assigns preference to collective bargaining[47] (for its symbolic value, rather than for its practical value, limited by making numerous legal provisions mandatory). Similarly, in identifying the scope of the contract, it is used an expression more appropriate to its historical function.[48]

Nonetheless, employment in the public sector is still largely subject to special rules.

Take for example the disciplinary area, among those in which the legislative re-application in 2009 has been more intrusive and limiting with respect to freedom of negotiation. Following a substantial early uniformity, there has been a radical transformation that has not only resulted in a strong expansion and prevailing regulation of legislative source over negotiating source, but has also seen disciplinary action become compulsory, attributing responsibility to those who fail to exercise it. This has led to the question of whether the nature of the disciplinary power of the public employer has been transformed, with a return to public law, and over the direction of the changes introduced by Legislative Decree No. 75 of 2017.

At present, the answers are cautious. In fact, the "restrictions on operations and on the exercise of disciplinary power" are confirmed, if not reinforced.[49] But there are elements that lead to still consider the disciplinary area regulated by private law: the explicit reference to Article 2106 of the Civil Code; the reserve to collective

[46]According to Ricci (2014), pp. 461 et seq., the regulatory exceptions and differences with respect to private employment are now such that there is no longer mention of the uniqueness of employment relationships. Rather, today there would be three distinct types of employment: that under public law, that which is strictly private, and "in the middle that with public administrations (. . .) less and less privatised and increasingly characterised (. . .) by the retrieval of elements typical of the public relationship for emphasising authority and control".

[47]In the provision on repealability of the law by successive contracts, the wording "only if expressly provided for by law" is deleted.

[48]Which eliminates the "distrust" attributable to the 2009 text "reopening the theoretical physiological spaces of collective autonomy" (Natullo 2018, p. 34).

[49]Quaranta (2018), pp. 234 et seq.

bargaining for establishing infringements and imposing penalties related to certain cases of absence; and, moreover, the authority of judicial protection attributed to the labour court.

On the other hand, the push arising from the resumption of union relations and negotiations must not be underestimated. Staying with the disciplinary field, a look at recently signed national contracts reveals numerous measures concerning "employee obligations", "disciplinary penalties", "disciplinary code", "precautionary suspension" during disciplinary proceedings and in case of criminal proceedings, "relationship between disciplinary proceedings and criminal proceedings", and "agreed determination of penalties". And it is not unreasonable to expect that the renewed negotiations will lead to a more general re-appropriation of the role and the spaces by collective bargaining.

Ultimately, the overall state of the matter reveals an imperfect linearity, uncertainties and ambiguities. The reform was conceived by assigning perspectives and expectations to the abandonment of the public model and the adoption of the private model in terms of quality of staff regulation and policies, organisational and managerial improvements, greater attention to productivity and efficiency, and a reduction and control of spending. If the forecasts only partially translated into effective results,[50] played a significant role the fluctuations and uncertainties of the reform process, the weakness in its application—thanks in part to insufficient adaptation and reinforcement of the professional skills of the staff involved—as well as unavoidable resistance to change. But the solution, rather than returning to a not bright past, would likely mean having to maintain and stabilise the regulatory framework which, in light of the indications of the Constitutional Court, should balance commonality and specificities of public and private work. This must be accompanied by a strong commitment to preparing the conditions necessary to ensure a consistent operational translation (not least, strategies aimed at strengthening and realigning to the new regulatory contest the professional skills of personnel).

References

Apicella EA (2016) Pubblico impiego: poteri organizzativi e gestionali. In: Cavallo Perin R, Police A, Saitta F (eds) L'organizzazione delle pubbliche amministrazioni tra Stato nazionale e integrazione europea. Firenze University Press, Firenze

Carinci F (1998) Una nuova rivista per una riforma *in itinere*. Lav pubbl amm: 1 et seqq

Carinci F (2013) Contrattazione e contratto collettivo nell'impiego pubblico "privatizzato". Lav pubbl amm: 493 et seqq

Carloni E (2013) Il nuovo codice di comportamento ed il rafforzamento dell'imparzialità dei funzionari pubblici. Istituzioni del federalismo: 377 et seqq

Cassese S (1997) Presentazione. In: Battini S, Cassese S (eds) Dall'impiego pubblico al rapporto di lavoro con le pubbliche amministrazioni. Giuffrè, Milano

[50]Gasparrini and Mastrogiuseppe (2017), pp. 85 et seq.

Cavallo Perin R (2009) L'etica pubblica come contenuto di un diritto degli amministrati alla correttezza dei funzionari. In: Merloni F, Cavallo Perin R (eds) Al servizio della Nazione. Franco Angeli, Milano, p 147 et seqq

D'Antona M (1998) Lavoro pubblico e diritto del lavoro: la seconda privatizzazione nel pubblico impiego nelle "Leggi Bassanini". Lav pubbl amm: 35 et seqq

Gasparrini S, Mastrogiuseppe P (2017) La contrattualizzazione nel lavoro pubblico: i suoi risultati, le sue prospettive. In: Dell'Aringa C, Della Rocca G (eds) Lavoro pubblico fuori dal tunnel? il Mulino, Bologna, p 85 et seqq

Melis G (2015) La burocrazia. il Mulino, Bologna

Natullo G (2018) Tra legge e contratto: l'"equilibrio instabile" del sistema delle fonti del lavoro pubblico. In: Esposito M, Luciani V, Zoppoli A, Zoppoli L (eds) La riforma dei rapporti di lavoro nelle pubbliche amministrazioni. Giappichelli, Torino, p 15 et seqq

Orsi Battaglini A (2007a) Fonti normative e regime giuridico dei rapporti di impiego con enti pubblici. In: Orsi Battaglini A, Scritti giuridici. Giuffrè, Milano, p 1475 et seqq

Orsi Battaglini A (2007b) Impiego pubblico e lavoro privato: per un nuovo statuto comune. In: Orsi Battaglini A, Scritti giuridici. Giuffrè, Milano, p 1355 et seqq

Quaranta M (2018) Illeciti rilevanti e tipologia di sanzioni. In: Esposito M, Luciani V, Zoppoli A, Zoppoli L (eds) La riforma dei rapporti di lavoro nelle pubbliche amministrazioni. Giappichelli, Torino, p 234 et seqq

Racca GM (2009) Disciplina e onore nell'attuazione costituzionale dei codici di comportamento. In: Merloni F, Cavallo Perin R (eds) Al servizio della Nazione. Franco Angeli, Milano, p 250 et seqq

Ricci M (2014) Lavoro privato e lavoro pubblico; rapporti tra le due ipotesi di riforma, estensione delle regole e modelli. Lav pubbl amm: 461 et seqq

Romeo C (2012) La legge "Fornero" e il rapporto di impiego pubblico. Lav pubbl amm: 713 et seqq

Rusciano M (1978) L'impiego pubblico in Italia. il Mulino, Bologna

Rusciano M (2015) Contrattazione collettiva nel pubblico impiego. 1. Profili generali. In: Diritto on line – Treccani

Saitta F (2016) L'organizzazione delle pubbliche amministrazioni e lo Stato nazionale: i profili evolutivi. In: Cavallo Perin R, Police A, Saitta F (eds) L'organizzazione delle pubbliche amministrazioni tra Stato nazionale e integrazione europea. Firenze University Press, Firenze

Zanobini G (1958) Corso di diritto amministrativo, vol III. Giuffrè, Milano

Chapter 15
The Management of Healthcare in Italy: The Situation 150 Years Since Administrative Unification

Fabio Saitta

Contents

Abstract The research is aimed at identifying the faults of the Italian Health Service (S.S.N.) in the light of recent legislative developments and upcoming reforms. It stems from an analysis of the underlying reasons of the substantial failures of law No. 833 of 1978, the following reform in 1992–1993 presents several elements of a sharp break with the past legal regime and institutional set up, although it did not sweep away the whole pre-existing system. Then, on the one hand, the 1999 reorganisation adopted by the so-called "Bindi Decree" has completed the process started in 1992 and, on the other hand, reintroduced some elements of the 1978 Law. Furthermore, the research highlights that the shift from traditional administrative model to that of the current hospital authorities with a company's form has created more issues than any other privatization process in Italy. Indeed, in this context, health service agents deal with social rights and entitlements and, most of all, with the protection and promotion of the right to health being the social right par excellence. Finally, the paper analyses the "variables" which are the grounds for

---

F. Saitta (✉)
Magna Graecia University of Catanzaro, Catanzaro, Italy
e-mail: fsaitta@unicz.it

D. Sorace et al. (eds.), *The Changing Administrative Law of an EU Member State*,
https://doi.org/10.1007/978-3-030-50780-0_15

any further reform plan of the national health system and identifies possible legislative proposals which would improve the issues constantly at the crux of any health system reform over the years.

15.1 The Organizational Evolution of the Italian Healthcare System, Starting with the Administrative Unification Laws

At the end of 1859, when Italy had already embarked on the path towards unification, our country's first comprehensive healthcare law[1] was enacted, the wording of which was replicated several years later in Annex C to the administrative unification law of 20 March 1865, whose 33 articles unified the management of the public healthcare system throughout the Kingdom according to the model used by the Kingdom of Sardinia from 1847 to 1851.[2] This consisted of a multifaceted regulatory framework "without any actual healthcare organization criteria; in fact, healthcare was one of the many functions of the civilian government, and was operated by its hierarchically dependent bodies":[3] responsibility for healthcare essentially lay with the Minister of the Interior and, under its dependence, was entrusted to the prefects, sub-prefects, and mayors, who were assisted by advisory bodies appointed by the crown or the ministries, and, at a lower level, nominated by municipal councils.[4]

Having replaced the draft "Public healthcare code" introduced in 1885 by Agostino Bertani (which, envisaging a technical-healthcare pyramid entirely independent of the administrative authorities [prefects and mayors], was certainly of interest due to its progressive political leaning, but was premature, precisely for this reason, due to the conditions afflicting the Italian State at the time),[5] the provisions of Annex C and its subsequent regulatory amendments remained in force until the so-called "Rattazzi Law",[6] which—despite maintaining "the joint interest of society" in public healthcare—left the administrative structure responsible for the continuity of the public healthcare system established by the first unification law largely unaltered.[7]

[1]Law no. 3793 of 20 November 1859.

[2]Soresina (2015), p. 180.

[3]see Giannico (1984), p. 75.

[4]More information, see Soresina (2015), pp. 180–185.

[5]see Giannico (1984), p. 77.

[6]Law no. 5849 of 22 December 1888.

[7]see Soresina (2015), p. 185; Giannico (1984), pp. 78–80.

A major turning point came just 70 years later, when, upon the creation of the Ministry of Health,[8] the technical and administrative autonomy already envisaged at the time of Bertani, *ergo* "the definitive and solemn politicization of public healthcare issues", was achieved:[9] the health authorities were identified, on a provincial level, as the provincial physician, and on a municipal level, as the medical health officer, both of whom were considered peripheral subjects of the newly instituted Ministry.[10]

Meanwhile, art. 32 of the Constitution had intervened, which, in stating that "the Republic safeguards healthcare as a fundamental individual right and collective interest, and guarantees free medical care to the needy", had rendered "positive action on the part of the public authorities in this field constitutionally necessary."[11]

It took nearly two more decades, however, for the constitutional provision to be implemented via comprehensive healthcare reform: in fact, the first step in this process was the hospital reform of 1968, approved by the so-called "Mariotti law",[12] which completed the process of publicizing the hospitals by creating the hospital authority, the public legal entity with which the public health and charitable institutions were associated, the other public authorities operating exclusively in the field of hospital care, and the hospitals belonging to other public authorities serving other purposes. Under this first reform, "the residual charitable/volunteer nature that still characterized the operations in question was overcome, with the establishment of a more stable configuration as a public service intended for all of society."[13] Once the right of all citizens to be admitted to hospital had been recognized (subject only to the individual's need, regardless of any assessments concerning the payment of the hospital costs),[14] the right of all citizens to receive healthcare couldn't help but follow: at this point, only a short step remained towards real healthcare reform.[15]

With the transfer of the "healthcare and hospital care" functions to the ordinary-statute regions,[16] which took place following the first regionalization,[17] and the division of the functions among various institutional levels, which took place with the second,[18] the groundwork was laid for the comprehensive reform of the system:

[8]Law no. 296 of 13 March 1958.

[9]As highlighted by Arru (1967), p. 37.

[10]see Giannico (1984), p. 80; Soresina (2015), p. 185.

[11]Aicardi (2003), p. 629; in similar terms, De Cesare (1989), p. 246, according to whom "the wording of this article of the Constitution is to be understood as the proposition of a particular healthcare intervention policy, in order to determine the State's intervention priority."

[12]Law no. 132 of 12 February 1968.

[13]Aicardi (2003), p. 636; according to De Cesare (1989), p. 249, the hospital law "ironically originated from the fact that the charities and hospitals had since become mere service providers, whose financial independence was provided by mutual aid societies."

[14]Art. 41, letter *a)*, Law no. 132/1968.

[15]De Cesare (1989), p. 249.

[16]This is the definition of regional ownership contained in the original art. 117 of the Constitution.

[17]Italian Presidential Decree No. 4 of 14 January 1972.

[18]Italian Presidential Decree No. 616 of 24 July 1977.

Law no. 833 of 23 December 1978 established the national health service and fully implemented the constitutional precept envisaging a public service based on the principles of universality, equality, and globality. Regardless of the delay with which it was approved (due also to an oversimplification of the constitutional precept),[19] and the defects and contradictions that it certainly contained,[20] this law represented the "culmination of an evolution that, having begun with the old nineteenth-century style liberal State, ultimately reached the point of comprehensively handling people's most vital needs."[21]

The law of 1978 was based on new dedicated bodies, the local health units, whose uncertain legal status was likely one of the main reasons for the general failure of the law itself.[22] In fact, with a decision upheld by arbitration,[23] which removed the regions from their healthcare management role and relegated them to act as mere planners and service regulators,[24] the legislature established the local health office (USL), on the one hand, as an independent administration with its own bodies and functions,[25] and, on the other hand, as "an operational structure of the individual or partnering Municipalities, and mountain communities":[26] on a more analytical level, it consisted of "all the various units, offices and services of the individual or partnering municipalities and mountain communities that fulfil the duties of the National Health Service within a specific area."[27] It was therefore an entity that played a dual role: a functional role, with regard to its broader health protection duties; and an organizational role in relation to the local authorities, to whom the function itself was, in principle, entrusted.[28] This led to an initial complication due to the fact that the USLs weren't necessarily constituted for each individual municipality, but rather for zones or areas determined by the regions based on State law[29] and political/administrative decisions largely expressed in regional laws: it therefore followed that, when the area identified by the region was broader than the boundaries of an individual municipality, the instrumental relationship between the municipality and the USL tended to change and become more complex.[30]

---

[19] Morana (2009), p. 321 et seq.

[20] Which will be discussed in greater detail further ahead.

[21] Catelani (2010), p. 45.

[22] According to Cazzola (1994), p. 138, the establishment of the USLs was "one of the most unique legal solutions to a political problem": the assignment of all administrative healthcare and hospital functions not entrusted to the State and the regions directly to the municipalities.

[23] The debate on this topic is nicely summed up by Aicardi (2003), p. 639, even in a footnote, to which reference is even made for the relative bibliographical references.

[24] Poggi (2014), p. 89.

[25] Art. 14 of Law no. 833/1978.

[26] Art. 15, paragraph 1 of Law no. 833/1978.

[27] Art. 10, paragraph 2 of Law no. 833/1978.

[28] Falcon (1984), pp. 587–588.

[29] Art. 14 of Law no. 833/1978.

[30] see Falcon (1984), pp. 591–592.

The USL was also established by the Law of 1978 as a structure governed by bodies that weren't of a technical nature, but instead had democratic legitimacy, or rather political bodies indirectly representing the local electoral body, which were tasked with ensuring the connection between the USL and the individual or partnering municipality or mountain community: the general assembly, which had general functions, made up of the municipal council or the representatives of the partnering municipalities, and the management committee, elected by the same assembly with a limited vote.[31]

Nevertheless, it was difficult to argue that it acted as a tool of the subject political/administrative authority, since, for that purpose, it was lacking both the powers exercised by a representative assembly in relation to a smaller body with a specifically administrative function, and, above all, the ability to divide the representative assembly from the administrative body, and to attribute them to different organizations: the representative assembly didn't act as a body of the local authority, but seemed to have been "cropped" from the authority itself, to which it basically belonged, in order to act as a representative assembly of the USL while at the same time maintaining its own identity: therefore, from a strictly legal standpoint, the USL did not seem to be conceived as a technical/administrative part of a broader local organization that encompassed it and utilized it, but rather as a comprehensive and complete local organization in its own right.[32] This ambiguous configuration of the USLs from an organizational standpoint, as well as the limited guidance and control exercised over them by the municipalities, meant that these new bodies would establish themselves as autonomous local powers, which essentially weren't responsible for their operating results.[33]

The failure of the Law of 1978 was also due to the excessive politicization of the bodies, which had been appointed according to "political criteria, or rather development criteria",[34] and the unlimited and indiscriminate extent of the services, also due to the lack of approval of the healthcare plans. This approval process was unwisely entrusted to a law that was extremely difficult to draft,[35] and caused the system's costs to increase in an unsustainable manner,[36] thereby forcing the legislature to frequently intervene in order to cover the USLs' budget deficits, thus substantially reducing the scope of the principles of globality and free service envisaged by the law itself.[37]

In an attempt to remedy the inefficiency of the system established by the 1978 reform, which gradually proved to be increasingly unmanageable, the legislature first made some minor adjustments to the internal organization of the USLs—namely

[31]Art. 15 of Law no. 833/1978. On this topic, see Aicardi (2003), p. 639.

[32]see Falcon (1984), pp. 593–596.

[33]Aicardi (2003), p. 641.

[34]Giannini (1991), p. 33.

[35]On this point, *amplius*, Mattioni (2009), pp. 272–273.

[36]Effectively defined by Merusi (1982), p. 13, as "with rigid funding and anarchical management."

[37]see Aicardi (2003), p. 641.

including the insertion of a board of auditors among its bodies,[38] the abolition of the general assembly, and the reduction of the number of the management committees' member–[39] and, later, with the so-called bridge-law of 1991, replaced the political bodies with a special administrator appointed by the region, who was vested with "all powers of management, including legal representation", but was still supported by a board of trustees appointed by the municipality, with general guidance functions.[40]

The time was ripe for a total reorganization, which was launched with legislative decree no. 502 of 30 December 1992, and—following a Constitutional Court ruling[41]—corrective legislative decree no. 517 of 7 December 1993.

While not entirely overturning the framework of the instituting law of 1978, the 1992–1993 reorganization contained several clear points of divergence from the same:

- the near complete exclusion of the municipalities from healthcare management, and the configuration of the USL as a regional body;
- the reduction of the number, the corporatization, and the depoliticization of the USLs through the creation of a single management body chosen by the region based on technical competence;
- the autonomy of the main area hospitals, which remained separate from the USLs;
- the financial empowerment of the regions;
- the configuration of a system of competition between public and private facilities based on accreditation, and the rate-based financing of the facilities themselves.[42]

Especially with regard to the corporatization of the USLs—which was carried out during the course of the more general process of privatizing numerous administrative bodies during the 1990s—and the changed relationship with the private healthcare operators, i.e. upon the reconstruction of the public health service according to tendentially equal rules and principles, the profound correction of original model becomes clear, to the extent that "we move from a purely public service outlook to a set of values and practical and operational rules (and, therefore, a real philosophy) rooted in the cultural *humus* of the market economy."[43] But major new developments also took place with regard to the provision of services, which by this point was objectively conditioned by the financial resources believed able to be rendered

[38]Art. 13 of Law No. 181 of 26 April 1982.

[39]Law no. 4 of 15 January 1986 (the so-called "Degan mini=reform").

[40]Art. 1 of Legislative Decree no. 35 of 6 February 1991, converted into Law No. 111 of 04 April 1991. On this latter reform, see Clarich (1991), p. 6 et seq.; Rampulla (1991), p. 933 et seq.; Speranza (1992), p. 776 et seq.

[41]Judgement no. 355 of 28 July 1993, in *Foro it.*, 1995, I, 62.

[42]see Aicardi (2003), p. 643.

[43]Ferrara (2007), p. 117.

available to the N.H.S.,[44] and the misappropriation of the national healthcare plan[45] to Parliament,[46] albeit within the scope of an overall design in which the planning continued to represent a prominent central institute.

The reorganization of 1992–1993 was followed by the continued organizational restructuring of the N.H.S.: in fact, with Legislative Decree no. 229 of 19 June 1999 (the so-called "Bindi Decree"), a new reform was approved, which, on the one hand, brought to a close the processes already begun in 1992, and, on the other hand, brought back aspects more similar to the instituting law of 1978.[47] With regard to the former, the process of the corporatization and privatization of the bodies and activities undertaken just a few years earlier became more radical and far-reaching, emphasizing both the strategic role played by the healthcare corporation's general director, thanks to the corporate private-law act,[48] as well as generally subjecting the activities of the corporation itself to private law; on the other hand, "a somewhat moderate public configuration, primarily with regard to the types of legal relationships between the institutions of the public service and the accredited private sector operators",[49] was somehow recovered, and the healthcare services were reorganized as the "expression of a public function, supported by funding of the same nature suitable for satisfying the subjective right of the universality of the subjects."[50]

15.2 Public and Private Healthcare in Italy (and Europe)

Having completed our historical-legislative *excursus*, the first variable to be investigated regards the relationship between the public and private facilities, a topic that would require a much broader analysis than that which can be provided herein. In fact, while it is generally true that the relationships between the public and private facilities is one of the main issues in every sector of administrative law,[51] it is also true that, with regard to the healthcare sector in particular, that which has been authoritatively defined as the "great dichotomy"[52] takes on a unique value and lends itself to different perspectives of observation.[53]

According to a generally acceptable reconstruction, there are at least three models of legal relationships between the public and private sectors: a first model, of an

---

[44]Mattioni (2009), p. 280. On this point, *amplius*, *infra*, § 6.

[45]Which, therefore, as noted by Liguori (1996), p. 58, remained "the core of the system."

[46]see Mattioni (2009), pp. 283–286.

[47]Poggi (2014), p. 90.

[48]This aspect will be discussed again further ahead: *infra*, §§ 3 and 4.

[49]see Ferrara (2007), p. 118.

[50]see Mattioni (2009), p. 299.

[51]For everyone, Napolitano (2003b).

[52]Bobbio (1985), p. 3 et seq.

[53]Conticelli (2012), p. 4.

organizational type, characterized by a decidedly public philosophy, according to which private healthcare workers play a mere supporting role, almost as if adhering to the horizontal principle of subsidiarity; a second model, in which public management is significantly reduced; and a third so-called mixed model, in which the public and private sectors coexist in a balanced manner.[54]

Looking at the most important European countries, one might say that their national healthcare systems are based on two distinct models: the "Bismarck" model, which is derived from the model of solidarity initially introduced for the Prussian soldiers, and is based on mandatory insurance, and the "Beveridge" model, which is characterized by universal coverage, with financial resources derived from general taxation. Despite the differences between the various countries' national health services, at least two unifying elements have been able to be identified: the overall consistency of the political dynamics, with an increasing "healthcare demand" directed at the State, which practically monopolizes the provision of healthcare services; and technological innovation, which meets the healthcare demand, but at the same time allows it to increase.[55]

Italy is the only EU country to have changed its medical *welfare* model during the last century from a Bismarck type system to a Beveridge type.[56]

France, in turn, tried to offer universal and nearly free healthcare coverage to its population after the second world war, specifically by creating a mandatory "health insurance" scheme, whereby the State, thanks to monopolistic conditions, found itself with a forced 'clientele', as the insured individuals were legally obliged to fund everything with their contributions.[57] This system, however, had to contend with limited economic resources, and ultimately generated *deficits* from the very outset. Government leaders were consequently forced to increase the rate of the taxes used to sustain the general healthcare scheme; for this reason, its prospects do not appear to be reassuring.[58]

Germany has adopted a different system, in which the provision of hospital services is heavily regulated by the State, especially since the 1972 law on hospital funding, and with the individual *Länder* being responsible for directly steering the offering and the hospitals' investments.[59] Aside from the differing positions expressed by the German public regarding the privatization of the former public hospitals, the *trend* of privatization has been reinforced, and leads us to anticipate

[54] see Ferrara (2007), p. 149.

[55] Pelissero and Mingardi (2010), pp. 24–25.

[56] see Pelissero (2010), p. 45.

[57] Petkantchin (2010), p. 81.

[58] see Petkantchin (2010), pp. 82–83 and 103, who notes how the increasing role played by taxation in funding the system is not aimed at controlling healthcare costs, but is rather aimed at having broader political and bureaucratic control over the system itself.

[59] Neubauer and Beivers (2010), p. 107.

more purchases of public hospitals by private firms in the future, accompanied by an increasing demand for healthcare and hospital services.[60]

It is also worth noting the healthcare system adopted by the *Netherlands*, which, after a series of reforms, has opted for private management (the system is no longer public), but with the obligation for all Dutch citizens to be insured (as well as foreign residents who work and pay taxes in the Netherlands). A "two-headed system" (one private and the other public) run by private insurance companies that are required to offer at least the basic package to every citizen, who in turn have the possibility of choosing from among several competing insurance companies located in their area, regardless of their age or health status. Allowances for partial coverage are available for citizens whose income is below a certain threshold.[61]

Another interesting healthcare system is that of *Switzerland*, which is based on the same "three-pillar principle" as the Swiss Social Security system, which in turn is founded upon: (i) an age-based public pension scheme, which guarantees all citizens a minimum pension once they have reached the legal retirement age; (ii) a second mandatory pillar that hinges upon the employer and is offered to employees; (iii) optional savings accounts with tax benefits and long-term life insurance capitalization schemes. A system which, as noted, works pretty well, although some circumstances have resulted in poor quality services and a limitation of choices.[62]

The English and Spanish systems, on the other hand, are based on the universal model.

The system adopted in *England* represents the European prototype for the universal model: on the one hand, public healthcare services are funded by taxes, and are provided to the entire population; on the other hand, the system is characterized by a high degree of centralization and integration.[63] However, the system has also undergone major reforms,[64] which have incentivized the separation of the operators (funders and providers of primary and secondary healthcare services), the users' freedom to choose, and the awareness of their needs and rights, all with the aim of increasing competition on the market, thus improving cost control and service quality.[65]

The system adopted by *Spain* represents a particular application of the English system, and has elements that integrate the funding, management, and provision of the services under the public system.[66] The operators qualified to provide services under the public system are both public and private facilities affiliated with the

[60]see Neubauer and Beivers (2010), pp. 124–125.

[61]For further information, see the lengthy essay by Mingardi (2010), p. 127 et seq.

[62]On this topic, *amplius*, Crespo (2010), p. 171 et seq.

[63]D'Angelosante (2012), pp. 41–42.

[64]For more information in this regard, please refer to Civitarese Matteucci (2011a); Id. (2011b) (2), p. 381 et seq.

[65]On this point, *amplius*, Toth (2009a), p. 69 et seq.

[66]As highlighted by D'Angelosante (2012), p.51 set seq., to which reference is even made for the relative bibliographical references.

public system itself, even if the former are much more prevalent. With respect to the English system, however, it is decidedly more regionalized and provides for a greater decentralization of the responsibilities.[67]

In short, while one might say that the European Countries are considerably different in terms of their methods of organizing, regulating, funding, and using healthcare services, all of them nevertheless dedicate considerable resources to healthcare.[68]

Getting back to Italy, in analysing the history of our healthcare legislation, historians and political scientists warn of the inability to reduce the matter of public healthcare to the context of the socialized State, since the healthcare practices always bring private players into the field, even in the most highly advanced public systems of our times.[69] The art. 32 of the Constitution, on the other hand, is limited to the establishment of a health service that's "mandatory for necessary activation", but doesn't seem to require its implementation through public facilities,[70] thus leaving several possibilities open, from the establishment of a public health system, to the promotion of a mixed system, or the funding of private entities.[71]

In our opinion, even if we cannot entrust the management of healthcare "more or less completely to facilities that are at risk of being strongly permeated by a logic of *Gemeinschaft*, and not *Gesellschaft*", and even if "we have to make an effort to at least preserve a space (structurally public, but ethically civilian) where the citizen *sans phrase* can be heard and taken care of as a simple individual",[72] we must nevertheless consider the fact that the functionality of the private sector, given the presence of a public sector, can serve to improve the overall efficiency of the healthcare system, and to guarantee equal access to healthcare services.[73]

15.3 The Privatisation of the Healthcare System: A Difficult Comparison of Diverse Values

As noted,[74] one of the fundamental innovations contained in the reorganization of 1992–1999 regards the organization of the services, which has now taken on a corporate logic and a managerial form of administration: the selected organizational format is that of a corporation, with a clear separation of the management duties, which are entrusted to the managerial component of the organization, and the

[67]see D'Angelosante (2012), p. 57, and the broad bibliographical indications contained therein.

[68]For more information, see Sigismondi (2004).

[69]see Soresina (2015), pp. 188–189.

[70]Aicardi (2003), p. 630.

[71]Corso (1997), p. 410.

[72]Romano Tassone (2003), pp. 643–644.

[73]Clerico (2009), p. 75.

[74]Among the many, see Liguori (1996), p. 66.

guidance duties, which are entrusted to outside political representatives. The USLs, whose numbers have been reduced until a territorial scope that generally coincided with that of the province was obtained, have become "corporations with public legal personality and business autonomy",[75] which "base their activities on the principles of effectiveness, efficiency, and profitability, and are required to respect budgetary constraints, by balancing costs and revenues, including transfers of financial resources."[76] They "conduct themselves according to private-law acts",[77] and even "their organization and functionality are governed by a corporate private-law act."[78]

With good reason, this was immediately seen as a "Copernican revolution that took place within the healthcare system [...]: the managers of the service—the local health units—were transformed from ambiguous and poorly defined "facilities" of the individual or partnering municipalities, to their current state as "corporations" with public legal personality and business autonomy."[79] In particular, in combination with the organisational autonomy with which it is now vested, the latter allows the USLs to define their organizational structures based on the local requirements, thus bridging the previous gap between the formal structure and the actual structure.[80]

In general, it's safe to say that, combined with service-based payment, privatization represented the most original innovation within the context of Beveridge-type healthcare systems. In fact, it was only partly anticipated by the Thatcher Trusts of the English NHS, and was potentially capable of introducing elements of efficiency and competition within a system that largely constituted a public oligopoly.[81]

Elements of considerable originality are also found in the corporate private-law act,[82] which "identifies the operational facilities vested with management or technical/professional autonomy, subject to analytical reporting", and is exclusively bound to "respect the principles and criteria established by [...] regional law":[83] in fact, it

---

[75] Art. 3, paragraph 1-*bis*, legislative decree no. 502/1992, inserted by legislative decree no. 229/1999.

[76] Art. 3, paragraph 1-*ter*, legislative decree no. 502/1992, inserted by legislative decree no. 229/1999.

[77] Art. 3, paragraph 1-*ter*, legislative decree no. 502/1992, inserted by legislative decree no. 229/1999.

[78] Art. 3, paragraph 1-*bis*, legislative decree no. 502/1992, inserted by legislative decree no. 229/1999.

[79] Ferrara (2003), pp. 2500–2501.

[80] Ruffini (1999), Bergamaschi (editor) (2000); Hinna (editor) (2001).

[81] Pelissero (2010), p. 56.

[82] An example of how private law is increasingly also applied to internal structural profiles, which have traditionally been considered the exclusive domain of the public sphere, and the lowest common denominator of the public authority's general institute: Napolitano (2003a) (2), p. 820; interesting and more recent considerations on this topic can also be found in Pioggia (2013), p. 481 et seq.

[83] Art. 3, paragraph 1-*bis*, legislative decree no. 502/1992, inserted by legislative decree no. 229/1999. Therefore, this does not constitute an approval per se, but rather a verification of

allows the public health system's managers to free themselves (even if somewhat relatively, since they fall under the "protective umbrella" of the organizational principles and criteria established by the regional legislature, which not only serve to guide the strategic decisions of the general director, but also to "safeguard" them, or rather to cover them and legitimize them politically, especially when they're painful and unpopular because imposed for budgetary reasons) from the political body in charge of the management itself (the region), and therefore represents "the true centre of gravity of the healthcare sector's business system."[84]

However, as noted by the more acute interpretations, the corporatization of the USLs creates problems far greater than those posed by the privatization of any other facility or public entity: "in fact, the real problem is that the healthcare operators—and therefore the system's overall management—are operating within the sensitive area of social rights, or rather for the protection and promotion of the greatest social right of all, a social right that's even considered to be fundamental, absolute, and irrefutable [. . .]. Which certainly helps to portray the problems of the national health service's organization and management in the entirely unique light of a universal service; a service in which (and in relation to which) the known objectives in terms of effectiveness and efficiency, cost-revenue balance, etc., must be evaluated based on a comparison of values that cannot be mechanistically limited to the mere issue of management, to the simple evidence of a measurable outcome based on the principles of a cost-benefit analysis or analytical accounting, and therefore without regard for the relational and social impact that it ultimately produces (upon both the individual and society as a whole)."[85] This would suggest that the USL is set up as a corporation, or rather an entity that organizes itself and works to provide the service as a business, in a very specific manner.[86] That of the healthcare corporation essentially remains an atypical model that cannot be compared to any other corporate format: in fact, it consists of a public body, which, by virtue of its business autonomy, uses the private sector's tools to guarantee healthcare as a fundamental individual right and collective interest.[87] It is therefore safe to say that the autonomy of the healthcare corporations is only instrumental because the framework of the objectives is entirely determined from outside,[88] and because they are required to operate according to the principles of profitability, but only a "partial profitability", in the sense that the legal regime is not inspired by criteria of complete privatisation, since the service provided is too important and essential: the function of

compliance with the general guidelines indicated the region by, on the part of the regional government: Pieri (2009), p. 40.

[84]see Ferrara (2003), p. 2506.

[85]see Ferrara (2003), pp. 2502–2503.

[86]Clarich (1993), p. 6 et seq.; more recently, with the support of the case law, Rinaldi (2007), p. 1922 et seq.

[87]Pieri (2009), p. 38.

[88]Adami (2013), p. 1422.

safeguarding the public's health cannot be subject to entirely private-sector principles.[89]

15.4 The Political and Technical Management of Healthcare: The Legislature's Hesitations, and Persistent Problems Within the System

As well evidenced by the more thorough interpretations,[90] in abstract terms, healthcare organization systems can be vastly different from one another: with regard to the "overall scope of power", the possibilities range from politics to technocracy[91] (with several intermediate variants like democracy).

Following the overall failure of law no. 833 of 1978 (due also to the excessive politicisation of the USLs, as mentioned above), the legislature wanted to make a fresh start, by changing from an organization based mainly on political/representative models, to a structure inspired by technical/corporate criteria, mainly centred around an individual and intentionally-monocratic management figure: the general director.[92] Representing a complete break from the previous outlook, as it was clearly intended to give a more technical character to the local management of healthcare, which at this point was based on a public service no longer managed by pseudo party experts, but by *managers*, who, although still connected to the political world, were nevertheless held accountable based on principles of efficiency, productivity and profitability, in a system of business-like competition,[93] this decision certainly resulted in a considerable decrease in the degree of democracy in the governance of the matter,[94] but, at least abstractly, appeared to be consistent. This was mainly because the legislature, both in 1992 and, perhaps to an even greater extent, in 1999, had taken care to vest the top management figure of the reorganized USLs with such a broad range of powers as to render him an absolute *dominus*,[95] like

[89]Bottari (2011), p. 46; in similar terms, Catelani (2010), pp. 112–118, which even identifies the managerial efficiency criteria with the public-sector requirements of fairness and good performance pursuant to art. 97, paragraph 1, of the Constitution, which characterizes the public-sector management of these instrumental organizations: therefore, it has absolutely nothing to do with truly private management.

[90]Ferrara and Vipiana (1999), pp. 64–65.

[91]As highlighted, with regard to the USLs, by Romano Tassone (1997), p. 387 et seq.

[92]Cilione (2003), p. 167.

[93]Cappucci (2001), pp. 1249–1250.

[94]On this point, see Constitutional Court, 24 June 2003, no. 220, in *Ragiusan*, 2003, no. 233-4, 77. On the need for citizens to participate in the determination of healthcare choices, by helping to identify the objectives of the NHS, Tallacchini (2006), p. 23.

[95]Gallo (1999), p. 213.

the actual head of a company.[96] This statement is supported by several legislative indications:

(a) first and foremost, there's the corporate private-law act, which, as previously noted, allows the general director to independently organize the entire functionality of his operational structures, and uniquely assigns both the political/governmental duties, and those more typically considered to be of a management nature, to a single individual;[97]
(b) of equal importance is the fiduciary nature of the relationship between the general director and his coadjutors, the administrative director and the medical director;[98]
(c) finally, note should also be made of the similar broad discretion enjoyed by the general director up until just a few years ago, when he was called upon to grant and revoke assignments for the management of both simple and complex facilities.[99] And, in fact, the new medical directors—who are no longer exclusively responsible for the management of the medical procedures, but also administer the *budgets* for achieving their assigned objectives[100]—were initially appointed by the general director outside the scope of a comparative assessment procedure, as the case law unambiguously stated, in contrast to certain interpretations,[101] that art. 15-*ter* of Legislative Decree no. 502 of 1992, introduced by Legislative Decree no. 229 of 1999, in its original version, included the provision for granting the aforementioned assignment as an act of negotiation, based on fiduciary assessments rather than a competitive procedure.[102] The general director was essentially free to choose from a list of suitable candidates prepared by a special commission (without the attribution of scores and without establishing a ranking), with the assignment being granted based on a fiduciary

[96]As defined by Rebora (2005), p. 35 et seq., highlighting how he plays the top management role in the corresponding institutional structure, with full oversight over all the other internal figures, and complete power over the organization and coordination of the main strategic and operational choices. Regarding the top management, with several proposals for rendering the management more collegial, see also Carpani (2010), p. 451 et seq.

[97]Jorio (2006), p. 13.

[98]In fact, the case law unanimously supports the assertion that art. 3, paragraph 7, of Legislative Decree no. 502/1992, as amended by art. 4 of Legislative Decree no. 517/1993, entrusts the general director with discretional and essentially fiduciary decision making power with regard to the appointment of his close associates (specifically the administrative and medical directors), with the sole caveat that the appointees must meet the necessary requirements in terms of professionalism and maximum age, which cannot exceed the age of sixty-five: *ex multis*, Cass., Sec. lav., 3 August 2005, no. 16281, in *CED Cassazione*, 2005; and prior, T.A.R. Puglia-Bari, Sec. II, 28 September 1998, no. 775, in *Trib. amm. reg*, 1998, I, 4232.

[99]In this regard, for all, see Montini (2004), p. 157 et seq.

[100]Lambertucci (2006), p. 825 et seq.; Mazzotta (2003), p. 471 et seq.

[101]Ferrara (2003), p. 2509; Gallo (1999), p. 219.

[102]T.A.R. Lazio-Roma, Sec. III, 31 January 2006, no. 677, in www.giustizia-amministrativa.it.

decision entrusted to his sense of managerial responsibility.[103] Considering also that, by virtue of the previously cited art. 15-*ter*, par. 2, the aforementioned commission called upon to prepare the shortlist of candidates was nominated by the same general director, was chaired by the medical director (therefore, a close associate), and also included two staff managers of the National Health Service, in charge of a complex structure defined by the relative legislation, one of whom was, once again, appointed by the general director, and one by the Board of directors, of which the medical and administrative directors were also members,[104] one becomes aware of the immense power given to the general director in this regard. Although without any legal basis, the general director was also considered to have the power to revoke the aforementioned facility management positions,[105] and was therefore free to confer and revoke positions that, in addition to holding considerable powers and professional prestige, also provided for considerable benefits. Therefore, it certainly wouldn't be illogical to assume that the line of contact between the political leadership and the management lay not between the region and the general director, but rather between the general director and the healthcare management.[106]

However, while being vested with these broad management powers, the general director was rarely able to govern independently, and to exercise the full extent of his powers. This was not only due to actual statutory provisions, which, more or less intentionally, hedged his boundaries of intervention, but was also due to reasons of a somewhat more pathological nature, or rather the persistent control exercised over him by the political parties (as we have previously attempted to demonstrate).[107] The latter, first and foremost, inevitably ended up influencing the regional choices relating to the assessment of the general director's work and his confirmation in his post:[108] the considerable amount of discretion that permeated this process[109] ensured that the decision constituted a means of exerting pressure upon the corporation's top management figure, who could have been compelled to "earn" his confirmation by engaging in less than exemplary conduct.

---

[103]Cass., Sec. un., ord. 8 November 2005, no. 21593, in *CED Cassazione*, 2005; Cons. St., Sec. V, 29 November 2004, no. 7747 and 10 June 2002, no. 3199, in *Foro amm. – CdS*, 2004, 3246 and 2002, 1454; Trib. Avellino, 19 April 2004, in *Ragiusan*, 2004, no. 248, 490; T.A.R. Calabria-Reggio Calabria, 30 October 2002, no. 1511, in *Foro amm. – TAR*, 2002, 3398; TAR Campania-Napoli, Sec. V, 13 June 2002, no. 3448, *ibidem*, 2151.

[104]Art. 17 of Legislative Decree no. 502/1992, as replaced by art. 15 of Legislative Decree no. 229/1999.

[105]Saitta (1999), p. 953.

[106]As highlighted by Mazzotta (2003), p. 483; similarly, see Tuccillo (2012), p. 156.

[107]Saitta (2007), p. 5 et seq.; see also Tuccillo (2012), p. 151.

[108]Art. 3-*bis*, paragraph 6, legislative decree no. 502/1992, inserted by legislative decree no. 229/1999.

[109]Cons. St., Sec. V, 3 October 2003, no. 5746, in *Risorse umane*, 2003, 836.

But the general director shouldn't always be seen as the blameless victim of politicians with their own interests at stake: in fact, in many cases it is the general director himself who carries the heavy burden of a debt of gratitude towards the politicians throughout his entire mandate; a debt that must be paid back when deemed appropriate by the latter. This alludes to the fact, which is well-known among all the industry's operators, that most of the general directors' appointments were made in a far from objective and impartial manner, and not with the aim of choosing the best *manager* for the job, but rather of placing... the right person in the right post. It should be pointed out that this was not only due to the legal provisions governing the issue,[110] but was also due to the backing of the administrative case law, which had consistently upheld that, in view of their purely fiduciary nature, the provisions for the appointment of the general directors were subject to a high level of discretion, to the point of being considered as acts of high administration, and therefore did not require any comparative assessment of the various candidates.[111] Ultimately, many general directors (naturally there were some exceptions) took office by issuing some sort of "blank cheque" in favour of the politicians who supported their appointment, thus severely restricting their independent decision-making power:[112] in fact, the subsequent adoption of the corporate act, the selection of the medical and administrative directors, and even the individual granting of simple and complex facility management positions ended up becoming occasions to return past favours (and, for the politicians who had sponsored them, to cash in!). They were therefore nothing more than operations managers, often securely in the hands of the politicians, and as such were unable to effect the much-desired change in healthcare management. In fact, not even the case law on the so-called *spoil system*, which was allegedly intended to provide a certain stability and autonomy to their employment relationship,[113] was able to render them truly free to allocate resources and to manage them in such a way as to best pursue the objectives, while at the same time respecting their assigned constraints. The resulting picture, which is truly distressing in some respects, is that of a "technocratic" Government that's significantly distorted by persistent over-politicization, and, worse yet, without the political system itself (intended in the noblest sense possible) receiving any

[110]Consider the aforementioned art. 3-*bis*, paragraph 1, which stated that the previously mentioned provisions "are adopted exclusively with reference to the requirements set forth under paragraph 3." As we will see further ahead, the legislation governing the appointment procedure changed several years ago.

[111]In this sense, *ex plurimis*, T.A.R. Campania-Napoli, Sec. V, 9 October 2003, no. 12580 and 13 June 2002, no. 3448, in *www.giustizia-amministrativa.it* and in *Foro amm. – TAR*, 2002, 2151; Cons. St., Sec. IV, 3 July 2000, no. 3649, in *Ragiusan*, 2000, no. 197, 37. In the legislation, for all, Barilà (1999), p. 565 et seq.

[112]This point is eloquently elaborated by Carpani (2010), p. 457: "The fiduciary nature of the relationship [...] can be fertile ground for exploiting the broad powers of a Director who does not respect the rules of impartiality and good administration, as well as for requests to be submitted to the corporate *management* by the responsible regional bodies in order to obtain decisions or forms of conduct that are not consistent with the law."

[113]Ceresetti (2009), p. 1655 et seq.

benefit whatsoever; which would have at the very least led to a greater participation of the citizens in corporate decisions, and therefore a more democratic process. Hence the need to learn from past experiences (that of 1978, and that undertaken from 1992 to 1999, which is still relevant today), in order to find the right dosage of politics and practicality that will finally allow healthcare to be adequately managed.

In this sense, there has recently been positive legislative action concerning the procedure for the general director's appointment (which now involves a comparative assessment and adequate justification), as well as his job assessment criteria, and the procedure for the appointment of complex facility managers, which is now set up as an actual competition.[114]

However, after over 20 years of experience, during which the regions and the general directors did not show themselves to be competent at appointing, respectively, the general directors themselves and the complex facility managers, the Balduzzi reform would likely have done better to make a definite choice, thereby completely eliminating any remaining fiduciary aspects of the procedures for appointing positions.

With regard to the top management, this alludes to the fact that, after legislative decree no. 171 of 2016 was corrected by legislative decree no. 126 of 2017, the national procedure is now entirely independent of the subsequent local procedure, which is no longer in any way required to acknowledge the reasons for which the top management intends to give priority to a suitable candidate holding a much lower score than the other candidates, whether during the creation of the shortlist of candidates, or during the assignment of the position (a task which is now performed by a regional commission appointed by the president of the region).[115]

Not to mention the fact that the public healthcare and healthcare organization training required for aspiring directors is somewhat perplexing, as it is entrusted to a course organized by the region, without any involvement on the part of the university system.[116]

Although it would have been better to entrust the entire process of appointing the senior complex facility managers to an actual contest, at the present time the general

---

[114]Art. 3-*bis*, paragraph 3 of legislative decree no. 502/1992, as amended by art. 4 of legislative decree no. 158/2012, converted into law no. 189/2012. For more details, see Niglio (2012), Tuzza (2012) and Fragale (2013), p. 567 et seq.

[115]Critical considerations in this regard are raised by Monaco (2017), p. 699 et seq., spec. 704–705, according to which the latest legislative decisions "seem to bring together the reform process and the particular political logics that should have been done away with in favour of more meaningful meritocratic criteria." More recently, however, see T.A.R. Valle d'Aosta, Sec. I, 14 February 2018, no. 14, in *www.lexitalia.it*, no. 2/2018, which reiterates how, in light of the clear provisions of art. 2, paragraph 2, of legislative decree no. 171/2016, any appointment of a general director, on the part of the regional council, that does not in any way indicate the reasons for his/her appointment, should be regarded as illegitimate.

[116]Jorio (2018).

director is still entitled to choose "even the lowest ranking candidate" identified by the commission, or even to forego filling the positions entirely.[117]

Moreover, in light of the well-established constitutional case law concerning the assignment of management positions, it doesn't appear that the new medical directors (despite now being required to handle the administration of their respective budgets, as well as the management of the medical procedures) can be considered as equal to the corporation's top management (or rather, the administrative and medical directors), within the circle of the so-called fiduciary management,[118] and can therefore be excluded from the meritocratic logic that now permeates the entire system for granting management positions that do not involve direct cooperation with the political body.[119]

15.5 State and Regional Healthcare Management

The "variables" upon which any further healthcare management reform project will have to be based does not, however, exclusively regard that which was initially defined as the "overall scope of power", but also the problem of allocating and dividing the tasks and functions between the State and the regions. This problem must now be reviewed in light of Title V, Part Two, of the Constitution, which has certainly broadened the scope of the regional legislative competence, by replacing the original item "health and hospital care" with that titled "healthcare", which is now included among the current body of legislation in art. 117, paragraph 3, of the Constitution.[120] This represents another strategic option that will have to be reflected in any future legislative decisions aimed at improving the current system, and which we therefore intend to examine, even within the limitations of the space available.[121]

The question essentially concerns, on the one hand, the implied reinterpretation of the managerial and organizational aspects of the NHS within the scope of the more general matter of "healthcare" and, on the other, their already successful transfer under the exclusive legislative jurisdiction of the regions.[122] In this respect, it should first be noted that a part of the legislation and the case law were vested with an organizational competence from the state's supposed jurisdiction over the

[117]As highlighted by Cerbo (2015), who notes the difficulty of identifying a steady equilibrium between the binding nature of the ranking established the commissioners and the fiduciary nature of the choice made by the top management, who naturally want to ensure a certain degree of subjectivity in a choice concerning the corporation's management.

[118]For indications regarding the differentiation criteria for fiduciary and non-fiduciary management, see, if you will, Saitta (2008), pp. 299–303.

[119]On this point, more recently, Ieva (2016), p. 1702.

[120]Morana (2018), p. 3.

[121]Limitations that preclude a description of the non-unique pathway of decentralization undertaken by the NHS from 1978 up until the present, thus forcing us to defer to Griglio (2009), p. 223 et seq.

[122]As highlighted by Bottari (2011), pp. 9–10.

"determination of essential performance levels",[123] *i.e.* the power to dictate the basic principles of the NHS's organizational framework.[124] The State, however, does not appear to be able to go any further, because, by virtue of the inclusion of "healthcare" as a matter of joint jurisdiction, with regard to which the state legislation is only able to deal with the "determination of the basic principles",[125] every fundamental legislative power relating to healthcare organization must be allocated to the regional legislation.[126] However, there is no doubt that the constitutional system inferred by the laws currently in place have attributed broader organisational autonomy to the regions.[127] And while it's true that it's difficult to find the right balance between the need for healthcare uniformity and the now differentiated organizational models, in relation to which broad regional autonomy is granted,[128] it is also true that the decisive effort to regionalize the NHS has long given rise to regional situations that are considerably different from one another, even in terms of the rules governing the organization and functionality of the regional health service and the relationships between the various institutions:[129] in 2013, for instance, there was a consolidated trend of establishing health corporations on a provincial level (ASPs), which are now found in almost every region, while there is also no shortage of unified corporations on a regional level (Marche, Molise, Aosta Valley and the autonomous provinces of Trento and Bolzano).[130] However, this complete organisational autonomy has not yet been effectively utilized, as the healthcare organizations of the various regions still have rather uniform organizational models, which basically reflect the provisions of the legislative decrees of 1992 and 1999.[131] There are also several regions (e.g. Lombardy) whose healthcare systems constitute true alternatives to those of all the other regions.[132]

---

[123]Art. 117, paragraph 2, letter *m)* of the Constitution.

[124]For all, Molaschi (2003), p. 523 et seq.; similarly, see Ferrara (2007), pp. 123–124. On the "'possible' differentiation" of the LEAs, Antonelli (2018), spec. § 3.

[125]Art. 117, paragraph 3 of the Constitution. On this point, for all, see D'Angelosante (2007), p. 30 et seq.

[126]In the sense that "the organization of healthcare services falls within the scope of the Region's duties", Constitutional Court, 15 February 2000, no. 63 and 22 July 1999, no. 351, in *Giur. cost.*, 2000, I, 484 and in *Reg.*, 1999, 1152. In the legislation, Ferrara (2007), pp. 129–130; according to Nicolazzi (2002), p. 1745 et seq., the experience of the regionalization of healthcare services is precisely one of the reasons that has led the constitutional legislature to include the subject of "healthcare" on the current legislative agenda.

[127]Bottari (2011), p. 12.

[128]Miglioranza (2005), p. 2445.

[129]On this topic, most recently, see Fares (2018).

[130]For more details, see *Relazione sullo Stato Sanitario del Paese 2012-2013*, p. 15.

[131]Cicchetti (2013), p. 107 et seq.; Balduzzi (2005), p. 717 et seq.

[132]Pelissero (2010), p. 47.

De iure condendo, the text of the constitutional amendment approved at first reading by the Parliament several years ago must also be taken into account. In fact, in providing for the outright elimination of the concurrent legislation, this amendment granted the State exclusive legislative authority over "general and common provisions relating to healthcare, social policies, and food safety", and limited the legislative power of the regions to the "planning and organisation of healthcare and social services."[133]

15.6 The Right to Healthcare During the (Economic) Crisis: The Legislature's Decisions and the Indications Provided by Constitutional Case Law

It's no secret that the so-called right to healthcare[134] does not constitute an intangible presumption in terms of legislative choices, as its recognition must take other constitutionally protected values and principles into account, including the need to balance public funding:[135] in other words, each individual's claim to medical treatment is guaranteed to the extent of the objective limitations that the legislature encounters in relation to the organizational and financial resources at the system's disposal.[136] We're therefore talking about a situation that's vastly different from the era when the law instituting the NHS was passed, or rather when the "unlimited faith in the magnificent and progressive destiny of the rightful social State" caused the citizens' performance expectations to be increased, "in the same manner as somewhat absolute subjective legal situations."[137] From this standpoint, one might say that the reorganization of 1992–1999 provided for a radical renewal, as it replaced a healthcare system that was based on the detection of needs whose satisfaction was ensured with a system conditioned by pre-established financial parameters.[138]

Today, this raises the question as to whether it would be better to have improved management *performance* at the cost of a relative sacrifice in terms of the citizen/user's performance expectations, or else an end product that better corresponds to the latter's expectations, but characterized by a certain budget *deficit*.[139] If the end, this question regards the (political) decision for the central administration to determine

[133]For the first indications in this regard, see Jorio (2015a), p. 1.

[134]With regard to its varied contents, for all, Police (2003), p. 1173 et seq.

[135]T.A.R. Campania-Napoli, Sec. I, 18 March 2008, no. 1372, in *Foro amm. – TAR*, 2008, 783.

[136]T.A.R. Lazio-Roma, Sec. III *ter*, 2 December 2002, no. 10892, in *Foro amm. – TAR*, 2002, 4019.

[137]see Ferrara (2007), p. 155.

[138]see Mattioni (2009), p. 280.

[139]see Ferrara (2007), p. 169.

the *budget* to be allocated to the NHS,[140] and therefore entails the more general problem of the difficulty of applying the criterion of profitability to certain areas of administrative activity.[141] This problem is effectively conveyed by the question as to whether it is better to "producing health or DRGs".[142] Therefore, during these times of economic crisis, the prospects for intergenerational equity are particularly critical, and it becomes necessary to explicitly clarify the levels of assistance that the NHS will be able to continue to ensure on a universal basis.

From the perspective of the organization, which also "constitutes the decisive meeting point of the inevitable tension between essential performance levels and available resources",[143] without prejudice to the possible implementation of various models in terms of funding,[144] the constant decline in the financial resources available to the regions to fund the healthcare systems requires the corporations to develop every possible organizational formula aimed at identifying sources of funding other than regional transfers and the revenues linked to the provision of ordinary services (tickets), i.e. the ability, typical of private businessmen, to delve into dynamic market contexts in order to obtain additional sources of funding.[145]

In this regard, however, the Constitutional Court's recent open-mindedness should be noted, as it has clearly stated that "the budget is affected by the assurance of our inalienable rights, which cannot be denied due to the need to balance the budget itself."[146]

It's a statement that clearly stands out,[147] and should serve to reaffirm the existence of certain fundamental rights that still cannot be touched by policies of reducing public expenditure:[148] that area that, nearly a decade ago, the Constitutional Court itself had defined as an "unfailing nucleus of guarantees",[149] which

---

[140]That is to say, the extent to which the citizens are willing to pay to maintain it: Testi (2009), pp. 434–435. On the procedural relationship between the LEAs and the available resources in healthcare, see Balduzzi (2013), pp. 25–28.

[141]On these issues, it is permissible to defer to Saitta (2001), p. 491 et seq. With specific regard to public health, the difficulty of obtaining the concrete ability to exercise the right to healthcare in the presence of a poor definition of LEAs is well noted by Spandonaro (2013), p. 39 et seq. Recently, in the sense that the LEAs consist of the set of activities, services and benefits that the National Health Service provides to all citizens, whether free of charge or upon the payment of a *ticket*, regardless of income or place of residence, T.A.R. Veneto, Sec. III, 7 May 2015, no. 491, in *Giurisd. amm.*, 2015, II, 774.

[142]Catanati (2010), p. 529 et seq., who, in an intentional and openly provocative manner, inserts the antithesis between quality of care and the corporate vision of the hospital, which is represented by the notorious DRGs.

[143]Balduzzi (2013), p. 29.

[144]Broad indications in this regard can be found in Petretto (2012), pp. 6–9.

[145]Sammartino (2015), p. 1.

[146]Judgement 16 December 2016, no. 275, in *www.giurcost.org*.

[147]Di Donato (2017), p. 25.

[148]Madau (2017), p. 11; Ardizzone and Di Maria (2017), p. 185.

[149]Judgement 04 July 2008, no. 251, in *www.giurcost.org*.

could call back into question the concept of the financial conditioning of fundamental rights.[150]

And the conditional is not used by chance, as the State Council recently reiterated, on the one hand, that "with regard to healthcare, in the presence of inevitably limited resources, the possibility of unlimited spending, having regard exclusively for the needs, regardless of the severity and urgency, is unthinkable, as the expense must be commensurate to the actual availability of the financial resources, which affect the quantity and the level of the healthcare services";[151] and, on the other hand, that the definition itself of the LEAs "is not only aimed at offering a catalogue of services that the State is required to guarantee in order to ensure the effectiveness of the right to healthcare, but is also to be regarded as the limit that the individual regions must respect in order to avoid creating an imbalance in their financial resources."[152]

Nevertheless, if the Constitutional Court considered it inconceivable that the legislature might violate that boundary of undeniable assets, which "include the school transport service and assistance, since, for students with disabilities, it constitutes an essential element for ensuring the effectiveness of the right in question",[153] why then *preclude* possibility that the right to healthcare might be insusceptible to financial conditioning?[154]

On the other hand, if it is true that the most recent constitutional case law gives rise to the obligation of the regions to guarantee these inviolable right under all circumstances (or rather, "no matter what sacrifices or by whom"), including healthcare,[155] and that the administration case law, in turn, has shown some sensitivity in admitting the justifiability of the LEAs,[156] a certain degree of optimism can perhaps be retained.

If we then broaden our outlook to include all of Europe, we cannot help but notice that Italy's NHS costs less than those of many European countries that are similar in terms of economic development, such as France, Germany, Sweden, Austria and

---

[150]In this sense, see Lucarelli (2016), p. 8; Grasso (2017), pp. 7–8.

[151]Sec. III, 22 February 2017, no. 836, in *www.giustizia-amministrativa.it*.

[152]Sec. III, 23 January 2017, no. 267, in *www.giustizia-amministrativa.it*.

[153]Judgement no. 275/2016, cit.

[154]see Saitta (2017), p. 10.

[155]Bergo (2017), p. 13.

[156]Among the decided cases, see Bergo (2017), pp. 17–25, specifically makes note of the judgement whereby the closure of the Hospital in Bracciano was deemed to be incompatible with the so-called *golden hour*, or rather the maximum time limit within which patients must be guaranteed access to basic treatments for survival, such as emergency room services (Cons. St., Sec. III, 30 May 2012, no. 3242, in *www.giustizia-amministrativa.it*). Most recently, on the illegitimacy of the closure of an emergency room for financial reasons, without considering the needs of the population affected and the limit of 60 min indicated by law, T.A.R. Umbria, Sec. I, 7 February 2018, no. 98, in *www.lexitalia.it*, no. 2/2018.

Great Britain,[157] and that Italy's healthcare spending to GDP ratio is now lower than that of Greece, and is similar to that of Mexico.[158]

It therefore goes without saying that the issue of healthcare spending[159] is part of the broader issue of guaranteeing social rights at a time of severe economic crisis, which can only be briefly addressed herein.[160]

15.7 Current Competition in the Healthcare Sector

As we have seen,[161] the public/private relationship of the NHS was already controversial during the post-unification period, became progressively more complicated with approval of the Constitution, and subsequently with the instituting law of 1978, appeared to turn in the direction of integration during the reorganization of 1992, and once again became problematic. This is especially due to the fact that the private sector is now competing with the public sector in the distribution of resources and budgetary allocations, under the Bindi Decree, with which the legislature, concerned about the indiscriminate increase in healthcare spending (which is also to be contained via greater control of the private facilities operating under the NHS), introduced limits to the principles of freedom of choice and equality among the facilities that provide services to the public.[162]

In fact, a series of provisions upon which we cannot dwell here prevent us from considering the public and private facilities as having equal positions, from allowing actual competition in the healthcare sector,[163] and, therefore, from granting the user freedom of choice.[164] In short, it might be said that the so-called "third reform" (legislative decree no. 229 of 1999) was characterized, on the one hand, by the strengthening of the principles of planning and the introduction of harsh restrictions on freelance medical professionals, and, on the other hand, by the acceleration of the corporatization of the public service providers, and the establishment of a detailed

[157]For more specific references, see Frittelli (2017), Pelissero (2010), p. 63 et seq., according to whom Italy's problem is, rather, due to "moderate public health spending in a State with an overall public spending and public debt that are already too high due to the harmful spending policies implemented by the governments over the past decades"; Montella and Mostacci (2014).

[158]Antonini (2017), p. 5.

[159]On this point, more recently, see D'Angelosante and Tubertini (2016), pp. 113–117.

[160]On this topic, more recently, see Poggi (2017); Di Marco (2017), pp. 8–12.

[161]*Retro*, § 2.

[162]Conticelli (2012), pp. 237–240, 245 and 249–253; Liguori (2012), pp. 13–14, according to whom, with the intervention of 1999, the opening of the market that characterized the legislation of 1992–1993 gave way to opposing logics marked by rigid planning, with the effect of protecting the private sector operators who had already joined the NHS in a reserve role.

[163]On this topic, *amplius*, D'Angelosante (2012), p. 303; Id. (2013), p. 1.

[164]Lottini (2008), p. 2553 et seq.

pathway for rendering them equal to the private service providers, based on the accreditation/contract mechanism.[165]

The result was a healthcare market characterized by a sort of "administered competition",[166] which could pose compatibility problems with the European competition forecasts:[167] in fact, it is well known that the European Union considers services of a general/economic interest, pursuant to the Treaty, to also include healthcare services (even if it concerns itself with the same insomuch as their organization and provision must be compliant with the competition and internal market regulations, and they must not diverge from the their specific assigned mission[168]), and therefore this subject matter, which is generally reserved for the individual Member States, becomes relevant to the European system in terms of access to market operators, the existing market's operating rules, the connections between the *providers* operating on the market, and the systems for funding and remunerating the services provided.[169]

Ultimately, however, despite considering healthcare services as economic services, the European Court of Justice itself cannot help but acknowledge that the European tradition is largely based "upon the guarantee of healthcare according to a public framework that ensures tendentially universal health services."[170]

15.8 In Conclusion: The Future of Healthcare Services in Italy and Europe

In a recent interesting book, an authoritative scholar, who had dealt with healthcare systems several years earlier,[171] tried to use specific parameters to verify whether the Italian healthcare system can truly be considered one of the world's best, as indicated by a survey conducted by the World Health Organization at the beginning of this century.[172] The Ministry of health also recently published a *Report on the State of the Nation's Healthcare 2012-2013*, which states from the very beginning that "the Italian scenario paints a complex picture from both an economic/financial and

[165]As highlighted by Pelissero (2010), p. 57, according to whom all of this is an expression of an centralistic and government-controlled vision that's bound to fail. In the sense that accreditation, in particular, should be regulated differently, Cerrina Feroni (2012), p. 113.

[166]Antoniazzi (2004), p. 603 et seq. The same formula is used by Sigismondi (2004), p. 2.

[167]Füßer and Oss (2008), p. 48 et seq.

[168]D'Angelosante (2012), p. 73, who clarifies that the competition system's incompatibility with the mission of general/economic interest must be proven by those who intend to disregard the competitive market statute.

[169]Civitarese Matteucci and D'Angelosante (2011), p. 219 et seq., spec. 221.

[170]Civitarese Matteucci (2008), p. 361 et seq., to which reference is also made for a broad overview of the European case law on the economic nature of services of general interest.

[171]Toth (2009b).

[172]see Toth (2014), reviewed by D'Angelosante (2014), 721 et seq.

clinical/support standpoint, one which requires considerable effort" and for which "a strengthening of the entire healthcare *governance* system" is required, namely "an optimization of the resources and the organizational structure, even with a rethinking of the roles and the integration of the public and private sectors, a strengthening of integrative healthcare, a revival of the Nation's excellence, even from the perspective of cross-border healthcare, and a constant reinvestment in healthcare of that which is gained from the spending review."

At the end of the inevitably incomplete description of the Italian NHS's organizational models, in light of the legislative developments over the past one hundred and 50 years, it should have been revealed that, as since noted by the more thorough interpretations, the most critical factors that were constantly focused upon by the legislators of each era (as a confirmation of the relevance of the "paradox of the eternal reformer") are the creation of a more or less public or private sector management model and the relationship between public and private facilities.[173]

As for the first aspect, with the myth of privatization being a cure for all evils having long been discredited,[174] and with proof having been obtained that corporatization doesn't always guarantee the "depoliticization of the management model",[175] the solution certainly cannot once again consist of the politicization of the management body itself, but rather the elimination of any political pollution from the technical aspects by relying upon meritocracy. And this seems to be the direction in which our legislature began moving, albeit timidly, when it regulated the procedure for appointing the general director, the relative job assessment criteria, and the procedure for appointing the complex facility managers, even at the cost of downsizing the vast power of the top management body and redefining several spheres of activity.[176]

With regard to the relationship between the public and private sectors, in addition to cultivating the idea that non-public institutions can also serve "a function of ethical/cultural pluralism that's useful for the choices of the subject with a personalized interpretation",[177] which began gaining ground in 1999, it is necessary to immediately eliminate the continuing impediments to freedom of choice and the effective equality of these facilities in order to allow for effective competition in the healthcare sector.[178] The so-called "system of the 3As" (authorization, accreditation, and contractual agreement) must be radically overhauled "in an effort to guarantee the presence and the provision of truly excellent healthcare practices, and not the

---

[173]Ferrara (2007), pp. 153–154.

[174]On this point, with specific regard to the organization of the public administrations, see D'Orta (2011), p. 391 et seq.

[175]As stated by Mattioni (2009), p. 312.

[176]Tuzza (2012), pp. 16–17; Niglio (2012), p. 8; a favourable opinion on this legislative intervention is also provided by Jorio (2015b) (2): 1, who blames the so-called "healthcare *managers*" for excessive accounting uncertainties, the formation of an enormous public debt, and the establishment of decidedly inappropriate LEAs throughout half the Country.

[177]see Mattioni (2009), p. 317.

[178]On this point, *amplius*, Caruso (2017), p. 157 et seq.

type that are replicated everywhere, which have such a negative impact upon the treatment outcomes and the citizens' pocketbooks."[179]

In broadening our horizons to include the entire European context, it seems useful to note that the *Euro Health Consumer Index* (EHCI) published in 2014 highlights the consolidation of the "Bismarck beats Beveridge" paradigm: the systems based on mandatory social insurance policies continue to surpass those based on national healthcare services, like the Italian, English, and Spanish systems (even in terms of *performance*); however, when the top five Bismarck countries are compared to the top five Beveridge countries, it becomes clear that, when faced with a much greater *per capita* healthcare expenditure, the health results obtained by the Bismarck systems are slightly superior to those of the Beveridge systems.

It should also be noted that, unlike that which takes place among the regional Italian systems, patients cannot yet freely circulate among the various countries of the European Union, meaning that, despite the presence of an overall trend towards greater competition in the healthcare sector,[180] there currently aren't any elements of competition between healthcare systems organized in different manners, even if the big question of universal and readily accessible medical *welfare* will likely arise once a sense of European citizenship has been established, along with the relative rights.[181] Obviously, the European healthcare markets would inevitably change if the European Court of Justice were to decide once and for all that healthcare security systems are also economic organizations that operate like service providers.[182]

More generally, one cannot help but note how all countries, despite having taken the necessary corrective measures with regard to the significant increase in healthcare spending taking place everywhere due to medical advancements and ageing populations,[183] have reaffirmed the suitability of their original organizational models, as if everyone were to be ultimately jealous of their own healthcare system.[184]

Although it is still uncertain which model of national and European healthcare coexistence might prevail, Europe's role in healthcare politics seems destined to

[179]see Jorio (2015c) (3), pp. 8–9.

[180]As highlighted by Neubauer and Beivers (2010), p. 125. In the sense that international competition between healthcare systems nevertheless exists, and can help the more enlightened politicians to look beyond their borders," Crespo (2010), p. 195.

[181]Pelissero (2010), pp. 78–79.

[182]As highlighted, at the end of a lengthy legal *excursus*, by Füßer and Oss (2008), p. 56.

[183]On this point, for all, Tanzi and Schuknecht (2007), p. 35: "the pressure being placed upon the "healthcare budgets" is likely to increase. Technical progress will probably increase the costs of healthcare services more than in any other sector, and the increased life expectancy and the ageing population will make the improved and cost-efficient use of public resources all the more urgent." Interesting considerations regarding the ageing population's impact upon the future trend of healthcare costs can be found in Sigismondi (2004).

[184]Galli (2010), p. 7.

grow,[185] especially due to at least two shared requirements: keeping costs down, and simultaneously maintaining a high level of healthcare services.[186]

To sum up, it may seem bold to imagine what the future of healthcare in Italy and Europe might hold: however, it is certainly no coincidence that, in a recent authoritative report, the *Economist Intelligence Unit* identified seven *trends*, and consequently five extreme scenarios, which, in its view, describe the potential European healthcare scenario in the year 2030:

- the triumph of technology in the treatment of chronic diseases;
- the creation of a single pan-European healthcare service;
- the promotion of healthy lifestyles and prevention as priorities for the treatment of diseases;
- greater attention to more vulnerable subjects;
- the privatisation of all treatments and healthcare services, including their funding.

This latter possibility unfortunately cannot be discarded, since (as recently noted) if the minimum and inalienable nucleus of the right to healthcare isn't "fixed and relatively stabilized",[187] the possibility of healthcare once again becoming a private affair, like in the times of Annex C to the law of 1865, cannot be excluded.[188]

Whatever the case, even if it is difficult to say whether these scenarios will ultimately materialize, these considerations can hopefully serve to enrich the debate.

References

Adami P (2013) Aziende sanitarie e affidamenti in house, in Giur. merito

Aicardi L (2003) La sanità, in Trattato di diritto amministrativo, a cura di Cassese, S., 2[a] ed., Milano, t. 1

Antonelli V (2018) La garanzia dei livelli essenziali di assistenza nei primi 40 anni del Servizio sanitario nazionale: dall'uniformità all'appropriatezza, in www.federalismi.it, n. 7

Antoniazzi S (2004) Servizio sanitario nazionale e principio comunitario di libera prestazione di servizi, in Riv. it. dir. pubbl. com

Antonini L (2017) Il diritto alla salute e la spesa costituzionalmente necessaria: la giurisprudenza costituzionale accende il faro della Corte, in www.federalismi.it, n. 22

[185]D'Angelosante (2012), p. 73 et seq., notes a two-fold emphasis, on a European-wide scale, indicative of an nascent inclination on the part of the European legal order to come up with its own social model (both with regard to competition in the provision of healthcare services, as well as the free circulation of patients, with the charges being borne by the healthcare systems to which the displaced users belong).

[186]Civitarese Matteucci (2008), pp. 388–389.

[187]Bin (2010). p. 721 et seq.

[188]Feliziani (2017), p. 399. With regard to the inexorable devaluation of the right to healthcare due to the economic crisis, see Ferrara (2013), p. 489, who describes this as an "ineffable and unexpected return to the recent past."

Ardizzone L, Di Maria R (2017) La tutela dei diritti fondamentali ed il "totem" della programmazione: il bilanciamento (possibile) fra equilibrio economico-finanziario e prestazioni sociali (brevi riflessioni a margine di Corte cost., sent. 275/2016), in Dir. reg
Arru L (1967) L'organizzazione sanitaria sul piano centrale, in L'ordinamento sanitario. L'amministrazione sanitaria, a cura di Alessi R., Vicenza (I.S.A.P., Atti del Congresso celebrativo del centenario delle leggi amministrative di unificazione, 11 voll., Vicenza, 1967-1969)
Balduzzi R (2005) Cinque anni di legislazione sanitaria decentrata, in Reg
Balduzzi R (2013) Aziendalizzazione, livelli essenziali, risorse disponibili, in Efficacia ed equità nell'assetto federale del Servizio sanitario nazionale (Atti del Convegno di Roma del 19 maggio 2011), a cura di Cicchetti, A., Milano
Barilà E (1999) La nomina ed il rapporto di lavoro del direttore generale delle aziende sanitarie e ospedaliere nella riforma del servizio sanitario nazionale, in Lav. pubbl. amm
Bergamaschi M (a cura di) (2000) Manuale di organizzazione delle aziende sanitarie, Milano
Bergo M (2017) I nuovi livelli essenziali di assistenza. Al crocevia fra la tutela della salute e l'equilibrio di bilancio, in Riv. A.I.C., n. 2
Bin R (2010), Verso il "federalismo fiscale" o ritorno al 1865?, in Reg
Bobbio N (1985) La grande dicotomia: pubblico/privato (1980-1982), in Id., Stato, governo, società. Per una teoria generale della politica, Torino
Bottari C (2011) Tutela della salute ed organizzazione sanitaria, 2ª ed., Torino
Cappucci A (2001) La configurazione giuridica delle aziende sanitarie locali e loro profili autonomistici, in San. pubbl
Carpani G (2010) La sanità, in La corruzione amministrativa. Cause, prevenzione e rimedi, a cura di Merloni F, e Vandelli L, Firenze
Caruso E (2017) L'accreditamento nei servizi sanitari e socio-sanitari fra esigenze di sistema e prospettive di liberalizzazione, in Ist. fed
Catanati C (2010) L'ospedale: produrre salute o DRG?, in Il governo dell'azienda sanitaria, a cura di Vanara, F., Bologna
Catelani A (2010) La sanità pubblica, Padova
Cazzola G (1994) Lo stato sociale tra crisi e riforme: il caso Italia, Bologna
Cerbo P (2015) L'affidamento degli incarichi per la dirigenza sanitaria (Relazione al Convegno su: "La gestione del Servizio sanitario nazionale dopo il Patto per la salute 2014-2016" – Osimo, 12-13 giugno 2015)
Ceresetti G (2009) Spoil system in ambito sanitario tra fiduciarietà ed imparzialità, in Foro amm. – CdS
Cerrina Feroni G (2012) Pubblico e privato nella erogazione delle prestazioni sanitarie: una comparazione con la Germania e con la Svizzera, in Munus
Cicchetti A (2013) Innovazione organizzativa e dinamiche regionali: evidenze da studi sul campo, in Efficacia ed equità nell'assetto federale del Servizio sanitario nazionale (Atti del Convegno di Roma del 19 maggio 2011), a cura di Cicchetti, A., Milano
Cilione G (2003) Diritto sanitario, Rimini
Civitarese Matteucci S (2008) Servizi sanitari, mercato e "modello sociale europeo", in Oltre l'aziendalizzazione del servizio sanitario. Un primo bilancio, a cura di Pioggia., Dugato M, Racca G, Civitarese Matteucci S, Milano
Civitarese Matteucci S (2011a) La riforma del NHS inglese. Evoluzione o rivoluzione?, in Pioggia A, Civitarese Matteucci S, Racca G, Dugato M. (a cura di), I servizi sanitari: organizzazione, riforme e sostenibilità. Una prospettiva comparata, Rimini
Civitarese Matteucci S (2011b) Quadrare il cerchio tra efficienza, qualità e accesso universale alla sanità. La riforma Tory del National Healthcare System inglese, in Munus
Civitarese Matteucci, S, D'Angelosante M (2011) Concorrenza e sperimentazioni gestionali nella prospettiva comunitaria, in La sanità in Italia. Organizzazione, governo, regolazione, mercato, a cura di De Vincenti C, Finocchi Ghersi R, Tardiola A, Bologna

Clarich M (1991) I rapporti tra organi dell'azienda sanitaria: verso il modello della società per azioni?, in Ragiusan, n. 85-6
Clarich M (1993) Le nuove aziende sanitarie tra ente pubblico e impresa, in Ragiusan, n. 9-10
Clerico G (2009) Teoria economica e produzione sanitaria, Milano
Conticelli M (2012) Privato e pubblico nel servizio sanitario, Milano
Corso G (1997) Welfare e stato federale: uguaglianza e diversità delle prestazioni, in Federalismo, regionalismo, welfare state (Atti del Convegno di Roma del 9-10 maggio 1996), Milano
Crespo A (2010) Regolamentazione, cartelli, qualità e scelta: un mix svizzero insostenibile, in Pelissero G, Mingardi A (a cura di), Eppur si muove. Come cambia la sanità in Europa, tra pubblico e privato, Torino
D'Angelosante M (2007) La tutela della salute è competenza concorrente... ma riservata allo Stato, in Foro amm. – CdS
D'Angelosante M (2012) Strumenti di controllo della spesa e concorrenza nell'organizzazione del servizio sanitario in Italia, Rimini
D'Angelosante M (2013) Fallimenti dello Stato e sussidiarietà inclusiva del mercato nel governo della salute ai tempi della crisi economica. Report annuale 2013 Italia, in www.ius-publicum.com
D'Angelosante M (2014) Discorrendo su uno dei migliori sistemi sanitari al mondo (dibattito su La sanità in Italia, di Federico Toth), in Ist. fed
D'Angelosante M, Tubertini C (2016) Cittadinanza amministrativa, salute e sanità, in Cittadinanze amministrative, a cura di Bartolini A, Pioggia A, Firenze
D'Orta C (2011) L'organizzazione delle p.a. dal diritto pubblico al diritto privato: il fallimento di una riforma, in Lav. pubbl. amm
De Cesare G (1989) Sanità (dir. amm.), in Enc. dir., XLI, Milano
Di Donato G (2017) Crisi economica, sovranità statale e diritti sociali nell'era dell'austerity di bilancio e del neoliberismo europeo, in Osserv. cost., n. 1
Di Marco C (2017) La difesa dei diritti fondamentali, beni comuni incomprimibili dello Stato sociale. In margine alla Sent. n. 275/2016 della Corte costituzionale, in www.federalismi.it, n. 6
Falcon G (1984) Unità sanitaria locale, in Giannini MS, De Cesare G (a cura di), Dizionario di diritto sanitario, Milano
Fares G (2018) Principi erogativi ed elementi organizzativi del Servizio sanitario italiano – La prospettiva del giurista, in www.giustamm.it, n. 3
Feliziani C (2017) Sostenibilità finanziaria e servizi pubblici. Corsi e ricorsi storici nel finanziamento del servizio sanitario, in Munus
Ferrara R (2003) Organizzazione e principio di aziendalizzazione nel servizio sanitario nazionale: spunti problematici, in Foro amm. – TAR
Ferrara R (2007) L'ordinamento della sanità, Torino
Ferrara R (2013) Il diritto alla salute oggi: verso la decadenza di un diritto assoluto?, in Dir. e proc. amm
Ferrara, R, Vipiana PM (1999) Principi di diritto sanitario, Torino
Fragale N (2013) La dirigenza delle aziende sanitarie dopo la c.d. riforma Balduzzi, in Ist. fed
Frittelli T (2017) Spunti di riflessione sul sistema di finanziamento del Servizio Sanitario nazionale, in www.federalismi.it, n. 21
Fü߀er K, Oss G (2008) Sanità pubblica e privata; profili italiani ed europei, in www.fuesser.de
Galli G (2010) Prefazione, in Pelissero G, Mingardi A (a cura di), Eppur si muove Come cambia la sanità in Europa, tra pubblico e privato, Torino
Gallo CE (1999) La dirigenza e il personale del servizio sanitario nazionale, in San. pubbl
Giannico L (1984) Amministrazione sanitaria: storia, in Giannini MS, De Cesare G. (a cura di), Dizionario di diritto sanitario, Milano
Giannini MS (1991) L'organizzazione sanitaria dalla legge di riforma sanitaria alla l. 15.1.1986 n. 4, in AA.VV., Lineamenti di organizzazione sanitaria, Milano
Grasso G (2017) Appunti su reddito di inclusione, assistenza socio-sanitaria e vincoli sulle risorse disponibili, in Osserv. cost., n. 3

Griglio E (2009) La sanità "oltre" le regioni. Il superamento della dimensione territoriale statica e la riscoperta del ruolo dei comuni, in Balduzzi, R. (a cura di), Trent'anni di servizio sanitario nazionale. Un confronto interdisciplinare, Bologna
Hinna L (a cura di) (2001) Management in sanità, Roma
Ieva L (2016) Gli incarichi dirigenziali nel lavoro pubblico, in Foro amm
Jorio E (2006) L'atto aziendale e i suoi contenuti, in San. pubbl
Jorio E (2015a) La revisione costituzionale e la salute, in www.astrid-online.it
Jorio E (2015b) La sanità che ci vuole alla luce del fabbisogno reale e delle verità emerse dai conti della Salute, in www.astrid-online.it
Jorio E (2015c) Convenzioni, accreditamento e contratti: una disciplina da rivedere per la sostenibilità del SSN, in www.astrid-online.it
Jorio E (2018) Nella sanità si pretende una governance di qualità ma si snobba la formazione, in www.astrid-online.it, n. 4
Lambertucci P (2006) Dirigenza sanitaria, responsabilità dirigenziale e gestione delle risorse umane: brevi appunti, in Lav. pubbl. amm
Liguori F (1996) Impresa privata e servizio sociale nella sanità riformata, Napoli
Liguori F (2012) Flessibilità e modelli organizzativi del S.S.N., in Liguori, F. – Zoppoli, A. (a cura di), La sanità flessibile, Napoli
Lottini M (2008) Il concorso dei privati al servizio sanitario nazionale: alternativi al pubblico o succedanei al pubblico?, in Foro amm. – TAR
Lucarelli A (2016) Il diritto all'istruzione del disabile: oltre i diritti finanziariamente condizionati. Nota a Corte Cost. n. 275 del 2016, in Giur. cost
Madau L (2017) "È la garanzia dei diritti incomprimibili ad incidere sul bilancio, e non l'equilibrio di questo a condizionarne la doverosa erogazione". Nota a Corte cost. n. 275/2016, in Osserv. cost., n. 1
Mattioni A (2009) Le quattro riforme della sanità. Una lettura sinottica di nodi istituzionali fondamentali, in Balduzzi R (a cura di), Trent'anni di servizio sanitario nazionale. Un confronto interdisciplinare, Bologna
Mazzotta O (2003) Attribuzioni e poteri del dirigente sanitario, in Lav. pubbl. amm
Merusi F (1982) Introduzione, in Unità sanitarie e istituzioni, a cura di Merusi F, Bologna
Miglioranza M (2005) Sanità e principi fondamentali: la programmazione regionale, in Foro amm. – CdS
Mingardi A (2010) Per una eguaglianza più libera: il sistema sanitario olandese, in Pelissero G, Mingardi A (a cura di), Eppur si muove. Come cambia la sanità in Europa, tra pubblico e privato, Torino
Molaschi V (2003) Sulla "determinazione dei livelli essenziali delle prestazioni": riflessioni sulla vis espansiva di una "materia", in San. pubbl
Monaco MP (2017) La dirigenza sanitaria: il "correttivo" rende effettiva la riforma, in Giorn. dir. amm
Montella M, Mostacci F (2014) Austerità, sistemi sanitari europei e diritto alla salute, in www.economiaepolitica.it
Montini M (2004) Gli incarichi di direzione di struttura complessa dei dirigenti medici: questione di giurisdizione e natura degli atti della relativa procedura, in Foro amm. – CdS
Morana D (2009) Dal 1948 al 1978: l'interpretazione (riduttiva) dell'art. 32 Cost. nel primo "trentennio sanitario", in Balduzzi R (a cura di), Trent'anni di servizio sanitario nazionale. Un confronto interdisciplinare, Bologna
Morana D (2018) La tutela della salute fra competenze statali e regionali: indirizzi della giurisprudenza costituzionale e nuovi sviluppi normativi, in Riv. A.I.C., n. 1
Napolitano G (2003a) Soggetti privati "enti pubblici", in Dir. amm
Napolitano G (2003b) Pubblico e privato nel diritto amministrativo, Milano
Neubauer G, Beivers A (2010) Variazioni strutturali e crescente privatizzazione del mercato ospedaliero tedesco, in Pelissero G, Mingardi A. (a cura di), Eppur si muove. Come cambia la sanità in Europa, tra pubblico e privato, Torino

Nicolazzi T (2002) I livelli essenziali di assistenza, in Foro amm. – TAR

Niglio N (2012) La procedura di nomina dei direttori generali presso le ASL alla luce delle novità introdotte dalla legge n. 189 dell'8 novembre 2012 (Un primo commento all'articolo 4 della legge n. 189/2012), in www.lexitalia.it, n. 11

Pelissero G (2010) Il sistema sanitario italiano: una realtà in continua evoluzione, in Pelissero G, Mingardi A (a cura di), Eppur si muove. Come cambia la sanità in Europa, tra pubblico e privato, Torino

Pelissero G, Mingardi A (2010) Introduzione, in Pelissero G, Mingardi A. (a cura di), Eppur si muove. Come cambia la sanità in Europa, tra pubblico e privato, Torino

Petkantchin V (2010) Il sistema sanitario francese sulla strada della burocratizzazione, in Pelissero G, Mingardi A (a cura di), Eppur si muove. Come cambia la sanità in Europa, tra pubblico e privato, Torino

Petretto A (2012) Organizzazione sanitaria, finanziamento e incentivi, in Munus

Pieri M (2009) Le aziende sanitarie, in Le aziende sanitarie pubbliche, a cura di Miriello, C., Padova

Pioggia A (2013) L'amministrazione pubblica in forma privata. Un confronto con la Francia e una domanda: che fine ha fatto il "pubblico servizio" in Italia?, in Dir. amm

Poggi A (2014) I diritti delle persone, Milano

Poggi A (2017) Crisi economica e crisi dei diritti sociali nell'Unione europea, in Riv. A.I.C., n. 1

Police A (2003) Le situazioni giuridiche soggettive degli utenti del servizio sanitario, in San. pubbl

Rampulla FC (1991) La gestione transitoria delle usl tra aziendalizzazione ed amministrazione pubblica tradizionale, in San. pubbl

Rebora G (2005) Profili dei direttori generali nelle aziende sanitarie, in San. pubbl

Rinaldi F (2007) L'incerta natura giuridica dell'azienda sanitaria locale, in Giur. merito

Romano Tassone A (1997) L'azienda sanitaria tra tecnocrazia e democrazia, in San. pubbl

Romano Tassone A (2003) Sussidiarietà "orizzontale" e tutela della salute, in San. pubbl

Ruffini R (1999) Logiche di progettazione dell'assetto organizzativo delle aziende sanitarie pubbliche, in Mecosan, n. 29

Saitta F (1999) Prime considerazioni sull'ultima riforma del servizio sanitario nazionale: la dirigenza, in San. pubbl

Saitta F (2001) Interrogativi sul c.d. divieto di aggravamento: il difficile obiettivo di un'azione amministrativa "economica" tra libertà e ragionevole proporzionalità dell'istruttoria, in Dir. e soc

Saitta F (2007) Governo della sanità e falsa "tecnocrazia": cronaca di un fallimento annunciato, in San. pubbl

Saitta F (2008) Burocrazia e indirizzo politico: il modello della Corte costituzionale (Relazione al Convegno su: "Il diritto amministrativo nella giurisprudenza della Corte costituzionale" – Bologna, 27-28 settembre 2007), in Dir. e proc. amm

Saitta F (2017) La tutela della salute nelle isole minori: il punto della situazione (Relazione alle Giornate di studi su: "Le isole minori: un laboratorio di iniziative e di promozione del territorio, dall'ambiente al paesaggio, dai beni culturali al turismo, dalla sanità all'accoglienza alla luce della legislazione e della giurisprudenza nell'ultimo decennio. Esperienze a confronto"" – Lampedusa, 15-17 giugno 2017), in San. pubbl. e priv

Sammartino M (2015) Attività "imprenditoriali" delle aziende sanitarie nell'ambito dell'art. 43 della legge n. 449/1997, in www.lexitalia.it, n. 5

Sigismondi F (2004) Sistemi sanitari europei, i problemi e le tendenze in comune (Comunicazione alla Conferenza nazionale su: "Per il diritto alla salute un sistema di qualità. Cultura, politica, contrattazione" – Roma, 29-30 gennaio 2004), in www.cgil.it

Soresina M (2015) Sanità pubblica (all. C), in Storia Amministrazione Costituzione, Annale ISAP, n. 23

Spandonaro F (2013) Federalismo ed equità nel Sistema sanitario nazionale, in Efficacia ed equità nell'assetto federale del Servizio sanitario nazionale (Atti del Convegno di Roma del 19 maggio 2011), a cura di Cicchetti, A., Milano

Speranza N (1992) Unità sanitarie locali, in Enc. dir., XLV, Milano

Tallacchini M (2006) Democrazia come terapia: la governance tra medicina e società, in Politeia, n. 81
Tanzi V, Schuknecht L (2007) La spesa pubblica nel XX secolo: una prospettiva globale, Firenze
Testi A (2009) Sostenibilità economica e tenuta unitaria del Ssn, in Balduzzi, R. (a cura di), Trent'anni di servizio sanitario nazionale Un confronto interdisciplinare, Bologna
Toth F (2009a) Le riforme sanitarie in Europa: tra continuità e cambiamento, in Riv. it. pol. pubbl., 2
Toth F (2009b) Le politiche sanitarie. Modelli a confronto, Bari-Roma
Toth F (2014) La sanità in Italia, Bologna
Tuccillo S (2012) Il ruolo del dirigente medico tra politica e amministrazione, in La sanità flessibile, a cura di Liguori, F., e Zoppoli, A., Napoli
Tuzza A (2012) La governance degli Enti del Servizio Sanitario Nazionale. Dalla legge n. 833 del 23 dicembre 1978, alla riforma Balduzzi, in www.lexitalia.it, n. 11

Chapter 16
Civil Protection: The Fight Against Earthquakes

Umberto Allegretti

Contents

Abstract This essay examines Civil Protection as one of the public functions that assumed most importance in the last 50 years as defense of Italian territory and community from social risk. Its importance depends on the fragility of our territory, especially from seismic as well as hydrogeological point of view. A 1992 statute ruled for a long time civil protection after many previous developments and received many amendments and additions. It has recently been replaced by the "Code of Civil Protection" (here: The Code) approved by legislative decree n. 1 of 2018. Such function is very complex: forecasting, prevention, risk mitigation, emergency management and overcoming are its principal components. Prevention has the maximum importance; it is a consequence of the prevision of a damaging event, and must be reciprocally coordinated with laws concerning the different matters (land use, cultural heritage and so on). The organization for carrying out civil protection function is equally complex. It is the task of a National Service, including not just

U. Allegretti (✉)
University of Florence, Florence, Italy
e-mail: allegretti@unifi.it

D. Sorace et al. (eds.), *The Changing Administrative Law of an EU Member State*,
https://doi.org/10.1007/978-3-030-50780-0_16

State agencies, but also regional, municipal and other public and private agencies. However, civil protection is not only an institutional task, but also a social one: the Code and practice provide a role of the science, forms of self-protection by people, participation of the affected citizens in the decisions and intervention of volunteers.

16.1 A Definition

In the present situation of "*Risiko Gesellschaft*",[1] "Civil Protection" (in Italian *Protezione Civile*) is a big issue in the context of Italian public policies and administrative system as well as those of other countries.

Civil Protection (*Sécurité civile* in French, *Protecciòn Civil* in Spanish, *Protecção civil* in Portuguese, *Bevölkerungsschutz* or *Katastrophenhilfe* in German) is an expression that has fairly recently entered Italian law and common use in our language to mean defense from a public or social risk (*rischio*). There are of course many risks tied to natural events (earthquakes, volcanic eruptions, hydraulic and hydrogeological phenomena of various characters) and others phenomena resulting from human activities (industrial, chemical, nuclear, a number of factors causing pollution etc.). Furthermore, there are different levels of risks and Italian law (see the Civil Protection Code—*Codice della Protezione civile*—Legislative Decree n. 1 of 2 January 2018, referred to hereinafter as the *Code*, composed of 50 articles) distinguishes among national, regional and local emergencies, corresponding to different levels of authority and different proceedings. In this essay, we generally limit our attention to earthquakes and to the national level.

In order to correctly interpret the juridical concept of the word *risk*, we should note that it derives from the scientific use of the same word, expressed as product of three factors through the formula:

$$\mathbf{R} = \mathbf{H} \times \mathbf{V} \times \mathbf{E}$$

In this formula **H** corresponds to hazard (*Pericolosità*), that is to say the probability of occurrence of a dangerous event, implied in natural or artificial conditions. **V** means vulnerability (*Vulnerabilità*), that is the degree of susceptibility to damage of a structure or an infrastructure following an event. **E** exposure (*Esposizione*), points out the amount of persons or goods (buildings, structures, infrastructures, productive activities, historic and cultural heritage etc.) which can be damaged by the event.

The aims of civil protection are very complex, but they can be summarized by reference to the classic formula introduced by the Roman architect Vitruvius, who maintained that the required characteristics of buildings are stability, utility and

[1]Beck (1986).

beauty (*firmitas, utilitas and venustas*).[2] Obviously, stability is the primary concern and involves the preservation of human life, or the protection of the human beings from death, injury or other direct harm. But it would be improper to limit the aims of civil protection to these essential priorities, it being also very important to ensure the community life and to safeguard the functionality of urban and territorial services, jobs and other human activities, before and after hazardous events (utility). As well as it is important to preserve architecture, art, landscape and historical artefacts (beauty), so characteristic of the Italian context, for the benefit of present and future generations. Therefore, compared with other countries, reduction of risks is more complex. Some authors[3] propose a true "Italian model" of responding to earthquakes as inherently different from the US and Japanese models, considering the peculiarity of our country.

16.2 A Brief History of State Intervention in a Fragile Territory

Still, the origin of what we now call civil protection is not as recent as the term used. Seismic disasters and other catastrophes of major or of minor entity have always occurred throughout time, due to the exposure of the Italian peninsula, whose "fragility" is high, to such events.

It has been calculated that about 1700 earthquakes have occurred in Italy in the past millennium. Special mention can be made of the earthquake that destroyed a great number of towns in east Sicily (Catania included) in 1693; another great disaster occurred in Calabria in 1783 and Messina and Reggio Calabria were destroyed by a tremendous seismic and tsunami event in 1908.

Strong seismic motions affect about 44% of the entire Italian territory. Their frequency is very high on the Apennines chain from southern Calabria to Central-Northern Italy, in Sicily and in the north-eastern region of Friuli, the highest probability of occurrence (70%) being concentrated in the Apennines. Even if their intensity does not often exceed a magnitude of 7 on the Richter scale, Italy is prone to a strong earthquake hitting one or more regions every 4 or 5 years. In the last approximately 150 years since the foundation of the unitary state (1861), 36 strong earthquakes have affected 21 million people and provoked about 150,000 casualties. In the last 50 years, the number of strong seismic events has amounted to 12, with about 5000 casualties.[4] Every earthquake hits an average number of 70 settlements.

Another strong risk impends on Italian territory and community, without exceptions, from a hydrogeological point of view; harmful landslides of different gravity

---

[2]Inter alia Giuffrè (1987).

[3]De Marco (2017) and Crespellani (2018).

[4]Guidoboni (2018). For an in-depth history of earthquakes in Italy, see Guidoboni and Valensise (2011).

are often generated in at least 10% of the whole territory. In the last 50 years the victims of landslides are estimated to be about 1500 and 5 million people are at risk. These numbers show that among the different natural disasters, earthquakes pose the most severe risk and legislation is frequently called on to deal with them. That is why in principle the subject of this chapter will be the efforts to respond to seismic problems, without omitting some references to other kinds of disasters faced by civil protection authorities.

The most common form of State intervention is special national and regional statutes enacted after each earthquake. These statutes, as well as the intervention of the public authorities, follow rather than prevent the occurrence of the single events. Very rarely could one say that there are sufficient forms of prevention "before" the event, even though after a period of intensive studies we know many methods of forecasting and of preparedness for addressing seismic risk.[5] This habit has continued even in important cases of the last 50 years, such as those of Belice (1968), Friuli (1976), Irpinia (1980), Umbria and Marche (1997), L'Aquila (2009), Emilia (2012) and the sequence that hit four regions of Central Italy in 2016–2017.

In view of the considerable likeness between the consequences of each event and the ways to confront them in general, similar but not identical means are adopted in response. Nevertheless, as each event may give rise to special problems, their concrete management may include the issuance of special orders (*ordinanze*) by general or special authorities, which may also derogate, within certain limits, from general administrative regulations.[6] Reliance on this method is not always justifiable and is the object of frequent abuses.

Over the course of time, have been enacted general statutory provisions. Among them, after an important act of 1970, Act of Parliament n. 225 of 24 February 1992 (composed of 21 articles) was for many years the fundamental source of rules concerning the system of State organization and the single agencies authorised to act during and after events. However, it did not address the substantial aspects of the individual issues tied to every event. Quite recently, the previously mentioned Legislative Decree n. 1 of January 2018 replaced that act and is today the fundamental text governing civil protection. This text has the great merit of laying down general guidelines on *organization* and *proceeding* in this area, incorporating the multiple changes introduced by amendments to the previous fundamental Act, even though it does not contain the *substantial* rules to apply for solving the problems created by the damage resulting from disastrous events.[7] It is accompanied by regional statutes approved by the single Regions.

In addition to Italian law, we must consider the legislation of the European Union, which is based on the Lisbon Treaty (Articles 6 f and 196 TFEU). It is only supportive in nature, that is, the action of the European Union is limited to supporting, coordinating and complementing the action of Member States. Through

[5]Aversa and Crespellani (2017).

[6]Cardone (2011).

[7]Allegretti (2018a).

Decision n. 1313/2013, the EU created a Union Mechanism of Civil Protection (EERC) whereby, on the request of a Member State hit by a catastrophe, it would provide support to the different functions of Member States in this field.[8]

16.3 The Classification of Territorial Zones and the "Seismic Code" (norme tecniche)

The present state of knowledge does not enable us to identify with precision the time, location and magnitude of the single earthquake events; it is only possible, through seismic history and seism-genesis supported by technical instruments to approximately identify these three elements for assessing the probability of an earthquake.

Two kinds of forecasting and prevention means have been introduced. Firstly, the classification of the different zones within the national territory distinguishes, according to the different degree of severity of the earthquake that one could predict on the base of the seismic history and the geological conditions of the soil, four categories of zones of different severity (*zonazione*).

Secondly, as the technical components of legal regulations are generally complex, legislative acts are not sufficient to provide a complete set of rules appropriate to the various situations. A seismic code (*norme tecniche*) is necessary: this code is highly detailed and takes account of advances in scientific and technical knowledge as well as the lessons of experience. Its adoption is entrusted to a set of administrative authorities and it is of course legally mandatory.

Initially, some technical standards were included in specific statutes following the earthquakes of Messina Strait (1908) and Avezzano (1913), and they were limited to those zones. Later, the conviction that all the territories exposed to seismic events require the adoption of prevention measures in order to avert future damage led to the introduction of more general rules. These were introduced for the first time in 1927 and then in the following years, culminating in the important set of standards promulgated in 1974 on the base of an Act of Parliament, whereby they were extended to the entire Italian territory. After many studies, a 1996 decree provided a new body of technical standards.

The following decade was a period marked by true uncertainty. Following the 2003 earthquake of San Giuliano di Puglia, under the leadership of the Prime Minister and the technical guidance of the Civil Protection Department, hurriedly a new body of rules was issued through an initially improper procedure, which resulted in multiple technical errors. After many modifications, a definitive body of rules (Ministerial decree of 14 January 2008; now Ministerial Decree of 17 January 2018) was issued by the Minister of Infrastructure and is now the fundamental basis

[8]The 2018 Code (art. 29) provides the Italian participation to the EERC; furthermore, authorizes the Service to emergencies and rescue activities in foreign countries all over the world in disaster events. In several occasions (as Haiti 2010) this kind of solidarity has just been experimented.

in this field. However, the rules seem too complex and many problems in their interpretation and application continue to give rise to a number of difficulties among professionals and the administrative experts responsible for their application and oversight.[9]

These are the two classic instruments addressing prevention measures, but these cannot be limited therein. Other protection measures are: ordinary land-use planning, the activities of "microzoning" (*microzonazione*),[10] aseismic design of buildings and careful design of these to reduce their vulnerability, citizen preparedness to be ensured through a proper education, etc.[11]

16.4 The "Cycle" of Civil Protection Functions

The task of civil protection is very complex. One might speak about a whole "*cycle*" or a coherent sequence of different activities, with many successive stages of a complete action aimed at tackling the problems related to the unleashing of a calamity and the consequent disaster.

Article 2 of the Code lists the different stages of this cycle. The principal elements outlined as necessary in order to manage risks and deal with events are: prediction and forecasting, prevention, risk mitigation and emergency management and overcoming. In principle, this cycle excludes reconstruction, considering that the latter corresponds to a different task, which will follow at a later time. However, that is only partially true: one could distinguish between a narrow and a broad concept of civil protection, the former including just functions for restoring minimum living conditions, the latter including attainment of a definitive revival of the region struck by the calamity.

The decisions concerning reconstruction depend on many elements and have to be evaluated by actors other than those responsible for civil protection activities; they generally take a longer time to be implemented. However, confusion has arisen between reconstruction and decisions regarding civil protection in a strict sense in more than one case. Reconstruction is too decisive for the future life of the people concerned to be entrusted to the activities and individuals who are mainly acting for civil protection purposes in the strict sense. The Code rightly limits itself in this respect, but at the same time—as a real connection exists between the risks and activities involved in the first stages of civil protection and the complete revival of

[9]The procedure bypassed the competence of the Ministry of Infrastructure. It may be noticed that the Prime Minister was Silvio Berlusconi and the head of Civil Protection Department was Guido Bertolaso. For a critique concerning the different stages of those chaotic events see Crespellani (2003, 2005, 2009).

[10]Crespellani (2014). Microzoning is the technical identification of the response of sites and soils to ground motion due to the different nature and properties of the local soils, which influence the severity of the hazard ("*pericolosità locale*").

[11]Crespellani (2014).

normal life—points out the necessity of a tie between reconstruction and civil protection measures and vice-versa. That is why Article 18.3 establishes the necessity of coordination between ordinary planning and civil protection planning.

Besides, the Code has definitively abandoned, after a long period of extension culminated in the first decade of this century,[12] the extension of civil protection to tasks to which it had nothing to do. It was the handling of so-called "major events" (*grandi eventi*) of the most heterogeneous nature (national, international, even local events concerning police, culture, health etc.) which have to be addressed by different public functions.

The Code provides (Article 2) an analytic definition of the different moments of civil protection. So, forecasting concerns the identification and study of possible risk scenarios for planning the intervention of civil protection authorities. Prevention includes many "structural" and "not-structural" activities aimed at avoiding or reducing damage, based on the results acquired through forecasting. Article 2 lists structural and non-structural activities. The former include risk management and mitigation policies. Unfortunately, even if theory and practice are rapidly growing, the Code fails to mention microzonation. Not structural activities include alerting the population as to the probability of events, disseminating knowledge aimed at building the resilience of communities and the adoption of self-protection measures by citizens, and many others. Emergency management consists in help and assistance provided to the population through urgent measures such as the provision of tents, provisional shelters etc.; while the actions to overcome an emergency include the mitigation of residual risk, the restoration of the most essential services, the recovery of production and jobs, and the urgent safeguard of cultural heritage and residential property.

A consequence of the complexity of these functions and of the links existing between them is the need for a planning method. Each phase has to be the object of a plan (Article 18 of the Code), as it cannot be reduced to isolated acts. The plans outline the "scenario" for their application.

16.5 Prevention: A Problem Not Solved

Within the civil protection cycle, traditionally the maximum importance is granted, generally speaking, to the phase of managing and overcoming an emergency, including of course rescue. That is normal. The life and integrity of people are, according to a long classical tradition corresponding to human nature, the focus of required protection.

[12]This period largely coincided with that of the government led by Silvio Berlusconi and the direction of the Civil Protection Department by Guido Bertolaso. After much criticism, the category of major events had been restricted by a presidential directive of 27 July 2010 and suppressed by law n. 27 of 24 March 2012.

However, in many countries exposed to earthquake risk, such as the US, Japan and Chile, prevention has been drawing maximum attention, as also shows the small proportion of victims produced by strong earthquakes. The importance given to prevention is the ripest fruit of the interpretation of the earthquakes, as we shall see, by the Enlightenment. In Italy, this concentration on prevention is late. It is stressed in many recent documents, such as the "Casa Italia" program devised by a special mission "structure" of the Prime Minister's office (June 2017), now abandoned. We may suspect that all the present talk about prevention is merely rhetoric and does not really correspond to true and efficient engagement by public institutions and to the sensitivity of society. The Code itself is attentive to the definition of the problem, as we saw in the previous paragraph, but fails to provide concrete long-term policies to face it.

The recent specific legislation, such as that introduced following the L'Aquila seismic event, while providing resources for prevention, does not establish criteria for the distribution of financial instruments to the most hazardous, vulnerable and exposed zones of the country. A random distribution of resources across the whole territory is the clear temptation to which such legislation exposes the administration and which politicians, bureaucrats and professionals really prefer to more difficult but objectively justifiable funding criteria (as authors like De Marco 2018 critically underline).

Recent initiatives are now in progress in expert milieu to raise within scientific, political and social world the persuasion of the central position of prevention. Up to now, this movement has not conquered the attention that it deserves and it would be necessary a strong and long fight to impose in a society prone to removal of disasters the conscience of future required by prevention.

16.6 Organization: The National Civil Protection Service

Given the complexity of civil protection activities, one should easily understand why the organization itself of the respective functions is equally complex. This is the subject of chapter III of the Code.

Its form is peculiar: an entire system of public and private institutions whose name is the National Civil Protection Service (*Servizio nazionale della protezione civile*, hereinafter referred to as "the Service"), was created by the Act of 1992. This act largely modified previous simpler models, as the name "Servizio nazionale" shows: it is composed by a number of institutions pertaining to different levels of public authorities (central, regional and local) as direct political members and other public and private entities, as operative and concurrent members, unified by a common task. Previously, different individual ministers (Minister of Public Works, Minister of the Interior, special delegated ministers or secretaries) were authorised to take charge of what is now civil protection. The present Code has maintained and perfected the Service (Article 3 et seq.). In view of the extreme complexity of this system, this essay will just consider the most important components.

The political head of the Service is the Prime Minister (*Presidente del Consiglio dei Ministri*). This occurs in other western democratic countries such as—due to the federal division of the service, whose activities are not within the broad competence of the states—in Germany and in the United States, where the supreme authority is the chief of the executive of the Federal State. In the UK the general policy of civil protection is based in the Cabinet Office. In France, and similarly in Spain, the supreme responsibility lies with the Minister of the Interior; the Portuguese agency works within a *Sistema integrado de operação e Socorro*. In Italy, the reasons for the present choice, adopted in recent decades, are political as well as juridical. Juridical, because many ministers are directly involved, so a strong power of coordination among them is required. But above all political, because the structure of the executive is collegial, but civil protection involves great political sensitivity and is used with a high degree of discretion lying with the chief of the executive.[13]

The second fundamental political actors are the Regions, in the persons of their Presidents: this derives from the fact that the Constitution divides legislative power in matters of civil protection, as "concurrent" power, between the State and Regions. Therefore, many of them act through statute law and administrative action and have created specialised agencies for this purpose. The Code provides that the Regions must govern the organization of the civil protection system in their territory, possibly using the Provinces for services extending to a large area.

The third essential actor of the system are the Municipalities (the Code declares that civil protection is a "fundamental function" of the Municipality), which act primarily through the Mayor (*sindaco*) and the mayor of metropolitan cities (where they exist), as well as through the resolutions of their Councils. The Prefect (*Prefetto*), a state authority formerly acting as the sole local representative of the State, still has a residual power of coordination at the provincial level.

Administrative agencies have a big role in the concrete exercise of the functions of civil protection. It is a role of an essentially technical nature, and their composition is in itself very peculiar, including in the staff seismologists, seismic engineers with different specialisations (structural engineers, geotechnical experts etc.), land planners and possibly sociologists, anthropologists etc. There was a period in which the greatest importance within this division of public power was assigned to the Seismic Service (*Servizio sismico*), which had considerable independence from the Government and acted with technical autonomy in a field requiring a specific role within the State machine. The core of the present organization is the Civil Protection Department (*Dipartimento della protezione civile*—hereinafter referred to as the Department—which, as the principal instrument of the office of the Prime Minister, exercises the power of support and coordination pertaining to the supreme authority.

[13]For instance, during his long term in this capacity, Prime Minister Berlusconi posed the maximum accent on this political power, using it as a means to exercise a strong primacy within public institutions and before society.

In Germany an analogous authority is the *Bundesamt für Bevölkerungsschutz und Katastrophenhilfe*—BBK. In the Unites States the F.E.M.A. In France, the highest authority collaborating with the Ministry of Interior is the *Direction générale de la sécurité civile et de la gestion des crises*; in Spain the *Direcciòn General de Protecciòn Civile y Emergencia.* In Portugal, a specific agency works within the previously mentioned *Sistema integrado*.

In a first stage, the Department was the product of creation by a simple administrative act, whereby it was under the direct leadership of the chief of the executive. However, the responsibility of the important political personality[14] of a Subsecretary (*Sottosegretario*) and then Minister charged of the effective leadership (Friuli 1976, and Irpinia 1980 earthquakes) assured that the necessary autonomy was given to that delicate branch of the government. Just for a brief period (1999–2001), the Department was replaced by an independent agency that was autonomous from the direct leadership of the executive. But in 2001 the agency was suppressed and the Department was recreated, with the precise intent to make this organization directly politically dependent on the Prime Minister himself.[15]

As a result of all these circumstances, this government branch emerged as an important actor in the conduct of public policy and has remained in this condition. That has led to the positioning of this administrative entity inside the core of the State's political and administrative organization and conferred on it a central role in the complex State machine, as well as drawing social attention to the entire political and administrative tableau, something that had never occurred in the past. The Code (art. 8) lists the tasks of the Department as the principal instrument of the Prime Minister and the whole Service. The indoor organization of the Department is very complex and corresponds to its functions. However, one can observe that the function of prevention is not organized adequately inside the Department's structure.[16] It is to notice that for every national emergency the Department creates by order of its head an entity named Di.Coma.C. This special organization, grouping representatives of the different agencies members of the Service, operates, for a limited number of months, as the direction of command and control which acts on the place to coordinate the technical operations necessary for the emergency time, concerning particularly the appreciation of the residual risks.[17] A long-time tradition is the appointment of a special commissioner to oversee administrative activities in the wake of a single earthquake, or a "commander and comptroller in situ" (if one wishes to use an American expression) who answers for the Department. One can read with great pleasure the suggestive description in "Italian Journey" by Wolfgang

[14]Giuseppe Zamberletti.

[15]It was one of the first acts of the Berlusconi Government in 2001 (Law n. 401 of 9 November 2001).

[16]The Casa Italia program proposed the institution within the Prime Minister's office of a second "Department for the promotion and safety of housing" (a duplication of departments that raised some perplexities).

[17]Marsan and Corazza (2018).

Goethe concerning the activity of an Englishman as commissioner for the earthquake in Messina in 1783, but there are other examples in Sicily in the seventeenth century. Nowadays, the head of the Department itself sometimes is appointed as commissioner but this task is frequently given to the president of the respective region (or to one of them in the case of many regions hit by the catastrophe), as representative of the local authorities, and may be sub-delegated by him or her to other local authorities, especially the president of the province. The commissioner should provide for contingent powers to be exercised on behalf of the government in managing the consequences of dramatic events and may approve orders subordinated to the Prime Minister's or Department's acts. The utility of this role depends on the constant presence the commissioner might have on the territory, as compared to the greater distance in space and time of the other authorities. But the actual success of commissioners in different situations has varied; sometimes they exercise few substantial powers, and sometimes they are faded figures.

For operations of aid during the period of emergency, the fire-fighters corps (*Corpo nazionale dei vigili del fuoco*) serves as the traditional and very valuable actor, exhibiting high expertise and personal dedication to saving human life and minimising damage.

16.7 The Role of Science

In addition to the special institutions, all of society is involved in confronting earthquakes.

First of all, the role of the scientific community is of utmost importance (Article 19 of the Code), in terms both of the dissemination of knowledge about earthquakes and the participation in missions entrusted to it by civil protection authorities.

Many branches of science are involved: principally geophysics (in the specific application of seismology), geology and engineering (structural engineering, geotechnics and so on). After the terrible and amply documented seismic event that occurred in Lisbon in 1755 and the large debate surrounding it (Voltaire, Rousseau, Kant were the leaders of enlightened opinion on this subject), the supremacy of the religious and theological interpretation of seismic events as God's punishment for human sins was overcome during the Enlightenment. Nevertheless, in the middle of nineteenth century this view was still present in religious milieus and even in the pronouncements of Pope Pius IX.[18] Gradually, scientific research intervened in the study of ground motion phenomena and developed very useful theories and practices. In present times, no outdated religious interpretations should be widespread in the ideas of our society, as we are conscious that the causes of catastrophes are the result of a combination of natural conditions and human behaviours.

[18]Camaiani (1976).

In the past century, great advances were made in Italy in the Sixties and afterwards, in close relationship with global scientific progress. This was the important result obtained by the group of academic scientists and other experts participating in the *Progetto finalizzato Geodinamica*[19] within the National Research Council, followed by the "National Group for Defence against Earthquakes"—GNDT), both entrusted with conducting dedicated research on behalf of public institutions to enhance protection against seismic events. This research produced substantial progress in Italian knowledge in this field and provided an important body of data to the official authorities. Today, the *INGV* ("National Institute for Geophysics and Volcanology") is an important centre for applied research in the same field.

It must be underlined that, in order to obtain a genuine scientific contribution to the management of earthquake risk, the relationship of science with the work of public authorities (above all the Civil Protection Department) must meet at least three requisites.

The first requisite is the willingness of members of the scientific community to conduct their research not in the perspective of an abstract and purely theoretical method, but rather with a view to its application to the characteristics and problems of the Italian territory and context and the nature of seismic phenomena within this territory. The second requisite, tied to the previous one, is the willingness of scientific researchers to choose and conduct their research for the purpose of meeting the needs and requests of the institutional bodies responsible for the relevant areas. The third requisite, which is not in contradiction with the second just mentioned, is that scientific collaborators maintain their autonomy in the formulation of methods and in respect of the results of their activity. Public institutions must meet similar requisites in the formulation of their requests.

These requisites were observed in the previously recorded practice, but some scientists note that at this precise moment they are not being fully observed, which diminishes the genuine role of the relationship between institutional and scientific development.

A constant institutional bond was established between public institutions and the scientific community, and a National Committee for Forecasting and Prevention of Major Risks (*Commissione Grandi Rischi*) was set up. It was given the tasks of a government consulting body supplying instructions and fulfilling requests for studies and research. It is made up of experts specialized in the different kinds of risks and its organization is governed by a specific decree of the Prime Minister (art. 20 of the Code).

Furthermore, the Code (art. 21) provides that collaboration between public authorities and the scientific community may be achieved through the establishment of centres of competence ("*Centri di competenza*") inside universities and other scientific institutions and in several branches of the public administration. These centres have to be governed by decrees of the head of the Department and

[19]This project was led by the prominent scientists Giuseppe Grandori and Franco Barberi.

agreements may be arranged between the centres and the Civil Protection Service agencies.

Unfortunately, in the case of L'Aquila the Commission Grandi Rischi met on the 31st of March 2009 but failed in its task, which was to punctually examine and draw up guidelines for forecasting shocks and alerting the population so that people could take at least the simplest self-protection measures. Instead, in a public statement the Committee reassured the population, notwithstanding the repeated previous shocks, thereby contributing to the dramatic consequences of the emergency. As six days after that meeting the last shock resulted in more than 300 victims and a large amount of destruction, a criminal proceeding followed. After a conviction by the L'Aquila tribunal, in the second and third instances of the judicial proceeding all members of the committee, except one, were acquitted. This outcome of this process gave rise to strong criticism[20] and its final result can be considered as a prominent example of the widespread but unjustified conviction that "science cannot be put on trial".

16.8 Volunteers

Volunteers are another important social actor in civil protection. They are persons who, by personal choice, wish to participate in civil protection activities; in Italy there is an old, widespread tradition reflecting this attitude. This is particularly true for anti-seismic protection and a set of articles of a special chapter of the Code (Chapter V) has been dedicated mostly to rules concerning volunteers.

Volunteers participate in civil protection activities in two ways. The most important is through organizations of special voluntary services engaged in civil protection activities, which also have to be fostered by the public authorities in accordance with the rules of section II of the chapter concerned. The second is the occasional participation of individual persons during an emergency. In both cases, the volunteers must acquire the knowledge and abilities necessary in order for them to be able to collaborate and act according to the directives of the competent authorities of the Service.

Volunteers are a form of spontaneous and rich participation very frequently to be seen on the occasion of recent Italian disasters. In some cases there has been a strong presence of foreign citizens (for instance after the flooding in Florence in 1966 and the seismic event in L'Aquila in 2009).

[20]See Allegretti (2017).

16.9 The Participation of the Population

As is clear, seismic events (we might say more than other calamities) are not merely technical facts, but also social ones.[21] They involve not only the country's institutions, but also, and one should say mostly, individual citizens and society as a whole. Attitudes of citizens and society are especially useful in non-structural prevention activities, as well as in the projects for reconstruction, which strongly affect the future of communities.

Strong earthquakes may change the life—not only the economy and financial situation—of an entire region; in Italy, a country rich in urban heritage and landscape beauty, and full of economic problems, in just a few minutes they can alter the whole context of national life for a long period. How might one ignore the fact that Italian territory and society are frequently subject to major problems provoked by a big earthquake?

The major impact is of course on the areas directly involved and their populations. If this is true, it is a necessary consequence that the local communities should be closely involved in dealing with the consequences of a calamity. That is why Article 31 of the Code states that the Service is required to inform citizens about risk scenarios and the organization of civil protection and disseminate knowledge and a culture of civil protection in order to favour the community's resilience, the adoption of measures of self-protection and its participation in the planning of the different civil protection activities.[22]

However, in this respect the proposals for action and their implementation are very remote from each other; therefore, the effectiveness of civic participation is less than claimed. In the case of Friuli (1976), the participation of people, in the form of consultation and through the decisions of local authorities and meetings of the population, was high and new, if compared to the hierarchical planning in Belice (1968) and Irpinia (1990). A similar level of public consultation occurred in Umbria and Marches following the 1997 earthquake. In San Giuliano di Puglia (2003) and above all in the L'Aquila case (2009), the hierarchical model was largely dominant, despite the multiple spontaneous efforts of action in the city of L'Aquila. Most important decisions, like the relocation of 15.000 inhabitants of L'Aquila into villages known as C.A.S.E., Anti-seismic Eco-compatible Complexes (*Complessi Antisismici e Ecocompatibili*), were the fruit of an autocratic decision of the Prime Minister.[23] A remarkable participation of the communities about the reconstruction, led by the Special Office for Reconstruction created by statute and by Mayors, seems to be in progress in several towns of Central Italy severely hit by the 2016–2017 seisms, like Amatrice and Accumoli. However, in many small settlements

[21]Solbiati and Marcellini (1983) and Crespellani (2012).

[22]For a global survey of participation all over the world, see Allegretti (2016).

[23]The Prime Minister was still Silvio Berlusconi, fully supported by Guido Bertolaso, head of the Department, and Professor Calvi, founder of the Pavia centre.

participation is intended, above all, to information of citizens and training of the municipal staff.

Participation and the models of its implementation are not, generally speaking, a primary concern either of legislation or as reflected in the ideas prevailing in the scientific community and society. However, the mention of many forms of participation in the legislation passed on Central Italy reveals a tendency of the legislator to accept participation as a principle to be followed in civil protection and reconstruction activities.

Unfortunately, a different model has been adopted with the recent "seism bonus", a type of financial incentive based on substantial State aid provided to homeowners and the owners of production facilities who invest in reinforcing buildings in order that they can better withstand future ground motions. At present, this new State contribution, in the form of an income tax allowance of up to 85% of expenses appears to have a remarkable success, especially in the more active urban contexts, under the strong lobbying of owners and professional associations. However, it is a subject that has given rise to opposing views in the public debate. This form of State intervention has been criticised[24] because of its individualistic nature and disregard for public planning, as well as its being extended to almost all of Italy, including zone 3, which has the lowest degree of seismicity, instead of favouring aid to the most dangerous zones 1 and 2. Is it a serious measure of anti-seismic prevention, as it ought to be, or a means to encourage the building industry?

16.10 The Rights of Citizens Affected: A Gap in the Code

Rights of participation and financial contributions are a delicate subject for citizens affected by a calamity, but also other rights are necessary in order to improve their situation. A true scheme of their rights ("*cittadini del giorno dopo*", or "citizens of the day after", according to a valid definition)[25] should be formulated.

Laws concerning civil protection and its implementation should include a complete set of provisions governing the rights of affected persons, up to the stage of reconstruction.

However, following a long tradition, general legislation limits itself to defining functions and the organization of the response to an emergency and does not directly consider the rights of the community or of citizens. This task is left to specific statutes (generally more than one) issued separately for each calamity. Therefore, for instance, we have statutory acts for L'Aquila, Emilia, and Central Italy.

The rights commonly granted to citizens relate to the extension of terms for legal actions and some kinds of contracts, as well as to the partial suspension of the payment of some taxes and other charges etc. They are very similar in every special

---

[24]De Marco (2018) and Crespellani (2018).

[25]De Marco (2013).

statute; thus they could be reproduced in the Code according to a uniform scheme valid for all earthquakes. The assignment of provisional housing to families that have suffered damage must be adapted to the characteristics of the individual event, but general criteria could be laid down in the general statute. Exceptionally, some variations could be introduced in a special statute only if strictly necessary.

16.11 Some Principles of the Activities in View of Reconstruction

The civil protection cycle in a broad sense does not necessarily end here. The real end, in fact, is the restoration of the normal conditions of life of the community and individual citizens through the reconstruction of the region destroyed or damaged by the calamity.

As already stated, reconstruction of what the earthquake damaged is not truly a part of the civil protection process as strictly conceived. The decision to rebuild depends on many elements and has to be evaluated by actors other than those charged with the different activities of civil protection in a strict sense. That is why cases (such as L'Aquila) in which activities of permanent reconstruction have been confused with civil protection functions in a strict sense at the time of an emergency need to be avoided.

Therefore, it may appear correct that the Code does not directly rule this matter. However, one might think that civil protection, broadly understood, should include reconstruction. Some provisions in this respect should thus be included in the general statute. In this perspective, the Code might briefly outline some general principles guiding post-earthquake policies; such principles do appear in the Code itself, but are principally tied to reflections on culture and practice.

First of all, one of the prevention activities mentioned in the Code (Article 2.4. i) entails coordination between civil protection planning and land-use planning and management. There are two aspects of this coordination. On the one hand, civil protection planning ought to observe, where possible, the directives of the pre-existing land-use planning of the region where reconstruction will take place. On the other hand, these directives have to be adapted to the necessities of civil protection planning, which implies making any necessary modifications to the pre-existing planning policies. The principal technical tools for achieving these aims are damage maps and microzonation maps, which are used in order to reach the maximum possible stability consistent with the various land-use planning requirements. Article 18.3 addresses this point, establishing the need for coordination between ordinary planning and civil protection decisions.

Secondly, the special identity of the locality and community involved in the reconstruction ought to be respected. Delocalisation should be an extreme and exceptional measure; many mistakes have been made in their application in reconstruction following seismic as well as hydrogeological events, as is shown by the historical examples of Belice and Irpinia. Anthropologic factors suggest a different approach; some studies of anthropology[26] show that populations and territories may be damaged for life where delocalisation is imposed. A number of disadvantages result from the alteration of the *venustas* of places and their history. A good criterion was applied in the Friuli reconstruction: rebuild where it was and how it was ("*dove era e come era*"). A criterion naturally to be applied with a sense of measure.[27]

The Friuli example also suggests a further criterion in relation to the timeframe of reconstruction: "first the factories, then the homes and then the churches". This was established as a requirement in the highly productive region of Emilia, where typical forms of local industry were damaged (the production of Parmigiano-Reggiano cheese, pharmaceutical devices manufacturers). It should be established that some provisions might be included in the general statute. Of course, a number of principles have to be observed according to the different situations, including those related to projects of economic recovery and development. For instance, one might imagine that an artistic, landscape, culinary and tourist itinerary should be promoted in the central Apennine region so severely hit by the 2016–2017 earthquakes to favour the recovery of an already poor economy exposed to depopulation, as has occurred in areas of Calabria, hit on many occasions by seismic and hydrological events.

16.12 Funding, the Possibility of Corruption, the Issue of Efficiency

Obviously, the burden of seismic calamities is so high that it may justify the appeal of the Italian government for the European Union's help (provided for under a regulation of 2002 updated in 2014). It may also justify the proposal of the exemption of the country from the restrictions on the budgetary deficit, as permitted both under the EU Fiscal Compact and Article 81 of the Italian Constitution.

In the Code (Chapter VI) three principal funds have been set up within the Prime Minister's budget to meet this burden: a national fund for forecasting activities and prevention, a fund for national emergencies and a regional civil protection fund; the amounts of the latter are transferred to the regions hit by the calamitous events. Special statutes approved by Parliament, very often after a long time, generally provide more specific resources for each individual event.

Many problems in managing the consequences of seismic events arise from the nature of the large financial commitments and the inevitable rush to act in emergency, recovery and reconstruction activities. One of these problems is the risk of political and bureaucratic corruption in public procurement, as has been shown in cases like Belice, Irpinia and L'Aquila. Mafia infiltration is the highest and most dangerous risk.

---

[26]Teti (2014).

[27]Nimis (2009).

The normal application of statutory rules on public contracts and controls is not a sufficient remedy. That is why some years ago a special agency for general prevention of corruption was created: the National Anti-Corruption Agency (ANAC), headed by a judge who is appointed by the government but fully independent. In any case, the courts are the inevitable ultimate recourse.

One could also mention many cases in which a substantial amount of money was spent on projects of little utility: for instance, in Belice Valley large modern buildings completely out of line with the traditional architecture of that region were erected and proved not to be really useful to the population.

An even greater defect of our general administrative system is the scarce effectiveness of many projects, which should ensure consistency with the local history and landscape, and (most notoriously) the practical and economic inefficiency of many bodies involved in administration. The consequences of the Irpinia catastrophe (1990) are still partially felt today; the centre of the town of L'Aquila, despite being of special artistic and historical value, is still encumbered by ruins or impacted by works progressing at an excessively slow pace 9 years after its destruction.

And secrecy, much favoured among government agencies, may be one of the worst obstacles in the fight against inefficiency and corruption.

We would like just to mention another tragic disaster (not seismic in nature) that may serve as a true example of what can happen under certain conditions: the recent event that occurred on the 14th August 2018 in one of the great Italian cities: Genoa. The collapse of an important and daring bridge, considered a masterpiece of Italian engineering of the Sixties, produced more than 40 victims and resulted in what will be a long crisis of the entire transport network and production across a large part of Northern Italy. The bridge had long been suspected of having many deficiencies and the construction of an alternative roadway along the same route ("*Gronda di Ponente*") had been planned. The decision regarding this alternative roadway had been the focus of an important experiment of "débat public"[28] which has now been introduced as an obligatory proceeding for major public works (*grandi opere*) by the recent Code of Public Procurement (Article 22 Legislative Decree n. 50 of 18 April 2018, and Regulation n. 76 approved with a Prime Minister's Decree on 10 June 2018[29]). This form of public debate, a genuine model of public participation, produced important results in 2009, showing the erroneousness of the idea that participation is a cause of slowdown in decision*s* on public works. In fact, almost 10 years later, the new project is at a standstill, providing evidence that the very dangerous deficiency of our administration is the slowness of administrative approval procedures and in the execution of works. It should be added that, just in this case, as newspaper reports revealed,[30] the secrecy of sensitive data was a privileged instrument used to avoid providing information to the public about the

[28]Bobbio (2010).

[29]Allegretti (2018b).

[30]La Repubblica, 28 and 29 August 2018. The Executive admitted guilt and published the secret clauses.

relationships between public administration and private operators of the highway system and probably favoured the collapse probably due to deficiency of maintenance.

Therefore, the true reform of public works needed in Italy in order to acquire a better degree of civil protection is the complete but arduous restructuring of the entire practical system of public administration.

16.13 Conclusions

We may conclude briefly by highlighting the main developments of the last 50 years and the present state of Italian law concerning the problems of civil protection.

A significant progress has been made and among other things we may mention:

(1) Extensive knowledge about the seismic characteristics of the territory as a whole, its seismic classification and more precise information about the seismic characters of several zones;
(2) The refinement of technical standards, despite some defects arising from their complexity and difficulties in their application;
(3) An increase in the practice of microzonation;
(4) A clarification of the role not only of the central government but also of the regional authorities and the initiatives on the part of some of them as regards the seismic discipline in theory and in practice.

Nevertheless, there exist important gaps both in legislation and in practice. Among them we have to mention:

(1) The abuse of specific statutes instead of the formulation of more general rules, especially regarding the rights of citizens affected by calamities;
(2) The lack of concern about prevention and its deformation through isolated initiatives (such as the seism bonus system);
(3) Insufficient citizen participation;
(4) A use of techniques not precisely linked to land-use planning.

References

Allegretti G (2016) Emergenze e partecipazione dei cittadini, Mirandola, Convegno "Terremoti e riduzione del rischio sismico: conoscere per partecipare"

Allegretti U (2017) The Italian civil protection Service. Present situation and prospects of reform, "Forum di Quaderni costituzionali"

Allegretti U (2018a) Il Codice della Protezione Civile (d.lgsl. 2 Gennaio 2018, n. 1), "Aedon", n. 1-2018

Allegretti U (2018b) Un caso di attuazione del principio costituzionale di partecipazione: il regolamento del dibattito pubblico sulle grandi opere, "Rivista AIC", n. 3-2018

Aversa S, Crespellani T (2017) Seismic microzonation: an essential tool for urban planning in seismic areas, "Upland", n. 1/2016
Beck U (1986) Risikogesellschaft. Auf dem Weg in eine Moderne, Frankfurt am Main, Suhrkamp Verlag
Bobbio L (2010) Il dibattito pubblico sulle grandi opere. Il caso dell'autostrada di Genova, "Rivista Italiana di politiche pubbliche", n. 1
Camaiani PG (1976) Castighi di Dio e trionfo della Chiesa. Mentalità e contrasti dei cattolici nell'età di Pio IX, "Rivista storica italiana", n. 4
Cardone A (2011) La "normalizzazione" dell'emergenza; Contributo allo studio del del potere extra ordinem del Governo, Turin, Giappichelli
Crespellani T (2003) Il nuovo modello di difesa dai terremoti, "Democrazia e Diritto", n. 2
Crespellani T (2005) Difesa dai terremoti e normative tecniche: un'eredità difficile, "Democrazia e Diritto", n. 3
Crespellani T (2009) La "resistibile ascesa" della Protezione Civile, "Democrazia e Diritto", n. 1
Crespellani T (2012) Il terremoto "evento naturale ed "evento sociale", Cagliari, Festival Scienza-L'alfabeto della scienza, V ed., http://www.iav.it/flex/cm/pages/ServeBLOB.php/L/IT/ID page 277
Crespellani T (2014) Seismic microzoning in Italy: a brief history and recent experience, "Ingegneria Sismica", XXXI, n. 2
Crespellani T (2018) Sisma bonus: uno strumento problematico, "Il Giornale dell'Ingegnere", n. 9
De Marco R (2013) Il cittadino del giorno dopo. Formulazione di una carta per la tutela del cittadino colpito da calamità, "Convegno Nazionale Protezione civile 'Una carta dei diritti per il cittadino'". Rome, Palazzo Valentini, 23 July 2013
De Marco R (2017) Report to the Seminar I terremoti che verranno, Rome, Department of Architecture, University of Rome 3
De Marco R (2018) The "day after prevention" and that for the new century "Geologia dell'ambiente", n. 1/2018, suppl
Giuffrè A (1987) L'ingegneria sismica in Italia, paper presented at the conference "L'ingegneria sismica in Italia", Rome
Guidoboni E (2018) Seismic disasters in Italy: a review of social and cultural response in the long term, "Geologia dell'Ambiente, n. 1, suppl
Guidoboni E, Valensise G (2011) Il peso economico e sociale dei disastri sismici in Italia negli ultimi 150 anni, Bologna, Bononia University Press
Marsan P, Corazza A (2018) The emergency management of earthquake-induced phenomena: the cases of earthquakes occurred in Abruzzo (2009), in Emilia-Romagna (2012) and in Central Italy (2016-2017), "Geologia dell'ambiente" n. 1/2018, suppl
Nimis GP (2009) Terre mobili. Dal Belice al Friuli, dall'Umbria all'Abruzzo, Rome, Donzelli
Solbiati R, Marcellini A (1983) Terremoto e società, Milan, Garzanti
Teti V (2014) Quel che resta. L'Italia dei paesi, tra abbandoni e ritorni, Rome, Donzelli

Chapter 17
Territorial Policies and Urban Dimension

Gabriella De Giorgi Cezzi

Contents

Abstract The paper is focused on the examination of the "state of the territories" in Italy, in particular on how the core-periphery relationship has evolved. With the decision to extend the Savoy 1859 legislation to the new unitary State many consequences have derived, such as the centralization, guaranteed by the reunion into one person of the function of Prime Minister and the function of Minister of the Interior and by a rigid system of controls. The Republican Constitution of 1948 has dismissed the model in favor of institutional pluralism. Only at the end of twentieth century decades of profound changes in administration have started. First, the institution of the Regions (1970): regional laws, in fact, immediately register the change and use a new language. The change is based on the awareness that the cities have become the engines of economic growth, thanks to their policies of welcoming, job opportunities, and others. The new method is articulated in different areas: social housing policies, urban regeneration policies, landscape care. The housing need pushes the State lawmakers to draw up plans, such as the 2009 National Housing Plan. In the spaces left by the State intervention, the Regions can elaborate programs of urban regeneration. Landscape and territory, once considered antagonistic, are reconciled in the Code of Cultural heritage and landscape approved in 2004. The Code sets out now a relationship between landscape protection and urban law in more complex and profound terms, very far from the original indifference, and open

---

G. De Giorgi Cezzi (✉)
University of Salento, Lecce, Italy

D. Sorace et al. (eds.), *The Changing Administrative Law of an EU Member State*,
https://doi.org/10.1007/978-3-030-50780-0_17

an essential dialogue for the implementation of the EU principle of political and territorial cohesion.

17.1 Introduction. The "State of the Territories" and the Urban Question

An examination of the "state of the territories" in Italy in the last 50 years is only possible through the comparison of the new European Union regulation with the original laws that governed the administration of the new Italian State born in 1865. The so-called "urban question"—which nowadays is a cornerstone of the policies of the European Union—seems to be a useful observation point to study how the core-periphery relationship has evolved. The core-periphery formula can synthesize different problems, among these:

- the condition of the municipalities at the time of the unification and the republican order of 1948;
- the territory vs. the *territorial heritage;*
- the role of the municipalities according to the EU principle of territorial cohesion.

17.2 The State of Municipalities at the Time of the Unification (1865) and at the Time of the Republican Constitution of 1948

The birth of the State—as a new type of general concept—shattered the "culture of the city" typical of the municipalities of the Middle Ages. For that culture, the municipality was not only a political body, but was identified with the same general order of the community, while the super-communal orders appeared external and set to a degree similar to the current international system or in general to the superstate ones (Giannini 1967, p. 3).

With the disappearance of the municipal culture and its peculiar juridical and political characteristics, the cities of the modern State would have been quite different organisms, although the *Risorgimento* culture continued to ideally recall that experience.

The history of the Italian municipalities thus appears the story of a double break: the first coincides with the end of the Middle Ages experience, with the consequent loss of continuity between the regulations of this period and the subsequent ones; the second follows the reception of the French imperial legislation, which has given a new order to the territorial jurisdictions (Giannini 1967, p. 15).

The *Risorgimento* culture retains the territories in ideal continuity with the medieval experience, but without realizing that the life of the municipalities in the pre-unification Sates had nothing in common with that experience, nor with the ideals of the *pouvoir municipal* so much inspired by the *Risorgimento* momentum.

This sort of 'squint' will be at the base of the decision to extend to the new unitary State, with a few adaptations, the Savoy 1859 legislation (see the so-called Rattazzi Bill), that was a reception, even less liberal, of the Albertine legislation of 1848.

This legislation was based on the principle of centralization, guaranteed by the union into one person of the function of Prime Minister and the function of Minister of the Interior (which holds the monopoly of relations with local authorities) and by a rigid system of controls.

This allowed the Prime Minister to concentrate in his hands all the relations with the peripheries, first through the Intendant and then through the Prefects, representatives of the public authorities in the province "for the implementation of their political objectives" (Ghisalberti 1963).

The extension of the Savoy model to the very different territorial realities—what has been defined as the *piemontesizzazione* of the Italian State—resulted in the disruption of what was still alive and vital in those territories, with the undeniable consequence of delaying the progress, and in the complete defeat of the regional vision of Marco Minghetti that so much inspired the *Risorgimento* culture.

The municipal and provincial Bill of 1865 will remain in force in Italy until 1990, i.e. until the approval of the new legislation on territorial autonomy, the first approved by the Parliament and not by the Government (as happened in 1865 for the needs of unification, in 1911 for the Libyan war, and in 1934 with the special powers of the Fascist regime). Accordingly, through dictatorial powers (Cattaneo 1864) readjustments and overlapping, a very long time frame unites modern Italy with the Albertine kingdom of 1848.

The core-periphery relationship developed "without shocks, slipping (...) rather than moving" (Cassese 1986, p. 595), still anchored to a rigid system of administrative controls that over the time were transformed from a defense weapon against feudal abuses to "an instrument of protection of established privileges against new needs and new social forces that (...) appeared in local communities" (Petracchi 1962, p. 386). This explains the apathy and impotence of the false autonomies granted by the national monarchy, which by necessity (as in the South, that didn't have a lively and vital bourgeoisie) or by choice (as for the northern bourgeoisie) preferred the far and comfortable state control to the uncomfortable and close self-government through autonomous institutions (Sepe 1967).

17.3 Territory vs. Territorial Heritage

The Republican Constitution of 1948 dismisses that model in favor of institutional pluralism.

The choice, however, does not immediately translate into new core-periphery relationships, that will be governed by the nineteenth century legislation, inspired by the principle of centralization, until the end of twentieth century when decades of profound changes in administration started, with the institution of the Regions (1970) and the relative transformation of the system.

Consequences of the regional system, however, are the profound inequalities that reflect strengths and weaknesses of the cities that have become the engines of economic growth, through their policies of welcoming, job opportunities and, above all, through the discipline of the territory, considered as specific responsibility of the municipalities since the Middle Ages, which the Constitution merely recognizes.

It is thanks to the territory and its discipline that the municipality becomes the master of its physical and functional form.

In the last fifty years, therefore, the task of urban planning has been to describe the 'state of the territories', with methods, objectives and a language that the changing and the multiplication of needs and interests of the territories have contributed to profoundly shape.

The state urban planning legislation, dating back to 1942, however, appears completely inadequate to register this change (Stella Richter 2002) and the territory appears to be slowed down by traditional urban planning mechanisms and by the overlapping of sectorial interventions typical of the urban culture of the 1960s.

The restraint of urban development—which was the objective of that culture, due to the economic crisis—becomes less urgent than other problems, such as land consumption and housing dispersion.

Regional laws, on the other hand, immediately register the change and use a new language: the choice of terms like *territorial heritage* (*patrimonio territoriale*) instead of territory (e.g., Tuscany Regional Law 10 November 2014, No. 65, *Rules for territorial government*) is expression of a politics that look not only at quantitative profiles (e.g., how much soil can be consumed), but also at qualitative ones (the compatibility of interventions, the problems of social inclusion, the preservation of cultural identity and economic development).

The new method is articulated in different areas: social housing policies; urban regeneration policies; landscape care.

The housing need—which now touches new social groups (single-income families, young people, women, etc.) in addition to the traditional ones—pushes the State lawmakers to draw up plans, such as the 2009 national housing plan, to meet the right to housing, guaranteed by the Constitution in a uniform way on the national territory (Sorace 1977, p. 1035; Corso 1981, p. 756), involving more subjects (Regions, municipalities, institutions for the popular construction, partnerships) and more instruments (project financing, subsidies to real-estate cooperatives, real estate funds, etc.).

In the spaces left free by the State intervention, the Regions elaborate programs of urban regeneration (e.g., Puglia Law, July 29, 2008, No. 21, *Rules for urban regeneration*) that reflect the national model in force in the 90s (Salvia 2012, p. 153), with the aim of framing the housing problem into a more general design of the urban territory and of the related needs, according to a logic of equalization and compensation, capable of giving a new face to the cities, and to its 'public' features in particular.

Even national objectives change, along with the language.

Landscape and territory, once considered antagonistic (as the interest in conservation and in development), are reconciled in the Code of cultural heritage and landscape approved in 2004 (D.Lgs. 22 January 2004, No. 42) that replaces the 1930s legislation and at the same time combines landscapes and cultural heritage into the notion of *cultural heritage* (Art. 2) which implements Art. 9 of the Constitution.

The synthesis is useful to describe the most profound nature of the landscape: it represents the identity of the specific population and the result of the interaction of human and natural factors.

Problems related to the center-periphery relationship still remain open.

Landscape planning is elaborated and approved jointly by the Ministry and the Regions, which are now less free than in the past.

Municipalities are allowed only to participate in regional-state landscape choices, which prevail over territorial ones.

The role of private subjects is even more undermined: they are the users but also the "creators" of the landscape (one can think of the agrarian landscape, Sereni 1961). Participation in the related choices is only possible (as in the case of public inquiries), in the landscape planning procedure and only if regulated by the Region.

However, also integration models of landscape management are being used.

The so-called river and landscape contracts arise from voluntary initiatives, based on the consensus and cooperation between local authorities and private entities (Brocca 2018, p. 331).

These are models of active participation related to the landscape management of local institutions and resident populations, according to the indications of the Art. 5 of the European Landscape Convention, which the Code overlooks.

Despite these problems, the Code sets out now a relationship between landscape protection and urban law in more complex and profound terms, very far from the original indifference, and opens an essential dialogue for the implementation of the EU principle of political and territorial cohesion.

17.4 The Role of the Municipalities According to the EU Principle of Territorial Cohesion

Even when the rapid overlapping of the political-social issues that press on the city will lead to dismiss the idea that town planning can represent the discipline for a stable and lasting use of the territory—its new mission is being outlined: to offer a synthesis of the many functions and the many interests that are concentrated in a city and to offer that general vision of the possible 'functioning' of a territory, with needs that affect not only the destinations of the areas, but also the mobility system of things and people; the protection of valuable assets; the discipline of commerce; the water service; the waste cycle etc.

Cities thus become the natural places of promotion and development that require active urban rehabilitation policies: a driving and incentive action described by the new concept of the *political-territorial cohesion* (Massera 2016, p. 453), according to the principle set by the Lisbon Treaties and in particular by Art. 3, par. 3 TEU, Articles 4,14,174-178 TFEU and protocol no. 28, and art. 36 EU Charter of Fundamental Rights.

The expression describes the interest, not only in the subjects and their mutual relations, but above all in the actions and their quality, inspired by the principles of fairness, efficiency, solidarity and equalization. It is the research for a "different way to unify": unifying not the territory, but through the territory (Tuccari 2016, p. 62).

The new policies of the Union start from the idea that only within territorial defined areas it is possible to overcome any conditions of disadvantage of the territory, looking for new solutions for socio-economic and environmental imbalances, especially with regard to social inclusion, public services supply, promotion of renewable energy sources, development of green areas, land consumption containment, contrast to the economic crisis and the climate change.

The centrality of the urban issue arises from this new awareness and the formula of the *sustainable city* summarizes the new territorial policies that aim at quality (i.e., quality of spaces, networks, suburbs and urban environment, mobility and local labor market) for the personal progress of citizens and social inclusion: and this is possible only through "a harmonious and sustainable development of all the territories through the conscious use of their resources and their characteristics" (European Commission, *Sixth Progress Report on economic and social cohesion,* SEC2009, 828).

The issue transcends the relationships between the different levels of territorial government, because social imbalances are also recorded in the same urban context, between urbanized and non-urbanized parts, between center and periphery, and policies of "approaching" citizens to social contexts and services and institutional places cannot but affect local authorities.

The implementation of the principle touches other important aspects of the 'state of the territories' such as the question of financial autonomy necessary to implement cohesion policies.

The modification of Art. 119 of the Constitution was conceived with the aim of enhancing and empowering municipalities towards forms of financial self-sufficiency.

The inequalities between Regions, however, have exasperated—as demonstrated by health protection programs, a strategic matter to implement the values of solidarity and cohesion, constrained between purposes of restraint and restoration of public deficit and needs to promote quality and efficiency of the services.

The paradoxical effect is a new push towards the center, in terms of cohesion and overall stability of the health system.

More generally, the territories are diversified and disintegrated, and the request of some Regions to obtain special forms of autonomy is the certification of a reality (the so-called two-speed-Italy) featured by moralism (only the 'virtuous' Regions can obtain more autonomy).

The basic approach remains that of a national "guide" on public finance and, even more deeply, that of a substantial hierarchy of public interests, in which the protection of public finances precedes and prevails over the others (De Siano 2016, p. 409).

The two profiles are linked: it seems that the State, with the quality of financial backer, becomes a regulator, deciding—or at least conditioning—the main policies of public intervention, with the effect of undermining the aspiration of the territorial bodies to be interpreters and bearers of their territory's interests.

Similar considerations can be made with reference to policies on the management of public assets (estate divestitures, securitizations, federal property).

The new concept of public real estate assets—no longer considered as a good to be statically preserved, but also as a resource to be managed according to efficiency criteria—has progressively led to the belief that the assets are also a source of fiscal consolidation, thanks to their valorization but also to their sale.

New models are created for an effective management of these assets, first in State, then in the Regional sphere, but the formulas are struggling to establish themselves and to be translated into factors of cohesion and territorial development (Accettura 2015, p. 210).

The attention is therefore brought back to the basic question: rather than seeking specific organizational and functional solutions to individual problems, it is essential to identify "places" and "policies" able to ensure a full connection and an effective composition of the interests involved: it is a perspective that primarily requires urban planning—and this requirement confirms the flexibility of the planning instrument and, at the same time, its vitality, its capacity for updating, but also the "fidelity" to its more intimate vocation.

References

Accettura B (2015) Valorizzazione del patrimonio culturale e nuovi modelli per lo sviluppo dei territori. Jovene, Napoli

Brocca M (2018) Interessi ambientali e decisioni amministrative. Profili critici e nuove dinamiche. Giappichelli, Torino

Cassese S (1986) Centro e periferia in Italia. I grandi tornanti della loro storia. Rivista trimestrale di diritto pubblico 2:549

Cattaneo C (1864) Lettera prima sulla Legge comunale e provinciale. Il diritto

Corso G (1981) I diritti sociali nella Costituzione italiana. Riv. trim. dir. pubbl. 3:756

De Siano A (2016) Autonomia finanziaria degli enti territoriali e politiche pubbliche di coesione. In: De Giorgi Cezzi G, Portaluri PL (a cura di) La coesione politico-territoriale, II, A 150 anni dall'unificazione amministrativa italiana. In: Ferrara L, Sorace D (a cura di) Studi, 195. Firenze University Press, Firenze

Ghisalberti C (1963) Contributo alla storia delle amministrazioni preunitarie. Giuffrè, Milano

Giannini MS (1967) I comuni. In: Id. (a cura di) Atti del congresso celebrativo del centenario delle leggi amministrative di unificazione. Neri Pozza, Vicenza

Massera A (2016) La coesione politico-territoriale: una 'nuova' formulazione nella dimensione europea di una 'vecchia' questione nazionale. In: De Giorgi Cezzi G, Portaluri PL (a cura di) La coesione politico-territoriale, II, A 150 anni dall'unificazione amministrativa italiana. In: Ferrara L, Sorace D (a cura di). Studi, 451. Firenze University Press, Firenze

Petracchi A (1962) Le origini dell'ordinamento comunale e provinciale italiano, I, 1962. Neri Pozza, Venezia

Salvia F (2012) Manuale di diritto urbanistico. Cedam, Padova

Sepe O (1967) Il sistema del controllo ed i vari controlli sui comuni. In: Giannini MS (a cura di) Atti del congresso celebrativo del centenario delle leggi amministrative di unificazione. Neri Pozza, Vicenza

Sereni E (1961) Storia del paesaggio agrario italiano. Laterza, Roma-Bari

Sorace D (1977) A proposito di «proprietà dell'abitazione», «diritto all'abitazione» e «proprietà (civilistica) della casa». In: Scritti in onore di Costantino Mortati, III, 1035. Giuffrè, Milano

Stella Richter P (2002) I principi del diritto urbanistico. Giuffrè, Milano

Tuccari FF (2016) Politiche europee di coesione territoriale e processi di unificazione nazionale. In: De Giorgi Cezzi G, Portaluri PL (a cura di) La coesione politico-territoriale, II, A 150 anni dall'unificazione amministrativa italiana. In: Ferrara L, Sorace D (a cura di) Studi, 59. Firenze University Press, Firenze

Part III
Voices from Across the EU

Chapter 18
150 Years of Administrative Law in Italy and in France: Some Comparative Insights

Jean-Bernard Auby

Contents

Abstract French and Italian administrative laws are brothers. They were not very distant from each other at the origin. They were faced with many similar difficulties. This did not prevent them from following slightly different paths on certain issues, in particular: the scope of administrative law and of administrative judges' juridiction, the pace of constitutionalisation and Europeanisation, the organisation of judicial review, the development of administrative procedure.

18.1 Introduction

The idea that most commonly comes to the mind of anyone comparing the modern political-administrative histories of Italy and France is that there is a large asymmetry between them: where the French system would rely on a coherent state

J.-B. Auby (✉)
Sciences Po, Paris, France
e-mail: jeanbernard.auby@sciencespo.fr

D. Sorace et al. (eds.), *The Changing Administrative Law of an EU Member State*,
https://doi.org/10.1007/978-3-030-50780-0_18

framework and a strong feeling of national unity, Italy would be looking indefinitely for these two elements.

This opposition is certainly exact for a significant part, but, at least from the French point of view which is mine, it deserves to be nuanced.

In France, a strong French national sentiment has certainly existed since the 1789 Revolution and the Napoleonic wars that followed it, but it was not until the end of the nineteenth century and the 1914–1918 war that it took its full strength: one of the priority tasks of school education in the first half of the "Third Republic", that is to say from 1870 to 1940, was to impose French as a common language whereas, in the countryside at least, people spoke mostly local languages. Today, without suffering from a high degree of fragmentation, France still shelters strong regionalisms—sometimes turning to separatism—in Brittany, in Alsace, in the Basque Country, in Corsica, in some overseas territories like New Caledonia.

As for the State itself, it certainly still constitutes a strong administrative framework, supported by a public service firmly structured on the national level although in three sub-groups—the governmental public service, the territorial public service, the public hospital function—. But this strong framework has been impacted by repeated decentralization reforms since the 1980s.

In addition, it should not be forgotten that until the beginning of the Fifth Republic (1958), the administrative stability contrasted with a high level of governmental instability. Only the semi-presidential system set up in 1958 managed to move away from the "ministerial waltz" that existed before, governments generally not lasting more than a few months.

The same nuanced mixture of similarities and differences makes itself discover between the Italian and French administrative laws.

Italian administrative law is usually considered to have taken deep roots in French administrative law, before unification as well as later.[1] However, their trajectories were not to be identical, Italian administrative law making here and there different major choices—that of the unity of jurisdiction, at the beginning—and drawing on other inspirations, notably that of German law.[2]

The truth is that their respective evolutions led them to intersect and move away alternately. We would like to illustrate it through four common issues: the scope of administrative law (I), the incorporation of supra-legal norms—constitutionalisation and Europeanisation—(II), the emergence and development of judicial review (III), and theories on the administrative act and evolution of the administrative procedural law (IV).

[1]Mattarella (2017), pp. 329 sq.—There are, however, commentators attributing to Gian Domenico Romagnosi, who published in 1814 his "Principi fondamentali del diritto amministrativo", the true paternity of administrative law in Europe: E.A. Albertoni, Per conoscere Romagnosi, Ed. Ghringhelli-Invernici, 1982.

[2]Sandulli (2009), pp. 52 sq.

18.2 The Scope of Administrative Law

On the face of it, from the point of view of their understanding of administrative law field, the Italian system and the French system are structurally similar. They are both based on the idea that it is the administrative decision—the right to create rights and obligations unilaterally—that constitutes the characteristic reality justifying the existence of a "public" administrative law, distinct from private law and the existence of special administrative jurisdictions: the two systems are indeed dualistic and possess special administrative jurisdictions, distinct from civil, commercial, etc. courts.

But behind this general convergence, things are more complicated.

On the understanding of what is specific to the administration and justifies the application of special rules, the two systems have experienced fluctuations between which there is no true symmetry

In the aftermath of the unification, Italian administrative law, inspired by liberal ideas, favoured a broad application of the common law to the administration. Then, around the beginning of the twentieth century, there was a "grande pubblicizzazione", to which the fascist period will later bring its reinforcement.[3]

However, the criteria defining the border between administrative and private law have never been formally clarified.[4]

The second half of the twentieth century saw the pendulum return to private law. The notion of private law act of the administration was then widening.[5] But it is the civil service that happened to be most strongly affected by the privatization movement: in the 1990s, the majority of it was moved into a system of labour law and collective agreements.[6]

At the beginning of the period we are analyzing here, French administrative law relied on the idea that the administration had to be subjected to special rules when it appeared in the form of public power, of authority—"puissance publique"—. A very important change occurred towards the end of the nineteenth century, when jurisprudence began to link the application of special rules to the concept of public service—"service public"—: this was what did the most famous judgment in French administrative law, the *Blanco* judgment of 1873.[7]

What followed was more complicated. Some decades later, the case-law turned back to consider that some of the public services—the industrial and commercial ones—should in fact be essentially subject to common law.[8] On the contrary, after

---

[3]Napolitano (2007), pp.4 sq.

[4]Mattarella (2017), cited, p. 358.

[5]See, in this book, C. Marzuoli's contribution.

[6]See, in this book, A. Police and A. Corpaci contributions.

[7]Tribunal des Conflits, 8 février 1873: see for eg. Lachaume et al. (2017), p. 6.

[8]Tribunal des Conflits, 22 janvier 1921, Société commerciale de l'ouest africai.

the Second World War, the case-law re-emerged in the other direction by reinforcing the role of the notion of public service as a criterion for applying special rules of public law.[9]

The privatization and deregulation movements that France has experienced, like all comparable systems, since the 1980s, have not really made the balance swing in the other direction. The field of public law in administrative matters remains very wide: we will come back to it.

18.3 The Incorporation of Supra-Legal Norms: Constitutionalisation, Europeanisation

Naturally, in both systems, the supremacy of the Constitution and European law over the proper sources of administrative law has never been discussed. But the concrete constitutionalisation and Europeanization of French administrative law has been delayed for reasons that can be explained.

18.3.1 The Constitutionalization of Administrative Law

Penetration of administrative law by constitutional norms, feeding of the first by the seconds, came earlier in Italy for two sorts of reasons.

The first one is that the Italian Constitution contains a significant number of rules that concern administrative law directly and specifically: that of the "buon andamento", for example.[10]

The second is that Italy was earlier than France endowed with an efficient and dynamic constitutional review.

The result is that constitutional law of the administration has fostered in the Italian law.

The French system has evolved on quite different bases.

On the one hand, the French Constitution of 1958 contains few standards of direct and explicit interest in administrative law: essentially rules concerning the organization of national and local public authorities.

On the other hand, the constitutional review was slow to take off: it did not really until it incorporated the standards of fundamental rights protection attached to the preamble of the Constitution (1974) and until it was admitted that the Constitutional Council could be appealed to by ordinary citizens, first through members of

[9]Notably: Tribunal des Conflits, 28 mars 1955, Effimieff—Conseil d'Etat, 19 octobre 1956, Epoux Bertin.

[10]Even if the practical impact of these constitutional provisions was limited: Mattarella (2017), already mentioned.

Parliament (1974), then directly by the way of "questions prioritaires de constitutionnalité" raised before a judge and transmitted to the Constitutional Council (2008).

Today, there is a substantial constitutional case law on administrative law issues, but this is a recent phenomenon.[11]

18.3.2 The Europeanization of Administrative Law

The incorporation of European law within administrative law seems to have been rather natural in Italy, even though the Constitutional Court remained attached to the idea that between national law and European law, the relationship had to be conceived as a coordination one rather than an integration one.[12]

French administrative law, on the other hand, has for a long time been in a position, if not of resistance to European law, in any case of maximum supervision of its effects. The most marked symptom of this attitude: it was not until 1989[13] that the Council of State accepted the primacy of European norms over posterior legislation.

Nevertheless, it must be said that since that date, a real release has occurred and the French administrative judge has become rather Europhile today.

18.4 Emergence and Development of Judicial Review

18.4.1 The Organization of Administrative Litigation

The two systems, Italian and French, are dualistic and house specialized administrative jurisdictions. However, while it is a very old feature of French administrative law, which had appeared much earlier than the period covered by our comparison, Italian administrative law first made the choice of the unity of jurisdiction when the country was unified, to rally later to dualism.[14]

The structure of administrative jurisdiction is similar in the two systems: administrative tribunals at the bottom, the Council of State at the top. The essential difference lies in the fact that in 1987, France set up an intermediate level of "cours administratives d'appel": the aim was to relieve the Council of State, which was heavily congested.

---

[11]See eg: Stirn (2019).

[12]Torchia (1998), p. 137.

[13]Conseil d'Etat, 20 octobre 1989, Nicolo.

[14]Cassese (2014), pp. 115 sq.; Fromont (2006), pp. 29 sq.

On the other hand, there are fairly clear differences in the way jurisdiction is divided between administrative and ordinary courts. This is mainly due to the fact, recalled above, that the Italian administrative law borrowed from the German tradition the principle according to which administrative disputes which are of a patrimonial character—those which concern the contracts, the administrative assets, administrative liability- normally fall to the judicial judge and not to the administrative judge.

This has led in particular Italian administrative law to draw a very original distinction between administrative disputes concerning "subjective rights" and those concerning "legitimate interests",[15] the equivalent of which does not exist in French administrative law. In the latter, when the distribution of powers is not fixed by statute—which is becoming more and more frequent—it is established on the basis of various criteria which make it possible to determine that the particular litigation situation falls within the scope of public law or private law: for example, a contract—not qualified by statute—is a public law one if it includes provisions which could normally not be found in private contracts—"clauses exorbitantes du droit commun"—or if it entrusts the execution of a public service.[16]

18.4.2 The Powers and Methods of Judges

In both systems, the core of the administration's judicial supervision is the review of the legality of administrative decisions.

On the whole, the Italian and French administrative judges carry out this supervision according to comparable methods. However, nuances appear on various points. In the control of discretion, the Italian administrative judge seems in general more reserved than the French administrative judge.[17] However, the principle of proportionality, which is not formally recognized in French administrative law, has been recognized as a general principle in Italian law.[18]

The respective importance of controlling the formal elements and controlling the content of the decisions may not be exactly the same, the French administrative judge being traditionally more willing to draw consequences of formal illegalities.[19]

There are notable differences in the treatment of the administration's responsibility. The cleavage "subjective rights"/"legitimate interests" has curbed the development of it in the Italian administrative law, which was not the case in the French

[15]Napolitano (2007), already mentioned, pp. 15 sq².

[16]Frier and Petit (2018), pp. 448 sq.

[17]See, in this book, Gian Domenico Comporti's contribution.

[18]Consiglio di Stato, 13 February, 1998, La Betulla.

[19]See, in this book, Gian Domenico Comporti's contribution—Auby (2016b), pp. 843 sq.

system, where it is most often for the administrative judge itself to adjudicate on administrative liability disputes.[20]

18.5 Theories on the Administrative Act and Evolution of the Administrative Procedural Law

Here are two aspects on which, although they start from similar premises, Italian and French administrative laws followed rather divergent paths.

18.5.1 The Administrative Act Theory and Its Link with Administrative Procedure[21]

Certainly, both administrative laws place the administrative act—unilateral: the administrative decision—at the center of their construction. For both, it is the existence of the administrative power to create rights and obligations unilaterally that explains and fundamentally justifies the existence of a special law for the administration.

But a divergence came from the fact that while the French administrative law remained polarized on the isolated administrative act, in its singularity, the Italian administrative law became interested more and more in the procedural context in which administrative acts are placed.

The Italian administrative law made a theoretical turn which led it from a major attention to the act to a greater attention to the proceedings—"procedimento"–,[22] where the French administrative law remains poor in concepts that take into account the continuity and consistency of procedural frameworks.

18.5.2 The Construction of Procedural Administrative Law[23]

The different viewpoints which have been just mentioned have had consequences in the development of procedural administrative law in both systems.

[20] See, in this book, C. Marzuoli's contribution—On corresponding French administrative law, see eg: Frier and Petit (2018), already mentioned, pp. 653 sq.

[21] Auby (2016b), already mentioned, pp. 85 sq. and 71 sq.

[22] See in this book C. Marzuoli's contribution.

[23] Auby (2016a).

The reflection begun early in Italy on the procedural processes, beyond the act in its individuality, made it possible to elaborate since 1990 a general statute on administrative procedure.

In France, after various attempts that came up against reluctance, either from ministries or from the Council of State, it was not until 2015 that a "code des relations entre le public et l'"administration" was adopted, in which the essential procedural administrative rules were regrouped.

The two texts are not identical either. Among other things, Italian law includes mechanisms that are not found in French law, such as the exercise of administrative power through agreements or the "conferenze di servizi".

French and Italian administrative laws are brothers. They was not very distant from each other at the origin. They were faced with many similar difficulties. This did not prevent them from following different paths on certain issues. Anyone who practices comparative law knows this dialectic of the Other and the Same well.

References

Auby J-B (ed) (2016a) Codification of administrative procedure. Bruxelles, Bruylant

Auby J-B (ed) (2016b) Droit comparé de la procédure administrative. Comparative law of administrative procedure. Bruxelles, Bruylant

Cassese S (2014) Governare gli italiani. Storia dello Stato. Il Mulino, Bologna, p 115 sq.

Frier P-L, Petit J (2018) Droit administratif. Librairie Générale de Droit et de Jurisprudence, Paris

Fromont M (2006) Droit administratif des Etats européens. Librairie Générale de Droit et de Jurisprudence, Paris

Lachaume J-F, Pauliat H, Braconnier S, Deffigier C (2017) Droit administratif. Les grands arrêts de la jurisprudence. Presses Universitaires de France, Paris

Mattarella BG (2017) Evolution and *Gestalt* of the Italian state. In: von Bogdandy A, Huber P, Cassese S (eds) The administrative state. Oxford University Press, Oxford, p 329 sq

Napolitano G (2007) Diritto amministrativo comparato. Giuffrè, Milan, p 4 sq

Sandulli A (2009) Costruire lo Stato. La scienza del diritto amministrativo in Italia (1800–1945). Giuffrè, Milan, p 52 sq

Stirn B (2019) Les sources constitutionnelles du droit administratif. Librairie Générale de Droit et de Jurisprudence, Paris

Torchia L (1998) Developments in Italian administrative law through cross-fertilisation. In: Beatson J, Tridimas T (eds) New directions in European public law. Hart Publishing, Oxford, p 137

Chapter 19
Administrative Jurisdiction in Federal States

Dian Schefold

Contents

Abstract In this volume, the article gives a comment, from a German point of view, to the contribution of Giandomenico Comporti. It remembers the different origin of Italian unity, based on the expansion of the Kingdom of Piemonte and its legal order, and of the German unification, based on treaties without unifying the internal, esp. administrative organization and procedure of the member States. Only slowly these fields were influenced by the Federation, and only after the Nazi period, protection of individual rights was an essential aim of the Basic Law (GG) and thus of constitutional and legal development. Under these aspects, the Code of Administrative Court Procedure (VwGO) and the Code of Administrative Proceedings (VwVfG) are presented, and the similarity of this development to that of the European Union is underlined.

19.1 Italian Unity, German Unification, European Union

When I received the invitation to participate in the study covering 150 years of Italian administrative unification, adding insight from a German point of view, my mind immediately went to the origin of the nation's unification and its impact on the

D. Schefold (✉)
University of Bremen, Bremen, Germany
e-mail: schefold@uni-bremen.de

D. Sorace et al. (eds.), *The Changing Administrative Law of an EU Member State*,
https://doi.org/10.1007/978-3-030-50780-0_19

structure of administrative law. Going over the contributions, I realised how many different topics they covered and began to think of recent developments quite distant from the historical dilemma. Nevertheless, the existence of the issue seems unquestionable, and important once again for the process of unification that has happened and is still happening with the European Union. I'll use Gian Domenico Comporti's comprehensive, in-depth essay on Italian administrative judges as a model, permitting myself a few observations on the topic in comparison with Germany.

The fact that Italian unification stemmed from a uniform administrative and legal system already in place before unification, in my opinion, is essential. As such, the Italian judiciary system was at the very origins of the unitary state, including the promise to encompass the protection of rights, excluding protections according to older models of administrative law. However, the Consiglio di Stato (Council of State) remained, and given the insufficiency of protecting rights solely through the courts, Crispi's reforms created additional way to keep the Council of State in check, though separate from the judiciary. This separation shaped the developments that ensued, up to the present day, and characterised the issue of jurisdictional power in Italy.

As for German unification, it is true that there were annexations by Prussia that could have introduced comparable solutions, though the overall unification method was different. Despite the conflicts, including war, unification took place via treaties and accords, and the resulting constitution was essentially a way for Prussian powers and other federated states to co-manage the empire through a few shared bodies. Without going into too much detail, the co-existence of these states is visible in the way they are organised, without the decisive influence of the central state on their internal administrative and legal structures. In terms of imperial legislation, jurisdictional structure and civil and criminal procedures were important, but the organisation of single jurisdictional authorities remained in the hands of the member states. Especially when it came to new tasks, administration required specific central authorities, but traditional, already-existing administrative structure as a whole was not impacted by the integration of member states into the federal state. Thus, even judicial protection against the administration was not established and regulated by the empire, but remained the exclusive power of the states. The separation of ordinary jurisdictional power (civil and criminal) and administration was complete.

It is upon the basis of such experiences that we can examine the development of the European Union. The initial goals of the confederation of member states were, first and foremost, the creation of an economic community, free trade, a single market and the regulations required to meet these goals. The need for a more perfect union was secondary. On the other hand, the organisation of the single states, and administrative and judicial procedures, have remained unchanged. It is up to the member states to regulate them, perhaps as an exception to ensure an 'effet utile' of the substantial rules. This is also true for national jurisdictional powers, despite attempts at standardisation. Yet, the influx of guarantees in art. 6 and 13 of the European Convention on Human Rights and art. 47–50 of the European Charter of Fundamental Rights impacts the courts in order to protect the principles of the rule of law.

19.2 Heterogeneity in Systems of Administrative Jurisdiction and Administrative Procedures

In Germany administrative law systems remained diverse because of the limited jurisdiction of the empire. While § 182 of the Frankfurt Constitution of 28 March 1849 abolished administrative justice and re-routed judgements on rights violations to the courts[1] (a model for Annex E to Italian law n. 2248 of 1865), after its failure, the controversy had begun, asserted in the writings of Otto Bähr and Rudolf Gneist.[2] While the former sustained the idea anchored in the Frankfurt Constitution, in favour of the total jurisdiction of ordinary courts in all conflicts with the administration, the latter argued for the jurisdiction of decentralised honorary commissions to keep the administration in check, connecting participation in self-administration with control over the rule of law. Thanks in part to Gneist's influence, this system shaped what happened in Prussia. The solutions in other member states of the empire were quite different, often closer to ordinary courts. In terms of the empire and its constitution, the issue was not exactly decided upon; instead practical needs required the creation of a number of special administrative courts for matters regulated and managed by the central power.

The situation did not change in any significant manner in the Weimar Republic. Though it is true that the Constitution (art. 107) established and guaranteed the creation of administrative courts on the level of the *Reich* and the *Länder*, it did not dictate the models and details, and the debate between supporters of a model close to the administration (including Gerhard Anschütz) and one close to ordinary courts (including Walter Jellinek, in principle also Hugo Preuß) continued. By then the legislative power of the Reich on the matter was not beyond doubt: power, according to art. 7 no. 3 of the Constitution covered ordinary (not administrative) jurisdiction, and an extension of the rules of the Reichsverwaltungsgericht (provided for in art. 107) on administrative jurisdiction in the Länder would have limited them without a constitutional basis. It is therefore understandable if the job of regulating administrative jurisdiction and creating an administrative court for the Reich was left unfinished. The special administrative courts of the Reich increased in number, such as the creation of a central finance court for tax matters, but there was no court with general jurisdiction. Administrative procedures were even less covered by central legislation. The Austrian model had little effect on Germany, with a law in Thuringia and a draft law in Wurttemberg, but nothing on a central level.

---

[1]See 'Costituzione di Francoforte' (1849), *Monitore Costituzionale* 17, Macerata 2018, with my introduction.

[2]Otto Bähr, *Der Rechtsstaat*, Kassel 1864; Rudolf Gneist, *Der Rechtsstaat und die Verwaltungsgerichte in Deutschland*, Berlin 1872, 2a ed. 1879.

19.3 The Influence of the Nazi Period

Divided jurisdictions came to a halt upon the arrival of the Nazis, with the *Gleichschaltung* (levelling) of the Länder and the centralisation the Reich's power via the law of 30 January 1934. In this unified, totalitarian state, federalist motives against a united judicial system disappeared, and a uniform administrative jurisdiction system was possible.

Nevertheless, such a model would have been contrary to Nazi ideology. To them, the free rein of state power, especially the police, was essential. Therefore, judicial protection against police measures (practically illusory already with the path opened to interventions in fundamental rights suspended with the early measures of the Nazi state) was formally repealed with the *Gestapo* law of 10 February 1936. Once the war began, early laws to simplify administration included a drastic reduction in the administrative jurisdiction that remained, now accessible only if the administrative authority so allowed. Yet, with a decree from the *Führer ('Führererlass')* on 3 April 1941, an administrative court of the Reich (*Reichsverwaltungsgericht*) was officially created.[3] It was a formal merger with the Prussian administrative court, the Austrian administrative court and some special administrative courts with centralised power—far from a protection of rights, alien to the totalitarian state.

19.4 The Jurisdictional Model of the Basic Law (GG)

It is against this background that we must evaluate the solution offered by the Basic Law (Grundgesetz—GG) the development of liberated Germany. 'Moved by the annihilation that the authoritarian government of the National Socialists, scorning personal freedom and human dignity, has caused in the old free Hanseatic city of Bremen...',[4] the protection of rights was the main scope of the new system. The expression of rights was part of it, as was the means of protection: art. 19, par. 4 of the Basic Law guarantees legal recourse (*Rechtsweg*) if one's rights are violated. Unlike art. 24, par. 1 of the Italian Constitution, however, there is no distinction between rights and legitimate interests, and jurisdiction is taken as a precise concept. The section of the Basic Law on jurisdiction entrusts it to judges (art. 92) and establishes, in this way, a substantial understanding of what jurisdiction is: beyond civil and criminal law is an element, the protection of rights. Certainly the definition of what is included in jurisdiction was not beyond doubt; the current doctrine defines it as a binding authoritative state decision in cases of violated or contested rights

[3]For more details, see Wolfgang Kohl, *Das Reichsverwaltungsgericht*, Tübingen 1991.

[4]As stated in the preamble to the Constitution of the Land of Bremen of 1947; other Länder constitutions are similar.

through independent, neutral third parties in a separate procedure.[5] All these matters are entrusted to judges, and no other state power may claim activities in these areas: a penal authority or one of decisions on civil conflicts of the administration is equally excluded as a limitation to the access to the judge against administrative measures and executive power. As such, judicial power is the guardian of freedom and the rule of law, while the democratic guarantees of the Basic Law, though provided for in principle, are less concrete.

This model of course implies problems of limitation. Jurisprudence has tolerated disciplinary measures against officials, sanctions for administrative violations, wire tapping for the protection of the constitutional system, etc., but the principle is maintained and has fundamentally influenced the German system, especially the position of the citizen before the administration.

Singularity of power follows the organisation of judicial protection. One cannot, like in Italy, talk of judicial function exercised by the judiciary and of separated protection against the administration, nor a monopoly of the ordinary courts. For that reason, freeing oneself from nineteenth-century models, one seeks a new solution. Depending on the character of the conflicts, there is a subdivision of the jurisdictions, in the matters of civil and labour law, and also public law, with the connection of criminal law to civil law, but also constitutional, administrative, tax and social security law. To guarantee this structure, the Basic Law includes, for single topics [in addition to the Federal Constitutional Court organised in a more complete manner (art. 93/94)], the five federal supreme courts mentioned in art. 95 par. 1: the federal court (civil and criminal), the federal administrative court, the federal finance court, the federal labour court and the federal social security court. For coordination in the event of differences, there is a common senate (art. 95, par. 3). In addition, the jurisprudence of the Constitutional Court, important thanks to the possibility of direct appeal in case of rights violations, even against last instance judgements, is necessary in order to coordinate the entire jurisdiction. Each supreme court is at the apex of a subject-specific jurisdiction with lower courts and appellate courts in the Länder. All of these jurisdictions are regulated by federal laws. Today, unlike in the Weimar Republic (above, par. 2), the coherence of the jurisdictions means that the federal regulation of court proceedings (art. 74, no. 1 GG) relates to all the jurisdictions.

Therefore, it is truly a unified, cohesive jurisdictional power, even with a certain degree of administrative independence in the single jurisdictions. Yet there is still the counter-argument and issue that Germany, unlike Italy, has not created a independent council of the judiciary, leaving certain organisational powers to ministers (though often with the participation of mixed commissions)—especially when it comes to the appointment and promotion of judges. It is indisputable that these march-in rights limit the independence of judges and there are critiques of this situation in related legal theory. On the other hand, however, it is important to

---

[5]See Morlok/Michael, *Staatsorganisationsrecht*, 4th ed. Baden-Baden 2019, p. 394, with references.

note that there is a need for judges to be rooted in state procedures that are democratically legitimised, and that not even the Italian solution of the Supreme Judicial Council avoids the tension between independence, compliance and necessary legitimacy.[6]

19.5 The Code of Administrative Court Procedure (Verwaltungsgerichtsordnung: VwGO)

Indeed, the solution chosen by the Parliamentary Council of Bonn was prepared by legislation in the Länder, drawn up by German experts (including, importantly, Walter Jellinek) and with the support of occupation forces. In this way, courts and administrative appellate courts were created for the majority of the Länder. After the issuing of the Basic Law, the first step was the creation of the Federal Administrative Court (first in Berlin, upon reunification, and then in Leipzig) to monitor the application of the law (*Revision*, comparable to cassation in Italian law). The first two levels of judicial protection remained, on the other hand, entrusted to administrative courts and administrative appellate courts in the Länder.

However, after the adaptation of the laws on ordinary, labour and social security jurisdiction, came the preparation of an administrative process code in 1960 and, at the same time, a tax process code in 1965. In this way, the German jurisdictional system, structured in principle by the Basic Law, was elaborated. Of course there were differences that perhaps weren't always justified, but with similar structures that would allow citizens to access the court with jurisdiction for all conflicts pertaining to their rights. The jurisdiction of each court is defined by codes. For the administrative courts, this means all non-constitutional public rights conflicts that aren't handled by another court. The provision thus implies the general clause of legal jurisdiction, guaranteed by the Basic Law. In detail, the definition is complicated, thanks to stipulations (in part constitutional) of certain matters, such as compensation for expropriations and the liability of officials, to ordinary jurisdiction (§ 40, VwGO). If the claimant chooses the wrong court, the latter must send the case to the court with jurisdiction (now § 17a of the law on the legal organisation—Gerichtsverfassungsgesetz).

The general clause for public law conflicts corresponds to a second general clause, concerning forms of appeal. Although an appeal against administrative acts with the aim of annulment is the most common, in the case of rejected, delayed or omitted acts, the claimant may request a sentence for the administration to issue a certain act, or a specific service to which he is entitled. Even investigation or

[6]As an in-depth, recent comparative study, see Martin Minkner, *Die Gerichtsverwaltung in Deutschland und Italien*, Tübingen 2016; but also see the critique by Hans-Ernst Böttcher, Justizverwaltung in Europa, in: *Verdikt* 2.18, p. 25 et seq.

verification is possible (§§ 42 and 43, VwGO). In these respects, the administrative process resembles the civil process.

However, the problem remains of discretionary administrative power that, even in Germany, cannot be controlled by a judge, § 114 VwGO. Judges are thus limited to ordering the administration to decide in accordance with the legal aspects established in the sentence. Yet the judge can verify if the discretionary limits have been observed and if discretionary power has been used according to its intended purpose. In addition, open-ended legal notions are normally interpreted by the judge, and are usually special fields where, for example, the technical nature of the decision and the probability of prognosis in cases of uncertainty or personal evaluation open up a broader decision-making space for the administrative authority.

As a system, the described model of administrative jurisdiction has worked and works well in terms of providing citizens with access to rights protections and also reinforcing awareness about the legality and the responsibility of the administration. Meanwhile, the influence of the German model on the enactment of the administrative procedure code seems obvious, and the observations made by Comporti on the 'full protection against public power' similarly characterise the German situation. On the other hand, it can be said that the modern administration's resources are so broad in information, science and culture to cope with the actual tasks at hand.

The problem instead is the enormous quantity of court cases and, as a consequence, the increase in the number of judges, with its own cost to the system. Already with the legal processes relating to the environment and infrastructure, then through the enormous increase in conflicts in civil service, education (both schools and universities) and in relation to social security benefits, and finally with the issues of immigration and asylum, administrative courts are under such pressure that they no longer are able to deal with all the work before them. For that reason, since 1960 textual amendments to the law code have mainly limited the number of and access to the means of appeal, thereby decreasing protections across three jurisdiction levels. Administrative recourse options before the lawsuit, appeal, then recourse at the court of cassation (*"Revision"*) have been reduced or tied to admission according to different procedures, while cases within the jurisdiction of appellate courts or the first instance federal court have been increased. From the point of view of the rule of law and the legal system established by the Basic Law, such reductions are problematic, though at least partially inevitable to ensure the effectiveness of the system.

19.6 Regulations on Administrative Proceedings

With such a matter, the problem of regulating administrative procedures is ambivalent. Based on the division of power and accenting the legal protection of rights, one might argue in favour of the freedom of the administration to complete its tasks, as part and parcel with the exercising of discretion, though controlled by the judge. It is clear that, with the effectiveness of jurisdictional protection, administrative appeals established in the administrative processes before access to the judge have lost their importance and are often limited or even repealed. While the law code on administrative processes had established, as a rule (albeit one with exception by law), hierarchical appeals to the administration before the legal case (§ 68 VwGO), legislation, even in the Länder, had introduced an ever-increasing number of exceptions, reducing the number of bottom-up appeals.

On the other hand, such a tendency diminishes internal control over the administration, even over opportunity of administrative action, uncontrolled by the judge, and gives him an additional responsibility, often more costly than an internal check. Then, many issues in the administrative process, under the rule of law, need precise regulations, often elaborated in the courts, but better yet if based on formal laws. The models of Austrian law from 1925, adopted later in Thuringia and in a draft in Wurttemberg, recommended such a path.

In consideration of such topics, and after the initial years of the Federal Administrative Court's legal practice, the interior ministers of the Federation and the Länder decided, in the late 1950s, to create a law on administrative proceedings. After a broad discussion, the federal law was issued in 1976, its influence on the drafting of Italian law n. 241 of 1990 being fairly obvious.

However, the two laws differ in character. The Italian law, according to its title, contains 'new regulations', including access to administrative documents, and its first point establishes principles for administrative reform. The German law, on the other hand, is broadly based on jurisprudential experience and attempts to give it precise wording to ensure legal certainty. Of course, this difference is not absolute, and it has been mitigated with modifications to both laws in recent decades. Italian law has even adopted regulations on the efficiency, revocation, invalidity and the voidability of legal cases, similar to the analogous provisions of the German law. For its part, recent changes to the German law have introduced rather programmatic regulations, such as on early public participation (§ 25, sect. 3).[7] Obviously however, a legislative guide to the administrative process has proven to be useful.

A specifically German problem, however, is the legislative power in the matter. While federal jurisdiction in judicial proceedings is undisputed today (see above, par. 2 and 4), administrative proceedings take place both federally and in the Länder, and there is no federal authority regulating the process in the Länder, with the exception of the execution of federal laws attributed to the Länder if the federal legislation so determines, with the consent of the Bundesrat.[8] The implementation of the laws of the Länder is up to their authorities, exclusively according to Länder legislation. Considering this situation, parallel legislation has been implemented, starting from the early proposals onward. Alongside federal law, there are parallel Länder laws, and thanks to the cooperation of administrations and parliaments, the

[7]See in Augsberg, *Herausforderungen und Innovationen im Verwaltungsverfahrenschrecht*, in Sfide e innovazioni nel diritto pubblico, eds. Luca de Lucia/Ferdinand Wollenschlägen, Torino-Baden-Baden 2019, p. 84 (97–98).

[8]See art. 84, par. 1 GG, section 1, 2 par. of the law on federal administrative proceedings.

content of these laws is identical, also including changes to them. Thus, in the administrative process, the Federal Administrative Court, which is normally limited to ensuring the application of federal law, also ensures the application of laws in cases in the Länder (§ 137, sect. 1, nr. 2 VwGO). As such, it also standardises general administrative law. This system works without serious issues, on the condition that both sides are willing to cooperate.

19.7 The Influence of the European Union

The development and limitation of central power in Germany begs for comparison with the European Union. It too was formed by member states that had and have maintained their systems to protect rights and administrative processes. The European Court of Justice, established to rule on conflicts on rights and duties based on treaties, does not have the ability to rule on the means of appeal against decisions made by national courts. On this matter, it defers to the European Court of Human Rights that, thanks to the Convention (art. 34), can make decisions on appeals against measures taken by national supreme authorities. Yet in both cases, it is not a matter of a homogeneous jurisdiction system. Instead, these are complete national systems that are still being expanded by international remedies according to European Courts.

However, as Comporti's research proves, all guarantees to protect the rights of the ECHR substantially amplify the protection system in Italy. In Germany, it has less influence. The interjections of the Court of Strasbourg remain even in the interpretation and application of rights in Germany, e.g. in the conflict between the freedom of expression and the right to personal identity,[9] but the techniques used to protect those rights are less controversial and modified, if ever, primarily in criminal proceedings.[10] In relation to the administrative process, on the other hand, the German system is less influenced by European courts.

The relationship with EU power is much more important and aggravated by problems. It is true that even the EU, a product of the union of states with different rights protection systems, though with the claim of being complete, cannot impose its own supplementary system. Based on the jurisdiction of the union in specific matters (such as the common market, freedom of movement, legal cooperation, competition, the environment, etc.), there are many rules that impact administrative procedures and the protection of rights. But those influences produce, and require of national policy makers, special sector-based rules, far from a codified system.

[9]See the deep-seated conflict in the cases brought by Caroline of Monaco, BVerfGE 101,361 et seq., then ECHR sent. 24-6-2004 – 59320/00, BVerfGE 120,180 et seq., see also Dian Schefold, “Convergenze e divergenze tra le Corti europee e le Corti tedesche”, in: Giancarlo Rolla (edited by), *Il sistema europeo di protezione dei diritti fondamentali e i rapporti fra le giurisdizioni*, Milan 2010, p. 189 et seq.

[10]E.g.: BVerfGE 131,268 (296 et seq.); 133,40 et seq..; 134,33 et seq., on safe custody procedures.

One classic issue is the guaranteed application of European law on state aid, today regulated by art. 107–109 of the Treaty on the Functioning of the EU (TFEU). German law on administrative procedures had, based on administrative case law, regulated the annulment by the public authority of an unlawful administrative act in favour of the citizen, with certain limits to protect the interests of the addressee (§ 48, VwVfG). The solution is comparable to art. 21-nonies of law n. 241 of 1990. Therefore, measures that offer financial aid, granted in contradiction to art. 107–109 TFEU, cannot necessarily be annulled, and the amounts are not always to reimburse. In a fundamental case on 21 September 1983, the Court of Justice recognised this protocol in principle, confirming that the principles of protection of trust and legal certainty are also part of European law. But it has excluded the application of national procedural law that discriminates against the application of European law, and insisted on the weight of the European Union's interests in balancing interests.[11] In this way, it insisted, while maintaining national authority to regulate the matter, on the regulation of its implementation and application.

The essential tool for such authority is the primary ruling (today art. 267 TFEU) as a procedural tool comparable to adjournment for control over the constitutionality of laws and, in the federal state, in the form of adjournment to ensure the uniform interpretation of the constitutional system.[12] This is not, however, a matter of a means of appeal in a unified judicial system. It is not the interested citizen who lodges an appeal, but the cooperation of the courts with jurisdiction that, maintaining their independence and separation, avoids divergences in grave cases and arrives, in this way, at cooperation, no matter how informal.

19.8 Jurisdictional Cultures, Tolerated Differences and Dialogue

In Europe, we therefore find ourselves amid a uniform jurisdictional and administrative system like that which Italy created 150 years ago. The European states all have their legal and administrative preferences, with different organisational structures, traditions and procedural solutions, and the unification of Europe does not claim to remove these differences and level out all systems. The situation is similar to that in Germany in 1871, but differs in that, in this case, the civil and criminal process and jurisdictional organisation were codified and unified rather quickly. Only in public law have the differences been maintained for a lengthy amount of time and, in certain respects, up until today.

[11] Court of Justice, sent. of 21-9-1983 – 205-215/83, *Neue Juristische Wochenschrift* 1984, p. 2024 et seq.

[12] A classic example from Germany: the standardisation of constitutional jurisprudence of the Länder according to art. 100, sect. 3 GG. See Daniela Poli, *Bundesverfassungsgericht e Landesverfassungsgerichte: un modello "policentrico" di giustizia costituzionale*, Milan 2012.

This example teaches us the potential of a pluralist system, even in this regard. It would of course take a standardisation of national solutions in order to defend European constitutional values, but perhaps more importantly to guarantee the implementation of European law and the policies that it shapes. Naturally, regulations to this end cannot help but be complicated, and thus the compromise between simplification, standardisation and respect for the varied solutions is an ongoing process that is the subject of constant debate and controversy. Of course, the guarantee of equality, an essential value of the EU pursuant to art. 2 of the TEU is to be respected, as is the equality of the member states and of their national identities pursuant to art. 4, 2nd par. TEU.

Yet it isn't the isolated problem of respect when facing national solutions that relativises and limits the idea of a unified system. In national law, limited resources for the protection of rights have required restrictions on appeals and means of redress, for example, according to the value of the case or its legal relevance, with procedures for the admission of certain means of appeal or simplified, summary procedures. For access to the supreme courts, appeals for rights violations require limitations, in the American 'certiorari' just as in the admission procedures for direct appeal to the German Constitutional Court. For this reason, it's quite natural that there is a need to select the cases of appeal at the European Court of Human Rights.

As a result, the perfect unity of jurisprudence remains a goal and perhaps an ideal, though unreachable in broad, complex jurisdictional systems. Taking account of these limits is tantamount to recognising juridical pluralism, an essential element of the systems in question. However, it is still possible to reduce divergences, beyond the legally-established tools for standardisation, like primary rulings and transmissions in cases of divergences or doubts of the superior courts, through cooperation and informal dialogue between them. The development of such cooperation mitigates pluralism and brings the courts closer to the ideal of equality, an irrefutable value of the European Union.

Chapter 20
The Roller Coaster Ride of English Administrative Law

Peter Leyland

Contents

Abstract This chapter discusses the main trends in English administrative law. It begins by seeking to define administrative law in a UK context before moving on to discuss the role of 'red light' and 'green light' theory as competing approaches to understanding the contribution of administrative law from the latter part of the nineteenth century. An assessment of the common law development is approached by explaining the significance of prominent case law with particular attention to the famous *Wednesbury* case, the decision in *Ridge v Baldwin* and the *GCHQ* case. However viewed from a different perspective the rising importance of administrative law is attributed to procedural reforms which relaxed the rules of standing and swept away other procedural impediments to making claims. An assessment of the contribution of the Human Rights Act 1998 follows as this not only incorporated the ECHR but also further increased the profile of the courts. The heightened judicial profile calls for a discussion in outline of the conceptual debate between legal and political constitutionalism concerning the extent of the judicial role. The final section of the chapter adopts a 'bottom up' approach by briefly assessing the contribution of alternatives to the judge centred approach, with reference to alternative dispute resolution and the new system of tribunals. It is argued that recent rule changes to

P. Leyland (✉)
School of Oriental and African Studies (SOAS), University of London, London, UK
e-mail: pl3@soas.ac.uk

D. Sorace et al. (eds.), *The Changing Administrative Law of an EU Member State*,
https://doi.org/10.1007/978-3-030-50780-0_20

reduce legal aid costs and impose court fees are having a radical impact on the number of cases, with drastic implications for claimants.

20.1 Introduction

Within days of the Brexit referendum in 2016, the pivotal importance of Judicial Review was brought to general attention in spectacular fashion in the *Miller* case.[1] The claimant argued that triggering Brexit without prior parliamentary approval was unlawful, because it would inevitably result in the loss of a number of existing rights enjoyed under the European Union Act of 1972 and other related statutes. On final appeal this fundamental question of legality was referred to the UK Supreme Court to decide. The matter before the court was of great importance, not because the court's decision was likely to prevent or even delay the Brexit process, but because of its constitutional significance. The Brexit referendum was not legally binding under the relevant statute.[2] Had ministers alone taken the decision to trigger Brexit Parliament would have been, in effect, side lined from a decision with far reaching implications for the nation. The UK Supreme Court held that such radical constitutional change must be 'effected in the only way the UK constitution recognises, namely by Parliamentary legislation.'[3] The government, of course, complied with the judgment and the ruling duly resulted in an enabling Act of Parliament granting the government authority to signal withdrawal from the EU.[4] In one sense *Miller* might be regarded as an exemplary judicial challenge. It involved a question of legality which arose when the government sought to use the prerogative power without the consent of Parliament, and the courts by resolving the issue of legality were not only setting legal limits, but also arbitrating between the executive and legislative branches of the state, and in this sense, the *Miller* case offered a 'rigorous defence of the traditional constitution'.[5] To what extent can this outcome be taken to reflect the more general condition of English administrative law?

This chapter offers a selective thematic survey of important trends in administrative law.[6] In approaching the task it is first relevant to point out that there is no universally agreed definition of what administrative law consists of. The subject is sometimes defined mainly in terms of the legal control of public power. Some of the best known academic studies adopt a court centred perspective which concentrates

---

[1] *R (Miller) v Secretary of State for Exiting the European Union* [2017] UKSC 5.

[2] See the European Union Referendum Act 2015.

[3] Poole (2017), pp. 696–710 and 702.

[4] See European Union (Notification of Withdrawal) Act 2017.

[5] Poole (2017), p. 710.

[6] In this chapter many important areas of administrative law are not discussed. For example, privatization and regulation.

on judicial review.[7] While others consider the wider functioning of the administrative state and address the field of public administration more generally.[8] Our discussion begins by revisiting 'red light' and 'green light' theory as the traffic light dichotomy highlights contrasting but at the same time influential trends, and it also introduces a historical trajectory to the analysis that follows. The following sections investigate the reasons for the emergence of judicial review as a remedy of major constitutional significance from a number of standpoints. It is argued that the emergence of the courts is attributed, in part, to substantive principles developed in landmark cases; in part, to greater ease of access facilitated by key procedural reforms that assisted litigants in making a claim; and, in part, to the impact of the Human Rights Act which allows citizens to challenge public authorities in the domestic courts for infringing rights enjoyed under the ECHR. The section on judicial review ends by briefly evaluating the wider conceptual debate between advocates of legal and political constitutionalism. In order to consider the more general accountability of the public administration the remainder of the chapter is concerned with assessing the contribution of the full range of available remedies, including the emergence of Alternative Dispute Resolution (ADR), ombudsmen and tribunals. As a metaphor a roller coaster ride conveys the impression of the apparently uninterrupted upward trend in the profile of judicial review and the consolidation of tribunals into a system now in some ways resembling administrative courts. However, notwithstanding recent prominent judgments such as the *Miller* case, in the last 5 years this rise has been followed by a steep decline in take up. A spectacular drop in the throughput of cases can be attributed partly to the progressive imposition of resource constraints, and, partly to a revision of the rules at the behest of government that apply to judicial review claimants.

20.2 Red Lights, Green Lights and the Rise of the Modern Administrative State

Harlow and Rawlings began their landmark study of '*Law and Administration*' first published in 1984 by stating that behind every theory of administrative law lies a theory of the state.[9] The famous 'red light' and 'green light' dichotomy is then artfully deployed to explain that the growth of the administrative state is accompanied by two contrasting, and, at times, conflicting trends. On the one hand, there is what is termed the 'red light' approach which reverts to Dicey's notion of the rule of law. 'In England the idea of legal equality, or the universal subjection of all classes to law administered by the ordinary courts, has been pushed to its utmost limit'.[10] The

[7] See e.g. Wade and Forsyth (2014) and Craig (2016).

[8] See e.g. Harlow and Rawlings (1984) and McEldowney (2016).

[9] Harlow and Rawlings (1984), p. 1.

[10] Dicey (1959), p. 193.

law is conceived in a negative sense as primarily concerned with curbing or controlling the state. In fact the approach is characterised by 'suspicion of the growing power of the administration, emphasis is on control and ancient liberties and the fear that government will run amok'.[11] Apprehension over the encroachment of bureaucracy on public life was elaborated further by the Lord Chief Justice, Lord Hewart, a generation later.[12] From this standpoint the application of the rule of law has the effect of qualifying the core principle of parliamentary sovereignty by providing a crucial element of judicial control of the executive. In particular, by placing limits on the discretionary power granted to officials. According to this view this is because under the uncodified British constitution common law developed by judges recognises, and by implication, defends the rights of individuals by upholding the rule of law in the courts.

On the other hand, the 'Green Light' view represents a markedly different approach to the emergent administrative state, and later the so called 'welfare' state, in which the emphasis changed from judge made law to legislation and regulation.[13] The reform minded supporters of this trend, such as Laski, Robson and Jennings from the London School of Economics drew upon the work of Bentham, Durkheim and Duguit (among others) in developing a 'functionalist method' which is concerned to maximise the practical application of the law so that 'administrative law became all the law relating to administration and not merely that concerned with the control of executive power'.[14] The emphasis is upon an administration centred definition of administrative law recognising that it is the law in the form of primary and secondary legislation which determines the organisation, powers and duties of administrative authorities. Rather than viewing progressive social policy from the standpoint of the encroachment of the liberty of some individual citizens, the extension of collective economic and social rights to pensions, benefits, education, public housing has become *the* central goal of contemporary governance. The trend of modern administrative law shifts towards improving the quality of rule-making as part of an overall legislative framework. It favours the use of specialised administrative agencies, such as tribunals, as the main form of control, with court centred adjudication deliberately side-lined. Green light commentators were also aware of the contribution of parliamentary oversight mechanisms and other forms of dispute resolution in providing accountable government.[15] This approach adopts a much wider definition of administrative law which potentially includes all the law relating to public administration.

---

[11]Harlow and Rawlings (1984), p. 13.

[12]Hewart (1929).

[13]Harlow and Rawlings (1984), p. 41.

[14]Harlow and Rawlings (1984), p. 36.

[15]Jennings (1959).

A succession of statutes in many different policy areas[16] demonstrated a trend of increasing legislative complexity with widespread reliance on delegated powers, but this was not a systemic feature based on any general principles. In fact functionalist critics tended to stress the shortcomings of the Donoughmore Committee Report.[17] The reliance on statutory schemes was merely the approach adopted by Parliament to achieve specific policy objectives. Instead of anything resembling continental style administrative courts, dispute resolution fell under individual government departments in the form of appeals procedures and tribunals.[18] In consequence, there was a notable absence of any separation between executive and judicial powers.

For the first seven decades of the twentieth century administrative law is characterised by this tension until the emergence of an "amber light view" suggested that there was a gradual accommodation between these two contrasting positions. For instance Harlow and Rawlings state: 'It would be wrong to leave the subject, however, without any mention of a growing consensus over administrative law values. This has crystallised around a trilogy of values—transparency, participation and accountability—that reflect the "good governance" programmes of international institutions.'[19]

While much attention is devoted to judicial review in the scholarly literature, it is crucial to stress the importance of re-adjusting the focus of administrative law to reflect momentous changes in the political climate. For example, the 'Thatcher' revolution was in full swing by the time of the publication of the second comprehensively re-written edition of *Law and Administration* which has a new chapter entitled 'Blue Rinse' to assess the impact of New Public Management techniques, privatisation and a 'contract culture'.[20] Of course it was argued by successive governments that wasteful public services could be transformed by adopting private sector ideas associated with privatisation and New Public Management. As the in house delivery of services at the level of central and local government has been replaced with contractual agreements, so established forms of accountability to Parliament and the courts were placed under threat. For example, there might be less scope for legal challenge given the distinction drawn under the application for judicial review procedure between public and private powers.[21] In essence, these reforms have changed the relationship between the government and the citizen. As Harlow and Rawlings themselves explain: 'The structural and managerial revolution clearly establishes a strong framework for the future role and development of

[16]See e.g. National Insurance Acts 1911 and 1965, Housing Acts 1925, 1930, 1985, National Health Service Act 1946, Town and Country Planning Act 1947 to name but a few.

[17]See Report of the Committee on Ministers' Powers, Cmnd (1932); See Loughlin (1992), chapter 6 and p. 235.

[18]See Report of Committee on Administrative Tribunals and Enquiries, 1957 (Cmnd 218) mentioned below.

[19]Harlow and Rawlings (2009), p. 46.

[20]Harlow and Rawlings (1997), chapter 5.

[21]Davies (2013), p. 350.

government. Its all pervasive ethos and vocabulary has been adopted at home by both political parties. Its discourse has spread throughout Europe, reinforced by the market ideology entrenched at constitutional level by the EC Treaty'.[22]

20.3 Judicial Oversight: The Rising Profile of the Courts?

The origins of administrative law in terms of the common law response were rooted in the nineteenth century. This was largely because of the activation of Parliament as a legislative body. New laws were imposing obligations on factory owners and boards set up to regulate railways, docks and canals and this was often perceived by property owning classes as a dangerous invasion of their individual liberty. Orders of *certiorari* were granted by the courts as remedies to quash regulatory decisions. Also *mandamus* was used to compel reluctant local justices to convict authorities for breaching regulatory provisions.[23] We have already observed that the 'red light' perspective prioritises a court centred view of administrative law. In *Cooper v Wandsworth*[24] it was recognised that a person deserves to be given notice and a hearing before being deprived of their property. Even in the absence of legislative provisions Mr Justice Byles affirmed that 'The justice of the common law [will] supply the omission of the legislature'. Common law attempts to uphold fairness and natural justice were barely apparent in other judgments however, and the extent of judicial protection during the first half of the twentieth century was in fact minimal.[25] For example, in the well known case of *Local Government Board v Arlidge*[26] the court neglected to act in a robust fashion to order the publication of a crucial report and thus 'failed to keep abreast of the standard of fairness required'.[27]

Indeed, the express purpose of the Wednesbury test was to avoid merits review and it sets a high threshold for judicial intervention which went beyond enforcing the boundaries of a conferred power.[28] The general use of the word "unreasonable" is applied as a broad description of things which must not be done. For instance, (paraphrasing Lord Greene) a person entrusted with a discretion must, direct himself properly in law. He must call his own attention to matters which he is bound to consider. He must exclude from his consideration matters which are irrelevant to what he has to consider. If he does not obey those rules, he may truly be said to be acting "unreasonably". But unreasonable is meant here in a general rather than strong sense. Of course, in the Wednesbury case itself the drafting of the statutory

[22]Harlow and Rawlings (1997), pp. 138ff and 149.

[23]Sedley (1997), pp. 17 and 18.

[24](1863) 14 CB (NS) 180, 194.

[25]Sedley (2015), p. 27.

[26][1915] AC 120.

[27]Wade and Forsyth (2014), p. 412.

[28]*Associated Provincial Picture Houses Ltd v Wednesbury Corporation* [1948] 1 KB 223 (CA).

power under the Sunday Entertainments Act 1932 allowed for: 'such conditions as the authority think fit to impose' and thus conferred a very wide discretion, one to be exercised executively by the local authority as the responsible body, not judicially by the courts. The strong Wednesbury standard of "unreasonableness" recognised by Lord Greene MR attaches a special, administrative law meaning to the term unreasonable. Wednesbury unreasonableness meant 'something so absurd that no sensible person could ever dream that it lay within the powers of the authority' or a decision 'so unreasonable that no reasonable authority that no reasonable authority could ever come to it.'[29] In order to avoid merits review this hurdle had to be overcome as the court should be considering the legality of the decision, not the subject matter under consideration which is for the decision-maker to determine.

Sir Stephen Sedley has recently remarked that: 'Much of the development of modern public law has been a struggle to escape from Lord Greene's straitjacket'.[30] In practice, the level of the Wednesbury threshold has been adjusted by the courts upwards or downwards to take account of policy or human rights implications raised by the case in hand.[31] Sir John Laws has argued that the Wednesbury standard embodies an underlying moral principle. It is that the law presumes against interference with individual liberty and that like cases should be treated alike. This is a translation of Kant's imperative into legal principle and it embodies the tension between the rule of law and democracy.[32]

On the other hand, the case of *Ridge v Baldwin*[33] can be seen as emblematic of a fresh wave of judicial activism dating from the 1960s.[34] The judgment swept aside what had been regarded as a previous impediment in the form of the limitation of the prerogative writs of mandamus, prohibition and certiorari to those decision makers having a duty act judicially. Lord Reid held that wherever any person or body of persons has authority conferred by legislation to make decisions it is amenable to a remedy, either for error of law in reaching it, or for failure to act fairly towards the person who will be adversely affected by it.[35] Three decades before the *Miller* case (discussed in the introduction) illegality, irrationality and procedural impropriety were explained as the main grounds of judicial review by Lord Diplock in the GCHQ case.[36] Lord Diplock employs language which in defining illegality and irrationality

---

[29]Taggart (2003), p. 320.

[30]Sedley (2015), p. 25, n. 8.

[31]See for "super" Wednesbury *R v Secretary of State for the Environment, ex p Nottinghamshire CC* [1986] AC 240 and for sub Wednesbury/anxious scrutiny test see e.g. *R v Secretary of State for the Home Office, ex p Bugdaycay* [1987] 1 AC 514.

[32]Laws (1998), pp. 191ff.

[33][1964] AC 40.

[34]Other landmark cases included: *Padfield v Minister of Agriculture Fisheries and Food* [1968] AC 997 (established that a wide statutory discretion must promote the policy and objects of the act) and *Anisminic Ltd v Foreign Compensation Commission* [1969] 2 AC 147 (recognised limits to statutory ouster clauses).

[35]Wade and Forsyth (2014), p. 412.

[36]*Council of Civil Service Unions v Minister for the Civil Service* [1985] AC 374.

resembles Lord Greene's formulation of general unreasonableness and strong Wednesbury unreasonableness respectively. In common with *Miller* the GCHQ case also concerned the exercise of the prerogative power and it is clear that the unions would have enjoyed a legitimate expectation to be consulted in advance of the decision being taken, but in view of the security implications raised by the government the decision to prohibit civil servants working at the covert government communications centre from remaining trade union members was not set aside by the court.[37] Nevertheless, it was recognised that decisions of central government, whether under statute or the prerogative, could be subjected to judicial scrutiny, and this amenability to review was regarded as essential for the maintenance of the rule of law.

20.4 Procedural Reforms and Opening Up Access

The decisions discussed above refer to some of the key conceptual tools developed by the courts as grounds of review when considering the legality of decisions by public authorities. However, the far reaching procedural changes which followed in the wake of a report by the Law Commission in 1976 were undoubtedly a highly significant factor in increasing the availability of judicial review.[38] In fact shortly after the procedural reforms were implemented, Lord Diplock, one of the architects of these innovations, famously remarked that progress towards a comprehensive system of administrative law was 'the greatest achievement of the English courts in my lifetime'.[39] In order to fully grasp the impact of these reforms it is crucial to understand that the courts have a supervisory jurisdiction. An application for judicial review depends on seeking a remedy and that 'Prior to the reforms of 1977 damages, injunctions and declarations were sought in an ordinary action, as in private law; but the prerogative remedies had to be sought by a procedure of their own, which could be combined with an ordinary action'.[40] The Law Commission recommended the fusion of the public and private law remedies as part of a revised two stage application for judicial review procedure.[41] Following the implementation of the reforms the appellate committee of the House of Lords in *O'Reilly v Mackman*[42] set out the so called 'exclusivity principle'. This approach recognises that all the remedies for the infringement of rights protected by public law could now be obtained by judicial review. In consequence, as a general rule it would be contrary to public policy and an abuse of process for a litigant complaining of a public

[37]Drabble (2017), p. 97.

[38]Remedies in Administrative Law, Cmnd 6407 (London, 1976).

[39]See *O'Reilly v Mackman* [1983] 2 AC 237 at 279.

[40]Wade and Forsyth (2014), p. 478.

[41]Remedies in Administrative Law, Cmnd 6407 (London, 1976), para 59.

[42][1983] 2 AC 237, 238.

authority's infringement of a public law right to seek redress by private law action. In English law, subject to certain exceptions, decisions by public bodies or bodies performing public functions with public consequences[43] were made subject to judicial review.

In the second place, access was facilitated by a change in the interpretation of the rules of standing. As part of the procedure the court rules of standing specify that a claimant must have *sufficient interest* in order to proceed with a judicial review case.[44] Before the reforms this requirement differed according to the remedy which was sought and was frequently interpreted as requiring direct personal interest. In the *Fleet Street Casuals Case* Lord Diplock stated on final appeal in the House of Lords that: 'it would be a grave lacuna in our system of public law if a pressure group, ... or even a single public-spirited taxpayer, were prevented by out dated technical rules of *locus standi* from bringing the matter to the attention of the court to vindicate the rule of law and get the unlawful conduct stopped.'[45] This statement marked a change in judicial policy towards a more flexible approach allowing challenges from legal persons such as pressure groups and trade unions.[46] This liberalisation of the rules of standing represents a change from a drainpipe (private interest) model to a funnel (public interest advocate) model of judicial review.[47] Certainly, judicial review has assumed a higher profile and the appearance of the publication the 'Judge Over your shoulder'[48] intended as a kind of handbook for civil servants setting out best practice in administrative decision-making, testifies to the lingering spectre of judicial review in the background as a potent remedy if officials fail to act in accordance with the law.[49] In the mid 1990s it was observed that 'These reforms have for the first time given English administrative law the characteristics of Continental legal systems. Most notably, a system of public law, distinct and procedurally separate from private law.'[50]

[43]In turn this raises further issues in defining a public body. See *R v Panel on Take-overs and Mergers, ex p Datafin* [1987] QB 815.

[44]Order 53,T.

[45]*R v Inland Revenue Commissioners, ex parte National Federation of Self-Employed and Small Business* [1982] AC 617, 644.

[46]The victim requirement under the Human Rights Act was recently considered by the Supreme Court which held that 'where the Northern Ireland Human Rights Commission is intervening in human rights proceedings, the person instituting the proceedings must be a an actual or potential victim of an unlawful act ...' for standing requirements to be satisfied. Lord Mance para 56. See *In the matter of an application by the Northern Ireland Human Rights Commission for Judicial Review, Reference by the Court of Appeal in Northern Ireland pursuant to Paragraph 33 of Schedule 10 to the Northern Ireland Act 1998 (Abortion) (Northern Ireland)* [2018] UKSC27.

[47]Harlow and Rawlings (2009), pp. 672ff.

[48]This first appeared in 1987, for the latest version see 'Judge Over Your Shoulder: A Guide to good decision making' (Government Legal Department, 2016); https://www.gov.uk/government/publications/judge-over-your-shoulder.

[49]Ibid, 'Appendix 3: Checklist for making decisions'.

[50]Boyle (1994), p. 88.

In one sense the progressive increase in litigation demonstrates the heightened profile of judicial review. Measured in terms of raw statistics the simplification of the procedure with the reform of Order 53 of the Rules of the Supreme Court in 1977 has led to a surge in the number of applications for JR.[51] There were 160 cases in 1974, 685 cases in 1982, 2439 cases in 1992, 5298 cases in 2001 and by 2010 the total had risen to more than 10,600 cases.[52] Of course, the statistics do not take account of how the threat of JR has operated as a deterrent and impacts on the approach of officials to the day to day practice of public administration.[53]

20.5 Administrative Law and Rights Protection

The upward surge of judicial review was boosted further by the passage of the Human Rights Act 1998. Certain rights have been recognised since Magna Carta[54] and some rights are protected under individual statutes[55] but the United Kingdom constitution is distinctive because it is unwritten and lacks any formal definition of fundamental citizen rights. The Labour government when elected in 1997 was committed to introducing HR legislation because of a perception that fundamental rights had been gradually eroded in response to increasing crime and threats of terrorism. This ground breaking statute in constitutional terms did not directly provide the United Kingdom with new citizen rights. To achieve the goal of upholding rights it incorporated into domestic law an international treaty, the European Convention on Human Rights, and the rights already set out therein. The profile of the courts was undoubtedly heightened to a significant extent with the passage of the Human Rights Act 1998 (HRA). When it came into force in the year 2000 the HRA made it unlawful for public authorities to act in a way that is incompatible with convention rights.[56] A citizen whose rights were allegedly infringed was now able to make a claim using the judicial review procedure in UK domestic courts against the public body concerned rather than having to take the case to Strasbourg.

As Paul Craig observes:

> The most significant difference between the earlier system of review and the current regime is in relation to rights based review. We have grown rapidly accustomed to the Human Rights Act 1998, and the way in which it has altered judicial review by giving greater weight to rights, more especially so since the Convention rights brought into UK law accord the status of rights to some interests that would not have been so regarded in the seventeenth or

---

[51]The reform was later enacted as Section 31 of the Senior Courts Act 1981.

[52]Leyland and Anthony (2016), p. 198.

[53]See Sunkin and Bondy (2016), p. 337.

[54]Blick (2015), p. 47.

[55]See e.g. The Police and Criminal Evidence Act 1984.

[56]HRA 1998, section 6.

> eighteenth centuries. Insofar as interests such as free speech and the like were protected, it was in the form of negative residual liberties . . .[57]

The Act granted the courts formidable new powers. The purposive interpretation of legislation allowed judges to read in words to render measures convention compatible[58] and where they were not able to interpret legislation in a convention compliant way the court could issue a declaration of incompatibility.[59] This does not invalidate the offending legislation but the effect is to refer the matter back to Parliament, thereby establishing a form of dialogue between the courts and Parliament.[60] It is notable that it was not the common law but the Human Rights Act which opened the way for the adoption of a proportionality test in place of *Wednesbury*[61] for cases involving convention rights.[62] Proportionality review requires the courts to conduct a balancing exercise to assess whether the alleged interference with a claimant's convention rights was justified.[63]

The famous *Belmarsh* case[64] best epitomises the willingness of the courts to defend convention rights even in the sensitive policy area of the government's anti-terrorism policy. A group of Algerian nationals challenged their indefinite detention in a high security prison as terror suspects under the Anti-terrorism Crime and Security Act 2001. On final appeal, notwithstanding the attempted derogation from Article 5, the court held 'that the measure did not rationally address the threat to security, was not a proportionate response, was not strictly required by the exigencies of the situation and unjustifiably discriminated against foreign nationals on grounds of their nationality'.[65] However, despite the heavy judicial censure the Belmarsh detainees remained in prison until the offending legislation was repealed by Parliament with the passage of the Prevention of Terrorism Act 2005.[66]

The Human Rights Act had a profound impact on the functioning of the entire judicial system. In particular, with the separation of powers requirements of Article 6 the ancient office of Lord Chancellor appeared outmoded. It was no longer feasible for the minister running the government department with responsibility for running the courts and appointing judges to preside over the House of Lords as legislature while also retaining the right to sit as a member of the highest appellate court.[67] The legislative response in the form of the Constitutional Reform Act 2005 not only addressed the absence of separation of powers by establishing a duty to uphold

[57]Craig (2015), p. 42.

[58]HRA 1998, section 3.

[59]HRA 1998, section 4.

[60]Cohn (2013).

[61]See e.g. *R v Secretary of State for the Home Department, ex p Brind* [1992] AC 696.

[62]See e.g. *R v Home Secretary, ex p Daly* [2001] 2 AC 532.

[63]See Hickman (2008), p. 694.

[64]*A v Home Secretary* [2005] 2 AC 68.

[65]Bingham (2010), p. 149.

[66]See Clayton (2017).

[67]Woodhouse (2001), pp. 12ff.

judicial independence[68] but also introduced a Supreme Court for the United Kingdom outside of Parliament in place of the appellate committee of the House of Lords[69] and it reformed the system of judicial appointments.[70] Nevertheless, the UK Supreme Court was not designed as a constitutional court in a continental sense with the power to invalidate primary legislation.

20.6 Political Versus Legal Constitutionalism: Bridging the Gap Between Theory and Practice

In identifying the wider constitutional implications it is helpful to mention the vigorous scholarly debate concerning the relative virtues of what has been termed 'political' and 'legal' constitutionalism.[71] In one sense there is a consensus over the need for a core legality principle of some kind. The rule of law was explained by Dicey in relation to the sovereignty of Parliament and the constitution.[72] More recently its essence was summarised by Lord Bingham:

> The core of the existing principle [of the rule of law] is, . . . that all persons and authorities within the state, whether public or private, should be bound by and entitled to the benefit of laws publicly made, taking effect in the future and publicly administered in the courts.[73]

Even John Griffith as an arch exponent of 'political constitutionalism' accepted that: 'If the Rule of Law means that there should be proper and adequate machinery for dealing with criminal offences and for ensuring that public authorities do not exceed their legal powers, and for insisting that official penalties may not be inflicted save on those who have broken the law, then only an outlaw would dispute its desirability.' This acknowledges the importance of a limited judicial role but he then went on to state that '. . . when it [referring to the rule of law] is extended to mean more than that, it is a fantasy invented by Liberals of the old school in the late nineteenth century. . . . Then it is become a new metaphysic, seeming to resolve the doubts of the faithful with an old dogma'.[74]

The case for a higher judicial profile and an expanded role for the courts has been promoted by influential academic commentators and judges[75] but the approach is hotly disputed by others.[76] Broadly speaking, legal constitutionalists regard

[68]CRA 2005, Section 3.

[69]CRA 2005, Part 3.

[70]CRA 2005, Part 4.

[71]For a detailed up-to-date overview see Craig (2015), pp. 166ff.

[72]Dicey (1959), p. 188.

[73]Bingham (2010), p. 8.

[74]Griffith (1979), p. 15.

[75]See e.g. Allan (2001), Dworkin (1986) and Raz (1979).

[76]See e.g. Griffith (1979), pp. 1–21; Poole (2003), p. 453; Tomkins (2005); Bellamy (2007).

administrative legality or accountability to law as entailing the judicial enforcement of rule of law-based values of fair or just treatment. In a sense such an approach echoes the third meaning attributed to the rule of law by Dicey, namely that the constitution is pervaded by general principles, including the right to personal liberty which resulted from judicial decisions brought before the courts.[77] As Trevor Allan puts it:

> . . . the values of individual autonomy and human dignity are *internal* to law, basic assumptions critical to its meaning in specific cases. And so far from the rule of law being merely a safeguard against the abuse of law itself – a shield against a political oppression imposed by assertion of law – it is, on the contrary a basic protection against arbitrary power from whatever quarter it appears . . . The rule of law is the ideal of government according to *law* insulating the individual citizen against the unfettered discretion of officials, on the one hand, and the depredations of other persons or private organizations, on the other.[78]

In practical terms this law amounts to judicially created standards of public behaviour now enforced through the application of the modern grounds of judicial review developed by the judges.[79]

John Griffith, on the other hand, adopted a starkly positivistic view of the constitution. To paraphrase his position, he maintained that ministers and others in high positions of authority are individuals who happen to exercise political power but without any such right to that power which could give them a superior moral position. The laws made by those in authority derive validity from no other fact or principle. They do not impose a moral obligation of obedience on others. Furthermore, for Griffith individual rights or human rights are no more and no less than political claims made by individuals on those in authority. The upshot is that 'any society is endemically in a state of conflict between warring interest groups, having no consensus or unifying principles sufficiently precise to be the basis of a theory of legislation.'[80]

Professor Bellamy, a more recent exponent of a revised brand of political constitutionalism, states that 'the true protection of rights, the rule of law and even democracy comes from democracy—the power of individual citizens to claim and frame their rights and demand that they be treated on equal terms with others.'[81] In fact the suitability of courts as decision-making bodies is called into question by political constitutionalists for a number of well rehearsed reasons. To take but a few, it is misleading to imply that the common law embodies a particular view of morality. Very often in common with the wider community judges disagree with one another about many issues, including individual and minority rights (as well as other political issues) and this disagreement affects how judgments are formulated

[77] Dicey (1959), p. 195.

[78] Allan (2013), p. 78.

[79] Craig (2015), pp. 22ff.

[80] Griffith (1979), p. 19.

[81] Bellamy (2007), p. 141.

and applied.[82] Further, apart from not being accountable in a democratic sense, judges responsible for developing the common law in special policy fields may not be equipped to take the decisions that come before them. Judges are neither representative of society nor directly politically accountable for the decisions they take.[83]

Moreover, while the relative independence of courts and judicial reasoning in one sense might be desirable when considering rights questions, the complex underlying issues are frequently refined into narrow points of law as part of an adversarial process which results in a clear winner and loser. As Professor Waldron puts it: 'By the time cases reach the high appellate levels . . . almost all trace of the original flesh-and-blood right holders has vanished, and argument, such as it is, revolves around the abstract issue of the right in dispute.'[84] For instance, a difficult question for judges to answer is how polycentric disputes might be resolved satisfactorily in a situation where competing views and the wider context are not represented. A court room by its very definition lacks the features of the republican model of active citizenship.[85] In *R (Rogers) v Swindon NHS Primary Care Trust*[86] the court intervened to grant a remedy when the claimant was refused an expensive new treatment for breast cancer by her local hospital which was available under the NHS in other areas of the country. The argument in this case naturally concerned, in narrow legal terms, the rationality of this individual decision. The case was confined to examining the decision-making process, but the court was not in a position to address the impact in terms of the allocation of scarce resources as part of a publicly funded health system.[87] Given the discussion about judicial disagreement above, it is also worth pointing out that a decision which had been considered lawful by a judge in the high court at first instance was overturned on appeal. In response to such objections it has been observed that 'The general thrust of political constitutionalist thought has been to limit legal constitutionalism in the form of judicial review and to extol in its place political oversight'.[88]

Of course, in the final analysis it comes down to whether the courts should be the ultimate controlling factor and have the last say as part of the constitutional order. The *Jackson* case considered, among other things, the validity of an act of Parliament to ban hunting passed under the Parliament Acts 1911 and 1949 without the assent of the House of Lords. In giving judgment Lord Steyn claimed authority for legal constitutionalism as an autonomous concept by arguing that the Supremacy of Parliament itself is a judge made principle, and that in extreme circumstances it

---

[82] Waldron (2006), pp. 1346 and 1366.

[83] Tushnet (2013), pp. 60ff.

[84] Waldron (2006), pp. 1379ff.

[85] See e.g. Poole (2003), pp. 435–454.

[86] [2006] 89 BMLR 211. See Leyland and Anthony (2016), p. 298.

[87] Syrett (2006), pp. 664–673 at 667.

[88] Craig (2015), p. 180.

could be qualified by the courts.[89] This claim was and remains very controversial. As Professor Geoffrey Goldsworthy points out: 'If it is true that Parliaments authority must come from somewhere it must be equally true of the judges authority. But they, too, cannot pull themselves up by their own bootstraps by conferring authority on themselves.'[90] As Professor Martin Loughlin puts it: 'Contrary to the views of those such as Dicey and Jennings who acknowledged the distinction between constitution and law and therefore the conventional nature of "constitutional law" ... [this approach promotes] law over practice, a normative version of constitutional ordering over institutional description, and 'legal constitutionalism' over the inherited practices of the 'political constitution''.[91]

Where, as we noted above when considering green light approaches and will see in the final section of this chapter, political constitutionalism sees law as a tool for the execution of political goals related to efficient policy implementation, legal constitutionalism promotes accountability to law as a moral vision related to the idea that liberty and justice are integral to the common law. A question remains over whether such ideas can ever provide a convincing account of how to address the practical questions which come before the courts. In their critique of courts and support for an approach based on parliamentary supremacy political constitutionalists have taken for granted certain assumptions about the good health and efficient functioning of democratic institutions which are regarded as an alternative to courts.[92] Such foundations, particularly relating to the effectiveness of Parliament as an oversight body, are perhaps more questionable than ever, given current political volatility and the deep divisions within political parties as well as between parties in the present political climate.[93]

20.7 Administrative Law Bottom Up: ADR, Ombudsmen and Tribunals

The debate between these rival schools of thought in part depends on different understandings of the concept of law, and, in turn, the type of executive accountability to law. It will be apparent in this final section that an altogether different picture of administrative law comes into view if the grievance chain, with judicial review at its apex, is viewed from the bottom up.[94] At base level in seeking a remedy a potential claimant may be able to take advantage of various types of Alternative

[89] *Jackson v Attorney General* [2005] UKHL 56, para 102. See also the judgment of Lord Hope.
[90] Goldsworthy (2010), p. 51.
[91] Loughlin (2013), pp. 99ff.
[92] Waldron (2006), p. 1360.
[93] Leyland (2016), p. 305.
[94] See Harlow and Rawlings (2009), chapter 10; Birkinshaw (1994).

Dispute Resolution (ADR),[95] including informal complaints mechanisms, Citizen's Charter/Chartermark initiatives[96] and compliant/appeal schemes available under a statutory framework.[97] Over the past two decades where heavy constraints have been placed on the grant of legal aid, there has been a marked change of emphasis, often motivated by cost cutting. Lord Woolf's CJ stated that:

> . . . even in disputes between public authorities and the members of the public for whom they are responsible, insufficient attention is paid to the paramount importance of avoiding litigation whenever this is possible. Particularly in the case of these disputes both sides must by now be acutely conscious of the contribution alternative dispute resolution [ADR] can make to resolving disputes in a manner which both meets the needs of the parties and the public and saves time, expense and stress.[98]

The implication here is that a tribunal should first ensure that the possibility of streamlining the process has been explored as an option prior to proceeding with a hearing.[99] Proportional dispute resolution[100] is the wider principle that results from such an approach.[101] There is an assumption that the formality of the proceedings and procedural protection offered will depend on the subject matter under consideration and is related to the outcome which the claimant wishes to achieve by pursuing the matter.[102] In many situations an internal complaints mechanism or one of the available forms of ADR might provide at more rapidly and at lower cost a satisfactory resolution of the grievance in question.[103]

Turning briefly to the domain of Parliament and oversight of central government, the Parliamentary Ombudsman was introduced in 1967 to fill another perceived gap in grievance handling. The office was created as 'an independent upholder of the highest standards of efficient and fair administration'.[104] More than a decade earlier the Crichel Down Affair (1954) had exposed the manifest limitations of MPs in pursuing cases of maladministration against government departments on behalf of their constituents.[105] While the Parliamentary Commissioner for Administration

---

[95](Alternative Dispute Resolution). Such as Mediation, Adjudication, Arbitration, Conciliation. https://publiclawproject.org.uk/what-is-public-law/guides-public-law-2/; Roberts and Palmer (2005).

[96]Willet (1996).

[97]See e.g. Part VII of the Housing Act 1996, section 202.

[98]*Cowl v Plymouth City Council* [2001] EWCA 1935.

[99]The JR procedure requires claimants to state that they have exhausted existing remedies before proceeding. /publiclawproject.org.uk/resources/mediation-in-judicial-review-a-practitioners-handbook/.

[100]*Transforming Public Services: Complaints, Redress and Tribunals*, Cm 6243, (HMSO, 2004), section 2.

[101]Adler (2006), pp. 958–985.

[102]Le Sueur (2007), p. 320.

[103]Alternative Dispute Resolution processes include: adjudication, arbitration, conciliation.

[104]See *The Citizen and Administration: The redress of grievances* (Wyatt Report) 1961 the UK parliamentary ombudsman tended towards the Danish model.

[105]Leyland and Anthony (2016), p. 133.

(Parliamentary Ombudsman) was granted considerable investigatory powers, at first, the jurisdictional remit of the office was relatively narrow, although the scope was later extended to include the Health Service and local government.[106] Further, the requirement that all complaints had to be referred through an MP was an impediment which prevented the ombudsman from routinely patrolling the territory of public administration in order to root out instances of bad practice. The MP filter was inserted in the legislation, in part, to discourage wasteful investigation of unworthy cases, but also to prevent the new office from usurping the role of MPs as investigators in their own right.[107] The filter has been removed for health service complaints[108] and does not apply to the Local Government ombudsman (and other subsequent ombudsman schemes), but it otherwise remains in place for the Parliamentary Ombudsman. Ombudsmen in general if they find in favour of the complainant may only make recommendations, including for the payment of compensation, but with the exception of the Financial Services Ombudsman, they do not have the power to grant a mandatory remedy. In the vast majority of cases the department concerned will acknowledge its own shortcomings and follow the recommendations.[109] In recent years the office of Parliamentary Ombudsman has evolved significantly from acting mainly as an individual remedy towards the conduct of investigations into systemic defects in public administration.[110] Perhaps of even greater significance has been the more recent concern to develop in a preventative context universal values to apply generally to the public service at national and local level in the form of Principles of Good Administration, Principles of Good Complaint Handling and Principle of Remedy.[111]

At the beginning of this chapter it was pointed out that tribunals have been regarded as the classic 'green light' remedy. At an intermediate level in the grievance chain (between JR and ADR) tribunals continue to hear the vast majority of administrative cases, more than 540,000 were pending at the time of writing. Over the same quarterly period there were 122,400 receipts of new cases and 103,800 disposals.[112] However, it is important to remember that these adjudicative bodies were first introduced under a range of different statutes as part of the haphazard growth of the administrative state.[113] On the one hand, as alternatives to courts tribunals were intended to be more accessible, less formal, cheaper, with a much

[106]Parliamentary Commissioner Act, schedule 2 and 3.

[107]Parliamentary Commissioner Act 1967, section 5.

[108]See the Health Service Commissioners Act 1993.

[109]A notable exception were the occupational pension cases in 2005 involving more than 750,000 potential claimants which led to protracted litigation before any concession was made by the government on granting compensation. See Leyland and Anthony (2016), p. 153.

[110]Abrahams (2011), p. 10.

[111]Ibid, 22; https://www.ombudsman.org.uk/publications/corporate-publications?page=2.

[112]Tribunals and Gender Recognition Statistics Quarterly, January to March 2018, *Ministry of Justice* 14 June, 2018.

[113]Cane (2009), pp. 42ff.

more rapid throughput of cases.[114] On the other, the introduction of statutory mechanisms for grievance resolution and appeals outside the ordinary courts was at variance with the traditional judge centred view of the rule of law.[115] Many of the decision-making processes of officialdom were deliberately placed beyond judicial oversight by an *intra vires* remedy (resort to a tribunal), except when a dispute arose over how a tribunal interpreted the law or its own jurisdictional limits. In terms of the overall conception of administrative justice, it is highly significant that an assortment of heterogeneous tribunals which hear the vast majority of cases have been transformed into nationwide system. One that resembles in certain respects administrative courts in continental Europe.[116]

The changes were introduced following the publication of Sir Andrew Leggatt's comprehensive report in 2001 which was critical of the absence of any institutional structure across the 70 existing tribunals and it identified a marked lack of uniformity in the procedural rules adopted by tribunals.[117] By the time Leggatt reported and the subsequent White Paper was published[118] the protection of fundamental rights under the Human Rights Act 1998 required both a clear demarcation of separation of powers[119] and a standardisation of procedural rules in line with Article 6 of the ECHR.[120] The new framework meant that most of the tribunals, previously falling under individual sponsoring government departments, were arranged as part of a single system of tribunals with structural coherence. It comprised of a First Tier (FT) and an appellate Upper Tier (UT). According to the then Lord Chancellor the 2007 legislation was intended to put 'it beyond doubt that the tribunal judiciary are independent from the Executive and the tribunals themselves are independent of the departments which make the decisions under review'.[121] The Ministry of Justice (MOJ)[122] which was already responsible for the administration of the courts was given overall responsibility for the National Tribunal Service (NTS) which was created as an executive agency. The agency itself is headed by an appeal court judge, designated the Senior President of Tribunals.[123] Further reinforcing separation of

[114]Cane (2011), p. 319.

[115]The constitution and workings of tribunals was considered by the Frank's report. See Report of Committee on Administrative Tribunals and Enquiries, 1957 (Cmnd 218).

[116]Cane (2009), p. 72.

[117]See 'Tribunals for Users: One System, One Service' (London, TSO, 2001), The Leggatt Report.

[118]*Transforming Public Services: Complaints, Redress and Tribunals*, Cm 6243, (HMSO, 2004).

[119]The importance of tribunals as judicial bodies being formally independent of the body responsible for the decision under review was recognized in the Franks Report of 1957. See Richardson and Genn (2007), p. 119.

[120]For example, the right of access to an impartial hearing in reasonable time; the public pronouncement of reasoned judgment; the right of parties to be personally present; the compliance with principle of equality of arms.

[121]Lord Falconer, Lord Chancellor, HL Hansard, 29 Nov 2006, col 761.

[122]Prior to its present existence as the Ministry of Justice this department was called the Department of Constitutional Affairs (2003–2007) and before that the Lord Chancellor's Department.

[123]Tribunals, Courts and Enforcement Act 2007, Schedule 1.

powers, the NTS now draws upon its own tribunal judiciary[124] which has been given increased security of tenure. Under the provisions of the Constitutional Reform Act 2005 the independent Judicial Appointments Commission has responsibility for the appointment of tribunal judges by open competition.[125]

Any reform, however, needed to retain the highly specialised character of particular tribunals.[126] This objective was achieved by forming both the First Tier and the Upper Tier into individual 'chambers' to consider cases according to the nature of the subject matter of the claim.[127] The main task of the First Tier tribunals is to hear appeals directly from administrative decisions while the Upper Tribunal deals with general appeals from the First Tier. The Upper Tribunal also has a judicial review jurisdiction of decisions of first tier tribunals when points of law arise.[128] In *R (Cart) v Upper Tribunal*[129] the Supreme Court was required to consider the scope for judicial review of decisions by the Upper Tier tribunal where there is no further right of appeal. This includes cases where the Upper Tribunal refuses permission to hear an appeal as the final appellate body. The argument advanced by the government that, as a superior court of record, the Upper Tribunal should be immune from review was firmly rejected. It was held that decisions by the Upper Tribunal should not be subject to routine judicial oversight but, in principle, they would be amenable to review. This was made subject to the proviso that a case raises important point(s) of principle or practice.[130]

Lastly, in regard to this judicial review jurisdiction, it is important to note that the Upper Tribunal Immigration and Asylum Chamber (UTIAC) has now become a specialist public law court responsible for a substantial volume of JR claims resulting from the indifferent quality of Home Office decision-making in the sensitive field of immigration and asylum law.[131] From 2013 a high proportion of immigration judicial reviews have been channelled from the Administrative Court to the Upper Tribunal.[132] The case load of the UTIAC amounts to 90% of immigration judicial reviews, comprising 75% of all JR claims. This routing of cases to the UTIAC was an attempt to deal with the build up of delays in the throughput of immigration cases

---

[124]Until the reforms post Leggatt the adjudicators at tribunals were not referred to as judges.

[125]Constitutional Reform Act 2005, Part IV and Schedule 12.

[126]For example, tax, mental health, immigration and asylum.

[127]First Tier tribunals include: Asylum Support, Care Standard, Criminal Injuries Compensation, General Regulatory Chamber, Immigration and Asylum Chamber, Mental Health, Primary Health Lists, Property Chamber, Social Security and Child Support, Special Educational Needs and Disability, Tax Chamber, War Pensions and Armed Forces Compensation. Upper Tribunal: Administrative Appeals Chamber, Immigration and Asylum Chamber, Lands Chamber, Tax and Chancery Chamber. Some important tribunals, such as the Employment and Employment Appeal Tribunal, fall under the NTS but are not included as part of the main two tier system.

[128]Tribunals, Courts and Enforcement Act 2007, Ss 15–18.

[129][2011] UKSC 28.

[130]See Leyland and Anthony (2016), p. 174.

[131]Thomas (2015), pp. 652–678.

[132]Radcliffe (2007), pp. 197–203 and 199.

resulting from the severe resource constraints on the administrative court[133] but the rationing effect is also linked to recent changes to the procedural rules for JR discussed in the conclusion.

As a result of these changes, the citizen is given access to a single, overarching structure, comprising the majority of administrative tribunals.[134] And in a positive sense the new structure is 'more rational, less haphazard, potentially more efficient, and has a clearer and more consistent pathways through it in terms of rights of appeal'[135] This response to the procedural shortcomings exposed by the HRA combined with the Leggatt reforms placed tribunals clearly within the judicial branch, functioning as adjudicative court like bodies, often with an adversarial procedure. In order to ensure that equivalent cases are treated in an equivalent manner the system tended to be more rule bound[136] and decisions of the Upper Tribunal were legally binding for first tier tribunals.[137] However, this trend towards increased formality conflicts with other important objectives, particularly that of providing accessible and participatory justice. For instance, the White Paper which preceded the 2007 legislation had identified the need to not only provide formal hearings and authoritative rulings but also recognised: 'a mission to resolve disputes fairly and informally either by itself or in partnership with the decision-making department ...'[138] One of the obvious advantages of an oral hearing is that it provides open justice but as legal aid is usually not available unrepresented tribunal claimants using an increasingly rule bound system are in danger of finding any such hearing a daunting experience.[139]

20.8 Conclusion: Administrative Justice in Retreat?

Our discussion of English Administrative Law ends with an account of the downward plunge of the roller coaster by addressing a deliberate backlash against judicial review, the Human Rights Act and access to justice. The policies implemented by successive governments suggests that the exalted position of the courts as an oversight mechanism have been undermined and continues to be undermined in important ways.[140] This resistance to judicial intervention has been manifested through outright opposition to the HRA, particularly from within the Conservative

[133]Thomas (2015), p. 652.

[134]Cane (2016), p. 331.

[135]Elliott (2013a), p. 240.

[136]Elliott (2013a), pp. 241ff.

[137]Radcliffe (2007), p. 203.

[138]Department of Constitutional Affairs, Transforming Public Service: Complaints, redress and tribunals, Cm 6243 (July 2004).

[139]Richardson and Genn (2007), pp. 116–141 and 130.

[140]See Harlow and Rawlings (2016).

party, and it has been encouraged by some sections of the media. For instance the Conservative Party fought the 2010 general election promising to repeal the Act and replace it with a British Bill of Rights. PM Cameron's government lacked an electoral mandate to follow through with this reform. However, under the coalition deal reached in 2010 a Commission on a Bill of Rights was established. Far from serving as a blueprint for a replacement for the HRA the subsequent report exposed extreme divisions in approach and failed to make any clear recommendations.[141] In the frenetic political atmosphere following the Brexit referendum result there is little immediate prospect of proceeding with repeal or replacement of the Act.

Nevertheless, the heightened prominence of JR has elicited a deliberate reaction from government in the form of a raft of statutory measures which have the effect of rationing access to justice. In the course of the preceding analysis there has already been reference to the Judge Over Your Shoulder which alerted civil servants to the possibility of being brought before the courts. More recently, government has responded to the increased prominence of the courts by changing the ground rules to the detriment of potential claimants, and also with recourse to retrospective legislation to nullify the effects of unfavourable decisions.

In particular, the Criminal Justice and Courts Act 2015 rebalances the internal dynamics of the JR process in favour of public authorities. Public interest litigation as commonly practised by expert "repeat players" has been a prime target.[142] First, at the entry point the conditions for granting permission for a judicial review have been restricted by amending the section 31 of the Senior Courts Act 1981. For example, now if it appears to the High Court, or to the Upper Tribunal exercising its JR jurisdiction, to be highly likely that an outcome would not be substantially different, the court is required not to grant leave for a judicial review to go ahead at the permission stage (unless there are circumstances of exceptional public interest).[143]

In addition, this reduction in throughput has been achieved by introducing financial disincentives to litigate.[144] Not only has there has there been a radical curtailment in the general entitlement to legal aid[145] but the approach to awarding costs has been modified. The rule derived from private law has been adopted so that if a claim is lost the claimant must pay the costs of the defendant and, potentially, also of any interested party. As Tom Hickman points out: 'Even if an individual acts as a litigant in person or negotiates a no-win-no-fee (or reduced fee) arrangement with lawyers, they have no control and no visibility over the level of potential adverse costs.'[146] Ministers justified these reforms as necessary to reduce the pursuit of weak claims but the imposition of these financial constraints to limit the costs

[141] See Ministry of Justice, *Commission on a Bill of Rights: A UK Bill of Rights? The Choice Before Us* (London 2012); Elliott (2013b), pp. 137–151.

[142] Harlow and Rawlings (2016), p. 313.

[143] See Mills (2015), pp. 582–595.

[144] Harlow and Rawlings (2016), pp. 312ff.

[145] Civil Legal Aid (Remuneration) (Amendment) (No 3) Regulations 2014.

[146] T Hickman 'Public Law's Disgrace' UK Const L Blog (9th Feb 2017).

which can be awarded has meant that claimants risk more but receive less.[147] In practice, the legislation has been drafted in such a way[148] that cost capping provisions operate as a statutory bar on access to justice for many deserving claimants and these provisions may also infringe Article 6 ECHR and Article 47 of the EU charter of rights.[149] As a consequence, the vast majority of the population are, in effect, denied access to judicial review. This outcome is particularly significant as we began the discussion by referring to importance of the *Miller* case and earlier sections of this chapter charted what appeared to be an inexorable rise in the profile of judicial review claims, with the figure reaching its apogee of 15,594 cases in 2013.[150] The latest statistics bear witness to a dramatic plunge. By 2017 the total figure had fallen back to below 4000 cases a year, demonstrating the severity of the dip in the roller coaster ride.[151]

References

Abrahams A (2011) The Parliamentary Ombudsman and administrative justice: shaping the next 50 years. *Justice.* Tom Sargant memorial lecture, p 10

Adler M (2006) Tribunal reform: proportionate dispute resolution and the pursuit of administrative justice. Mod Law Rev 69(6):958–985

Allan T (2001) Constitutional justice: a liberal theory of the rule of law. Oxford University Press

Allan T (2013) Accountability to law. In: Bamforth N, Leyland P (eds) Accountability in the contemporary constitution. Oxford University Press, p 78

Bellamy R (2007) Political constitutionalism: a republican defence of the constitutionality of democracy. Cambridge University Press, Cambridge

Bingham T (2010) The rule of law. Allen Lane, London

Birkinshaw P (1994) Grievances remedies and the state, 2nd edn. London, Sweet & Maxwell

Blick A (2015) Beyond Magna Carta: a constitution for the United Kingdom. Bloomsbury, p 47

Boyle A (1994) Sovereignty, accountability, and the reform of administrative law. In: Richardson G, Genn H (eds) Administrative law and government action: the courts and alternative mechanisms of review. Oxford University Press, p 88

Cane P (2009) Administrative tribunals and adjudication. Hart, Oxford

Cane P (2011) Administrative law, 5th edn. Oxford University Press, Oxford, p 319

Cane P (2016) Controlling administrative power. Cambridge University Press, Cambridge, p 331

Clayton R (2017) A v Secretary of State for the Home Department [2005]: The Belmarsh Case. In: Juss S, Sunkin M (eds) Landmark cases in public law. Hart, Oxford

[147]Craig (2015), pp. 162ff.

[148]Criminal Justice and Courts Act 2015, section 88(1).

[149]T Hickman 'Public Law's Disgrace: Part 2' UK Const L Blog (26 Oct 2017).

[150]Civil Justice Statistics Quarterly, England and Wales (incorporating Privacy Injunction Statistics July to December 2014), Ministry of Justice, October to December 2014.

[151]The published figures for 2017 indicate the Home Office had 1500 applications, down 18% from the previous year. While there were 1400 claims against the Ministry of Justice of which 878 were against tribunals, a 17% increase, 713 applications were against local authorities down 6% from the previous year. Civil Justice Statistics Quarterly, England and Wales, January to March 2018 (Ministry of Justice, 7 June 2018), 10.

Cohn M (2013) Sovereignty, constitutional dialogues, and political networks: a comparative conceptual study. In: Rawlings R, Leyland P, Young AL (eds) Sovereignty and the law. Oxford University Press, Oxford

Craig P (2015) UK, EU and global administrative law: foundations and challenges. Cambridge University Press, Cambridge

Craig P (2016) Administrative law, 8th edn. Sweet & Maxwell, London

Davies A (2013) Beyond new public management: problems of accountability in the modern administrative state. In: Bamforth N, Leyland P (eds) Accountability in the contemporary constitution. Oxford University Press, p 350

Dicey A (1959) An introduction to the study of the law of the constitution, 10th edn. Macmillan, London

Drabble R (2017) Council of Civil Service Unions v Minister for the Civil Service [1984]: reviewing the prerogative. In: Juss S, Sunkin M (eds) Landmark cases in public law. Hart/ Bloomsbury, p 97

Dworkin R (1986) Laws empire. Fontana, London

Elliott M (2013a) Ombudsmen, tribunals, inquiries: refashioning accountability beyond the courts. In: Bamforth N, Leyland P (eds) Accountability in the contemporary constitution. Oxford University Press

Elliott M (2013b) A damp squib in the long grass: the Report of the Commission on a Bill of Rights. Eur Hum Rights Law Rev (2):137–151

Goldsworthy G (2010) Parliamentary sovereignty: contemporary debates. Oxford University Press, p 51

Griffith J (1979) The political constitution. Mod Law Rev 42(1):1–21

Harlow C, Rawlings R (1984) Law and administration. Weidenfeld and Nicolson, London

Harlow C, Rawlings R (1997) Law and administration, 2nd edn. Butterworths, London

Harlow C, Rawlings R (2009) Law and administration, 3rd edn. Cambridge University Press

Harlow C, Rawlings R (2016) "Striking Back" and "Clamping Down": an alternative perspective on judicial review. In: Bell J, Elliott M, Varuhas JNE, Murray P (eds) Public law adjudication in common law systems: process and substance. Hart

Hewart L (1929) The new despotism. Ernest Benn, London

Hickman T (2008) The substance and structure of proportionality. Public Law 694

Jennings I (1959) The law and the constitution, 5th edn. University of London Press, London

Laws J (1998) Wednesbury. In: Forsyth C, Hare I (eds) The Golden Metwand and the Crooked Cord. Clarendon Press, Oxford, pp 191ff

Le Sueur A (2007) Courts, tribunals, ombudsman, ADR: administrative justice, constitutionalism and informality. In: Jowell J, Oliver D (eds) The changing constitution, 6th edn. Oxford University Press, p 320

Leyland P (2016) The constitution of the United Kingdom: a contextual analysis. Hart, Oxford, p 305

Leyland P, Anthony G (2016) Textbook on administrative law, 8th edn. Oxford University Press

Loughlin M (1992) Public law and political theory. Oxford University Press

Loughlin M (2013) The British Constitution: a very short introduction. Oxford University Press, p 99ff

McEldowney J (2016) Public law, 4th edn. Sweet & Maxwell, London

Mills A (2015) Reforms to judicial review in the Criminal Justice and Courts Act 2015: promoting efficiency or weakening the rule of law? Public Law 582–595

Poole T (2003) Back to the future? Unearthing the theory of common law constitutionalism. Oxf J Leg Stud 23

Poole T (2017) Devotion to legalism: on the Brexit case. Mod Law Rev

Radcliffe C (2007) The tribunals revolution. Judicial Rev 197–203

Raz J (1979) The authority of law: essays on law and morality. Clarendon Press, Oxford

Richardson G, Genn H (2007) Tribunals in transition: resolution or adjudication? Public Law 116–141

Roberts S, Palmer M (2005) Dispute processes: ADR and the primary forms of decision-making. Cambridge

Sedley S (1997) The common law and the constitution. In: Nolan M, Sedley S (eds) The making and remaking of the British Constitution. Blackstone Press, London, pp 17 and 18

Sedley S (2015) Lions under the throne. Cambridge University Press, Cambridge, p 27

Sunkin M, Bondy V (2016) Use and effects of judicial review. In: Bell J, Elliott M, Varuhas JNE, Murray P (eds) Public law adjudication in common law systems: process and substance. Hart, p 337

Syrett K (2006) Opening eyes to the reality of scarce health care resources. Public Law 667

Taggart M (2003) Reinventing administrative law. In: Bamforth N, Leyland P (eds) Public law in a multi-layered constitution. Hart, Oxford, p 320

Thomas R (2015) Mapping immigration judicial review litigation: an empirical legal analysis. Public Law 652–678

Tomkins A (2005) Our Republican Constitution. Hart, Oxford

Tushnet M (2013) Judicial accountability in comparative perspective. In: Bamforth N, Leyland P (eds) Accountability in the contemporary constitution. Oxford University Press, Oxford, p 60ff

Wade W, Forsyth C (2014) Administrative law, 11th edn. Oxford University Press, Oxford

Waldron J (2006) The core case against judicial review. Yale Law J 115

Willet C (1996) Public sector reform and the citizen's charter. Blackstone Press, London

Woodhouse D (2001) The Office of Lord Chancellor. Hart, Oxford, pp 12ff

Chapter 21
The Spanish Administrative Law Transformation in the Last 50 Years and the Challenges for the Future

José-Luis Piñar

Contents

Abstract The modern Spanish Administrative Law has its origin in the doctrinal and legal contribution that was carried out in the middle of the twentieth century, above all by the hand of the Generation of Masters of Administrative Law led by Eduardo García de Enterría. The 1978 Constitution brought with it the need to revise the foundations of Administrative Law. It establishes an entirely new model of State that defines the bases on which Public Administration and Administrative Law must be based: a social and democratic State of law (arts. 1 and 9), based on the human dignity and the recognition of individual rights and freedoms (art. 10), strongly decentralized (art. 2 and Title VIII), integrated into the European Union (art. 93), which recognises freedom of enterprise and public initiative in the economy (arts. 38 and 128), which requires taking into account the principle of budgetary stability (art. 135), and which guarantees full judicial control of the entire activity of the Public Administration (art. 106.1) and the principle of the responsibility of the Administration (art. 106.2). The technological revolution and the digital society raise the need to question whether the current regulatory framework is capable of

J.-L. Piñar (✉)
CEU San Pablo University of Madrid, Madrid, Spain
e-mail: jlpinar@ceu.es

D. Sorace et al. (eds.), *The Changing Administrative Law of an EU Member State*,
https://doi.org/10.1007/978-3-030-50780-0_21

adapting to this new reality, especially as regards the recognition of the rights of so-called digital citizenship, or whether, on the contrary, it is necessary to carry out a new regulation of new rights. The Public Administrations must undoubtedly face a process of renewal that implies assuming the new scenario of the digital revolution in which the challenge of the full guarantee of rights by them is assumed.

21.1 The Origins of Modern Spanish Administrative Law. The "Generation of the *Revista de Administración Pública*" and the Laws of the Mid-Twentieth Century

It is often said that, after a few years of passionate struggle between Anglo-Saxon and French models,[1] Spanish Administrative Law emerged as such in the mid-nineteenth century, with the creation of the Contentious-Administrative Jurisdiction and the judicialization of the control of the Administration. In the end, a model was imposed that was clearly aligned[2] with the French continental model.

But the truth is that when in 1950 Professor Eduardo Garcia de Enterria (1923–2013) created the *Revista de Administración Pública* (*RAP*),[3] published by the Centro de Estudios Políticos, he was laying the foundations of the new Spanish Administrative Law. These were the foundations that, together with an extraordinary Generation of Masters,[4] were even able to adapt to the constitutional framework that emerged from the 1978 Constitution[5] and to some extent to the present day. A group of young jurists (almost all of them under the age of 30) set up, in the midst of Franco's dictatorship, a forum for debate (the *RAP*, which of course continues to be published today),[6] discreet but of enormous influence in its field, to promote a new Administrative Law, which also drank in the most advanced doctrines of Italy, France and Germany.

Given that the jurisprudence of the Courts applied and interpreted laws that were clearly obsolete and that the *Consejo de Estado* (Council of State, of an exclusively

[1]Vid. Santamaria (2006) (reedition of the original 1972 edition).

[2]On the formation of the Spanish Administration after the Old Regime, vid. Garcia de Enterria (1999). On the influence of the French Revolution on the Administration in general and on the Municipal Administration in particular, by the same author, Garcia de Enterria (1981b).

[3]Since 2019, access to the entire collection of the Journal, in its electronic edition, is free: http://www.cepc.gob.es/publicaciones/revistas/revistaselectronicas?IDR=1&IDN=ALL.

[4]José Luis Villar Palasi (1922–2012), Jesús Gonzalez Perez (1924–2019), Manuel Ballve (1920–1961), Fernando Garrido Falla (1921–2003), Manuel Clavero (1926) and Laureano Lopez Rodo (1920–2000).

[5]On the contribution of the great Masters of Spanish Administrative Law, see the different reviews contained in "La aportación doctrinal de los grandes Maestros del Derecho Administrativo contemporáneo", in Zambonino (2011), pp. 147–264.

[6]The last issue, at the time of publishing this paper, is 208, January–April 2019.

administrative nature) lacked room for manoeuvre in that authoritarian model, it was necessary to opt for an enormously risky option but then the only possible one: to promote the new Administrative Law that those young people wanted to implement through the approval of new laws that would regulate the most important issues of the Public Administration regime: its organisation, action, control and relations with the "administered". Laws that in order to coexist with the dictatorship could only be based on an impeccable technical quality that would allow incorporating guarantees for citizens that not infrequently went unnoticed by the Franco's apparatus itself. Laws that were written almost entirely by that unrepeatable generation of Masters. The 1954 *Ley de Expropiación Forzosa* (Compulsory Expropriation Act), the 1956 *Ley reguladora de la Jurisdicción Contencioso-Administrativa* (Contentious-Administrative Jurisdiction Act), the 1956 *Ley de Régimen del Suelo y Ordenación Urbana* (Land Regime and Urban Planning Act), the 1957 *Ley de Régimen Jurídico de la Administración del Estado* (State Administration Legal Regime Act), or the 1958 *Ley de Procedimiento Administrattivo* (Administrative Procedure Act) thus emerged. Of all of them only the Compulsory Expropriation Act remains in force, but certainly not a few of the principles incorporated into all the others are still valid and some of them were included in the Constitution of 1978.[7]

Consequently, contrary to what happened in France or Italy, the current Spanish Administrative Law had its origin not in the jurisprudence or in the doctrine of the Council of State, but in the laws, sometimes unconsciously approved by the legislator in the middle of the last century, but with an impeccable technical invoice, which managed to impose, in full dictatorship, principles that even inspired the 1978 Constitution. Once the laws were approved, it was the scientific doctrine (made up of the drafters of the laws themselves) who were in charge of betting on the most generous possible interpretation of their articles. The *Revista de Administración Pública* was the appropriate forum for promoting legal debate, and later, also, the *Revista Española de Derecho Administrativo* (*REDA*), also founded and directed by García de Enterría.

The pre-constitutional regime, in which political freedoms were not recognised, was rigidly centralist,[8] with a strong presence of the Public Administration even in the sphere of economic initiative, mainly through the National Institute of Industry, (*Instituto Nacional de Industria, INI*), created in 1941[9] on the model of the Italian IRI. Despite some attempts to enter the European Community at the end of the Franco era, Spain was on the fringe of European construction, with what this implied, in what we are now interested in, in relation to Administrative Law and Public Administration.

---

[7]Vid Martin Rebollo (2018), p. 1204. On the principles of Administrative Law, Santamaría (2011).

[8]Not even the mayors were elected, but appointed by the central power.

[9]Created by law of September 25, 1941, whose article 1.° indicated that the purpose of the INI was "*to propel and finance, in service of the Nation, the creation and resurgence of our industries, especially those that propose as main purpose the resolution of the problems imposed by the demands of the defense of the country or that are directed to the development of our economic autarchy*".

21.2 The Impact of the 1978 Constitution. The Constitutional Bases of Administrative Law

After Franco's death in 1975, the exemplary Transition from Franco's dictatorship to democracy brought with it a new transformative revolution of Spanish Administrative Law under the 1978 Constitution.[10] As Carlo Esposito warned (in reference to the Italian Constitution, but transferable to the Spanish one), whoever wants to know how the Administration is regulated in the Constitution should not read one or two articles but the entire Constitution. This is indeed the case, since Administrative Law and Public Administration are absolutely conditioned and defined by the entire Constitution. The constitutional bases of Administrative Law became full respect for the Rule of Law, the configuration of our State as a social and democratic State of Law, the definition of a strongly decentralized State, with full European vocation, and the guarantee of full jurisdictional control of administrative activity. All of this is based on the full recognition of the dignity and equality of the individual and of fundamental rights and public freedoms.

Within this framework, certain constitutional precepts are absolutely essential.

Article 10 clearly states that "the human dignity, the inviolable and inherent rights, the free development of the personality, the respect for the law and for the rights of others are the foundation of political order and social peace"[11] and article 14 recognizes the right to equality before the law.[12] Article 1 provides that "Spain is a social and democratic State governed by the rule of law, which advocates freedom, justice, equality and political pluralism as the highest values of its legal system". Article 9 (2) (clearly inspired by Article 3 of the Italian Constitution) concretizes the social state clause by stating that "it is incumbent upon the public authorities to promote conditions which ensure that the freedom and equality of individuals and of the groups to which they belong may be real and effective, to remove the obstacles which prevent or hinder their full enjoyment, and to facilitate the participation of all citizens in political, economic, cultural and social life".[13]

The constitutional option for a decentralized model is found in article 2 according to which "the Constitution is based on the indissoluble unity of the Spanish nation, the common and indivisible country of all Spaniards; it recognises and guarantees

[10]It is very easy to access the texts of the Constitution and all the laws and regulations cited in this work. There are many existing repertoires and Internet resources. In any case, the series of "Codes" offered on the website of the "Boletín Oficial del Estado" is extremely useful, where Spanish legislation can be consulted, more often than not updated: https://www.boe.es/legislacion/codigos/.

[11]For the English text of the constitutional precepts I use the unofficial translation published by "Boletín Oficial del Estado" Editions: https://www.boe.es/legislacion/codigos/codigo.php?id=158_Constitucion_Espanola_The_Spanish_Constitution_&modo=1.

[12]Spaniards are equal before the law and may not in any way be discriminated against on account of birth, race, sex, religion, opinion or any other personal or social condition or circumstance.

[13]On the social and democratic rule of law in general and in the 1978 Constitution in particular it is essential Garcia Pelayo (1988), 2ª ed.

the right to autonomy of the nationalities and regions of which it is composed, and the solidarity amongst them all.". Title VIII of the Constitution regulates the territorial organisation of the State, designed around municipalities, provinces and Autonomous Communities, the latter with legislative powers, but without the right to self-determination, which resides in the Spanish people as a whole, the sole holder of national sovereignty. I'll talk about it later.

For its part, article 103, a key piece in the constitutional configuration of the Public Administration, provides in its first paragraph that "the public Administration serves the general interest with objectivity and acts in accordance with the principles of efficiency, hierarchy, decentralisation, deconcentration and coordination, being fully subject to justice and the law". The constitutional function of the administration is defined: the service which is the objective of the general interest; the principles of its action are laid down (in a list, which is certainly not exhaustive, since the principle of cooperation must also be taken into account) and the full application of the rule of law is once again underlined. To this end, it is essential to ensure that all administrative activity is subject to full judicial control. Article 106 recalls: "The Courts control the power to issue regulations and to ensure that the rule of law prevails in administrative action, as well as to ensure that the latter is subordinated to the ends which justify it".

On the other hand, the Constitution enshrines the principle of patrimonial responsibility of the Administration, in very broad terms. At this point, what it has done is to transfer to its articulate the foundations of the responsibility that already fixed in its moment the Compulsory Expropriation Act of 1954 and gathered the Legal Regime of the Administration of the State Act of 1957.[14] A system of strict liability that today includes Article 106(2) of the Constitution: "Private individuals shall, under the terms established by law,[15] be entitled to compensation for any loss that they may suffer to their property or rights, except in cases of force majeure, whenever such loss is the result of the operation of public services."

The constitutional model designed in 1978, which conditions the entire Public Administration, is also based on belonging to Europe. Article 93 provides that "by means of an organic law, authorisation may be granted for concluding treaties by which powers derived from the Constitution shall be vested in an international organisation or institution". Without naming them, the precept undoubtedly refers to the European Communities, today the European Union, to which the Member States must cede part of their competences, on the basis of the very model that arose in 1957 with its creation. In Spain, Organic Law 10/1985 of 2 August 1985

[14]Once again it was essential in this point the contribution of Garcia de Enterria to consecrate in very generous terms the patrimonial responsibility of the Administration. Vid. *Los principios de la nueva ley de expropiación forzosa*, Instituto de Estudios Políticos, Madrid, 1956. There are subsequent editions. For example, Thomson Civitas, Madrid, 2007.

[15]At present, the regime of patrimonial responsibility of the Administration is regulated in Laws 39/2015, of administrative procedure (arts. 64, 67, 96.4) and 40/2015, of legal regime of the Public Sector (arts. 32 and following).

authorised the ratification of the Treaty of Accession, which allowed our entry, together with Portugal, with effect from 1 January 1986.

Finally, the economic model of the Constitution (what some call the Economic Constitution) is based on the freedom of enterprise and the recognition of public initiative in the economy. According to Article 38 "free enterprise is recognised within the framework of a market economy"; but adds that "the public authorities shall guarantee and protect its exercise and the safeguarding of productivity in accordance with the demands of the economy in general and, as the case may be, of its planning". Article 128(2) recognizes "public initiative in economic activity". In any case on this point, as on so many others, European Union law is a key conditioning factor, which has led to the adoption of one of the few amendments to the Constitution. Due to the economic crisis of 2008, in September 2011 Article 135 of the Constitution was modified, imposing the principle of budgetary stability in the actions of all Public Administrations. Paragraph 2 of the aforementioned article provides that "neither the State nor the Autonomous Communities shall enter into a structural deficit beyond the limits stipulated, if applicable, by the European Union for its Member States". It adds that "an organic law shall set the structural deficit ceiling allowed for the State and for the Autonomous Communities according to their Gross Domestic Product". The Constitution is therefore more demanding now with the State and the Autonomous Communities, but it is much more demanding with the Local Authorities, since in relation to them it states that they must necessarily "present a balanced budget". In application of the new article 135, Organic Law 2/2012 of 27 April on Budgetary Stability and Financial Sustainability[16] has been approved. According to his Explanatory Memorandum, "the three objectives of the Law are: to guarantee the financial sustainability of all public administrations; to strengthen confidence in the stability of the Spanish economy; and to reinforce Spain's commitment to the European Union in terms of budgetary stability".

In conclusion, the Constitution of 1978, only 3 years after Franco's death, establishes an entirely new model of State that defines the bases on which Public Administration and Administrative Law must be based: a social and democratic State of law (arts. 1 and 9), based on the human dignity and the recognition of individual rights and freedoms (art. 10), strongly decentralized (art. 2 and Title VIII), integrated into the European Union (art. 93), which recognises freedom of enterprise and public initiative in the economy (arts. 38 and 128), which requires taking into account the principle of budgetary stability (art. 135), and which guarantees full judicial control of the entire activity of the Public Administration (art. 106.1) and the principle of the responsibility of the Administration (art. 106.2).[17]

[16]Amended by Organic Laws 2/2012 of 27 April, 4/2012 of 28 September, 9/2013 of 20 December and 6/2015 of 12 June.

[17]On the Spanish Constitution, Martín-Retortillo (1991). On the constitutional bases of Administrative Law, vid. Parejo (2018), pp. 83 and following; Sánchez Morón (2018), pp. 73–112.; Martin Rebollo (2018), pp. 288–359; Santamaría (2016), pp. 53–116.

Once the Constitution was approved, the first challenge was to make clear its normative nature, its value as a true legal norm, invocable even before the Courts, to which all public powers should be subject. Once again the work of Garcia de Enterria was essential.[18] In addition, it was essential to immediately set up the Constitutional Court, and this was done by means of Organic Law 2/1979, of 3 October.

The machinery of the 1978 Constitution was already in place: a framework of freedoms in an environment of total attachment of the Administration to the principle of legality and to the rule of law with full submission to jurisdictional control. It was then necessary to develop what the Constitution had imposed.

With regard to the system of rights and freedoms, there was hardly any need for far-reaching regulatory reforms, since the Constitution was and is directly applicable and binding in this respect. The normative value of the Constitution so requires.[19] Thus, all the pre-constitutional norms contrary to the model of rights and freedoms enshrined in the Constitution were repealed with the stroke of a pen and all its precepts recognizing such rights and freedoms, mainly in articles 10 to 38, were directly applicable. It was necessary to guarantee the effective protection of fundamental rights, which was carried out through the regulation of the appeal for protection (*recurso de amparo*) in Organic Law 2/1979, on the Constitutional Court, and the special appeal for the protection of fundamental rights regulated by Law 62/1978, of 26 December, on the Jurisdictional Protection of the Fundamental Rights of the Individual. The International Covenant on Civil and Political Rights, the International Covenant on Economic, Social and Cultural Rights, both done in New York on 19 December 1966,[20] and the Convention for the Protection of Human Rights and Fundamental Freedoms, done in Rome on 4 November 1950,[21] were also ratified. Something capital given the scope of article 10 (2) of the Constitution, according to which "the principles relating to the fundamental rights and liberties recognised by the Constitution shall be interpreted in conformity with the Universal Declaration of Human Rights and the international treaties and agreements thereon ratified by Spain".

21.3 The Territorial Organization of the State

What was essential was to adapt the territorial and decentralization structure to the new constitutional framework.

---

[18]García De Enterría (1981a). See also Muñoz Machado (2015). volume 5, on *La Constitución como norma*.

[19]Garcia de Enterria (1981a), op.cit.; Muñoz Machado (2015), Vol. V, op. cit.

[20]Both were signed by Spain on 28 September 1976 and ratified on 13 April 1977.

[21]It was signed on 24 November 1977 and ratified on 4 October 1979.

The recognition of the autonomy of local entities was soon made manifest by the Constitutional Court in its early Judgment of 2 February 1981, which declared the "supervening unconstitutionality" of the regulations on Local Authorities prior to the Constitution and in which it already established its doctrine on the scope of local autonomy:

> Autonomy refers to limited power. Indeed, autonomy is not sovereignty – and even this power has its limits – and given that each territorial organization endowed with autonomy is a part of the whole, in no case can the principle of autonomy be opposed to that of unity, but it is precisely within this that it reaches its true meaning, as expressed in article 2 of the Constitution.

The regime of Local Authorities (mainly municipalities and provinces) is now included in Law 7/1985, of 2 April, Regulating the Bases of the Local Regime, subject to multiple modifications and revisions (the last, by Royal Decree-Law 9/2018, of 3 August), of which perhaps the most relevant is that which was carried out by Law 27/2013, of 27 December, on the rationalisation and sustainability of local administration, with the aim, above all, of adapting the local regime to the model of budgetary stability imposed by the new article 135 of the Constitution, in order, above all, to adapt the local regime to the model of budgetary stability imposed by the new article 135 of the Constitution. The Constitutional Court, for its part, has had occasion to pronounce itself on multiple occasions in relation to local autonomy.[22] Local Authorities also have a specific resource for the defence of local autonomy before the Constitutional Court: the conflict in defence of local autonomy, regulated in articles 75 bis and following of the Organic Law of the Constitutional Court, in accordance with the modification approved by Organic Law 7/1999, of 21 April.

The Autonomous Communities, for their part, were formally set in motion with the gestation and approval of the Statutes of Autonomy (the first to be approved was that of the Basque Country, through Organic Law 3/1979 of 18 December).[23] The current 17 Autonomous Communities were created on the basis of the dispositive principle, with a very notable level of self-government. Not all Communities are equal. Navarre and the Basque Country have a different financing regime based on historical precedents that are reflected in the Constitution of 1978 itself. The rest of the Autonomous Communities have a similar level of competence, although special reference should be made to Catalonia, to which I will immediately refer.

The challenges facing the political decentralisation model in Spain are innumerable. Some are already recurrent, such as the questioned reform of the Senate in order to convert it into a real Chamber of territorial representation (in the image of the German *Bundesrat*), the lack of a stable financing model or the lack of reform of the

---

[22]For example, only Law 27/2013 has been the subject of Judgments of the Constitutional Court (SSTC) 41/2016 of 3 March, 111/2016 of 9 June, 168/2016 of 6 October, 180/2016 of 20 October, 44/2017 of 17 April, 45/2017 of 17 April, 54/2017 of 11 May, 93/2017 of 6 July, 101/2017 of 20 July and 107/2017 of 21 September.

[23]And the "Autonomous Cities" of Ceuta and Melilla.

Administration, which gives rise to multiple organizational duplicities. Others have a deeper scope, and question the constitutional model itself. Should we move towards a federal model? Should the system of distribution of competences between State and Autonomous Communities be reviewed? Above all, is there a right to self-determination in the 1978 Constitution?

This last question brings us back to Catalonia in particular. Without entering now into the origins of the current situation nor into the political component that it undoubtedly has, the truth is that the Constitution does not recognize a hypothetical right to self-determination at all. Catalonia has a notable degree of self-government and autonomy based on the current Statute of Autonomy, approved by Organic Law 6/2006, of 19 July, which was the subject of an appeal for unconstitutionality, giving rise to Constitutional Court Decision 31/2010, of 28 June.[24] The process that was gradually set in motion after the ruling, which was very badly received by part of Catalan society, gave rise to the attempt to proclaim Catalonia's independence on the basis of a supposed right to self-determination that would correspond to the "Catalan people". The Constitution, however, does not admit any national sovereignty other than that of the Spanish people as a whole. The Constitutional Court, in its Sentence 114/2017, of 17 October, issued in the Appeal against the Law of the Parliament of Catalonia 19/2017, of 6 September, called "the referendum of self-determination", affirms it categorically:

> For none of the "peoples of Spain", to use the words of the preamble to the Constitution, exists a "right of self-determination", understood, in the manner of Law 19/2017, as a "right" to promote and consummate their unilateral secession from the State in which Spain is constituted (art. 1.1 Spanish Constitution-CE-). Such a "right" is clearly "not recognised in the Constitution" [STC 42/2014, FJ 3.b), and ATC 122/2015, 7 July, FJ 5]... nor can it be argued ... that it forms part of our international treaty system to which Spain is a party (art. 96 CE)", nor is it based on international law. Respect for 'national unity', for the 'fundamental political and constitutional structures' and for the 'territorial integrity' of the Member States are principles which are expressly proclaimed, and with the highest rank, in European law (art. 4.2 of the Treaty on European Union).
>
> The Court reiterates this categorical doctrine in Sentence 124/2017, of 8 November, issued on the occasion of the appeal of unconstitutionality filed against the Law of the Parliament of Catalonia 20/2017, of 8 September, on the "legal and foundational transitory nature of the Republic".

21.4 The Reform of Civil Service

The public employees of the Spanish Public Administration have a very solid training as a result of the rigorous and very professional system of entry into the public service. The reforms carried out in connection with the Civil Servants Act of 7 February 1964 (still partially in force) succeeded in significantly modernising

[24]The text of the Statute of Autonomy with reference to the sections or incisors declared unconstitutional can be consulted at https://www.boe.es/buscar/act.php?id=BOE-A-2006-13087&b=93&tn=1&p=20100716#a76.

public employment. But once again the model of State that emerged with the 1978 Constitution forced a profound transformation of public employment. Not only as a consequence of the creation of the Autonomous Communities, which have passed their own public employment laws, but because the Francoist public administration was based on a rigidly statutory model, with a highly flexible incompatibility regime (really almost non-existent) and which did not recognize the rights of unionization and strike of public employees. These circumstances made it very difficult, almost impossible, to address a modernization and rejuvenation of public employees, as there were many vested interests and very strong resistance to change.

It was the first socialist government of Felipe Gonzalez that faced such a situation. In 1984, Law 30/1984 of 2 August on measures for the reform of the civil service was passed, and shortly thereafter Law 53/1984 of 26 December on Incompatibilities of Personnel in the Service of Public Administrations. Three years later, Law 9/1987 of 12 June 1987 on the representation and participation of public employees was passed.

Law 30/1984 was intended to facilitate the transition from the Francoist civil service to that of the new public administration of democracy. In order to do so, among other measures, it wished to undertake a profound "laborization" of public employment, but the Constitutional Court, through Ruling 99/1987, of June 11, was forced to declare unconstitutional several of its precepts based fundamentally on the fact that article 103 (3) of the Constitution[25] opted for a statutory and non-labour model of public employment.[26] For its part, Law 53/1984, on incompatibilities, wanted to put an end once and for all to generalized situations of accumulation of two or even more jobs in the Public Administration, even in different cities. On this occasion the Constitutional Court supported the full constitutionality of the Law through its Judgement 178/1989, of 2 November. For its part, Law 9/1987 took an important but short step in the recognition of the trade union rights of public employees.

This whole system is today fundamentally regulated in the Revised Text of the Law on the Basic Statute of Public Employees of 30 October 2015,[27] which consolidates the statutory, non-labour model of public employment in Spain. Article 9(2) provides that "in any event, the exercise of functions involving direct or indirect participation in the exercise of public authority or in safeguarding the general interests of the State and public administrations shall be the exclusive responsibility of public officials". Moreover, the incompatibility regime remains very strict[28] and the trade union rights of public employees have been widely recognized.

---

[25]Article 103 (3) provides: "The law shall regulate the status of civil servants, entry into the civil service in accordance with the principles of merit and ability, the special features of the exercise of their right to union membership, the system of incompatibilities, and guarantees regarding impartiality in the exercise of their duties".

[26]The ruling of the Constitutional Court led to the approval of Law 23/1988, of 28 July, which has subsequently also been repealed, as indicated in the text.

[27]Approved by Royal Legislative Decree 5/2015 of 30 October.

[28]It is still regulated by Law 53/1984.

21.5 The Reform of the Administrative Procedure. Technological Innovation. Cross-Border Procedures

With public employment reformed and adapted to the constitutional framework, the administrative procedure needed to be reformed.

The Administrative Procedure Act of 1958 had more than served its purpose, but the Constitution required changes that could not be delayed. On the one hand to bring the Administration closer to citizens, on the other hand to adapt the regulation of the procedure to the framework of distribution of competences between the State and the Autonomous Communities: Article 149.1.18 gives the State exclusive competence to regulate "the common administrative procedure, without prejudice to the special features of the Autonomous Community's own organisations". So it was necessary to regulate this "common administrative procedure".

This gave rise to Law 30/1992, of 26 November, on the Legal System for Public Administrations and Common Administrative Procedure. The law initially received harsh criticism,[29] which led to several amendments, the most important of which was Law 4/1999, of 13 January. In any case, the changes of 1992 and 1999 were more formal than substantive. Moreover, one of the main intentions of the legislator, which was the unification or at least simplification of procedures, was not achieved, as special procedures continued to proliferate.

More than 20 years later, Law 39/2015 of 1 October on Common Administrative Procedure for Public Administrations was passed. The intention of the legislator on this occasion was to modernise the procedure somewhat and to incorporate some provisions to regulate the e-Government (the so-called "electronic administration"). The impact of technological innovation was regulated by Law 11/2007, of 22 June, on citizens' electronic access to Public Services, which established the right of citizens to interact with the Public Administration by telematic means.[30] This law has been repealed by Law 39/2015 and now it is Law 40/2015, of 1 October, on the Legal Regime of the Public Sector, which in its articles 38 to 46 regulates the "Electronic Functioning of the Public Sector". There has undoubtedly been a notable boost to the use of electronic media by Public Administrations, but much remains to be done. Even the implementation of the electronic register, the Administration's general electronic access point and the electronic single file will not take place until October 2020.[31]

In conclusion, the regulation of the administrative procedure and the e-Government is still far from being complete and in line with what the application

---

[29]Because of the bad regulation of "administrative silence" regime, or of administrative appeals, as well as because of its not good legislative technique in some points of its text.

[30]On e-Government, among others, vid. Aguirreazkuenaga and Chinchilla (2001); Bauza (2003); Garcia Rubio (2004); Ochoa (2000); Ortega (1993), pp. 211 and following; Martinez (2009); Piñar (2011); Valero (2004); Valero (2013); AA.VV. (2004).

[31]As established by Royal Decree-Law 11/2018 of 31 August amending Law 39/2015 of 1 October on Common Administrative Procedure for Public Administrations.

of information technologies can mean for what a new public administration could be. Unfortunately, issues such as the lack of resources or the lack of guarantees of interoperability[32] between the different Administrations (even more so in a decentralised State such as Spain) are slowing down the effective implementation of e-Government. Without forgetting the debate on the formation of the will of the Administration on the basis of artificial intelligence techniques.[33]

In any case, neither Law 39/2015 nor Law 40/2015 have faced the great challenges of the administrative procedure, which derive not only from the implementation of information and communication technologies, but also from the impact of globalization on the procedure.[34] This is, however, taken into account when regulating cross-border procedures in the area of personal data protection by Regulation (EU) 2016/679 of the European Parliament and of the Council of 27 April 2016 on the protection of individuals with regard to the processing of personal data and on the free movement of such data and repealing Directive 95/46/EC: General Data Protection Regulation.[35] Articles 60 to 67 regulate in detail the principle of cooperation and the so-called coherence mechanism. The aim is to ensure cooperation between the data protection authorities of the Member States and with each other and with the European Data Protection Board when they are called upon to act in relation to cross-border data processing involving more than one Member State.[36] Organic Law 3/2018, of 5 December, on data protection and guarantee of digital rights regulates in articles 60 to 62 the coordination within the framework of the procedures regulated in the General Data Protection Regulations, while in articles 63 to 69 it regulates the procedures in case of violation of data protection regulations, with references to the specialities to be applied in the case of processing of cross-border procedures.[37] This is an example that once again comes to us from European Union law and that must make us reflect on the necessary revision of procedures in a global or, at least, transnational world.

[32]Regarding interoperability, Royal Decree 4/2010, of 8 January, which regulates the National Interoperability Scheme in the field of Electronic Administration, is of great importance.

[33]On it vid. Piñar (2007); Ponce (January 2019).

[34]Vid. Barnes (2008).

[35]*DOUE,* L 119, from 4-5-2016.

[36]About it vid. Irurzun, Fernando, "Cooperación y coherencia entre autoridades de control", in Piñar (2016), pp. 513–526; Lopez Calvo (2018), pp. 609–632.

[37]On the new sanctioning regime in the field of data protection vid. Hernández Corchete (2019).

21.6 Transparency and Access to Information

One of the pending subjects of Spanish administrative law until a few years ago was that of transparency. Evidently the pre-constitutional Public Administration was absolutely opaque, which in addition, throughout the years, had generated a culture of opacity deeply rooted in public employment but also in the administrative doctrine that, with some exceptions, hardly paid attention to the subject.

Article 105 (b) of the Constitution provides that the law shall regulate "the access of citizens to administrative files and records, except as they may concern the security and defence of the State, the investigation of crimes and the privacy of individuals". This timid provision was initially developed by the legislation on administrative procedure (Law 30/1992)[38] but did not materialize into a law on transparency. It was not until Law 19/2013 of 9 December on Transparency, Access to Public Information and Good Governance that there was specific legislation on the subject.[39] But it is a Law that has not responded to the expectations that had been placed in it, fundamentally because it does not recognize the right of access as a fundamental right but as a right of citizens that derives from transparency as a principle of action of the Administration.[40] The transparency laws approved by all the Autonomous Communities move in the same direction. So although an important (albeit belated) step has been taken in favour of transparency, the fact is that a magnificent opportunity has been missed to establish a truly transparent administration. This is without prejudice to the existence of sectoral laws regulating more specific aspects of transparency, such as Law 27/2007, of 18 July, regulating the rights of access to information, public participation and access to justice in environmental matters, and Law 37/2007, of 16 November, on the reuse of public sector information.

21.7 Consolidation of Full Jurisdictional Control of the Public Administration's Activity

As I pointed out, as early as 1956 a very good Law on Contentious-Administrative Jurisdiction was passed which allowed for more or less effective control of the Administration. Although on several occasions the Constitutional Court itself accepted that it could be interpreted in accordance with the 1978 Constitution, the truth is that there were some questions that were difficult to accept: judicial control was essentially limited to administrative acts, the so-called "political acts" of the Government were beyond control, there was a lack of adequate regulation of

[38]On the subject vid., among others, Rams (2008).

[39]Vid, Among others, Wences et al. (2014).

[40]Garcia Macho (2010); Piñar (December 2014), pp. 1–19.

precautionary measures and the regulation of the execution of sentences left much to be desired. The Constitution, moreover, is categorical in pointing out in its article 106(1), which I have already transcribed earlier, that "The Courts control the power to issue regulations and to ensure that the rule of law prevails in administrative action, as well as to ensure that the latter is subordinated to the ends which justify it".

It was therefore necessary to approve a new Jurisdictional Law, and this was done through Law 29/1998, of 13 July, on Contentious-Administrative Jurisdiction.[41]

The law represented a notable advance in the full jurisdictional control of Public Administrations. In addition to extending control also to political acts, the object of jurisdiction has extended the entire activity of the Administration. As the "Exposition of Reasons" (Preamble) for the Law points out: "it is nothing less than overcoming the traditional and restricted conception of contentious-administrative recourse as a judicial review of previous administrative acts, that is, as a recourse to the act, and definitively opening the doors to obtain justice in the face of any unlawful behaviour of the Administration". It also regulates with greater precision and guarantees the regime of precautionary measures and guarantees the enforcement of judgments. On the other hand, the organs of the Jurisdiction are modified and the process and appeals are regulated.

This is a technically very correct law, but it has not succeeded in achieving rapid and effective administrative justice. Matters inevitably continue to pile up. On the other hand, recently a reform has been approved (Organic Law 7/2015, of July 21) that reaches among other extremes to the appeal of cassation before the Supreme Court that is generating not few criticisms.

In short, the jurisdictional control of public administrations is fully guaranteed on the basis of the 1998 Jurisdiction Act, although the degree of efficiency and speed that would be advisable has not yet been achieved.

21.8 Digital Society and New Rights

The technological revolution and the digital society raise the need to question whether the current regulatory framework is capable of adapting to this new reality, especially as regards the recognition of the rights of so-called digital citizenship, or whether, on the contrary, it is necessary to carry out a new regulation of new rights. The Public Administrations must undoubtedly face a process of renewal that implies

[41]The bibliography on Law 29/1998 is abundant. Among others, the works included in the special edition of the *Revista Española de Derecho Administrativo,* n. 100, dedicated monographically to the aforementioned Law; likewise, issue 100 of the *Revista Andaluza de Administración Pública* is dedicated monographically to *Twenty years of Law 29/1998, of 13 July, regulating the Contentious-Administrative Jurisdiction: balance and perspectives*. Also, Cano (2009); Cosculluela (2018); Esteve (2018); Fernandez Farreres (2018); García De Enterría (2010); García De Enterría and Fernández (2017); Martín-Retortillo (2007); Parada (2015); Santamaría (2010).

assuming the new scenario of the digital revolution[42] in which the challenge of the full guarantee of rights by them is assumed.[43] But first we have to consider whether it is necessary to recognize new rights of digital citizenship.

As I have already pointed out elsewhere,[44] the 1978 Constitution undoubtedly admits for an interpretation that allows the recognition of rights to be extended to the digital environment when, by their very nature, they so require. The rights and freedoms recognised in Article 14 and Section One of Chapter Two of Title I ("Fundamental Rights and Public Freedoms") are undoubtedly extendable to the digital environment. As well as, of course, respect for the dignity of the individual (art. 10). And not a few of the "Governing Principles of Economic and Social Policy" contained in Chapter Three of the same Title I admit recognition or protection in the digital environment. In any case, the clause of Article 9(2) operates, according to which, as we know, "it is incumbent upon the public authorities to promote conditions which ensure that the freedom and equality of individuals and of the groups to which they belong may be real and effective, to remove the obstacles which prevent or hinder their full enjoyment, and to facilitate the participation of all citizens in political, economic, cultural and social life". This precept does not have to be limited to the effectiveness of rights in the physical world, and undoubtedly extends to the digital environment, in which rights, all of them, have to be equally real and effective. Article 79 of Organic Law 3/2018, of 5 December, on Data Protection and the Guarantee of Digital Rights, states that "the rights and freedoms enshrined in the Constitution and in the International Treaties and Conventions to which Spain is a party are fully applicable on the Internet". Information society service providers and Internet service providers will help to ensure its implementation. Consequently, it is possible to consider that fundamental rights have to be considered as fully recognized in the digital environment and that their enjoyment has to be real and effective.

However, it may be thought that certain rights require an updated or clarifying regulation of their content and scope in the digital society. This would be the case, for example, of the right of access to the Internet, the right to respect for digital identity or the right of access to knowledge. As regards the right of access to the Internet, it can be said that it is a question of recognising it as a new right that also increasingly conditions the exercise of other rights, such as the right to electronic access to public services. In this sense, it is very noteworthy that article 81 of Organic Law 3/2018 has recognized the right to universal access to the Internet regardless of the personal, social, economic or geographical status of individuals.

The regulation of rights in the digital environment is, in any case, a risky venture that would merit in-depth reflection and debate, since we are talking about the

---

[42]Barnes (2006); Muñoz Machado (2011), pp. 191–237, De La Quadra-Salcedo (2018, 2019); Parejo (2012); Martín (2018), pp. 179–202; Gamero (2015); Piñar (2018a), pp. 95–112, and (2018b), pp. 11–30.

[43]Valero (2018), pp. 375–396.

[44]Piñar (2019).

regulation of the future and new law. In Spain, the regulation of digital rights guarantees has been included in Title X (articles 79 to 97) of the aforementioned Organic Law 3/2018.[45]

The addition of this Title has been controversial (in my opinion the regulation of fundamental rights in the digital society deserves a specific Organic Law that honors the importance of the subject,[46] and not a Title of a very specific Law whose main purpose is to adapt Spanish law to the General Data Protection Regulations; Title, moreover, which was incorporated by way of amendment in the Congress of Deputies). But the truth is that the Law regulates issues of enormous importance and interest for the development of fundamental rights in the digital society. This regulates the right to Internet neutrality (art. 80), the right to universal access to the Internet (art. 81), the right to digital security (art. 82), the right to digital education (art. 83), the protection of minors on the Internet (art. 84) and the data protection of minors on the Internet (art. 92), the right to rectification on the Internet (art. 85), and the right to update information in digital media (art. 86), the right to be forgotten in Internet searches and in social network services and equivalent services (arts. 93 and 94 respectively), the right to portability in social network services and equivalent services (art. 95) or the so-called right to a digital will (art. 96). In addition, Title X devotes special attention to digital rights in the workplace (also extendable to public employment in the Public Administrations) such as the right to privacy and the use of digital devices in the workplace (art. 87), the so called "right to disconnection" in the workplace (art. 88), the right to privacy as opposed to the use of video surveillance and sound recording devices in the workplace (art. 89), the right to privacy as opposed to the use of geolocation systems in the workplace (art. 90) and digital rights in collective bargaining (art. 91). Finally, the law regulates public policies to promote digital rights (art. 97).

In any case, the regulation of rights in the digital society must be done by placing the individual at the centre of it, on the basis that the rights recognised in the physical environment must be reflected in the digital environment and with the perspective of rules that are capable of overcoming their obsolescence in spite of innovation, for which it is essential to establish a new dialogue between regulation and self-regulation.

21.9 Future Challenges for a Social Administrative Law

Without prejudice to the great challenges that Public Law faces (rather the Law in general), such as the possible or necessary reform of the Constitution or the clarification of the territorial model of the State, I believe that the great challenge of contemporary Administrative Law is, nothing more and nothing less, to achieve a

[45] Rallo Lombarte (2019), pp. 23 and following; Barrio (2019).

[46] On this, see de la Quadra Salcedo and Piñar (2018).

better Public Administration within the framework of the social and democratic State of Law. Citizens have the right to a good administration that meets their needs and fulfils the constitutional function that, with simplicity and forcefulness, is included in article 103 of the Constitution: to serve the general interest with objectivity.[47] It must devote all its efforts and resources to this.

Administrative Law, which has probably been too absent when it comes to seeking solutions before, during and after the economic crisis,[48] must be the right to social regulation, to the guarantee of rights and liberties, to the provision of services by the State in accordance with the principles of effectiveness and efficiency. Even more so in a scenario of technological innovation.

It seems that after moments of excessive use of Private Law as a supposed mechanism to increase the efficiency of the Public Administration and therefore to guarantee the fulfillment of the constitutional purposes that correspond to it, the Administrative Law is vindicated once again. As I had the opportunity to say a few years ago on the occasion of the XIX Italian-Spanish Congress of Administrative Law,[49] we must claim not the Administrative Law of privileges, but that of the general interest, the interest of all. A simplified Administrative Law, adapted to the new social realities, but which, in spite of everything, continues to be an instrument and a channel for solving problems, not for raising them. And what is certain is that, with a few exceptions, neither Administrative Law nor scholars of Administrative Law have had, at least in Spain, the presence and protagonism that would have been expected during the crisis. The challenges posed have been, are and will be many and of the first order: administrative organization, financing of the Administration, use of the sources of Law and in particular the use and abuse of the Decree-Law, restructuring of the public service, distribution of territorial power, new regulations and deregulations, access to justice, and many more issues that directly affect Administrative Law.

However, in times of uncertainty it is necessary to have clear ideas and keep them. The greater the uncertainty, the greater the clarity of ideas. These ideas must also be present in the institutional, juridical and doctrinal debate. Despite the situation of uncertainty (that uncertainty that is present today in science, as Werner Heisenberg has shown), it is necessary to provide some island of certainty, to paraphrase Edgar Morin[50] ("We should learn to navigate on a sea of uncertainties, sailing in and around islands of certainty"), in Administrative Law.

This being the case, it must be denounced that the exceptional situation in which we find ourselves (already for years) aims to justify the adoption of exceptional

[47]About it vid. Nieto (1991), pp. 2188 and following.

[48]On the crisis and the Administrative Law are numerous now the contributions, although, with exceptions, they have surely arrived late. For example Blasco (2011); Piñar (2013). In particular, in this collective work, Martín-Retortillo (2013), pp. 25–41; Jordano Fraga, Jesús, "El Derecho Administrativo de la crisis", pp. 71–146; Tornos Mas, Joaquín, "Crisis del Estado de Bienestar. El papel del Derecho Administrativo", pp. 171–221.

[49]"Reivindicando el Derecho Administrativo", in Piñar (2013), pp. 13 and following.

[50]Morin (1999), p. 3 and others.

measures, such as the use of the Decree-Law as an almost usual normative instrument to regulate the most varied matters on the occasion of the adoption of measures supposedly necessary to face situations of extraordinary and urgent need. The impact of the crisis on the system of sources is therefore unquestionable and criticizable.

> In the meantime, public administration control systems have become increasingly inoperative; supervisors seem to have failed in the exercise of their functions; the provision of public services (those that remain) is left in the hands of private entities; public employment is demotivated; transparency models do not meet the minimum standards of any advanced model of access to public information; territorial models are in question and the financing of public administrations is suffering cuts that are causing irreversible consequences. This also generates a serious crisis of public credibility. The economy has occupied positions that the law has ceded. Unfortunately. Who regulates who? The law to the economy or the economy to the law?

Alejandro Nieto, already highlighted years ago the crisis in which the Administrative Law is: "Today everything has changed, nothing is comfortable, we do not know exactly where we are, we must start again".[51] We must definitely vindicate Administrative Law: the Law of the general interest (a topic that was addressed at the Italian-Spanish Congress held in Bologna in 2010),[52] of public service, of effectiveness and efficiency in the provision of services, of the guarantee of social rights. An Administrative Law that is capable of resolutely facing the crisis, despite the fact that it seems that we are overcoming it.

References

AA.VV (2004) Administración electrónica y procedimiento administrativo. Ministerio de Economía, Madrid

Aguirreazkuenaga I, Chinchilla C (2001) El uso de los medios electrónicos, informáticos y telemáticos en el ámbito de las Administraciones Públicas. Revista Española de Derecho Administrativo (109)

Barnes J (ed) (2006) Innovación y Reforma en el Derecho Administrativo. Global Law Press Global Law Editorial, Seville

Barnes J (ed) (2008) La transformación del Procedimiento Administrativo-transforming administrative procedure. Global Law Press Global Law Editorial, Seville

Barrio M (2019) Garantía de los derechos digitales en la LOPDGDD (Título X). In: Lopez Calvo J (ed) La adaptación al nuevo marco de protección de datos tras el RGPD y la LOPDGDD, Bosch. Wolters Kluwer, Madrid

Bauza FJ (2003) Procedimiento Administrativo Electrónico. Comares, Granada

Blasco A (ed) (2011) El Derecho Público de la Crisis Económica. Transparencia y Sector Público. Hacia un nuevo Derecho Administrativo. INAP- Asociación Española de Profesores de Derecho Administrativo, Madrid

Cano T (2009) Lecciones y materiales para el estudio del Derecho Administrativo. Iustel, Madrid, 8 volumes

Cosculluela L (2018) Manual de Derecho Administrativo. Parte General. Civitas, Madrid

---

[51] Nieto (1986), p. 9.

[52] Roversi-Monaco et al. (2012).

De La Quadra-Salcedo T (2018) Retos, riesgos y oportunidades de la sociedad digital. In: De La Quadra-Salcedo T, Piñar J-L (eds) Sociedad Digital y Derecho. BOE-Red.es, Madrid, pp 21–86
De La Quadra-Salcedo T (2019) Derechos fundamentales, democracia y mercado en la edad digital. In: Revista Derecho Digital e Innovación-digital law and innovation review. Wolters Kluwer, Alphen aan den Rijn, n. 1
De La Quadra-Salcedo T, Piñar J-L (eds) (2018) Sociedad Digital y Derecho. BOE-Red.es, Madrid
Esteve J (2018) Lecciones de Derecho Administrativo, 8th edn. Pons, Madrid
Fernandez Farreres G (2018) Sistema de Derecho Administrativo, vol I and II, 4th edn. Thomson Reuters-Civitas, Madrid
Gamero E (2015) Desafíos del Derecho Administrativo ante un mundo en disrupción. Comares, Seville
García De Enterría E (1981a) La Constitución como norma y el Tribunal Constitucional. Civitas, Madrid
García De Enterría E (1981b) Revolución Francesa y Administración Contemporánea, 2nd edn. Taurus, Madrid
García De Enterría E (1999) La Administración Española, 6th edn. Civitas, Madrid
García De Enterría E (2010) Le trasformazioni della Giustizia Amministrativa. Giuffrè Editore, Milan
García De Enterría E, Fernández T-R (2017) Curso de Derecho Administrativo, vol I, II, 18th and 15th edn. Thomson Reuters-Civitas, Madrid
García Macho R (ed) (2010) Derecho administrativo de la información y administración transparente. Marcial Pons, Madrid
García Pelayo M (1988) Las transformaciones del Estado contemporáneo. Alianza Universidad, Madrid
Garcia Rubio F (2004) El régimen jurídico de la e-Administración. El uso de medios informáticos y telemáticos en el procedimiento administrativo. Comares, Granada
Hernández Corchete JA (2019) Exhaustividad del RGPD y estándares de protección del principio de legalidad sancionadora. In: Revista Derecho Digital e Innovación-Digital Law and Innovation Review. Wolters Kluwer, n. 2
Lopez Calvo J (2018) Cooperación y coherencia. In: Lopez Calvo J (ed) El nuevo marco regulatorio derivado del Reglamento Europeo de Protección de Datos. Bosch-Wolters Kluwer, Madrid, pp 609–632
Martín Rebollo L (2018) Manual de las Leyes Administrativas, 2nd edn. Thomson Reuters Aranzadi, Cizur Menor
Martín I (2018) El acceso electrónico a los servicios públicos: hacia un modelo de Administración digital auténticamente innovador. In: De La Quadra-Salcedo T, Piñar J-L (eds) Sociedad Digital y Derecho. BOE-Red.es, Madrid, pp 179–202
Martínez R (2009) Administración pública electrónica. Thomson-Civitas, Madrid
Martín-Retortillo S (ed) (1991) Estudios sobre la Constitución Española. Libro homenaje al Profesor Eduardo García de Enterría. Civitas, Madrid
Martín-Retortillo S (2007) Instituciones de Derecho Administrativo. Civitas, Madrid
Martín-Retortillo L (2013) El Derecho Administrativo ante la Crisis. In: Piñar J-L (ed) Crisis Económica y crisis del Estado de Bienestar. El papel del Derecho Administrativo. Actas del XIX Congreso Italo-Español de Profesores de Derecho Administrativo. REUS, Madrid, pp 25–41
Morin E (1999) Seven complex lessons in education for the future. UNESCO, Paris. Available on https://unesdoc.unesco.org/ark:/48223/pf0000117740
Muñoz Machado S (2011) Hacia un nuevo Derecho Administrativo. In: Blasco A (ed) El Derecho Público de la Crisis Económica. Transparencia y Sector Público. Hacia un nuevo Derecho Administrativo. INAP-Asociación Española de Profesores de Derecho Administrativo, Madrid, pp 191–237
Muñoz Machado S (2015) Tratado de Derecho Administrativo y Derecho Público General. BOE, Madrid. 14 volumes

Nieto A (1986) Estudios históricos sobre Administración y Derecho Administrativo, Colección Estudios de Historia de la Administración. INAP, Madrid
Nieto A (1991) La Administración sirve con objetividad los intereses generales. In: Martin-Retortillo S (ed) Estudios sobre la Constitución Española. Libro homenaje al Profesor Eduardo García de Enterría, vol III. Civitas, Madrid, p 2188 and following
Ochoa J (2000) ¿Hacia la ciberadministración y el ciberprocedimiento? In: Sosa Wagner F (ed) El derecho administrativo en el umbral del siglo XXI. Homenaje al Prof. Ramón Martín Mateo, vol I. Tirant lo Blanch, Valencia
Ortega L (1993) Nuevas tecnologías y procedimiento administrativo. Revista Jurídica de Castilla-La Mancha (18):211 and following
Parada J-R (2015) Derecho Administrativo, vol I and II. Open Editorial Universitaria, Madrid
Parejo L (2012) Transformación y ¿Reforma? del Derecho Administrativo en España. INAP-Global Law Press Editorial Derecho Global, Seville
Parejo L (2018) Lecciones de Derecho Administrativo, 9th edn. Tirant Lo Blanch, Valencia
Piñar J-L (2007) Revolución tecnológica, Derecho Administrativo y Administración Pública. Notas provisionales para una reflexión. In: La autorización administrativa. Administración Electrónica. La enseñanza del Derecho Administrativo hoy. Thomson Aranzadi-Asociación Española de Profesores de Derecho Administrativo, Cizur Menor, pp 51–92
Piñar JL (ed) (2011) Administración electrónica y ciudadanos. Civitas, Madrid
Piñar J-L (ed) (2013) Crisis Económica y crisis del Estado de Bienestar. El papel del Derecho Administrativo. Actas del XIX Congreso Italo-Español de Profesores de Derecho Administrativo. REUS, Madrid
Piñar J-L (2014) Transparencia y derecho de acceso a la información pública. Algunas reflexiones en torno al derecho de acceso en la Ley 19/2013, de transparencia, acceso a la información y buen gobierno. Revista Catalana de Dret Públic (49):1–19
Piñar J-L (ed) (2016) Reglamento General de Protección de Datos. Hacia un nuevo modelo europeo de privacidad. Reus, Madrid
Piñar J-L (2018a) Identidad y Persona en la Sociedad Digital. In: De La Quadra-Salcedo T, Piñar J-L (eds) Sociedad Digital y Derecho. BOE-Red.es, Madrid, pp 95–112
Piñar J-L (2018b) Derecho, ética e innovación tecnológica. Revista Española de Derecho Administrativo (195):11–30
Piñar J-L (2019) ¿Qué regulación de los derechos en la sociedad digital? In: Revista Derecho Digital e Innovación-Digital law and innovation review. Wolters Kluwer, Alphen aan den Rijn, n. 1
Ponce J (2019) Inteligencia artificial, Derecho administrativo y reserva de humanidad: algoritmos y procedimiento administrativo debido tecnológico. Revista General de Derecho Administrativo (Iustel) (50). Also at http://laadministracionaldia.inap.es/noticia.asp?id=1509505
Rallo Lombarte A (2019) Del derecho a la protección de datos a la garantía de nuevos derechos digitales. In: Rallo Lombarte A (ed) Tratado de Protección de Datos. Tirant lo Blanch, Valencia, p 23 and following
Rams L (2008) El derecho de acceso a archivos y registros administrativos. Reus, Madrid
Roversi-Monaco F, Cammelli M, Vandelli L (eds) (2012) Forme Private e Interessi Generali: quale ruolo per le Fondazioni?, Atti del XVIII Congresso dell'Associazione italo-spagnola dei professori di Diritto Amministrativo. Bologna, 27–29 mggio 2010. Bononia University Press, Bologna
Sánchez Morón M (2018) Derecho Administrativo. Parte General, 14th edn. Tecnos, Madrid
Santamaría JA (2006) Sobre la Génesis del Derecho Administrativo Español en el Siglo XIX. Iustel, Madrid, pp 1812–1845
Santamaría JA (2010) La Ley reguladora de la Jurisdicción Contencioso-Administrativa. Iustel, Madrid
Santamaría JA (2011) Los principios jurídicos del Derecho Administrativo. La Ley Wolters Kluwer, Madrid
Santamaría JA (2016) Principios de Derecho Administrativo General, vol I and II, 4th edn. Iustel, Madrid

Valero J (2004) El régimen jurídico de la e-Administración. El uso de los medios informáticos y telemáticos en el procedimiento administrativo. Comares, Granada

Valero J (2013) Derecho, innovación y Administración electrónica. Global Law Press-Editorial Derecho Global, Sevilla

Valero J (2018) La necesaria configuración de las garantías jurídicas en el contexto de la transformación digital del Sector Público. In: De La Quadra-Salcedo T, Piñar J-L (eds) Sociedad Digital y Derecho. BOE-Red.es, Madrid, pp 375–396

Wences I, Kölling M, Ragone S (2014) La Ley de Transparencia, Acceso la información Pública y Buen Gobierno. Una perspectiva académica. Centro de Estudios Políticos y Constitucionales, Madrid

Zambonino M (2011) Nacimiento y desarrollo de la Administración moderna. La libertad de comercio. Pasado y presente: los grandes maestros del Derecho Administrativo Contemporáneo. Instituto Andaluz de Administración Pública-Asociación Española de Profesores de Derecho Administrativo, Seville

Chapter 22
Greece: A State with Weak Institutions, in Continuous Crisis

Spyridon Flogaitis

Abstract The author aims at answering the following question: why Greek institutions are that weak? In the first part, the chapter illustrates the historical reasons which prevented the development of strong state institutions. In the second part, it focuses on the consequences of the entry of Greece into the European Communities and, then, into the Eurozone.

The idea occurred to me to write about the theme: 'Greece: a state with weak institutions, in continuous crisis'. I wanted to deal with this theme only because I have the feeling that our leadership, the leadership of Greece, fails to talk to the friendly nations in terms of truth, at least the way I understand the truth, and to remind them who we are, where we come from, what we are trying to do in our part of the world and why and what this crisis is leading us to. I have divided my chapter into two parts, honoring my French education. The first part will deal with Greece, a state with weak institutions. We have to understand that Greece has never developed into a state like every other state on the European continent and this is why history has made this country a state with weak institutions. Having explained that, the second part of this paper deals more in particular with the Greek crisis we have been through for almost a decade.

To begin with, Greece is a state with weak institutions. All the states in Europe, especially in Western Europe, are the result of the institutional and societal evolution from the times of the late feudalism up to the present. Around the fourteenth century, European societies started developing institutions which gradually led to the concept of the state. In this evolution, England, France, Portugal, Spain, Germany—Germany in those days did not exist, but the German states—all of them participated and

S. Flogaitis (✉)
University of Athens, Athens, Greece
e-mail: sflogaitis@eplo.int

D. Sorace et al. (eds.), *The Changing Administrative Law of an EU Member State*,
https://doi.org/10.1007/978-3-030-50780-0_22

contributed to this development, but Greece was absent from this. Greece back then was still one of the provinces of the Ottoman Empire. We had lived without political independence, self-determination, practically since the crusades. This started in the eleventh century but it was concluded, at least symbolically, with the fall of New Rome, Constantinople in 1453. When the rest of Europe's societies were evolving, Greece was not there.

In 1814—that is, four centuries later—in Odessa, on Russian soil, three merchants established the so-called Society of the Friends. Their idea was to prepare a national revolution in the name of the Greeks, bringing together the enlightened Hellenic diaspora of those days and all the local Greek populations. The idea did not come just like that. We must not forget that the Greeks in those 400 years had started many revolutions and participated in all the Christian battles against the Ottomans, trying to finally gain our independence but all of those attempts had failed ... and then it was 1814. This is a very important date because it is just one year before the resolutions of the Congress of Vienna and it must be remembered that the Congress of Vienna put a straightforward principle: no change of monarchies, no change of borders of the states. And only a year before, while the Congress of Vienna was taking place and reaching resolutions, three Greeks, and behind them all of the Greeks, were fool enough to believe that they could go against the dogma and the doctrine of Vienna.

It is not a coincidence that this happened in Odessa. Actually, the national dream to have an independent Greek state for the Greek people crossed in the last more or less two centuries, from the seventeenth to the eighteenth/nineteenth century, a very specific Russian project. It must be remembered that the Russians had developed since the early days the idea that they were the successors of the Roman Empire of Constantinople. They, in Moscow, would be the so-called 'third Rome'. Russians had the imperialist dream of moving to the South and protecting the Greek Orthodox populations along with other populations of the region. So, there was this Russian project and the Greeks who constituted the Society of the Friends were hoping that the Tsar would back this struggle. As a matter of fact, there were rumors among the Greek populations about a superior authority behind this project, letting everybody understand that it was the Tsar.

In 1821, they organized a revolution in the name of the Greeks and the Tsar did not appear. The Russian foreign minister then was a Greek, Graf Ioannis Capodistrias. He was asked by the Tsar what to do. He was bound by the Vienna doctrine and Capodistrias, who was the true head of this movement behind the scenes, advised him, "Go to war, Majesty". But the Tsar did not go to war; so the Greeks were left alone. In this Greek war of independence, the societies of Western Europe were excited with the desperate Greek struggle. For the first time ever, Western European societies came up and said, "Look, we exist as societies and we want to support this". So they started offering help and sending people to fight for Greece. Lord Byron was the most famous of them who came over to fight and died for the Greek cause.

The Greeks then made a declaration—the famous Declaration of Independence. The first paragraph is the Greek nation's mandate. It is what they wanted to do and what brings people to talk about this issue today. They said "we were the descendants of the wise, ancient, Greek people, the descendants of the ancient and wise Greeks; we were ashamed of the situation of barbarism and the tyranny which we had lived with and we wanted to create a state similar to the one of our Christian, friendly, civilized European nations". That's the mandate of the revolution. The problem is that being typically Greeks, when the revolutionaries started this revolution—that is, as soon as they started existing politically—they went into civil wars; one, two, three civil wars—because the Greeks are political animals. They want to know who is going to lead. They don't want to be behind the leader. They want to be the leader. So, Greeks started killing each other and the revolution was in great danger, and this great danger was avoided because of an international intervention. Now, the word "intervention" should not be forgotten, because it is useful in order to understand the weakness of the Greek state. As a matter of fact, one of the reasons for the weakness of the Greek state is that, before establishing the state, the Greeks started killing each other.

The second truth is that, at the end of the day, the heroic people of Greece needed a foreign intervention in order to regain their place in history again, and this intervention was the naval battle of Navarino in 1827. The British, the French and the Russians came together and, with the responsibility of the British Admiral Codrington, they sunk the Turkish-Egyptian fleet, so Greece started hoping for independence. The French army came to clean the territory from the enemy troops and started liberating the land. It is a mystery why Codrington did that, since he had a very specific order to follow the situation but not to intervene. Nevertheless, he did intervene—that's why one of the main streets in downtown Athens bears his name. He was sanctioned by the British later, but Greece still needs to remember that we owe our independence to the British nation and to Admiral Codrington who did that for the Greeks. Finally, in 1830 we had a new state borne on ancestral Greek soil, all thanks to the Protocol of London.

In the Protocol of London, the three powers which had intervened in Navarino declared themselves "protectors" of Greece. Now, this was not a protectorate; it was a very original form of protection. But it legally lasted over a century and it had specific political importance, since the three powers which intervened in Navarino had done so because their societies wanted them to intervene but also for specific strategic reasons. Every single one of them wanted Greece to be under its influence. So, in Greece, we ended up back then having three political parties: the British, the French and the Russian. It's not that the Greeks were not patriots but there were three ways of thinking as to whom we should ally to in order to bring the country ahead.

In 1832, the first king came to Greece. He was the second son of Ludwig von Wittelsbach, King of Bavaria. The revolution was republican but the three powers wanted the state to be a kingdom. What the three powers really wanted was someone to have the possibility to liaise with in a country of unpredictable people. We have seen this again in several moments of the Modern Greek history.

A dream was coming true. We finally had the possibility to create a state like the ones of every civilized nation of Europe and to build a state, very original for those days when state building had started, since the Bavarians who came over to Greece started transplanting the Napoleonic state in the country. It was pure transplantation. State building in Greece was not the result of a centuries-long evolution like in Western Europe. Nothing of this had been heard of on Greek soil for four centuries. Nobody knew what a Prime Minister was. Nobody was accustomed to obey a public administration; there was no public administration. There were no true courts. There was nothing of the kind in the memory of the population. Actually, at a certain moment, Ludwig asked Rudhardt—Rudhardt had been a high official of the public administration of Bavaria—to serve as prime minister in Greece. Rudhardt wrote memoirs, and in his memoirs wrote how disappointed he was by his service in Greece because (in my words) "in my country I was director general of a ministry and everybody respected me, and now in Greece everybody comes to my office whenever they want, they shout at me, I am in continuous danger. What country is this?". Greek people did not know any of those things then. Everyone lived with his own affairs or of their little village or with the people who run the village, nothing that you know of, but still the Greeks wanted to create a state, and so they did. They transplanted state institutions, together with the Bavarians. We owe a lot to Georg Ludwig von Maurer, a professor of French public law at the University of Munich, who came to Greece with King Otto and transplanted the Napoleonic state in Greece.

In fact, the era launched by the Bavarians in the newly independent Greek State turned out to be much more sustainable than usually thought, since the central and local institutions introduced then in Greece lasted until the 1909 movement and thereafter. For example, a Royal Decree adopted by the Bavarians in 1833 was one of the laws that constituted the internal structure of the Greek Kingdom of that era. It reflected the legal thought of Maurer. The most important innovation of that Bavarian piece of legislation concerned the size of municipalities. It disregarded the preexisting situation and structure of local administration and reorganized municipalities from scratch in order to create local institutions of an operative size. Nevertheless, the creation of large municipalities attracted harsh criticism. Years later, Eleftherios Venizelos gave an end to this development. With a Law in 1912, he disempowered mayors by creating smaller municipalities, thus smaller political bases, hence freeing the parliament from local dependencies. It was a crucial step in state building.

However, the Bavarian-transplanted institutions had no memory, and no past. They were very weak since their very conception, and then there was the famous east/west issue. What is Greece? Do we belong to the east or to the west? The revolution was giving the answer. We belonged to Europe, meaning to the west, the western way of doing things, but society had a great distrust for the west—a distrust which, interestingly, dates back to the days of the crusades.

Greeks had lost their political autonomy for many reasons. One of them is the infiltration of our region by the Franks, which started in the eleventh century and which made Greeks in 1453 to prefer the Ottomans than Western societies, and then we had the church working on it—because the church had to explain why it was better to be with the Ottomans. They said that we did it to save our souls, because the Pope wanted us to change our credo; we did it because they were stealing our properties. The looting of Constantinople was never forgotten. So, however crazy it may seem to talk about it nowadays, Greeks are a historic nation and whenever you start talking about anything, they start with Homer and then they come to the present. Whether they have the right to do that or not, that's who we are, and our distrust towards the west influences the perception of the institutions brought from the west. Are those institutions better, or perhaps could we have developed our own institutions? We could have developed the local government that existed under the Ottoman Empire according to all sorts of unrealistic political theories. Those theories in fact are not pro-modernization, and we had a specific forward-looking mandate by the Greek revolution.

If somebody asked any Greek today who was the leader of the Greek revolution, they will name Kolokotronis. He was not. He was one of the leaders of the revolution. He was perhaps the one whom all the enemies were afraid of, because he was still in the mountains when Ibrahim was devastating Peloponnese and just before Navarino he was still fighting and he's Greece's glory. However, the true leader of the revolution was Demetrios Ypsilantis, a prince from Russia, a Greek prince of the Russian order appointed by the secret Society of the Friends as the leader of the Greek revolution. Was he highly regarded during the revolution? No. Do the Greeks always recognize him as the most valiant, the most virtuous of the Greeks? Yes. At the end of the day, though, he, the one who symbolized modernity, was overshadowed by others—the brave warriors—who were not symbolizing modernity. Yet, this might be an understatement, since Kolokotronis too was a product of the west: he had been exposed to the British traditions as a lieutenant of the British army in the Ionian Islands and this had helped him a lot to understand his glorious Greek past, the tactics and the war.

The Greek state created in 1830 was small. The new state was meant to be small and weak. The state was meant to be small for international reasons, but the Greek dream was to liberate all of the ancestral land of the nation. Thus, from 1830 up to 1947, every generation went to war to claim and to acquire what is now the Greek territory. This is the first generation which did not go to war—at least up until now. But this is the result of a country, this is the result of a nation which did not spare money or effort and did not hesitate to go to war in order to create Greece.

Thus, Greece has been in steady turmoil throughout its modern history. In 1897, it went bankrupt for similar reasons as today, because of a prime minister called Harilaos Trikoupis. He found low interest rates in those times and he made many infrastructure works in Greece, but then the interest rates went up and Greece was forced to bankruptcy. So, it will never be forgotten that Greece went bankrupt, but had he not taken the loans needed, Greece would have been far worse off than it is today. Later, in 1909 Eleftherios Venizelos comes to power, the man who takes Greece, as small as it was, and makes of it a country five times bigger. How? Because from 1910 to 1912 he takes a bankrupt country, he brings a French mission and reorganizes the public administration and the state. He allies himself to the British, he goes to the Balkan Wars and then to the First World War. This went on until 1919 and then follows the adventure of Asia Minor, leading up to the destruction of the Greek populations of Asia Minor in 1922.

In fact, prewar Greece, from 1910 onwards, has been a unique example of a state in constant political instability, for numerous reasons. It was very hard, if not impossible, for a country that lacked state tradition and institutions to sustain all of the adventures that Greece suffered for much of the twentieth century without its administrative mechanism falling apart. For instance, in 1922 about two million Greeks came from the Asia Minor to build a new life in Greece; again, this was a state and institutions which had to work in a much bigger space with parts of Greece that had forgotten what political autonomy was for five centuries ... and then two million people were arriving here. That's Greece. It's not like England. It's not like France. None of Europe's societies had ever been exposed to a situation like that. And then Greece had the Second World War, where it should be remembered that it never surrendered. Greece is a small state that never surrendered to the Italians whom we fought in Albania. Then the Germans arrived through Yugoslavia and Bulgaria. The government went along with the British to the Battle of Crete and then to the Battle of El Alamein. Greeks went to Normandy. Greece was one of the winning powers, but the Greeks were barefoot—and the only possibility not to be barefoot was thanks to the shoes the British sent to the army. Later on, when every other nation started recovering, Greeks did not forget that they were the best in civil wars. So, Greece had a civil war from 1946 to 1949 and we destroyed whatever had been left by the Germans.

Speaking of the Germans, it should never be forgotten that Greeks are the only nation among all of the occupied nations which lent money to the Germans. We lent money to the Germans because the Germans wanted our gold, and the Quisling government—despite the fact that it was a Quisling government—did not accept to do it. So, they went to Rome and signed a contract and the Germans took the gold on the promise to pay it back with interest after the pacification. This is one of the biggest traumas in the memory of modern Greeks, because we know that we owe a lot to Germany today, but we cannot forget that they never paid back that money. It is crucial that they never paid that contracted money, because that winter the Athenians died in the streets by thousands, as there was literally no drachma left to support them in such difficult times for the nation.

In 1947, with the peace treaty signed with the Italians, Greece acquired the Dodecanese. Therefore, the Greek territory as we know it only dates since 1947. Then, in 1967 Greece had a military dictatorship, which pushed Greece even more backwards, and in 1974 the Cyprus drama came. This completes, in a few words, who the Greeks are. That's exactly who they are. *They are a state with weak institutions, because they have never had the time to develop better and stronger institutions*. Never, almost never, because Greece has lived a 'normal' political life for only the past 40–45 years.

Moving to the second part of this chapter, it is needed to look into the crisis which is the result of what has happened in the past 45 years in Greece, ever since 1974. The dictatorship of 1967 in Greece aimed to stop the democratization process of the Greek society leading to its homogenization and brought a very severe coup to the weak institutions of the country. As a matter of fact, from 1952 up to 1967 a very important restructuring process had started. The need for administrative reform after the end of the Civil War was evident. Greece had a public administration which was not bad. Its only problem was that it belonged exclusively to the winners of the civil war, not to the others, but the structure existed and it could have been democratized. The dictatorship stopped this democratization process and later on it collapsed in the Cyprus crisis. The day when nobody knew where the ministers were will always be remembered. When the dictatorship provoked the Turkish invasion—because they gave Turks the pretext to intervene in Cyprus and to ultimately occupy a third of the island—Greek ministers were nowhere to be found. They did not go to the ministries, there was no government in the country; nothing. The need for reform came up.

The Greeks had, at least as late as 1974, the strong need to reorganize, to create a modern Greek state through reform. Administrative reform called for legislative modernization, organizational reform as well as human resources reform. A new political class comes into existence after 1974—the so-called '*metapolitefsi*' era. The old political class disappears. New people come up and they are the new society; they represent the new society of modern Greece. Actually, the political class born during the dictatorship that governed the country in this new era originated from the core of the ordinary people, middle or poorer middle classes. So, in a sense a new society was coming to power.

And then in 1981, Greece acceded to the European Communities. This was a big achievement. In order to understand the importance of this turning point, it must be remembered that, since the division of the Roman Empire in eastern and western, Greece—whatever Greece is today—had never been, during all this time, with the west, ever. It is the first time since the fourth century that Greece sided with that other part of the old Roman empire. As said above about the west/east division, this was a revolution for the Greeks; a happy revolution, indeed, because they were again within the mandate of the Declaration of Independence of Greece. That's what our ancestors had wanted. They wanted Greece to be there. Nevertheless, the Greek entry into the European Communities created a very original inertia in the political class because everything had to be decided by Brussels. Greece was meant to be part of this decision process. Nobody knows how good the political class was in truly participating in this decision making process, but little by little they started acting as the local administrators of policies decided elsewhere. Money was pouring in. Everybody was happy, but Greek-made policies, one could not see. Greek platforms for reform, one could not see; only whatever was decided by the European Communities in Brussels.

In 1981, the socialists came to power. It was a new party born after 1974 representing all this new society born before, during and after the dictatorship. The years 1982–1984 were reform years. However, the reforms which took place in 1982–1984 were long delayed reforms: they were reforms which should have taken place in the sixties or the seventies, rather introverted, and not taking advantage of expert knowledge. Then it was too late. For example, the new forms of participation into local government, when they were brought to Greece from Italy—because many of our expatriates during the dictatorship had found refuge in Italy—they had already been abandoned in Italy because society had changed. They were long delayed reforms, not always of excellent quality. In addition, they were reforms that followed the traditional pattern. What was the traditional pattern? That the state has to do everything. Literally, that the state has the means to do everything.

Those were the years when Greeks started borrowing more and more money. The state budget had been more or less in good balance until then, but after 1981 Greece started borrowing money, perhaps way more than it could ever afford to pay back. Until one day, in the 1990s, the new policy for the Euro and the creation of a common monetary union in Europe came from Brussels. Should Greece have joined the Eurozone? Of course it should—the political class wanted it to be in the Eurozone for many reasons. Sharing the same currency with the Germans, it could never be believed that this would ever happen, because most of the people lived in the fifties in extreme poverty—and few years later Greeks became members of a rich community sharing the same currency with the Germans! And in this unfounded euphoria, we forgot that the Euro was a currency created on a specific platform. Europe wanted us to have specific prerequisites and in order to have specific prerequisites, the appropriate reforms had to be done.

They say Greece lied to Europe. Greece did not lie to Europe. This is not true. Europe knew very well what Greece did. We did a swap and we sent a part of our public deficit 20 years later. It was legal. It was announced. It was done by a well-known international company. The problem of Greece is that we did not read the document when we signed. It's not just a Greek problem, but Greece was a problem for Euro, and it is a problem for Greece, because, as said in the first part, Greece is the only state among the states of Europe, which has truly weak institutions. Portugal was present in the fourteenth century. Spain was present in the fourteenth century. But Greece was nothing in those days, under Ottoman occupation, rather than a dream. And so the question is: *what reform*? My answer is, *any* reform. Let us do something. It is needed to create the state from scratch, because the one we have created cannot go on any more.

To conclude, Greece, a state with weak institutions, a relatively young state, needs once again to adapt its structures to the stark new realities of today. This adaptation needs to put together the best practices from other countries, as well as mobilize the best national forces. Greeks are a very well-educated nation. They need to finally put all of these forces to work for this country to move fast forward. Greeks feel truly offended when they see that they send us experts from Europe to explain this or that. We have all the forces needed to reform the country, but we need the platform. We need somebody to start reforming in any way. What we have, it cannot go on. What we have today is a state which was created in 1910/1912, with adaptations. After 80 years with no reforms, even the Soviet Union collapsed.

This state needs continuous reform and we, the Greeks, we can reform our country. But: we need a strategy and a strategy can only be given by the political class. And I'm confident that our political class will guide Greece to better days in the future. We the Greeks, we have all the forces needed to reform this country, but we need a platform. Perhaps the platform is given by Europe, by the little letters. This will be decided by the politicians, but let them do whatever they want, very quickly. Time flies!

The manufacturer's authorised representative in the EU is Springer Nature Customer Service Centre GmbH, Europaplatz 3, 69115 Heidelberg, Germany. If you have any concerns regarding our products, please contact ProductSafety@springernature.com

Printed and bound by CPI Group (UK) Ltd, Croydon, CR0 4YY
30/09/2026
02225696-0020